DEFENSE, SECURITY AND STRATEGIES

THE NATIONAL NETWORK OF FUSION CENTERS

EFFECTIVENESS, CAPABILITIES, AND PERFORMANCE

DEFENSE, SECURITY AND STRATEGIES

Additional books in this series can be found on Nova's website
under the Series tab.

Additional E-books in this series can be found on Nova's website
under the E-book tab.

DEFENSE, SECURITY AND STRATEGIES

THE NATIONAL NETWORK OF FUSION CENTERS

EFFECTIVENESS, CAPABILITIES, AND PERFORMANCE

NANCY C. LINCOLN
AND
JANET B. SEEGMILLER
EDITORS

nova publishers
New York

For permission to use material from this book please contact us:
Telephone 631-231-7269; Fax 631-231-8175
Web Site: http://www.novapublishers.com

Library of Congress Cataloging-in-Publication Data

ISBN: 978-1-62948-138-8

Published by Nova Science Publishers, Inc. † New York

CONTENTS

PREFACE

This book provides a comprehensive study of the National Network of Fusion Centers in an effort to understand current strengths and gaps and provide recommendations for improvement.

Chapter 1 – In the aftermath of the information sharing failures leading to the September 11, 2001 terrorist attacks that killed nearly 3,000 people in New York City, at the Pentagon, and in a Pennsylvania field, States and localities across the United States established what are known today as State and Major Urban Area Fusion Centers (fusion centers). Collectively known as the National Network of Fusion Centers (National Network), many of these – now numbering 78 – fusion centers are still in their infancy.

The Homeland has been attacked five times since 2001: the Little Rock Recruiting Station shooting (2009); the Fort Hood shooting (2009); the attempted bombing of Northwest Airlines Flight 253 on Christmas Day (2009); the attempted car bombing in Times Square (2010), and the Boston Marathon bombings (2013). In the wake of these attacks, we have come to understand that homeland security, including counterterrorism efforts, must be a National responsibility – a true and equal partnership across all levels of government, and inclusive of the American people themselves. A top down, wholly Federal approach simply does not and cannot suffice. Fully integrating State and local law enforcement and emergency response providers as National mission partners requires a grassroots intelligence and analytic capability. Stakeholders rely upon fusion centers to provide that capability.

The *Implementing Recommendations of the 9/11 Commission Act of 2007* (Pub. L. 110-53) defines fusion centers as: "a collaborative effort of 2 or more Federal, State, local, or tribal government agencies that combines resources, expertise, or information with the goal of maximizing the ability of such agencies to detect, prevent, investigate, apprehend, and respond to criminal or terrorist activity." The October 2007 *National Strategy for Information Sharing* further specifies that "State and major urban area fusion centers will be the focus, but not exclusive points, within the State and local environment for the receipt and sharing of terrorism information, homeland security information, and law enforcement information related to terrorism."

During the 112th Congress, then-Committee on Homeland Security (Committee) Chairman Peter T. King, currently the Chairman of the Subcommittee on Counterterrorism and Intelligence, directed Committee Majority staff to conduct a comprehensive study of the National Network in an effort to understand current strengths and gaps and provide recommendations for improvement. This work continued into the 113th Congress under the additional direction of current Committee Chairman Michael T. McCaul. Over the course of nineteen months (January 2012-July 2013), the Committee logged 147 meeting hours during visits to 32 fusion centers, in addition to numerous briefings and discussions with various Federal partners, representatives of the National Fusion Center Association, and follow-up conversations with fusion center directors and personnel.

Chapter 2 – Threats to the homeland are persistent and constantly evolving. Domestic and foreign terrorism and the expanding reach of transnational organized crime syndicates across cyberspace, international borders, and jurisdictional boundaries within the United States highlight the continued need to build and sustain effective intelligence and information sharing partnerships among the federal government; state, local, tribal, and territorial (SLTT) governments; and the private sector. These partnerships are the foundation of a robust and efficient homeland security intelligence enterprise that goes beyond shared access to information and intelligence to foster sustained collaboration in support of a common mission. This collaboration enables the fusion process and provides decision makers across all levels of government and within the private sector with the knowledge to make informed decisions to protect the homeland from a variety of threats and hazards.

State and major urban area fusion centers (fusion centers) are the nexus of the homeland security intelligence enterprise at the state and local level. They serve as focal points for the receipt, analysis, gathering, sharing, and safeguarding of threat-related information between the federal government and SLTT and private sector partners. As such, fusion centers provide a state and local context that enhances the national threat picture and enables local officials to better protect their communities. They also provide critical information and subject matter expertise that allows the Intelligence Community (IC) to more effectively "connect the dots" to prevent and protect against threats to the homeland.

In: The National Network of Fusion Centers
Editors: Nancy C. Lincoln and Janet B. Seegmiller
ISBN: 978-1-62948-138-8

Chapter 1

THE NATIONAL NETWORK OF FUSION CENTERS*

Majority Staff of the U.S. House Homeland Security Committee

EXECUTIVE SUMMARY

> "[B]ut the truth of the matter is, nobody bats 1,000, and I think as a nation we need to come to terms with it and do everything we can to prevent it, but also recognize that fusion centers and intelligence analysis…are part of our future."
>
> - Boston Police Commissioner Edward Davis,
> Testifying before the House Committee on Homeland Security,
> May 9, 2013

In the aftermath of the information sharing failures leading to the September 11, 2001 terrorist attacks that killed nearly 3,000 people in New York City, at the Pentagon, and in a Pennsylvania field, States and localities across the United States established what are known today as State and Major Urban Area Fusion Centers (fusion centers). Collectively known as the National Network of Fusion Centers (National Network), many of these – now numbering 78 – fusion centers are still in their infancy.

The Homeland has been attacked five times since 2001: the Little Rock Recruiting Station shooting (2009); the Fort Hood shooting (2009); the attempted bombing of Northwest Airlines Flight 253 on Christmas Day (2009); the attempted car bombing in Times Square (2010), and the Boston Marathon bombings (2013). In the wake of these attacks, we have come to understand that homeland security, including counterterrorism efforts, must be a National responsibility – a true and equal partnership across all levels of government, and inclusive of the American people themselves. A top down, wholly Federal approach simply does not and cannot suffice. Fully integrating State and local law enforcement and emergency response providers as National mission partners requires a grassroots intelligence and analytic capability. Stakeholders[1] rely upon fusion centers to provide that capability.

The *Implementing Recommendations of the 9/11 Commission Act of 2007* (Pub. L. 110-53) defines fusion centers as: "a collaborative effort of 2 or more Federal, State, local, or

---

* This is an edited, reformatted and augmented version of the U.S. House of Representatives, dated July, 2013.

tribal government agencies that combines resources, expertise, or information with the goal of maximizing the ability of such agencies to detect, prevent, investigate, apprehend, and respond to criminal or terrorist activity."[2] The October 2007 *National Strategy for Information Sharing* further specifies that "State and major urban area fusion centers will be the focus, but not exclusive points, within the State and local environment for the receipt and sharing of terrorism information, homeland security information, and law enforcement information related to terrorism."[3]

During the 112th Congress, then-Committee on Homeland Security (Committee) Chairman Peter T. King, currently the Chairman of the Subcommittee on Counterterrorism and Intelligence, directed Committee Majority staff to conduct a comprehensive study of the National Network in an effort to understand current strengths and gaps and provide recommendations for improvement. This work continued into the 113th Congress under the additional direction of current Committee Chairman Michael T. McCaul. Over the course of nineteen months (January 2012-July 2013), the Committee logged 147 meeting hours during visits to 32 fusion centers, in addition to numerous briefings and discussions with various Federal partners, representatives of the National Fusion Center Association, and follow-up conversations with fusion center directors and personnel.

> "We have intelligence estimates that look at threats to the Homeland. But what do we have where you have a legitimate homegrown threat? ... The world over here has an effect over there, and vice versa. So I would argue the emphasis should be pushing out our capabilities to support and enable our fusion centers on the front lines. State and local law enforcement is ultimately best positioned and, in many cases, most competent to deal with these issues."
>
> - Frank Cilluffo, Testifying before the Committee on Homeland Security, September 20, 2012

Summary of Findings

- ***The Committee strongly believes that the National Network is a National asset that needs to realize its full potential to help secure the Homeland.*** Based on the Committee's long history of oversight of the fusion centers' development, it appears that the National Network is on a path of continued growth, improvement, and increasing value to both the Federal Government and the fusion centers' individual customers. In addition to significant numbers of State and local partners represented, site visits revealed over 20 different Federal offices and agencies with personnel assigned across the 32 visited fusion centers, suggesting that fusion centers provide value to a wide variety of Federal agencies.
- ***The strength of the National Network lies in individual fusion centers' unique expertise; their independence from the Federal Government; and their ability to leverage the State and local perspective on behalf of the National homeland security mission, which includes counterterrorism.*** Formally standardizing all aspects of fusion center operations would be disadvantageous. Over the past three years, the Department of Homeland Security's (DHS) efforts have been targeted to assist fusion centers in developing plans, policies, and standard operating procedures. The goal has been to achieve capacity and standardized capability – namely the

Critical Operational Capabilities – across the National Network, while allowing individually tailored processes for each fusion center. Although much work remains, these efforts appear to have improved consistency and standardization, and have helped to establish a common "language" across the National Network.

- ***The Federal Government should continue to facilitate and enable fusion center development in order to ensure that centers have the capacity necessary to fulfill their role as National mission partners.*** This must include continued improvements in information sharing. However, State and local stakeholders, including the fusion centers themselves, must take ownership and be a driving force behind much of the requisite growth moving forward. In order for the National Network to develop fully, a greater level of commonality and unified direction is necessary.
- ***The lack of a comprehensive State and locally-driven National Strategy for Fusion Centers reflecting the equities of fusion centers' diverse stakeholders is a barrier to the National Network reaching its full potential.*** A comprehensive Federal Strategy for Fusion Centers is also necessary to explain how and why the Federal Government engages with fusion centers, guide Federal planning, serve as the foundation to develop additional performance and value- based metrics, and drive Federal resource allocation to fusion centers. The lack of these two strategies stands in the way of maximum efficiency, effectiveness, and the ability of the National Network to provide full benefit to the National homeland security mission.
- ***Thus far, fusion center metrics have primarily focused on measuring capacity and capability rather than "bang for the buck."*** Due to the inherent difficulty in determining the success of prevention activities, stakeholders struggle with how to accurately, adequately, and tangibly measure the value of fusion centers to the National homeland security mission, and particularly the counterterrorism mission. Although great strides have been made, the current metrics – including the five performance measures included in the 2012 annual Fusion Center Assessment – are only a partial measure, and do not alone demonstrate overall success or failure of the National Network. Future metrics should reflect the values articulated in a comprehensive National Strategy for Fusion Centers and companion Federal Strategy for Fusion Centers. Further, there are not currently any tracking mechanisms in place to provide a complete picture, even quantitatively, of how fusion center-gathered information affects Federal terrorism or criminal cases or other homeland security mission areas. This is a significant gap that must be corrected in the short term in order to show the value of the National investment.
- ***Challenges remain across the National Network itself, particularly with the lack of individual fusion centers' operational activities being universally inclusive of strategic counterterrorism threat analysis.*** Participation in the National Network should carry with it the expectation of National mission partnership, including the production of strategic counterterrorism threat analysis. Mature fusion centers utilize their analytic expertise, understanding of the nuances of their local environment, and unique information to look for potential ties to terrorism, in addition to fulfilling their other State, local, and homeland security missions. However, as a true National partner, fusion centers must fulfill their individual missions in a way that trains and requires analysts to view State and local crime with an eye toward strategic National counterterrorism and threat analysis.

- ***There should be continued enhancement and growth in the areas of analysis, Terrorism Liaison Officer programs, partnerships with first responders and public health officials, and Critical Infrastructure and Key Resources sectors.***
- ***Owned and operated by States and localities, the bulk of Federal investment in fusion centers is limited to funds subgranted to the fusion centers through the DHS preparedness grants,*** specifically the State Homeland Security Grant Program and the Urban Area Security Initiative, and through the deployment of computer systems, training, and personnel, primarily from DHS's Office of Intelligence and Analysis and the Federal Bureau of Investigation (FBI).
- ***Stakeholders must undergo a thorough discussion to determine the next steps to ensure the National Network continues to develop as a partner in the National and Homeland Security Enterprises.*** Lack of action at this juncture could have a negative, and potentially debilitating impact on the National Network, which in turn could undermine homeland security.

Particularly in light of the current fiscal climate, the National Network is at a crossroads. Many fusion centers are struggling to maintain their operational tempo due to drastically changing annual budgets. As a result, some fusion centers are facing the possibility of closing or having to make significant changes to their staffing or operations. Fusion center directors consistently noted that if Federal grant funding were to disappear their individual fusion center would likely remain, but its focus would turn inward toward exclusively State and local mission needs. This would reduce those fusion centers' potential value to the National homeland security mission, possibly leaving the Homeland less secure.

SUMMARY OF RECOMMENDATIONS

Comprehensive Strategies & Measures of Success

1. ***National Strategy for Fusion Centers and Federal Strategy for Fusion Centers-*** Driven by the State and locals, stakeholder groups should collaborate to establish a National Strategy for Fusion Centers. As a companion to the National Strategy for Fusion Centers, the Federal Government should develop a comprehensive Federal Strategy for Fusion Centers to steer Federal coordination and support to fusion centers and the National Network.
2. ***Performance Metrics-*** Stakeholders, including I&A and the Federal Emergency Management Agency should develop additional performance metrics to further guide fusion center-related grant expenditures within the States, and the Federal resource allocation process. The metrics should be tied to a National Strategy for Fusion Centers and a Federal Strategy for Fusion Centers.
3. ***Fusion Center Information Tracking-*** The FBI and other Federal partners should more fully track their use of information gathered by fusion centers to better understand its affects on Federal counterterrorism and criminal cases at various points in the investigative lifecycle.

Funding

4. ***National Network Funding-*** DHS should engage in a thorough discussion with stakeholders – including but not limited to, the fusion centers, States and Major Urban Areas, the FBI, the Program Manager for the Information Sharing Environment, and Congress – to conclude whether the Federal Government should more directly and/or more fully fund all or a subset of fusion centers. This should be done with guidance from a National Strategy for Fusion Centers.
5. ***Funding Model-*** DHS should carefully examine other grant and funding models to determine if a different model would be more effective to support the long-term needs of the National homeland security mission, as fulfilled by the National Network.
6. ***Period of Performance-*** The Federal Emergency Management Agency should carefully examine the current environment in which the ultimate intended recipient of grants must operate, and determine whether it may be necessary to return the period of performance to three years, or make other changes.

Fusion Center Analysis

7. ***Statewide Analysis-*** In States with multiple fusion centers, one of the fusion centers should be responsible for the integration of analysis from across all fusion centers within the State, establishing a statewide threat picture.
8. ***National Mission Analysis Units-*** Stakeholders should further explore the possible establishment of specialized analytic units within fusion centers to enhance the identification and analysis of information to meet national mission requirements.
9. ***Suspicious Activity Reporting Trend Analysis-*** Fusion centers should increase Suspicious Activity Reporting trend analysis, including the creation and dissemination of such an analytic product to its customers. I&A should then use that State and local analysis to regularly produce Nationwide Suspicious Activity Reporting trend analysis.
10. ***Fusion Center Analyst Career Path & Training Roadmap-*** The National Network and the Federal Government should continue to work with stakeholders to examine options and implement a plan to address the need for State and local analyst career paths and a training roadmap.
11. ***Analytic Coordination Programs-*** Fusion centers should establish formal, regional or statewide analytic coordination programs to enhance collaboration, deconfliction, and planning.
12. ***Critical Infrastructure and Key Resources-*** Fusion centers with limited Critical Infrastructure and Key Resources (CIKR) programs should work to enhance these programs in the short term. Fusion centers not currently engaging in CIKR analysis should make this an immediate priority.

Outreach

13. ***Statewide Outreach-*** In States with a single fusion center, that center should gather and analyze threats from across its entire area of responsibility – presumably the entire State. A robust Terrorism Liaison Officer program and a greater proliferation of fusion center nodes may be methods to achieve this goal.
14. ***Terrorism Liaison Officer Programs-*** The fusion centers and DHS should work together to strengthen Terrorism Liaison Officer (TLO) programs across the National Network. Further, the fusion centers, DHS, the FBI, and other stakeholders should come together and determine what, if anything, may lend itself to further TLO standardization across the National Network. Fusion centers currently lacking a TLO program should work to establish one in the short term.
15. ***Fusion Partnerships-*** Fusion centers lacking robust fusion partnerships outside of the law enforcement community should make this an immediate priority, particularly focusing on partnerships with the fire, emergency medical services, and public health sectors.

Access to Information & Systems

16. ***Security Clearances***- In order to understand the disparity in security clearances granted to State and local personnel, DHS, the FBI, and the Program Manager for the Information Sharing Environment should complete a thorough review. Federal partners should take steps to further equalize security clearances among the State and locals to foster increased information sharing between Federal, State, and local law enforcement agencies and policymakers.
17. ***White List-*** DHS should identify fusion centers that currently make significant use of classified information and work with them to further test the recently-established procedures to request additional accesses. DHS and the Department of Defense (DOD) should also immediately work to reduce the current best-case timeframe required for access approval. Additionally, DOD, with the help of I&A and fusion centers, and in consultation with other Intelligence Community partners, should be more proactive in identifying information sets that meet fusion centers' missions and further their ability to assist Federal partners.
18. ***FBINet-*** The FBI should undergo a thorough review to understand current State and local access to FBINet, establish standards to support more consistent access to FBINet for fusion center personnel, and ensure a broad awareness of those standards among its homeland security partners. Additionally, the FBI and DHS should work together to establish a formal policy and process regarding I&A Intelligence Officers' (IO) access to FBINet in the field.
19. ***National Sensitive-But-Unclassified System-*** In an effort to establish a National primary Sensitive-But-Unclassified information sharing system, the Executive Branch should work with Congressional oversight committees and State and local stakeholders to determine an appropriate path forward, potentially merging similar Federal systems.

Office of Intelligence and Analysis, Department of Homeland Security

20. ***Analytic Production Approval Process-*** I&A should address issues surrounding the analytic production approval process that inhibits timely joint-seal products with fusion centers.
21. ***Intelligence Officers-*** I&A should continue to work with the fusion centers, other stakeholders, and the Committee to determine what, if any, changes should be made to the IO program as individual fusion centers and the National Network continue to mature.
22. ***Reports Officers-*** I&A should work with Congressional oversight committees to determine whether there are appropriate areas to expand Reports Officers' responsibilities that may benefit both the DHS and National missions.
23. ***Intelligence Analysts-*** I&A should undergo a thorough cost-benefit analysis, and work with Congressional oversight committees, to determine whether restructuring its Office of Analysis to increase intelligence analyst deployment to the field is in the best interest of homeland security.
24. ***Management of Field Officers-*** I&A should examine the current management structure surrounding its field officers – Regional Directors, Intelligence Officers, Reports Officers, Senior Reports Officers, and Intelligence Analysts – to determine whether consolidating field management could be more effective.

Federal Bureau of Investigation

25. ***Information Sharing-*** FBI Headquarters should conduct more stringent oversight, including audits, of information sharing occurring between its field offices and the fusion centers. As an element of that oversight, FBI Headquarters should make a more concerted effort to ensure its field offices are held accountable for robust cooperation and information sharing with fusion centers and State and local law enforcement.

BACKGROUND

"[T]he term 'fusion center' means a collaborative effort of 2 or more Federal, State, local, or tribal government agencies that combines resources, expertise, or information with the goal of maximizing the ability of such agencies to detect, prevent, investigate, apprehend, and respond to criminal or terrorist activity."

- "Homeland Security Act of 2002," As Amended by the "Implementing Recommendations of the 9/11 Commission Act of 2007"
Pub. L. 110-53, Aug. 3, 2007, §511, 121 STAT. 322. Amends Homeland Security Act of 2002 by adding §210A(j).

Between 2003 and 2005, in the aftermath of the information sharing failures leading to the terrorist attacks of September 11, 2001, States and localities stood up what are known individually as State and Major Urban Area Fusion Centers (fusion centers) and collectively as the National Network of Fusion Centers (National Network). Established to break down agency barriers and analyze State and locally held information, the Federal Government identifies fusion centers as the primary conduit to share Federal terrorism-related information with State, local, tribal, and territorial (SLTT) partners. Today, there are 78 designated Fusion Centers that make up the National Network, across 49 States, three territories, and the District of Columbia. Forty-nine of the 78 fusion centers are operating within jurisdictions currently or previously eligible for Urban Area Security Initiative (UASI) funding.[4]

> "At that time [2004-2005], no standards or guidelines were in existence to assist with interoperability and communication issues with other centers at the state, regional, and federal levels. As a result, centers designed to share information were actually silos of information, incapable of information exchange."
>
> - Fusion Center Guidelines, 2006

In January 2006, the Department of Homeland Security (DHS) began direct engagement with fusion centers, including the first deployment of a DHS Office of Intelligence and Analysis (I&A) Intelligence Officer (IO) assigned to the Joint Regional Intelligence Center in Los Angeles, California. By the end of 2006, there were approximately 40 fusion centers across the country, and DHS and the Department of Justice (DOJ) collaborated with stakeholders to develop the *Fusion Center Guidelines*, in an effort to help shape fusion center development. This was supplemented by the September 2008 *Baseline Capabilities for State and Major Urban Area Fusion Centers* document.[5]

The term "National Network of Fusion Centers" became common in 2010, and describes the association of individual fusion centers to serve the National homeland security mission, including counterterrorism. Also in 2010, a number of fusion center directors came together to establish the National Fusion Center Association (NFCA) in an effort to increase education and awareness of the National Network and fusion centers.

Legislative History

In July 2007, Congress passed, and in August 2007, the President signed, the *Implementing Recommendations of the 9/11 Commission Act of 2007* (Pub. L. 110-53), which included language amending the *Homeland Security Act of 2002* (Pub. L. 107-296) to establish the "Department of Homeland Security State, Local, and Regional Fusion Center Initiative."[6] In September 2008, Congress passed the *Personnel Reimbursement for Intelligence Cooperation and Enhancement of Homeland Security Act of 2008* (the *PRICE of Homeland Security Act)* (Pub. L. 110-412), clarifying that State Homeland Security Grant Program (SHSGP) and UASI funds could be used for fusion center intelligence analysts.

Additionally, in October 2011 the Committee on Homeland Security in the US House of Representatives (Committee) ordered to be reported H.R. 3116 as amended, the *Department of Homeland Security Authorization Act for Fiscal Year 2012,* which included a provision establishing the "Department of Homeland Security National Network of Fusion Centers Initiative," in recognition of the significant growth and transformation of fusion centers since 2007. The whole House did not consider the bill.

On May 8, 2012 the Committee favorably reported, and on May 30th the House passed, H.R. 3140, the *Mass Transit Intelligence Prioritization Act*, directing the Secretary of Homeland Security to prioritize sending Transportation Security Administration (TSA) officers and intelligence analysts to fusion centers located in high-risk jurisdictions with mass transit systems. However, the bill was not taken up by the Senate during the 112th Congress. Subsequently, this bill (now H.R. 1210) was reintroduced in March 2013 and referred to the Committee's Subcommittee on Counterterrorism and Intelligence.

COMMITTEE RESEARCH METHODOLOGY

The Committee has consistently advocated that State and local law enforcement, emergency response providers, and fusion centers are a significant part of the National homeland security mission. Further, the Committee has a long history of oversight over the fusion centers and DHS support to them. During the 112th Congress, under the direction of then-Committee Chairman Peter T. King (now Chairman of the Subcommittee on Counterterrorism and Intelligence), Committee Majority staff designed and executed a comprehensive review of the National Network. This work continued into the 113th Congress under the additional direction of current Committee Chairman Michael T. McCaul. It is important to note that the Committee's study was not intended to be an investigation to uncover waste, fraud, or abuse. Its purpose was to identify and understand the strengths, weaknesses, and gaps in fusion center development, the National Network, and the Federal role.

Specifically, the Committee sought to understand:

- Fusion centers' development individually and as a part of the National Network;
- How well the National Network operates to fulfill a National need, including Federal, State, and local priorities and the National homeland security mission, particularly the counterterrorism mission;
- Changes to fusion centers' overall mission space, and how those changes have affected their ability to meet Federal, State, and local customer requirements;
- The impacts of having 78 designated fusion centers across the country, and multiple fusion centers within a single State;
- The current Federal Government role in the fusion centers' and the National Networks' development, and the role it should play moving forward;
- State and local security clearances and access to classified information;
- Fusion center analysts' training and development, and fusion centers' analytic production;
- Leveraging non-traditional partners as fusion partners, specifically fire, emergency medical services (EMS), and public health;
- The current funding environment and possible future funding models for fusion center and National Network sustainment; and
- DHS's and the Federal Bureau of Investigation's (FBI) relationship with fusion centers.

Between January and August 2012, the Committee visited 32 fusion centers across 20 States and the District of Columbia, logging 147 meeting hours with personnel assigned to the fusion centers. In April 2013, the Committee sent a follow up questionnaire to each of the visited fusion centers, requesting updated data. Additionally, between January 2012 and July 2013 the Committee received regular briefings from Federal partners, met with various stakeholder groups, and conducted follow-up calls with fusion center directors and personnel. The Committee also held a number of hearings in which it received testimony relevant to the subject of the study.

For a detailed description of the Committee's research methodology, please see Appendix II.

FINDINGS AND RECOMMENDATIONS

> "The ultimate goal is to provide a mechanism through which government, law enforcement, public safety, and the private sector can come together with a common purpose and improve the ability to safeguard our homeland and prevent criminal activity. It is critical for government to accomplish more with less."
>
> - Fusion Center Guidelines, 2006

Today, in many States and localities, fusion centers serve a critical Federal, State, local, and regional information sharing and analytic function, and are a force multiplier for the Federal Government to understand local and regional threats in a more holistic way. They are the established tie by which SLTT information can be fused with Federal information and shared with partners to protect the Homeland, while simultaneously protecting citizens' privacy and civil liberties.

There has been significant change and growth across the National Network over the past three years, largely a result of DHS' efforts to assess fusion center capabilities, provide training, technical assistance, dedicate resources to enhance fusion center operations, and target grant funding to mitigate gaps in fusion centers' capabilities.

However, there remain challenges, including the lack of a comprehensive National Strategy for Fusion Centers and a Federal Strategy for Fusion Centers, and the lack of individual fusion centers' operational activities being universally inclusive of strategic counterterrorism threat analysis. Additionally, there is much room for continued enhancement and growth, particularly in the areas of analysis, Terrorism Liaison Officer (TLO) programs, and partnerships with first responders, public health, and the Critical Infrastructure and Key Resources (CIKR) sectors.

The strength of the National Network lies in the diversity of expertise, individual fusion centers' unique identities, and operational independence from the Federal Government; a cookie-cutter approach would be detrimental to the National Network. However, there must be a greater level of consistency than currently exists in order for individual fusion centers to operate most efficiently and effectively within the National Network, and for the National Network to function most successfully as a National asset. The 2008 *Baseline Capabilities for State and Major Urban Area Fusion Centers* document offers a place to start. It does not establish standardized processes, but rather places a premium on fusion centers developing standard operating procedures in an effort to obtain standardized National Network- wide capability.

> "On October 8, 2010, the New York Police Department sent out an advisory concerning a suspicious tractor-trailer whose driver reportedly diverted its route to Times Square in New York City in exchange for $10,000. New York informed several fusion centers in the affected area. Subsequently, the Rhode Island State Fusion Center (RISFC) discovered that the original owner of the truck was a California native and asked the Northern California Regional Intelligence Center (NCRIC) to run a background check based on the owner's information. Within two hours of the advisory's release, information from these two fusion centers was used to coordinate with the Connecticut Intelligence Center (CTIC), which enabled Connecticut State Police to locate the tractor-trailer before it reached its reported target in New York City. The Connecticut State Police searched the vehicle and questioned the driver and passenger. Ultimately, officials concluded that the vehicle was not a threat, but the fact that these fusion centers were able to turn this incident from a Suspicious Activity Report (SAR) to resolution in a matter of three hours shows the value of the National Network of Fusion Centers."
>
> \- Provided by the FBI to the Committee, October 23, 2012

A greater level of standardization in strategic homeland security threat analysis, technology, analyst training, TLO programs, security clearances, access to and use of Federally-owned computer networks, and funding would significantly add to the efficiency and effectiveness of individual fusion centers and the National Network as a whole. Additionally, increased commonality in these areas would help to further break down barriers and establish a common language between Federal, State, and local homeland security partners.

The Federal Government should continue to facilitate fusion center development and activities to ensure the capacity to meet National mission needs, but ultimately should not be the primary force behind much of the necessary standardization. The fusion centers must take ownership and be the driving force to achieve much of the necessary commonality across the National Network. The Committee notes that the NFCA's plan to host the 2013 Fusion Center Annual Training Event for the first time, a job previously held by the Federal partners, is a significant milestone in the National Network's development.

The following pages contain detailed research findings and recommendations.

A National Strategy for Fusion Centers & Measuring Success

> "Although each fusion center will have unique characteristics, it is important for centers to operate under a consistent framework – similar to the construction of a group of buildings where each structure is unique, yet a consistent set of building codes and regulations are adhered to regardless of the size or shape of the building."
>
> \- Fusion Center Guidelines, 2006

As stated earlier, the fundamental strength of the National Network is individual fusion centers' unique identities, expertise, experiences, and partnerships coming together, and the

State and local vantage point lending itself to the National counterterrorism mission and the broader National homeland security mission. However, if there is to be true growth, there must be common agreement on what fusion centers are and should be, where the National Network should be headed in the future, and a plan to get there.

Fusion Center Strategies

A number of existing National strategies and policy documents are inclusive of or targeted toward fusion center development.[7] In particular, the 2007 National Strategy for Information Sharing's "Appendix 1: Establishing a National Integrated Network of State and Major Urban Area Fusion Centers" currently serves as a primary source for the limited strategic guidance for the National Network's development. However, there is currently no "one stop shop" articulating all of the strategic and fundamental goals, intentions, objectives, and expectations for fusion centers or the National Network.

The lack of a National Strategy for Fusion Centers (National Strategy) is a significant barrier to the National Network reaching its full potential, and hinders the National Network's sustainment long-term. Closing this gap would allow individual fusion centers and the Federal Government to implement long-term development and investment strategies, founded with nationally agreed-upon goals in mind. A National Strategy would also enable the Federal Government to develop more value-based metrics to understand, guide, and measure its investment in fusion centers. Without a firm foundation, such as a National Strategy, on which to develop performance metrics, it is difficult to determine whether current measures are adequately assessing relevant progress. A National Strategy would answer the question of "what are we progressing toward," and help stakeholders – including Congress – understand actual progress toward a clearly defined set of goals.

As all levels of government continue to face a difficult fiscal environment, calls from State and local stakeholders for Federal sustainment funding for fusion centers have grown louder. However, it is impossible to responsibly engage in a dialogue about sustainment funding until State and local stakeholders – including those chiefs, colonels, sheriffs, and other senior policymakers with authority over fusion centers – and the Federal Government have first articulated, to a greater extent, the value proposition for fusion centers, the specific capabilities needing preservation or development to meet National needs, and the roadmap to get there.

Based upon briefings provided by I&A and discussions with fusion center directors, the Committee is aware that a high level strategic outline for the National Network exists. This is an important first step toward a formal strategy, but it does not go far enough. Led by State and locals, stakeholders should come together, collaboratively, to establish a formal and comprehensive National Strategy.

While this National Strategy must be developed with the context of the current homeland security threat environment at the forefront, it must establish a system with the agility to adapt to an ever-changing environment. This National Strategy should include a National Network mission statement; long-term goals, objectives, and priorities for fusion centers and the National Network; and Federal expectations for the National Network and visa versa. It should also contain a comprehensive definition of what is and is not a fusion center, which should include a mission space and operational activity that is universally inclusive of strategic counterterrorism threat analysis and National mission partnership. This National

Strategy should acknowledge the inherent differences between fusion centers' State and local missions and their National homeland security mission, both of which a mature fusion center in the National Network should serve. The National Strategy should be used to guide resource allocation and planning, and individual fusion center and National Network-wide assessments moving forward. The National Strategy should provide a framework by which to measure success by first defining success.

In conjunction with this State and locally driven National Strategy, Federal Government stakeholders should develop a separate Federal Strategy for Fusion Centers to steer Federal coordination and support to fusion centers. Led by DHS, a Federal Strategy for Fusion Centers should clearly spell out the roles and responsibilities of various Federal agencies; priorities and objectives in their interaction with fusion centers; definitions of success and appropriate measures; and a clear mechanism to hold Federal partners accountable. A Federal Strategy for Fusion Centers should outline how and why the Federal Government will support the National Strategy described above, and help fusion centers meet National mission objectives.

Metrics

The 2010 Baseline Capabilities Assessment was the Federal Government's first attempt to measure progress in the development of fusion centers. In 2011, DHS became the Federal lead for fusion center assessments and introduced a new, annual Fusion Center Assessment (Assessment) to measure identified Critical Operational and Enabling Capabilities. The 2011 Assessment also introduced a National Network Maturity Model (Maturity Model) to measure the development of the National Network.[8] The Maturity Model aligns 46 Attributes to the Critical Operational and Enabling Capabilities.

With the 2012 Assessment, the Committee notes the first time inclusion of performance metrics in addition to the Capability measures. Developed collaboratively between DHS, fusion center directors, and other stakeholders, these new metrics represent a significant step forward in the Federal Government and National Network's ability to understand the maturation of the National Network and individual fusion centers. However, the 2012 performance metrics are limited and highly quantitative. While quantitative metrics are important data points, they alone do not demonstrate success or failure.

Quantitative metrics can provide a level of tangible insight into the relationship between fusion center-gathered information and Federal terrorism and criminal cases. Particularly in the current climate wherein stakeholders are still working to understand not only the full value of fusion centers but also the growth in information sharing and the Homeland Security Enterprise as a whole, the FBI and other Federal partners should make a concerted effort to track the disposition of information received from mission partners. Information from DOJ and the FBI suggests that tracking is done to some extent, but there appear to be significant gaps preventing a clear picture of how fusion center-gathered information affects FBI investigations at various points in the investigative lifecycle. The FBI should take steps to correct this shortcoming in the near term.

Although it's critical that the Assessments continue, it is also imperative that additional value- based performance metrics be developed to further guide Federal investment, including fusion center-related grant expenditures. These metrics should be focused to help

Federal stakeholders understand the "bang for the buck." The Committee acknowledges the inherent difficulty in developing qualitative metrics, particularly in the prevention discipline, and recommends that DHS and the fusion centers seek outside expertise to aid in this process. According to a briefing with representatives from I&A and the Federal Emergency Management Agency (FEMA), Assessment results will influence allowable fusion center expenditures of SHSGP and UASI funds, once awarded to the States.[9] The goal is to further target Federal grant funds to identified areas of weakness within individual fusion centers.

The Committee is aware that additional performance metrics are in development for the 2013 Assessment. While the inclusive process and efforts to measure performance are noteworthy and there are undoubtedly standard measures of performance that are common among analytic organizations, the Committee is nonetheless concerned that these metrics are being developed in a partial vacuum. As stated earlier, beyond assessing the Critical Operational and Enabling Capabilities, performance should be measured against long-term strategic goals and objectives, as should be identified in a National Strategy for Fusion Centers and a Federal Strategy for Fusion Centers like those discussed in the *A National Strategy for Fusion Centers & Measuring Success* section of this report. The Committee will continue to work closely with DHS and the National Network to ensure overall developmental goals are met.

Fusion Centers & the National Mission

> Fusion centers "foster a culture that recognizes the importance of fusing 'all crimes with national security implications' and 'all hazards' information (e.g., criminal investigations, terrorism, public health and safety, and emergency response) which often involves identifying criminal activity and other information that might be a precursor to a terrorist plot."
>
> - National Strategy for Information Sharing, October 2007

All Crimes Approach

In recent years, the National Network has seen a mass migration away from individual fusion centers exercising a strict counterterrorism mission focus, as was the case in the early days of fusion centers, and toward an "all crimes" mission space. While all of the 32 visited fusion centers described themselves as having a strong emphasis on counterterrorism, 10 of the 32 visited fusion centers describe themselves as having an "all crimes" mission, while the majority, 21, describe themselves as having an "all crimes-all hazards" mission. Only one of the visited fusion centers described itself as currently having a "counterterrorism" mission with "all crimes" as a secondary mission. This mass movement seems to be a result of several primary factors discussed below.

First, an "all crimes" approach utilizes and expands upon existing State and local law enforcement processes to identify and analyze suspicious activity. According to fusion center personnel, this approach, supplemented with additional training for line officers and first responders, better enables them to support the National homeland security mission. Building on the principle that terrorist plots often include precursor criminal activity (including financing, gathering materials, etc.), fusion centers are able to help identify possible signs of terrorist activity through their analysis of broad criminal information and gathering Suspicious Activity Reports (SAR).

> "In October 2011, the Alaska Information and Analysis Center (AKIAC), in coordination with the Alaska JTTF, issued an Officer Safety Bulletin on two potentially violent individuals believed to be illegally armed and departing for Canada. The AKIAC used liaisons with the Royal Canadian Mounted Police and U.S. Customs and Border Protection (CBP) to ensure that the Canadian Border Security Agency (CBSA) received this information and was on alert. As a result, CBSA conducted a high-risk inspection at a port of entry, and discovered a weapon. The suspect was denied entry into Canada, turned around, and was then stopped at the CBP checkpoint, where he was arrested by Alaska State Troopers."
>
> - Provided by the FBI to the Committee, October 23, 2012

According to information provided by the FBI and DOJ, 176 SARs entered by fusion centers into the eGuardian or Shared Spaces SAR databases between December 2008 and December 4, 2012 resulted in the FBI opening a new terrorism investigation.[10] This represents 20% of all those SARs entered into eGuardian or Shared Space resulting in the initiation of a new FBI investigation. ***Additionally, 289 Terrorist Watchlist encounters reported by fusion centers enhanced existing FBI cases.***[11] It is important to note that the Committee's research suggests that, due to the variety of other means by which SARs and other fusion center-gathered information are shared with the FBI, this number is most likely significantly lower than the totality of SARs from fusion centers leading to or enhancing an FBI investigation. As discussed earlier in this report, there does not appear to be any mechanism currently in place that provides a complete picture of how fusion center-gathered information affects Federal terrorism or criminal cases.

Second, fusion center personnel maintain that this expanded mission space increases and encourages awareness of the fusion process across all levels, making law enforcement agencies, first responders, and other non-traditional partners more likely to participate, thereby increasing involvement in the National homeland security mission.

Third, although counterterrorism is a National mission, and thus a shared responsibility of partners across all levels of government, fusion centers' individual customers and supporting agencies have a much broader mission space. The "all crimes" and "all crimes-all hazards" approach is representative of the fusion centers' individual State and local mission space, and their status as partners in broader homeland security mission areas. Fusion centers increase their relevance to their SLTT customers and Federal partners by leveraging the National Network to identify and combat nationwide criminal enterprises and to identify otherwise undetected State, local, regional, or National trends. This relevance can also have a major impact on State and local resources dedicated to the fusion centers. Congress demonstrated support for the fusion centers' engagement in the broader homeland security mission space through the "Border Intelligence Priority," established in the *Implementing Recommendations of the 9/11 Commission Act of 2007* (Pub. L. 110-53), and the 2012 House of Representatives-passed *Mass Transit Intelligence Prioritization Act* (H.R. 3140; reintroduced in 2013 as H.R.1210).

Lastly, this "all crimes" approach enables fusion centers to serve as partners in the broader homeland security mission, beyond the counterterrorism mission. Although DHS – including I&A, TSA, Customs and Border Protection (CBP), Immigrations and Customs Enforcement (ICE), US Coast Guard, US Secret Service, US Citizenship and Immigration Services (USCIS), National Protection and Programs Directorate (NPPD), and the Federal Protective Service – and the FBI are the largest supporting Federal partners, many other Federal agencies appear to have identified fusion centers as valuable mission partners. According to reporting from the thirty- two visited fusion centers, seven are collocated with High Intensity Drug Trafficking Area (HIDTA) analysts. The Bureau of Alcohol, Tobacco, Firearms, and Explosives (ATF) has personnel assigned to twelve of the fusion centers, and one fusion center is collocated with a local ATF Field Division. Seven fusion centers have representatives assigned from the National Guard or other Department of Defense (DOD) element. The Drug Enforcement Administration (DEA) has representatives assigned to four of the visited fusion centers, and one DEA Division is collocated with a fusion center. Other agencies with representatives assigned to visited fusion centers include, but are not limited to the: US Attorney's Office (3); Department of State (3); US Marshals (2); Internal Revenue Service (1); Treasury Department/FinCEN (1); Social Security Administration (1); National Park Service (1); and Amtrak (1). Nearly all of the fusion centers reported having, at a minimum, close working relationships with Federal partners beyond DHS and the FBI.

Operating fusion centers with an "all crimes" or "all crimes-all hazards" focus is a positive development for the National Network provided that it is done in a way that ultimately encourages and preserves a robust strategic counterterrorism analytic capability. Although individual fusion centers serve State and local needs and play a significant role in the broader National homeland security mission areas, Federal investment in fusion centers has primarily been intended to support the National need to detect and prevent terrorist attacks on the Homeland. Therefore, as National counterterrorism mission partners, mature fusion centers should leverage their "all crimes" focus to understand criminal activity and analyze it in such a way as to identify possible indicators of terrorist activity. Some fusion centers describe this as an "all crimes approach to counterterrorism."

The National Response and Recovery Mission

Twenty-one of the visited fusion centers identified themselves as "all crimes-all hazards" centers. According to fusion center personnel, the formal move to "all crimes-all hazards" reflects a center's growing relationship with first responders and an increasing focus on CIKR. Further, nine of the visited centers (five of which consider themselves as "all crimes-all hazards") are collocated with their State or local Emergency Operations Center (EOC), and stated that they play a supporting role when the EOC is activated. The full extent to which individual fusion centers are involved with their local EOC operations varies.

This expanded mission space provides a clear link between the fusion centers and FEMA's National response and recovery mission. For example, in the aftermath of Hurricane Sandy, New Jersey's fusion center, the Regional Operations Intelligence Center

(ROIC), completed Preliminary Damage Assessments (PDAs) of critical infrastructure sites – including police and fire stations, hospitals, and schools – in conjunction with FEMA. Additionally, the ROIC served as the conduit for information flow between the New Jersey EOC, front line officers, and policymakers. Further, briefings and products from the ROIC enabled Federal, State, and local partners to maintain a common operating picture and broad situational awareness in the aftermath of Hurricane Sandy.

In the event of a terrorist attack or natural disaster, all available resources are leveraged to aid in response and recovery. At the Federal level, DHS recently released three of the five National Preparedness System's Frameworks that, among other things, explore options for the integration of prevention and response efforts.[12] The relationship between fusion centers and State and local response organizations is discussed further in the *Fusion Centers & Emergency Response* section of this report.

National Mission Partnership

Mature fusion centers utilize their analytic expertise, understanding of the nuances of their local environment, and unique information to serve the National homeland security mission. As discussed in the previous section, a National Strategy for Fusion Centers should require that participation in the National Network carry with it the expectation of National mission partnership.

> "[T]errorist financiers are increasingly shifting to criminal activity. Earlier this year, U.S. authorities indicted a vast Hezbollah network for money laundering, cocaine deals and more exposing 30 U.S. –based car dealerships that helped the group move cash .... If this trend continues, it's reasonable to assume that criminal investigations will play an increasingly prominent role in U.S. efforts to counter terror finance."
>
> - Jonathan Schanzer, Testifying before the House Committee on Homeland Security, Subcommittee on Counterterrorism and Intelligence, May 18, 2012

Of those visited, the more mature fusion centers generally appeared to embrace the idea of an "all crimes approach to counterterrorism." Although the vast majority are still developing their advanced analytic capabilities, fusion centers engage in analysis surrounding prison radicalization, border security, human trafficking and human smuggling, identity theft, gangs, drug trafficking, weapons smuggling, transnational criminal organizations, cigarette smuggling, and cybersecurity, among other things. Through their analysis of criminal enterprises and local crime information, mature fusion centers look for potential ties to terrorism, both foreign and domestic, including pre- operational activities and financing.

As true National partner, fusion centers must fulfill their individual missions in a way that trains and requires analysts to view State and local crime with an eye toward strategic National counterterrorism and threat analysis. The ability to balance State, local, and National needs is a sign of fusion center maturity.

In many small fusion centers the resources simply do not exist to have a large cadre of strategically focused analysts. Further, immature centers have yet to develop a more advanced analytic capability. However, true participation in the National Network requires participation as a National mission partner. Fusion centers should ensure that all of its analysts understand the National mission space, and that it has personnel assigned to perform strategic level homeland security analysis, and particularly counterterrorism analysis.

At the time of the site visits, a number of fusion centers remained primarily focused on tactical intelligence and investigative support, rather than strategic threat analysis. In most of these cases fusion center leadership acknowledged this as a shortcoming and voiced a desire to continue the move toward more strategic analysis, citing a lack of resources, training, and center immaturity as the primary inhibitors. Further, particularly when a center is fully or near-fully funded by State and/or local funds, the Committee recognizes that it may be difficult for fusion centers to sell a value proposition for participation in the National homeland security mission to their sponsoring agencies. However, awo of the visited fusion centers were so focused on local criminal and tactical analysis and investigative support that they apparently do not engage in strategic threat analysis, nor did they have plans or desire to expand their analysis. This is a significant gap.

Regardless of the reason, strictly inward-looking, tactical or investigative support-focused fusion centers are not genuine fusion centers at all. These are crime analysis centers. The Committee observed that these centers generally have limited partnerships beyond their parent agency, further limiting their ability to conduct strategic, all-source threat analysis. While local crime analysis centers serve an important function for State and local mission partners, these centers are not robust National mission partners. DHS should take fusion centers' partnership in the National homeland security mission into consideration upon the dedication of resources, including SHSGP and UASI funds and assignment of IOs and other personnel.

Information Sharing

> "What all these [pre-9/11 Intelligence Community] stories have in common is a system that requires a demonstrated 'need to know' before sharing. This approach assumes it is possible to know, in advance, who will need to use the information. Such a system implicitly assumes that the risk of inadvertent disclosure outweighs the benefits of wider sharing. Those Cold War assumptions are no longer appropriate. The culture of agencies feeling they own the information they gather at taxpayer expense must be replaced by a culture in which the agencies instead feel they have a duty to the information – to repay the taxpayers' investment by making that information available."
>
> - The 9/11 Commission Report, 2004

Although significant strides have been made in information sharing across the Federal, State, and local levels since 2001, information access, collaboration, and sharing continue to be plagued by individuals holding fast to pre-9/11 organizational paradigms. The September 11, 2001 attacks ushered in a period of swift and drastic change across all levels of government, particularly within the areas of intelligence, information sharing, and homeland security. However, as we move further from September 11, 2001, momentum has slowed. As demonstrated most recently in the aftermath of the terrorist attacks in Boston, improvements in information sharing today are often reactive instead of proactive, which can inhibit the necessary continued growth and refinement. In a couple of isolated instances, the fusion center site visits resulted in concern that the relationships between the Federal, State, and local law enforcement agencies in those areas may even be moving backwards, at least partially the result of a system still dependent upon personal relationships.

Further, the Committee is aware that in the last 18 months the FBI pulled both its analysts and its network connectivity out of four separate fusion centers, including three State primary centers. Although there are legitimate reasons for the FBI to pull out of a given fusion center, the Committee is greatly concerned by this development, particularly in the aftermath of the terrorist attack in Boston. The Committee will continue to closely monitor and conduct oversight of the FBI's engagement with fusion centers, including as part of its ongoing investigation into the terrorist attack in Boston.

Historical distrust and competition between law enforcement agencies continues to stand in the way of truly breaking down the walls between them. In some cases there remains a lack of individuals' understanding and willingness to take part in the symbiotic relationship that can, and should, exist between the fusion centers and the Federal Government. Agencies, at all levels, need to continue moving away from the historical ownership model of information sharing, and toward one focused on what the Program Manager for the Information Sharing Environment (PM-ISE) calls "information stewardship;" the idea that all of the information collected is a National asset.[13]

This discussion of an "information stewardship" model was never more timely than in the wake of the recent terrorist attack in Boston. Although the Committee is currently conducting an investigation to fully understand what did and did not happen, it appears clear that local law enforcement was unaware that the FBI was investigating an individual identified as a possible terrorist. The results of the Committee's investigation and final recommendations are pending. However, there must be immediate action to improve the sharing of potentially vital terrorism investigative information with State and local law enforcement and the fusion centers.

> "[P]eople generally will share now, but they will generally share once they determine that something is relevant to a terrorism investigation that someone else might be able to help them on. And that's too late. The fact is, you have to share volumes of information … but there are often disputes about that, because they say, 'Well, it's just travel information. It's not counterterrorism information.' And the answer is, you don't know if it's counterterrorism information until you have it, until you can compare it to other information and find connections between those dots."
>
> - Michael Leiter, Former Director, National Counterterrorism Center Testifying before the House Committee on Homeland Security, July 10, 2013

A large body of anecdotal evidence suggests that the FBI's, and to some extent even the DHS components', relationship with individual fusion centers remains largely based on personal relationships established in the field. In many cases field leadership appear to have bought in to the idea that partnership is mutually beneficial and serves the greater good. Although excellent personal relationships have, in most instances, proven to equal excellent working relationships, this is an unsustainable model. A change in leadership in any one organization and the relationships risk collapse. This cannot be the foundation for information sharing in an era that requires robust information sharing to secure the Homeland.

The Committee recognizes the good work being led by the PM-ISE to continue to break down barriers at the National level. It is vital that work continue aggressively, not only at the

Federal headquarters' level, but at the field level, and organizational leaders must hold their staffs accountable for sharing information and partnering across the Homeland Security Enterprise. We must not allow the successes made since September 11th to degrade, and we must continue moving forward.

The Number of Fusion Centers in the National Network

> "The Federal Government does not dictate where fusion centers should be built and maintained, nor does it designate fusion centers. However, the Federal Government has a shared responsibility with state and local governments to promote the establishment of a national network of fusion centers to facilitate effective information sharing."
>
> - Information Sharing Environment Guidance Federal Resource Allocation Criteria
> June 3, 2011 (ISE-G-112)
> *See Appendix VII

As a result of State and local ownership of fusion centers, and the established process by which governors designate centers and establish eligibility for Federal resource support, the Federal Government has limited ability to impact the total number of fusion centers in the National Network.

As of September 1, 2007, 58 fusion centers were either operating or being established.[14] By the end of 2011, there were 77 fusion centers within the National Network, and with the January 2013 designation of a fusion center in Guam, there are now 78: 52 State and territorial and 26 Major Urban Area fusion centers.

There is a strong argument for each State and territory to have a minimum of one fusion center to ensure that individual States' information is leveraged to the fullest extent practicable, and that local, State, and National policymakers have the most complete threat picture possible. Additionally, given the dense population and higher threat risk, it is also reasonable for certain Major Urban Areas to have dedicated fusion centers.

However, significant questions remain as to the ideal number of fusion centers that the Federal Government should financially support to meet National homeland security mission objectives.[15] Simply, the questions include: Do we have a stronger National Network by relying on Federal grant dollars to support fusion centers at individual States' and Urban Areas' discretion, as is the case under the current grant structure? Or do we have a stronger National Network by ensuring that a minimum number of fusion centers, in carefully identified locations, can operate on steady financial footing? Does having more fusion centers, although somewhat starving and unfocused on the National mission, yield a safer Homeland than having slightly fewer, but very strong and focused fusion centers?

With limited financial resources, and the significant reduction of SHSGP and UASI funds over the years, DHS should engage in a thorough discussion with stakeholders – including but not limited to the fusion centers themselves, States and Major Urban Areas, the FBI, the PM-ISE, and Congress – to conclude whether it makes more sense for the Federal Government to more directly and/or more fully fund a subset of fusion centers to ensure the "net" is widely cast and is healthy across the entire country, likely with additional funding to supplement areas of higher risk.

The National Network is at a crossroads. If 78 (or more) fusion centers are necessary to fully support National homeland security mission needs, then the funding and resources should be dedicated from a variety of Federal, State, and local sources to fully support them. If 78 fusion centers are deemed unnecessary to carry out the National homeland security mission, then decisions must be made regarding which ones will be left up to States and localities to fully fund or let close. The National Network is far too important to homeland security to allow it to struggle for basic survival, and it must be allowed to realize its full potential. Hard decisions must be made, and they must be made in the short term.

Multi-Fusion Center States

The Committee visited States with multiple fusion centers, in particular California and Texas, in an effort to understand how well those fusion centers coordinate within their States, and the need – or lack thereof – for multiple designated fusion centers within a single State. Prior to visiting all six of California's fusion centers and four of Texas' seven, including two of its newest, the Committee was exceedingly skeptical of the need for six or seven fusion centers in a single State.

Given the sheer size of California and Texas, significant variation exists not only in local partnerships and environment, but also in the nature of the threat itself. ***The Committee concludes that regionalizing fusion centers across large States is reasonable, provided it is done in a thoughtful way, that demands close collaboration, coordination, and deconfliction in an established Statewide network.*** Further, all of the fusion centers in a statewide network must be fully resourced and supported, since it will only be as strong as its weakest link.

- **California:** In 2004, California developed a "State Threat Assessment System" (STAS) seeking to: "create a statewide information sharing network of trusted partners throughout all public safety, public agency, critical infrastructure, and key resource private sector partner organizations within California," and "provide those trusted partners with the training and resources they need to assist the national homeland security enterprise with detecting, deterring, and preventing threats to California and its citizens while protecting their privacy, civil rights, and civil liberties".[16]

  California's STAS consists of four regional fusion centers, a Major Urban Area fusion center, and the State Threat Assessment Center. With a formal concept of operations, the STAS establishes structure for coordination across all six fusion centers within the State. In particular, the statewide TLO training and certification program, and the Lead Analyst Working Group, are highlights of the relationship developed through the STAS.
- **Texas:** Upon the designation of four additional fusion centers, bringing the Texas total to seven, in 2011 the Texas Legislature passed a law establishing general guidelines for fusion centers operating inside the State. Specifically, it establishes that the Texas Fusion Center (the State's primary fusion center), part of the Texas Department of Public Safety (DPS), "shall serve as the state's primary entity for the planning, coordination, and integration of government communications capabilities to help implement the governor's homeland security strategy and ensure an effective response in the event of a homeland security emergency."[17] The law also requires

DPS to establish a "Texas Fusion Center Policy Council … to assist the department in monitoring fusion center activities" in Texas.[18] The Council is made up of representatives from all of Texas' designated fusion centers, and is charged with making recommendations to DPS, which is then required to "adopt rules to govern the operations of fusion centers" in Texas.[19]

At the time of the visits to Texas, the Fusion Center Policy Council had only convened a handful of times, therefore the Committee is unable to comment on its impact. However, the Committee recognizes this as a significant step toward establishing a coordinated statewide network.

In States with multiple fusion centers, it is imperative that there be statewide harmonization. One of the fusion centers should be tasked to integrate analysis from the other centers, creating a statewide threat picture. In turn, this statewide analysis should help drive regional and urban area threat analysis.

Without a strong State center fusing analysis from across an established statewide network, adding to it, and bridging stovepipes within the State, policy makers are left with an incomplete threat picture. Additionally, a lack of coordination inevitably leads to duplication, redundancy, and an increased likelihood of things falling through the cracks; outcomes that neither the States nor the Federal Government can afford.

Single Fusion Center States and Nodes

In States with a single fusion center, it is not uncommon to find that center located within the most populated area. This causes a tendency for that fusion center to become consumed by the immediate surrounding area rather than looking in depth across the entire State, particularly if the host major metropolitan area is the primary resource partner. Further, single statewide centers generally continue to struggle with outreach into the more remote areas of their State. This is due to a variety of factors, but primarily resource constraints and proximity.

It is imperative that statewide fusion centers find a way to collect and analyze threats from across their entire area of responsibility (AOR). This may be most easily achieved through a robust TLO program and with a greater proliferation of fusion center nodes.

An increase in the identification of nodes, fusion center "satellite offices," would further incorporate outlying areas into the statewide fusion process and, through their linkage with the fusion centers, into the National fusion process. Therefore, rather than establishing additional independent fusion centers, States should consider leveraging existing resources, such as county sheriffs' or cities' intelligence units, and selectively establish small fusion center nodes to help reach outlying areas. These nodes should coordinate TLOs and SAR collection, provide locally tailored analysis, and increase communication and partnerships across the State. Functioning much like a cell phone repeater, nodes can amplify the fusion center message and increase signal strength across a State. These nodes should be part of the organizational structure of the nearest State or Major Urban Area fusion center insomuch as they are carrying out the fusion center's State and National mission, while also respecting the independence of the host agency.

Funding

"[T]hat's one of the concerns we have. When we look at budgets, there are those who look at things like [fusion centers] as the first thing to go. I don't think it ought to be the first thing to go. I think it ought to be one of the things that we try and make even better. Because in the area of terrorism, as in so much other things, much of the intelligence is gathered by people who weren't looking for terrorists as their first objective.... There are so many more eyes and ears with local law enforcement than there are federal agents. And part of our job is to make sure we give the expertise, share the expertise, on the federal level with those at the local and state level .... And I fear that when we run into these tough budget times that's the first thing to go because it's not a fancy gadget ...."

- Former Congressman Dan Lungren, Committee on Homeland Security, Full Committee Hearing, September 20, 2012

Fiscal Year 2012 Fusion Center Funding

Of the 32 fusion centers visited, funding profiles differ across the entire spectrum, from those centers that are predominately funded through State or local funds, to those centers relying heavily on Federal funding for general operating expenses (See Figures 1 & 2).[20]

In fiscal year 2012, all of the visited centers expended State and/or local funds. Additionally, most fusion centers expended Federal funds, allocated through DHS preparedness grants, HIDTAs, and several DOJ grant programs. Two fusion centers expended solely State and/or local funds in fiscal year 2012. SHSGP and UASI grants were used to cover 23% of the combined total expended operating funds of the 32 visited fusion centers.[21]

Three of the visited fusion centers are located in areas that were eligible to receive fiscal year 2012 UASI funds, but will no longer be eligible to receive funding under the new fiscal year 2013 UASI structure (five fusion centers in the National Network fall into this category). These fusion centers will consequently lose this as a future funding source. Since fiscal year 2010 and as of fiscal year 2013, 28 fusion centers within the National Network have lost UASI as a funding source.

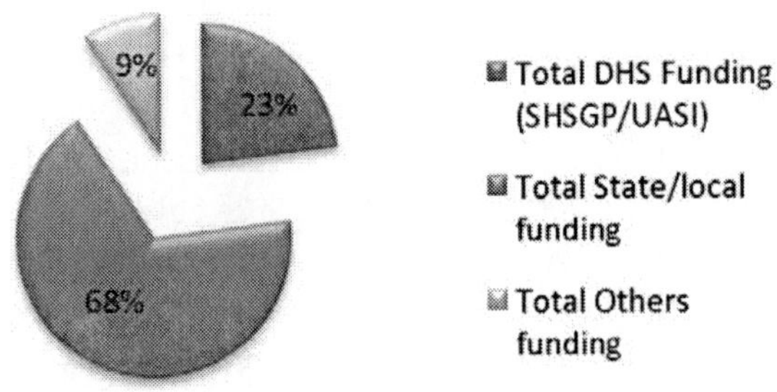

* This reflects the total combined funding expended in Fiscal Year2012.

Figure 1. Visited Fusion Centers' Combined Fiscal Year 2012 Operating Budget Funding Sources.

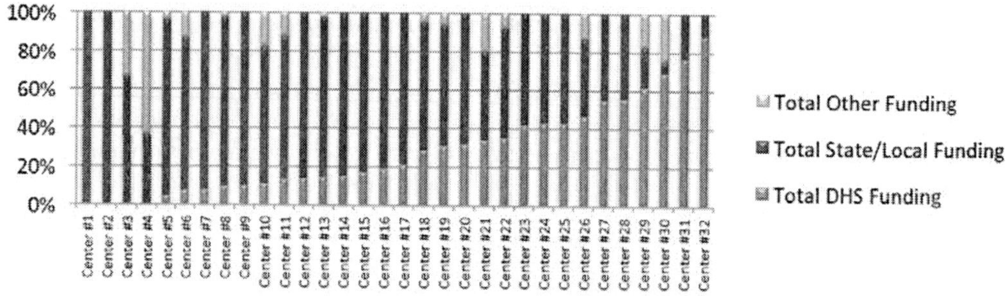

Figure 2. Fiscal Year 2012 Visited Fusion Centers' Funding Expended Sources.

The Current Grant Process

Since 2005, grantees have been able to expend SHSGP and UASI funds to support fusion centers. Beginning in fiscal year 2007, and in each successive year, grant guidance has recognized fusion center enhancement as a priority, and the Federal Government has used the grant process to drive certain initiatives.

In fiscal year 2010, the SHSGP and UASI guidance included strict language prohibiting the use of those funds to support a fusion center, "unless the fusion center is able to certify that privacy and civil rights/civil liberties (CR/CL) protections are in place that are determined to be at least as comprehensive as the ISE Privacy Guidelines by the ISE Privacy Guidelines Committees within 6 months of the award date on this FY10 award."[22]

In fiscal years 2011 and 2012, the grant guidance required States applying for SHSGP funds and urban areas applying for UASI to include at least one investment justification (IJ) directed toward the State or urban area's fusion center, if one exists. Additionally, fusion center IJs submitted for fiscal years 2011 and 2012 were specifically required to prioritize the allocation of funds to any gaps in Critical Operational or Enabling Capabilities, identified during the 2010 Baseline Capabilities Assessment or 2011 Assessment.[23]

In the recently released fiscal year 2013 grant guidance, DHS continues to place fusion center maturation and enhancement among the Nation's priorities for SHSGP and UASI funds. Similar to fiscal years 2011 and 2012, the fiscal year 2013 guidance requires grantees to work with fusion centers to ensure that the IJ is directly aligned to capability gaps identified during the center's 2012 Assessment. Additionally, the fiscal year 2013 guidance recommends that fusion centers continue to mature their analytic capabilities.

In a briefing provided to the Committee, representatives from FEMA's Grant Programs Directorate (GPD) stated that since adding the IJ requirement, grant dollars requested for fusion centers have increased.[24] ***However, FEMA has long acknowledged significant gaps in its ability to provide an accurate accounting of grant funding going to fusion centers. FEMA's inability to accurately account for these funds is unacceptable, and the Committee has been closely monitoring FEMA's progress to correct this serious deficiency.***

In fiscal year 2011, FEMA, in coordination with I&A, developed a new function in the Grant Reporting Tool allowing grantees to check a box indicating projects that support fusion centers. According to GPD, this additional check box improves accuracy and provides a more complete picture of grant funds expended on fusion centers.[25] Unfortunately, while an improvement over previous years, this "self reporting" check box still does not accurately reflect the total amount of grant funds allocated to fusion centers. The Committee is extremely disappointed with these results and will continue to work with FEMA to ensure further improvement in accounting.

In addition to the check box, the fiscal year 2013 grant guidance requires States and urban areas to consolidate all fusion center related projects into a single IJ. The Committee hopes that this new requirement will further enhance FEMA's ability to provide an accurate accounting of grant funds allocated to fusion centers.

Funding Challenges

The Committee spent significant time during the site visits discussing the challenges faced by individual fusion centers due to the current grant process, the most common of which are identified below.

- **Uncertainty of Funding:** The principal budgetary challenge cited by fusion center personnel was uncertainty of funding. Although all of the fusion centers recognize the difficult budget climate at both the State and Federal levels, the inability to budget with a reliable expectation of a fusion center's top line operating budget from year to year reduces the ability to engage in strategic or long term budget planning, or introduce new capabilities into the center.

  Personnel from three fusion centers told the Committee that when their fusion center opened, they immediately implemented a plan to reduce, and eventually eliminate, dependence on Federal grants over a period of years. However, significant, unexpected cuts to the grants were a "shock to the system" and, in at least two of those cases, the States did not have the ability to provide additional funding to make up for the reduced Federal funds. Therefore, a reduction in fusion center capability was the only available solution.

  The continued maturation of the National Network, and its ability to meet the National mission needs, requires a level of sustained base funding to ensure that individual fusion centers are able to grow and maintain capabilities, and adapt to the changing nature of the threat environment. As discussed in The Number of Fusion Centers in the National Network section of this report, the Federal Government should undergo a thorough examination to determine whether grant funds should be targeted to a narrower subset of fusion centers.

  Additionally, DHS should carefully examine other grant and funding models to determine if another would be more effective.

> "It is vital to the security of our homeland that States and localities are able to continue to receive funding for the participation of State and local analysts in fusion centers.... While fusion centers are increasingly seen as national assets given their central role in sharing information across the country, the cost of their operation has been a continuing concern.... Congress, in the Implementing Recommendations of the 9/11 Commission Act of 2007 (P.L. 110-53) ... recognized that sustainment funding for fusion centers necessarily involves Federal support for the hiring and retention of intelligence analyst at fusion centers."
>
> - House Committee on Homeland Security's Committee Report on the "PRICE of Homeland Security Act"
> House Report 110-752, July 10, 2008

- **Period of Performance:** In fiscal year 2012, FEMA reduced the period of performance for SHSGP and UASI from three years to two in an effort to expedite the drawdown of funds. Due to internal State processes, personnel from many fusion centers stated that they often do not receive grant funds until 10 to 12 months after the grant is awarded. Further, in order for State and local grant managers to meet their deadlines, the subgrantees (i.e. the fusion centers) are often required to close their books one to two months prior to the official period end. According to fusion center personnel, this leaves centers with a year or less to actually expend the funds. For many fusion centers, this prohibits or inhibits the ability to use grant funds to hire contract analysts or engage in service agreements, particularly once contract approval time is factored in, which could, in reality, leave only months. Despite the concerns raised by many stakeholders, FEMA kept the period of performance at two years for fiscal year 2013.

  It is unclear what other unintended consequences grantees and subgrantees may be experiencing from the change in the period of performance. FEMA should carefully examine the current environment in which the ultimate intended recipient of grants must operate, to determine whether a return to a three-year period of performance, or other changes, may be necessary. At a minimum, FEMA should guarantee that fusion centers will receive waivers for analyst expenditures.
- **Grant Distribution Process:** According to fusion center personnel, one of the biggest challenges they face is their State's individual processes for SHSGP and UASI fund competition and distribution. Fusion centers are by their very nature in the "prevention business." However, the District of Columbia and 12 of the 20 States visited (representing 19 fusion centers) have emergency management agencies serving as the State Administrative Agency (SAA), the agency designated by the governor to administer homeland security grants.[26] According to personnel at many of the fusion centers, the result has been a tendency to favor response and recovery over prevention and protection in State grant distribution processes.

  DHS's recent grant guidance shows a clear desire to recommit Federal funds to prevention and protection, in addition to response and recovery. However, many fusion center personnel suggested that while the current grant guidance is good, it is not strong enough to ensure fusion centers are fully supported by the States. For example, the guidance requires that one IJ be directed to fusion centers, but does not require a specific amount or percentage of funds to be expended. Therefore, in theory, a State that provides just $1.00 to its fusion center will be in compliance with this requirement.

  Fusion centers that have a close relationship with their State's SAA, and those with SAAs who are well-educated about what the fusion center is and does, appear to fare better in the State grant process. Fusion centers should do everything possible to ensure the SAA is fully educated as to the fusion center's mission and value to the State and/or urban area. The National Network should continue to make education and outreach to State leadership a priority.
- **Future Grant Cycles:** The President's fiscal year 2013 budget request for FEMA proposed a new, consolidated, National Preparedness Grant Program (NPGP). This program would replace a number of the terrorism preparedness grant programs, including SHSGP and UASI. However, the proposal lacked sufficient detail on how

high risk urban areas would apply for funding, a major concern for fusion centers currently receiving UASI funding. The lack of clarity raised further questions as to whether or not fusion centers would remain a National priority under the NPGP.

Given the insufficient level of detail in both the request and further discussions with FEMA officials, and the lack of stakeholder engagement in the proposal's development, there was bicameral, bipartisan concern in Congress with, and opposition to, the NPGP proposal. As a result, the *Consolidated and Further Continuing Appropriations Act of 2013* (Pub. L. 113-6) prohibited FEMA from implementing the NPGP in the absence of authorization by Congress.

Despite this explicit instruction, the Committee was frustrated to see that the President's fiscal year 2014 budget request re-proposed the NPGP, again failing to provide sufficient detail or proposed legislative language for the program's authorization. As a result, the *Fiscal Year 2014 Department of Homeland Security Appropriations Act* (H.R. 2217), which passed the House on June 6, 2013, again prohibits FEMA from using funds to implement this program.

Moving forward, FEMA needs to conduct proper outreach to all stakeholders, including law enforcement agencies and Congress, when considering whether to restructure the grant program. Further, in the coming years, and whether or not there are changes to the grant program, it is imperative that fusion centers remain a National priority in the grant guidance.

Other Grant Sources

With the reduction in available SHSGP, UASI, and State funding, some fusion centers have started to explore non-DHS grant sources. For example, four of the visited centers receive grants from DOJ's Bureau of Justice Assistance. Because of its public health representatives, one fusion center qualifies for Centers for Disease Control and Prevention grants. Further, five of the visited fusion centers benefit from funding through collocation with HIDTA analysts.[27]

The Committee was surprised to learn that many fusion centers had not explored grant sources beyond SHSGP and UASI. The National Network should establish a mechanism by which the individual fusion centers are able to share information regarding nontraditional funding sources.

Analysis & Training

> "[T]he successful use of the legal system to address the first World Trade Center bombing had the side effect of obscuring the need to examine the character and extent of the new threat facing the United States.... The law enforcement process is concerned with proving the guilt of persons apprehend and charged.... The process was meant, by its nature, to mark for the public the events as finished ... It was not designed to ask if the events might be harbingers of worse to come. Nor did it allow for aggregating and analyzing facts to see if they could provide clues to terrorist tactics more generally – methods of entry and finance, and mode of operation inside the United States."
>
> - The 9/11 Commission Report, 2004

Analysis is an area that continues to need significant attention across the National Network. In addition to a generally recognized need to increase the caliber of State and local analysis, healthy and mature fusion centers should look beyond local crime analysis, local criminal investigative support, and the traditional "law enforcement process." As vital players in the Homeland Security Enterprise, and the strategic intelligence component of a given State or region, fusion centers engaging in crime analysis to support tactical and operational intelligence needs, should do so through a lens of strategic threat analysis. As members of the National Network, fusion centers' strategic threat analysis should ultimately be driven by and include a counterterrorism focus.

Fusion centers should be hubs of State and local strategic analysis, "aggregating and analyzing facts to see if they could provide clues to terrorist tactics," asking if events "might be harbingers of worse to come."[28] Ultimately, it is the FBI's responsibility to conduct counterterrorism investigations. However, no single government entity has the mission and capacity to coordinate, gather, and look comprehensively across the massive volume of State and locally owned crime data and SARs and connect those "dots," particularly those related to local crime and, potentially, the nexus between those criminal activities and terrorist activity. This is the principal value proposition for the National Network.

National Mission Analysis

As discussed earlier in this report, membership in the National Network must carry with it certain requirements and expectations; most importantly a partnership in the National mission. ***However, many fusion centers struggle to strike the right balance between meeting State and local mission priorities and National ones, often leaning more heavily toward the State and local priorities. As a result, the National Network, the Federal Government, and therefore the National mission, are not receiving the maximum potential benefit from many of the fusion centers.***

The Committee is aware of stakeholder discussions regarding the possible establishment of special analytic units within fusion centers in an attempt to increase the value derived for the National mission from State and locally held information. The idea of some form of specialized analytic unit has merit as a possible means to achieve greater concentration on National mission areas, provided it could be accomplished without establishing artificial barriers between the fusion center mission sets. The success of any such unit would be contingent upon a mature and healthy fusion center foundation, and any special analytic unit should remain fully entwined with the host fusion center's broader mission space. Such a unit could serve as the primary focal point within the fusion center to engage on Intelligence Community (IC) issues and priorities, while leveraging existing capabilities, resources, and expertise resident in the center. Prior to standing up any such specialized units, stakeholders should comprehensively map out the concept, path forward, and desired end state, and determine metrics to demonstrate success. The Committee will continue to work with stakeholders, to determine whether this or a similar concept, would benefit the National mission.

Further, as discussed in the *DHS and the Fusion Centers* section of this report, the Committee believes that deployment of additional I&A Intelligence Analysts to the fusion centers may enhance National mission-focused analysis derived from State and locally-held information.

Areas for Increased Analytic Focus

As noted earlier, many fusion centers must move beyond tactical analysis and toward greater strategic and counterterrorism analysis, and the need remains for further development of general analytic capability and tradecraft. There is, none-the-less, marked improvement in the analysis performed and products produced by fusion centers in recent years. Two specific areas where the National Network should increase its analytic focus are SAR trend analysis, and CIKR threat and vulnerability analysis. SAR trend analysis is discussed below and CIKR is discussed in the *CIKR, Cybersecurity, & Private Sector Outreach* section of this report.

Suspicious Activity Reporting Trend Analysis

Fusion centers are in the best position to perform SAR trend analysis for their AOR and, ideally, work with other centers regionally to form a comprehensive picture. Most of the fusion centers visited receive and vet SARs in a clearinghouse fashion and, if a potential nexus to terrorism is identified, pass them along to the FBI for possible investigation. While a number of those fusion centers visited regularly publish a "SAR Report," highlighting SARs for law enforcement and first responders, only three engage in more advanced SAR analysis and reporting.[29] SAR trend analysis is an important next phase in fusion center analytic development. I&A should then use that State and local analysis to regularly produce National SAR trend analysis.

To highlight one regional developing best practice, the four fusion centers covering the National Capital Region (NCR) – the Virginia Fusion Center, Northern Virginia Regional Intelligence Center, Washington Regional Threat and Analysis Center, and the Maryland Coordination and Analysis Center – partner to publish a monthly SAR awareness report for the entire NCR. Importantly, given the high threat nature of the region and the high volume of Federal, State, and local law enforcement agencies operating in extremely close proximity, this product helps to provide common situational awareness.

SAR collection is discussed in the *Terrorism Liaison Officer Programs & Suspicious Activity Reporting Collection* section of this report.

Fusion Center Production

The overwhelming majority of visited fusion centers publish specific product lines on a regular basis. Many have a wide variety of products ranging from general situational awareness to officer safety bulletins. In more advanced centers, production includes strategic pieces focusing on terrorist groups, gangs, drugs, and SARs, and their relevance to the fusion centers' AOR.

Not surprisingly, the analysis produced by more mature fusion centers is often more strategic, maintains a more balanced production approach, and demonstrates greater depth than the analysis produced by less mature centers. Generally speaking, the more mature fusion centers are also partnering more frequently with DHS and the FBI to produce joint products, both classified and unclassified.

According to the 2012 National Network of Fusion Centers, Final Report, (2012 Final Report), which published the findings of the 2012 Assessment,"77.9% of the National Network (60 fusion centers) have analytic production plans," an increase from 68.1% in 2011.[30] Formal planning is a significant accomplishment in a fusion center's maturation, and demonstrates a more deliberative approach to analysis. ***These plans should be oriented to***

ensure that fusion centers' production serves their State and local missions as well as the National counterterrorism and broader homeland security missions, and should encourage the continued growth and development of strategic analysis.

In an effort to increase and encourage fusion centers' use of common information sharing platforms, in fiscal year 2013, centers that are leveraging SHSGP and/or UASI funds will be "evaluated based upon compliance with ... [posting] 100 percent (100%) of distributable analytic products (as defined by the annual Assessment process) to the Homeland Security Information Network's (HSIN's) Homeland Security State & Local Intelligence Community of Interest (HS SLIC) as well as any other applicable portals, such as LEO, RISS, their agency portal, etc."[31] The Committee notes DHS's use of the grant guidance to enhance standardization and further improve information sharing across the National Network, and encourages the fusion centers to comply with this requirement in the short term.

Fusion Center Analytic Training

According to the 2012 Final Report, the National Network has, as a whole, reached the second stage in the Maturity Model, the "Emerging Stage."[32]

Although this demonstrates growth in the National Network since 2011, some fusion centers have reached more advanced stages of analytic capability, and require specialized training to sustain and continue to grow their workforce. ***Additionally, many fusion centers still require a significant basic training on analytic tradecraft to improve basic competencies. When asked, fusion center personnel most often stated that the training provided by I&A is excellent, but more is needed, particularly advanced analytic training.***

> "This environment also requires analysts to have the necessary experience, expertise, and training on crime and intelligence analysis functions; tactical, operational, and strategic products; and Intelligence Community oversight of the use of data from sensitive sources."
>
> - Common Competencies for State, Local, and Tribal Intelligence Analysts, June 2010

I & A currently deploys a number of select courses across the country via its Mobile Training Teams (MTT). However, budgetary constraints have limited I&A's ability to deploy the MTTs more broadly. Fusion center analysis will not continue to grow to fully meet National needs without additional and advanced analyst training.

Limited numbers of State and local fusion center analysts have attended the Washington, DC- based in-residence Basic Intelligence Threat Analysis and Mid-level Intelligence Threat Analysis Courses (BITAC & MITAC), developed by I&A primarily for DHS intelligence analysts. Further, I&A has worked with the IC to make some IC-wide training opportunities available to State and local analysts.

Having State and local intelligence analysts trained to Federal analytic standards will go a long way in continuing to break down the divide between Federal and State and local analysis, and would likely increase the utility of fusion center analysis to the National homeland security mission. However, the ability for fusion center analysts to travel to Washington, DC for training can be an obstacle. I&A should continue working with National Network representatives to determine whether alternate combinations of in-residence and virtual coursework, or other models, would better serve the needs of fusion center analysts. The Committee was encouraged to learn recently of I&A's plan to pilot the BITAC as a combination online and in-residence course in fiscal year 2013, and looks forward to learning the results of that pilot.

Fusion center personnel expressed a need for increased Federal training opportunities in CIKR threat and risk analysis and cybersecurity analysis. DHS should explore further incorporating fusion center analysts into DHS's broader cybersecurity workforce training programs, and developing supplementary CIKR training modules to ensure the fusion centers have the capability to be full mission partners.

Fusion Center Analyst Career Path and Training Roadmap

State and local intelligence analysts come from a wide variety of backgrounds including sworn officers, crime analysts, recent graduates, contract analysts, and seasoned former DOD and IC analysts. ***However, as with any career, the best and brightest are often poached by agencies offering more money and greater career advancement potential. In many cases it appears the fusion centers have become a training ground for future Federal intelligence analysts.***

Throughout the visits, the Committee heard consistent pleas for aid to increase the quality, pool, and retention of fusion center analysts. Increased and advanced training opportunities and analyst career paths are essential to achieve National Network analytic capability and capacity improvements. Further, established State and local intelligence analyst career paths are necessary to grow and retain talented fusion center analysts, and develop future fusion center leaders.

The Federal Government and stakeholders should continue efforts to examine options and implement a plan to address these issues. Federal assistance could include further expansion of training opportunities and guidance in establishing an analyst training roadmap defining analytic competencies. Any such roadmap should be focused to ensure a level of commonality and interoperability between Federal, State, and local intelligence analysts. The National Network is also encouraged to develop its own specialized, training programs for fusion center analysts nationwide.

Partnerships and Coordination

An important opportunity for growth in the National Network is the partnership between analysts in different fusion centers. Sharing locally-gathered information between analysts, bringing together expertise, and challenging assumptions are at the heart of intelligence analysis. There are many ongoing joint projects, not only among fusion centers in a single region, but also across the country. More should be done to increase and encourage these partnerships.

Opportunities for analytic mentorship both within and between fusion centers should be exploited to the fullest extent possible and formalized across the National Network. Although not a complete substitute, paring senior analysts with junior analysts, and establishing analytic partnerships between mature and immature fusion centers could go a long way toward mitigating current training gaps.

Organized analytic coordination between fusion centers is an area beginning to show growth within the National Network, and should be further enhanced. The Northeast Fusion

Center Region's effort, where all nine fusion centers are working to establish a program of analysis to identify regional threats and guide production, should serve as a model for regional coordination. The program facilitates collaboration and deconfliction, while also serving as a mechanism to ensure regional threats are analyzed by assigning fusion center "leads" to specific topics. California's Lead Analyst Working Group serves a similar function across the State's six fusion centers. Other regions should consider similar models.

Terrorism Liaison Officer Programs & Suspicious Activity Report Collection

> "TLOs are a vital link in keeping those engaged in public safety professions aware of current terrorist tactics, techniques, and practices. Through the diligent performance of their duties, public safety personnel are alerted to terrorism indicators and warnings that might otherwise go unreported."
>
> - Terrorism Liaison Officer Information Network
> Joint Regional Intelligence Center, www.TLO.org

Terrorism Liaison Officers

One of the greatest value propositions for the National Network, and also an area recommended for immediate growth, are the TLO, and TLO-like, programs.[33] TLO programs are vehicles that enable police officers, emergency response providers, public health officials, the private sector, and other fusion partners to achieve broader situational awareness and become formally trained partners in the National counterterrorism mission. TLOs are the conduit between the fusion centers and their home agencies, and should ultimately number enough to cover all of a fusion centers' AOR. Further, some fusion centers also leverage their TLO network to serve broader homeland security mission needs. TLO networks can be an effective tool for communication and information sharing, although counterterrorism should remain the primary focus of the TLO programs.

In addition to quantity and training, diversity is key to strong and effective TLO programs. Law enforcement is the most well represented constituency in the majority of TLO programs, primarily a result of fusion centers' law enforcement roots. However, fusion centers that do not incorporate other, non-law enforcement, sectors into their TLO program are leaving a significant gap. TLO programs should include fire, EMS, public health, and the private sectors. Given that a primary National Network function is outreach to, and two-way communication with, the front lines, it is impossible for fusion centers to be robust National counterterrorism mission partners without a strong TLO program. In the most basic programs, TLOs serve as a point of contact to disseminate fusion center information and products to the field. This is a first step in TLO program development. In many States, TLOs are also the primary link to report SARs to the fusion centers. In more advanced programs, TLOs receive significantly more training to educate their home agencies on threats and trends, and conduct outreach to critical infrastructure owners and community groups.

The Committee observed a number of very strong TLO programs and identified best practices, but notes that many TLO programs are in their infancy, have been slow to roll out, are too small to provide adequate coverage, or are limited in the sectors involved (i.e. only law enforcement). At the time of the site visits, seven fusion centers were in the very early stages of developing their TLO programs.

Additionally, six fusion centers do not have a formal TLO program and also do not appear to have plans to develop one.[34] Further, some centers with formal programs had not conducted the broad outreach necessary to establish TLOs throughout their entire AOR.

The disparity in TLO programs, including training requirements that range from a single course that lasts only a few hours, to one that lasts several days and includes frequent supplemental training, would likely benefit from a thorough Network- wide review. There may be opportunities for States to combine training elements, reduce costs, and increase overall effectiveness and awareness of best practices.

Given the Federal benefit from a strong nationwide network of TLOs, the Federal Government should continue to work with fusion centers to strengthen the TLO programs across the National Network. The Committee notes current Federal efforts in this regard – including sponsoring the March 2012 National Fusion Liaison Officer Program Workshop, the Fusion Liaison Officer (FLO) Technical Assistance Program, and bimonthly calls with FLO coordinators – as a step forward in this effort. The fusion centers, DHS, the FBI, and other stakeholders should come together and determine what, if anything, may lend itself to TLO standardization across the National Network. This is also an area DHS could explore as a possible initiative in future years' grant guidance.

> "In June 2011, the Lakewood, Colorado Police Department received information that an individual had placed two improvised explosive devices at a Borders bookstore at the Colorado Mills Mall. Due to the nature of the crime, the Lakewood Police Department notified the FBI of the incident, who in turn activated the JTTF. Agents from the JTTF and the Bureau of Alcohol, Tobacco, Firearms, and Explosives (ATF) responded to the scene and began collecting information, which they passed to the Colorado Information Analysis Center (CIAC). A few hours later, the CIAC sent information to fusion centers nationwide and Terrorism Liaison Officers (TLO) statewide, requesting information that may relate to the incident. Less than 15 minutes after sending this information to Colorado TLOs, the CIAC received vital information from a State Trooper. Approximately twenty-four hours earlier, the suspect crashed his vehicle and was taken into custody for Felony Menacing and Driving Under the Influence of Alcohol. After receiving the information from the CIAC, the arresting officer believed the suspect he arrested was also the suspect in the bookstore- bombing attempt. Concurrently, and while the investigation was still active, the CIAC received another lead from a different TLO which linked the suspect to yet another device that partially detonated near a hotel a short distance from the bookstore. The CIAC in turn passed this information to the FBI JTTF to further support the investigation and the subject was arrested."
>
> - Provided by the FBI to the Committee, October 23, 2012

Although best practices can be drawn from elements of many different TLO programs, a few highlights are below:

- Central Florida Intelligence Exchange (CFIX) Intelligence Liaison Officers' (ILOs) responsibilities include further analyzing CFIX products and tailoring them to the

ILOs' individual county prior to further distribution. Additionally, the CFIX assigns ILO Coordinators to track ILO work and ensure they are, in fact, further disseminating CFIX information. CFIX ILOs are nominated and selected based on gaps in a discipline (law enforcement, fire, health, etc.) to ensure broad coverage. Florida is currently in the final stages of developing a statewide concept of operations to harmonize ILO programs across the State.

- California's STAS includes a coordinated statewide TLO program. Although TLOs are recruited by individual fusion centers, training and certification are managed jointly across the STAS, increasing opportunities for all.
- The New Hampshire Information & Analysis Center (NHIAC) ties its ILO program to grant expenditures. ILOs' home agencies receive salary reimbursements for the certified time their officers spend working with the NHIAC in an ILO capacity, namely improving information sharing between the NHIAC and the ILOs' home agencies in line with National priorities and capabilities.
- Robust TLO programs should recruit beyond traditional law enforcement, and incorporate partners from a variety of disciplines. Many fusion centers have, or are in the early stages of incorporating, fire services and EMS TLOs. Of the fusion centers visited, 15 have emergency response TLOs (fire, EMS, health, and emergency managers). Nine fusion centers have programs that train private sector/CIKR representatives in a similar capacity, and seven have also partnered with DOD.
- As standard operating procedure, the vast majority of visited fusion centers consistently reach back to TLOs in an effort to "close the loop" following receipt and vetting of SARs. Letting TLOs (or other reporting agencies) know the disposition of SARs is vital to maintaining an active TLO Network and encourages further reporting and information sharing. This should be standard practice across the National Network, and those fusion centers not currently doing so should immediately take steps to conduct this follow-up.
    - This recommendation also applies to the FBI when it receives SARs passed from the fusion centers. Closing the loop is an important practice to maintain strong partnerships. Additionally, this type of feedback may help the FBI establish a more detailed tracking methodology for the disposition of information it receives from the fusion centers or other State and local partners.

Suspicious Activity Reporting Collection and Vetting

Enabled by robust TLO programs, SAR collection and vetting, awareness bulletins, and trend analysis are an important part of fusion center operations. No single government entity has the capacity or mission to vet the volume and broad array of SARs reported nationwide by State and locals. Although the FBI is ultimately responsible for investigating terrorism-related SARs, incoming reporting to fusion centers also includes drug, gang, and other crime-related activities that fall within the fusion centers' jurisdiction. ***Therefore, fusion centers should be the primary collection point and should be staffed to vet all incoming SARs within their AOR.*** It is absolutely vital, however, that a system be in place to ensure that the FBI immediately receives any SAR deemed to have a possible nexus to terrorism. Insofar as the Committee assessed, timely transmission of SARs to the FBI appears to be occurring in all of the visited fusion centers.

During the site visits, 30 fusion centers were identified as the primary collection point for SARs in their area, and two had limited or no official SAR collection, vetting, or analysis program. Subsequently, as of the April 2013 survey, one of those two fusion centers had taken steps toward developing a SAR collection and vetting program. The Committee is extremely concerned that a lack of SAR collection, vetting, and analysis by fusion centers may result in missed opportunities and a heightened security risk.

As noted in the *Analysis & Training* section of this report, SAR trend analysis is an area needing increased fusion center attention.

Shared Space and eGuardian

Ongoing FBI and Nationwide SAR Initiative (NSI)-Program Management Office (PMO) efforts to address interoperability challenges between eGuardian and the Shared Spaces appear to be having a positive effect. During the site visits, the Committee noted significant remaining challenges, particularly ensuring that information entered into one system fully populated into the other. Additionally, due to individual State laws regarding retention of information or relationships with the FBI, several fusion centers had chosen to exclusively enter SARs into one system over the other. The result appeared to be a continued risk that neither the Shared Spaces nor eGuardian included all vetted SARs, despite efforts to eliminate that risk, which the Committee then-noted as a significant gap.

At the time of the Committee's site visits, 15 fusion centers reported entering SARs into both systems; 11 reported entering SARs into only one of the two systems, for various reasons; and five did not enter SARs into either system. According to survey data received in April 2013, 17 fusion centers reported that they now enter SARs into both systems; 12 enter SARs into one of the two systems; and three still do not enter into either system.

Based upon information received from DOJ and the FBI on July 15, 2013, the NSI-PMO and the FBI's Guardian Management Unit appear to have fully addressed the concerns noted above by recently fully automating the push of SARs between the systems.[35] The Committee notes this as a significant milestone in breaking down barriers to information sharing.

DHS, DOJ, and stakeholders demonstrated a significant effort to improve commonality in SAR reporting and sharing through the development of "A Call To Action: A Unified Message Regarding the Need to Support Suspicious Activity Reporting and Training."[36] Nonetheless, the Committee continues to question the prudence of having two separate systems for sharing terrorism-related SARs. In December 2011, then-Chairman King, along with Ranking Member Bennie Thompson, and Senate Committee on Homeland Security and Governmental Affairs Chairman Joseph Lieberman and Ranking Member Susan Collins, asked the Government Accountability Office (GAO) to review the NSI, including Shared Space and eGuardian. The results of that study were published in March 2013.[37]

The Committee is aware that the NSI is currently undergoing a significant overhaul, with an anticipated plan release expected in the August-September 2013 timeframe. The Committee looks forward to receiving a briefing on the new proposal, and will continue to conduct oversight of the NSI to ensure SARs are being collected, shared, and disposed of in the most effective and efficient manner to protect the Homeland.

Customers & Leveraging the Power of the National Network

Individual Fusion Centers

The diversity of individual fusion centers' customer sets varies widely. The Committee observed that fusion centers "owned" by a single organization, with little outside representation in the center, are often narrowly focused on a small subset of customers or even a single primary customer. These fusion centers also tend to be more focused on tactical crime analysis and investigative support rather than strategic threat analysis. ***As these fusion centers continue to mature they should incorporate nontraditional partners, thereby strengthening and expanding their analysis and its applicability to additional customers.***

A mature fusion center should be incorporated into its State's broader statewide information sharing plan, and its customer base should be multi-layered to include State and local leadership, law enforcement, emergency response providers, critical infrastructure, the private sector, the National Network, and the Federal Government. In the case of States with a single statewide fusion center, that center must include not only its immediate local area, but the entire State within its customer set. A wide variety of relevant customers leads to an increased general awareness of the fusion center and its mission. Many fusion centers have seen this yield increased formal partnerships, and greater information sharing and reporting to the fusion center. In many cases, this appears to have also led to an increase in resources dedicated to the fusion center from State and local fusion partners.

Fusion center threat analysis should be used to assist State and local leaders in prevention and preparedness resource allocation. Since many governors, State homeland security advisors, and local law enforcement leaders hold security clearances, fusion centers should not shy away from utilizing the classified information available to them to create the most comprehensive threat picture possible for cleared customers.

The extent to which fusion centers should utilize classified information and publish classified products continues to be a subject of some debate, and is discussed further in the *Access To and Use Of Classified Networks and Information* section of this report.

The National Network

The National Network's customer set should mirror that of individual fusion centers. Meaning, the entire Network can and should be leveraged for the benefit of all those operating within it. ***Participation in the National Network as a true National mission partner should mean having the power of the other 77 fusion centers across the country readily available and accessible to any individual center.***

When asked about their interactions with other centers, fusion center personnel consistently gave a strong, positive response. Most fusion center personnel noted a subset of other centers they partnered with more frequently than others, often due to shared analytic interest, expertise, or threat. Fusion center personnel frequently commented that even without a personal relationship with another center, participation in the National Network means having a trusted partner on the other end of the phone.

The National Network should continue its efforts to strengthen partnerships between fusion centers, to include joint training opportunities and analytic collaboration across the National Network, like that discussed in the *Analysis & Training* section of this report.

Security Clearances

> "Results from the 2012 Assessment indicate that all 77 fusion centers (100%) have personnel with at least a Secret-level security clearance. Furthermore, of the 1,966 SLTT personnel identified by fusion centers as needing security clearances, 1,618 (82.3%) have been granted a clearances. Of the remaining SLTT personnel identified as needing a clearance, 210 (10.7%) have submitted clearance requests and are awaiting final adjudication. Despite their success in clearing staff and retaining cleared staff, fusion centers reported that they anticipate the need to submit approximately 500 new SLTT clearance requests within the next 12 months, mainly because of staff turnover."
>
> - 2012 National Network of Fusion Centers, Final Report
> June 2013

All of the 32 visited fusion centers have State and/or local analysts cleared to at least the Secret level, while 18 have at least one State and/or local staff member cleared to Top Secret (TS) or TS//SCI.[38] At least two of the fusion center directors did not currently hold a security clearance, but were in process of applying at the time of the Committee visit. In at least seven instances, the fusion center director holds a lower level clearance than individuals reporting to him or her, usually occurring when local detectives assigned to the Joint Terrorism Task Force (JTTF) fall within the fusion center chain of command. Additionally, due to a recent high turnover of fusion center directors across the National Network, the Committee believes the number of directors currently without a clearance, or holding a lower level clearance, may be much higher.

DHS appears to be doing a capable job clearing State and local fusion center personnel to the Secret level; the Committee heard surprisingly few complaints about the process from fusion center personnel. As a matter of general policy, DHS does not clear any fusion center staff higher than the Secret level; when granted, it is the FBI that provides TS or TS//SCI clearances to fusion center personnel. Insofar as the Committee could ascertain from field research, these higher-level clearances are generally sponsored as a result of a positive existing relationship between the fusion center and the local FBI, rather than a concerted effort from FBI Headquarters to clear fusion center personnel.

The Committee requested additional information from FBI Headquarters regarding the formal policies surrounding granting TS and TS//SCI clearances to fusion center personnel. However, there appears to be a significant disconnect between the information provided by FBI Headquarters and the field situation described by fusion center personnel. The Committee will work closely with the FBI and fusion centers to ensure a common policy is implemented, and stakeholders are aware of that policy.

Additionally, as a matter of practice, DHS grants governors and State homeland security advisors TS clearances, further expanding a gap in information sharing with the very organizations designed to support State and local policymakers- the fusion centers. DHS should revisit its State and local clearance policies to determine whether it has inadvertently set up a wall between the fusion centers and policymakers, making it more difficult for fusion centers to fully support State leadership.

Given the complexity of threats facing the Nation, and the need for collaboration across all levels of government, it seems reasonable for at least one individual within each fusion center, ostensibly the director, to hold a TS or TS//SCI clearance. This would allow increased awareness of threats and encourage greater interaction and information exchange between State and local leadership and the FBI field offices and JTTFs. Even if fusion center directors are unable to further disseminate the detailed information to their analysts, enhanced awareness would allow them to better focus their center's analysis and resources to address current threats, better support their customers, and serve as stronger National mission partners.

In an effort to understand the disparity in security clearances granted to State and local personnel and therefore their access to classified information, DHS, the FBI, and the PM-ISE should complete a thorough review of security clearances held not only by fusion center personnel, but also by all State and local government personnel. Additionally, TS and TS//SCI security clearances for State and local fusion center personnel, and consistent and enhanced access to classified information, should be part of the conversation surrounding the National Strategy for Fusion Centers and the Federal Strategy for Fusion Centers, discussed in the A National Strategy for Fusion Centers & Measuring Success section of this report.

Access to and Use of Classified Networks and Information

> "[T]he biggest impediment to all-source analysis – to a greater likelihood of connecting the dots – is the human or systemic resistance to sharing information."
>
> - The 9/11 Commission Report, 2004

The Wikileaks case remind us that the post-9/11 era's vital "need to share" must be carefully balanced with accountability, reasonable restrictions on information sharing. The Committee is cognizant of the extreme difficulty in achieving this balance, both in terms of general policy and technological hurdles. ***However, although greatly improved since September 11, 2001, State and local access to, and use of, classified information continues to be a challenge.***

Not surprisingly, advanced fusion centers with well-trained, career intelligence analysts – many former IC or DOD analysts – voiced the greatest concern over the limitations of classified information access in the fusion centers. Additionally, and troublingly, several of the fusion centers visited make little or no regular use of classified information in their analysis. Some fusion center personnel went so far as to note that they see little value in it beyond general situational awareness, because they are operating at the Unclassified or Sensitive-But-Unclassified (SBU) level to serve their uncleared law enforcement customers.

Although fusion centers should operate primarily at the Unclassified or SBU level to meet the majority of their customers' needs, the ability to utilize classified information to guide analytic priorities, shape Unclassified or SBU production, and create classified threat analysis, is a sign of fusion center maturity. Fusion centers should ensure analysts understand how to use classified information in developing a comprehensive threat picture for State and local leadership and National mission partners. This local picture should then be fused with other information to create statewide and multi-State regional analysis, and used by I&A, the FBI, and other Federal partners to develop a National threat picture.

Homeland Secure Data Network (HSDN)

Twenty-nine of the visited fusion centers have DHS' HSDN Secret network installed on site, and two others have off-site access due to recent facilities moves. As of July 15, 2013, 66 fusion centers across the National Network currently have access to HSDN either within the center or onsite.[39]

Fusion centers without HSDN, or other classified network connectivity, are at a disadvantage and are a weak link in the National Network. It not only leaves State and local personnel without classified access, but also leaves the IO without onsite access, thus compounding the information gap. IOs at those fusion centers have creatively developed workarounds (for example, coordinating with local Federal field offices for classified connectivity), but they are cumbersome and far less than ideal.

Given a variety of factors, DHS is currently unable to predict when it will complete HSDN deployment to the fusion centers, although it has tentative plans to deploy HSDN to five additional centers across fiscal years 2013 and 2014.[40] DHS should work to further prioritize and accelerate the HSDN deployment schedule, and achieve full installation at fusion centers as quickly as possible. DHS should also continue rigorous development of analytic and collaborative tools, and requisite training, to further encourage the use of classified information for advanced analysis.

The White List

At nearly every fusion center visited, the Committee heard concerns about the "White List" – a relatively short list of classified webpages accessible by cleared State and local fusion center personnel via the HSDN interconnection to DOD's Secret network, SIPRNet.

The Committee received a briefing from DHS and DOD regarding efforts underway to increase State and local access to information on SIPRNet.[41] As laid out, between the DHS vetting and DOD approval processes, each request will take approximately four weeks before users are granted access (if granted), assuming there aren't extenuating circumstances requiring additional steps. The Committee recognizes the difficult hurdles DOD faces in clearing information with content managers and originators, but believes this delay is potentially dangerous to homeland security. In many cases, waiting a month for access may be a frustration, but not a problem. In other instances, information may be of depreciating value as time passes, or potentially cause an increased risk to the Nation. By its very nature, intelligence is perishable. Although there are important reasons to restrict access, there is clear value in well-trained State and local intelligence analysts having access to a broader subset of Federally-held classified information than is currently available to them.

DHS should identify fusion centers that currently maximize classified information in its analysis and work with them to test the new access request system. Additionally, DHS and DOD should immediately work to reduce the current best-case timeframe required for access approval.

Further, DOD, with the help of I&A, and in consultation with other IC partners, should be more proactive in identifying information sets residing on SIPRNet that meet fusion centers' National mission objectives, and further their ability to assist Federal partners. DOD should also consult experienced fusion center analysts (particularly those former-IC and former DOD intelligence analysts), and the new Joint Counterterrorism Assessment Team for assistance in identifying relevant information.[42]

Following an apparent breakdown earlier this year, the Committee understands that DOD and DHS are again making progress to improve the process, and notes the recent addition of several sites to the White List. The Committee expects to receive a briefing on the updated process in the coming weeks, and will continue to exercise rigorous oversight over the White List processes to ensure its effectiveness in information sharing.

FBINet

According to the June 2012 Information Sharing Environment, Annual Report to the Congress, the FBI's Secret network, FBINet, is installed in 47 fusion centers.[43] ***However, the Committee found that direct State and local access is inconsistent across the 32 visited fusion centers.***

According to data provided by DHS that was collected as part of the 2012 Assessment, 17 of the visited fusion centers have at least one State and local partner with access to FBINet. However, the data collected as part of the Assessment process does not differentiate between State and local personnel working in a fusion center and fusion center personnel assigned to a JTTF. This is a gap in understanding fusion center access to FBINet. Due to restrictions in information sharing outside of the JTTFs and the disparity in security clearances, State and local access to FBINet within a JTTF is not equivalent to fusion center personnel having onsite access. The Committee is continuing to investigate information sharing processes between the FBI and the fusion centers as part of its ongoing investigation into the recent terrorist attack in Boston.

The Committee heard at least three different versions of what fusion center personnel believe to be the "Official FBI Headquarters Policy" for State and local access to FBINet. Specifically: State and local access requires that the individual be deputized as a JTTF Task Force Officer; access requires direct line supervision of an FBI analyst (for example, if a fusion center's lead analyst is an FBI analyst, then local analysts falling in that chain of command could have access); or no one other than an FBI analyst or agent is allowed direct access to FBINet.

A similar disparity existed in IO access to FBINet located within the visited fusion centers. In some cases the IO was allowed to complete requisite training and access FBINet. In other cases, there appeared to be no mechanism for the IO to be granted access. This leads the Committee to conclude that the personal relationships between State, locals, DHS, and FBI in the field continue to be a driving factor in information sharing between them. The Committee applauds those individuals who continue to initiate information sharing improvements but, as noted earlier in this report, personal relationships cannot be the foundation for vital homeland security information sharing.

In an effort to ensure pre-9/11 paradigms and personal biases do not stand in the way of information sharing, the FBI should undergo a thorough review to understand current State and local access to FBINet. Further, the FBI, in consultation with State and local partners, DHS, and the PM-ISE, should establish standards to support more consistent access to FBINet for fusion center personnel and ensure a broad awareness of those standards among its homeland security partners. Additionally, the FBI and DHS should work together to establish a formal policy and process regarding IO access to FBINet in the field.

HSIN and Technology Standardization

Homeland Security Information Network

DHS is currently in the process of rolling out "HSIN 3.0." In June 2013, DHS completed full migration of State, local, and territorial users onto the new HSIN platform, and is currently working to complete the migration of Federal users. DHS anticipates complete migration of all users by July 31, 2013.[44]

> "The mission of HSIN is to provide stakeholders across the Homeland Security Enterprise with effective and efficient collaboration tools for decision making, secure access to data, and accurate, timely information sharing and situational awareness."
>
> - DHS Briefing to the Committee
> April 2012

It is well known that HSIN was plagued by constant criticism from its inception and DHS continues to work toward significant improvement. ***To date, however, the Committee has received word of relatively few issues following the recent user migration, despite inquires to a number of State and local fusion center representatives.***

At the time of the site visits, the majority of visited fusion centers utilized HSIN, but to varying degrees. Some fusion centers queried it as an information source only, others maintained a local portal, and for others HSIN is their primary information sharing and analytic platform. Only a few fusion centers stated that they made little to no use of HSIN because of the system's historic problems.

Almost all fusion centers expressed concern about the ongoing HSIN issues at the time of the site visits, but those familiar with the HSIN 3.0 pilot seemed hopeful for the future. Many fusion centers said that they would consider increasing their HSIN usage, potentially even migrating from their current systems to HSIN, but were waiting to be sure HSIN 3.0 delivers all of the necessary capabilities.

By most State and local accounts, DHS has done significant outreach to the fusion centers over the past 18-24 months to solicit user feedback on HSIN capabilities. DHS must continue its efforts to ensure that all users are fully trained on its use and new capabilities, and solicit user feedback. DHS should further leverage its field representatives currently working with fusion centers – particularly the IOs and I&A's Regional Directors (RD), component intelligence analysts, and Protective Security Advisors (PSA) – to serve as HSIN mission advocates.

The Committee heard from some fusion centers that had realized significant cost savings by increasing HSIN usage; for example, utilizing the virtual meeting capability in order to cut down on travel costs. There may be ways to leverage HSIN capability, for both cost savings and programmatic outreach, that fusion centers simply have not considered. Fusion centers are encouraged to highlight their unique uses and cost savings to inform and educate other fusion centers across the National Network.

According to DHS, it is working to develop measures of HSIN success. The Committee is gratified to know that the HSIN Program Management Office recognizes that numbers of users alone does not measure the platform's viability and value to its users.[45] The Committee looks forward to receiving updates from DHS and stakeholders on its use and growth across the National Network.

Technology Standardization

A level of technology standardization is necessary to allow interoperability between Federal, State, and local analysts. The proliferation of fusion center investments in proprietary software and systems has grown considerably over the years. Many private companies have developed fixes to a lack of interoperability and disparate datasets, and many fusion centers have purchased one of any number of those fixes. Some centers have even developed their own in house, closed, statewide information sharing system while others primarily utilize Federal systems.

The situation is not significantly different at the Federal level, where any number of information sharing systems exist across all classification levels. Agencies developed similar yet different systems with the stated goal of enhancing information sharing and break down stovepipes, but this has resulted in there being no single National system for comprehensive nationwide counterterrorism and threat information sharing.

There are clear technological hurdles involved with user access controls, data security, and privacy protection requirements that would come from merging systems. However, in the current fiscal climate, Federal, State, and local governments cannot afford to fund and maintain numerous nearly duplicative systems. Additionally, the continued proliferation of databases and information sharing platforms continues to challenge intelligence analysts at all levels and, in the end, makes the Homeland less safe.

The Committee notes the inclusion of a single SBU platform as an Attribute of a "mature" National Network in the Maturity Model, and agrees that this must be a goal.[46] However, fusion centers likely cannot achieve this on their own, and the need for real leadership is clear. The Executive Branch should work with Congressional oversight committees and State and local stakeholders to determine an appropriate path forward, potentially merging similar Federal systems.

Fusion Centers & Emergency Response

> "The need for first responders to receive vital intelligence information to mitigate, respond to, and recover from terrorist attacks or natural disasters is far too great to limit the Intelligence and Information Sharing core capability to the prevention and protection frameworks."
>
> - Chairman Peter T. King, Congressman Gus Bilirakis, & Former Congressman Robert Turner, June 27,2012 Letter to Secretary Janet Napolitano, advocating for the inclusion of the intelligence and information sharing core capability to the Mitigation, Response, and Recovery Frameworks required by Presidential Policy Directive - 8

First Responders & Public Health in the Fusion Centers

The value of incorporating the first responder and public health communities into fusion centers must not be understated. The fire, EMS, and public health sectors can be

invaluable fusion partners, proving tailored expertise as analysts, and distinctive insight as TLOs. Further, the situational awareness and safety information provided by the fusion centers should be an important factor in emergency planning and response.

Given that most fusion centers were born out of law enforcement agencies, the inclusion of fire analysts, fire liaisons, and public health officials in fusion centers is a relatively new phenomenon. While the vast majority of the visited fusion centers are taking steps to partner with local fire services and some are also partnering with their local health sector, the Committee was disheartened that a small handful of fusion centers remain resistant to establishing those partnerships. At one fusion center, personnel went so far as to note that because they do not consider themselves an "all hazards" center, fire and EMS are not necessary fusion partners. This is shortsighted.

By their nature, fusion centers are intended to gather, analyze, and share information from and with a variety of sources. Further, given the wide range of threats and terrorist tactics for which the Homeland must be prepared, fusions centers should not so easily dismiss nontraditional partners such as fire or EMS. Fusion centers lacking robust partnerships outside of the law enforcement community should make obtaining such partnerships an immediate priority.

Of the 32 visited fusion centers, 21 currently have at least one fire analyst or representative assigned either part or full time to the fusion center and 13 have at least one part- or full-time public health analyst assigned. As noted earlier, 15 fusion centers have emergency services TLOs (fire, EMS, public health, and emergency management). The Committee identified the exceptionally strong relationship between law enforcement and fire services existing at the Orange County Intelligence Assessment Center as a best practice.

Several visited fusion centers regularly publish products for the emergency services community, including descriptions of events and their applicability to fire and EMS, and articles specifically tailored for their operating environment. The Committee identified bulletins published by the San Diego Law Enforcement Coordination Center and the Northern Virginia Regional Intelligence Center among current best practices.

Fusion centers should work to increase outreach to the fire, EMS, and public health sectors, and bring them into the centers as full fusion partners. Fusion centers should also work with first responders to increase suspicious activity recognition and reporting, while protecting privacy and civil liberties.

> "When I served as US Attorney for the Southern District of Indiana, I very proudly helped establish the Indiana Intelligence Fusion Center. I recently had the opportunity to visit it again as a Member of Congress. I was then, and I remain, a firm believer in the value of both individual fusion centers and the National Network of Fusion Centers. Fusion centers are a vital partner in the vast national homeland security mission space including, in many cases, a partner in emergency response and recovery efforts."
>
> - Congresswoman Susan W. Brooks, Question for the Record, Committee on Homeland Security, Full Committee Hearing, April 18, 2013

Disaster Response & Recovery

As noted in the *Fusion Centers & the National Mission* section of this report, some fusion centers have become an important part of State and local disaster response and recovery efforts. For example, the New Jersey ROIC – which is collocated with the New Jersey EOC –

recently played a significant role in information sharing and establishing a common operating picture for New Jersey's Hurricane Sandy response and recovery efforts.

According to information provided by the ROIC, FEMA, and I&A, during New Jersey's Hurricane Sandy response the fusion center became more aligned with the EOC and the State leveraged the fusion center's established communications channels – including the FLO program – to distribute information from the EOC to law enforcement, first responders, public health, and State and local emergency managers. The ROIC disseminated over 700 situational awareness reports to over 9,000 customers in the three weeks immediately following the hurricane, on topics ranging from providing the location of operational gas stations, shelters, and food distributions sites, to gathering and analyzing information on storm-related criminal activities, with the goal of enabling a more effective deployment of resources.

The Committee notes the Colorado Information Analysis Center's (CIAC) significant role in response and recovery efforts during the State's 2012 wildfires as another best practice. According to information provided by the CIAC, in June 2012 the CIAC deployed two Mobile Analytical Response Teams to Incident Command Posts around the High Park Fire and Waldo Canyon Fire. These teams helped streamline the communications flow, providing decision- makers with timely information. Additionally, these teams produced tailored "Flash Reports" summarizing Incident Command Post briefings, and disseminated them to the decision-makers, including the Governor's office. Further, during the wildfires emergency managers and firefighters from the affected and surrounding areas, who were not already TLOs, were added to CIAC dissemination lists to improve the information flow. Over the course of the 2012 wildfire season, CIAC analysts produced and disseminated over 300 Flash Reports.

The CIAC noted that Mobile Analytic Response Teams also supported the arson investigations surrounding some of the wildfires. According to the CIAC, these deployed analysts utilized information gathered from tips, leads, and Incident Command Post briefings to produce predictive analysis that assisted law enforcement officials during the investigation.

> "The goal is to rapidly identify emerging threats; support multidisciplinary, proactive, and community-focused problem-solving activities; support predictive analysis capabilities; and improve the delivery of emergency and nonemergency services."
>
> - Fusion Center Guidelines, 2006

A lack of communication and coordination between prevention and response organizations can impede the Nation's preparedness and response efforts. Although many fusion centers and emergency managers are actively working to establish or improve these relationships, there are still many States and urban areas where there appears to be a continued general lack of understanding of how these disciplines can come together to better serve their communities. In addition to the analytic collaboration described above, it is essential to the Nation's preparedness that fusion centers and State and local emergency managers clearly define – in advance – the roles and responsibilities of each participating partner in an active disaster or steady state. Even those States and urban areas maintaining strictly counterterrorism or "all crimes" analytic fusion centers may find it helpful to explore the potential benefits of a formal response and recovery engagement strategy between their fusion center and emergency response agencies.

The Committee will continue to work with fusion centers, I&A, FEMA, and other stakeholders to better understand the current and potential relationship between prevention and response agencies at the Federal, State, and local levels, during both a steady state and active disasters, and explore how various levels of integration or coordination may affect response and recovery efforts nationwide. At a minimum, it appears that even non-"all hazards," purely analytic- focused, fusion centers – perhaps through their TLO networks – could help facilitate an additional level of communications and outreach with law enforcement and first responders during the response and recovery phases of a natural disaster or terrorist attack. The Committee was encouraged to learn of plans for an upcoming meeting, hosted by I&A and FEMA, to bring fusion center directors together with emergency managers to discuss best practices, challenges, and opportunities for enhanced collaboration. The Committee looks forward to receiving an after action report from this meeting.

Stakeholders should explore these relationships and fusion centers' potential role when establishing a National Strategy for Fusion Centers and Federal Strategy for Fusion Center, discussed in the *A National Strategy for Fusion Centers & Measuring Success* section of this report.

CIKR, Cybersecurity & Private Sector Outreach

> "CIKR-related capabilities in the fusion center should center on the development of analytical products, such as risk and trend analysis. This analysis should combine CIKR-specific information with federal, state, and local criminal and homeland security information and intelligence and will contribute not only to protection of CIKR but to the combined missions of federal, state, and local partners within each center."
>
> - CIKR Protection Capabilities for Fusion Centers
> December 2008

Critical Infrastructure and Key Resources

The Homeland Security Act of 2002 (Pub. L. 107-296) charges DHS with reducing the vulnerability of the United States to terrorism. Guided by the *National Strategy for Physical Protection of Critical Infrastructure and Key Assets and the National Infrastructure Protection Plan (NIPP),* DHS's Office of Infrastructure Protection leads the National effort to reduce the risk and vulnerability posed to CIKR. However, if elements of the *NIPP* or the *National Strategy for Physical Protection of Critical Infrastructure and Key Assets* are to be executed to the fullest, fusion centers must be a key part of the effort.

CIKR coordination and partnership between DHS and fusion centers can lead to a more effective effort overall, and further National goals. First, critical infrastructure within a fusion centers' AOR is significantly more than that which is included in any of the National plans. DHS simply is not, nor should it be, resourced to meet all CIKR analytic needs across the country. Further, fusion centers' operating environments enable the development of the State and local relationships necessary to gather and properly contextualize threat and vulnerability information. This serves their State and local customers, and adds to a pool of analysis that can be fused nationally. One fusion center director called CIKR the "sweet spot for fusion center analysis." Of the visited fusion centers, 26 stated that they have at least 1 analyst working CIKR; a number of those have a single part time analyst.

Fusion centers with limited CIKR programs should work to enhance these programs in the near- term. Fusion centers not currently engaging in CIKR analysis should make this an immediate priority. As noted in the *Analysis & Training* section of this report, DHS should make additional CIKR threat and vulnerability training opportunities available to fusion center analysts.

Cybersecurity

Cybersecurity is a relatively new addition as a fusion center analytic discipline, and a major focus area for the Committee in the 113th Congress. Twelve of those fusion centers visited currently have an established cyber program, and 14 are in the process of developing or implementing a cyber program or partnership. It should be noted that six out of the fourteen centers that are developing or implementing a cyber program currently have a dedicated cyber analyst. As noted earlier, in an effort to establish a common operational and analytic language and strengthened partnerships, DHS should explore the further incorporation of fusion center analysts into DHS broader cybersecurity workforce training programs.

As part of the Committee's ongoing focus on cybersecurity, it will seek to gain a deeper understanding of fusion centers' developing cybersecurity programs and how State and local analysts fit into the broader National homeland security cyber mission.

Private Sector Outreach

In addition to work with CIKR on vulnerability assessments, private sector outreach is a valuable fusion center contribution to both the National homeland security mission and State and local missions. This is an area needing further growth across the National Network.

As of April 2013, 27 of the visited fusion centers have outreach programs in place, to varying degrees, aimed at information sharing and situational awareness; an increase from the 22 that were identified during the January-August 2012 site visits. These programs generally include tailored, unclassified, private sector bulletins, and many fusion centers hosted regular private sector threat briefings, usually in partnership with the IO and the local DHS PSA. Making private partners aware of sector-specific threats should be a key objective for every fusion center.

Nine of the visited fusion centers have private sector TLOs, and some centers have developed training specifically for the private sector (versus law enforcement). This specialized training is an important step to maintain the line between what is asked of law enforcement TLOs versus the private sector.

At the time of the site visits, the Committee noted a lack of private sector outreach programs at 10 of the visited fusion centers, suggesting that this may be a significant gap across the entire National Network. Upon receipt of supplemental data in April 2013, that number had reduced to five among visited fusion centers, demonstrating significant improvement.

Fusion centers cannot wait until a problem arises to begin the dialogue with the private sector; those relationships must be established early and built on a history of trust. Fusion centers should make private sector outreach an immediate priority.

Tribal Fusion

> "There continue to be some recognized gaps in tribal information sharing. PM-ISE's efforts are focused on addressing and improving some of the foundational policy, governance, relationship, and capacity issue related to tribal information sharing. While not all fusion centers allow tribal representation at this point in time, progress in this area continues."
>
> \- Information Sharing Environment, Annual Report to the Congress, June 2012

Although the PM-ISE, DHS, the former Interagency Threat Assessment Coordination Group, and others have taken active steps to improve information sharing between the Federal Government and tribes, it remains a significant gap.

There are 56.2 million acres of tribal lands (representing 566 separate Federally recognized tribes and 326 Federally administered Indian reservations) inside the United States, including 200 linear miles along the Northern, Southwest, and maritime borders. Eleven of the States visited have 193 Federally-recognized tribes within their borders. At the time of the site visits, none of the fusion centers visited had a tribal representative on staff. Furthermore, only four of the visited fusion centers (of the fifteen with tribes in their AOR) actively engage in significant outreach efforts with the tribal community.

The *2011 Final Report* states that 31.9% of the then-72 fusion centers have access to tribal subject matter experts; the 2012 Assessment and *2012 Final Report* do not include this specific measure.[47] The 2011 metric does not, however, measure the level of actual interaction, engagement, or information sharing. The Committee's research suggests that across the National Network significant interaction and information sharing is severely lacking. Of those fifteen visited centers with tribes within the vicinity of their AOR, only four stated that they currently have tribal representation within their TLO program. As of April 2013, only one fusion center currently has embedded tribal representation. That same center also hosts a specialized tribal TLO training course and is the only center with tribal representation on its executive board.

The Committee recognizes that there are significant challenges that inhibit or prevent fusion centers' attempts to partner with sovereign tribal nations. However, those challenges should not be allowed to stand in the way of attempts to develop strong relationships. The Committee was encouraged to learn of the upcoming fusion center-tribal partners roundtable exchange meeting planned for this fall, and looks forward to receiving an after action report. The PM-ISE and DHS should continue to work with fusion centers to further encourage and enhance outreach to tribes.

Additionally, stakeholders should include tribal outreach as part of the National Strategy for Fusion Centers, discussed in the *A National Strategy for Fusion Centers & Measuring Success* section of this report.

> "The Arizona Counter Terrorism Information Center (ACTIC) supported a five-month investigation led by a tribal partner, the Tohono O'odham Nation (TON) Police Department and the Bureau of Indian Affairs Division of Drug Enforcement. This investigation led to the arrest of 10 suspects and the apprehension of weapons, cash, vehicles, cocaine, marijuana, and ecstasy in May 2010 – the largest drug enforcement operation in TON history. The investigation marked a key opportunity to collaborate with tribal partners and opened information sharing initiatives between several other agencies, including the FBI, ATF, and other police departments in the area."
>
> Provided by the FBI to the Committee, October 23, 2012

Privacy, Civil Rights & Civil Liberties Protections

> "[T]hank you for recognizing the importance of information sharing; Fusion Centers. Mr. Keating, my Ranking Member, we've both looked at Fusion Centers. Sometimes they're given a bit of a bad name. And I think that privacy protection piece is important to preserve the integrity of what -- the work that they're doing. And to make sure that privacy interests are protected."
>
> - Chairman Michael T. McCaul, Committee on Homeland Security Subcommittee on Oversight, Investigations, and Management Hearing, September 14, 2012

Over the past three years, the Federal Government utilized the grant programs as a way to drive privacy, civil rights, and civil liberties (P/CRCL) standardization and compliance across the National Network.

In 2010, the SHSGP and UASI guidance required fusion centers to have a DHS-certified privacy policy in place that is at least as comprehensive as the Federal Information Sharing Environment (ISE) guidelines, as a prerequisite to the receipt of grant funds. Fusion centers that failed to meet that requirement were only permitted to spend fiscal year 2010 SHSGP or UASI funds to establish a privacy policy.[48] ***All fusion centers at that time met the deadline, and today all of the current 78 fusion centers have approved privacy policies in place.***[49]

Following the identification in the 2011 Assessment that only 34 (47.2% of then-72 centers) fusion centers "underwent annual P/CRCL compliance review," the 2012 SHSGP and UASI guidance further required that all fusion centers "conduct an annual audit of their P/CRCL policy in accordance with the Privacy Civil Rights and Civil Liberties Compliance Verification for the Intelligence Enterprise."[50] According to the 2012 Assessment, 54 (70.1% of 77 centers) fusion centers conducted a compliance review between August 1, 2011 and July 31, 2012.[51]

It is imperative that DHS and the Federal Government continue to work with fusion centers to ensure compliance to National P/CRCL minimum standards, including the provision of training for fusion center personnel.

DHS and the Fusion Centers

> "The Federal Government may need to provide financial and technical assistance, as well as human resource support, to these fusion centers if they are to achieve and sustain a baseline level capability."
>
> - National Strategy for Information Sharing, October 2007

Almost without exception, State and local fusion center personnel were exceedingly complementary of the work, dedication, and contribution of the I&A IOs, RDs, Reports Officers (RO), and Intelligence Analysts (IA) assigned to their individual fusion centers. The Committee held lengthy private conversations with State and local fusion center personnel to understand their perspectives on DHS support to the National Network. General observations and findings are included below.

Intelligence Officers[52]

IOs appear to be successfully serving as the primary intelligence linkage between State and local law enforcement, DHS, and the IC, as the IO program intends. In nearly all cases, fusion center personnel said that they could not operate as effectively without their resident IO. Some fusion center directors went so far as to state that they "would be lost" without the IO, and that the IO program is "the best thing DHS has ever done." As of the date of this report's publication, there are 69 IOs deployed to the field.

> "It's a homerun for I&A when they have the right IO assigned to a fusion center."
>
> - A Fusion Center Director

Notably, I&A has left a level of discretion in the roles and responsibilities for IOs in the field. This allows them the vital flexibility to adapt to the particular operating environment and needs of each unique fusion center and other State and local homeland security partners. Although flexibility is necessary, the IO's primary focus should remain DHS's homeland security mission space, particularly its counterterrorism mission; capacity building; and the facilitation of intelligence and information sharing between the Federal, State, and local levels.

The Committee believes that the IOs' role in the development of individual fusion centers has been vital to the National Network's growth. ***However, as fusion centers' capacity and information sharing processes continue to mature, it may be in the mission's best interest to refine the IOs' job description and restructure the program, particularly in light of the current fiscal climate.*** For example, I&A might consider some form of regionalization with the IOs serving a number of mature fusion centers and State leadership, while maintaining a surge capacity to provide onsite fulltime assistance to less mature centers for a set period of time, or to fulfill a special need. I&A could then couple the above with a significantly increased number of deployed IAs and ROs in an effort to further increase homeland security mission value. I&A should continue to work with the fusion centers, other stakeholders, and the Committee to determine what, if any, changes should be made to the IO program moving forward. In any case, the IOs' duties should be reflective of and tied to the National Strategy for Fusion Centers and the Federal Strategy for Fusion Centers outlined in the *A National Strategy for Fusion Centers & Measuring Success* section of this report.

> "In late 2010, a DHS Intelligence Officer, with the assistance of fusion center analysts assigned to the Alaska Information and Analysis Center (AKIAC), analyzed and reported on a series of threats being made against government officials and law enforcement by an Alaska militia leader. This information proved crucial to the subsequent investigation and arrest of the militia leader and several associates by the Anchorage JTTF on suspicion of plotting the murder of State police officers and municipal judges."
>
> Provided by the FBI to the Committee, October 23, 2012

Regional Directors[53]

I&A's RDs are DHS's most senior field intelligence officers. The Committee observed that individual RDs have a tremendous impact on the growth of fusion centers and on relationships between fusion centers in their assigned region. In addition to their management responsibilities, these individuals are positioned to support fusion centers' policy development and implementation, identify best practices, and help drive increased coordination and collaboration between fusion centers. It is important that the RDs continue to keep an open dialogue amongst themselves and with I&A Headquarters to increase National coordination and continue to drive regional collaboration.

Reports Officers[54]

I&A ROs are an important addition to DHS' field presence. However, they are likely too few in number (18 at the time of this report's publication) to fully accomplish the mission. ***Further, the Committee questions whether their scope may be too limited, particularly with respect to their interaction with DHS components and access to the components' information.*** There are significant questions as to whether component reports officers are adequately representing IC requirements in their reporting, given their limited resources and need to meet component tactical requirements. Given their unique role in the IC, I&A ROs may be able to offer additional expertise and value to DHS component-gathered and held information. Therefore, I&A should work with Congressional oversight committees to determine whether there are appropriate areas to expand I&A RO training and responsibilities, as well as their access to and reporting of component-held information, which may benefit both the DHS and National missions.

The Committee will continue to work with DHS on the development of its RO's, both within I&A and the DHS components.

Intelligence Analysts[55]

Fusion centers consistently highlighted a need for an IA of which only two are currently deployed from I&A's Office of Analysis. Whether to almost exclusively house IAs at I&A Headquarters, as is currently the case, or forward-deploy them en masse, has been a topic of debate for years.

As I&A continues to refine its mission and its unique contribution to its State, local, DHS, IC, and private sector customers, it should fully explore the possibility of expanding its analytic footprint in the field, presumably reducing the number of analysts assigned to I&A Headquarters. ***I&A may better meet its overall analytic mission objectives with significant numbers of IAs forward-deployed.*** Further, the Committee feels strongly that I&A should increase its use of State and local information in its analysis and believes that an expanded analytic presence in the field would significantly aid in this effort. Embedding Federally trained analysts alongside State and local analysts may also have a secondary effect of helping to improve fusion center analysis.

Given I&A's mission to analyze intelligence and threats specific to the Homeland, and its role in the IC as the primary linkage with SLTT information and intelligence functions, I&A should undergo a thorough cost-benefit analysis and work with Congressional oversight committees to determine whether a restructuring of the Office of Analysis is in the best interest of homeland security moving forward.

I&A Management of Field Officers

I&A forward-deployed staff all report to different divisions within the organization. Specifically, the IOs and RDs report to I&A's State and Local Program Office (SLPO), the ROs and Senior ROs report to the Collections and Requirements Division, and the IAs report to the Office of Analysis. The Committee is concerned that this disparate structure perpetuates the very lack of mission unity that I&A is working to correct. Further, the Committee heard anecdotal evidence that the current structure causes a lack of cohesion among I&A's officers in the field. It seems logical that a more consolidated structure would help harmonize I&A's field activities and increase effectiveness. I&A should carefully examine the current model to determine whether further consolidating field management might be more effective.

I&A Analytic Production

During the site visits, the Committee heard a combination of praise and concern regarding I&A products distributed to the fusion centers. ***The many contradictory comments regarding I&A's products reveals I&A's significant challenge in meeting all of its customers' analytic needs and expectations.*** For example, some fusion centers noted a decline in the number of products distributed, stating that they need more. In contrast, other fusion centers had the opposite perspective and noted that I&A, quite simply, produces too many products. Some fusion center personnel commented that I&A's products were always extremely helpful and very timely, while others stated that product utility was hit and miss or rarely helpful, and that I&A needed to be more timely in their releases. In general, the DHS-FBI Joint Intelligence Bulletins and threat briefings delivered by the IOs received praise from the fusion centers.

The Committee notes and shares the widespread concern among the fusion centers that I&A's production approval process greatly inhibits fusion centers' ability to produce joint-seal products with I&A. The Committee is cognizant of the history behind I&A's internal process, and acknowledges I&A's extreme caution in the protection of individuals' privacy and civil liberties, and its efforts to meet analytic tradecraft standards. However, changes should be considered to enable more expeditious approval for joint field production.

The Committee will continue to conduct rigorous oversight and work with I&A to address analytic production concerns, and ensure its products meet the needs of its State, local, DHS, IC, and private sector customers, recognizing that these partners all have different expectations and requirements.

Field Analytic Support Taskforce (FAST)

In an effort to increase collaboration and analytic focus on its State and local partners' homeland security intelligence requirements, I&A recently established the FAST at I&A Headquarters.[56] Under the current design, the FAST consists of a full time Federal Government employee serving as the director, and staffing from SLTT fellows and personnel from I&A's Office of Analysis and SLPO. Additionally, I&A's FAST analysts are deployable on temporary duty to work directly with State and locals in the field on joint analytic products.

It is laudable that I&A is working to improve its ability to meet mission objectives, particularly given that I&A's mission to support and produce analysis relevant to its State and local partners is second only to its mission to support the Secretary of Homeland Security. There is significant value in direct State and local input into I&A's National analytic production process, and also in State and local analysts having the experience of a rotation at I&A Headquarters. It is also noteworthy that the FAST is not being established as a separate division but as a taskforce, which implies some level of flexibility in function and staffing.

The Committee has heard anecdotally that the FAST is already yielding positive returns for I&A's State and local customers. However, questions remain as to whether the FAST will serve to truly integrate I&A across its own divisions and enhance its focus on State and local analytic requirements, or further segregate I&A's divisions from one another, and establish an artificial barrier between its State and local mission and Departmental intelligence support mission. It is also unclear that State and local partners are able to support the FAST to the level necessary to enable its full functionality long-term. The Committee will closely monitor the development of the FAST to ensure it provides actual benefit, and improves I&A's focus on its State and local analytic and information sharing mission space.

Protective Security Advisors[57]

There are currently 93 PSAs deployed across the 50 states and Puerto Rico. The Committee heard from many fusion centers that the assigned PSA coordinates closely with their CIKR analysts, not only deconflicting site assessments but also often conducting joint site surveys, thus reducing the disruption to infrastructure owners and operators. One fusion center noted that, at the host State's request, CIKR assessments were coordinated through the State's primary fusion center, allowing full visibility into CIKR efforts and coordination across the State, and maximization of resources. This is a model that other States and DHS may wish to explore.

Nine of the visited fusion centers noted having little to no interaction with the area's assigned PSA. The DHS Office of Infrastructure Protection should ensure that all PSAs work with the fusion centers to avoid duplication of effort, burden on the private sector, and to make the most of limited resources.

DHS Components in the Fusion Centers

The relationship between fusion centers and the DHS component agencies in the field – specifically CBP, ICE, TSA, USCIS, US Secret Service, and the US Coast Guard – continues to be inconsistent. At the time of the site visits, 15 of the 32 fusion centers had personnel assigned at least part time from a non-I&A DHS component. Data collected in

April 2013 indicated that number had grown to 24; 12 of those 24 fusion centers having more than one component represented either part or full time.

In some cases, the component officials assigned are not representatives from the components' intelligence offices, but from operational divisions. Although this interaction is valuable, the components should prioritize placing trained intelligence analysts in the fusion centers, and the strategic collocation of DHS component personnel within the fusion centers should be further enhanced in general.

Additionally, a close working relationship between component field intelligence officers and IOs, and between I&A ROs and component ROs, is extremely important to ensure coordinated DHS messaging, information sharing, and reporting. Yet, site visits revealed a number of instances where that coordination does not regularly occur. In one location, the Committee was even presented with anecdotal evidence of component field intelligence personnel refusing to partner with an IO. If true, this is inexcusable. DHS cannot operate with hostility towards itself in the field, and must immediately work to improve these relationships.

Numerous fusion center personnel noted that, from their perspective, DHS as a whole is dysfunctional and driving in too many directions. While DHS is charged with an extraordinarily difficult task of coordinating across its multitude of mission areas, this on-the-ground perspective from DHS partners and customers is noteworthy. DHS, regardless of the component or headquarters element, is one department, and must present itself as such even while fulfilling its diverse mission sets.

The Committee will continue to research this issue, examining, in particular, the extent to which components' field intelligence staffs and ROs, and I&A's IOs and ROs partner, coordinate, and collaborate, and determine whether legislative action may be necessary to compel closer coordination.

The FBI & Fusion Centers

> "The Federal Bureau of Investigation (FBI) has approximately 100 personnel (Special Agents and Intelligence Analysts) assigned to 55 fusion centers nationwide, 16 of which are co-located within the FBI's Joint Terrorism Task Forces (JTTF) ... or Field Intelligence Groups (FIG). The FBI's classified computer network (FBINet) is installed in 47 fusion centers."
>
> \- Information Sharing Environment, Annual Report to the Congress, June 2012

With more than 18,000 State and local law enforcement agencies in the United States, the FBI should embrace the fusion centers' capabilities, and look on them as assets and law enforcement force multipliers.[58]

FBI Headquarters has frequently and publicly stated the value proposition brought by fusion centers, and the importance of strong, positive FBI-fusion center relationships. Unfortunately, the Committee's research suggests this message has not been universally embraced in the field, leaving the Federal Government without the full benefit of a State and local partnership, and some fusion centers without the benefit of FBI expertise and analytic mentorship and, more strikingly, the full value of Federal information relevant to potential threats to their AOR.

Of the 32 fusion centers visited, 22 have one or more FBI agent, analyst, or reports officer assigned either full time or part time, and 9 of those centers have two or more FBI employees embedded. Additionally, two of the visited fusion centers told the Committee that they were in the process of onboarding an FBI analyst. Further, one of the fusion centers visited is among the four previously noted within the National Network as having recently lost their FBI onsite presence. Relationships between the visited fusion centers and the FBI varied wildly.

> "The FBI continues to recognize the importance and commitment of sharing intelligence with our federal, state, local, tribal, territorial and private partners. Through the network of state and local fusion centers, we work together to ensure information is shared between these partners and the FBI, especially the FBI's Joint Terrorism Task Forces. The FBI supports the fusion centers through close interaction and an everyday working relationship."
>
> - FBI Headquarters email to FBI Field Offices
> October 10, 2012

In general, the most effective FBI-fusion center relationships appear to be those in which:

- The fusion center retains its autonomy from the local FBI field office and JTTF;
- At least one FBI analyst is assigned to the fusion center full time;
- FBI and State and local fusion center analysts have onsite access to FBINet;
- The local FBI leadership encourages and empowers its personnel to engage in proactive information sharing with fusion center personnel, and the assigned analyst takes the initiative to do so;
- Regular meetings or briefings with local FBI leadership and analysts are held to discuss current threats and relevant, ongoing and closed cases;
- The local FBI and fusion center deconflict and assist each other with ongoing threat analysis; and
- The FBI and fusion center both receive mission-value in having an FBI analyst and/or agent embedded in the fusion center.

It should not be understated that in the majority of the fusion centers visited, the FBI-fusion center relationships, while often needing improvement, outwardly appeared to be on a positive path forward. ***There has clearly been a lot of headway made in recent years, and the FBI and State and local partners should be applauded for that. However, that is not the case everywhere, and there are still considerable gaps that suggest a serious disconnect between FBI Headquarters' public policy statements and the field, and suggest that FBI Headquarters may not be doing enough to hold field offices accountable.***

Additionally, some of the visited fusion centers appear, on first glance, to have particularly healthy relationships with the local FBI field office: constant interaction, collocation, and robust information sharing and collaboration. However, a few of those fusion centers left the Committee concerned that the FBI and the fusion center are so closely tied together that there may be suppression of the independent State and local perspective. The greatest value of a mature fusion center is gained through a close collaboration with the Federal Government, but in an environment where the fusion center maintains its autonomy and ability to contribute as a fully independent, equal partner.

In one instance, the fusion center-FBI relationship is best described as toxic. The animosity and distrust from both sides is pervasive and has created a thoroughly dysfunctional and ineffective relationship, even with an FBI analyst assigned to the fusion center. During a separate visit, a different fusion center director noted that his center is "doing good work despite the FBI."

In still another visited location, where the fusion center and FBI field office had historically been collocated, the FBI moved out of the building. In doing so, the FBI not only took all of its personnel, but also pulled all of the cable for its computer networks. The Committee acknowledges the security rationale behind pulling the cable when it removed its staff, but the result remains that if the FBI were to decide to put an analyst back at the fusion center, it would have to start from scratch to provide system access. According to fusion center personnel, the fusion center and the FBI had regularly published joint products, but that ceased when the FBI moved. Upon further inquiry to the FBI, the Committee was told that the move was required to collocate FBI personnel in the area. However, it remains unclear why the FBI did not leave a single analyst at the fusion center, even part time, and apparently does not have any plan to assign anyone to the center in the foreseeable future.

There is certainly blame to go around, and the Committee recognizes these examples are extremes. However, these anecdotes demonstrate that the situation is still far from perfect. It just takes one terrorist to slip through, or one plot to fall through the cracks to put the Homeland in danger. FBI Headquarters should make a more concerted effort to ensure its field offices and JTTFs are held accountable for robust cooperation and information sharing with fusion centers. Strongly worded statements are not enough to assure field compliance or continued improvement to information sharing and analytic partnerships.

Since concluding the site visits in August 2012, the FBI has pulled out of three additional fusion centers within the National Network; three of these four fusion centers are State primary centers, and two were from one State. As noted earlier, the Committee fully agrees – as the FBI responded upon inquiry – that the mission value of a detailed FBI agent must be reciprocal.[59] However, the Committee is greatly concerned that this may be an indication of a rising trend. In light of the current threat environment, the Federal Government should be leaning further forward to work with State and locals, not backward.

The Committee strongly encourages the FBI and State and local law enforcement leaders and policy makers to continue building bridges between their organizations, and reminds all stakeholders that the relationships between the Federal Government and fusion centers should be a symbiotic partnership with the common goal of securing the Homeland.

The Committee again stresses the need for a National Strategy for Fusion Centers and Federal Strategy for Fusion Centers as outlined in the *A National Strategy for Fusion Centers & Measuring Success* section of this report, to help deconflict mission requirements, expectations, and better guide Federal resource support to individual fusion centers and the National Network.

Joint Regional Intelligence Groups (JRIG)

The Committee notes the recent establishment of JRIGs, overseen by the FBI. In addition to numerous discussions with Federal, State, and local stakeholders involved in the development process, the Committee received formal briefings from the FBI, DHS, and the Office of the Director of National Intelligence.[60]

Given that the JRIGs are expected to enhance stakeholders' understanding of regional threats, there are still significant concerns that the JRIGs will not be sufficiently aligned with fusion centers. A lack of alignment would increase the likelihood of redundancy, information stovepiping, lack of coordination with State and local partners, and potential degradation of the very local-level analytic infrastructure that the JRIGs would theoretically depend upon for their own analysis.

The Committee will continue asserting a high degree of scrutiny over JRIG program development, including how it uniquely improves counterterrorism and domestic security information sharing and analysis.

I&A & FBI in the Field

In most fusion centers, the assigned IO and FBI analyst relationship was described as good or excellent: working together, holding joint briefings, and sharing information between them. ***However, even in centers where the assigned individuals get along, the prevailing perspective of the fusion center personnel is that DHS and the FBI are in constant battle.*** In one fusion center, this allegedly goes so far as the FBI analyst withholding information and refusing to brief fusion center personnel if the IO is in the room.

> "There is an uneasy truce between DHS and the FBI."
>
> \- A Fusion Center Director

DHS and FBI Headquarters must hold the field accountable and send a clear, unmistakable message that internal disputes threaten the security of the Homeland, and will not be tolerated. The Committee will continue rigorous oversight to ensure the Federal Government is not perpetuating or returning to pre-9/11 turf wars.

CONCLUSION

> "After [the Boston Marathon bombings], a point was made – there was no chatter, there was no international intelligence coming. I think that's going to be the wave of the future is going to be attacks that are under the radar screen, and it's more important than ever that the local police be involved, because no one has a better feel for the community than the local police."
>
> \- Congressman Peter T. King, Committee on Homeland Security
> Full Committee Hearing, May 9, 2013

The terrorist attacks of September 11, 2001 ushered in an era that dramatically changed the United States' approach to securing the Homeland. We have come to understand that homeland security, including counterterrorism efforts, must be a National responsibility – a true and equal partnership across all levels of government, and inclusive of the American people themselves. A top down, wholly Federal approach simply does not and cannot suffice. The surge of homegrown radicalization in the United States over the last several years reinforces that this new approach is an imperative. As threats to the Homeland become more diverse and decentralized, the full participation of State and local law enforcement is critical to prevention. The April 2013 terrorist attacks in Boston demonstrate just how far we have come and how far we have yet to go.

In the wake of this horrible attack that left 4 dead and 260 wounded, Boston's response serves as a National model. By all accounts, training, exercises, and communications and emergency response equipment – significantly funded through the Homeland Security Grant Program – saved perhaps hundreds of lives that day as people lay severely wounded on Boylston Street, steps from the Boston Marathon finish line. However, the revelation that Federally-held information about one of the would-be bombers wasn't shared with local law enforcement demonstrates a continued substantial gap in information sharing.

There is currently no evidence indicating that local awareness of the would-be bomber would have affected the outcome. However, it is certainly possible that additional scrutiny would have been applied to the information, if only by virtue of inviting another organization's perspective. As former National Counterterrorism Center Director Mike Leiter recently stated, "people generally will share now, but they will generally share once they determine that something is relevant to a terrorism investigation that someone else might be able to help them on. And that's too late.... [Y]ou don't know if it's counterterrorism information until you have it, until you can compare it to other information and find connections between those dots."[61] The terrorist attack in Boston demonstrates that there is still a long way to go before all parties are viewed as truly equal members of the team and information sharing reaches its full potential.

No one agency has the capability or capacity to single-handedly detect, deter, or prevent all potential terrorist attacks or other threats to the Homeland. It requires a comprehensive, National effort, from the boots on the ground local law enforcement, to emergency response providers, to Federal law enforcement and intelligence agencies. The ability to gather, analyze, and share critical information between partners, in a secure and timely matter, is essential. In the post-9/11 Homeland we cannot afford to let information slip by unnoticed and unanalyzed. Comprehensively sharing threat information with fusion centers, and fusion centers analyzing that information in a local context must become the norm. Fusion centers are uniquely positioned to be the facilitator of information sharing between the Federal Government and State and local officials, and analyze threat information in a local context. The Federal Government must continue to increase its commitment to improving information sharing. Without fulsome analysis that can only be achieved through robust information sharing, prevention and protection will be a constant hurdle.

The National Network has been built from the ground up since September 11, 2001, and the newest fusion center was designated only seven months ago. There is unquestionably significant room for improvement, particularly as it relates to fusion centers' support to the National counterterrorism mission. At this stage, Federal support to the fusion centers and the National Network remains as focused on capability and capacity building, as it is about building partnerships and information sharing.

Although much work remains to enhance their capability and refine the careful balance between fusion centers' State and local, and National missions, the ability to analyze and understand State and local information in a National homeland security mission context is vital. Further, ensuring that State and local partners have the intelligence capability necessary to enhance line officers' ability to serve as mission partners is essential in today's ever-changing threat environment.

The progress made in fusion centers' and the National Network's development is critical to the Nation's prevention efforts, and fusion centers closing or withdrawing as National mission partners due to budget constraints could be a detriment to our Nation's security. The Federal Government and State and local stakeholders must continue to provide the support that fusion centers require to continue to grow and develop, enabling the National Network to reach its full potential as a National asset and homeland security partner.

APPENDIX I. "DEPARTMENT OF HOMELAND SECURITY STATE, LOCAL, AND REGIONAL FUSION CENTER INITIATIVE," FROM THE IMPLEMENTING RECOMMENDATIONS OF THE 9/11 COMMISSION ACT OF 2007 (PUB. L. 110-53)

Subtitle B--Homeland Security Information Sharing Partnerships

SEC. 511. Department of Homeland Security State, Local, and Regional Fusion Center Initiative

(a) In General- Subtitle A of title II of the Homeland Security Act of 2002 (6 U.S.C. 121 et seq.) is further amended by adding at the end the following:

Sec. 210A. Department of Homeland Security State, Local, and Regional Fusion Center Initiative.

(a) Establishment- The Secretary, in consultation with the program manager of the information sharing environment established under section 1016 of the Intelligence Reform and Terrorism Prevention Act of 2004 (6 U.S.C. 485), the Attorney General, the Privacy Officer of the Department, the Officer for Civil Rights and Civil Liberties of the Department, and the Privacy and Civil Liberties Oversight Board established under section 1061 of the Intelligence Reform and Terrorism Prevention Act of 2004 (5 U.S.C. 601 note), shall establish a Department of Homeland Security State, Local, and Regional Fusion Center Initiative to establish partnerships with State, local, and regional fusion centers.

(b) Department Support and Coordination- Through the Department of Homeland Security State, Local, and Regional Fusion Center Initiative, and in coordination with the principal officials of participating State, local, or regional fusion centers and the officers designated as the Homeland Security Advisors of the States, the Secretary shall--

  (1) provide operational and intelligence advice and assistance to State, local, and regional fusion centers;

  (2) support efforts to include State, local, and regional fusion centers into efforts to establish an information sharing environment;

  (3) conduct tabletop and live training exercises to regularly assess the capability of individual and regional networks of State, local, and regional fusion centers to integrate the efforts of such networks with the efforts of the Department;

(4) coordinate with other relevant Federal entities engaged in homeland security-related activities;
(5) provide analytic and reporting advice and assistance to State, local, and regional fusion centers;
(6) review information within the scope of the information sharing environment, including homeland security information, terrorism information, and weapons of mass destruction information, that is gathered by State, local, and regional fusion centers, and to incorporate such information, as appropriate, into the Department's own such information;
(7) provide management assistance to State, local, and regional fusion centers;
(8) serve as a point of contact to ensure the dissemination of information within the scope of the information sharing environment, including homeland security information, terrorism information, and weapons of mass destruction information;
(9) facilitate close communication and coordination between State, local, and regional fusion centers and the Department;
(10) provide State, local, and regional fusion centers with expertise on Department resources and operations;
(11) provide training to State, local, and regional fusion centers and encourage such fusion centers to participate in terrorism threat-related exercises conducted by the Department; and
(12) carry out such other duties as the Secretary determines are appropriate.

(c) Personnel Assignment-
(1) IN GENERAL- The Under Secretary for Intelligence and Analysis shall, to the maximum extent practicable, assign officers and intelligence analysts from components of the Department to participating State, local, and regional fusion centers.
(2) PERSONNEL SOURCES- Officers and intelligence analysts assigned to participating fusion centers under this subsection may be assigned from the following Department components, in coordination with the respective component head and in consultation with the principal officials of participating fusion centers:
(A) Office of Intelligence and Analysis.
(B) Office of Infrastructure Protection.
(C) Transportation Security Administration.
(D) United States Customs and Border Protection.
(E) United States Immigration and Customs Enforcement.
(F) United States Coast Guard.
(G) Other components of the Department, as determined by the Secretary.
(3) QUALIFYING CRITERIA-
(A) IN GENERAL- The Secretary shall develop qualifying criteria for a fusion center to participate in the assigning of Department officers or intelligence analysts under this section.
(B) CRITERIA- Any criteria developed under subparagraph (A) may include--

(i) whether the fusion center, through its mission and governance structure, focuses on a broad counterterrorism approach, and whether that broad approach is pervasive through all levels of the organization;
(ii) whether the fusion center has sufficient numbers of adequately trained personnel to support a broad counterterrorism mission;
(iii) whether the fusion center has--
(I) access to relevant law enforcement, emergency response, private sector, open source, and national security data; and
(II) the ability to share and analytically utilize that data for lawful purposes;
(iv) whether the fusion center is adequately funded by the State, local, or regional government to support its counterterrorism mission; and
(v) the relevancy of the mission of the fusion center to the particular source component of Department officers or intelligence analysts.

(4) PREREQUISITE-
(A) INTELLIGENCE ANALYSIS, PRIVACY, AND CIVIL LIBERTIES TRAINING- Before being assigned to a fusion center under this section, an officer or intelligence analyst shall undergo--
(i) appropriate intelligence analysis or information sharing training using an intelligence-led policing curriculum that is consistent with--
(I) standard training and education programs offered to Department law enforcement and intelligence personnel; and
(II) the Criminal Intelligence Systems Operating Policies under part 23 of title 28, Code of Federal Regulations (or any corresponding similar rule or regulation);
(ii) appropriate privacy and civil liberties training that is developed, supported, or sponsored by the Privacy Officer appointed under section 222 and the Officer for Civil Rights and Civil Liberties of the Department, in consultation with the Privacy and Civil Liberties Oversight Board established under section 1061 of the Intelligence Reform and Terrorism Prevention Act of 2004 (5 U.S.C. 601 note); and
(iii) such other training prescribed by the Under Secretary for Intelligence and Analysis.
(B) PRIOR WORK EXPERIENCE IN AREA- In determining the eligibility of an officer or intelligence analyst to be assigned to a fusion center under this section, the Under Secretary for Intelligence and Analysis shall consider the familiarity of the officer or intelligence analyst with the State, locality, or region, as determined by such factors as whether the officer or intelligence analyst--
(i) has been previously assigned in the geographic area; or
(ii) has previously worked with intelligence officials or law enforcement or other emergency response providers from that State, locality, or region.

(5) EXPEDITED SECURITY CLEARANCE PROCESSING- The Under Secretary for Intelligence and Analysis--

(A) shall ensure that each officer or intelligence analyst assigned to a fusion center under this section has the appropriate security clearance to contribute effectively to the mission of the fusion center; and

(B) may request that security clearance processing be expedited for each such officer or intelligence analyst and may use available funds for such purpose.

(6) FURTHER QUALIFICATIONS- Each officer or intelligence analyst assigned to a fusion center under this section shall satisfy any other qualifications the Under Secretary for Intelligence and Analysis may prescribe.

(d) Responsibilities- An officer or intelligence analyst assigned to a fusion center under this section shall--

(1) assist law enforcement agencies and other emergency response providers of State, local, and tribal governments and fusion center personnel in using information within the scope of the information sharing environment, including homeland security information, terrorism information, and weapons of mass destruction information, to develop a comprehensive and accurate threat picture;

(2) review homeland security-relevant information from law enforcement agencies and other emergency response providers of State, local, and tribal government;

(3) create intelligence and other information products derived from such information and other homeland security-relevant information provided by the Department; and

(4) assist in the dissemination of such products, as coordinated by the Under Secretary for Intelligence and Analysis, to law enforcement agencies and other emergency response providers of State, local, and tribal government, other fusion centers, and appropriate Federal agencies.

(e) Border Intelligence Priority-

(1) IN GENERAL- The Secretary shall make it a priority to assign officers and intelligence analysts under this section from United States Customs and Border Protection, United States Immigration and Customs Enforcement, and the Coast Guard to participating State, local, and regional fusion centers located in jurisdictions along land or maritime borders of the United States in order to enhance the integrity of and security at such borders by helping Federal, State, local, and tribal law enforcement authorities to identify, investigate, and otherwise interdict persons, weapons, and related contraband that pose a threat to homeland security.

(2) BORDER INTELLIGENCE PRODUCTS- When performing the responsibilities described in subsection (d), officers and intelligence analysts assigned to participating State, local, and regional fusion centers under this section shall have, as a primary responsibility, the creation of border intelligence products that--

(A) assist State, local, and tribal law enforcement agencies in deploying their resources most efficiently to help detect and interdict terrorists, weapons of mass destruction, and related contraband at land or maritime borders of the United States;

(B) promote more consistent and timely sharing of border security-relevant information among jurisdictions along land or maritime borders of the United States; and

(C) enhance the Department's situational awareness of the threat of acts of terrorism at or involving the land or maritime borders of the United States.

(f) Database Access- In order to fulfill the objectives described under subsection (d), each officer or intelligence analyst assigned to a fusion center under this section shall have appropriate access to all relevant Federal databases and information systems, consistent with any policies, guidelines, procedures, instructions, or standards established by the President or, as appropriate, the program manager of the information sharing environment for the implementation and management of that environment.

(g) Consumer Feedback-

(1) IN GENERAL- The Secretary shall create a voluntary mechanism for any State, local, or tribal law enforcement officer or other emergency response provider who is a consumer of the intelligence or other information products referred to in subsection (d) to provide feedback to the Department on the quality and utility of such intelligence products.

(2) REPORT- Not later than one year after the date of the enactment of the Implementing Recommendations of the 9/11 Commission Act of 2007, and annually thereafter, the Secretary shall submit to the Committee on Homeland Security and Governmental Affairs of the Senate and the Committee on Homeland Security of the House of Representatives a report that includes a description of the consumer feedback obtained under paragraph (1) and, if applicable, how the Department has adjusted its production of intelligence products in response to that consumer feedback.

(h) Rule of Construction-

(1) IN GENERAL- The authorities granted under this section shall supplement the authorities granted under section 201(d) and nothing in this section shall be construed to abrogate the authorities granted under section 201(d).

(2) PARTICIPATION- Nothing in this section shall be construed to require a State, local, or regional government or entity to accept the assignment of officers or intelligence analysts of the Department into the fusion center of that State, locality, or region.

(i) Guidelines- The Secretary, in consultation with the Attorney General, shall establish guidelines for fusion centers created and operated by State and local governments, to include standards that any such fusion center shall--

(1) collaboratively develop a mission statement, identify expectations and goals, measure performance, and determine effectiveness for that fusion center;

(2) create a representative governance structure that includes law enforcement officers and other emergency response providers and, as appropriate, the private sector;

(3) create a collaborative environment for the sharing of intelligence and information among Federal, State, local, and tribal government agencies (including law enforcement officers and other emergency response providers), the private sector, and the public, consistent with any policies, guidelines, procedures, instructions, or standards established by the President or, as appropriate, the program manager of the information sharing environment;

(4) leverage the databases, systems, and networks available from public and private sector entities, in accordance with all applicable laws, to maximize information sharing;
(5) develop, publish, and adhere to a privacy and civil liberties policy consistent with Federal, State, and local law;
(6) provide, in coordination with the Privacy Officer of the Department and the Officer for Civil Rights and Civil Liberties of the Department, appropriate privacy and civil liberties training for all State, local, tribal, and private sector representatives at the fusion center;
(7) ensure appropriate security measures are in place for the facility, data, and personnel;
(8) select and train personnel based on the needs, mission, goals, and functions of that fusion center;
(9) offer a variety of intelligence and information services and products to recipients of fusion center intelligence and information; and
(10) incorporate law enforcement officers, other emergency response providers, and, as appropriate, the private sector, into all relevant phases of the intelligence and fusion process, consistent with the mission statement developed under paragraph (1), either through full time representatives or liaison relationships with the fusion center to enable the receipt and sharing of information and intelligence.

(j) Definitions- In this section--
(1) the term `fusion center' means a collaborative effort of 2 or more Federal, State, local, or tribal government agencies that combines resources, expertise, or information with the goal of maximizing the ability of such agencies to detect, prevent, investigate, apprehend, and respond to criminal or terrorist activity;
(2) the term `information sharing environment' means the information sharing environment established under section 1016 of the Intelligence Reform and Terrorism Prevention Act of 2004 (6 U.S.C. 485);
(3) the term `intelligence analyst' means an individual who regularly advises, administers, supervises, or performs work in the collection, gathering, analysis, evaluation, reporting, production, or dissemination of information on political, economic, social, cultural, physical, geographical, scientific, or military conditions, trends, or forces in foreign or domestic areas that directly or indirectly affect national security;
(4) the term `intelligence-led policing' means the collection and analysis of information to produce an intelligence end product designed to inform law enforcement decision making at the tactical and strategic levels; and
(5) the term `terrorism information' has the meaning given that term in section 1016 of the Intelligence Reform and Terrorism Prevention Act of 2004 (6 U.S.C. 485).

(k) Authorization of Appropriations- There is authorized to be appropriated $10,000,000 for each of fiscal years 2008 through 2012, to carry out this section, except for subsection (i), including for hiring officers and intelligence analysts to replace officers and intelligence analysts who are assigned to fusion centers under this section.'.

(b) Training for Predeployed Officers and Analysts- An officer or analyst assigned to a fusion center by the Secretary of Homeland Security before the date of the enactment of this Act shall undergo the training described in section 210A(c)(4)(A) of the Homeland Security Act of 2002, as added by subsection (a), by not later than 6 months after such date.

(c) Technical and Conforming Amendment- The table of contents in section 1(b) of the Homeland Security Act of 2002 (6 U.S.C. 101 et seq.) is further amended by inserting after the item relating to section 210 the following:

Sec. 210A. Department of Homeland Security State, Local, and Regional Information Fusion Center Initiative.'.

(d) Reports-

(1) CONCEPT OF OPERATIONS- Not later than 90 days after the date of enactment of this Act and before the Department of Homeland Security State, Local, and Regional Fusion Center Initiative under section 210A of the Homeland Security Act of 2002, as added by subsection (a), (in this section referred to as the `program') has been implemented, the Secretary, in consultation with the Privacy Officer of the Department, the Officer for Civil Rights and Civil Liberties of the Department, and the Privacy and Civil Liberties Oversight Board established under section 1061 of the Intelligence Reform and Terrorism Prevention Act of 2004 (5 U.S.C. 601 note), shall submit to the Committee on Homeland Security and Governmental Affairs of the Senate and the Committee on Homeland Security of the House of Representatives a report that contains a concept of operations for the program, which shall--

(A) include a clear articulation of the purposes, goals, and specific objectives for which the program is being developed;

(B) identify stakeholders in the program and provide an assessment of their needs;

(C) contain a developed set of quantitative metrics to measure, to the extent possible, program output;

(D) contain a developed set of qualitative instruments (including surveys and expert interviews) to assess the extent to which stakeholders believe their needs are being met; and

(E) include a privacy and civil liberties impact assessment.

(2) PRIVACY AND CIVIL LIBERTIES- Not later than 1 year after the date of the enactment of this Act, the Privacy Officer of the Department of Homeland Security and the Officer for Civil Liberties and Civil Rights of the Department of Homeland Security, consistent with any policies of the Privacy and Civil Liberties Oversight Board established under section 1061 of the Intelligence Reform and Terrorism Prevention Act of 2004 (5 U.S.C. 601 note), shall submit to the Committee on Homeland Security and Governmental Affairs of the Senate and the Committee on Homeland Security of the House of Representatives, the Secretary of Homeland Security, the Under Secretary of Homeland Security for Intelligence and

Analysis, and the Privacy and Civil Liberties Oversight Board a report on the privacy and civil liberties impact of the program.

APPENDIX II. COMMITTEE RESEARCH METHODOLOGY

The Committee has consistently advocated that State and local law enforcement, emergency response providers, and the fusion centers are a significant part of the National counterterrorism and broader homeland security mission. Under the direction of then-Committee Chairman Peter T. King, now Subcommittee on Counterterrorism and Intelligence Chairman, Committee Majority staff worked to identify and understand the strengths, weaknesses, and gaps in fusion center development, the National Network of Fusion Centers (National Network), and the Federal role. This work continued into the 113th Congress under the additional direction of current Committee Chairman Michael T. McCaul.

Specifically, the Committee sought to understand:

- Fusion centers' development individually and as a part of the National Network;
- How well the National Network operates to fulfill a National need, including Federal, State, and local priorities and the National homeland security mission, particularly the counterterrorism mission;
- Changes to fusion centers' overall mission space, and how those changes have affected their ability to meet Federal, State, and local customers' requirements;
- The impacts of having 78 designated fusion centers across the country, and multiple fusion centers within a single State;
- The current Federal Government role in the fusion centers' and the National Networks' development, and the role it should play moving forward;
- State and local security clearances and access to classified information;
- Fusion center analysts' training and development, and fusion centers' analytic production;
- Leveraging non-traditional partners as fusion partners, specifically fire, emergency medical services (EMS), and public health;
- The current funding environment and possible future funding models for fusion center and National Network sustainment; and
- The Department of Homeland Security (DHS) and the Federal Bureau of Investigation's (FBI) relationship with fusion centers.

The findings and recommendations discussed in this report are based on the following series of official meetings and the Committee's history of fusion center, DHS Office of Intelligence and Analysis (I&A), and the DHS Intelligence Enterprise programmatic oversight.

Between January 2012 and August 2012, the Committee visited 32 fusion centers across 20 States and the District of Columbia (*See Figure 3*), specifically:

- Tennessee Fusion Center, Tennessee;
- Georgia Information and Strategic Analysis Center, Georgia;

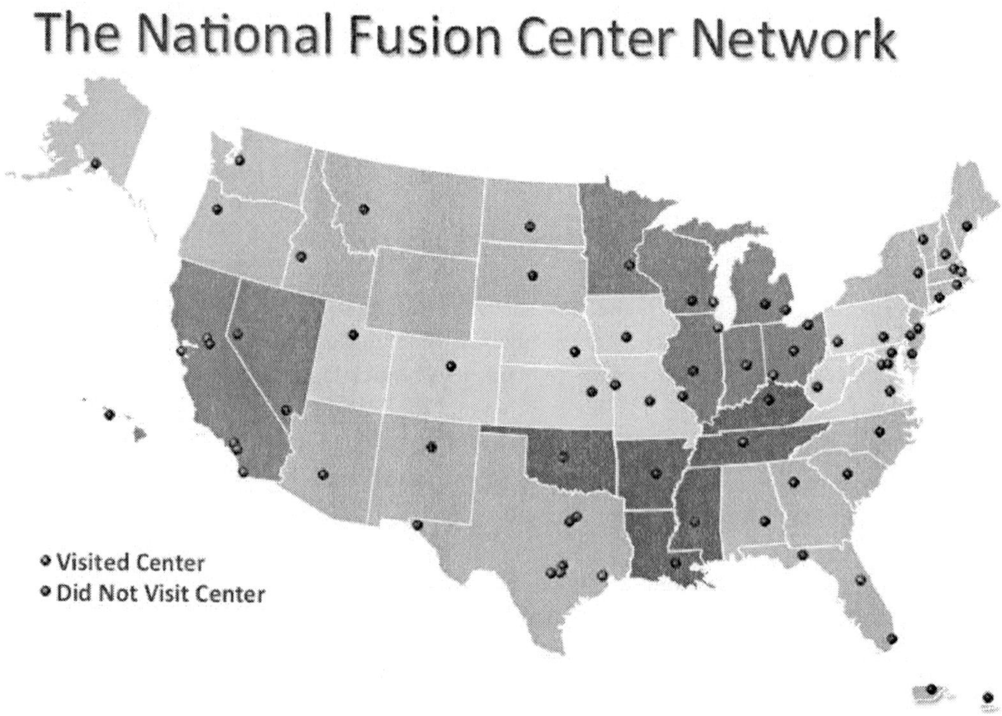

Figure 3. Location of visited centers.

- Ohio Strategic Analysis and Information Center, Ohio;
- Cincinnati/Hamilton County Regional Terrorism Early Warning Group, Ohio;
- Indiana Intelligence Fusion Center, Indiana;
- Arizona Counterterrorism Information Center, Arizona;
- Maryland Coordination and Analysis Center, Maryland;
- New Jersey Regional Operations Intelligence Center, New Jersey;
- Pennsylvania Criminal Intelligence Center, Pennsylvania;
- Rhode Island Fusion Center, Rhode Island;
- Massachusetts Commonwealth Fusion Center, Massachusetts;
- Boston Regional Intelligence Center, Massachusetts;
- New Hampshire Information and Intelligence Analysis Center, New Hampshire;
- New York State Intelligence Center, New York;
- Northern California Regional Intelligence Center, California;
- Central California Intelligence Center, California;
- California State Threat Assessment Center, California;
- Los Angeles Joint Regional Intelligence Center, California;
- Orange County Intelligence Assessment Center, California;
- San Diego Law Enforcement Coordination Center, California;
- Virginia Fusion Center, Virginia;
- Washington Regional Threat Analysis Center, District of Columbia;
- Chicago Crime Prevention and Information Center, Illinois;
- South Eastern Wisconsin Threat Analysis Center, Wisconsin;

- Northern Virginia Regional Intelligence Center, Virginia;
- Washington State Fusion Center, Washington;
- Colorado Information Analysis Center, Colorado;
- Central Florida Intelligence Exchange, Florida;
- Southwest Texas Fusion Center, Texas;
- Austin Regional Intelligence Center, Texas;
- Texas Fusion Center, Texas; and
- Houston Regional Information Service Center, Texas.

These specific fusion centers were chosen to achieve an understanding of a representative sample, based on a variety of factors including, but not limited to: at least one fusion center in each of the nine fusion center regions; a mixture of small, medium, and large-sized fusion centers; collocation with a Federal agency field office; collocation with a State emergency management agency and/or emergency operations center; varying host agencies (law enforcement; emergency management; or no single "parent" agency); fusion center age; centers located within an Urban Area Security Initiative (UASI)-eligible urban area; centers located within an urban area that was previously deemed eligible for UASI funding; and States with multiple centers.

Individual visits ranged between 2.5 hours to 7.5 hours in length, for a total of 147 meeting hours and an average of 4.6 meeting hours per fusion center.

State and local representation at each meeting varied, but generally included the: fusion center director; lead analyst(s); grants specialist; privacy officer; security officer; fire service analyst; critical infrastructure & key resource analyst(s); I&A Intelligence Officer; I&A Regional Director; I&A Reports Officer (RO) or Senior RO, if assigned; I&A Intelligence Analyst, if assigned; and the FBI analyst or agent(s), if assigned.

Some of the meetings additionally included the: State Homeland Security Advisor; DHS Protective Security Advisor; emergency management agency director or deputy; and/or additional members of a fusion center's governance board. In a few instances, the Committee had the opportunity to meet with all personnel assigned to the given fusion center.

During all visits, the Committee met with State and local fusion center representatives and Federal partners (DHS, FBI, etc.) jointly, as well as with State and local fusion center representatives privately. In most cases, the Committee also had the opportunity to meet with DHS and/or other Federal representatives privately. Additionally, in three locations the Committee had the opportunity to meet with the local FBI Special Agent in Charge.

Between January 2012 and July 2013, the Committee received regular briefings from officials in the DHS I&A State and Local Program Office. Additionally, the Committee received briefings from the Federal Emergency Management Agency Grant Programs Directorate; DHS Chief Information Office (CIO); I&A CIO; I&A Office of Analysis; DHS National Security Systems Joint Program Management Office (PMO); Homeland Security Information Network PMO; Department of Defense; FBI; the Program Manager for the Information Sharing Environment; and the Government Accountability Office.

In April 2013, the Committee sent a follow up questionnaire to each of the visited fusion centers, requesting data to update information previously collected as part of the site visits. The Committee also received data collected by I&A as part of the 2012 annual Assessment process, and data collected by the National Fusion Center Association (NFCA). Additionally, the Committee met on numerous occasions with various members of the NFCA Board of Directors, and held follow-up telephone conversations with fusion center directors and personnel, and the Office of the Director of National Intelligence.

Further, from April 2-5, 2012, Committee staff attended the National Fusion Center Training Event, in Phoenix, Arizona.

The Committee also held a number of hearings in 2012 and 2013 in which it received testimony relevant to the subject of the study, including:

- Subcommittee on Counterterrorism and Intelligence: *Federal Government Intelligence Sharing with State, Local and Tribal Law Enforcement: An Assessment Ten Years After 9/11,* February 28, 2012;
- Subcommittee on Emergency Preparedness, Response, and Communications: *Ensuring the Transparency, Efficiency, and Effectiveness of Homeland Security Grants (Part 1 and Part 2)*, March 20, 2013 and April 26, 2012;
- Subcommittee on Emergency Preparedness, Response, and Communications: *The National Preparedness Report: Assessing the State of Preparedness*, June 6, 2012;
- Subcommittee on Oversight, Investigations, and Management: *Lessons From Fort Hood: Improving our Ability to Connect the Dots,* September 14, 2012;
- Full Committee: *The Department of Homeland Security: An Assessment of the Department and a Roadmap for its Future,* September 20, 2012;
- Subcommittee on Emergency Preparedness, Response, and Communications: *Homeland Security Grants: Measuring Our Investments*, March 19, 2013;
- Subcommittee on Counterterrorism and Intelligence: *Counterterrorism Efforts to Combat a Chemical, Biological, Radiological, and Nuclear (CBRN) Attack on the Homeland*, April 25, 2013;
- Full Committee: *The Boston Bombings: A First Look*, May 9, 2013;
- Full Committee: *Assessing Attacks on the Homeland: From Fort Hood to Boston*, July 10, 2013

On December 9, 2011, then-Chairman King, joined by Ranking Member Bennie Thompson, and the Senate Homeland Security and Governmental Affairs Committee Chairman Joseph Lieberman and Ranking Member Susan Collins, requested that the Government Accountability Office (GAO) examine the Nationwide Suspicious Activity Reporting Initiative, including a look at the relationship between the Shared Space and eGuardian systems.[62]

On June 4, 2012, then-Chairman King, joined by Chairman Lieberman, Ranking Member Thompson, and Congressmen Patrick Meehan and Brian Higgins, requested that the GAO examine field intelligence organizations – specifically High Intensity Drug Trafficking Areas, Joint Terrorism Task Forces, FBI Field Intelligence Groups, and State and Major Urban Area Fusion Centers – in an effort to further understand the relationships between each, and identify areas of actual mission duplication or overlap.[63]

On April 24, 2012, now-Committee Chairman Michael McCaul joined Senator Tom Coburn in his request that the GAO examine intelligence analysis within the DHS Intelligence Enterprise.

Appendix III. Fiscal Year 2011 HSGP Guidance

Fusion Center Investment. As maturation of the national network of fusion centers is one of the Department's highest priorities in FY 2011, DHS is requiring that at least one (1) fusion center Investment from a State to provide funding support to the State's primary fusion center, as designated by the Governor.

Additionally, FY 2011 eligible UASI applicants will be required to provide an Investment to the DHS-recognized fusion center within the Urban Area. Grantees must coordinate with the fusion center when developing a fusion center Investment prior to submission.

Priority Three – Maturation and Enhancement of State and Major Urban Area Fusion Centers

One of the Department's priorities in FY 2011 is to support recognized State and major Urban Area fusion centers and the maturation of the Information Sharing Environment (ISE). Fusion centers serve as focal points within the State and local environment for the receipt, analysis, gathering, and sharing of threat-related information between the Federal government and State, local, Tribal, territorial (SLTT) and private sector partners. Building a National Network of Fusion Centers (National Network) empowers law enforcement and homeland security personnel by helping them understand local implications of national intelligence, thus enabling them to better protect their communities.

A National Network also provides a mechanism for the Federal government to receive information from SLTT partners, which helps create a more complete intelligence picture at the National level. With timely, accurate information on potential terrorist threats, fusion centers can also directly contribute to and inform investigations initiated and conducted by Federal entities, such as the Joint Terrorism Task Forces led by the Federal Bureau of Investigation (FBI).

The *2010 National Security Strategy* identifies fusion centers as critical in enlisting all of our intelligence, law enforcement, and homeland security capabilities to prevent acts of terrorism on American soil.

In support of this strategic vision, the Department is requiring recognized State and Major Urban Area fusion centers to participate in an annual assessment of their achievement of baseline capabilities, as outlined in the Global Justice Information Sharing Initiative's (Global) *Baseline Capabilities for State and Major Urban Area Fusion Centers*. The results from this assessment will help fusion centers identify gaps in their operational capabilities.

As maturation of the National Network is one of the Department's highest priorities in FY 2011, DHS is requiring that at least one (1) of the Investment for State or Urban Areas, in which the 72 DHS-recognized fusion centers reside, address funding support for the recognized fusion center.

Grantees must coordinate with the fusion center when developing a fusion center Investment prior to submission. All efforts should be made to address gaps that are identified by taking advantage of the service deliveries made available through the joint DHS and Department of Justice Fusion Process Technical Assistance Program.

Additionally, any jurisdiction or agency that leverages HSGP-related funds to support intelligence- or fusion process-related activities (i.e., intelligence unit, real time crime information and analysis centers, etc.) must ensure these efforts are integrated and/or coordinated with the respective recognized State or Urban Area fusion centers.

Background

The *Baseline Capabilities for State and Major Urban Area Fusion Centers* (September 2008) identifies the baseline capabilities for fusion centers and the operational standards necessary to achieve each of the capabilities across the National Network of Fusion Centers. Fusion centers, in partnership with the Federal Government, prioritized four critical operational capabilities (COCs)1, which align to the steps in the intelligence cycle. During the Baseline Capabilities Assessment (BCA)2, fusion centers are assessed on their ability to perform the COCs.

Objective One

Baseline Capabilities. Fusion centers leveraging SHSP and/or UASI grant funds must prioritize the allocation of these grant funds to address any capability gaps identified as a result of the BCA. This will ensure the implementation of common and consistent operational standards across the National Network of Fusion Centers.

Fusion center priorities for FY 2011 focus on enhancing and maintaining their ability to execute the COCs at a fundamental level, which means that, at a minimum, fusion centers have approved plans, policies, or standard operating procedures (SOPs) for each COC that codify their business processes.

No two localities are exactly alike, so each center should tailor its procedures to meet its local needs. However, it is essential that DHS gain a National perspective of fusion center network capabilities.

To achieve that end, individual fusion center SOPs, plans, and policies must be developed in a standardized fashion. Those centers that have approved plans, policies, or SOPs for each COC should also continue to fully implement these plans, policies, or SOPs, as well as other gaps identified during the fusion center‘s baseline capability assessment. FY 2011 fusion center priorities also focus specifically on maturing analytic capabilities as part of COC 2: Analyze.

Fusion centers leveraging SHSP and/or UASI grant funds are required to demonstrate, at a minimum, the following fundamental capabilities:

- *Receive:* A written plan, policy or SOP describing fusion center business processes for the receipt, handling, and storage of classified (SECRET) and unclassified information from Federal partners
- *Analyze:* A written plan, policy, or SOP describing fusion center business processes for assessing the local implications of threat-related information provided by Federal partners (DHS, FBI, etc.) through a formal risk analysis process. This process should determine what critical information needs to be provided to State, local, Tribal, and territorial (SLTT) and private sector partners to support prevention, protection, and other response- related operational planning efforts, and to inform these partners of

behaviors and circumstances that may serve as pre-incident indicators of an emerging threat

- *Disseminate:* A written plan, policy, or SOP describing fusion center business processes for disseminating critical information to SLTT and private sector partners in the fusion center's area of responsibility
- *Gather:* A written plan, policy, or SOP describing fusion center business processes for gathering locally generated information, participating in the NSI, and sharing pertinent information with the local JTTF for investigation and DHS for further analysis
- *Privacy, Civil Rights, and Civil Liberties (P/CRCL) Protections:* An approved P/CRCL policy to ensure that P/CRCL protections are in place that are at least as comprehensive as the ISE Privacy Guidelines, and that all staff receive training on both the center's P/CRCL policies and 28 CFR Part §23. The development and updating of such policies provide an opportunity to engage the whole community

Measurement Methods

- Percentage of fusion centers with documented plans, policies, or SOPs describing fusion center business processes for receiving, handling, and storing classified and unclassified information in accordance with the metrics established by the DHS Office of Intelligence and Analysis (I&A)
- Percentage of fusion centers with documented plans, policies, or SOPs describing fusion center business processes for assessing local implications of threat-related information in accordance with the metrics established by the DHS I&A
- Percentage of fusion centers with documented plans, policies, or SOPs describing fusion center business processes for disseminating information to SLTT and private sector partners in accordance with the metrics established by the DHS I&A
- Percentage of fusion centers with documented plans, policies, or SOPs describing fusion center business processes for gathering locally generated information and participating in the NSI in accordance with the metrics established by the DHS I&A
- Percentage of fusion centers with an approved P/CRCL policy
- Percentage of fusion centers that have conducted a audit of their P/CRCL policy in accordance with the *Privacy Civil Rights and Civil Liberties Compliance Verification for the Intelligence Enterprise4*

Reporting

- Achievement of these capabilities will be evaluated through the following methods:
  - IJ will be based upon the courses of action to fill identified gaps from the BCA, and these assessment results must be included as part of the IJ
  - The SAA must certify the fusion center's participation in the annual BCA process by reporting:
    - Percentage compliance with executing the critical operational capabilities at a fundamental level as a part of the IJ
    - Percentage of achievement of the critical operational capabilities must be regularly reported in the BSIR

- Exercises to evaluate the implementation of COCs and analytical proficiency, which will occur every two years. The SAA must certify the fusion center's participation in these exercises. This certification would be made to GPD as part of regular BSIR reporting.

Objective Two

Analytic Capabilities. All fusion center analytic personnel must demonstrate qualifications that meet or exceed competencies identified in the Common Competencies for State, Local, and Tribal Intelligence Analysts.

In addition to these training requirements, fusion centers should also continue to mature their analytic capabilities by addressing gaps in analytic capability identified during the fusion center's BCA.

Measurement Methods

- Percentage of fusion center analytic personnel funded out of SHSP and UASI that have received/participated in training deemed to be compliant with the *Common Competencies for State, Local, and Tribal Intelligence Analysts*
- Percentage of fusion center analysts that require SECRET clearances have them (or have submitted requests for them)
- Percentage of fusion center analysts with access to sensitive but unclassified (SBU) systems
- Percentage of fusion center analysts trained on 28 CFR Part §23
- Percentage of fusion center analyst with access to tools identified in the Analyst Toolbox6

Reporting

- Assessed through reporting methods identified in **Objective 1.**

Fiscal Year 2012 HSGP Guidance

Priority Three: Maturation and Enhancement of State and Major Urban Area Fusion Centers

One of the Department's highest priorities in FY 2012 remains support for recognized State and major Urban Area fusion centers and the maturation of the Information Sharing Environment (ISE).

Fusion centers serve as focal points within the State and local environment for the receipt, analysis, gathering, and sharing of threat-related information between the Federal government and State, local, tribal, territorial (SLTT) and private sector partners.

Building a National Network of Fusion Centers (National Network) empowers law enforcement, fire, emergency management and homeland security personnel by helping them understand local implications of national intelligence, thus enabling them to better protect their communities.

A National Network also provides a mechanism for the Federal government to receive information from SLTT partners, which helps create a more complete intelligence picture at the National level. With timely, accurate information on potential terrorist threats, fusion centers can also directly contribute to and inform investigations initiated and conducted by Federal entities, such as the Joint Terrorism Task Forces led by the Federal Bureau of Investigation (FBI). The 2010 National Security Strategy identifies fusion centers as critical in enlisting all of our intelligence, law enforcement, fire, emergency, management, and homeland security capabilities to prevent acts of terrorism on American soil.

In support of this strategic vision, the Department is requiring recognized State and major Urban Area fusion centers to participate in an annual assessment of their achievement of Critical Operational Capabilities (COCs) and Enabling Capabilities (ECs), as based upon the Global Justice Information Sharing Initiative‘s (Global) Baseline Capabilities for State and Major Urban Area Fusion Centers. The four COCs are: receive; analyze; disseminate; and gather.

The four ECs are: Privacy, Civil Rights, and Civil Liberties (P/CRCL) Protection; Sustainment Strategy; Communications and Outreach; and Security. The results from this assessment will help fusion centers identify gaps in their operational and enabling capabilities.

Mitigating these gaps will enhance fusion centers' capacity to improve the nation's ability to safeguard the homeland and prevent terrorist and criminal activity, while enabling local officials to better protect their communities.

As maturation of the National Network is one of the Department‘s highest priorities in FY 2012, DHS is requiring that all fusion center related funding requests be consolidated into a single (1) Investment for States or Urban Areas, in which recognized fusion centers reside, and this Investment must address funding support for the recognized fusion center. Grantees must coordinate with the fusion center when developing a fusion center Investment prior to submission, and Investment requests must directly align to and reference any capability gaps identified during the center's individual 2011 Fusion Center Assessment Report. In particular, each proposed project included in the fusion center Investment must reference the corresponding COC or EC, as well as associated attribute(s), the funding investment is intended to address.

Additionally, any jurisdiction or agency that leverages HSGP funds to support intelligence- or fusion process-related activities (i.e., intelligence unit, real time crime information and analysis centers, etc.) must ensure these efforts are integrated and/or coordinated with the respective State or major Urban Area fusion center(s).

Background: The Baseline Capabilities for State and Major Urban Area Fusion Centers (September 2008) identifies the baseline capabilities for fusion centers and the operational standards necessary to achieve each of the capabilities across the National Network. Fusion centers, in partnership with the Federal Government, prioritized four COCs, which reflect the operational priorities of the National Network, and four ECs, which provide a foundation for the fusion process.

During the annual fusion center assessment, fusion centers are assessed on their ability to execute the COCs and ECs.

Objective One: Baseline Capabilities. Fusion centers leveraging SHSP and/or UASI grant funds must prioritize the allocation of these grant funds to any capability gaps identified as a result of the 2011 Fusion Center Assessment and, only after identified capability gaps have been addressed, maintain and enhance capabilities in execution of the COCs and ECs. This will ensure the implementation of common and consistent operational standards across the National Network.

Objective Two: Analytic Capabilities. All fusion center analytic personnel must demonstrate qualifications that meet or exceed competencies identified in the Common Competencies for State, Local, and Tribal Intelligence Analysts. In addition to these training requirements, fusion centers should also continue to mature their analytic capabilities by addressing gaps in analytic capability identified during the annual fusion center assessment.

Measurement Methods (Fusion Center Reporting and Compliance)

In order to effectively measure implementation of this priority, recognized State and major Urban Area fusion centers leveraging SHSP and/or UASI grant funds will be evaluated based upon compliance with the following:

- Successful completion of the annual Fusion Center Assessment Program managed by the DHS Office of Intelligence and Analysis (I&A). The Fusion Center Assessment Program is comprised of the self assessment, validation, staffing and product tables, and cost assessment data and will evaluate each Fusion Center against the four COCs
- Have approved plans, policies, or SOPs and, per the Fusion Center Assessment Program, demonstrate improvement in each of the four COCs
- Have an approved P/CRCL policy that is determined to be at least as comprehensive as the ISE Privacy Guidelines
- Conduct an annual audit of their P/CRCL policy in accordance with the Privacy Civil Rights and Civil Liberties Compliance Verification for the Intelligence Enterprise (http://it.ojp.gov/docdownloader.aspx?ddid=1285)
- Ensure all staff receive annual training on both the center's P/CRCL policies and 28 CFR Part 23
- All fusion center analytic personnel must meet designated competencies, as identified in the *Common Competencies for State, Local, and Tribal Intelligence Analysts*, that have been acquired through experience or training courses Successfully complete an exercise to evaluate the implementation of the four COCs at least once every two years and address any corrective actions arising from the successfully completed exercises

Reporting

- For SHSP and UASI, fusion centers will report on the achievement of capabilities and compliance with measurement requirements within the Maturation and Enhancement of State and Major Urban Area Fusion Centers priority through the annual Fusion Center Assessment Program managed by DHS I&A and reported to FEMA

Fiscal Year 2013 HSGP Guidance

Priority Three: Maturation and Enhancement of State and Major Urban Area Fusion Centers

DHS preparedness grants continue to support designated State and major Urban Area fusion centers (see http://www.dhs.gov/fusion-center-locations-and-contact-information) and the maturation of the Information Sharing Environment (ISE). Fusion centers, a critical component of our Nation's distributed homeland security and counterterrorism architecture, provide grassroots intelligence and analytic capabilities within the state and local environment.

Fusion centers contribute to the ISE through their role in receiving threat information from the Federal government; analyzing that information in the context of their local environment; disseminating that information to local agencies; and gathering tips, leads, and SAR initiatives from local agencies and the public. Enhancing and sustaining these capabilities across the National Network of Fusion Centers (National Network) helps to empower law enforcement, fire service/emergency medical services (EMS), emergency management, public health and other public safety and homeland security personnel by helping them understand local implications of national intelligence, thus enabling them to better protect their communities.

A National Network also provides a mechanism for the Federal government to receive information from SLTT partners, which helps create a more complete threat picture at the National level. Participating in the Nationwide SAR Initiative enables fusion centers to receive and analyze suspicious activity reporting from frontline public safety personnel, the private sector, and the public, and ensure the sharing of SAR with the Federal Bureau of Investigation- led Joint Terrorism Task Forces for further investigation. *The 2010 National Security Strategy* identifies fusion centers as critical in enlisting all of our intelligence, law enforcement, fire service, emergency management, and homeland security capabilities to prevent acts of terrorism on American soil.

In support of this strategic vision, the Department of Homeland Security's Office of Intelligence & Analysis (DHS I&A) is requiring designated State and major Urban Area fusion centers to participate in an annual assessment of their achievement of Critical Operational Capabilities (COCs) and Enabling Capabilities (ECs), as detailed in the Global Justice Information Sharing Initiative's (Global) *Baseline Capabilities for State and Major Urban Area Fusion Centers.*

The results from this assessment, to be conducted in the fall of 2013, will help fusion centers identify gaps in their COCs and ECs and focus Federal investment so resources are targeted to mitigate any identified capability gaps and shortfalls and sustain existing capabilities.

This will enhance fusion centers' capacity to improve the nation's ability to safeguard the homeland and prevent terrorist and criminal activity, while enabling local officials to better protect their communities.

As maturation of the National Network continues to be a high priority in FY 2013, DHS is requiring that all fusion center related funding requests be consolidated into a single (1) Investment for States or Urban Areas in which designated fusion centers reside, and this Investment must address funding support for the designated fusion center. The single

Investment provides state and urban areas a means to centrally manage and report on fusion center related activities.

Grantees must coordinate with the fusion center when developing a fusion center Investment prior to submission, and the Investment must directly align to and reference any capability gaps and shortfalls identified during the center's individual 2012 Fusion Center Assessment Report. In particular, each proposed project included in the fusion center Investment must reference the corresponding COC or EC, as well as associated attribute(s), the funding investment is intended to address.

Additionally, any jurisdiction or agency that leverages HSGP funds to support intelligence- or fusion process-related activities (i.e., intelligence unit, real time crime information and analysis centers, etc.) must ensure these efforts are integrated and/or coordinated with the respective designated State or major Urban Area fusion center(s).

Background: The *Baseline Capabilities for State and Major Urban Area Fusion Centers* (September 2008) (http://www.dhs.gov/national-network-fusionidentifies the baseline capabilities for fusion centers and the operational standards necessary to achieve each of the capabilities across the National Network. Federal partners, in coordination with fusion center directors, prioritized four COCs, which reflect the operational priorities of the National Network Network, and four ECs, which provide a foundation for the fusion process. Enhancing and sustaining these capabilities across the National Network creates a national capacity to gather, process, analyze, and share information in support of efforts to protect the country.

During the annual fusion center assessment, fusion centers are assessed on their ability to execute the COCs and ECs.

Objective One: Baseline Capabilities. Fusion centers leveraging SHSP and/or UASI grant funds must prioritize the allocation of these grant funds to address any capability gaps and shortfalls identified as a result of the 2012 Fusion Center Assessment and maintain and enhance capabilities in execution of the COCs and ECs. This will ensure the implementation of common and consistent operational standards across the National Network.

Objective Two: Analytic Capabilities. All fusion center analytic personnel must demonstrate qualifications that meet or exceed competencies identified in the Common Competencies for State, Local, and Tribal Intelligence Analysts. In addition to these training requirements, fusion centers should also continue to mature their analytic capabilities by addressing gaps and shortfalls in analytic capability identified during the annual fusion center assessment.

Measurement Methods (Fusion Center Reporting and Compliance)

In order to effectively measure implementation of this priority, designated State and major Urban Area fusion centers leveraging SHSP and/or UASI grant funds will be evaluated based upon compliance with the following:

- Successful completion of the annual Fusion Center Assessment Program managed by the DHS I&A. The Fusion Center Assessment Program evaluates each Fusion Center against the COCs and ECs and is comprised of the self-assessment questions, staffing, product, and cost assessment data tables, and validation

- Maintain approved plans, policies, or SOPs and, per the Fusion Center Assessment Program, and, when applicable, demonstrate improvement in each of the four COCs
- Maintain an approved Privacy, Civil Rights, and Civil Liberties (P/CRCL) policy that is determined to be at least as comprehensive as the *ISE Privacy Guidelines*
- Conduct a compliance review of their P/CRCL policy in accordance with the *Privacy Civil Rights and Civil Liberties Compliance Verification for the Intelligence Enterprise (http://it.ojp.gov/docdownloader.aspx?ddid=1285)*
- Ensure all staff receive annual training on the center's P/CRCL policies
- Ensure all staff are trained on 28 CFR Part 23
- Ensure all Federally funded criminal intelligence databases comply with 28 CFR Part 23
- All fusion center analytic personnel must meet designated competencies, as identified in the *Common Competencies for State, Local, and Tribal Intelligence Analysts,* that have been acquired through experience or training courses
- Successfully complete an exercise to evaluate the implementation of the COCs at least once every two years and address any corrective actions arising from the successfully completed exercises within the timeframe identified in the each exercise' AAR
- Post 100 percent (100%) of distributable analytic products (as defined by the annual assessment process) to the Homeland Security Information Network's (HSIN's) Homeland Security State & Local Intelligence Community of Interest (HS SLIC) as well as any other applicable portals, such as LEO, RISS, their agency portal, etc.
- Have formalized process (as defined by the annual assessment process) to track incoming and outgoing Requests for Information (RFI), including send/recipient and actions taken
- For States that have multiple designated fusion centers, the primary fusion center has documented a plan that governs the coordination and interactions of all fusion centers within the state

Reporting

For SHSP and UASI, fusion centers will report on the achievement of capabilities and compliance with measurement requirements within the Maturation and Enhancement of State and Major Urban Area Fusion Centers priority through the annual Fusion Center Assessment Program managed by DHS I&A and reported to FEMA

APPENDIX IV. NATIONAL NETWORK MATURITY MODEL: EXCERPT FROM THE 2012 NATIONAL NETWORK OF FUSION CENTERS FINAL REPORT, P. 37.

National Network Maturity Model

The National Network Maturity Model (Maturity Model) is a multistage framework designed to evaluate and categorize the overall progress of the National Network as a whole—as opposed to individual fusion centers—in achieving the COCs and ECs. It defines a path for the National Network to move from the current state to a desired end state where a fully integrated, mature, and sustainable National Network strengthens efforts to protect the homeland. Using the Maturity Model, the fusion center stakeholder community can target resources and strategic planning efforts to support National Network capability maturation towards a defined goal with discrete intermediate capability targets.

Figure 14: The National Network of Fusion Centers has reached the Emerging Stage

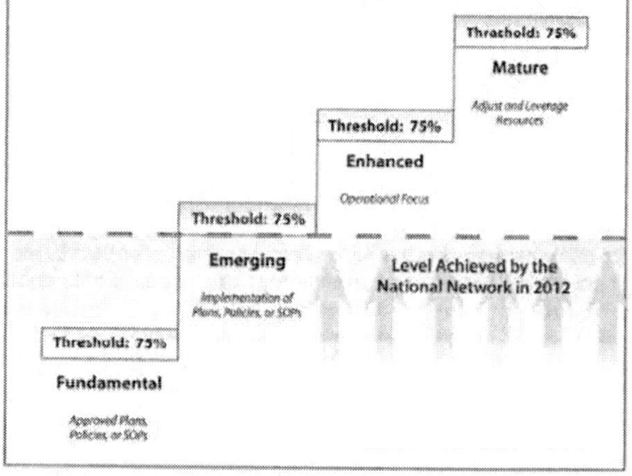

The Maturity Model consists of 46 attributes aligned to four distinct stages: Fundamental, Emerging, Enhanced, and Mature. For each stage of the Maturity Model, the fusion center stakeholder community established an outcome-oriented, qualitative definition and aligned capability attributes based on each attribute's contribution to the defined outcome for that maturity stage. Some of the attributes associated with the Maturity Model differ from those attributes aligned to individual fusion centers because the attributes needed for a fully capable fusion center are different from those needed for a fully capable National Network.

The National Network advances through each of the four stages of the Maturity Model when 75% of fusion centers achieve the attributes associated with that level of the Maturity Model. Each stage is equally important to achieving a fully integrated National Network.

Fundamental (Approved Plans, Policies, or SOPs): Fusion centers across the National Network have approved plans, policies, or SOPs for each of the four COCs and EC 1.

Emerging (Implementation of Plans, Policies, or SOPs): The National Network has the systems, mechanisms, and processes needed to implement the plans, policies, or SOPs and the COCs and ECs as a whole.

Enhanced (Operational Focus): The National Network has the operational capability to produce products and provide services to federal, state, and local customers.

Mature (Adjust and Leverage Resources): The National Network has the full capability to leverage the collective resources among individual fusion centers and adjust to both the changing threat environment and evolving requirements.

Appendix V. Executive Summary: GAO Study on Field-Based Information Sharing Activities, April 2013

Why GAO Did This Study

In 2007, DOJ and its federal partners developed the Nationwide Suspicious Activity Reporting Initiative to establish a capability to gather and share terrorism-related suspicious activity reports. GAO was asked to examine the initiative's progress and performance. This report addresses the extent to which (1) federal agencies have made progress in implementing the initiative, and what challenges, if any, remain; (2) the technical means used to collect and share reports overlap or duplicate each other; (3) training has met objectives and been completed; and (4) federal agencies are assessing the initiative's performance and results. GAO analyzed relevant documents and interviewed federal officials responsible for implementing the initiative and stakeholders from seven states (chosen based on their geographic location and other factors). The interviews are not generalizable but provided insight on progress and challenges.

What GAO Recommends

GAO recommends that DOJ implement formalized mechanisms to provide stakeholders feedback on the suspicious activity reports they submit, mitigate risks from supporting two systems to collect and share reports that may result in the FBI not receiving needed information, more fully assess if training for line officers meets their needs, and establish plans and time frames for implementing measures that assess the homeland security results the initiative has achieved. DOJ agreed with these recommendations and identified actions taken or planned to implement them.

What GAO Found

The Department of Justice (DOJ) has largely implemented the Nationwide Suspicious Activity Reporting Initiative among fusion centers—entities that serve as the focal point within a state for sharing and analyzing suspicious activity reports and other threat information. The state and local law enforcement officials GAO interviewed generally said the initiative's processes worked well, but that they could benefit from additional feedback from the Federal Bureau of Investigation (FBI) on how the reports they submit are used. The FBI has a feedback mechanism, but not all stakeholders were aware of it. Implementing formalized feedback mechanisms as part of the initiative could help stakeholders conduct accurate analyses of terrorism-related information, among other things.

The technical means that federal, state, and local entities use to collect and share terrorism-related suspicious activity reports—Shared Spaces servers that DOJ provides to most fusion centers and the FBI's eGuardian system—provide many overlapping or duplicative services. For example, both systems provide a national network for sharing the reports and tools to analyze them. The federal government is aware that duplication exists but supports both systems to enable fusion centers to control information on individuals, consistent with the centers' privacy requirements, and facilitate the FBI's investigative needs. However, the FBI was concerned that supporting two systems introduces risks that it will not receive all reports. For example, at the time of our review, many fusion centers were choosing not to automatically share all of their reports with the FBI's system—although they may have shared reports via phone or other means—and DOJ had not fully diagnosed why. In its March 2013 letter commenting on a draft of this report, DOJ stated that it had made progress on this issue. DOJ also had not formally tested the exchange of information between the two systems to ensure that the exchanges were complete. Taking additional steps to mitigate the risks that reports are not fully shared could help DOJ ensure that the FBI receives all information that can support investigations.

Stakeholders GAO interviewed generally reported that training fully or partially met objectives, such as making law enforcement more aware of the initiative. DOJ has mechanisms to assess the analyst training to help ensure that analysts have the information they need to review and share reports. However, DOJ had not fully assessed its training provided to officers on the front line, which could help ensure that officers receive sufficient information to be able to recognize terrorism-related suspicious activity. DOJ has provided training to executives at 77 of 78 fusion centers, about 2,000 fusion center analysts, and about 290,000 of the 800,000 line officers. DOJ is behind schedule in training the line officers but is taking actions to provide training to officers who have not yet received it.

DOJ and other agencies collect some data to assess the performance of the Nationwide Suspicious Activity Reporting Initiative—such as the number of reports submitted and resulting FBI investigations. These data show that stakeholders were increasingly submitting and using terrorism-related reports. However, DOJ had not yet established plans and time frames for implementing measures that assess the homeland security results achieved by the initiative and thus lacked a means for establishing accountability for implementing them.

Appendix VI. Executive Summary: GAO Study on Field-Based Information Sharing Activities, April 2013

Why GAO Did This Study

Federal agencies and state and local governments have established field- based entities (e.g., centers and task forces) nationwide that share terrorism- related information, among other things. GAO was asked to assess these entities. This report addresses (1) the extent to which these entities are distinct, fragmented, overlapping, or duplicative; (2) the extent to which DOJ, DHS, and ONDCP hold entities accountable for coordinating and have assessed coordination opportunities; and (3) how, if at all, DOJ, DHS, and ONDCP incorporate information on the results entities achieve when making funding decisions. GAO analyzed entities' missions, activities, and coordination efforts in eight selected urban areas that range in geographic dispersion and risk. Although not generalizable, this analysis provided insights. This is a public version of a sensitive report GAO issued in March 2013. Information the Federal Bureau of Investigations (FBI) deemed sensitive has been redacted.

What GAO Recommends

GAO recommends that ONDCP work with HIDTA officials to establish time frames to connect systems; DHS, DOJ, and ONDCP develop measures to hold entities accountable for coordination and assess opportunities to enhance coordination; and the PM-ISE report on the results of the agencies' efforts to assess coordination. DHS, ONDCP, and the PM-ISE concurred. DOJ generally agreed with the intent of the recommendations, but disagreed with their underlying premises that DOJ was not already taking such actions. GAO believes these actions do not fully address the recommendations as discussed further in this report.

What GAO Found

Five types of field-based information-sharing entities are supported, in part, by the federal government—Joint Terrorism Task Forces, Field Intelligence Groups, Regional Information Sharing Systems (RISS) centers, state and major urban area fusion centers, and High Intensity Drug Trafficking Area (HIDTA) Investigative Support Centers—and have distinct missions, roles, and responsibilities. However, GAO identified 91 instances of overlap in some analytical activities—such as producing intelligence reports—and 32 instances of overlap in investigative support activities, such as identifying links between criminal organizations. These entities conducted similar activities within the same mission area, such as counterterrorism, for similar customers, such as federal or state agencies. This can lead to benefits, such as the corroboration of information, but may also burden customers with redundant information. GAO also found that RISS centers and HIDTAs operate three different systems that duplicate the same function—identifying when different law enforcement entities may be conducting a similar enforcement action, such as a raid at the same location, to ensure officer safety—resulting in some inefficiencies. RISS and HIDTA have taken steps to connect two of the systems, but HIDTA does not have target time frames to connect the third system. A commitment to time frames would help reduce risks to officer safety and potentially lessen the burden on law enforcement agencies that are currently using multiple systems.

Agencies have neither held entities accountable for coordinating nor assessed opportunities for further enhancing coordination to help reduce the potential for overlap and achieve efficiencies. The Departments of Justice (DOJ) and Homeland Security (DHS), and the Office of National Drug Control Policy (ONDCP)—the federal agencies that oversee or provide support to the five types of field-based entities— acknowledged that entities working together and sharing information is important, but they do not hold the entities accountable for such coordination. A mechanism that enables agencies to monitor the results of coordination efforts could encourage more coordination, help reduce any unnecessary overlap and leverage resources. Officials in the eight urban areas said that practices such as having representatives from other agencies on governance boards and colocating entities where possible enhanced coordination, information sharing, and efficiencies—in their view, reducing the potential of unnecessary overlap. Federal agencies have not assessed the extent to which such practices could be further implemented and, therefore, may be missing opportunities to maximize benefits. The Program Manager for the Information Sharing Environment (PM-ISE)—which manages efforts to enhance sharing governmentwide—has not reported on specific coordination efforts across the entities. Including agencies' assessment progress in the annual reports to the Congress would enhance accountability.

The agencies collect information on entities' results, but vary in the extent to which they consider the results when they make decisions about future funding. For example, agencies may consider other factors—such as risk and threats— rather than results, or funding decisions may be determined by state grant recipients or set in part by statutory or other requirements.

APPENDIX VII. RESOURCE ALLOCATION CRITERIA

Information Sharing Environment Guidance (ISE-G)
Federal Resource Allocation Criteria (RAC)

Purpose

This document defines objective criteria to be used by federal agencies that provide direct support to state and major urban area fusion centers ("fusion centers") (herein referred to as federal fusion center support entities or FFCSE) when making federal resource allocation decisions to fusion centers.

Background

The Federal Government does not dictate where fusion centers should be built and maintained, nor does it designate fusion centers. However, the Federal Government has a shared responsibility with state and local governments to promote the establishment of a national network of fusion centers to facilitate effective information sharing. Since 2001, the Federal Government has provided significant grant funding, training, technical assistance, exercise support, federal personnel, and access to federal information and networks to support fusion centers. The Federal Government recognizes the importance and ability of state, local, tribal, and territorial (SLTT) governments to own operate, and/or participate in fusion centers and respects that a fusion center's mission should be defined according to its jurisdictional needs. To ensure that information sharing efforts are optimized and barriers minimized, SLTT governments should define and document how their jurisdictions intend to carry out intrastate coordination to gather, process, analyze, and disseminate terrorism, homeland security, and law enforcement information (the "fusion process").

The *National Strategy for Information Sharing (2007) ("NSIS")* provides a Federal Government-wide approach to interfacing and collaborating with fusion centers. In furtherance of the NSIS goals, the Federal Government must clearly define the parameters for the allocation of federal resources to fusion centers in order to provide support in a manner that:

- Collectively supports the development of a national network of fusion centers; and
- Effectively balances the need for supporting SLTT, as well as federal, imperatives.

The Federal Government can accomplish this task through the implementation of specific, objective criteria for resource allocation by FFCSEs to fusion centers. Not only will established criteria help bring transparency into the process of allocating federal resources to fusion centers; it will also enable FFCSEs to prioritize support in order to enhance the national network of fusion centers.

Criteria for Resource Allocation to Fusion Centers

FFCSEs will prioritize federal resource allocation across three categories. These categories (in order of primacy) and the corresponding prioritization criteria for resource allocation are detailed below.

Category 1: Criteria for Prioritization of Primary Fusion Centers

In each of the 50 states, the District of Columbia, and the five U.S. territories[64] there may be one primary fusion center. To be eligible for this category, a fusion center must be designated by the Governor[65] as the primary fusion center, pursuant to the joint Department of Homeland Security (DHS) and Department of Justice (DOJ) November 2007 fusion center designation letter, and this designation must be communicated to the Secretary of Homeland Security and the United States Attorney General.

A primary fusion center shall maintain the following criteria in order for FFCSEs to continue to prioritize it within this category for federal resource allocation:

- Designation as the primary fusion center by the Governor;
- Oversight and management by a state or local government agency;
- Receipt of DHS certification that privacy, civil rights, and civil liberties (P/CRCL) protections are in place that are determined to be at least as comprehensive as the Information Sharing Environment (ISE) Privacy Guidelines;
- Implementation of a plan and procedures to fulfill its responsibility as the focal point within the state and local environment for the receipt, analysis, gathering, and sharing of threat-related information[66], and for the coordination and execution of the statewide fusion process, including all fusion centers and other SLTT partners in its state or territory; and
- Achievement and maintenance of the *Baseline Capabilities for State and Major Urban Area Fusion Center (Baseline Capabilities),* as measured by the annual Baseline Capabilities Assessment (BCA).

Category 2: Criteria for Prioritization of Recognized Fusion Centers

The Federal Government respects the authority of state governments to designate fusion centers. Any designated fusion center, including major urban area fusion centers, not designated as a primary fusion center will be referred to as a recognized fusion center and included within this category for resource allocation, as appropriate.

A recognized fusion center shall maintain the following criteria in order for the fusion center to continue to be eligible for federal resource allocation within this category:

- Designation as a fusion center by the Governor;
- Oversight and management by a state or local government agency;
- Implementation of a plan and procedures to work in conjunction with the primary fusion center, as part of the statewide fusion process;
- Achievement and maintenance of the Baseline Capabilities; and
- Receipt of DHS certification that P/CRCL protections are in place that are determined to be at least as comprehensive as the ISE Privacy Guidelines.

Category 3: Criteria for Prioritization of Nodes

A state may leverage its criminal intelligence units, real-time crime analysis centers, and other law enforcement or homeland security analytic centers that have not been designated as fusion centers by state governments. These nodes can provide valuable support to the statewide fusion process by coordinating with the primary fusion center and recognized fusion centers in the geographic area, thereby participating in intrastate coordination. Nodes are encouraged to achieve the *Baseline Capabilities*, as they pertain to their operations. Additionally, nodes are encouraged to maintain all applicable P/CRCL protections.

Implementation of Resource Allocation Criteria

FFCSEs provide support and resources to fusion centers in order to achieve and sustain the Baseline Capabilities. These resources include, but are not limited to, deployed personnel, connectivity with federal data systems, training, technical assistance, exercise support, grant programs, and national and regional workshops and conferences. The goal of these criteria is to enable FFCSEs to prioritize resource allocation to fusion centers. Within the context of this policy, federal mission needs may also inform the allocation of resources provided by FFCSEs.

While prioritization for federal support and resources is dependent upon achieving and maintaining fusion center resource allocation criteria, meeting these criteria does not guarantee the provision of funding. Federal agency support will be contingent upon available resources.

Primary Fusion Centers

Because primary fusion centers are designated by state Governors as the focal points within the state and local environment for the receipt, analysis, gathering, and sharing of threat-related information and have additional responsibilities related to the coordination of critical operational capabilities across the statewide fusion process with recognized fusion centers and nodes, the highest priority for the allocation of federal resources to fusion centers shall be directed to primary fusion centers. FFCSEs are committed to deploying personnel and establishing connectivity with federal data systems to primary fusion centers with the understanding that once resources are obligated by federal partners, they may not be immediately replaceable if the fusion center moves or relocates. In addition, primary fusion centers will be eligible to receive joint DHSIDOJ Fusion Process Technical Assistance Program services, as well as other training and exercise services directly related to the fusion process. Primary fusion centers will also receive invitations to National Fusion Center Conferences and Regional Workshops. Primary fusion centers will remain eligible for state and Urban Areas Security Initiative (UASI) grant programs, as applicable. When available resources are limited, FFCSEs may prioritize the allocation of resources to those fusion centers within this category based on the fusion centers' demonstrated ability to achieve and maintain the *Baseline Capabilities* and collocation with existing federal resources at fusion centers.

Recognized Fusion Centers

Recognized fusion centers will be eligible to receive deployed personnel and connectivity to federal data systems, as available. They will be eligible to receive joint DHS/DOJ Fusion Process Technical Assistance Program services only when a request is submitted and approved through the primary fusion center or the Homeland Security Advisor. Recognized fusion centers will also be eligible to receive invitations to National Fusion Center Conferences and Regional Workshops only when a request is submitted and approved through the primary fusion center or the Homeland Security Advisor. Recognized fusion centers will remain eligible for state and UASI grant programs, as applicable. When available resources are limited, FFCSEs may prioritize the allocation of resources to those fusion centers within this category based on the fusion centers' demonstrated ability to achieve and maintain the *Baseline Capabilities* and collocation with existing federal resources at fusion centers.

Nodes

Nodes will receive access to deployed personnel and federal data systems through the primary and/or recognized fusion centers. They may be eligible to receive specialized fusion center training and technical assistance services, as applicable, and invitations to other conferences and workshops only when a request is submitted and approved through the primary fusion center or the Homeland Security Advisor. Nodes will remain eligible for state- and UASI grant programs, as applicable.

Effective Date and Expiration. This ISE-G is effective immediately and will remain in effect as the Federal Resource Allocation Criteria (RAC) until updated, superseded, or cancelled.

Kshemendra N. Paul Program
Manager for the Information
Sharing Environment
Date: June 3, 2011

Appendix VIII. List of Acronyms

2012 Final Report	*2012 National Network of Fusion Centers, Final Report, June 2013*
---- A ----	
AOR	Area of Responsibility
"Assessment"	Annual Fusion Center Assessment
ATF	Bureau of Alcohol, Tobacco, Firearms, and Explosives, Department of Justice
---- B ----	
BITAC	Basic Intelligence Threat Analysis Course
---- C ----	
CBP	Customs and Border Protection, Department of Homeland Security
CFIX	Central Florida Intelligence Exchange
CIKR	Critical Infrastructure and Key Resources
Committee	Committee on Homeland Security, US House of Representatives
---- D ----	
DEA	Drug Enforcement Administration, Department of Justice
DHS	Department of Homeland Security
DOD	Department of Defense
DOJ	Department of Justice
---- E ----	
EMS	Emergency Medical Services
EOC	Emergency Operations Center
---- F ----	
FAST	Field Analytic Support Taskforce
FBI	Federal Bureau of Investigation, Department of Justice
FEMA	Federal Emergency Management Agency, Department of Homeland Security
FLO	Fusion Liaison Officer, *similar to Terrorism Liaison Officer*
Fusion Centers	State and Major Urban Area Fusion Centers

----- G ----

GPD	Grant Programs Directorate, Federal Emergency Management Agency

---- H ----

HIDTA	High Intensity Drug Trafficking Area
HSDN	Homeland Secure Data Network
HSIN	Homeland Security Information Network

---- I ----

I&A	Office of Intelligence and Analysis, Department of Homeland Security
IA	Intelligence Analyst, Office of Intelligence and Analysis
IC	Intelligence Community
ICE	Immigrations and Customs Enforcement, Department of Homeland Security
IJ	Investment Justification
ILO	Intelligence Liaison Officer, *similar to Terrorism Liaison Officer*
IO	Intelligence Officer, Office of Intelligence and Analysis
ISE	Information Sharing Environment

---- J ----

JRIG	Joint Regional Intelligence Group

---- M ----

Maturity Model	National Network Maturity Model, introduced as part of the 2011 annual Fusion Center Assessment. See Appendix IV.
MITAC	Mid-Level Intelligence Threat Analysis Course
MTT	Mobile Training Team

---- N ----

National Network	The National Network of Fusion Centers
NCR	National Capital Region
NFCA	National Fusion Center Association
NHIAC	New Hampshire Information and Analysis Center
NIPP	*National Infrastructure Protection Plan*
NPGP	National Preparedness Grant Program
NSI	Nationwide Suspicious Activity Reporting (SAR) Initiative

---- P ----

P/CRCL	Privacy, Civil Rights, and Civil Liberties
PM-ISE	Program Manager for the Information Sharing Environment, Office of the Director of National Intelligence
PSA	Protective Security Advisor, Office of Infrastructure Protection

---- R ----

RD	Regional Director, Office of Intelligence and Analysis
RO	Reports Officer
ROIC	New Jersey Regional Operations Intelligence Center

---- S ----

SAA	State Administrative Agency
SAR	Suspicious Activity Report/Reporting
SBU	Sensitive-But-Unclassified
SHSGP	State Homeland Security Grant Program
SLPO	State and Local Program Office, Office of Intelligence and Analysis
SLTT	State, Local, Tribal, and Territorial
STAS	California's State Threat Assessment System

---- T ----

TLO	Terrorism Liaison Officer
TSA	Transportation Security Administration, Department of Homeland Security

---- U ----

UASI	Urban Area Security Initiative
USCIS	United States Citizenship and Immigration Services, Department of Homeland Security

End Notes

[1] National Network stakeholders include, but are not limited to: Federal partners; State and local law enforcement; State and local governments, officials, and agencies; the National Guard; Tribal; the private sector; and representative associations (ex: law enforcement associations, the NFCA, and the National Governors Association).

[2] "Homeland Security Act of 2002," as amended by the "Implementing Recommendations of the 9/11 Commission Act of 2007" Pub. L. 110-53, Aug. 3, 2007, §511, 121 STAT. 322. Amends Homeland Security Act of 2002 by adding §210A(j)(1).

[3] *National Strategy for Information Sharing*, October 2007, p. A1-1.

[4] "The UASI program addresses the unique risk driven and capabilities-based planning, organization, equipment, training, exercise needs, of high-threat, high-density Urban Areas based on the THIRA-generated capability targets process and associated assessment efforts, and assists them in building an enhanced and sustainable capacity to prevent, protect against, mitigate, respond to, and recover from acts of terrorism." *Fiscal Year 2013 HSGP Funding Opportunity Announcement*, May 21, 2013, p. 5.

[5] National Network stakeholders include, but are not limited to: Federal partners; State and local law enforcement; State and local governments, officials, and agencies; the National Guard; Tribal; the private sector; and representative associations (ex: law enforcement associations, the NFCA, and the National Governors Association).

[6] See Appendix I.

[7] Including, but not limited to: *The Homeland Security Act of 2002*, as amended by the *Implementing Recommendations of the 9/11 Commission Act of 2007 (Pub. L. 110-53); The National Criminal Intelligence Sharing Plan*, 2003; *Fusion Center Guidelines*, 2006; *The National Strategy for Information Sharing*, 2007; *Baseline Capabilities for State and Major Urban Area Fusion Centers*, 2008; *CIKR Protection Capabilities for Fusion Centers*, 2008; *Critical Operational Capabilities for State and Major Urban Area Fusion Centers, Short- Term Gap Mitigation Guidebook*, 2010; *Common Competencies for State, Local, and Tribal Intelligence Analysts*, 2010; *DHS/DOJ Fusion Process Technical Assistance Program and Services: Considerations for Fusion Center and Emergency Operation Center Coordination* (Comprehensive Preparedness Guide 502), 2010; *National Security Strategy*, 2010; *ISE-G Federal Resource Allocation Criteria*, 2011; *National Strategy for Information Sharing and Safeguarding*, 2012; and *National Prevention Framework*, 2013.

[8] See Appendix IV.

[9] FEMA and I&A briefing to the Committee, August 23, 2012.

[10] Information provided by DOJ and FBI, December 20, 2012.

[11] *Id.*

[12] On April 8, 2011, the Administration publicly released Presidential Policy Directive-8 (PPD-8). PPD-8 requires that the Secretary of Homeland Security develop a National Preparedness System, including the development of four new National Frameworks – Prevention, Protection, Mitigation, and Recovery – and update the National Response Framework. The Frameworks will help the Nation meet the National Preparedness Goal. DHS released the National Disaster Recovery Framework in September 2001; in May 2013 DHS released the Prevention, Mitigation, and Response Frameworks; and the Protection Framework remains outstanding. DHS recently informed the Committee that the Protection Framework is in the final development stages and will be released in the near future.

[13] Kshemendra Paul, Program Manager for the Information Sharing Environment, *Statement for the Record*, Testimony before the Subcommittee on Oversight, Investigations, and Management, House Committee on Homeland Security, "Lessons From Fort Hood: Improving our Ability to Connect the Dots." September 14, 2012.

[14] *National Strategy for Information Sharing*, October 2007, p. 20.

[15] Note: This is a separate question than that pertaining to whether the Federal Government should support fusion centers with other resources- HSDN, IOs, intelligence analysts, etc.

[16] California State Threat Assessment System, *Concept of Operations*, p. 1.

[17] Tex. Gov. Code §421.082 added by Acts 2003, 78th Leg., ch. 1312, Sec. 1, eff. June 21, 2003. amend. by Acts 2009, 81st Leg., R.S., Ch. 1350, Sec. 1, eff. June 19, 2009; Acts 2011, 82nd Leg., R.S., Ch. 1178, Sec. 5, eff. June 17, 2011.

[18] Tex. Gov. Code §421.083 added by Acts 2011, 82nd Leg., R.S., Ch. 1178, Sec. 6, eff. June 17, 2011.

[19] Tex. Gov. Code §421.084 added by Acts 2011, 82nd Leg., R.S., Ch. 1178, Sec. 6, eff. June 17, 2011.

[20] The Committee received fusion centers' fiscal year 2012 funding information on April 18, 2013.

[21] The calculated total of combined operating budgets reflects the funds expended by the fusion centers in fiscal year 2012.

[22] See Appendix III.

[23] Id.

[24] FEMA and I&A briefing to the Committee, August 23, 2012.

[25] Information provided by FEMA GPD, June 20, 2013.

[26] The SAAs for three States and the District of Columbia oversee both the State's homeland security and emergency management agencies.

[27] Types of HIDTA funding benefiting fusion centers include: staffing; information systems and technologies; training and exercises; and management and administration.

[28] *Final Report of the National Commission on Terrorist Attacks Upon the United States* (The 9/11 Commission Report), July 2004, p. 73.

[29] Based upon data collected during site visits, January-August 2012.

[30] *2012 National Network of Fusion Centers, Final Report*, June 2013, p. 16; 2011 *National Network of Fusion Centers, Final Report*, May 2012, p. 14.

[31] *FY2013 Homeland Security Grant Program (HSGP) Funding Opportunity Announcement*, p. 42.

[32] According to the Maturity Model, the "Emerging Stage" is reached when 75% of fusion centers in the National Network have the systems, mechanisms, and processes needed to implement the plans, policies, or SOPs and the COCs and ECs as a whole. See Appendix IV.

[33] TLOs are also known as Fusion Liaison Officers (FLO), Intelligence Liaison Officers (ILO), or by other names unique to individual host fusion centers.

[34] One of the fusion centers reporting that they do not have a TLO program did report an informal liaison program within its AOR.

[35] Information provided by FBI and DOJ to the Committee, July 15, 2013.

[36] "*A Call to Action: A Unified Message Regarding the Need to Support Suspicious Activity Reporting and Training*," 2011. http://nsi.ncirc.gov/documents/A_Call_to_Action.pdf

[37] See Appendix V.

[38] The total number of fusion centers with State and local personnel cleared to TS//SCI includes State or local personnel falling within the fusion center chain of command but are assigned to the local Joint Terrorism Task Force.

[39] Information provided by DHS to the Committee, July 15, 2013.

[40] *2012 National Network of Fusion Centers, Final Report*, June 2013, p13; DHS is unable to provide a final deployment timeline since deployment requires certified secure space and other requirements.

[41] DOD and I&A briefing to the Committee, September 6, 2012.

[42] The Joint Counterterrorism Assessment Team (JCAT) – a coordinated effort between the NCTC, I&A, and FBI – collaborates with members of the IC "to research, produce, and disseminate counterterrorism intelligence products for federal, state, local, and tribal government agencies and the private sector and advocate for the counterterrorism intelligence requirements and needs of these partners throughout the Intelligence Community." www.nctc.gov/jcat/jcat_roles_and_responsibilities.html

[43] *Information Sharing Environment, Annual Report to the Congress*, June 2012, p.4.

[44] Information provided by DHS to the Committee, July15, 2013.

[45] HSIN Program Management Office briefing to the Committee, April 15, 2013.

[46] *2011 National Network of Fusion Centers, Final Report*, May 2012, p. 53.

[47] *2011 National Network of Fusion Centers, Final Report*, May 2012, p. 15.

[48] See Appendix III.

[49] I&A briefing to the Committee, April 15, 2013.

[50] *2011 National Network of Fusion Centers, Final Report, May 2012, p. 22; and Fiscal Year 2012 HSGP Funding Opportunity Announcement*, February 2012, p. 32.

[51] *2012 National Network of Fusion Centers, Final Report*, June 2013, p. 48.

[52] Description provided by DHS: IO - I&A State and Local Program Office employee physically located at a fusion centers or other field site location, who is responsible for facilitating intelligence and information sharing relationships with federal, state, local, tribal, territorial and private sector stakeholders within their area of responsibility (AOR). IOs are the onsite lead for all I&A personnel within the assigned fusion center and AOR. The IO manages all functions of the intelligence cycle in a specific geography; supports fusion center directors' intelligence, information and resource requirements as they relate to Baseline Capabilities, especially Critical Operational Capabilities; and regularly conducts outreach to cultivate or strengthen relationships between I&A, DHS components, and State, Local, Tribal, Territorial personnel.

[53] Description provided by DHS: RD - Supervisory government employee assigned to the State and Local Program Office and physically located at a fusion center or other field site location. RDs are responsible for the development, direction, and facilitation of I&A goals and objectives within their respective areas of responsibility. As the senior I&A manager within a geographic region, the RD manages all assigned personnel, processes, and technologies to enable the National Network of Fusion Centers to meet U.S. Intelligence Community, DHS, and State, Local, Tribal, and Territorial requirements.

[54] Description provided by DHS: RO - An I&A Collections and Requirements Division Reporting Branch employee who is responsible for producing raw intelligence reports for dissemination to the Intelligence Community and other appropriate DHS stakeholders. The RO reviews, categorizes, stores, and retrieves highly sensitive information used in national security efforts. The RO writes, edits, vets, and disseminates raw intelligence reports based on information obtained through interaction with federal, state, local, tribal, territorial and private-sector partners in a geographic region.

[55] Description from information provided by DHS: IA - The two IAs assigned to fusion centers are responsible for organizing, planning, and conducting substantive, in-depth research and producing operational and strategic analysis that reflect regional subject matter knowledge. One of the IAs focuses strictly on border security analysis, and the other conducts broader homeland security analysis.

[56] I&A briefings to the Committee, November 19, 2012 & April 15, 2013.

[57] Description provided by DHS: PSA – Employees of DHS's National Protection and Programs Directorate's Office of Infrastructure Protection, PSAs are trained critical infrastructure protection and vulnerability mitigation subject matter experts who work with critical infrastructure owners and operators on a voluntary

basis. Overall, the PSAs focus on the Nation's most critical infrastructure as defined by the Level 1/Level 2 list. PSAs provide an on- the-ground perspective to the DHS national risk picture, facilitate information sharing among all levels of government and the private sector, conduct briefings and outreach meetings with critical infrastructure protection partners, support local exercises and planning initiatives, and disseminate critical infrastructure-related information. PSAs also coordinate requests from owners and operators concerning DHS programs and assistance, arrange for risk mitigation training, prepare critical infrastructure analytical reports and verification, and conduct security and resilience assessments.

[58] U.S. Department of Justice, Bureau of Justice Statistics, www.bjs.gov/index.cfm?ty=tp&tid=71

[59] FBI briefing to the Committee, May 28, 2013.

[60] FBI briefing to the Committee, August 21, 2012; I&A briefing to the Committee, September 5, 2012; FBI, I&A, & ODNI briefing to the Committee, January 24, 2013.

[61] Michael Leiter, Former National Counterterrorism Center Director, testifying before the House Committee on Homeland Security, July 10, 2013.

[62] See Appendix V.

[63] See Appendix VI.

[64] The five territories are American Samoa, Guam, the Northern Mariana Islands, Puerto Rico, and the U.S. Virgin Islands.

[65] For the District of Columbia, the Mayor may designate the primary fusion center.

[66] "State and major urban area fusion centers will be the focus, but not exclusive points, within the State and local environment for the receipt and sharing of terrorism information, homeland security information, and law enforcement Information related to terrorism." *National Strategy for Information Sharing. Al-l.*

In: The National Network of Fusion Centers
Editors: Nancy C. Lincoln and Janet B. Seegmiller
ISBN: 978-1-62948-138-8

Chapter 2

2012 National Network of Fusion Centers: Final Report*

U.S. Department of Homeland Security

Executive Summary

Overview

Threats to the homeland are persistent and constantly evolving. Domestic and foreign terrorism and the expanding reach of transnational organized crime syndicates across cyberspace, international borders, and jurisdictional boundaries within the United States highlight the continued need to build and sustain effective intelligence and information sharing partnerships among the federal government; state, local, tribal, and territorial (SLTT) governments; and the private sector. These partnerships are the foundation of a robust and efficient homeland security intelligence enterprise that goes beyond shared access to information and intelligence to foster sustained collaboration in support of a common mission. This collaboration enables the fusion process[1] and provides decision makers across all levels of government and within the private sector with the knowledge to make informed decisions to protect the homeland from a variety of threats and hazards.

State and major urban area fusion centers (fusion centers) are the nexus of the homeland security intelligence enterprise at the state and local level. They serve as focal points for the receipt, analysis, gathering, sharing, and safeguarding of threat-related information between the federal government and SLTT and private sector partners. As such, fusion centers provide a state and local context that enhances the national threat picture and enables local officials to better protect their communities. They also provide critical information and subject matter expertise that allows the Intelligence Community (IC) to more effectively "connect the dots" to prevent and protect against threats to the homeland.

* This is an edited, reformatted and augmented version of the U.S. Department of Homeland Security, dated June, 2013.

Background

Beginning in 2003, the federal government cooperated with state and local entities to develop and publish guidance to enable individual fusion centers to operate at a baseline level of capability and to form a robust and fully integrated National Network of Fusion Centers (National Network). To successfully perform these functions, fusion centers must develop and mature capabilities that enable efficient and effective information sharing, safeguarding, and analysis across the National Network and the broader Homeland Security Enterprise (HSE).[2] To guide the development of fusion center capabilities, Fusion Center Directors and the federal government jointly identified four Critical Operational Capabilities (COCs), which together reflect the operational priorities of the National Network, and four Enabling Capabilities (ECs), which provide a foundation for the fusion process.

In 2011, the U.S. Department of Homeland Security's (DHS) Office of Intelligence and Analysis (I&A), in coordination with federal and SLTT partners, began conducting an annual assessment of fusion centers to evaluate their progress in achieving the COCs and ECs and to collect additional data to better understand the characteristics of individual fusion centers and the National Network as a whole. DHS/I&A initiated the 2012 Fusion Center Assessment (2012 Assessment) in August 2012 as the second iteration of the annual assessment process and the first assessment to provide data on year-over-year progress in implementing the COCs and ECs. The 2012 Assessment was also the first assessment to collect National Network performance data based on an initial set of five performance measures adopted in 2011.

This *2012 National Network of Fusion Centers Final Report* (2012 Final Report) summarizes and characterizes the overall capabilities and performance of the National Network based on the results of the 2012 Assessment. This report does not include fusion center-specific capability or performance data. Instead, it uses aggregated data from the 2012 Assessment to describe the capability and performance achievements of the National Network.

This report also outlines ongoing efforts by National Network stakeholders to implement an outcome-based performance management framework to better understand the value and impact of the National Network in supporting national information sharing and homeland security outcomes.

Process

The 2012 Assessment measured fusion center capabilities in the following areas from August 1, 2011 through July 31, 2012:

- **Four COCs:** COC 1—Receive, COC 2—Analyze, COC 3—Disseminate, and COC 4—Gather.
- **Four ECs:** EC 1—Privacy, Civil Rights, and Civil Liberties (P/CRCL) Protections, EC 2—Sustainment Strategy, EC 3—Communications and Outreach, and EC 4—Security.

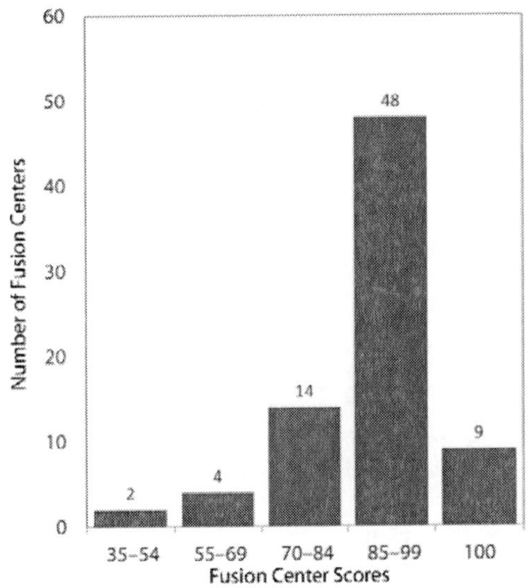

Figure 1. Overall Capability of the National Network of Fusion Centers.

The 2012 Assessment also measured National Network performance. Five initial performance measures developed jointly by federal and SLTT partners constitute a first effort to capture data on the value and impact of the National Network. Ongoing efforts by federal and SLTT fusion center stakeholders will define additional performance measures that reflect a broader range of National Network impacts on and contributions to national information sharing and homeland security outcomes. Future assessments will collect data on additional performance measures, once adopted.

As with the 2011 Assessment, the 2012 Assessment consisted of two phases. Phase 1 was a Self Assessment, and Phase 2 was a validation effort consisting of a comprehensive data quality review and interviews with Fusion Center Directors. All 77[3] fusion centers that constituted the National Network as of July 31, 2012 participated in the 2012 Assessment. Each fusion center received a score based on its validated Self Assessment responses. Individual fusion center scores were based on a 100-point scale.

SUMMARY OF FINDINGS

The overall capability scores for the 77 fusion centers that participated in the 2012 Assessment ranged from 38.4 to 100, with 9 fusion centers achieving scores of 100. The National Network average score was 88.4, which represents an increase of 11.6 points from the 2011 Assessment. More than one-third of the National Network—26 fusion centers—saw their overall scores increase by more than 20 points since last year.

DHS, in coordination with its interagency partners, analyzed the 50 individual attributes that contribute to full achievement of the COCs and ECs to understand the current capabilities within the National Network. DHS and interagency partners identified a number of significant findings that indicate noteworthy changes from last year (see Table 1).

Table 1. Summary of Findings

COC 1—Receive	All fusion centers (77 or 100%) have access to federally sponsored Sensitive But Unclassified (SBU) information sharing systems.
	Every fusion center (77 or 100%) has at least one person cleared to access Secret information, but regular staff turnover means that fusion centers will continue to request new clearances (approximately 500 new clearance requests in the next 12 months).
	A significant number of fusion centers have on-site access to classified information sharing systems (66 or 85.7%).
	Fusion center use of the DHS Secret Internet Protocol Router Network (SIPRNet) Whitelist (Whitelist) is limited (41 or 53.2%).
COC 2—Analyze	Fusion centers are highly involved in assessing threat and risk for their area of responsibility (AOR) (72 or 93.5%).
	Fusion centers are obtaining and using customer feedback on their analytic products (structured feedback: 65 or 84.4%).
	Analytic production plans are used widely across the National Network (60 or 77.9%).
	Critical infrastructure protection capabilities continue to expand across the National Network (75 or 97.4%).
COC 3—Disseminate	Despite progress since 2011, less than half (35 or 45.5%) of the National Network have a process in place to verify that customers are receiving their products.
	Fusion centers are increasingly designating a single, primary information sharing system (72 or 93.5%), but Homeland Security Information Network (HSIN) Intel is not frequently cited (23 or 29.9%) as the primary system for unclassified communication between fusion centers.
COC 4—Gather	The number of fusion centers that have developed Standing Information Needs (SINs) has increased (59 or 76.6%), but continued attention to SINs development is necessary.
	The National Network has a robust request for information (RFI) management capability (69 or 89.6%).
	A significant percentage of the National Network are involved in the Nationwide Suspicious Activity Reporting (SAR) Initiative (NSI), in particular in providing line officers with information on the behaviors identified in the Information Sharing Environment (ISE)-SAR Functional Standard (SAR line officer training: 66 or 85.7%).
EC 1—Privacy, Civil Rights, and Civil Liberties Protections	All but one of the fusion centers have a P/CRCL Officer (76 or 98.7%); however, turnover at this position is high across the National Network (37 or 48.1%).
	Fusion centers have made significant progress implementing P/CRCL protections (formal training of personnel: 71 or 92.2%), although compliance reviews (54 or 70.1%) and annual audits (53 or 68.8%) have not reached 100%.
	Coordinated outreach by fusion centers to stakeholders on P/CRCL issues is still lacking (P/CRCL outreach plans: 33 or 42.9%).
EC 2—Sustainment Strategy	The number of fusion centers with strategic plans has increased (54 or 70.1%), but almost 30% of fusion centers do not have an approved strategic plan.
	Fusion centers continue to address financial accountability (annual financial audit: 66 or 85.7%).
	The majority of fusion centers have adopted performance measures to evaluate progress in achieving programmatic outcomes (58 or 75.3%), although only about half connect performance measures to their strategic plans (36 or 46.8%).
	Fusion centers participate extensively in exercises (77 or 100%), although more exercises specifically focused on the fusion process, including the COCs and ECs, would benefit the National Network.
EC 3—Communications and Outreach	The number of fusion centers with approved communications plans has increased (51 or 66.2%), but a third of fusion centers still lack such a plan.
	Fusion centers are communicating their value, mission, and purpose through a documented process for capturing success stories and lessons learned (65 or 84.4%).

	Almost all fusion centers have a designated Public Information Officer or Public Affairs Officer to support communications and outreach (73 or 94.8%).
EC 4—Security	Fusion centers have developed plans, policies, or standard operating procedures (SOPs) to address physical, personnel, and information security (69 or 89.6%).
	Nearly all fusion centers have a designated Security Liaison (74 or 96.1%), but as with P/CRCL Officers, turnover among Security Liaisons is high (30 or 39.0%).
Cross-Cutting Capabilities	A large majority of fusion centers report to governance bodies (68 or 88.3%), and federal and SLTT partner representation on governance bodies is widespread.
	Fusion Center Director turnover is high (23 or 29.9%).
	Most fusion centers have established Fusion Liaison Officer (FLO) programs (58 or 75.3%) to broaden the scope of information sharing within their AOR.
	Most states with more than one fusion center have policies to guide coordination among fusion centers (10 of 12 states or 83.3%), but only half of fusion centers (41 or 53.2%) are part of plans that coordinate broader statewide information sharing.
	Fusion centers have significantly increased their capability to process National Terrorism Advisory System (NTAS) alerts (attained all NTAS attributes: 65 or 84.4%).

National Network Maturity

In addition to providing an evaluation of COC and EC achievements by individual fusion centers, data from the 2012 Assessment also allows an evaluation of the overall maturity of the National Network as a whole. DHS and its interagency partners employed a four-stage Maturity Model to describe how the National Network should progress as a unified system and what capabilities and resources are needed for the National Network to do so successfully. The National Network advances through a stage of the Maturity Model when 75% of fusion centers successfully achieve the attributes associated with that stage, as indicated by the percentage of positive responses to the corresponding question in that year's assessment.

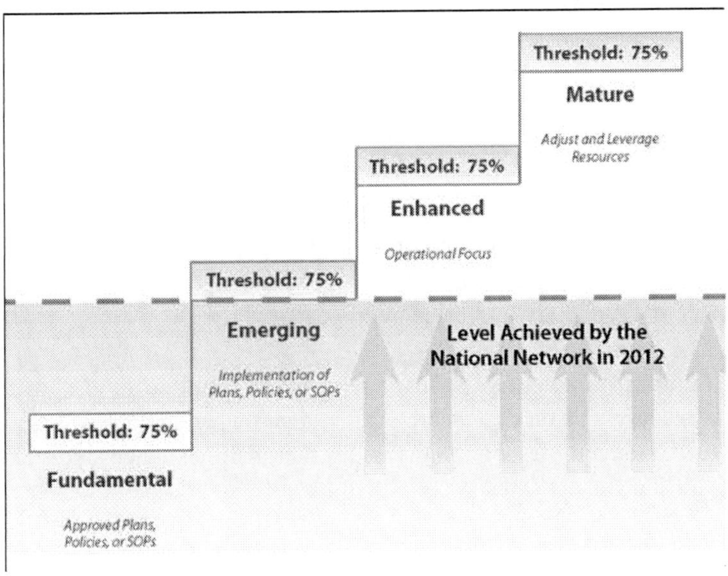

Figure 2. The National Network of Fusion Centers has reached the Emerging stage.

The results of the 2011 Assessment indicated that the National Network had reached the *Fundamental* stage, meaning that more than 75% of fusion centers have the requisite plans, policies, or SOPs to execute the fusion process. Over the last year, the fusion center stakeholder community has focused on ensuring continued improvement across the National Network in developing plans, policies, and SOPs and has also worked to reach the *Emerging* stage, which focuses on implementing effective fusion center business processes based on these plans, policies, and SOPs.

Results from the 2012 Assessment indicate that the National Network achieved the requisite threshold for each of the attributes associated with the *Emerging* stage, which include establishing the systems, mechanisms, and processes needed to implement their plans, policies, and SOPs and to execute the fusion process.

National Network Performance

National Network partners finalized the initial set of five performance measures in April 2012 (see Table 2).[4] These five performance measures reflect the shared benefits of a National Network, as well as the shared responsibilities of individual fusion centers and federal, state, and local partners in supporting and sustaining the National Network over time. These measures also start to characterize the effectiveness of the National Network, which reflects the implementation and institutionalization of the COCs and ECs and the fusion process in general. An expanded set of performance measures, which are currently under development, will provide a more comprehensive understanding of the broader value and impact of the National Network.

DHS, in close cooperation with federal and SLTT partners, will continue to help all fusion centers understand and implement the five initial performance measures in order to increase the quality and consistency of reported performance data and to ensure the broadest possible reporting of performance data across the National Network through future assessments.

Recommendations

Maturing and sustaining the National Network is a shared responsibility of federal and SLTT partners. Recognizing this shared responsibility, DHS has identified a number of recommendations intended to leverage the respective strengths of each partner to achieve desired end-states and capability implementation goals.

- **Use Standing Information Needs (SINs) as the foundation of a customer-driven fusion process:** Fusion centers are most relevant when they provide information and analysis that directly respond to the issues that their customers and stakeholders care about. Fusion centers should continue to identify and refine customer needs through a SINs management process and should build fusion process capabilities to effectively meet these needs. Fusion centers should build processes to tag products with SINs in order to effectively track the degree to which they are focusing on SINs—both their own internal SINs and the DHS Homeland Security (HSEC) SINs.

Fusion centers should also share their tagged products across the National Network and with other partners who have similar information needs. Federal partners should expand support to fusion centers through guidebooks, technical assistance, mentoring, and subject matter expertise to help fusion centers define and manage SINs and to more effectively and efficiently tag their products. Federal partners should also work to leverage technical solutions such as the Homeland Security Information Network (HSIN) IC of interest to help fusion centers automate SINs management processes and the sharing of analytic products across the National Network.

- **Minimize the impacts of staff turnover by documenting key business processes and ensuring consistent access to training:** High turnover in critical fusion center staff positions, including among Fusion Center Directors, P/CRCL Officers, and Security Liaisons, may limit the ability of fusion centers to build and maintain institutional knowledge. Effectively managing turnover supports key organizational partnerships, maintains fusion center productivity, and can strengthen oversight at critical steps in the fusion process. Fusion centers should ensure that all critical fusion center business processes are documented in approved plans, policies, and SOPs, not just for the COCs and P/CRCL, but for all elements of their operations. Federal partners should ensure that fusion center staff members have access to security and P/CRCL training, workshops, technical assistance, and other support. Federal partners should also facilitate exchanges and other opportunities to support these roles, such as peer-to-peer reviews and audits. At the same time, fusion centers should ensure that they take advantage of federal support and should cross-train fusion center staff members in critical business processes to minimize the impact of turnover when it does occur.
- **Implement organizational planning and evaluation processes to continuously improve fusion center operations:** Effective, high-performing organizations are guided by clearly defined missions, goals, and objectives, and they regularly and continuously evaluate themselves to determine whether they are achieving their intended outcomes. Fusion centers should clearly define their own mission, goals, and objectives by developing strategic plans and should use their strategic plans as the basis for measuring their performance. Fusion centers should also communicate their performance to governance bodies and other key stakeholders via mechanisms such as annual reports and demonstrate how investments in the fusion center result in tangible benefits within their areas of responsibility (AOR). Fusion centers should also continue to engage in broader National Network performance measurement efforts led by DHS to demonstrate how an organized, coordinated National Network supports national information sharing and homeland security outcomes. The federal government should provide technical assistance to fusion centers to support strategic planning efforts and should continue to lead performance planning and management on behalf of the National Network.

Table 2. Current Performance Measure Values and Targets for Future Years

		Assessment Year					
		2012	2013	2012	2012	2012	2012
1	**Percentage of fusion centers that conduct a privacy, civil rights, and civil liberties compliance review based upon the compliance verification tool (*Privacy, Civil Rights, and Civil Liberties Compliance Verification for the Intelligence Enterprise*) developed through the Global Justice Information Sharing Initiative (Global)** *(All fusion centers were able to provide the required data for this measure.)*						
	Actual/(Target)	**70.1%**	*(75%)*	*(80%)*	*(85%)*	*(95%)*	*(100%)*
2	**Number of Suspicious Activity Reporting that are vetted and submitted by fusion centers that result in the initiation or an enhancement of an investigation by the Federal Bureau of Investigation (e.g., Joint Terrorism Task Force investigations)** (*The FBI provided data for this measure for all fusion centers during the reporting period.*)						
	Actual/(Target)	**91**					
3	**Percentage of fusion center analytic products that reference fusion center Standing Information Needs (SINs)** *(Thirteen centers were able to provide full data, and 12 gave partial data for this measure.)*						
	Actual/(Target)	**14.3%**	*(40%)*	*(50%)*	*(60%)*	*(70%)*	*(80%)*
4	***Number of fusion center analytic products authored by two or more fusion centers*** *(All 77 fusion centers provided data for this measure.)*						
	Actual/(Target)	**80**	*(85)*	*(90)*	*(95)*	*(100)*	*(105)*
5	**Number of responses to fusion center-to-fusion center requests for information (RFIs)** *(Forty-four fusion centers provided full data, and 33 provided partial data for this measure.)*						
	Actual/(Target)	**15,356**					

INTRODUCTION

Both at home and abroad, the United States faces adaptive enemies in an asymmetric threat environment. To effectively address criminal and terrorist threats, the national security enterprise must reach beyond the capabilities of the federal government and the Intelligence Community (IC) to identify and warn about threats that impact the homeland, particularly when the individuals responsible for the threats operate within the United States and do not travel or communicate with others overseas.

Owned and operated by state and local entities, fusion centers serve as focal points for the receipt, analysis, gathering, and sharing of threat-related information between the federal government and state, local, tribal, territorial (SLTT), and private sector partners. By building trusted relationships and collaborating with SLTT and private sector partners, fusion centers can gather, share, and safeguard the information necessary to pursue and disrupt activities that may be indicators of or potential precursors to criminal and terrorist activity. Fusion centers are uniquely positioned to empower frontline law enforcement, public safety, fire service, emergency response, public health, and private sector security personnel and critical infrastructure owners and operators to understand the local implications of national intelligence, thus enabling local officials to better protect their communities from a variety of threats and hazards.

In order to achieve this strategic vision, individual fusion centers and the National Network of Fusion Centers (National Network) as a whole must institutionalize effective information sharing, safeguarding, and analysis business processes while demonstrating a commitment to protect and uphold the U.S. Constitution.

Background

Beginning in 2003, the federal government cooperated with state and local entities to develop and publish guidance to enable fusion centers to operate at a baseline level of capability and to form a robust and fully integrated National Network. To successfully perform these functions, fusion centers must develop and mature capabilities that enable efficient and effective information sharing and analysis across the National Network and the broader Homeland Security Enterprise (HSE).[5] To guide the development of fusion center capabilities, Fusion Center Directors and the federal government jointly identified four Critical Operational Capabilities (COCs),[6] which together reflect the operational priorities of the National Network, and four Enabling Capabilities (ECs),[7] which provide a foundation for the fusion process.

In 2011, the U.S. Department of Homeland Security (DHS) and interagency partners identified key attributes that are critical to successfully performing the fusion process for each COC and EC, regardless of the size, scope, geography, or mission of any individual fusion center. These attributes are defined primarily by the *Baseline Capabilities for State and Major Urban Area Fusion Centers* (2008) but are also derived from fusion center best practices, lessons learned, and success stories. DHS and its interagency partners identified 3 to 11 attributes for each COC and EC, for a total of 50 attributes. While not inclusive of all possible fusion center functions, the selected attributes provide a manageable and achievable set of targets that fusion centers—with the combined support of federal, state, and local stakeholders—can work to achieve in the near-term, while ensuring a reasonable degree of functional consistency in fusion centers across the National Network. Most important, these attributes form the basis against which all fusion centers will be assessed over time to demonstrate measurable progress from year to year.

Based on the COC and EC attribute framework, DHS implemented the Fusion Center Performance Program (FCPP) to measure the progress of individual fusion centers and the National Network as a whole in achieving the COCs and ECs.

The FCPP also expanded upon the capability-based framework to incorporate a performance component designed to evaluate how effectively the National Network as a whole uses its capabilities to support national information sharing and homeland security outcomes.

The FCPP consists of three interconnected elements:

- Measuring the capability and performance of the National Network through a structured, standardized annual assessment.
- Hosting and participating in prevention-based exercises that test fusion center capabilities against real- world scenarios.

- Mitigating identified gaps in order to increase capabilities, improve performance, and sustain fusion center operations.

Using Information Sharing to Manage Risks

National Strategy for Information Sharing and Safeguarding (NSISS) December 2012

The 2007 *National Strategy for Information Sharing* also highlights the importance of gathering and reporting locally generated information while emphasizing two-way flows of timely and actionable information among government, public, and private entities. To date, the concerted efforts of these partners have resulted in significant progress, including the establishment of a National Network owned and managed by state and local entities, which use the Nationwide Suspicious Activity Reporting Initiative to share terrorism information among all levels of government, and consistent policies to protect individual privacy, civil rights, and civil liberties. There have been increasing levels of collaboration among the fusion centers, the FBI JTTFs; Field and Regional Intelligence Groups; federal, state, and local law enforcement agencies; HIDTA programs; RISS Centers; intelligence and crime analysis units; and initiatives like the Fusion Liaison Officer Program, which includes tribal and non-law enforcement partners.

National Preparedness Report March 30, 2013

Overarching Findings: The National Network of Fusion Centers (National Network) and Joint Terrorism Task Forces (JTTFs) continued to mature. In addition, new national strategies and federal interagency governance structures emerged to provide a consistent and unified approach to guide the implementation of fusion center policies and standards.

National Prevention Framework May 2013

Having already established the ability to quickly collect, analyze, and further disseminate intelligence becomes critical in an imminent threat situation. In order to accomplish this, law enforcement, intelligence, homeland security professionals, and other members of the whole community must form engaged partnerships. These partnerships allow for the seamless acquisition and passage of information. In addition to Federal Bureau of Investigation (FBI) JTTFs and Field Intelligence Groups, as well as state and major urban area fusion centers, a variety of analytical and investigative efforts support the ability to identify and counter terrorist threats by executing these prevention support activities. These efforts include other state, local, tribal, territorial, and federal law enforcement agencies; various intelligence centers; and related efforts, such as High Intensity Drug Trafficking Areas (HIDTAs), Regional Information Sharing Systems (RISS) Centers, criminal intelligence units, real-time crime analysis centers, and others.

Each element of the FCPP is adjusted and repeated annually based on findings from the previous year, fusion center needs and national priorities, and the evolving threat environment.

DHS conducted the first annual Fusion Center Assessment in 2011, focusing on the capability element of the FCPP, pending the development of an initial set of National Network performance measures. The aggregate results of the 2011 Assessment were compiled in the *2011 National Network of Fusion Centers Final Report* (2011 Final Report), which was the first published report to provide a comprehensive National Network-level view of progress made in implementing the COCs and ECs. DHS initiated the 2012 Fusion Center Assessment (2012 Assessment) in August 2012 as the second iteration of the assessment process. The 2012 Assessment maintains consistent evaluation criteria and consistent data collection and validation processes from 2011 in order to provide an objective and standardized basis for evaluating National Network capability and performance over time. The 2012 Assessment is the first assessment to provide data on year-over-year progress in implementing the COCs and ECs and is also the first assessment to collect National Network performance data.[8] DHS defined five initial National Network performance measures through collaboration with fusion centers and a range of federal and SLTT partners. These measures are intended to help the fusion center stakeholder community better understand the value and impact of the National Network in supporting national information sharing and homeland security outcomes.

2012 National Network Snapshot

As of August 2012, 77 fusion centers supported the needs of federal, state, and local law enforcement and homeland security customers across the country. Fifty-one fusion centers operate at the state or territorial level, meaning that their areas of responsibility (AORs) encompass the entirety of these states or territories. The remaining 26 fusion centers operate within major urban areas, meaning that their AORs typically encompass smaller geographic areas in and around cities.

The average fusion center has been in existence for six years. When asked to characterize their broad mission focus, 97.4% of fusion centers indicated involvement in counterterrorism, 96.1% reported involvement in "all crimes," and 70.1% indicated involvement in "all hazards." Fusion centers were also asked to identify more specific mission focus areas within their center. These additional mission focus areas are listed in Table 3 on the next page.

Based on mission requirements and available resources, fusion center business hours vary across the National Network. Twenty-one fusion centers operate 24 hours a day, 7 days a week. Seventeen fusion centers have extended operating hours, typically over 10 hours a day or more than 5 days a week, but less than 24 hours a day, 7 days a week. Thirty-nine fusion centers operate only during core business hours, typically 10 hours or less a day, 5 days a week.

Fusion centers reported a total of 2,173 state, local, tribal, territorial, and private sector staff members working on either a full-time or part-time basis, which is an average of about 28 staff members per center. The median number of fusion center staff members is 18. Of the total SLTT and private sector staff members at fusion centers, 984, or about 13 per center, were identified as analysts.

Table 3. National Network Mission Focus Areas

Mission Focus Area	#	%
Border Security	24	31.2%
Chemical, Biological, Radiological, Explosive, & Nuclear	29	37.7%
Corrections, Parole, or Probation	33	42.9%
Criminal Finance	30	39.0%
Cyber Security	39	50.6%
Emergency Management/ Emergency Operations	35	45.5%
Emergency Medical Services	18	23.4%
Fire Service	32	41.6%
Gangs	54	70.1%
General Critical Infrastructure	71	92.2%
Human Trafficking	30	39.0%
Identity Theft/Document Fraud	29	37.7%
Maritime Security	26	33.8%
Narcotics	49	63.6%
Public Health and Healthcare	26	33.8%
Transnational Organized Crime	36	46.8%
Tribal	9	11.7%

As reported through the 2012 Assessment, the National Network developed and published more than 86,000 analytical products, 256 of which were produced jointly between multiple fusion centers or with federal partners.

Operational funding for the National Network is provided by a combination of federal, state, and local agencies. Federal funds, which account for approximately 48% of overall National Network funding, are divided between direct federal funding and federal grant funds, which are directed and controlled by state and local entities. Direct federal funding is primarily for federal personnel assigned to or directly supporting fusion centers, as well as federal information technology systems deployed to fusion centers. Federal agencies providing funding are identified in Table 4.

State and local agencies contribute approximately 51% of National Network operational funding and directly control the allocation of federal grant funds to fusion centers. As a result, state and local agencies are directly responsible for managing 76% of all National Network funding. Personnel costs account for approximately 80% of National Network operational costs. Despite a 7% increase in the number of fusion centers between 2011 and 2012, overall federal expenditures (direct and federal grants) in support of the National Network decreased by 25% from 2011 levels.

Table 4. Federal Dollars

Agency	Expenditures[9]	Percentage of Direct Federal Expenditures	Percentage of All Expenditures
DHS	$54,765,527	71.2%	18.0%
DOJ	$21,937,135	28.5%	7.2%
ODNI/PM-ISE	$186,000	0.2%	0.1%

2012 Snapshot National Network of Fusion Centers

Owned and operated by state, local, and territorial entities, fusion centers serve as focal points for the receipt, analysis, gathering, and sharing of threat-related information between the federal government and state, local, tribal, territorial, and private sector partners. Collectively, the capabilities of the National Network of Fusion Centers to conduct analysis and facilitate information sharing help homeland security partners prevent, protect against, and respond to crime and terrorism.

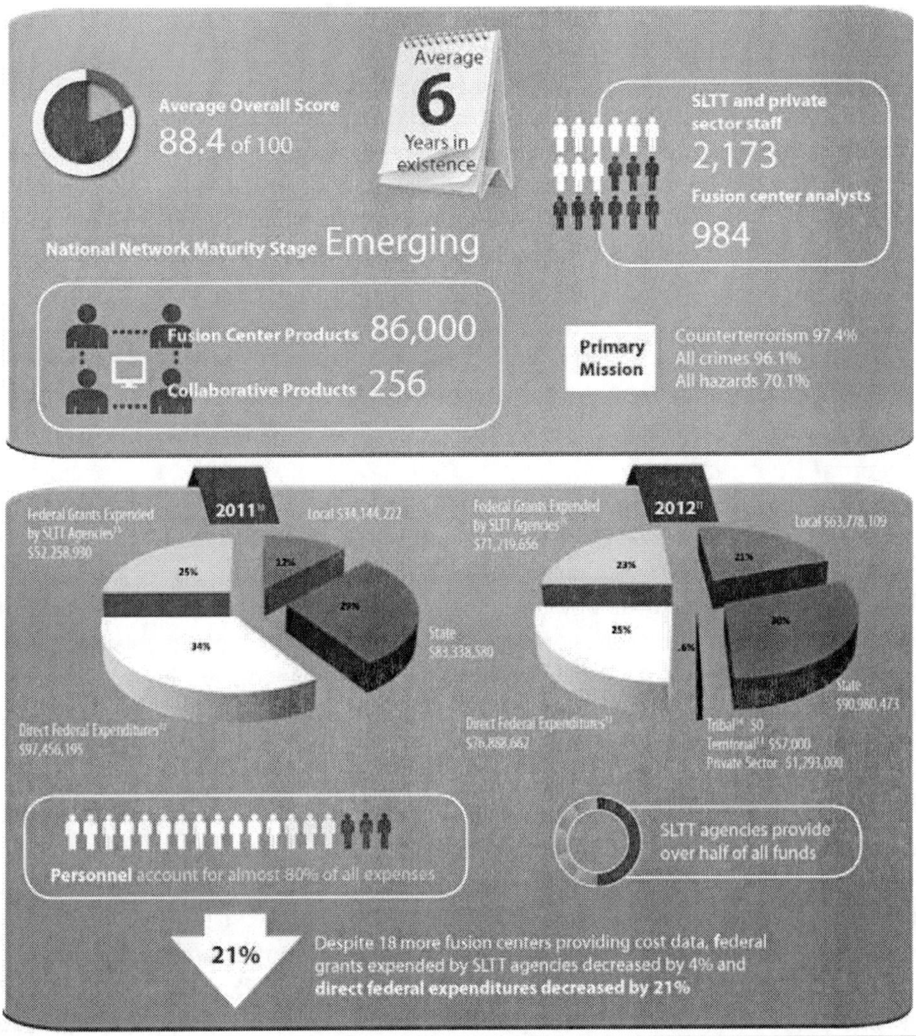

Reading This Report

The *2012 National Network of Fusion Centers Final Report* (2012 Final Report) summarizes and characterizes the overall capabilities and performance of the National

Network. The 2012 Final Report does not report fusion center-specific data; instead, it uses aggregated data from the 2012 Assessment to describe the capability and performance achievements of the National Network. It is structured by COCs and ECs, with additional sections dedicated to cross-cutting capabilities and the Maturity Model. Each of these sections includes:

- Significant findings since the 2011 Assessment, including supporting analysis, year-to-year comparisons, and data tables listing attribute achievement.
- Summary of significant statistics, with graphics indicating trends.
- Recommendations for both fusion centers and federal agencies to support continued capability improvements and sustainability.

The 2012 Final Report also addresses the initial performance measures adopted in 2012 and discusses next steps in applying an outcome-based methodology to demonstrate the impact of the National Network. An analysis of the effectiveness of federal support provided to fusion centers is also included based on data collected through the 2012 Assessment. Lastly, an overview of the FY 2012 Homeland Security Grant Program is provided, including compliance with fusion center-related requirements.

METHODOLOGY

Assessment Process

In 2011, DHS, in coordination with its interagency partners, designed a structured approach for assessing the National Network. This approach includes a standardized assessment and scoring methodology for individual fusion centers that accounts for both the complex operational realities of fusion centers and the strategic imperatives of national and homeland security priorities. It also enables DHS to report on the capabilities and performance of individual fusion centers and the National Network as a whole at specific points in time, as well as changes over time.

As in 2011, the primary data collection mechanism for the 2012 Assessment was an Online Self Assessment Tool that included numerous multiple-choice and "yes/no" questions focused on the 50 COC and EC attributes. In some cases, a single question was asked to determine whether a fusion center had achieved an attribute. In other cases, two or more questions were required to make this determination. Although the majority of questions were repeated from the 2011 Assessment, some were simplified and a limited number of new questions were included to refine the scope of data collected. Responses from the 2011 Assessment were uploaded whenever possible, further simplifying the 2012 Assessment process and significantly reducing the amount of time required to complete the assessment.

In addition to attribute-related questions, Fusion Center Directors were asked about the effectiveness of federal support received over the previous 12 months, as well as expected needs for the next 12 months. Finally, Fusion Center Directors were asked to answer questions and fill in data tables addressing cross-cutting capabilities, operational costs, demographic information, the National Network Maturity Model, and the initial performance measures. The 2012 Assessment captured the National Network's progress in these areas for the time period of August 1, 2011 to July 31, 2012.

Prior to the official start of the 2012 Assessment, DHS piloted the Online Self Assessment Tool with a representative sample of fusion centers. DHS provided electronic copies of the 2012 Assessment questions and tables to all fusion centers in early July to allow time for familiarization and initial data collection. The Online Self Assessment Tool was officially opened on August 1, 2012, and fusion centers were given until August 31, 2012 to submit responses.

Following the close of the Online Self Assessment Tool, DHS conducted validation activities from September through October 2012. Validation teams conducted detailed reviews of individual fusion centers' submissions to identify errors and inconsistencies and to minimize data discrepancies. Following these reviews, DHS conducted structured telephone interviews with Fusion Center Directors and staff to address any identified issues and to gather clarifying information, as necessary. After each interview, DHS provided Fusion Center Directors with proposed changes to their 2012 Assessment submissions based on the interview discussions, and Fusion Center Directors were given the opportunity to accept, reject, or otherwise comment on each item before any changes were finalized. All 77 designated[16] fusion centers that constituted the National Network as of August 1, 2012 completed the 2012 Assessment,[17] and the validated data is the basis for the scoring and analysis in this report.

Attribute Scoring Procedure

Within each COC or EC, individual attributes were assigned standard point values based on a simple calculation of the total possible COC or EC score divided by the total number of COC or EC attributes.[18] Since attributes are distributed unequally across the COCs and ECs because of the differing levels of complexity for each of the capabilities, the value of an attribute within each COC or EC varies.

To calculate COC and EC scores, the total number of attributes achieved within a COC or EC was multiplied by the standard point value for the COC and EC. Individual COC and EC scores were then combined to determine the fusion center's total score. Individual fusion center scores were based on a 100-point scale, with the four COCs worth 20 points each (4 x 20 = 80) and the four ECs worth five points each (4 x 5 = 20) (see Figure 3).[19]

Capability Findings and Recommendations

The following sections detail the National Network's achievement of capability attributes aligned to each COC and EC, as well as progress in cross-cutting areas such as governance. Each section includes identified National Network strengths and areas for continued improvement. Each section also includes recommendations for federal and SLTT fusion center stakeholders intended to promote continued achievement and sustainment of fusion center capabilities.

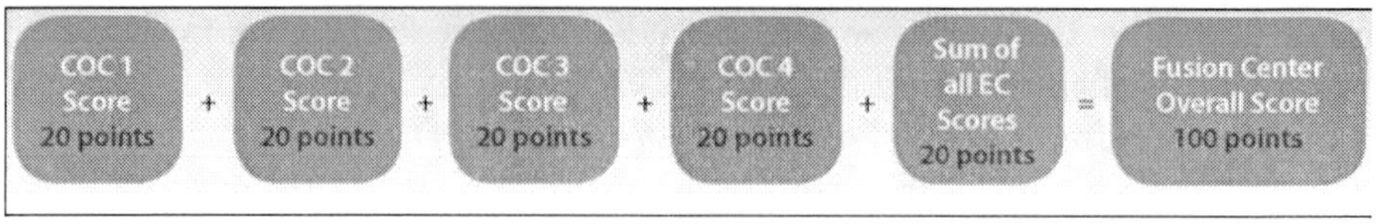

Figure 3. Fusion Center Scoring Methodology.

Overall Capabilities of the National Network

The overall capability scores for the 77 fusion centers that constituted the National Network during the 2012 Assessment reporting period ranged from 38.4 to 100. The average score of 88.4 represents an increase of almost 12 points over the 2011 Assessment.

Progress from the 2011 Assessment

As the second iteration of the repeatable annual assessment process, the 2012 Assessment provided the first opportunity to assess the year-over-year progress of the National Network in achieving the COCs and ECs. Overall fusion center capabilities increased significantly from 2011 to 2012. The scores for almost a third of the National Network (26 or 33.8%) increased by 20 points or more, while an additional 19 centers (24.7%) saw increases between 10 and 20 points. Scores for 24 fusion centers (31.2%) increased by less than 10 points. Overall scores for a small number of fusion centers (7 or 9.1%) decreased and one (1.3%) did not change.

Data collected through the 2011 Assessment indicated noteworthy strengths in 14 of the 50 attributes, as well as 11 attributes that would benefit from additional attention and investment. The 2012 Assessment data indicates continued improvements in the 14 most highly achieved attributes from 2011, with additional increases in 12 of those attributes. Even more significant, 2012 Assessment data indicates large gains in each of the 11 attributes noted in last year's assessment as requiring additional attention. Specifically, each of these 11 attributes saw increases ranging from 0.4% to 34.2% over last year. Additional details on these attributes are reported in the individual COC and EC sections.

Foundational Plans, Policies, and SOPs

Over the last several years, federal partners have placed significant emphasis on providing resources to help fusion centers develop the foundational plans, policies, and standard operating procedures (SOPs) to guide their operations. Plans, policies, and SOPs that document fusion centers' business processes enable them to execute the fusion process consistently over time and under a variety of circumstances. While fusion centers will tailor their policies according to state or local jurisdictional needs and requirements, having approved documentation in place is a crucial step toward the standardization of the fusion process across the National Network. Figure 5 indicates the progress made by the National Network in approving plans, policies, or SOPs for each of the COCs and for EC 1 since 2010, based on the 2012 and 2011 Assessments and the 2010 Baseline Capabilities Assessment (BCA). These are the five capabilities that were required to reach the Fundamental stage of network maturity.

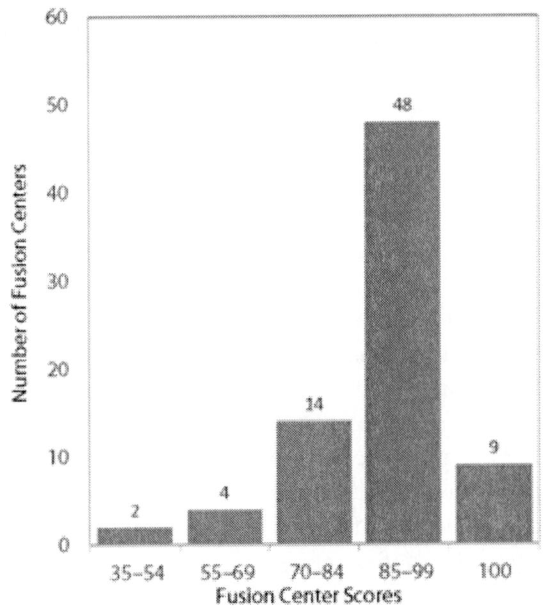

Figure 4. Overall Capability of the National Network of Fusion Centers.

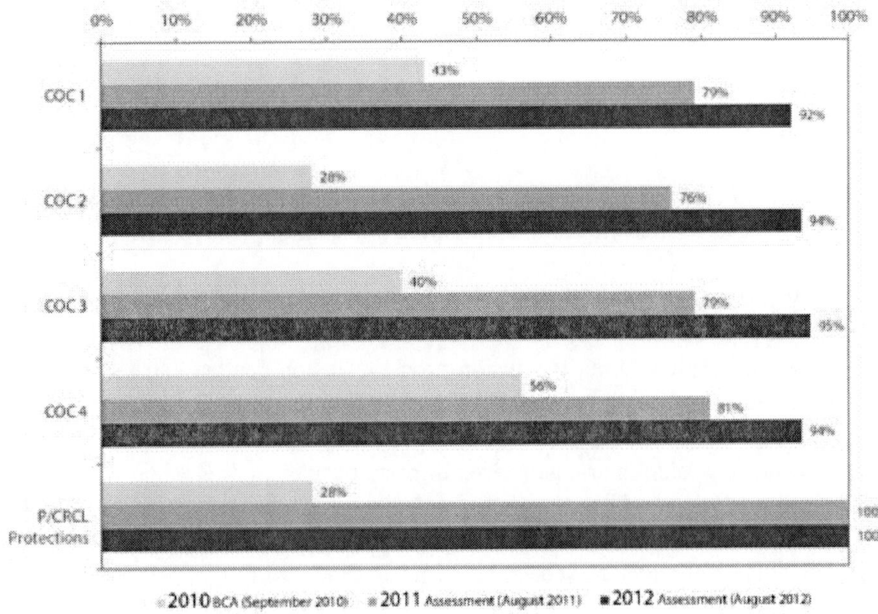

Figure 5. Progress of the National Network in Approving Plans, Policies, or SOPs: 2010–2012.

Overall, a total of 71 fusion centers (92.2%) have approved plans, policies, or SOPs for all four COCs and for EC 1. Results from the 2012 Assessment also show that fusion centers are making significant progress in implementing their plans, policies, and SOPs.

- **COC 1—Receive:** Seventy-one fusion centers (92.2%) have documented and approved plans, policies, or SOPs governing the receipt of federally generated information. Of these 71 fusion centers, 70 (90.9%) have implemented their plans, policies, or SOPs for COC 1.
- **COC 2—Analyze:** Seventy-two fusion centers (93.5%) have approved plans, policies, or SOPs for assessing the local implications of threat information. Of the 72 fusion centers with approved plans, 71 (92.2%) have implemented them, meaning that these plans, policies, and SOPs are communicated to internal and/or external partners; that staff are trained on them; or that they guide the day-to-day execution of analytic functions within these fusion centers.
- **COC 3—Disseminate:** Seventy-three fusion centers (94.8%) have approved plans, policies, and SOPs governing the procedures and communication mechanisms for the timely dissemination of products to customers within their AOR. Of these fusion centers, 71 (92.2%) have successfully implemented their plans by communicating the policies and procedures both internally and externally, training their staff, and/or monitoring the effectiveness of the plan, policy, or SOP.
- **COC 4—Gather:** Seventy-two fusion centers (93.5%) have a documented plan, policy, or SOP governing the gathering of locally generated information and/or are NSI-compliant. Sixty-nine fusion centers (89.6%) have implemented their plans and policies on gathering locally generated information.
- **EC 1—P/CRCL Protections:** All 77 fusion centers (100%) have an approved and documented P/CRCL policy that has been determined by DHS to be at least as comprehensive as the ISE Privacy Guidelines.

COC1—Receive

The ability to receive classified and unclassified information from federal partners

The ability to receive federal information (both classified and unclassified) to inform SLTT and private sector customers of threats relevant to their areas of responsibility (AOR) is a critical element of implementing the fusion process. Fusion centers can receive classified and unclassified information directly from federal agencies through federal systems and portals specifically designed to enable timely cross-jurisdictional information sharing. This allows fusion centers to keep their customers informed of relevant alerts and warnings and to develop focused analytic products that help customers make informed decisions regarding resource allocation and the implementation of appropriate protective measures.

The National Network average score for COC 1 is 18.6 out of 20, an increase of 9% from 2011. Of the five COC 1 attributes, 56 fusion centers (72.7%) achieved all attributes. There are four significant findings for COC 1.

All fusion centers have access to federally sponsored sensitive but unclassified (SBU) information sharing systems.

Fusion centers receive information from federal agencies in a variety of ways based on the type of information, the level of classification, and criticality. Federally sponsored SBU systems allow fusion centers to securely receive unclassified federally generated threat information. These systems also allow fusion centers to organize intelligence products, process requests for information and service, and disseminate information to federal, SLTT, and private sector partners. Data from the 2012 Assessment shows that access to federally sponsored SBU systems is widespread across the National Network:

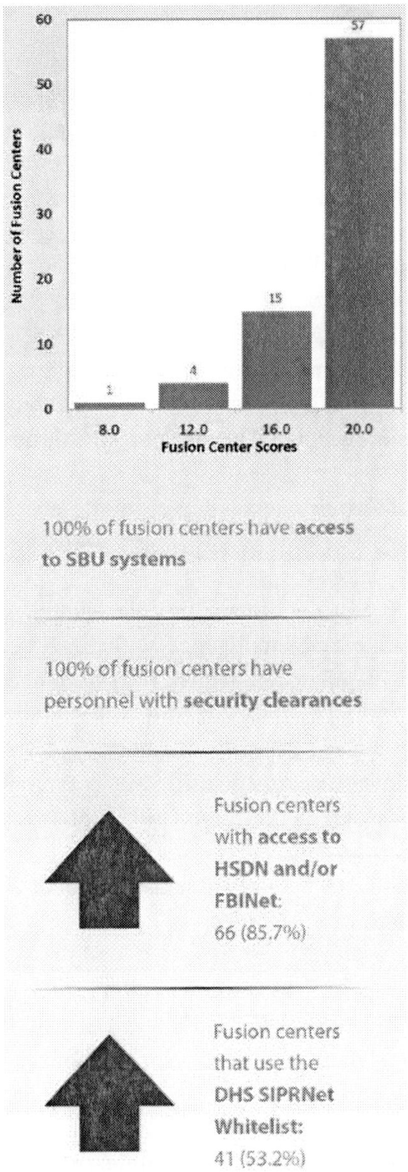

Figure 5. Capability of the National Network of Fusion Centers for COC 1—Receive.

- Homeland Security Information Network (HSIN)— 77 (100%)
- HSIN Intelligence (HSIN Intel)[20]— 76 (98.7%)
- Law Enforcement Online (LEO)— 77 (100%)
- Regional Information Sharing Systems® (RISS) Secure Cloud (RISSNET™)— 75 (97.4%)

Every fusion center has at least one person cleared to access Secret information, but regular staff turnover means that fusion centers will continue to request new clearances.

Clearing select fusion center staff to access classified information—and retaining cleared staff—is critical to ensuring that fusion centers can receive classified information and intelligence from the federal government. Classified information is a potentially vital source of detail and context that fusion centers can use to determine the relevance and credibility of potential threats to their AOR. Results from the 2012 Assessment indicate that all 77 fusion centers (100%) have personnel with at least a Secret-level security clearance. Furthermore, of the 1,966 SLTT personnel identified by fusion centers as needing security clearances, 1,618 (82.3%) have been granted a clearance. Of the remaining SLTT personnel identified as needing a clearance, 210 (10.7%) have submitted clearance requests and are awaiting final adjudication. Despite their success in clearing staff and retaining cleared staff, fusion centers reported that they anticipate the need to submit approximately 500 new SLTT clearance requests within the next 12 months, mainly because of staff turnover.

A significant number of fusion centers have on-site access to classified information sharing systems.

The federal government deploys and maintains classified systems to facilitate the timely sharing of classified information and intelligence with fusion centers. Data from the 2012 Assessment indicates that 85.7% of fusion centers (66) have access to the Homeland Secure Data Network (HSDN) and/or the Federal Bureau of Investigation Network (FBINet), either within the fusion center or on-site (i.e., in the same building but not in the center itself). The federal government will continue to deploy classified information systems to fusion centers in accordance with the Federal Resource Allocation Criteria policy.[21,22]

Fusion center use of the DHS Secret Internet Protocol Router Network (SIPRNet) Whitelist (Whitelist) is limited.

The Whitelist provides a mechanism to allow fusion center personnel to access classified information resident on SIPRNet via HSDN. Only 53.2% of fusion centers (41) reported using the Whitelist. The reasons most commonly reported for not using the Whitelist included a lack of access, difficulty accessing or using the sites, and a lack of awareness of the Whitelist. Only two fusion centers said they did not have a need for the Whitelist. Expanding content available via the Whitelist, making the Whitelist more user-friendly, and expanding marketing of the Whitelist among cleared fusion center personnel could result in increased usage and a more meaningful user experience.

Table 6. Attribute Data for COC 1—Receive

	COC 1 Attributes	#	%
1	Fusion center has approved plans, policies, or standard operating procedures (SOPs) for the receipt of federally generated threat information	71	92.2%
2	Fusion center has a plan, a policy, or an SOP that addresses the receipt and handling of National Terrorism Advisory System (NTAS) alerts	68	88.3%
3	Fusion center personnel with a need to access classified information are cleared to at least the Secret level	77	100%
4	Fusion center has access to sensitive but unclassified information systems	77	100%
5	Fusion center has access to the HSDN and/or the FBINet (i.e., within fusion center or on-site)	66	85.7%

Recommendations

- DHS should ensure that all distributable analytic products from the Office of Intelligence and Analysis (I&A) and other DHS components are both posted to HSIN Intel and tagged with appropriate DHS Homeland Security (HSEC) Standing Information Needs (SINs).
- Fusion centers should continue to ensure that the federal government is aware of personnel needing clearances for Secret-level systems and information.
- Fusion centers without access to HSDN should develop and implement the necessary security policies and protocols and identify secondary mechanisms to access classified information. All fusion centers should consider the potential impacts on access to classified systems that might arise if they move or change locations.
- The federal government should continue to facilitate the timely installation of classified systems at fusion centers that have met all appropriate security requirements.
- To assist fusion center analysts in developing and refining their analytic knowledge, skills, and abilities, the federal government should improve usability and increase content available on the Whitelist based on defined and validated fusion center needs. The federal government should also develop a Whitelist Resource Kit that describes current content and provides directions on how to request new content and report issues in accessing sites.
- Fusion centers should report lack of access to sites on the Whitelist or other technical issues to federal partners.

COC2—Analyze

The ability to assess the local implications of threat information through the use of a formal risk assessment process

Fusion centers develop timely and actionable intelligence products for their customers by overlaying national intelligence with locally gathered information. Defined analytical protocols and analytic tradecraft allow fusion centers to assess the local implications of threat information in order to define, prioritize, and recommend appropriate response actions and protective measures. A set of 11 attributes defines the overall capability of a fusion center to analyze threat information. These attributes include conducting and contributing to threat, vulnerability, consequence, and risk assessments within fusion center AORs; contributing to national-level risk assessments; ensuring that analysts are trained on core analytic competencies; and soliciting and responding to customer feedback on analytic products.

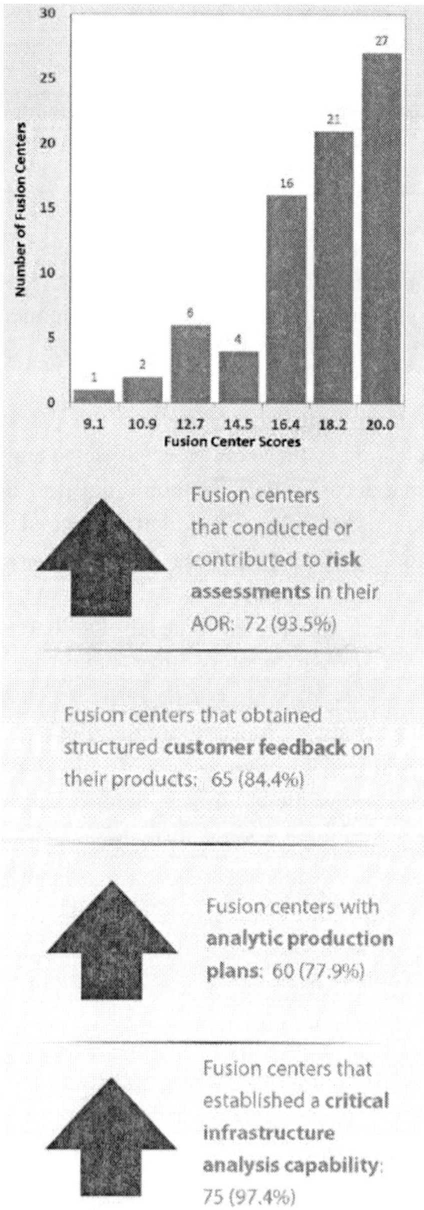

Figure 6. Capability of the National Network of Fusion Centers for COC 2—Analyze.

The National Network average score for COC 2 is 17.5 out of 20, which represents a slight increase over the 2011 Assessment average of 16.4. Overall, 26 of the 77 fusion centers in the National Network (33.8%) achieved all 11 attributes, and 48 (62.3%) achieved at least 10 attributes. There were four significant findings from the 2012 Assessment for COC 2.

Fusion centers are highly involved in assessing threat and risk for their AOR.

All 77 fusion centers (100%) reported that they conduct or contribute to threat assessments within their AOR. Seventy-three of these fusion centers (94.8%) conduct threat assessments for customers within their AOR, while the remaining four (5.2%) contributed to threat assessments developed by other entities. In supporting the understanding of overall risk to their AOR, 76 fusion centers (98.7%) conducted or contributed to vulnerability analyses and 70 fusion centers (90.9%) conducted or contributed to consequence analyses. Seventy-two fusion centers (93.5%) conducted or contributed to a risk assessment for their AOR, and 62 (80.5%) conducted or contributed to a Threat and Hazard Identification and Risk Assessment (THIRA).[23] However, only 41 fusion centers (53.2%) contributed to a national-level risk assessment (e.g., National Critical Infrastructure Prioritization Program or assessments for National Special Security Events). This is unchanged from the 2011 Assessment.

Fusion centers are obtaining and using customer feedback on their analytic products.

Sixty-five fusion centers (84.4%) reported using a structured mechanism (e.g., interviews, surveys, focus groups) to collect feedback from their customers on the relevance and value of their analytic products. A smaller number (48 or 62.3%) reported that they specifically used structured feedback request forms to collect customer feedback on some or all of their analytic products. This represents an increase from 2011, when 52.8% of fusion centers (38) reported having this capability. Furthermore, more than half of the National Network (41 or 53.2%) seek some form of structured feedback on all of their analytic products, and 24 centers (31.2%) seek structured feedback on some, but not all, of their analytic products. More notably, 79.2% of the National Network (61) have a process to review customer feedback and incorporate it into how their center conducts analysis and develops products.

Analytic production plans are used widely across the National Network.

An analytic production plan describes the types of analysis and products a fusion center intends to provide for customers and partners, how often or under what circumstances the products will be produced, and how each product type will be disseminated. As a best practice derived from the IC, analytic production plans help fusion centers plan appropriate analytic resources to address customer requirements. 2012 Assessment data indicates that 77.9% of the National Network (60 fusion centers) have analytic production plans, compared to 68.1% (49) in 2011.

Critical infrastructure protection capabilities continue to expand across the National Network.

Incorporating critical infrastructure protection activities into a fusion center's operations enhances the fusion process by increasing awareness of threats within a fusion center's AOR and by expanding the reach of fusion center information sharing networks. According to 2012 Assessment data, 27 fusion centers (35.1%) reported that they are the primary coordinating body overseeing critical infrastructure (CI) activities within their AOR, which is very similar to the 25 (34.7%) reported for 2011. All but one of the remaining 50 fusion centers (49 or 63.4%) currently support CI protection activities led by another agency, and the one remaining fusion center (1.3%) reported that it intends to support CI protection activities in the future. Seventy-five fusion centers (97.4%) reported having a CI analysis capability within their center, and the remaining two fusion centers (2.6%) indicated that they intend to establish this capability. A large majority of fusion centers (65 or 84.4%) reported having at least one full-time or part-time analyst assigned to CI issues, which represents a slight increase from 2011, when 73.6% of the National Network (53 fusion centers) reported analyst assignment to CI issues. Most fusion centers (61 or 79.2%) have established processes to use information from CI partners' risk assessments and other sources to inform their own analyses. In 2011, only 54.2% of fusion centers (39) had established these processes.

Table 7. Attribute Data for COC 2—Analyze

	COC 2 Attributes	#	%
1	Fusion center has approved plans, policies, or SOPs for assessing the local implications of time-sensitive and emerging threat information	72	93.5%
2	Fusion center has a documented analytic production plan	60	77.9%
3	Fusion center has access to multidisciplinary subject matter experts (SMEs) within AOR to inform analytic production	77	100%
4	Fusion center has access to multidisciplinary SMEs outside of its AOR to inform analytic production	76	98.7%
5	Fusion center has a process to provide DHS with information and/or intelligence that offers a local context to threat information in the event of an NTAS-related alert	77	100%
6	Fusion center conducts threat assessments within its AOR	73	94.8%
7	Fusion center contributes to or conducts a statewide risk assessment (threat, vulnerability, and consequence analysis)	67	87%
8	Fusion center contributes to national-level risk assessments	41	53.2%
9	Fusion center has a structured customer feedback mechanism for some or all of its analytic products	65	84.4%
10	Fusion center evaluates the effectiveness of the customer feedback mechanism for analytic products on an annual basis	66	85.7%
11	All fusion center analysts have received at least 20 hours of issue-specific training in the past 12 months	68	88.3%

Recommendations

- The federal government should provide additional guidance to assist fusion centers in contributing to a Threat and Hazard Identification and Risk Assessment for their AOR.
- The federal government should work with fusion centers to increase their participation in the development of national-level assessments and analytic products.

- The federal government should continue to support analytic exchanges to assist fusion centers in collaborating with field-based partners, such as High Intensity Drug Trafficking Areas (HIDTAs), RISS Centers, Field Intelligence Groups (FIGs), and Joint Terrorism Task Forces (JTTFs).
- The federal government should continue to offer fusion center analysts access to tools and assistance that build fusion center capabilities to conduct or contribute to a national risk analysis, such as a Risk Analysis Product Template and Risk Analysis Courses.
- The federal government should assist fusion center analysts to further expand their analytical skills and expertise by supporting exchanges, developing joint products, and mentoring.
- In order to collect customer feedback on analytic products, fusion centers should use a structured feedback process and should collect feedback data at least annually, but more often when possible.
- Fusion centers should continue to develop and regularly update analytic production plans.
- The federal government should continue to offer tools and resources that promote and improve risk analysis and understanding of threats to critical infrastructure through analysis, such as an Infrastructure Protection Field Resource Toolkit, Critical Infrastructure Capabilities Exchanges, and Risk Analysis Courses.

COC 3—Disseminate

The ability to further disseminate threat information to other state, local, tribal, and territorial entities within their jurisdictions

Fusion centers disseminate actionable, locally informed intelligence products to customers and stakeholders within their AOR. A successful dissemination process provides information in an organized, targeted, and timely manner to inform decision making and drive SLTT and private sector prevention, protection, and response activities. COC 3 has six attributes that focus on establishing the policies and processes related to the dissemination of time-sensitive information, including the use of dissemination matrices, the use of SBU systems for dissemination, verification of delivery of products, and handling NTAS alerts.

The National Network average score for COC 3 is 16.9, the lowest score of any COC. However, COC 3 is also the most improved COC from 2011, when the National Network average was 13.1. The COC average score increased by 28.4% from 2011 to 2012. Further, 39% of the National Network (30 fusion centers) achieved all six COC 3 attributes, and only 22.1% (17) achieved four attributes or fewer. There are two significant findings from the 2012 Assessment related to COC 3.

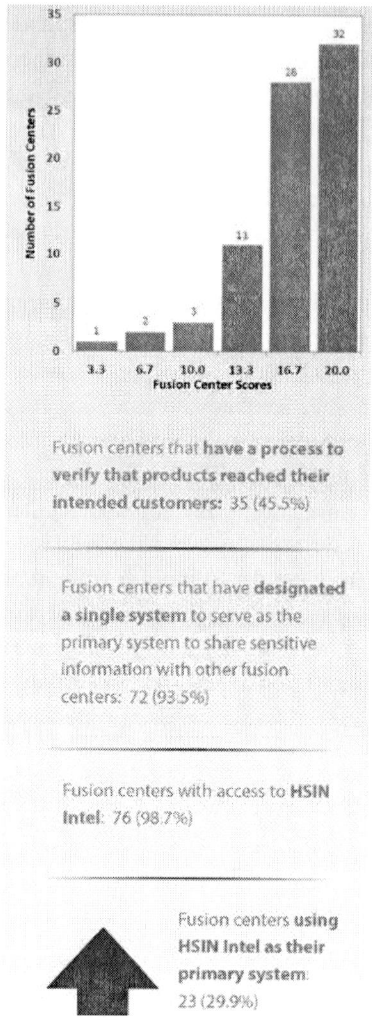

Figure 7. Capability of the National Network of Fusion Centers for COC 3—Disseminate.

Despite progress since 2011, less than half of the National Network have a process in place to verify that customers are receiving their products.

Fusion centers can more effectively and efficiently inform decision making when they can verify that their products reach their intended customers. 2012 Assessment data indicates that only 45.5% of the National Network (35 fusion centers) have established a process to verify the delivery of products to their intended customers, up 14.9% from a year ago. Processes to verify the delivery of products can be as simple as using e-mail read receipts for those centers using e-mail as a dissemination mechanism or can be more sophisticated, such as tracking product access through a secure online portal.

Fusion centers are increasingly designating a single primary information sharing system, but HSIN Intel is not frequently cited as the primary system for unclassified communication between fusion centers.

According to 2011 Assessment data, only 40 fusion centers (55.6%) were using a single SBU information sharing system as the primary means of disseminating SBU information to customers and partner agencies. The 2012 Assessment indicates that this number increased to 75 fusion centers (97.4%).

Relationship with Emergency Operations Centers

In accordance with *Comprehensive Preparedness Guide (CPG) 502: Considerations for Fusion Center and Emergency Operations Center Coordination*, many fusion centers support emergency operations centers (EOC) during manmade and natural incidents as well as in a steady state.

- 26% (20) are collocated with an EOC, up from 25% (18) in 2012.
- 92.2% (71) disseminate information to the EOC or its respective lead emergency management agency in their AOR, up from 76.4% (55) in 2012.

2012 Assessment data indicated that among the systems used as primary information sharing tools for communication between fusion centers, secure, encrypted e-mail and HSIN Intel are the two most common. However, while 76 fusion centers (98.7%) indicated that they have access to HSIN Intel, only 23 fusion centers (29.9%) cited this as their primary information sharing tool for unclassified communication between fusion centers, compared to 22 (28.6%) that cited secure, encrypted e-mail.

Table 8. Attribute Data for COC 3—Disseminate

COC 3 Attributes		#	%
1	Fusion center has approved plans, policies, or SOPs governing the procedures for the timely dissemination of products to customers within its AOR	73	94.8%
2	Fusion center has a dissemination matrix	64	83.1%
3	Fusion center has a primary SBU mechanism to disseminate time-sensitive information and products to its customers and partners	75	97.4%
4	Fusion center has a plan, a policy, or an SOP that addresses dissemination of NTAS alerts to stakeholders within its AOR	67	87%
5	Fusion center has a mechanism to disseminate NTAS alerts	76	98.7%
6	Fusion center has a process for verifying the delivery of products to intended customers	35	45.5%

Recommendations

- Fusion centers should engage customers to discuss preferred methods and timeliness of product dissemination.

- Fusion centers should ensure that all distributable analytic products are posted to HSIN Intel.
- The federal government should continue to ensure that HSIN Intel meets the functional needs of SLTT partners.

COC 4—Gather

The ability to gather locally generated information, aggregate it, analyze it, and share it with federal partners as appropriate

Fusion centers gather information—including tips, leads, and suspicious activity reports (SARs)—from local agencies and the public and share it across the National Network and with federal partners while ensuring appropriate security and P/CRCL protections. Developing and implementing well-defined processes for gathering information based on customer needs enables fusion centers to focus their efforts to capture the most relevant and accurate information. The ability to gather locally generated information that can supplement, enhance, or provide context for federally generated threat information places fusion centers in an indispensable position for identifying and mitigating potential threats.

The National Network average score for COC 4 is 18.1, an increase of 17.4% from the 2011 average of 15.4. With 62.3% of the National Network (48 fusion centers) achieving all eight COC 4 attributes and another 19.5% (15 fusion centers) achieving seven of eight attributes, the National Network has made significant progress in fully implementing COC 4. There are three significant findings from the 2012 Assessment for COC 4.

The number of fusion centers that have developed Standing Information Needs (SINs) has increased, but continued attention to SINs development is necessary.

SINs define the topics and issues that fusion center customers and stakeholders care about. Fusion centers use SINs to guide information gathering and intelligence production. Data from the 2012 Assessment indicates that the percentage of fusion centers with approved SINs increased from 54.2% (39) in 2011 to 76.6% (59) in 2012, leaving nearly a quarter of the National Network (18 or 23.4%) still without SINs. Among those centers with approved (or draft) SINs, engagement with partners in SINs development did not change significantly since 2011. In 2012 and 2011, respectively, fusion centers reported engaging with law enforcement (60 or 77.9% and 54 or 75%), emergency management (49 or 63.6% and 48 or 66.7%), fire service (47 or 61% and 43 or 59.7%), public health and health care (42 or 54.5% and 38 or 52.8%), and the private sector (38 or 49.4% and 34 or 47.2%). The number of centers reviewing and refreshing their SINs on an annual basis has increased from 69.4% (50) to 84.4% (65).

The National Network has a robust request for information (RFI) management capability.

An important measure of National Network maturity is the ability of fusion centers to request and respond effectively to RFIs from customers and partner agencies. RFI management processes help fusion centers target information-gathering efforts to respond to customer and partner needs. Sixty-nine fusion centers (89.6%) reported having an approved RFI management process. This represents a significant increase over 2011, when only 45 fusion centers (62.5%) reported having an approved process and an additional 15 (20.8%) reported having a draft process.

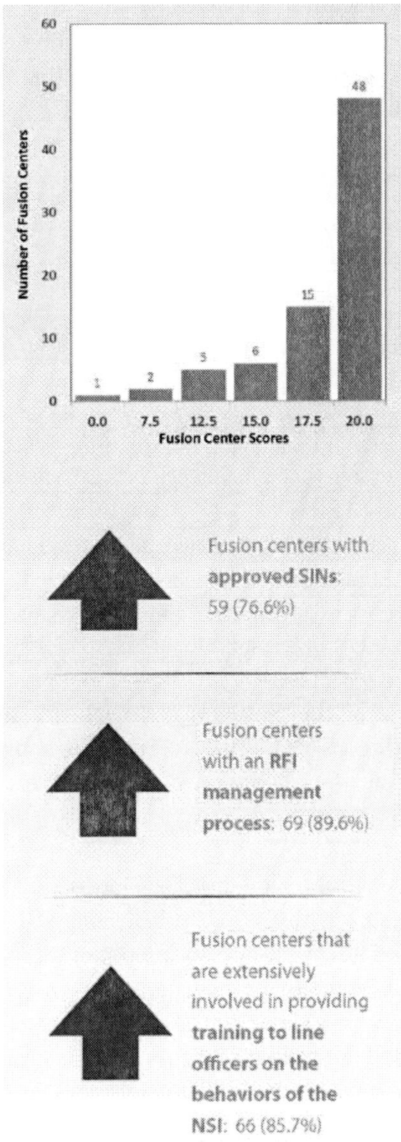

Figure 8. Capability of the National Network of Fusion Centers for COC 4—Gather.

HOMELAND SECURITY STANDING INFORMATION NEEDS (HSEC SINS)

HSEC SINs describe the full spectrum of enduring all-threats and all-hazards data and information needed by Homeland Security Community of Interest (COI) intelligence analysts to perform analytical work to answer their customers' intelligence questions. The HSEC COI includes DHS and its federal, SLTT, and private sector stakeholders and homeland security partners. Currently, 63 fusion centers (81.8%) report using the HSEC SINs in the development of their own SINs.

Table 9. Attribute Data for COC 4—Gather

	COC 4 Attributes	#	%
1	Fusion center is NSI-compliant OR has an approved plan, policy, or SOP governing the gathering of locally generated information	72	93.5%
2	Fusion center has a documented tips and leads process	71	92.2%
3	Fusion center has a process for identifying and managing information needs	74	96.1%
4	Fusion center has a process for managing the gathering of locally generated information to satisfy the fusion center's information needs	72	93.5%
5	Fusion center has approved SINs	59	76.6%
6	Fusion center has an annual process to review and refresh its SINs	65	84.4%
7	Fusion center has an RFI management process	69	89.6%
8	Fusion center has a process to inform DHS of protective measures implemented within its AOR in response to an NTAS alert	74	96.1%

A significant percentage of the National Network are involved in the Nationwide Suspicious Activity Reporting (SAR) Initiative (NSI), in particular in providing line officers with information on the behaviors identified in the ISE-SAR Functional Standard.

The NSI is a collaborative effort led by the U.S. Department of Justice's (DOJ) Bureau of Justice Assistance, in partnership with DHS, the FBI, and SLTT law enforcement partners. This initiative provides law enforcement with an important tool to help prevent terrorism and terrorism-related criminal activity by establishing a national capacity for gathering, documenting, processing, analyzing, and sharing SAR information. The NSI is a standardized process—including stakeholder outreach, privacy protections, training, and facilitation of technology—for identifying and reporting suspicious activity in jurisdictions across the ountry. The NSI also serves as the unified focal point for sharing SAR information among federal and SLTT partners.

Data collected through the 2012 Assessment indicates that fusion centers play an important role in the NSI, with 92.2% of centers (71) indicating that they play a role in vetting SAR information and 90.9% (70) indicating that they are involved in analyzing SAR information. Additionally, 2012 Assessment data indicates that fusion centers play a significant role in training line officers on the behaviors identified in the ISE-SAR Functional

Standard in order to improve the number and quality of submitted SARs. Sixty-six fusion centers (85.7%) indicated they provide SAR line officer training.

Recommendations

The federal government should continue to support fusion centers' efforts to develop and maintain SINs by deploying a resource kit that outlines processes for engaging with customers, identifying intelligence questions, identifying information needs, and developing collection requirements.

- Fusion centers should continue to develop, update, and approve SINs by soliciting input from key customers, including multidisciplinary partners.
- Fusion centers should ensure that all analytic products posted to HSIN Intel are tagged with appropriate DHS HSEC SINs and fusion center SINs, and the federal government should ensure that HSIN Intel tagging capabilities are easy to access and use.
- The National Network and the federal government should collaborate to develop processes and a template that would assist fusion centers in requesting information from SLTT and federal law enforcement entities, homeland security agencies, or other fusion centers.
- The federal government and fusion centers should expand training to non-law enforcement partners to further enhance both the gathering of information and the quality of SAR.

EC 1—Privacy, Civil Rights, and Civil Liberties Protections

The ability and commitment to protect the P/CRCL of all individuals

For fusion centers to engage in effective and meaningful information sharing, they must do so in a manner that protects individuals' privacy, civil rights, and civil liberties. Fusion centers implement safeguards to protect constitutional rights and to ensure that they are addressing their ethical and legal obligations while engaged in the fusion process. Fusion centers have demonstrated their commitment to this capability by ensuring that their personnel understand the importance of protecting P/CRCL and that intelligence systems are used in a manner that conforms to proper protocols and regulations.

The National Network average score for EC 1 is 4.4 out of 5, up from an average of 4.1 in 2011. Data from the 2012 Assessment indicates that 90.9% of the National Network (70) achieved at least five of the six EC 1 attributes and that no center achieved less than four attributes. All centers achieved the Homeland Security Grant Program (HSGP) requirement to have a P/CRCL policy that has been determined by DHS to be at least as comprehensive as the *Information Sharing Environment Privacy Guidelines*. There are three significant findings from the 2012 Assessment for EC 1.

All but one of the fusion centers have a P/CRCL Officer; however, turnover at this position is high across the National Network.

P/CRCL Officers play a critical role in ensuring that P/CRCL protections are fully integrated into fusion center operations. All but one of the fusion centers, which was established shortly before the 2012 Assessment began, reported having a designated P/CRCL Officer. However, turnover among fusion center P/CRCL Officers was high, with 48.1% of fusion centers (37) reporting turnover within the 12 months preceding the 2012 Assessment and another 16.9% (13) reporting that they expect turnover within the 12 months following the 2012 Assessment. Additionally, only 27.3% of fusion centers (21) reported that their P/CRCL Officer was experienced in P/CRCL issues before being assigned to the position within the fusion center, and 87% of fusion centers (67) reported that their P/CRCL Officer has additional duties beyond P/CRCL protections that account for the majority of his time.

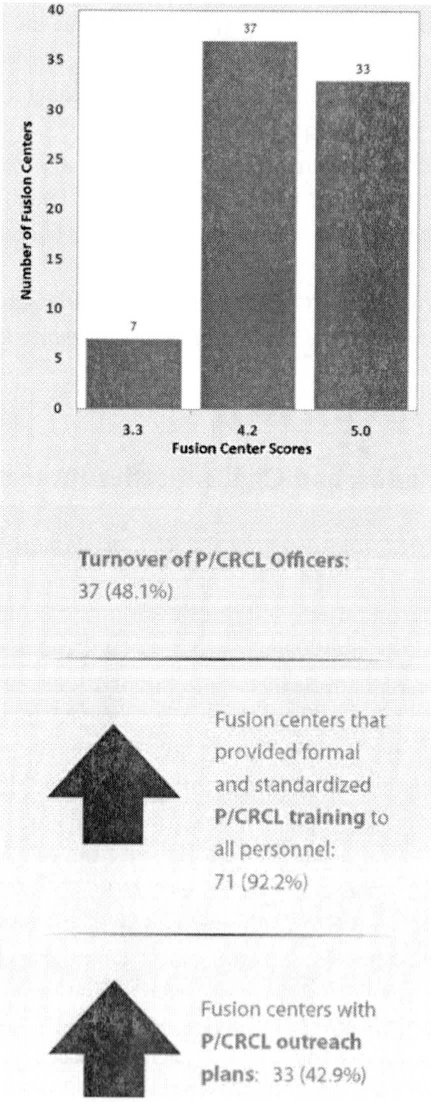

Figure 9. Capability of the National Network of Fusion Centers for EC 1—P/CRCL Protections.

Fusion centers have made significant progress in implementing P/CRCL protections, although compliance reviews and annual audits have not reached 100%.

Effective implementation of P/CRCL protections requires that all fusion center staff members receive training on their center's P/CRCL policies and procedures. Data from the 2012 Assessment shows that 92.2% of fusion centers (71) provide formal and standardized P/CRCL training to all personnel at least annually, up from 77.8% (56) last year. In addition to training, 96.1% of fusion centers (74) reported that they review analytic products for P/CRCL issues before dissemination. All but four fusion centers (73 or 94.8%) ensure that plans, policies, SOPs, and other mechanisms and processes in place are consistent with P/CRCL policies.

The *Privacy, Civil Rights, and Civil Liberties Compliance Verification for the Intelligence Enterprise* tool helps ensure compliance with all applicable P/CRCL protection laws, regulations, and policies. This tool was developed jointly by the Global Justice Information Sharing Initiative (Global), in coordination with DOJ and DHS, to provide guidance on implementing appropriate P/CRCL safeguards within a fusion center. Although the percentage of fusion centers that conduct compliance reviews increased by more than 20% compared to the previous year, 23 fusion centers (29.9%) had not conducted a compliance review. In contrast, a P/CRCL audit of fusion center operations identifies specific violations of a fusion center's P/CRCL policy. Twenty-four fusion centers (31.2%) had not undergone a P/CRCL audit within the 12 months covered by the 2012 Assessment.

Coordinated outreach by fusion centers to stakeholders on P/CRCL issues is still lacking.

A communications and outreach plan that addresses P/CRCL issues can help fusion centers engage with their customers and stakeholders regarding P/CRCL protections and promotes transparency on P/CRCL safeguarding efforts. While the National Network has made significant progress in implementing comprehensive P/CRCL protections over the last year, only 42.9% of the National Network (33 fusion centers) have a P/CRCL outreach plan.

Recommendations

- Fusion centers should take efforts to manage and reduce the potential impacts of P/CRCL Officer turnover so that their fusion center can maintain and build institutional knowledge regarding P/CRCL protections, especially during periods of transition.
- The federal government and appropriate partners (such as the Criminal Intelligence Coordinating Council) should continue to assist in training P/CRCL Officers at a level that ensures that all officers have a baseline understanding of their roles and responsibilities and at a level that enhances current P/CRCL Officers' efforts to support their fusion center.
- The federal government should provide guidance and templates to assist fusion centers in developing written implementation plans for their P/CRCL policies.

- Fusion centers should conduct P/CRCL compliance reviews that assess their policies and procedures related to P/CRCL protections through the use of the *Privacy, Civil Rights, and Civil Liberties Compliance Verification for the Intelligence Enterprise.*
- Fusion centers should audit operations against their approved privacy policy at least on an annual basis.
- Fusion centers should develop outreach plans, including outreach on P/CRCL policies and issues.

EC 2—Sustainment Strategy

The ability to establish and execute a sustainment strategy to ensure the long-term growth and maturity of the National Network

In order to ensure the long-term growth and maturation of the National Network, fusion centers and their federal and SLTT stakeholders must develop and execute strategies that demonstrate the value of the National Network to partners at all levels of government, as well as the private sector. Strategic plans enable fusion centers to more efficiently and effectively plan and allocate resources to implement and maintain COCs and ECs and to perform consistently over time. Evaluating operational effectiveness against defined priorities can be done by measuring fusion center performance, which helps identify ways to improve operational execution and overall management of the fusion process.

The National Network average score for EC 2 was 4.3 out of 5, compared to the score of 3.4 for 2011. More than half of the National Network (42 or 54.5%) achieved all five EC 2 attributes, and all (77 or 100%) fusion centers achieved the HSGP requirements to complete the operational cost assessment annually and participate in at least one exercise every two years. There are four significant findings from the 2012 Assessment for EC 2.

Table 10. Attribute Data for EC 1—P/CRCL Protections

	EC 1 Attributes	#	%
1	Fusion center has a P/CRCL policy determined by DHS to be at least as comprehensive as the Information Sharing Environment (ISE) Privacy Guidelines	77	100%
2	Fusion center provides formal and standardized training to all personnel on the fusion center's P/CRCL policy and protections annually	71	92.2%
3	Fusion center's policies, processes, and mechanisms for receiving, cataloging, and retaining information (provided to the center) comply with 28 Code of Federal Regulations (CFR) Part 23 when appropriate	77	100%
4	Fusion center trains all personnel who access criminal intelligence systems in 28 CFR Part 23	77	100%
5	Fusion center has identified a P/CRCL Officer	76	98.7%
6	Fusion center has a P/CRCL outreach plan	33	42.9%

The number of fusion centers with strategic plans has increased, but almost 30% of fusion centers do not have an approved strategic plan.

A strategic plan defines an organization's vision, mission, goals, and objectives and identifies programmatic and operational priorities and requirements. Strategic plans also help fusion centers demonstrate their commitment to long-term success and sustainment by defining and preparing for future opportunities and uncertainties. The percentage of fusion centers with a strategic plan increased by 21.5% from 2011 (35 or 48.6%) to 2012 (54 or 70.1%). However, 23 fusion centers (29.9%) still lack strategic plans. Linking strategic priorities to operational budgets further enables long-term planning and helps to justify funding requests. Although the number of fusion centers that link future-year budget requirements to their strategic plans has increased by 20.8% since last year, 31 fusion centers (40.3%) have not yet taken this step.

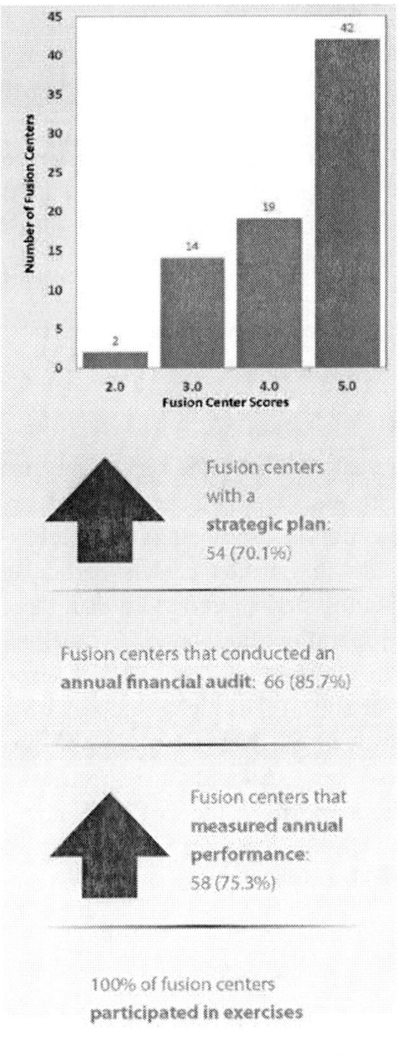

Figure 10. Capability of the National Network of Fusion Centers for EC 2—Sustainment Strategy.

Fusion centers continue to address financial accountability.

Fusion centers receive operational funding from a number of different sources, including SLTT governments, federal grants, and private sector entities. Fusion centers must effectively manage and account for operational funding in order to build trust and confidence among funding partners and to demonstrate how funding is used to achieve intended outcomes. Data from the 2012 Assessment indicates that 66 fusion centers (85.7%) conducted an annual financial audit, up from 46 (63.9%) in 2011.

The majority of fusion centers have adopted performance measures to evaluate progress in achieving programmatic outcomes, although only about half connect performance measures to their strategic plans.

Performance measurement allows organizations to evaluate whether they are achieving intended outcomes consistent with planned costs and within anticipated timelines. Fusion centers that measure their performance can quantify their impact and value in countering criminal and terrorism threats within their AOR and within the broader operating environment. In 2012, 75.3% of fusion centers (58) reported that they measure their performance, an increase of 14.2% from 2011. Of these fusion centers, 46.8% of the National Network (36 fusion centers) link performance measures to their strategic plan. Linking performance measures to a strategic plan helps ensure effective alignment of funding, performance targets, and strategic outcomes.

Fusion centers participate extensively in exercises, although more exercises specifically focused on the fusion process, including the COCs and ECs, would benefit the National Network.

Exercises provide fusion centers the unique opportunity to test specific capabilities, as well as the broader fusion process, within the context of realistic operational scenarios. Fusion centers reported participation in a wide range of exercises during the 2012 Assessment reporting period. Data indicates that fusion centers participated in an average of seven exercises each during the reporting period, and more than three-quarters of those exercises were specifically focused on prevention. Further, 2012 Assessment data indicates that all 77 fusion centers participated in either a discussion-based exercise (66 or 85.7%) or an operations-based exercise (77 or 100%). The high response rate for operations- based exercise participation is due largely to National Network-wide participation in the DHS-sponsored 2012 Communications Drill (see box). Although not specifically collected through the 2012 Assessment, fusion center feedback from the 2012 Communications Drill indicates that additional National Network-wide exercises and drills specifically focused on the COCs and ECs would help fusion centers identify and mitigate gaps in their ability to execute the fusion process.

Recommendations

- Fusion centers should develop strategic plans using existing guidebooks, templates, examples, and technical assistance resources.

- Fusion centers should continue to work with State Administrative Agencies and Urban Area Working Groups to increase fiscal efficiency and oversight of investment planning, grants management, and grants reporting.
- To demonstrate their value and impact in supporting mission requirements, fusion centers should develop performance measures aligned to strategic plans and report findings to stakeholders.
- Fusion centers should implement corrective actions identified in exercises.
- The federal government should conduct more exercises that test fusion center capabilities at the individual, regional, and national levels.

EXERCISES AND DHS'S FUSION CENTER READINESS INITIATIVE (FCRI)

The FCRI provides exercise-related tools and subject matter expertise to fusion centers, facilitates fusion center participation in prevention-focused exercises, and serves as a validation mechanism for the Fusion Center Assessment process. Under the auspices of the FCRI, I&A and its partners engaged in three noteworthy exercise activities in 2012:

- **2012 National Fusion Center Exercise (FUSION X)**—This tabletop exercise, hosted by DHS and other federal partners, included eight fusion centers and seven federal agencies and was solely focused on testing capability achievement and implementation. It provided fusion centers and federal partners with feedback on how to improve capabilities and refine operations.
- **2012 Communications Drill**—This drill evaluated the ability of 75 fusion centers to access and use federal classified and unclassified information systems to receive federally generated threat information (COC 1).
- **2012 DHS Chief Intelligence Officer (CINT) tabletop exercise (CINT TTX)**—The CINT TTX tested DHS's and fusion centers' information and intelligence sharing procedures. Fusion center participation in the CINT TTX demonstrated the value fusion centers have in contributing state and local context to prevention and protection operations. Furthermore, this exercise highlighted the critical role of fusion centers in sharing timely, actionable information and intelligence with SLTT customers.

Table 11. Attribute Data for EC 2—Sustainment Strategy

	EC 2 Attributes	#	%
1	Fusion center has an approved strategic plan	54	70.1%
2	Fusion center conducts an annual financial audit	66	85.7%
3	Fusion center completes an annual operational cost assessment	77	100%
4	Fusion center participates in an exercise at least once a year	77	100%
5	Fusion center measures its performance to determine the effectiveness of its operations relative to expectations it or its governing entity has defined	58	75.3%

EC 3—Communications and Outreach

The ability to develop and execute a communications and outreach plan

By establishing collaborative relationships with stakeholders, fusion centers can expand their customer base, better understand the needs of these customers, and improve the value of information sharing activities. Successful communications and outreach efforts also allow fusion centers to engage multidisciplinary partners in the fusion process. Interaction with a variety of external stakeholders at all levels of government and the private sector provides the opportunity to communicate the mission, purpose, and value of fusion centers.

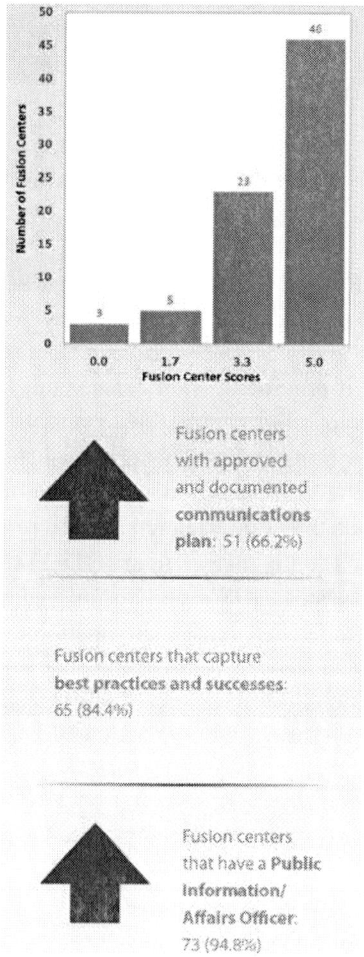

Figure 11. Capability of the National Network of Fusion Centers for EC 3—Communications and Outreach.

The National Network's average score for EC 3 is 4.1 out of 5, compared to 3.3 in 2011. Forty-six fusion centers (59.7%) achieved all three EC 3 attributes, and only eight fusion centers (10.4%) achieved one or no attributes. There are three significant findings from the 2012 Assessment for EC 3.

The number of fusion centers with approved communications plans has increased, but a third of fusion centers still lack such a plan.

A communications plan can help fusion centers define customers and stakeholder groups, outline key messages, and organize outreach and engagement activities to achieve intended communications objectives. A well-executed communications plan will enhance awareness of the fusion center's purpose, mission, functions, and value among customers and stakeholders and will help build and strengthen relationships through engagement and transparency. Fifty-one fusion centers (66.2%) have their own communications plan or one that falls within the scope of another agency's communications plan. However, 33.8% of fusion centers (26) still do not have an approved plan. The 2012 Assessment shows that fusion centers without communications plans typically conduct communications and outreach activities, but the absence of a clearly articulated plan for these activities could limit the consistency, scope, and effectiveness of fusion center outreach efforts.

FUSION CENTERS—COMMUNITY OUTREACH

Fusion Liaison Officer (FLO) Programs	76.6% (59)
"If You See Something, Say Something™" campaign	72.7% (56)
InfraGard	61.0% (47)
Open houses/community forums	32.5% (25)
Building Communities of Trust	31.2% (24)
Citizens Corps	18.2% (14)
Neighborhood Watch programs	10.4% (8)
Volunteers in Police Service (VIPS)	9.1% (7)

Fusion centers are communicating their value, mission, and purpose through a documented process for capturing success stories and lesson learned.

Capturing and sharing success stories and lessons learned improves awareness of the value and impact of fusion centers and helps identify and propagate fusion process best practices across the National Network. Data from the 2012 Assessment indicates that 65 fusion centers (84.4%) have developed and implemented a process for capturing success stories—an increase of 16.3% since last year. Expanding the number of success stories captured across the National Network will ensure that customers, stakeholders, and partners understand the wide range of roles that fusion centers play in criminal and terrorism information sharing and ultimately in preventing crime and terrorism in their communities.

Table 12. Attribute Data for EC 3—Communications and Outreach

EC 3 Attributes		#	%
1	Fusion center has a designated Public Information Officer or Public Affairs Officer	73	94.8%
2	Fusion center has an approved communications plan	51	66.2%
3	Fusion center has developed and implemented a process for capturing success stories	65	84.4%

Almost all fusion centers have designated a Public Information Officer or a Public Affairs Officer to support communications and outreach.

A Public Information Officer or a Public Affairs Officer can support the development and implementation of communications plans, act as a single point of contact for communications and outreach efforts, and help maintain consistent external messaging. Overall, the number of fusion centers that have designated an individual to serve as a Public Information Officer or a Public Affairs Officer rose from 87.5% (63) in 2011 to 94.8% (73) in 2012.

SHARING NATIONAL NETWORK SUCCESSES

The DHS Web site highlights the operational success and support provided by fusion centers (http://www.dhs.gov/fusion-center-success-stories). These stories highlight the unique role of fusion centers in protecting their communities, informing decision making, and enhancing information sharing activities among law enforcement and homeland security partners. These success stories and best practices illustrate the value of the National Network in preventing, protecting against, and responding to all-crimes and terrorism threats and all-hazards incidents.

Recommendation

- Fusion centers should develop documented communications outreach plans, including outreach guidance on P/CRCL issues, drawing on the *Communications and Outreach Guidebook: Considerations for State and Urban Area Fusion Centers* and associated technical assistance services.

EC 4—Security

The ability to protect the security of the physical fusion center facility, information, systems, and personnel

Fusion centers develop and implement appropriate security policies, procedures, and protocols to address physical, personnel, and information security within their centers. Implementing effective security practices enables fusion centers to appropriately collect, store, safeguard, and share classified and unclassified information. Effective security practices also provide federal partners with assurance that the information shared with fusion centers is safeguarded and shared appropriately.

The National Network average score for EC 4 is 4.4 out of 5, an increase of 11.2% since last year. Fifty-two fusion centers (67.5%) achieved all six EC 4 attributes, and 64 (83.1%) achieved at least five of the six EC 4 attributes. There are two significant findings from the 2012 Assessment for EC 4.

Fusion centers have developed plans, policies, or SOPs to address physical, personnel, and information security.

Effective security starts with developing plans, policies, and SOPs to safeguard information, personnel, and assets. Sixty-nine fusion centers (89.6%) reported that they have an approved security plan, policy, or SOP that addresses physical, personnel, and information security. In addition, 88.3% of fusion centers (68) train all personnel on their fusion center's security plan annually, and 84.4% (65) reported that their Security Liaison receives annual training in the areas of physical, personnel, and information security. Also of note, 68 fusion centers (88.3%) reported that their Security Liaison received training on the Central Verification System (CVS),[24] an increase of 27.2% since the last assessment.

Nearly all fusion centers have a designated Security Liaison, but as with P/CRCL Officers, turnover among Security Liaisons is high.

Fusion center Security Liaisons play a critical role in ensuring that physical assets, personnel, and information are properly protected. Seventy-four fusion centers (96.1%) reported that they have a Security Liaison who is working full-time on security issues or who may have additional duties beyond security. Although the average tenure of Security Liaisons across the National Network is 2.6 years, 39.0% of fusion centers (30) report turnover in this position in the 12 months preceding the 2012 Assessment, and 18.2% (14) expect to assign a new Security Liaison in the 12 months following the 2012 Assessment. Disproportional turnover in critical fusion center staff positions may disrupt business process management, force the continual rebuilding of institutional knowledge and relationships, and increase security risks.

Table 13. Attribute Data for EC 4—Security

	EC 4 Attributes	#	%
1	Fusion center has an approved security plan, policy, or SOP that addresses physical, personnel, and information security	69	89.6%
2	Fusion center trains all personnel on the fusion center's security plan annually	68	88.3%
3	Fusion center has identified a Security Liaison	74	96.1%
4	Fusion center's Security Liaison (or other organization's Security Liaison) completes annual security training	65	84.4%
5	Fusion center has access to the Central Verification System (CVS)	64	83.1%
6	Fusion center's Security Liaison (or other organization's Security Liaison) is trained on how to use CVS	68	88.3%

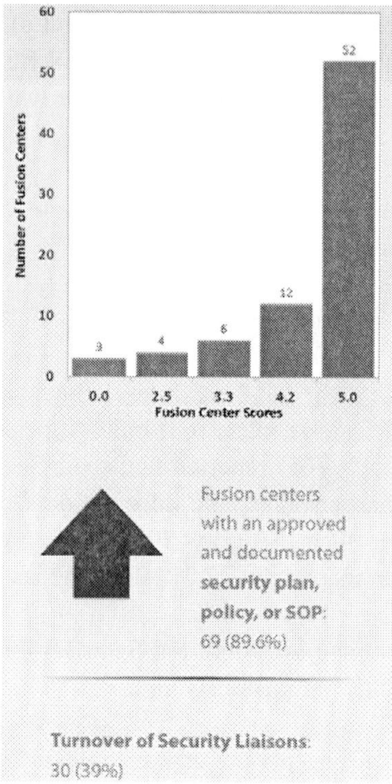

Figure 12. Capability of the National Network of Fusion Centers for EC—4 Security.

Recommendations

- Fusion centers should take efforts to manage and reduce the potential impacts of Security Liaison turnover so that their fusion center can build and maintain institutional knowledge regarding fusion center security.
- Fusion center Security Liaisons should conduct regular security inspections and annual security audits to identify and mitigate security risks within their fusion centers.
- Fusion centers should institutionalize their security-related plans, policies, and SOPs by participating in bimonthly conference calls with other fusion center Security Liaisons, attending annual security training, utilizing the resource kit for Security Liaisons, and requesting technical assistance.

Cross-Cutting Capabilities

Cross-cutting capabilities account for fusion center operational or programmatic functions that support multiple COCs and/or ECs or that relate to but do not cleanly align with a single COC or EC. These capabilities enable more effective fusion process management and more effective information sharing through the fusion process. In the 2011 Assessment, these capabilities were referred to as Additional Priority Areas–Governance. There are five significant cross-cutting findings from the 2012 Assessment.

Table 14. Collocation of Fusion Centers

Collocation of Fusion Centers	#	%
Collocated with one or more partners, including:	63	81.8%
State, county, or city EOC	20	26%
State, county, or city law enforcement	35	45.5%
State homeland security agency	17	22.1%
State, county, or city fire service	4	5.2%
FBI JTTF and/or FIG	15	19.5%
Real Time Crime Center	6	7.8%
HIDTA	9	11.7%
RISS Center or RISSafe™ Watch Center	1	1.3%

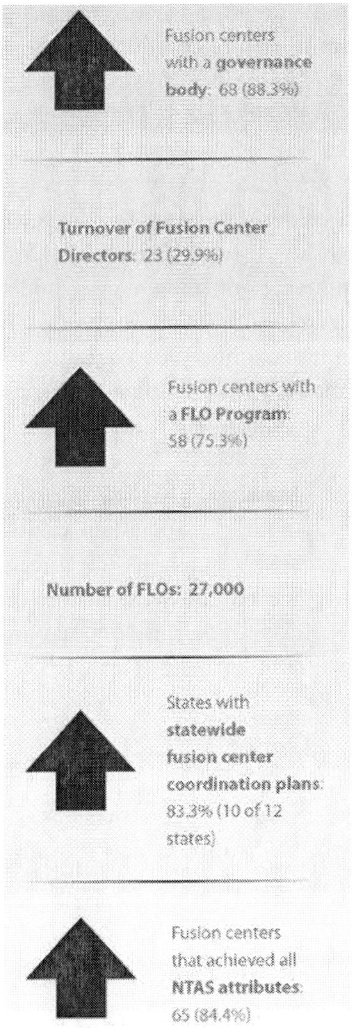

Figure 13.

Table 15. Representation on Fusion Center Governance Bodies

Entity	#	%
FBI FIGs and/or JTTFs	40	51.9%
HIDTA Investigative Support Centers	8	10.4%
RISS Centers	4	5.2%
United States Attorneys' Offices	18	23.4%

A large majority of fusion centers report to governance bodies, and federal and SLTT partner representation on governance bodies is widespread.

Fusion centers receive budgetary, programmatic, and operational guidance from governance bodies to ensure that they are meeting stakeholder expectations. Governance bodies also provide a mechanism to ensure coordination and deconfliction between agencies within a fusion center's AOR, including coordination and deconfliction between the fusion center and RISS Centers, HIDTAs, and FBI JTTFs and their FIGs. Often these parties are collocated with the fusion center.

The number and type of multidisciplinary partners involved in governance boards generally reflect the scope of a center's mission, the scope of support for the fusion center within its AOR, and the reach of a fusion center's information sharing network. The composition, mandate, and influence of governance bodies differ across the National Network, but 88.3% of fusion centers (68) reported that they have a governance body. These centers further indicated that multidisciplinary participation in their governance boards most frequently includes emergency management partners or agencies (39 or 50.6%), state or local homeland security agencies (45 or 58.4%), and Emergency Medical Services (16 or 20.8%). Additionally, many fusion centers indicated that their governance bodies have included formal roles for State Office of Homeland Security/ Homeland Security Advisors (40 or 51.9%), state police chiefs' and/or sheriffs' associations (39 or 50.6%), and State Emergency Management or Emergency Operations Center (EOC) Directors (26 or 33.8%). In order to ensure that field-based activities are coordinated, fusion centers also reported numerous instances in which federal agencies or other field-based information sharing entities are represented on governance bodies, as indicated in Table 15.

TRIBAL PARTNERS

Fusion centers continue to leverage tribal partnerships. A total of 32.5% (25) of fusion centers have access to tribal SMEs to inform analytic production, consistent with data collected in 2012 (31.9% or 23 fusion centers).

Fusion Center Director turnover is high.

Stability at the Fusion Center Director position increases the consistency of fusion process capability implementation and execution, and ensures common strategic direction for fusion center staff and partners. Data collected through the 2012 Assessment indicates that 29.9% of the National Network (23) experienced turnover at the Fusion Center Director position during the period covered by the 2012 Assessment, and an additional 29.9% of fusion centers (23) indicated that they expect turnover in the director position during the 12 months following the 2012 Assessment period. Further analysis of 2012 Assessment data indicates that 75.3% (58) of Fusion Center Director positions are filled by sworn law enforcement officers as opposed to civilians or codirectorships between sworn law enforcement officers and civilians.

Coordination of Field-Based Entities

Joint Terrorism Task Forces (JTTFs) are FBI-funded and -managed multijurisdictional task forces established to conduct terrorism-related investigations. JTTFs focus primarily on terrorism-related issues, with specific regard to terrorism investigations with local, regional, national, and international implications. Investigations conducted by JTTFs are focused on known threat actors or identified individuals who meet the thresholds established in accordance with the Attorney General Guidelines for Domestic FBI Operations to initiate assessments or investigations.

(http://www.dhs.gov/fusion-centers-and-joint-terrorism-task-forces)

FBI Field Intelligence Groups (FIGs) are located in each of the FBI's 56 field offices and are staffed with FBI intelligence analysts, language analysts, and special agents. FIGs are the primary mechanism through which FBI field offices develop human intelligence; identify emerging trends; identify, evaluate, and prioritize threats within their areas of responsibility; and support domain awareness and investigative efforts through the use of strategic and tactical analysis, linguists, subject matter experts, special operations groups, and specialized surveillance groups. FIGs are the hub of the FBI's Intelligence Program and serve as the FBI's conduit for information sharing and collaboration among the FBI; the U.S. Intelligence Community (IC); fusion centers; other federal, state, local, and tribal law enforcement, government, and private sector entities.

(http://www.dhs.gov/fbi-field-intelligence-groups-and-fusion-centers)

High Intensity Drug Trafficking Areas (HIDTA) Investigative Support Centers (ISC) are funded by the Office of National Drug Control Policy (ONDCP) and aim to support the disruption and dismantlement of drug trafficking and money laundering organizations through the prevention or mitigation of associated criminal activity. The ISC is responsible for collecting, analyzing, and disseminating drug-related law enforcement information and intelligence for the entire HIDTA but primarily supports ongoing cases or specific enforcement initiatives.

HIDTA enforcement initiatives include a variety of multiagency investigative, interdiction, and prosecution activities targeting drug trafficking and money laundering organizations, drug production organizations, drug gangs, drug fugitives, and other serious crimes with a drug nexus.

(http://www.dhs.gov/fusion-centers-and-hidta-investigative-support-centers)

Regional Information Sharing Systems (RISS) Centers provide services and resources to support regional law enforcement efforts to successfully resolve criminal investigations and prosecute offenders while providing the critical officer safety event deconfliction. RISS supports efforts against organized and violent crime, gang activity, drug activity, terrorism, human trafficking, identity theft, and other regional priorities, while promoting officer safety, and offers full-service delivery from the beginning of an investigation to the ultimate prosecution and conviction of criminals.
(http://www.riss.net/Default/Overview)

Most fusion centers have established Fusion Liaison Officer (FLO) Programs to broaden the scope of information sharing within their AOR.

FLO Programs vary in focus, complexity, and size, but all have the same basic goal of facilitating the exchange of information between fusion centers and stakeholders within the fusion center's AOR. According to 2012 Assessment data, 75.3% of the National Network (58) have established a FLO or comparable program, and another 20.8% (16) reported that they planned on establishing one by the end of calendar year 2012. Among those fusion centers with existing FLO Programs, the number of reported FLOs exceeded 27,000. Fusion centers identified the top three purposes of FLO Programs as gathering information, disseminating information to customers and partners, and conducting community outreach.

Most states with more than one fusion center have policies to guide coordination among fusion centers, but only half of fusion centers are part of plans that coordinate broader statewide information sharing.

State governments are responsible for determining the number of fusion centers necessary to execute the fusion process within their state. A total of 12 states have designated more than one fusion center in their state. Data collected through the 2012 Assessment shows that the fusion centers in these 12 states account for 48.1% of the National Network (37 fusion centers). Having more than one fusion center in a state means that state governments must ensure clear lines of communication between fusion centers and must encourage coordination to avoid duplication of effort and/or operational or analytic gaps. Of the 12 states with more than one fusion center, 10 (83.3%) have a documented statewide fusion center coordination plan, up from nine states (75%) in 2011.

Equally important to enabling the fusion process within states, including in those states with more than one fusion center, is developing and implementing intrastate coordination plans. These plans account for the broader collection of critical partners involved in the statewide information sharing environment, including law enforcement, fire, EMS, the private sector, public health, and a range of other entities. They can also account for coordination across all levels of government within a state, including with representatives from federal or national- level entities such as FBI FIGs and JTTFs, HIDTAs, RISS Centers, and other DHS components. Forty-one fusion centers (53.2%) representing a total of 27 of the 52 U.S. states and territories with a fusion center reported that their state or territory has a documented intrastate coordination plan. The absence of such plans among slightly less than half of states and territories with fusion centers (48.1%) represents a significant obstacle to effective statewide information sharing and poses additional challenges to effectively implementing a national information sharing enterprise.

Fusion centers have significantly increased their capability to process National Terrorism Advisory System (NTAS) alerts.

In April of 2011, the NTAS replaced the color-coded Homeland Security Advisory System. NTAS communicates information about terrorist threats by providing timely, detailed information to the public and federal, SLTT, and private sector partners. In addition to providing information and intelligence that may inform the decision to issue an NTAS alert, fusion centers play an important role in processing and sharing NTAS alerts once issued. Although all COC and EC attributes contribute to a fusion center's ability to support the NTAS process, five attributes address specific NTAS-related functions performed by fusion centers. Data collected through the 2012 Assessment indicates that 84.4% of fusion centers (65) achieved all five NTAS-related attributes. This represents a significant improvement from last year, when only 48.6% (35) of fusion centers had achieved these attributes. Of specific note, the National Network experienced a 28.6% increase from 2011 (59.7% or 43) to 2012 (88.3% or 68) in the percentage of fusion centers with an SOP that addresses the receipt of NTAS alerts and a 34.2% increase from 2011 (52.8% or 38) to 2012 (87.0% or 67) in the percentage of fusion centers with a documented plan, policy, or SOP for disseminating NTAS alerts to stakeholders within their AOR.

Recommendations

- Fusion centers should incorporate field-based partners, such as those supporting HIDTAs, RISS Centers, FIGs, and JTTFs, into governance bodies and intrastate coordination plans in order to improve fusion process coordination and avoid mission overlap.
- Fusion centers should expand multidisciplinary involvement in governance bodies in order to promote improved SLTT coordination and collaboration.
- Fusion centers should take advantage of technical assistance to develop and implement FLO Programs and a FLO Concept of Operations.
- All primary fusion centers should work with federal and SLTT intelligence, analytic, and investigative entities to develop a documented statewide information sharing plan.

National Network Maturity Model

The National Network Maturity Model (Maturity Model) is a multistage framework designed to evaluate and categorize the overall progress of the National Network as a whole—as opposed to individual fusion centers—in achieving the COCs and ECs. It defines a path for the National Network to move from the current state to a desired end state where a fully integrated, mature, and sustainable National Network strengthens efforts to protect the homeland. Using the Maturity Model, the fusion center stakeholder community can target resources and strategic planning efforts to support National Network capability maturation towards a defined goal with discrete intermediate capability targets.

The Maturity Model consists of 46 attributes aligned to four distinct stages: Fundamental, Emerging, Enhanced, and Mature. For each stage of the Maturity Model, the fusion center stakeholder community established an outcome-oriented, qualitative definition and aligned capability attributes based on each attribute's contribution to the defined outcome for that maturity stage. Some of the attributes associated with the Maturity Model differ from those attributes aligned to individual fusion centers because the attributes needed for a fully capable fusion center are different from those needed for a fully capable National Network.

The National Network advances through each of the four stages of the Maturity Model when 75% of fusion centers achieve the attributes associated with that level of the Maturity Model. Each stage is equally important to achieving a fully integrated National Network.

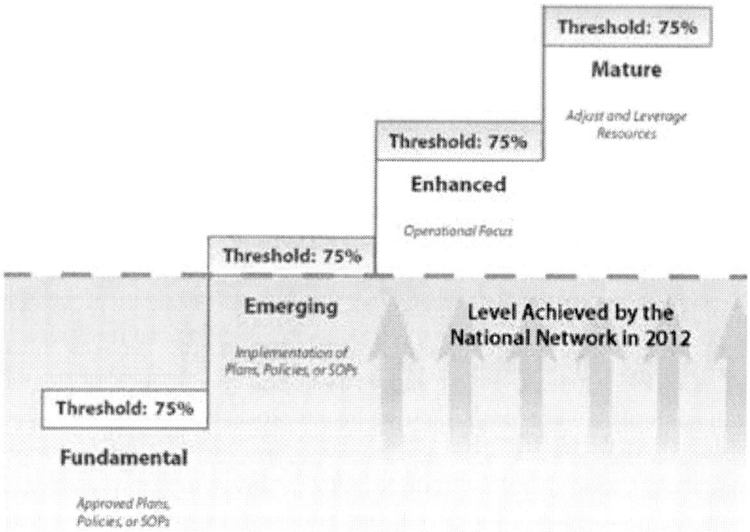

Figure 14. The National Network of Fusion Centers has reached the Emerging Stage.

Fundamental (Approved Plans, Policies, or SOPs): Fusion centers across the National Network have approved plans, policies, or SOPs for each of the four COCs and EC 1.

Emerging (Implementation of Plans, Policies, or SOPs): The National Network has the systems, mechanisms, and processes needed to implement the plans, policies, or SOPs and the COCs and ECs as a whole.

Enhanced (Operational Focus): The National Network has the operational capability to produce products and provide services to federal, state, and local customers.

Mature (Adjust and Leverage Resources): The National Network has the full capability to leverage the collective resources among individual fusion centers and adjust to both the changing threat environment and evolving requirements.

Current Status of the National Network—Emerging Stage

The results of the 2011 Assessment indicated that the National Network had reached the Fundamental stage, meaning that more than 75% of fusion centers have the requisite plans, policies, or SOPs to execute the fusion process. Written plans, policies, and SOPs memorialize business processes so fusion centers can sustain themselves through leadership and staff transition, changing customer requirements and, most important, evolving threats. The documents also encourage standardization and consistency in fusion process capability, terminology, and practice across the National Network, which is the basis for greater network integration.

As the National Network matures, its capabilities become more sophisticated and integrated. Over the last year, the fusion center stakeholder community has focused both on ensuring continued improvement across the National Network and on reaching the Emerging stage, which moves beyond developing plans, policies, and SOPs to implementing effective fusion center business processes based on these plans, policies, and SOPs. Results from the 2012 Assessment, as shown in Table 16 below, indicate that the National Network achieved the requisite threshold for each of the attributes associated with the Emerging stage, which includes establishing the systems, mechanisms, and processes needed to implement the COCs and ECs.

Next Stage of the Maturity Model

Looking forward, the National Network will focus on reaching the Enhanced stage, while continuing to build and sustain capabilities at the Fundamental and Emerging stages. At the Enhanced stage, the National Network is operationalizing the fusion process. Fusion centers create products and provide services in response to defined customer needs and work across organizational and jurisdictional boundaries to share information and collaborate in the fusion process.

Of the 13 attributes associated with the Enhanced stage, the National Network has reached the 75% threshold for 9, leaving 4 attributes to attain. Of these 4 attributes, the National Network has made significant progress towards the 75% threshold in 3 (*see Table 17)*. However, 2012 Assessment data shows that only 22.1% of fusion centers (17) tag all analytic products to HSEC SINs or their own fusion center SINs. As previously discussed, SINs define the topics and issues customers and stakeholders care about. Tagging fusion center analytical products to relevant SINs—both their own and the HSEC SINs—allows customers to easily identify relevant products. Tagging products also provides a way for fusion centers to track overall production and identify which customer needs are being met. At the national level, tagging enhances national information sharing efforts by enabling homeland security practitioners to research and retrieve intelligence products based on specific topics of interest.

Table 16. National Network Has Reached the Emerging Stage

Attributes in the Emerging Stage Achieved by the National Network		
1	The ability to conduct threat assessments within their AOR	94.8% (73)
2	A documented analytic production plan	77.9% (60)
3	Established critical infrastructure analysis capability	97.4% (75)
4	A structured customer feedback mechanism for some or all of their analytic products	84.4% (65)
5	A Fusion Liaison Officer (FLO) Program	75.3% (58)
6	Multidisciplinary partners in their SINs development process	79.2% (61)
7	An annual process to review and refresh their SINs	84.4% (65)
8	Participate in an exercise at least once a year	100% (77)
9	Conduct an annual financial audit	85.7% (66)

Table 17. Next Stage of the Maturity Model

Maturity Model Attribute for Enhanced Stage		Achieved
1	Conduct threat assessments within their AOR	✓
2	Have a documented analytic production plan	✓
3	Have established a critical infrastructure analysis capability	✓
4	Have a structured customer satisfaction mechanism for some or all of their analytic products	✓
5	Fusion centers have a FLO Program	✓
6	Have a FLO Concept of Operations	71.4% (55)
7	Have an annual process to review and refresh SINs	✓
8	Include multidisciplinary partners in their SINs development process	✓
9	Tag all analytic products to HSEC or fusion center SINs	22.1% (17)
10	Undergo a P/CRCL compliance review	70.1% (54)
11	Participate in an exercise at least once a year	✓
12	Conduct an annual financial audit	✓
13	Include multidisciplinary partners in governance bodies	72.7% (56)

Recommendations

The following recommendations are intended to support the National Network to achieve the four attributes remaining at the Enhanced stage.

- Fusion centers should ensure that all analytic products posted to HSIN Intel are tagged with appropriate DHS HSEC SINs and fusion center SINs.
- Fusion centers should conduct P/CRCL compliance reviews that assess their policies and procedures related to P/CRCL protections through the use of the *Privacy, Civil Rights, and Civil Liberties Compliance Verification for the Intelligence Enterprise*.
- Fusion centers should expand multidisciplinary involvement in governance bodies to promote improved SLTT coordination and collaboration.
- Fusion centers should take advantage of technical assistance to develop and implement FLO Programs and a FLO Concept of Operations.

Federal Support to Fusion Centers

Fusion centers are state and locally owned and operated entities that play a vital role in improving the nation's ability to prevent, protect against, and respond to threats to the homeland. Federal agencies provide support to fusion centers through grant funding, training, technical assistance, exercises, federal personnel, and access to federal information and networks. The 2012 Assessment gathered data from Fusion Center Directors to understand the effectiveness of federal support received during the period of August 1, 2011 through July 31, 2012, and to prioritize federal support requirements for the 12 months following the 2012 Assessment.

Fusion Center Directors were asked to identify the types of support they received during the assessment period to support each COC and EC, and then they were asked to evaluate the effectiveness of this support. Finally, they identified the types of assistance they would like to access in the future and rated the priority of that additional support. The categories of support included data systems, federal policy changes, guidebook and templates, personnel, technical assistance, and training. The effectiveness of federal support for each COC and EC and the priority of future federal support were rated on a scale from 1 (least effective/lowest priority) to 5 (highly effective/ highest priority). Only fusion centers that self-reported as leveraging federal support or needing future federal support were included in the evaluations and priority rankings. Seventy-six fusion centers provided data.

COC 1—Receive

Federal Support Received

During the period covered by the 2012 Assessment, the federal government provided support for COC 1 that included guidance on developing and implementing plans, policies, and SOPs; Secret-level clearances; and access to federally managed Secret-level information sharing systems. Assessment data revealed that granting Secret- level security clearances was the most effective support provided by the federal government for COC 1. Out of the 71 fusion centers that received this support, 90.1% identified it as highly effective. Additionally, 75.8% of the fusion centers that reported using federal support to access Secret-level information sharing systems ranked the support as highly effective, and 74.1% of the fusion centers that reported receiving federal support to develop plans, policies, or SOPs for COC 1 rated the support as highly effective.

Future Support Needed

Sixty-seven fusion centers identified obtaining security clearances to facilitate access to classified information as the highest priority for continued federal support over 12 months following the 2012 Assessment period, with 73.1% of those identifying this as a high priority. Out of the 68 fusion centers that identified a continued need for federal support to access classified systems or databases, 70.6% determined that this support was a high priority. Sixty-four fusion centers identified a need for federal training on classified and unclassified systems and databases, with 68.8% of these fusion centers identifying this as a high priority.

COC 2—Analyze

Federal Support Received

The federal government deployed resources that ensured that fusion centers obtain and sustain a robust analytic capability, including guidance, templates, training, and access to SMEs. Assessment data showed that this federal support effectively assisted fusion centers—most (60) indicated that they leveraged federal support to develop plans, policies, and SOPs for COC 2, and 80% of these indicated that the support they received was highly effective. Sixty fusion centers took advantage of analytic training opportunities, with 81.7% rating this training as highly effective. Additionally, of the 25 fusion centers that reported using federal support to access SMEs to inform analytic production, 76% found this support to be highly effective.

Future Support Needed

The 2012 Assessment data revealed that the types of federal support that fusion centers find effective are largely consistent with the types of federal support that fusion centers prioritize for the future. Projecting out 12 months, 67 fusion centers reported needing analytic training, with 94% of these centers identifying these services as a high priority. Sixty-one centers indicated a need for additional federal support to develop risk assessments, with 67.2% of these identifying this as a high priority. Additionally, 60 fusion centers indicated a need for additional federal support for developing strategic threat assessments, with 65% identifying this as a high priority.

COC 3—Disseminate

Federal Support Received

The federal government supported fusion centers' efforts to disseminate information to their customers by providing guidance, templates, and technical assistance to enable and enhance coordination and communication between fusion centers, multidisciplinary partners, and other customers and liaisons. The 2012 Assessment data revealed that federal support was effective in strengthening fusion centers' COC 3 capabilities. For example, 78.3% of the fusion centers that received federal assistance with developing and/or enhancing plans, policies, or SOPs ranked the support as highly effective. Of the 42 fusion centers that took advantage of federal support to develop dissemination matrices and protocols, 61.9% rated this support as highly effective.

Future Support Needed

The 2012 Assessment data revealed that 49 fusion centers anticipated needing federal support to ensure that a primary SBU mechanism was in place for disseminating information and products, with 67.3% of these fusion centers identifying this as a high priority. Additionally, 45 fusion centers indicated that they would need federal support to implement a standardized mechanism for verifying the delivery of products to their intended customers.

COC 4—Gather

Federal Support Received

The federal government supported fusion centers in building the capabilities needed to gather information while ensuring the protection of P/CRCL of individuals. In particular, the federal government facilitated fusion center participation in the NSI and supported fusion centers in identifying and documenting their SINs. Of the 58 fusion centers that took advantage of federal support to develop and implement NSI site plans or other associated plans, policies, or SOPs, 77.6% categorized this support as highly effective. Further, of the 48 fusion centers that indicated that they utilized federal support for identifying and documenting their SINs, 72.9% indicated that this support was highly effective.

Future Support Needed

When asked to prioritize future federal support, 53 fusion centers projected a need for additional support on identifying and managing their information needs, with 60.4% of these centers identifying this as a high priority. When asked more specifically about SINs, 55 fusion centers indicated a need for assistance in reviewing and refreshing their SINs, with 67.3% of these fusion centers identifying this as a high priority.

EC 1—Privacy, Civil Rights, and Civil Liberties Protections

Federal Support Received

The federal government is committed to assisting fusion centers in protecting the P/CRCL of all individuals, including through the provision of training and the facilitation of privacy policy compliance reviews. Fusion centers reported that the most effective federal support services for enhancing P/CRCL protections over the assessment period included assistance on developing and implementing policies, processes, and mechanisms for receiving, cataloging, and retaining information to comply with 28 CFR Part 23, as well as training provided to personnel who access criminal intelligence systems in compliance with 28 CFR Part 23. Both of these services were rated as highly effective by 85.2% of the fusion centers receiving such assistance. Additionally, federal support for policies related to privacy was favorably received, with 84.8% of fusion centers receiving this assistance identifying it as highly effective. Further, federal support for fusion center training on their privacy policy was rated highly effective by 76.1% of the fusion centers that received this assistance.

Future Support Needed

Assessment data revealed that most fusion centers anticipated needing continued federal support to ensure that all fusion center personnel who access criminal intelligence systems in 28 CFR Part 23 are appropriately trained. Of the 57 centers that indicated a need for this support, 71.9% rated it as a high priority. Additionally, 45 fusion centers identified the need for federal support on developing a P/CRCL outreach plan, with 64.4% rating this as a high priority.

EC 2—Sustainment Strategy

Federal Support Received

The federal government encouraged fusion centers to build sustainment capabilities by providing resources such as training for leadership and exercise support. Based on fusion center responses, the most effective federal sustainment support was training for fusion center leaders. This training was rated as highly effective by 44 of the 50 (88%) fusion centers that took advantage of it. Additionally, of the 49 fusion centers that utilized federal support to conduct exercises, 81.6% described it as highly effective.

Future Support Needed

2012 Assessment data indicated that training for fusion center leaders will continue to be important, with 62 of the 76 (81.6%) fusion centers indicating this need for the 12 months following the 2012 Assessment and 80.6% of these indicating it as a high priority. Fifty-eight fusion centers also indicated a need for support in conducting or participating in exercises, with 55.2% indicating it as a high priority. Forty-nine fusion centers projected an increased need for federal support in developing and/or enhancing their strategic plans, with 71.4% of these centers indicating it as a high priority.

EC 3—Communications and Outreach

Federal Support Received

To support capability development for communication and outreach to customers and stakeholders, the federal government provided guidance, templates, and technical assistance for capturing best practices and success stories and provided a communications and outreach guidebook to help fusion centers develop communications and outreach plans. The federal government also developed customized brochures and videos for the Building Communities of Trust initiative. Thirty-two fusion centers indicated that they took advantage of federal communication and outreach support offerings, and 62.5% of these centers indicated that this support was highly effective. Furthermore, 28 fusion centers took advantage of federal support for capturing success stories, with 64.3% rating the support as highly effective.

Future Support Needed

Forty-nine fusion centers foresaw a continued need for federal support in developing communications and outreach capabilities. Outreach to non-law enforcement partners was ranked the highest-projected need, with 59.2% of fusion centers identifying this support as a high priority. Additionally, 41 centers requested continued federal support for capturing best practices and success stories, with 56.1% indicating this as a high priority.

EC 4—Security

Federal Support Received

Federal government support enabled fusion centers to build and sustain security capabilities. Support offerings included training for Security Liaisons, access to security and clearance management systems, and security-focused technical assistance. Fusion centers rated the effectiveness of all EC 4 support from the federal government as high. Specifically, 89.4% of those fusion centers that reported receiving Security Liaison training indicated that this training was highly effective. Additionally, of the 43 fusion centers that took advantage of federal support in accessing the Central Verification System (CVS), 81.4% indicated that it was highly effective.

Future Support Needed

Fusion centers anticipated needing continued federal support over the next year to further build and sustain security capabilities, with a specific focus on training Security Liaisons and providing access to and training on CVS. Fifty-two fusion centers highlighted a need for continued Security Liaison training, with 71.2% percent of these indicating this as a high priority. Similarly, 54 fusion centers indicated a need for continued support for access to and training on CVS, with 59.3% identifying this as a high priority.

Fusion Center Performance

Beginning in 2012, DHS broadened the scope of the Fusion Center Performance Program from its focus on capability development to include an evaluation of the National Network's performance in contributing to the national information sharing and homeland security outcomes. National Network partners finalized the initial set of five performance measures in April 2012.[25] These five performance measures reflect the shared benefits of a National Network, as well as the shared responsibilities of individual fusion centers and federal, state, and local partners in supporting and sustaining the National Network over time. These measures also start to characterize the effectiveness of the National Network, which reflects the implementation and institutionalization of the individual COCs and ECs and the fusion process in general. An expanded set of performance measures, which are currently under development, will provide a more comprehensive understanding of the broader value and impact of the National Network.

DHS collected National Network performance data covering the same reporting period used for the 2012 Assessment (August 1, 2011 through July 31, 2012). Unless specifically noted in the below sections, the Online Self Assessment Tool was used to collect data for each measure. DHS worked with fusion center representatives and interagency partners to develop the targets by using 2012 data as a baseline.[26] These targets serve as goals for the National Network, defining achievable and incremental progress over a five-year period. These targets are not focused on individual fusion centers but instead are intended to encourage National Network- wide improvements. The percentage of the National Network that was able to provide data for each measure is indicated below.

Privacy Policy Compliance Review

Percentage of fusion centers that conduct a privacy, civil rights, and civil liberties compliance review based upon the compliance verification tool (Privacy, Civil Rights, and Civil Liberties Compliance Verification for the Intelligence Enterprise) developed through the Global Justice Information Sharing Initiative (Global)

This performance measure assesses verification of compliance with P/CRCL policies across the National Network and, by extension, the National Network's ability to protect P/CRCL. Specifically, this measure evaluates whether fusion centers conduct a review of their P/CRCL policies to ensure compliance with all applicable P/CRCL protection laws, regulations, and policies, as defined by the *Privacy, Civil Rights, and Civil Liberties Compliance Verification for the Intelligence Enterprise* tool. This tool was developed jointly by Global[27] and the Departments of Justice and Homeland Security to provide guidance on implementing appropriate P/CRCL safeguards within a fusion center. Completion of the compliance review was also included as a FY 2012 HSGP requirement. The level at which fusion centers comply with applicable policies indicates that they are able to effectively protect privacy, civil rights, and civil liberties. Conducting P/CRCL policy reviews is a requirement of the FY 2012 HSGP.

From August 1, 2011 through July 31, 2012, 70.1% (54) of the National Network conducted a P/CRCL compliance review. All fusion centers were able to provide the required data for this measure.

Assessment Year	**2012**	**2013**	**2014**	**2015**	**2016**	**2017**
Actual/*(Target)*	70.1%	*(75%)*	*(80%)*	*(85%)*	*(95%)*	*(100%)*

Contributions to Terrorism-Related Investigations

Number of Suspicious Activity Reporting that are vetted and submitted by fusion centers that result in the initiation or an enhancement of an investigation by the Federal Bureau of Investigation (e.g., Joint Terrorism Task Force investigations)

Fusion centers play a critical role in the SAR process by collecting, vetting, and analyzing SARs and by submitting approved SARs to the ISE Shared Space and/or the FBI's eGuardian for further federal review and analysis. This performance measure is intended to capture the contribution fusion centers make to both the Nationwide SAR Initiative (NSI) and the broader federal counterterrorism mission by identifying the number of terrorism-related SARs submitted by fusion centers that result the initiation or an enhancement of an investigation by the FBI, including JTTF investigations.[28]

During the period of review, fusion centers vetted and submitted 91 SARs that resulted in the initiation or an enhancement of an FBI investigation. The FBI provided data for this measure for all fusion centers during the reporting period.

Assessment Year	2012	2013	2014	2015	2016	2017
Actual/*(Target)*	91					

More collection and analysis is required in order to project appropriate benchmarks for future years. Although the number of SARs that lead to or enhance an existing JTTF investigation will continue to be reported out with anticipated increases from year to year, data will be studied for the next two years before determining viable performance target for 2015.

Analytic Products Tagged to Fusion Center Information Needs

Percentage of fusion center analytic products that reference fusion center Standing Information Needs (SINs)

SINs provide a formal, structured framework for categorizing issues and topics of interest for fusion centers. Fusion centers develop SINs through close coordination with customers and stakeholders and use SINs to help guide information-gathering and sharing efforts. As such, the tagging of analytic products with fusion center SINs demonstrates product relevance in the context of fusion centers' AOR. This performance metric is intended to evaluate the degree to which fusion centers are meeting the needs of customers within their AOR. Higher percentages indicate that fusion center analytic products are more relevant to customers and stakeholders.

For the purposes of this metric, *fusion center SINs* refer to draft or approved SINs. SINs do not have to align with DHS Homeland Security (HSEC) SINs. Additionally, *fusion center analytic products* are defined as finished intelligence products that include analytic conclusions derived from a review and assessment of available information and/or intelligence, including tactical, operational, and strategic analysis products.

During the period of review, 14.3% of fusion center analytic products referenced fusion center SINs. Thirteen centers were able to provide full data and 12 gave partial data for this measure.

Assessment Year	2012	2013	2014	2015	2016	2017
Actual/*(Target)*	14.3%	*(40%)*	*(50%)*	*(60%)*	*(70%)*	*(80%)*

Analytic Products Authored by Multiple Fusion Centers

Number of fusion center analytic products authored by two or more fusion centers

Information sharing and coordination across jurisdictional boundaries are critical to efforts to identify and mitigate threats to the homeland. In particular, collaboration between fusion centers strengthens the value and impact of analysis by leveraging disparate but specialized knowledge and skills resident across the National Network. This performance measure assesses the degree of collaboration across the National Network by measuring the number of analytic products authored by two or more fusion centers. For the purposes of this measure, *authored* means making a contribution to the product beyond simply providing raw reporting or other basic information. Authoring includes involvement in deriving the analytical conclusion of the product and/or producing all or a portion of the language in the product. Higher numbers of joint products indicate that the National Network is sharing and leveraging information and expertise from other fusion centers in order to enhance the strategic and tactical threat picture.

During the period of review, fusion centers reported producing 80 analytic products that were authored by two or more fusion centers. All 77 fusion centers provided data for this measure.

Assessment Year	**2012**	**2013**	**2014**	**2015**	**2016**	**2017**
Actual/*(Target)*	80	*(85)*	*(90)*	*(95)*	*(100)*	*(105)*

Fusion Center-to-Fusion Center Requests for Information

Number of responses to fusion center-to-fusion center requests for information (RFIs)

This performance measure assesses fusion center-to-fusion center coordination as a means of evaluating the functional effectiveness and responsiveness of the National Network. Specifically, this performance measure identifies the total number of RFIs sent and responded to amongst designated fusion centers. Qualifying RFIs include discrete requests for information, products, or services, including, but not limited to, name traces, database checks, threat or risk assessments, raw reports, subject matter expertise, finished intelligence products, or joint production. RFIs can be submitted or received through a purpose-built RFI management tool or via telephone, e-mail, or other communication mechanisms but should be tracked using a standardized RFI tracking process, such as a numbering system or date/time cataloging. Higher numbers of fusion center-to-fusion center RFIs indicate that the National Network is functioning effectively as a network to share information that enhances state and local preparedness conditions.

During the period of review, fusion centers responded to a total of 15,356 fusion center-to-fusion center RFIs. Forty-four fusion centers provided full data and 33 provided partial data for this measure.

Assessment Year	**2012**	**2013**	**2014**	**2015**	**2016**	**2017**
Actual/*(Target)*	15,356					

This number is expected to grow as more fusion centers refine their RFI tracking processes. Data for this performance metric will be collected and analyzed over the next two years to determine a viable target for 2015.

Recommendations

The following recommendations are intended to support the National Network to meet out-year targets and improve performance.

- Fusion centers should ensure that all analytic products posted to HSIN Intel are tagged with appropriate DHS HSEC SINs and fusion center SINs.
- The federal government should continue to support analytic exchanges to assist fusion centers in collaborating with field-based partners, such as HIDTAs, RISS Centers, FIGs, and JTTFs.
- The federal government should assist fusion center analysts to further expand their analytical skills and expertise by supporting exchanges, developing joint products, and mentoring.
- The federal government and fusion centers should expand training to non-law enforcement partners to further enhance both the gathering of information and the quality of SAR.

Next Steps

Moving forward, National Network partners are focused on two important efforts relating to the performance component of the broader FCPP. First, DHS, in close cooperation with federal and SLTT partners, will continue to help all fusion centers understand and implement the five initial performance measures in order to increase the quality and consistency of reported performance data and to ensure the broadest possible reporting of performance data across the National Network. These efforts will focus on adopting effective performance data collection mechanisms at fusion centers that minimize the time and effort associated with data tracking and reporting. Tied closely to this effort, DHS is developing guidance to assist fusion centers in implementing strategic plans and annual reporting processes that include fusion center-specific performance measures. When fusion centers implement performance-tracking processes to support AOR-specific annual reporting, they can more effectively demonstrate their AOR-specific value and impact to key partners and stakeholders, including their governance bodies. At the same time, they can more effectively track data aligned to the National Network performance measures.

The second important performance-related effort is the development of additional National Network performance measures. Starting in early FY2013, DHS began working with Fusion Center Directors, federal partners, and performance subject matter experts to define additional National Network performance measures, with the intent of formalizing these measures ahead of the start of the 2013 Fusion Center Assessment. Additional measures will examine a broad range of outputs and outcomes associated with fusion center operations. When combined with the five initial performance measures, the consolidated National Network performance measures will provide a more comprehensive understanding of the broad range of National Network impacts on national information sharing and homeland security outcomes. Once finalized, DHS will incorporate the new measures into the 2013 Fusion Center Assessment data collection process, where applicable, to minimize the reporting impact on individual fusion centers, and will work with National Network partners to determine other ways to collect relevant performance data.

HOMELAND SECURITY GRANT PROGRAM REQUIREMENTS

The FY 2012 Homeland Security Grant Program (HSGP), administered by the Federal Emergency Management Agency (FEMA's) Grant Programs Directorate, plays an important role in the implementation of Presidential Policy Directive 8 (PPD-8) by supporting the development and sustainment of core capabilities. Core capabilities are essential for the execution of each of the five mission areas outlined in the *National Preparedness Goal* (NPG). The development and sustainment of these core capabilities are not exclusive to any single level of government or organization but rather require the combined effort of the whole community. Intelligence and information sharing is identified in the NPG as a core capability, and the *National Prevention Framework* further identifies those capabilities, plans, and operations necessary to ensure the Nation has established the ability to collect, analyze, and further disseminate intelligence.

To support the development and sustainment of these capabilities, the FY 2012 HSGP guidance identified the maturation and enhancement of fusion centers as one of seven priority areas for HSGP funding. DHS identified fusion center-specific requirements necessary to support this priority area and used the 2012 Assessment to collect data to evaluate compliance.

Following completion of the 2012 Assessment, DHS analyzed assessment data to evaluate compliance status for all fusion centers. DHS notified fusion center leaders and their respective Homeland Security Advisors and State Administrative Agencies in those limited instances when requirements were not met and directed noncompliant states to provide a detailed explanation of their fusion center's current compliance status, along with a written plan detailing an approach for achieving full compliance. DHS will use the 2013 Fusion Center Assessment to validate explanations or justifications and to evaluate compliance with FY 2013 HSGP requirements.

The table on the next page details fusion center compliance with each of the 2012 HSGP requirements.

Table 18. 2012 HSGP Requirements Compliance

2012 HSGP Requirement	#	%
Successful completion of the Fusion Center Assessment Program, composed of the self assessment, validation, staffing and product tables, and cost assessment data	77	100%
Approved plans, policies, or SOPs for each of the four COCs		
Fusion center has approved plans, policies, or SOPs for the receipt of federally generated threat information	71	92.2%
Fusion center has approved plans, policies, or SOPs for assessing the local implications of time-sensitive and emerging threat information	72	93.5%
Fusion center has approved plans, policies, or SOPs governing the procedures and communication mechanisms for the timely dissemination of products to customers within its AOR	73	94.8%
Fusion center is NSI-compliant OR has an approved plan, policy, or SOP governing the gathering of locally generated information	72	93.5%
Approved P/CRCL policy that is determined to be at least as comprehensive as the ISE Privacy Guidelines	77	100%
Completion of a compliance review of the P/CRCL policy in accordance with the *Privacy, Civil Rights, and Civil Liberties Compliance Verification for the Intelligence Enterprise*	54	70.1%

2012 HSGP Requirement	#	%
All staff receive annual training on both the center's P/CRCL policy and 28 CFR Part 23	71	92.2%
All fusion center analytic personnel must meet designated competencies, as identified in the *Common Competencies for State, Local, and Tribal Intelligence Analysts*, that have been acquired through experience or training courses	68	88.3%
Completion of an exercise at least once every two years and address any corrective actions arising from the successfully completed exercises	77	100%

APPENDIX A. ACRONYMS

AOR	Area of responsibility
BCA	Baseline Capabilities Assessment
CFR	Code of Federal Regulations
CI	Critical infrastructure
CINT TTX	2012 DHS Chief Intelligence Officer (CINT) tabletop exercise
COC	Critical Operational Capabilities
COI	Community of Interest
CONOPS	Concept of Operations
CVS	Central Verification System
DHS	U.S. Department of Homeland Security
DOJ	U.S. Department of Justice
EC	Enabling Capabilities
EOC	Emergency operations center
FBI	Federal Bureau of Investigation
FBINet	Federal Bureau of Investigation Network
FCRI	Fusion Center Readiness Initiative
IC	Intelligence Community
ISE	Information Sharing Environment
IT	Information technology
FCPP	Fusion Center Performance Program
FIG	Field Intelligence Group
FLO	Fusion Liaison Officer
FTE	Full-time equivalent
Fusion X	2012 National Fusion Center Exercise
FY	Fiscal year
HIDTA	High Intensity Drug Trafficking Area
HSDN	Homeland Secure Data Network
HSE	Homeland Security Enterprise
HSEC	Homeland Security
HSGP	Homeland Security Grant Program
HSIN	Homeland Security Information Network
HSIN Intel	Homeland Security Information Network Intelligence Community of Interest
HSIN SLIC	Homeland Security Information Network Intelligence Community of Interest, now HSIN Intel
I&A	Office of Intelligence and Analysis
RFI	Request for information
RISS	Regional Information Sharing Systems
RISSNET	RISS Secure Cloud
SAR	Suspicious activity reporting

JTTF	Joint Terrorism Task Force	**SBU**	Sensitive but unclassified
LEO	Law Enforcement Online	**SIN**	Standing Information Needs
NSI	Nationwide Suspicious Activity Reporting Initiative	**SIPRNet**	Secret Internet Protocol Router Network
NTAS	National Terrorism Advisory System	**SLTT**	State, local, tribal, and territorial
ODNI	Office of the Director of National Intelligence	**SME**	Subject matter expert
P/CRCL	Privacy, civil rights, and civil liberties	**SOP**	Standard operating procedure
PM-ISE	Program Manager for the Information Sharing Environment	**THIRA**	Threat and Risk Identification and Risk Assessment
		Whitelist	DHS SIPRNet Whitelist

APPENDIX B. GLOSSARY

28 CFR Part 23—28 Code of Federal Regulations (CFR) Part 23 is a regulation and guideline for law enforcement agencies. It contains implementing standards for operating multijurisdictional criminal intelligence systems receiving federal grant funding. It specifically provides guidance in five primary areas: (1) submission and entry of criminal intelligence information, (2) security, (3) inquiry, (4) dissemination, and (5) the review-and-purge process. This regulation also helps ensure the protection of the privacy, civil rights, and civil liberties of individuals during the collection and exchange of intelligence information.

-A-

All-Crimes—An approach that incorporates terrorism and other high-risk threats into the existing crime- fighting framework to ensure that possible precursor crimes are screened and analyzed for linkages to larger- scale terrorist or other crimes. This approach recognizes that there is a nexus between types of criminal activity (for example, illegal drug operations, gangs, money laundering, fraud, identity theft, and terrorism). Using an all-crimes approach does not imply that a fusion center must address every single crime that occurs within its area of responsibility. Rather, the routine risk assessment that a fusion center develops or supports development of should assist in prioritizing which crimes and/or hazards a state or region should address and, in the development of a collection plan, identify what other sources of information may be useful for examining possible connections with other crimes.

All-Hazards—Refers to preparedness for terrorist attacks, major disasters, and other emergencies within the United States. Within the context of the fusion process, some fusion centers have defined their mission to include an all-hazards approach. While the application of this approach varies, in general, it means that the fusion center has identified and prioritized types of major disasters and emergencies, beyond terrorism and crime, that could occur within their jurisdiction and gathers, analyzes, and disseminates information which would assist the relevant responsible agencies (law enforcement, fire, public health, emergency management, critical infrastructure, etc.) with the prevention, protection, response, or recovery efforts of those incidents.

Analysis—An activity whereby meaning, actual or suggested, is derived through organizing and systematically examining diverse information and applying inductive or deductive logic for the purposes of criminal investigation or assessment.

Analytic Personnel—Fusion center personnel whose primary role is to conduct analysis or the research, writing, and review of information and/or intelligence products. All fusion center analytic personnel must meet designated competencies, as identified in the *Common Competencies for State, Local, and Tribal Intelligence Analysts*, that have been acquired through experience or training courses and must have successfully completed training to ensure baseline proficiency in intelligence analysis and production and/or previously served as an intelligence analyst for a minimum of two years in a federal intelligence agency, the military, or state and/or local law enforcement intelligence unit.

Analytic Product (may also be called Intelligence Product)—A report or document that contains assessments, forecasts, associations, links, and/or other outputs from the analytic process that may be disseminated for use in the improvement of preparedness postures, risk mitigation, crime prevention, target hardening, or apprehension of offenders, among other activities. Analytic products may be created or developed jointly with federal, state, and local partners.

Analytic Production Plan—A document that describes the types of analysis and products a fusion center intends to provide for customers and partners, how often or in what circumstances the products will be produced, and how each product type will be disseminated.

Approved Plan, Policy, or SOP—A documented plan, policy, or standard operating procedure (SOP) that has been approved by a fusion center's approval authority, as required by a fusion center's approval process. The plan, policy, or SOP may be further revised or updated (e.g., some centers view their plans, policies, or SOPs as living documents that are continually subject to updates), but in its current state, the plan, policy, or SOP is approved as a final document.

-B-

Building Communities of Trust—Initiative focused on developing relationships of trust among police, fusion centers, and the communities they serve, particularly immigrant and minority communities, to address the challenges of crime and terrorism prevention.

-C-

Collocation—Two or more organizations operating in the same building or office space.

Communications Plan—A plan to enhance awareness of the fusion center's purpose, mission, and functions with leaders and policymakers, the public sector, the private sector, the media, and citizens. A communications plan can help fusion centers define customers and stakeholder groups, outline key messages, and organize outreach and engagement activities to achieve intended communications objectives.

Concept of Operations (CONOPS)—A document that provides an overview of a program or system. For example, a CONOPS would usually include the program's mission, goals, and objectives. A CONOPS might also include roles and responsibilities of the program's key stakeholders and the high-level processes to achieve program goals and objectives.

Conduct—To lead or direct the performance or implementation of an activity (e.g., to conduct a threat assessment).

Consequence—The effect of an event, incident, or occurrence. The *2009 National Infrastructure Protection Plan* divides consequences into four main categories: public health and safety, economic, psychological, and governance impacts.

Consequence Analysis—Product or process of identifying or evaluating the potential or actual effects of an event, incident, or occurrence.

Contribute—To play a part in the planning or execution of an activity (e.g., to contribute analysis or intelligence that supports the development of a threat assessment).

Coordinating Body—The entity primarily responsible for organizing and directing a specific activity with multiple stakeholders or participants.

Counterterrorism—Practices, tactics, techniques, and strategies designed to prevent, deter, and respond to terrorism. Within the context of the fusion process, a fusion center with a counterterrorism mission is one that identifies and prioritizes potential terrorist threats that could occur within its area of responsibility and gathers, analyzes, and disseminates information which would assist the relevant responsible agencies (e.g., law enforcement, intelligence, and critical infrastructure) with the prevention, protection, response, or recovery efforts of those incidents.

Critical Infrastructure—Assets, systems, and networks, whether physical or virtual, so vital to the United States that their incapacitation or destruction would have a debilitating impact on security, national economic security, public health or safety, or any combination thereof.

Critical Infrastructure Protection Activities—These activities may include (1) efforts to understand and share information about terrorist threats and other hazards as related to critical infrastructure, (2) building security partnerships, (3) implementing a long-term risk management program, and (4) maximizing the efficient use of resources related to critical infrastructure protection. Examples include, but are not limited to (1) providing critical infrastructure owners and operators with timely, analytical, accurate, and useful information on threats to critical infrastructure; (2) ensuring that industry is engaged as early as possible in the development and enhancement of risk management activities, approaches, and actions; and (3) developing resources to engage in cross- sector interdependency studies through exercises, symposiums, training sessions, and computer modeling.

-D-

DHS SIPRNet Whitelist—The U.S. Department of Defense sites available to fusion centers via the Homeland Secure Data Network.

Dissemination Matrix—A document used by fusion center personnel to ensure the proper review, handling, and dissemination of products. Typically, a dissemination matrix identifies fusion center customers, classification, and handling caveats; details peer and supervisory reviews; and identifies the dissemination method for each fusion center product type.

Documented Plan, Policy, or SOP—A written or typed plan, policy, or SOP defined in document form.

Draft—Description of a document that has not yet been approved by a fusion center's required approval authority (e.g., fusion center governance body, homeland security advisor, Fusion Center Director).

-E-

EOC—Emergency Operations Center, a centralized management center for emergency operations.

Exercise—The employment of personnel and resources in a controlled environment to test, validate, and/or improve a specific plan or capability in pursuit of a stated objective. Exercises may include workshops, facilitated policy discussions, seminars, tabletop exercises, games, modeling and simulation, drills, functional exercises, and full-scale exercises.

-F-

Federal Resource Allocation Criteria Policy—A federal policy (Information Sharing Environment Guidance ISE-G-112) that defines objective criteria to be used by federal departments and agencies when making resource allocation decisions to fusion centers.

Federal Share—The share or amount of a fusion center cost that is paid for by an agency within the federal government (including grants).

Financial Audit—Verification of the financial statements of a legal entity, with a view to express an audit opinion. The audit opinion is a reasonable assurance that the financial statements are presented fairly, in all material respects, or give a true and fair view in accordance with the financial reporting framework. The purpose of an audit is to enhance the degree of confidence of intended users in the financial statements. No element of the annual Assessment process (including the Cost Assessment) is intended to serve the purpose of a financial audit.

Formal—Following or in accordance with an established form, custom, or rule (e.g., formal training is training that follows a specified format, such as activities designed to achieve targeted results versus informal training that might occur spontaneously and/ or casually).

Fusion Center Customers—Users, consumers, or recipients of fusion center analysis, information, or intelligence products. Customers can be individuals or organizations.

Fusion Liaison Officer (FLO)—Individuals who serve as the conduit for the flow of homeland security and crime-related information between the field and the fusion center for assessment and analysis. FLOs can be from a wide variety of disciplines, provide the fusion center with subject matter expertise, and may support awareness and training efforts. Fusion centers may use various names for FLOs, such as Terrorism Liaison Officer, Intelligence Liaison Officer, and Field Intelligence Officer.

FLO Program—FLO Programs vary in focus, complexity, and size, but all have the same basic goal of facilitating the exchange of information between fusion centers and stakeholders within the fusion center's area of responsibility.

Fusion Process—The overarching process of managing the flow of information and intelligence across levels and sectors of government and private industry. It goes beyond establishing an information/intelligence center or creating a computer network. The fusion process supports the implementation of risk-based, information-driven prevention, response, and consequence management programs. The fusion process turns information and intelligence into actionable knowledge.

-G-

Governance Body—An oversight entity composed of officials with decision-making authority, capable of committing resources and personnel to a fusion center.

-H-

High Intensity Drug Trafficking Areas (HIDTA)—A program created by Congress with the Anti-Drug Abuse Act of 1988 that provides assistance to federal, state, local, and tribal law enforcement agencies operating in areas determined to be critical drug trafficking regions of the United States.

Homeland Secure Data Network (HSDN)—Secret- level information network intended to provide Secret- level processing capability to fusion centers and other partners.

Homeland Security Grant Program (HSGP)— Composed of three interconnected grant programs— State Homeland Security Program (SHSP); Urban Areas Security Initiative (UASI); and Operation Stonegarden (OPSG)—which fund a range of preparedness activities, including planning, organization, equipment purchase, training, exercises, and management and administration.

Homeland Security Information Network (HSIN)—A U.S. Department of Homeland Security-managed national secure and trusted Web-based portal for information sharing and collaboration among federal, state, local, tribal, territorial, private sector, and international partners engaged in the homeland security mission.

Homeland Security Information Network Intelligence Community of Interest (HSIN Intel)—A subset of HSIN for state and local intelligence. It is a DHS-owned and -operated, user-driven, Web-based, unclassified sharing platform connecting homeland security mission partners.

Homeland Security Standing Information Needs (HSEC SINs)—Refers to the enduring all-threats and all- hazards information needs of DHS and its federal, state, local, tribal, territorial, and private sector stakeholders and homeland security partners.

-I-

"If You See Something, Say Something™" Campaign—A DHS program to raise public awareness of indicators of terrorism and violent crime and to emphasize the importance of reporting suspicious activity to the proper state and local law enforcement authorities.

Implement—To put into effect (i.e., to implement a plan by communicating it to internal and/or external stakeholders, training staff on it, and incorporating it into a fusion center's day-to-day activities).

Information—Pieces of raw, unanalyzed data that identify persons, evidence, or events or illustrate processes that indicate the incidence of a criminal event or witnesses or evidence of a criminal event.

Information Needs—The data and information needed by intelligence analysts in order to answer intelligence questions; types of information the intelligence unit needs and intends to gather from all available sources through passive and active collection and/or reporting.

Information Sharing Environment (ISE) Privacy Guidelines—Principles for federal departments and agencies to follow to ensure that the information privacy rights and other legal rights of Americans are protected as personally identifiable terrorism-related information is acquired, accessed, used, and stored in the ISE.

InfraGard—A partnership between the FBI and businesses, academic institutions, state and local law enforcement agencies, and other participants dedicated to sharing information and intelligence to prevent hostile acts against the United States. InfraGard chapters are geographically linked with FBI Field Office territories.

Intelligence—Actionable inference or a set of related inferences derived from some form of inductive or deductive logic. By combining information, analysis, and interpretation, intelligence helps to document a threat, ascertain its probability of occurring, and define a responsive course of action, all in a timely manner.

Issue-Specific Training—Training provided to fusion center analysts on issues (such as risk analysis, finance, critical infrastructure protection, counternarcotics, or gangs) that are consistent with the center's mission and analysts' roles and responsibilities.

-J-

Joint Terrorism Task Forces (JTTFs)—Small cells of highly-trained, locally-based investigators, analysts, linguists, SWAT experts, and other specialists from dozens of U.S. law enforcement and intelligence agencies. This multiagency effort is led by the U.S. Department of Justice (DOJ) and the FBI and is designed to combine the resources of federal, state, and local law enforcement.

-L-

Law Enforcement Online (LEO)—A virtual private network accredited and approved by the FBI for sensitive but unclassified information. Used by all levels of the law enforcement, criminal justice, and public safety communities to support investigative operations, send notifications and alerts, and provide an avenue to remotely access other law enforcement and intelligence systems and resources.

Local Context—The set of conditions or the environment associated with a geographic area or jurisdiction. A fusion center can apply a local context to any analysis it does that would involve considering local issues, conditions, implications, and other locally generated information. When considering federally generated information or other information received from outside of the local area, applying a local context would involve any additional analysis that would make that information more relevant, relatable, or actionable to stakeholders within a particular jurisdiction. For example, with national threat information, it could mean conducting analysis to determine potential impacts to a particular jurisdiction.

-N-

National-Level Risk Assessment—Product or process that collects information on issues of significant national concern and assigns values to risks for the purpose of informing national priorities, developing or comparing courses of action, and informing decision making.

National Terrorism Advisory System (NTAS)—NTAS replaces the color-coded Homeland Security Advisory System. Its purpose is to effectively communicate information about terrorist threats by providing timely, detailed information to the public, government agencies, first responders, airports and other transportation hubs, and the private sector.

Nationwide Suspicious Activity Reporting (SAR) Initiative (NSI)—A unified process for reporting, tracking, and accessing SARs in a manner that rigorously protects the privacy and civil liberties of Americans.

NSI Analyst Training—An eight-hour workshop format training focused on ensuring that SARs are properly reviewed and vetted to promote the integrity of information submitted; protect citizens' privacy, civil rights, and civil liberties; and successfully implement the SAR process.

NSI Compliance—Deemed by the NSI Program Management Office to be compliant with NSI requirements.

Neighborhood Watch Programs—Local crime prevention programs initiated either by the public or the police that involve citizens in crime prevention activities.

-P-

P/CRCL Outreach Plan—A plan for the engagement of a fusion center with internal and external stakeholders to promote the fusion center's privacy, civil rights, and civil liberties protections, processes, and efforts.

Primary Fusion Center—In each of the 50 states, the District of Columbia, and the five territories, a fusion center that is designated by the Governor as the primary fusion center, pursuant to the joint DHS and DOJ November 2007 fusion center designation letter and in accordance with the Federal Resource Allocation Criteria policy.

Private Sector—Includes business (both profit and nonprofit), commerce, associations, academia, and industry.

Public Affairs Officer/Public Information Officer—An individual designated by an appointing official or entity who is responsible for the initiation, development, production, and implementation of public relations and public communications plans, materials, and strategies.

-R-

Recognized Center—A center that has been designated as a fusion center by the Governor of the state but that has not been designated as the state's primary fusion center, in accordance with the Federal Resource Allocation Criteria policy.

Request for Information—A request initiated by the fusion center or a fusion center stakeholder (e.g., law enforcement agency or DHS) that could include, but is not limited to, requests for information or intelligence products or services such as name traces, database checks, assessments, subject matter expertise assistance, or finished intelligence products.

Risk—The potential for an unwanted outcome resulting from an incident, event, or occurrence, as determined by its likelihood and the associated consequences.

Risk Assessment—A product or process that collects information and assigns values to risks for the purpose of informing priorities, developing or comparing courses of action, and informing decision making.

RISSNET—Managed by the Regional Information Sharing Systems (RISS), RISSNET is a secure national intranet to facilitate law enforcement communications and information sharing nationwide.

-S-

Security Liaison—An individual designated by an appointing official or entity who is responsible for ensuring the security of the fusion center, including personnel, information, equipment, and facilities.

Standing Information Needs (SINs)—Enduring information needs about the homeland security threat or operational environment. SINs provide a formal, structured framework for categorizing issues and topics of interest for fusion centers.

Statewide Fusion Center Coordination Plan— Identifies the roles, responsibilities, and coordination efforts for each fusion center within a state in carrying out the fusion process within that state.

Strategic Plan— A plan that defines an organization or entity's vision, mission, goals, and objectives, identifying the strategic programmatic and operational priorities for a discrete period of time.

Subject Matter Expert—A person who is an expert in a particular area or topic.

Suspicious Activity Reporting (SAR)—Official documentation of observed behavior reasonably indicative of preoperational planning related to terrorism or other criminal activity.

-T-

Tag—To mark or provide with an identifying marker (e.g., to mark products with the Standing Information Needs they address).

Threat—Natural or man-made occurrence, individual, entity, or action that has or indicates the potential to harm life, information, operations, the environment, and/or property.

Threat and Hazard Identification and Risk Assessment (THIRA)—A comprehensive approach for identifying and assessing risks and associated impacts. It expands on existing local, tribal, territorial, and state Hazard Identification and Risk Assessments (HIRAs) and other risk methodologies by broadening the factors considered in the process, incorporating the whole community throughout the entire process, and by accounting for important community-specific factors. See FEMA's *Comprehensive Planning Guide 201: Threat and Hazard Identification and Risk Assessment* for additional information.

Threat Assessment—An assessment of a criminal or terrorist presence within a jurisdiction combined with an evaluation of the potential targets of that presence and a statement of probability that the criminal or terrorist will commit an unlawful act. The assessment focuses on the criminal's or terrorist's opportunity, capability, and willingness to fulfill the threat.

Tips and Leads—Information provided from fusion center stakeholders, the general public, or other sources regarding potentially criminal or illicit activity, but not necessarily or obviously related to terrorism.

-V-

Vulnerability—Physical feature or operational attribute that renders an entity, asset, system, network, or geographic area open to exploitation or susceptible to a given hazard.

Vulnerability Analysis—An analysis of possible criminal or terrorist group targets within a jurisdiction integrated with an assessment of the target's weaknesses, likelihood of being attacked, and ability to withstand an attack.

APPENDIX C. NATIONAL NETWORK OF FUSION CENTERS

State and major urban area fusion centers are owned and operated by state and local entities and are designated by the Governor of their state. The federal government recognizes these designations and has a shared responsibility with state and local governments to support the National Network of Fusion Centers (National Network). The following list includes the 77 fusion centers that made up the National Network as of August 2012.[29]

Primary Fusion Centers[30]

- Alabama Fusion Center
- Alaska Information and Analysis Center
- Arizona Counter Terrorism Information Center
- Arkansas State Fusion Center
- Nebraska Information Analysis Center
- New Hampshire Information and Analysis Center
- New Jersey Regional Operations Intelligence Center
- New Mexico All Source Intelligence Center

- California State Threat Assessment Center
- Colorado Information Analysis Center
- Connecticut Intelligence Center
- Delaware Information and Analysis Center
- Florida Fusion Center
- Georgia Information Sharing and Analysis Center
- Hawaii Fusion Center
- Idaho Criminal Intelligence Center
- Illinois Statewide Terrorism and Intelligence Center
- Indiana Intelligence Fusion Center
- Iowa Intelligence Fusion Center
- Kansas Intelligence Fusion Center
- Kentucky Intelligence Fusion Center
- Louisiana State Analytical and Fusion Exchange
- Maine Information and Analysis Center
- Maryland Coordination and Analysis Center
- Massachusetts Commonwealth Fusion Center
- Michigan Intelligence Operations Center
- Minnesota Fusion Center
- Mississippi Analysis and Information Center
- Missouri Information Analysis Center
- Montana All-Threat Intelligence Center
- New York State Intelligence Center
- North Carolina Information Sharing and Analysis Center
- North Dakota State and Local Intelligence Center
- Ohio Strategic Analysis and Information Center
- Oklahoma Information Fusion Center
- Oregon Terrorism Information Threat Assessment Network
- Pennsylvania Criminal Intelligence Center
- Puerto Rico National Security State Information Center
- Rhode Island State Fusion Center
- South Carolina Information and Intelligence Center
- South Dakota Fusion Center
- Southern Nevada Counter-Terrorism Center
- Tennessee Fusion Center
- Texas Fusion Center
- U.S. Virgin Islands Fusion Center
- Utah Statewide Information and Analysis Center
- Vermont Information and Analysis Center
- Virginia Fusion Center
- Washington Regional Threat and Analysis Center (DC)
- Washington State Fusion Center
- West Virginia Intelligence Fusion Center
- Wisconsin Statewide Information Center

Recognized Fusion Centers[31]

- Austin Regional Intelligence Center
- Boston Regional Intelligence Center
- Central California Intelligence Center
- Central Florida Intelligence Exchange

- Chicago Crime Prevention and Information Center
- Cincinnati/Hamilton County Regional Terrorism Early Warning Group
- Delaware Valley Intelligence Center
- Detroit and Southeast Michigan Information and Intelligence Center
- Houston Regional Intelligence Service Center
- Kansas City Regional Terrorism Early Warning Fusion Center
- Los Angeles Joint Regional Intelligence Center
- El Paso Fusion Center
- Dallas Fusion Center
- Nevada Threat Analysis Center
- North Central Texas Fusion Center
- Northeast Ohio Regional Fusion Center
- Northern California Regional Intelligence Center
- Northern Virginia Regional Intelligence Center
- Orange County Intelligence Assessment Center
- San Diego Law Enforcement Coordination Center
- Southeast Florida Fusion Center
- Southeastern Wisconsin Threat Analysis Center
- Southwestern Pennsylvania Region 13 Fusion Center
- Southwest Texas Fusion Center
- St. Louis Fusion Center

APPENDIX D. LISTS OF ATTRIBUTES

Table 19. Individual Fusion Center Attributes

COC 1: Receive; 5 Attributes	
1	Fusion center has approved plans, policies, or Standard Operating Procedures (SOPs) for the receipt of federally generated threat information
2	Fusion center has a plan, policy, or SOP that addresses the receipt and handling of National Terrorism Advisory System (NTAS) alerts
3	Fusion center personnel with a need to access classified information are cleared to at least the Secret level
4	Fusion center has access to sensitive but unclassified (SBU) information sharing systems
5	Fusion center has access to the Homeland Secure Data Network (HSDN) and/or the FBI Network (FBINet) (i.e., within fusion center or on-site)
COC 2: Analyze; 11 Attributes	
1	Fusion center has approved plans, policies, or SOPs for assessing the local implications of time-sensitive and emerging threat information
2	Fusion center has a documented analytic production plan
3	Fusion center has access to multidisciplinary subject matter experts (SMEs) within its area of responsibility (AOR) to inform analytic production
4	Fusion center has access to multidisciplinary SMEs outside of its AOR to inform analytic production

Table 19. (Continued)

COC 2: Analyze; 11 Attributes	
5	Fusion center has a process to provide the U.S. Department of Homeland Security (DHS) with information and/ or intelligence that offers a local context to threat information in the event of an NTAS-related alert
6	Fusion center conducts threat assessments within its AOR
7	Fusion center contributes to or conducts a statewide risk assessment (threat, vulnerability, and consequence analysis)
8	Fusion center contributes to national-level risk assessments
9	Fusion center has a structured customer feedback mechanism for some or all of its analytic products
10	Fusion center evaluates the effectiveness of the customer feedback mechanism for analytic products on an annual basis
11	All fusion center analysts have received at least 20 hours of issue-specific training in the past 12 months
COC 3: Disseminate; 6 Attributes	
1	Fusion center has approved plans, policies, or SOPs governing the procedures and communication mechanisms for the timely dissemination of products to customers within its AOR
2	Fusion center has a dissemination matrix
3	Fusion center has a primary SBU mechanism to disseminate time-sensitive information and products to its customers and partners
4	Fusion center has a plan, policy, or SOP for disseminating NTAS alerts to stakeholders within its AOR
5	Fusion center has a mechanism to disseminate NTAS alerts
6	Fusion center has a process for verifying the delivery of products to intended customers
COC 4: Gather; 8 Attributes	
1	Fusion center is Nationwide Suspicious Activity Reporting Initiative (NSI)-compliant OR has an approved plan, policy, or SOP governing the gathering of locally generated information
2	Fusion center has a documented tips and leads process
3	Fusion center has a process for identifying and managing information needs
4	Fusion center has a process for managing the gathering of locally generated information to satisfy the fusion center's information needs
5	Fusion center has approved SINs
6	Fusion center has an annual process to review and refresh its Standing Information Needs (SINs)
7	Fusion center has a request for information (RFI) management process
8	Fusion center has a process to inform DHS of protective measures implemented within its AOR in response to an NTAS alert
EC 1: P/CRCL Protections; 6 Attributes	
1	Fusion center has a P/CRCL policy determined by DHS to be at least as comprehensive as the Information Sharing Environment (ISE) Privacy Guidelines
2	Fusion center provides formal and standardized training to all personnel on the fusion center's P/CRCL policy and protections annually

EC 1: P/CRCL Protections; 6 Attributes	
3	Fusion center's policies, processes, and mechanisms for receiving, cataloging, and retaining information (provided to the center) comply with 28 CFR Part 23 when appropriate
4	Fusion center trains all personnel who access criminal intelligence systems in 28 CFR Part 23
5	Fusion center has identified a P/CRCL Officer
6	Fusion center has a P/CRCL outreach plan
EC 2: Sustainment Strategy; 5 Attributes	
1	Fusion center has an approved strategic plan
2	Fusion center conducts an annual financial audit
3	Fusion center completes an annual operational cost assessment
4	Fusion center participates in an exercise at least once a year
5	Fusion center measures its performance to determine the effectiveness of its operations relative to expectations it or its governing entity has defined
EC 3: Communications and Outreach; 3 Attributes	
1	Fusion center has a designated Public Information Officer or Public Affairs Officer
2	Fusion center has an approved communications plan
3	Fusion center has developed and implemented a process for capturing success stories
EC 4: Security; 6 Attributes	
1	Fusion center has an approved security plan, policy, or SOP that addresses physical, personnel, and information security
2	Fusion center provides security training to all personnel on its security plan and identified security measures, policies, and procedures annually
3	Fusion center has identified a Security Liaison
4	Fusion center's Security Liaison (or other organization's Security Liaison) completes annual security training
5	Fusion center has access to CVS
6	Fusion center's Security Liaison (or other organization's Security Liaison) is trained on how to use CVS

Table 20. National Network Attributes by Maturity Model Stage

Fundamental (Approved Plans, Policies, or SOPs): *Fusion centers across the National Network have approved plans, policies, or SOPs for each of the four COCs and P/CRCL protections.*	
COC 1—Receive	Fusion centers have approved plans, policies, or SOPs for the receipt of federally generated threat information
COC 2—Analyze	Fusion centers have approved plans, policies, or SOPs for assessing the local implications of time-sensitive and emerging threat information
COC 3—Disseminate	Fusion centers have approved plans, policies, or SOPs governing the procedures and communication mechanisms for the timely dissemination of products to customers within their AOR
COC 4—Gather	Fusion centers are NSI-compliant OR have an approved plan, policy, or SOP governing the gathering of locally generated information

Table 20. (Continued)

EC 1—P/CRCL Protections	Fusion centers have a P/CRCL policy determined by DHS to be at least as comprehensive as the *ISE Privacy Guidelines*
Emerging (Implementation of Plans, Policies, or SOPs): *The National Network has the systems, mechanisms, and processes needed to implement the plans, policies, or SOPs and the COCs and ECs as a whole.*	
COC 1—Receive	Fusion centers have implemented their approved plans, policies, or SOPs for the receipt of federally generated threat information
	Fusion centers have a plan, policy, or SOP that addresses the receipt and handling of NTAS alerts
	Fusion center personnel with a need to access classified information are cleared to at least the Secret level
	Fusion centers have access to the HSDN and/or the FBINet (i.e., within fusion center or on- site)
COC 2—Analyze	Fusion centers have implemented their approved plans, policies, or SOPs for assessing the local implications of time-sensitive and emerging threat information
	Fusion centers have processes to provide DHS with information and/or intelligence that offers a local context to threat information in the event of an NTAS-related alert
COC 3—Disseminate	Fusion centers have implemented their approved plans, policies, or SOPs for governing the procedures and communication mechanisms for the timely dissemination of products to customers within their AOR
	Fusion centers have a plan, policy, or SOP for disseminating NTAS alerts to stakeholders within their AOR
	Fusion centers have a mechanism to disseminate NTAS alerts
COC 4—Gather	Fusion centers are NSI-compliant OR have implemented their approved plan, policy, or SOP related to COC 4—Gather, governing the gathering of locally generated information
	Fusion centers have a process for managing the gathering of locally-generated information to satisfy the fusion centers' information needs
	Fusion centers have approved SINs
	Fusion centers have a process to inform DHS of protective measures implemented within their AOR in response to an NTAS alert
	Fusion centers have an RFI management process
EC 1—P/CRCL Protections	Fusion centers have implemented their P/CRCL policy
	Fusion centers' policies, processes, and mechanisms for receiving, cataloging, and retaining information (provided to their center) comply with 28 CFR Part 23 when appropriate
	Fusion centers train all personnel who access criminal intelligence systems in 28 CFR Part 23
	Fusion centers have identified a P/CRCL Officer
EC 4—Security	Fusion centers have an approved security plan, policy, or SOP that addresses physical, personnel, and information security
	Fusion centers provide security training to all personnel on their security plan and identified security measures, policies, and procedures annually
	Fusion centers have identified a Security Liaison

	Fusion centers have access to CVS
Enhanced (Operational Focus): *The National Network has the operational capability to produce products and provide services to federal, state, and local customers.*	
COC 2—Analyze	Fusion centers have a documented analytic production plan
	Fusion centers have established a critical infrastructure analysis capability
	Fusion centers conduct threat assessments within their AOR
	Fusion centers have a structured customer feedback mechanism for some or all of their analytic products
COC 3—Disseminate	Fusion centers have a Fusion Liaison Officer program
	Fusion centers have a documented Fusion Liaison Officer program Concept of Operations or plan
COC 4—Gather	Fusion centers include multidisciplinary partners in their SINs development process
	Fusion centers have an annual process to review and refresh their SINs
	Fusion centers tag all analytical products to one or more of their own SINs or the DHS HSEC SINs
EC 1—P/CRCL Protections	Fusion centers have undergone a P/CRCL compliance review using the *Privacy, Civil Rights, and Civil Liberties Compliance Verification for the Intelligence Enterprise* tool
EC 2—Sustainment Strategy	Fusion centers conduct an annual financial audit
	Fusion centers participate in an exercise at least once a year
	Fusion centers include multidisciplinary partners on their governance body
Mature (Adjust and Leverage Resources): *The National Network has the full capability to leverage the collective resources among individual fusion centers and adjust to both the changing threat environment and evolving requirements.*	
COC 2—Analyze	Fusion centers contribute to national-level risk assessments
	Fusion centers have a process to review and incorporate customer feedback into analytical processes and products
COC 3—Disseminate	Fusion centers are using the same SBU mechanism to disseminate products and time- sensitive information to other fusion centers
COC 4—Gather	Fusion centers have a process for prioritizing information needs
EC 2—Sustainment Strategy	Fusion centers have an approved strategic plan
	States with multiple fusion centers have a documented statewide fusion center coordination plan

APPENDIX E. SUMMARY OF FINDINGS AND RECOMMENDATIONS

Finding	Related Recommendation(s)
COC 1—Receive	
All fusion centers have access to federally sponsored SBU information sharing systems.	DHS should ensure that all distributable analytic products from the Office of Intelligence and Analysis (I&A) and other DHS components are both posted to HSIN Intel and tagged with appropriate DHS Homeland Security (HSEC) Standing Information Needs (SINs).

(Continued)

Finding	Related Recommendation(s)
Every fusion center has at least one person cleared to access Secret information, but regular staff turnover means that fusion centers will continue to request new clearances.	Fusion centers should continue to ensure that the federal government is aware of personnel needing clearances for Secret-level systems and information.
A significant number of fusion centers have on-site access to classified information sharing systems.	Fusion centers without access to HSDN should develop and implement the necessary security policies and protocols and identify secondary mechanisms to access classified information. All fusion centers should consider the potential impacts on access to classified systems that might arise if they move or change locations. The federal government should continue to facilitate the timely installation of classified systems at fusion centers that have met all appropriate security requirements.
Fusion center use of the DHS Secret Internet Protocol Router Network (SIPRNet) Whitelist (Whitelist) is limited.	To assist fusion center analysts in developing and refining their analytic knowledge, skills, and abilities, the federal government should improve usability and increase content available on the Whitelist based on defined and validated fusion center needs. The federal government should also develop a Whitelist Resource Kit that describes current content and provides directions on how to request new content and report issues in accessing sites. Fusion centers should report lack of access to sites on the Whitelist or other technical issues to federal partners.
COC 2—Analyze	
Fusion centers are highly involved in assessing threat and risk for their AOR.	The federal government should provide additional guidance to assist fusion centers in contributing to a Threat and Hazard Identification and Risk Assessment for their AOR. The federal government should work with fusion centers to increase their participation in the development of national-level assessments and analytic products. The federal government should continue to support analytic exchanges to assist fusion centers in collaborating with field-based partners, such as High Intensity Drug Trafficking Areas (HIDTAs), Regional Information Sharing Systems (RISS) Centers, Field Intelligence Groups (FIGs), and Joint Terrorism Task Forces (JTTFs). The federal government should continue to offer fusion center analysts access to tools and assistance that build fusion center capabilities to conduct or contribute to a national risk analysis, such as a Risk Analysis Product Template and Risk Analysis Courses. The federal government should assist fusion center analysts to further expand their analytical skills and

Finding	Related Recommendation(s)
	expertise by supporting exchanges, developing joint products, and mentoring.
Fusion centers are obtaining and using customer feedback on their analytic products.	In order to collect customer feedback on analytic products, fusion centers should use a structured feedback process and should collect feedback data at least annually, but more often when possible.
Analytic production plans are used widely across the National Network.	Fusion centers should continue to develop and regularly update analytic production plans.
Critical infrastructure protection capabilities continue to expand across the National Network.	The federal government should continue to offer tools and resources that promote and improve risk analysis and understanding of threats to critical infrastructure through analysis, such as an Infrastructure Protection Field Resource Toolkit, Critical Infrastructure Capabilities Exchanges, and Risk Analysis Courses.
COC 3—Disseminate	
Despite progress since 2011, less than half of the National Network have a process in place to verify that customers are receiving their products.	Fusion centers should engage customers to discuss preferred methods and timeliness of product dissemination.
Fusion centers are increasingly designating a single, primary information sharing system, but HSIN Intel is not frequently cited as the primary system for unclassified communication between fusion centers.	Fusion centers should ensure that all distributable analytic products are posted to HSIN Intel. The federal government should continue to ensure that HSIN Intel meets the functional needs of state, local, tribal, and territorial (SLTT) partners.
COC 4—Gather	
The number of fusion centers that have developed Standing Information Needs (SINs) has increased, but continued attention to SINs development is necessary.	Fusion centers should continue to develop, update, and approve SINs by soliciting input from key customers, including multidisciplinary partners. Fusion centers should ensure that all analytic products posted to HSIN Intel are tagged with appropriate DHS HSEC SINs and fusion center SINs, and the federal government should ensure that HSIN Intel tagging capabilities are easy to access and use.
The National Network has a robust request for information (RFI) management capability.	The National Network and the federal government should collaborate to develop processes and a template that would assist fusion centers in requesting information from SLTT and federal law enforcement entities, homeland security agencies, or other fusion centers.
A significant percentage of the National Network are involved in the Nationwide Suspicious Activity Reporting (SAR) Initiative (NSI), in particular in providing line officers with	The federal government and fusion centers should expand training to non-law enforcement partners to further enhance both the gathering of information and the quality of SAR.

(Continued)

Finding	Related Recommendation(s)
information on the behaviors identified in the ISE-SAR Functional Standard.	
EC 1—Privacy, Civil Rights, and Civil Liberties Protections	
All but one of the fusion centers have a P/CRCL Officer; however, turnover at this position is high across the National Network.	Fusion centers should take efforts to manage and reduce the potential impacts of P/CRCL Officer turnover so that their fusion center can maintain and build institutional knowledge regarding P/CRCL protections, especially during periods of transition. The federal government and appropriate partners (such as the Criminal Intelligence Coordinating Council) should continue to assist in training P/CRCL Officers at a level that ensures all officers have a baseline understanding of their roles and responsibilities and at a level that enhances current P/CRCL Officers' efforts to support their fusion center. The federal government should provide guidance and templates to assist fusion centers in developing written implementation plans for their P/CRCL policies.
Fusion centers have made significant progress in implementing P/CRCL protections, although compliance reviews and annual audits have not reached 100%.	Fusion centers should conduct P/CRCL compliance reviews that assess their policies and procedures related to P/CRCL protections through the use of the *Privacy, Civil Rights, and Civil Liberties Compliance Verification for the Intelligence Enterprise.* Fusion centers should audit operations against their approved privacy policy at least on an annual basis.
Coordinated outreach by fusion centers to stakeholders on P/CRCL issues is still lacking.	Fusion centers should develop outreach plans, including outreach on P/CRCL policies and issues.
EC 2—Sustainment Strategy	
The number of fusion centers with strategic plans has increased, but almost 30% of fusion centers do not have an approved strategic plan.	Fusion centers should develop strategic plans using existing guidebooks, templates, examples, and technical assistance resources.
Fusion centers continue to address financial accountability.	Fusion centers should continue to work with State Administrative Agencies and Urban Area Working Groups to increase fiscal efficiency and oversight of investment planning, grants management, and grants reporting.
The majority of fusion centers have adopted performance measures to evaluate progress in achieving programmatic outcomes, although only about half connect performance measures to their strategic plans.	To demonstrate their value and impact in supporting mission requirements, fusion centers should develop performance measures aligned to strategic plans and report findings to stakeholders.

Finding	Related Recommendation(s)
Fusion centers participate extensively in exercises, although more exercises specifically focused on the fusion process, including the COCs and ECs, would benefit the National Network.	Fusion centers should implement corrective actions identified in exercises. The federal government should conduct more exercises that test fusion center capabilities at the individual, regional, and national levels.
EC 3—Communications and Outreach	
The number of fusion centers with approved communications plans has increased, but a third of fusion centers still lack such a plan.	Fusion centers should develop documented communications outreach plans, including outreach guidance on P/CRCL issues, drawing on the *Communications and Outreach Guidebook: Considerations for State and Urban Area Fusion Centers* and associated technical assistance services.
Fusion centers are communicating their value, mission, and purpose through a documented process for capturing success stories and lesson learned.	
Almost all fusion centers have a designated Public Information Officer or Public Affairs Officer to support communications and outreach.	
EC 4—Security	
Fusion centers have developed policies, plans, or SOPs to address physical, personnel, and information security.	Fusion center Security Liaisons should conduct regular security inspections and annual security audits to identify and mitigate security risks within their fusion centers.
Nearly all fusion centers have a designated Security Liaison, but as with P/CRCL Officers, turnover among Security Liaisons is high.	Fusion centers should take efforts to manage and reduce the potential impacts of Security Liaison turnover so that their fusion center can build and maintain institutional knowledge regarding fusion center security. Fusion centers should institutionalize their security-related plans, policies, and SOPs by participating in bimonthly conference calls with other fusion center Security Liaisons, attending annual security training, utilizing the resource kit for Security Liaisons, and requesting technical assistance.
Cross-Cutting Capabilities	
A large majority of fusion centers report to governance bodies, and federal and SLTT partner representation on governance bodies is widespread.	Fusion centers should incorporate field-based partners, such as those supporting HIDTAs, RISS Centers, FIGs, and JTTFs, into governance bodies and intrastate coordination plans in order to improve fusion process coordination and avoid mission overlap. Fusion centers should expand multidisciplinary involvement in governance bodies in order to promote improved SLTT coordination and collaboration.
Fusion Center Director turnover is high.	

(Continued)

Finding	Related Recommendation(s)
Most fusion centers have established Fusion Liaison Officer (FLO) Programs to broaden the scope of information sharing within their AOR.	Fusion centers should take advantage of technical assistance to develop and implement FLO Programs and a FLO Concept of Operations.
Most states with more than one fusion center have policies to guide coordination among fusion centers, but only half of fusion centers are part of plans that coordinate broader statewide information sharing.	All primary fusion centers should work with federal and SLTT intelligence, analytic, and investigative entities to develop a documented statewide information sharing plan.
Fusion centers have significantly increased their capability to process National Terrorism Advisory System (NTAS) alerts.	
Maturity Model	
	Fusion centers should ensure that all analytic products posted to HSIN Intel are tagged with appropriate DHS HSEC SINs and fusion center SINs. Fusion centers should conduct P/CRCL compliance reviews that assess their policies and procedures related to P/CRCL protections through the use of the *Privacy, Civil Rights, and Civil Liberties Compliance Verification for the Intelligence Enterprise*. Fusion centers should expand multidisciplinary involvement in governance bodies to promote improved SLTT coordination and collaboration. Fusion centers should take advantage of technical assistance to develop and implement FLO Programs and a FLO Concept of Operations.
Fusion Center Performance	
	Fusion centers should ensure that all analytic products posted to HSIN Intel are tagged with appropriate DHS HSEC SINs and fusion center SINs. The federal government should continue to support analytic exchanges to assist fusion centers in collaborating with field-based partners, such as HIDTAs, RISS Centers, FIGs, and JTTFs. The federal government should assist fusion center analysts to further expand their analytical skills and expertise by supporting exchanges, developing joint products, and mentoring. The federal government and fusion centers should expand training to non-law enforcement partners to further enhance both the gathering of information and the quality of SAR.

APPENDIX F. 2013 GAP MITIGATION ACTIVITIES

Federal, state, and local fusion center stakeholders share a common goal of supporting a nationwide capacity for receiving, analyzing, disseminating, and gathering threat information. The purpose of gap mitigation is to assist fusion centers in fully achieving and maintaining their capabilities in the Critical Operational Capabilities (COCs), the Enabling Capabilities (ECs), and additional areas. In 2013, the federal government will continue to focus its support for fusion centers through the development and delivery of gap mitigation resources that will support fusion centers in obtaining the knowledge, skills, and tools necessary to execute the fusion process.

Leveraging the results of the 2012 Assessment described in this 2012 Final Report, the federal government identified those resources that can most effectively support fusion centers with mitigating identified capability gaps. As part of this process, federal interagency partners identified over 60 new or existing activities to support gap mitigation efforts. The tables below outline the menu of available gap mitigation activities for 2013, aligned to the four COCs, and the four ECs. These activities are not mandatory but are being made available to the National Network to assist fusion centers with mitigating identified capability gaps, as appropriate.

Overarching Gap Mitiagtion Activities	
Activity	**Description**
"COC Gap Mitigation Guidebook" Appendix with new resources*	The Resource Appendix contains additional sample policies to assist fusion centers in further developing and tailoring plans, policies, or standard operating procedures (SOPs) for the COCs as well as resources to assist with the implementation of these plans, policies, or SOPs. The Guidebook has also been updated to include additional guidance regarding how to incorporate National Terrorism Advisory System (NTAS) considerations into fusion centers' plans, policies, or SOPs for each of the four COCs.
Fusion Center Exchange Program*	This initiative facilitates the exchange of fusion center personnel. Exchanges connect fusion centers in need of operational support with subject matter experts (SMEs) from experienced fusion centers to help address specific operational topics in a workshop setting. Visiting personnel work with the host center on a variety of issues, such as but not limited to the following: • Exploring common operational or analytical issues, such as assessing threats to critical infrastructure, exploring border or maritime issues, or integrating non-law enforcement partners. • Developing a joint intelligence product focused on a regional issue or threat. • Using the *Privacy, Civil Rights, and Civil Liberties Compliance Verification for the Intelligence* • *Enterprise* resource. • Exploring fusion center organization or management structures. • Developing regional connectivity between fusion centers. • Developing and implementing a request for information (RFI) capture mechanism.
Technical assistance to support the development and maintenance of fusion centers' governance structure and authorities	The Fusion Center Governance Structure and Authority technical assistance service collaboratively facilitates the strategic planning for and development of a comprehensive fusion center governance structure.

(Continued)

Activity	Description
	COC 1—Receive
Homeland Secure Data Network (HSDN) resource kit	This resource kit helps fusion center personnel develop a more thorough understanding of the information to which they have access through HSDN.
Secret-level clearances	In accordance with Executive Order 13549, the U.S. Department of Homeland Security (DHS) sponsors appropriate fusion center personnel for security clearances.
Access to Secret-level systems (HSDN, Federal Bureau of Investigation Network [FBINet], etc.)	The federal government continues to provide fusion center personnel with Secret-level systems connectivity. For those centers where this is not yet feasible, the federal government will help identify access to Secret-level systems in nearby locations.
Guidance on how to formally request access to sites on the Secure Internet Protocol Router Network (SIPRNet)	This request form supports fusion centers' ability to request access to Secret-level information from federal partners. This request form is designed to provide a standard mechanism for fusion centers to request access to information that might not be currently available to them but is available through SIPRNet.
Basic sensitive but unclassified (SBU) training	This training assists fusion center personnel in fully leveraging existing platforms to access information at the SBU level.
Classified teleconference capability	The Classified Audio Bridge (CAB) is composed of technologies that enable the connection and standardization of several communication devices and encryption standards to ensure a secure multiuser conference capability at the Secret or Top Secret level.
	COC 2—Analyze
Template and guidance to assist with the development of an analytic production plan	The analytic production plan template will assist fusion centers in developing an analytic production plan that describes and prioritizes the types of analysis and products they intend to provide for their customers, how often or in what circumstances the products will be produced, and how each product type will be disseminated.
Fusion Center Risk Analysis Product Template	This template provides fusion center analysts with a flexible template for use in the development of risk products, to include threat, vulnerability, and consequence analysis, as well as recommendations regarding threat mitigation and risk reduction.
Suspicious activity reporting (SAR) Technical Assistance for Analysts and Nationwide SAR Initiative (NSI) Users Technical Assistance	The SAR Technical Assistance for Analysts and the NSI Users Technical Assistance services focus on how to access the shared space and on using the tools associated with the federated query. The technical assistance is provided to NSI sites subsequent to the NSI SAR Analytic Role Training deliveries and on an as-needed basis during NSI site visits.
Analytic peer mentorship opportunities	These mentorships support engagement and collaboration between fusion center and federal analysts via the Regional Analytic Advisor Program (RAAP) as well as analytic exchanges via conference calls and attendance of fusion center analysts at various workshops, conferences, and meetings to highlight and discuss successful fusion center analysis.
Access to analytic training courses	This training assists in building analytic capabilities within fusion center personnel. Specific courses are listed below:
	• Basic Intelligence and Threat Analysis Course (BITAC) • Critical Thinking and Analytic Methods Course (CTAM) • Introduction to Risk Analysis for Fusion Center Analysts Course • Intermediate Risk Analysis for Fusion Center Analysts Course • Mid-Level Intelligence and Threat Analysis Course (MITAC) • Open Source Intelligence Training (OSINT)

Activity	Description
	• Principles of Intelligence Writing and Briefing Course (PIWB) • SAR Analysis Training Course • Vulnerability, Threat, and Risk Assessments Course(VTRA) • Writing for Maximum Utility Course (WFMU) *Cyber Security Analysis Course*
MindLeap Critical Thinking Technical Assistance	*This service focuses on critical thinking and has been designed specifically to provide intelligence analysts with a structured, disciplined approach to causal analyses and evidence-based problem solving. This service enables analysts to recognize weaknesses and errors when undertaking causal analyses and identify how to guard against them.*
Specialized Analytic Seminar Series	*This seminar series has been developed to support advanced analytic training for fusion center analysts. The series addresses specialized threat topic areas and the associated patterns, trends, skills, and resources necessary to effectively monitor and evaluate potential threats in the analyst's area of responsibility. Topic areas include Transnational Organized Crime (Human Trafficking), Financial Crimes, All Hazards, All Crimes (Drugs), All Crimes (Gangs), Maritime, and Cybersecurity.*
Guidance on career development path for state and local analysts	In partnership with the Criminal Intelligence Coordinating Council, this effort will provide a road map and guidance to enhance analyst professional development and career advancement.
Risk analysis reach-back support	This initiative is intended to streamline access to and use of prioritized risk-related information to conduct time-sensitive analysis and enhance the overall capability to conduct risk analysis and produce associated products that are timely, rigorous, defensible, and actionable.
Infrastructure Protection (IP) Field Resource Toolkit	This initiative offers fusion centers a tailored, comprehensive presentation of the relevant Office of Infrastructure Protection tools and resources that are currently available. The IP Field Resource Toolkit provides the opportunity for fusion centers to gain access to IP critical infrastructure collection tools, training, and operational support to assist in the implementation of a strong and dynamic critical infrastructure protection capability. In addition, this initiative also directly supports efforts to achieve and maintain the COCs, including the ability to assess local implications of threat information through the use of formal risk assessment processes.
Template for threat input into a Threat and Hazard Identification and Risk Assessment (THIRA)*	*This template will assist fusion centers in providing input into the threat portion of the THIRA in a consistent and repeatable manner. THIRA is a requirement under the Homeland Security Grant Program.*
Considerations and templates for soliciting and incorporating feedback into analytic production and dissemination*	This initiative consists of considerations for the development and implementation of a standardized process to request customer feedback. Customer feedback mechanisms may include a product feedback questionnaire or structured, periodic meetings with key stakeholders. Fusion centers can then use this information to refine their analytical production processes and their dissemination plans and processes.
Critical Infrastructure/ Risk Analysis Workshop	The integration of critical infrastructure protection capabilities within fusion centers strengthens local, state, regional, and national infrastructure security and information sharing activities. The workshop is designed to accelerate the implementation of baseline critical infrastructure protection capabilities and will focus on practical learning objectives as well as the development of

(Continued)

Activity	Description
	operational skills, capabilities, and techniques. This event also provides a forum for discussing successful practices, available tools, and resources to support fusion center critical infrastructure capabilities.
Critical Infrastructure Protection Capabilities Exchange	This activity facilitates the implementation of baseline critical infrastructure protection capabilities in fusion centers that have chosen to support critical infrastructure protection activities, as well as the coordination between state and local critical infrastructure protection programs and their respective fusion centers.
Joint product development between fusion centers	This initiative facilitates the development of joint intelligence products between fusion centers. It helps to address cross-jurisdictional security issues, such as border-related crime, transnational organized crime, critical infrastructure assessments, and other strategic issues of mutual concern.
Joint product development between fusion centers and the federal government	This initiative supports the development of joint federal, state, and local analytic products and facilitates collaboration between federal and fusion center analysts on the development of analytic products.
Analytic supervisor and management courses	*This initiative sponsors fusion center analytic supervisors' attendance in management courses and enables collaboration across federal, state, and local arenas. Participants will get practical tips on managing collaborative projects; overcoming organizational, cultural, and behavioral obstacles; and applying structured analytic techniques to create an effective platform for collaboration.*
Checklist to assist in the review of analytic products to ensure P/CRCL protections*	Fusion centers create and disseminate different analytic products. This checklist identifies questions that should be addressed during the development, review, and dissemination of analytic products to ensure that P/CRCL protections are upheld in the product.
Activity	**Description**
National Fusion Center Analytic Workshop	*This workshop provides analysts with a current understanding of the threat environment. The workshop is designed to support the fusion centers' ability to assess local implications of threat information. The workshop also supports increased analytic competencies of fusion center analysts by enhancing their understanding of the role and importance of analytic methods and tradecraft and enhancing the consistency, quality, relevance, and defensibility of fusion center analytic products.*
COC 3—Disseminate	
Considerations and templates for soliciting and incorporating feedback into analytic production and dissemination*	This initiative consists of considerations for the development and implementation of a standardized process to request customer feedback. Customer feedback mechanisms may include a product feedback questionnaire or structured, periodic meetings with key stakeholders. Fusion centers can then use this information to refine their analytical production processes and their dissemination plans and processes.
Bimonthly conference calls with Fusion Liaison Officer (FLO) Coordinators*	*These regular conference calls with FLO Coordinators will assist with the standardization of the FLO Program across the National Network and will allow the sharing of best practices and lessons learned from implementation of FLO Programs by fusion centers.*
Fusion Center and Emergency Operations Center (EOC) Collaboration Symposium	*This symposium will facilitate discussions between EOCs and fusion centers as they coordinate and integrate functions into existing information sharing initiatives. The symposium will build upon the concepts outlined in Comprehensive Preparedness Guide (CPG) 502: Considerations for Fusion Center and Emergency Operations Center*

Activity	Description
	Coordination and will facilitate discussion of respective roles in receiving and transmitting critical operational information between fusion centers and EOCs.
Technical assistance to support coordination and communication among fusion centers, multidisciplinary partners, and other customers/ liaisons*	These services are designed to facilitate communication and coordination between fusion centers and their partners, including: • Emergency Operations Centers (EOC) • Public Health/Healthcare • Critical Infrastructure • Fire Service • FLO Program Development and Implementation
COC 4—Gather	
Guidance on identifying and documenting intelligence questions, information needs, and collection requirements	This initiative focuses on disseminating a resource kit that outlines a process for engaging with customers, identifying intelligence questions, identifying information needs, and developing collection requirements.
SAR training to homeland security partners (in partnership with the NSI)	This training enables homeland security and public safety partners to recognize behaviors, indicators, and other warnings that could be indicative of criminal activity associated with terrorism, while reinforcing the necessity of protecting privacy, civil rights, and civil liberties. • SAR Line Officer Training (law enforcement) • SAR Awareness for Hometown Security Partners (emergency management, fire/EMS, private sector security, parole/probation/corrections, and public safety telecommunications) • SAR indicator and warning training (e.g., State and Local Anti-Terrorism Training [SLATT®], Anti-Terrorism Intelligence Awareness Training Program [AIATP], and Information Collection on Patrol [InCOP])
NSI implementation to additional fusion centers (in partnership with the NSI)	Led by the NSI Program Management Office (PMO), this activity assists fusion centers in standardizing their processes in accordance with the Information Sharing Environment (ISE)- SAR Functional Standard, thus improving their ability to analyze and share SARs across the National Network and with the federal government.
Training and resources for identifying and reporting human trafficking	*This initiative is designed to enhance fusion centers' abilities to identify, report, and combat human trafficking by increasing training on recognizing human trafficking indicators; increasing partnerships between federal law enforcement agencies and their state, local, tribal, and territorial (SLTT) counterparts on human trafficking initiatives; providing guidance for fusion centers regarding the collection, analysis, and reporting of human trafficking information; and leveraging existing resources and protocols to improve information sharing.*
Technical assistance to support coordination and communication between fusion centers, multidisciplinary partners, and other customers/ liaisons*	These services are designed to facilitate communication and coordination between fusion centers and their partners, including: • EOCs • Public Health/Healthcare • Critical Infrastructure • Fire Service • FLO Program Development and Implementation
Bimonthly conference calls with Fusion Liaison Officer (FLO) Coordinators*	*These regular conference calls with FLO Coordinators will assist with the standardization of the FLO Program across the National Network and will allow the sharing of best practices and lessons learned from implementation of a FLO Program by fusion centers.*

(Continued)

Activity	Description
Template for requests for information (RFI)	*This standardized form, developed in collaboration with major city intelligence commanders and fusion centers, is designed to assist fusion centers in requesting information from other state, local, tribal, territorial, and federal law enforcement entities, homeland security agencies, or fusion centers.*
EC 1—Privacy, Civil Rights, and Civil Liberties (P/CRCL) Protections	
Checklist to assist in the review of products to	Fusion centers create and disseminate different analytic products. This checklist identifies questions that should be
ensure P/CRCL protections*	addressed during the development, review, and dissemination of analytic products to ensure that P/CRCL protections are upheld in the product.
Peer-to-peer P/CRCL compliance reviews	This initiative assists fusion centers, via a peer-to-peer process, as they review and assess their policies and procedures related to P/CRCL protections to ensure that these policies are comprehensive and are able to be implemented. The compliance review utilizes the *Privacy, Civil Rights, and Civil Liberties Compliance Verification for the Intelligence Enterprise*. This peer-to-peer process increases communication and coordination between fusion centers, identifies smart practices, and provides feedback and recommendations to mitigate potential implementation gaps.
Workshop for P/CRCL Officers	This workshop assists fusion center P/CRCL Officers in providing continuing training on P/CRCL issues to their own fusion centers.
P/CRCL training to fusion center staff	This on-site training delivers a "toolkit" approach that allows fusion centers to select from a list of available training modules to customize on-site training for fusion center personnel. This training is customized by working with local counsel (if available) and a local privacy point of contact to ensure that the presentation is as relevant as possible.
Conference call of fusion center Privacy Officers every two months	*These regular conference calls of Privacy Officers from fusion centers will allow the sharing of best practices and lessons learned from implementation of P/CRCL protections by fusion centers.*
Issue-specific P/CRCL guidance and training— First Amendment activities	*This guidance assists fusion center personnel and law enforcement officers as they prepare for, respond to, and follow up with events, activities, and assemblies that are protected by the First Amendment of the Constitution of the United States of America.*
Issue-specific P/CRCL guidance and training— social media	*This guidance assists fusion center personnel in the development of policies to guide personnel on the use of social media tools and resources as a part of their investigative and intelligence activities.*
Guidance in development of a Privacy Impact Assessment (PIA)	*This template will provide the format for a PIA and instructions for fusion centers on completing the sections of the PIA by examining the processes and authorities unique to their jurisdictions.*
EC 2—Sustainment Strategy	
Technical assistance to support the development and maintenance of a Concept of Operations (CONOPS) through strategic planning	This service provides subject matter expertise, templates, and samples to guide and facilitate the development of a viable, strategic CONOPS. This module is designed to provide flexible assistance using a phased Implementation approach. Each delivery is tailored for the individual needs of the requesting jurisdiction.
Technical assistance to assist with investment planning and grant portfolio management	The Investment Planning and Grant Portfolio Management Technical Assistance services provide subject matter expertise, templates, and samples to guide and facilitate the development of investment planning and associated grant portfolio management.

Activity	Description
A template for threat input into THIRA*	*This template will assist fusion centers in providing input into the threat portion of the THIRA in a consistent and repeatable manner. THIRA is a requirement under the Homeland Security Grant Program.*
Fusion Center Leaders Program	This graduate-level program examines key questions and issues facing fusion center leaders and their role in homeland security, public safety, and the ISE. This program is designed to enhance critical thinking related to homeland security and public safety issues at the federal, state, local, tribal, and territorial levels.
EC 3—Communications and Outreach	
Guidance and a template to assist fusion centers in capturing success stories	A key element of communicating the value and mission of fusion centers is sharing success stories of fusion center activities. Fusion center success-story guidance and templates provide Fusion Center Directors with standard topics, key information, and a standardized form. These success stories are shared at the appropriate classification levels to be leveraged to demonstrate the value of the National Network of Fusion Centers.
Building Communities and Relationships of Trust Guidance	This guidance provides advice and recommendations to community leaders on how to initiate and sustain trusting relationships that support meaningful sharing of information, responsiveness to community concerns and priorities, and the reporting of suspicious activities in a responsible manner.
Customized fusion center-specific brochures and videos	A service offered by the DHS/U.S. Department of Justice (DOJ) Fusion Process Technical Assistance Program provides the following services to fusion centers: • Customized trifold pamphlet including general information about fusion centers and a specific description of the fusion center's accomplishments and services • Fusion Center 101 video customized with the fusion center's contact information and logo • Customized "If You See Something, Say Something™" public awareness video
Technical assistance on communications and outreach	The Fusion Center Communications and Outreach Technical Assistance service supports fusion centers to communicate effectively with a unified voice, build advocates at all levels of government, and inform internal and external stakeholders of their mission, vision, and value. This workshop was developed from the *Communications and Outreach Guidebook: Considerations for State and Major Urban Area Fusion Centers.*
Annual Report sample kit	*This kit includes a collection of actual annual reports produced by fusion centers to serve as examples of what effective annual reports include. The purpose of this kit is to help fusion centers develop their own annual reports that demonstrate the value and impact of their centers in supporting mission requirements.*
Guidebook to assist engagement between fusion centers and private sector partners	This document will assist fusion centers and private sector partners to identify and tailor appropriate approaches to engage with each other based on identified best practices and lessons learned. Fusion centers can use this resource in conjunction with the *Critical Infrastructure and Key Resource Guidebook* when performing outreach to private sector partners.
Support for tribal participation in fusion centers	This service supports fusion centers to engage with Native Nations and tribal law enforcement via the Fusion Center Exchange Program.

(Continued)

Activity	Description
	EC 4—Security
Bimonthly conference call with fusion center Security Liaisons	*These regular conference calls of Security Liaisons from fusion centers will allow the sharing of best practices and lessons learned from implementation of security activities by fusion centers.*
Security technical assistance	This technical assistance service is designed to facilitate fusion center efforts to develop and implement appropriate security measures, policies, and procedures associated with the center's facility, including administrative, physical, information, systems, and personnel security. The service is also designed to support the fusion center's ability to collect, store, and share classified, controlled unclassified, and unclassified information to address homeland security and criminal investigations, while ensuring that all security plans and policies are coordinated with all privacy policies.
National Fusion Center Security Liaison Workshop	This workshop provides comprehensive security training for fusion center Security Liaisons, including training on clearance investigations, adjudications, and the Central Verification System (CVS); counterintelligence awareness; foreign disclosure; operational security; classified information technology systems; derivative classification and marking; security self- assessments and the security compliance review program; and classified meetings and closed storage areas. This workshop includes train-the-trainer materials to support Security Liaisons in training fusion center staff in security matters.
Counterintelligence Fundamentals Workshop	This one-day, on-site, regional workshop is intended to familiarize fusion center personnel with possible intelligence collection threats directed against their facility and enable them to recognize an elicitation attempt or recruitment pitch.
Assistance to help fusion centers understand how to access and use the CVS	CVS is a database that provides the status of active security clearances and security clearance history.
Security Liaison Resource Kit	*This resource kit is provided in accordance with the Classified National Security Information Program for State, Local, Tribal and Private Sector Entities Implementing Directive (March 2012) and is designed to provide newly appointed Security Liaisons with the knowledge and information necessary to fulfill their duties and responsibilities to implement and manage security requirements.*
Security Self-Inspection Checklist	*Pursuant to Executive Order 13549, Classified National Security Information Program for State, Local, Tribal, and Private Sector Entities, and its Implementing Directive, state and local entities must ensure that security standards governing access to and safeguarding of classified material are applied in accordance with the Executive Order. In keeping with these provisions, all state and local entities that create, handle, or store classified information must perform a self-inspection of their activities to ensure that classified information is marked, handled, and stored in accordance with governing directives. In support of this requirement, a self-inspection checklist and associated guidance will be provided to assist fusion centers.*

New resources for 2013 are indicated in italics in blue. Resources that support multiple COCs are indicated with an * in bold text.

Appendix G. Success Stories

Fusion Center Supports Colorado Wildfire Response Efforts

Colorado Information Analysis Center, March – July 2012

Between March and July 2012, Colorado experienced 25 major wildfires covering over 400,000 acres of land, resulting in the mandatory evacuation of over 44,000 people. Fighting the Colorado fires required every available state and federal resource and quickly became the focus of the entire country as other states and federal agencies provided resources to support the firefighting effort. Colorado's fusion center, the Colorado Information Analysis Center (CIAC), coordinated closely with the Colorado Division of Emergency Management (DEM) during the response to the wildfires, providing resources such as Mobile Analytical Response Teams, "Flash Reports," and investigative support to promote effective information sharing, support executive-level decision making, and reduce duplication of effort. The CIAC developed the Mobile Analytical Response Team concept to deploy assets and provide on-scene intelligence support for all-hazards incidents. The teams are composed of Colorado State Troopers and CIAC intelligence analysts who embed with emergency management to share information and produce intelligence to support the incident command. Additionally, the CIAC utilized its fire analyst, who resides within the fusion center, to provide subject matter expertise for the Mobile Analytical Response Teams as they processed information and developed products. The coordination and partnerships between the Colorado State Patrol, the CIAC, and DEM served to promote information sharing and collaboration that protected lives and property in Colorado.

Fusion Centers Collaborate to Assist in Opening a Homicide Investigation

Multiple Fusion Centers, March 2012

In March 2012, the Southern Nevada Counter-Terrorism Center (SNCTC) responded to a Las Vegas Metropolitan Police Department Terrorism Liaison Officer request for assistance in verifying identification information obtained from a local inmate, who claimed to be a soldier of the Gulf Cartel. After vetting information presented by the inmate—including details surrounding Gulf Cartel smuggling routes, tactics, techniques, and procedures, as well as specific information regarding an unsolved murder that took place in Texas several years prior—the SNCTC passed the information to the Texas Fusion Center (TFC).

Based on feedback from the TFC, SNCTC conducted a follow-up interview with the inmate, during which additional pertinent information was obtained and relayed to Texas. The follow-up interviews and continued research by the SNCTC led to the development of actionable intelligence that enabled the Hidalgo County Sheriff's Department to open a new investigation on an unsolved murder in Texas. Information received was also shared with the Intelligence Community to aid future federal counternarcotics efforts.

Fusion Center Assists in Homicide Investigation

Pennsylvania Criminal Intelligence Center, February 2012

In February 2012, the Pennsylvania State Police (PSP) conducted an investigation of a homicide. A suspect was interviewed in connection with the crime and denied having had any contact with the victim during the time frame of the offense. Cellular telephone records for both the victim and suspect were obtained and forwarded to the Pennsylvania Criminal Intelligence Center (PaCIC). Through the analytic support provided by the PaCIC, it was determined that the victim's and suspect's phones were at the same location at the same time, contradicting the suspect's statement. Following this discovery, the PaCIC prepared a map depicting the GPS coordinates of both phones and disseminated the map to investigators, thereby leading to the suspect's arrest for the homicide.

Fusion Centers Collaborate to Support Controlled Drug Seizure

Multiple Fusion Centers, January 2012

In January 2012, a Customs and Border Protection (CBP) officer at the Port of Cincinnati intercepted an opium- laced package from Great Britain bound for South Lake Tahoe, California. Seized after a CBP K-9 alerted law enforcement authorities to the suspicious nature of the package, the shipment was X-rayed, tested, and confirmed as containing opiate residue. As a partner agency at the Kentucky Intelligence Fusion Center (KIFC), the CBP officer asked the KIFC for additional information to support a controlled interstate delivery. Subsequently, they worked with the Central California Intelligence Center (CCIC) to provide support for the delivery. The team utilized the fusion center's trained Terrorism Liaison Officer (TLO) network and the Central Valley (California) High Intensity Drug Trafficking Area (HIDTA) to identify local points of contact to arrange a successful delivery to the California Department of Justice (DOJ) Narcotics Task Force. Acting on a search warrant on the same day, they seized 28 pounds of dried opium poppy pods and $26,000 in cash. This successful operation exemplifies the collaborative power that field-based information sharing entities leverage across their distinct networks to benefit the Homeland Security Enterprise.

Fusion Centers in Georgia and Virginia Collaborate to Solve Murder of Young Child

Multiple Fusion Centers, December 2011

In December of 2011, a young child was reported missing from an apartment complex in northern Georgia. After the Georgia Bureau of Investigation (GBI) identified a suspect in the case, the GBI analysts assigned to the Georgia Information Sharing and Analysis Center (GISAC), the Georgia fusion center, began developing information on the suspect. Upon determining that the subject had previously lived in Virginia, the GISAC contacted the Virginia Fusion Center and requested a check on the subject. The Virginia Fusion Center responded with an update that the suspect had previously been the subject of a local police report. Based on this information, the GISAC was able to request the full report from local

Virginia authorities and GBI Special Agents were sent to Virginia to reinterview the complainant documented in the report. Shortly thereafter, the subject was arrested and charged with murdering the child. This example demonstrates the importance of connectivity across the National Network of Fusion Centers, which provided investigators with critical information in real time that they otherwise would not have been able to access.

Fusion Center Provides Critical Information to International and Federal Partners Contributing to Arrest of Armed Suspects

Alaska Information and Analysis Center, October 2011

In October 2011, the Alaska Information and Analysis Center (AKIAC) issued an Officer Safety Bulletin informing state law enforcement of two potentially violent individuals believed to be illegally armed and possibly departing the state for Canada. This bulletin was informed by information provided by the Alaska Joint Terrorism Task Force. Leveraging liaisons with the Royal Canadian Mounted Police, a partnership with the U.S. Border Patrol Blaine Sector Intelligence Unit, and local Anchorage U.S. Customs and Border Protection (CBP) contacts, the AKIAC ensured that the Canadian Border Security Agency (CBSA) received this information and was on alert. As a result, CBSA conducted a high-risk inspection of the suspect's vehicle at the Beaver Creek Port of Entry, discovering a weapon. The suspect was denied entry, turned around, stopped at the CBP checkpoint, and arrested by the Alaska State Troopers.

Fusion Center Contributes to Decrease in Auto Theft

Colorado Information Analysis Center, October 2011

Auto-theft prevention has become a top priority in Colorado, given that it can be a "transitional crime," because stolen cars are often used in kidnappings, bank robberies, drug deliveries, and other violent felonies. Of the nearly 31,000 auto-theft cases in Colorado in the past five years, 75 percent involved another crime, including murder, robbery, assault, and sexual assault. The Colorado Information Analysis Center (CIAC) worked with the Colorado State Patrol to create and staff Colorado's Auto Theft Intelligence Coordination Center (ATICC). ATICC analysts have worked to analyze existing auto-theft data to produce products for law enforcement officers in Colorado and surrounding states. The CIAC has gathered, analyzed, and distributed data to local law enforcement to help identify stolen cars and potentially prevent thefts. These efforts, as well as partnerships with ten statewide task forces, have helped put the number of auto thefts in Colorado below the national average. ATICC is funded by a grant from the Colorado Auto Theft Prevention Authority, which is funded by a flat fee assessed on automobile insurance policies in Colorado. The goal of the partnership is to gather and analyze data in order to support local police departments with intelligence products and proposed countermeasures to prevent auto theft and related crimes.

Fusion Center Supports Apprehension of Armed and Dangerous Fugitives

Colorado Information Analysis Center, August 2011

In August 2011, three armed and dangerous siblings known as the Dougherty Gang were sighted in Colorado Springs. The FBI asked the Colorado Information Analysis Center (CIAC) to share intelligence across the state of Colorado to facilitate their search for the subjects. The FBI representative at the CIAC developed a "Be on the Lookout" (BOLO) alert for immediate distribution to Colorado law enforcement and the National Network of Fusion Centers. This alert, along with photographs of the subjects, was coordinated with the media for public dissemination; soon afterward, local law enforcement received a tip that the Doughertys were spotted in a rural area of southern Colorado. Members from the Colorado State Patrol and local law enforcement located the Doughertys there and took them into custody. Additional details about the CIAC's role in supporting this effort are located at *Fusion Center Supports Apprehension of Armed and Dangerous Fugitives.*

End Notes

[1] The fusion process is the overarching process of managing the flow of information and intelligence across levels and sectors of government and private industry. It goes beyond establishing an information/intelligence center or creating a computer network. The fusion process supports the implementation of risk-based, information-driven prevention, response, and consequence management programs. The fusion process turns information and intelligence into actionable knowledge.

[2] The Homeland Security Enterprise encompasses the federal, state, local, tribal, territorial, nongovernmental, and private sector entities and individuals, families, and communities who share a common national interest in the safety and security of America and the American population.

[3] Seventy seven designated fusion centers existed during the period covered by the 2012 Assessment—August 1, 2011 through July 31, 2012. The 78th designated fusion center, the Mariana Regional Fusion Center in Guam, was not officially recognized by DHS until after the close of the 2012 Fusion Center Assessment.

[4] Based on the date of final adoption of these measures, some fusion centers were unable to provide complete performance data for the entire period covered by the 2012 Assessment—August 1, 2011 through July 31, 2012. The performance data reported here, while not encompassing the entire National Network for the full reporting period, nevertheless provides a useful performance baseline to develop preliminary out-year performance targets. For measures 2 and 5, more collection and analysis are required in order to project appropriate benchmarks for future years.

[5] The Homeland Security Enterprise encompasses the federal, state, local, tribal, territorial, nongovernmental, and private sector entities and individuals, families, and communities who share a common national interest in the safety and security of America and the American population.

[6] The four COCs are COC 1—Receive, COC 2—Analyze, COC 3—Disseminate, and COC 4—Gather.

[7] The four ECs are EC 1—Privacy, Civil Rights, and Civil Liberties Protections; EC 2—Sustainment Strategy; EC 3—Communications and Outreach; and EC 4—Security.

[8] The definitions of four attributes were clarified for the 2012 Assessment:

- COC 2, Attribute 4: Access to multidisciplinary subject matter experts "outside of its state" was changed to "outside of its AOR" to account for major urban area fusion centers.
- COC 2, Attribute 9: The nature of the feedback mechanism was changed to "structured," excluding ad hoc and informal feedback. The scope was also narrowed to analytic products as opposed to all fusion center products and services, consistent with the intent of customer feedback mechanisms.
- COC 4, Attribute 1: The development of an NSI site plan was replaced with NSI compliance, a more rigorous and complete process that includes developing a site plan.
- EC 4, Attribute 2: Recognizing the need to provide fusion center personnel with periodic training on physical, personnel, and information security, the scope was broadened to include the fusion center's specific plans, security measures, policies, and procedures, and the frequency was clarified to annually.

[9] 2011 Federal Cost Inventory cost categories included Staff, Information Technology, Training & Exercises, Management & Administration, and Programmatic; federal staff costs are estimated.

[10] 2011 federal grant, state, and local expediture data for 60 of 72 fusion centers.

[11] 2011 federal grant, state, local, territorial, tribal, and private sector expenditure data for the 77 fusion centers designated at the time.

[12] 2011 Federal Cost Inventory cost categories included Staff, Information Technology, Training & Exercises, Management & Administration, and Programmatic; federal staff costs are estimated.

[13] FY12 estimates are from the 2011 Federal Cost Inventory and reflect only costs for the 72 centers designated at the time; federal staff costs are estimated.

[14] SLTT government FY varies and may include muliple-year grant awards.

[15] Territorial, tribal, and private sector cost data not collected in 2011.

[16] The Federal Resource Allocation Criteria policy (Information Sharing Environment Guidance ISE-G-112) defines the process by which states and territories designate fusion centers and defines objective criteria to be used by federal departments and agencies making resource allocation decisions regarding fusion centers.

[17] The 78th designated fusion center, the Mariana Regional Fusion Center in Guam, was not officially recognized by DHS until after the close of the 2012 Fusion Center Assessment.

[18] For a list of all COC and EC attributes, see Appendix D.

[19] Governance-related questions and responses were not included in the individual fusion center scoring process.

[20] After the close of the 2012 Assessment, the HSIN State and Local Intelligence Community of Interest (HSIN SLIC) was officially renamed HSIN Intel and was incorporated into the broader HSIN enterprise technical framework.

[21] Following the close of the 2012 Assessment reporting period, DHS deployed HSDN to two of the centers that reported not having access to a classified system. DHS has tentative plans to deploy HSDN to five of the remaining centers in FY13 and FY14.

[22] In June 2011, the federal government issued the Federal Resource Allocation Criteria (RAC) policy. The RAC policy defines objective criteria and a coordinated approach for prioritizing the allocation of federal resources to fusion centers. In addition, the RAC policy requires all fusion centers to achieve and maintain the Baseline Capabilities as measured by the annual Fusion Center Assessment to remain eligible for the allocation of federal resources.

[23] The THIRA allows a state or region to understand its threats and hazards and how their impacts may vary according to time of occurrence, seasons, locations, and community factors. This knowledge allows a jurisdiction to establish informed and defensible capability targets and commit appropriate resources drawn from the whole community to closing the gap between a target and a current capability or for sustaining existing capabilities.

[24] The Central Verification System (CVS) is the "reciprocity database." CVS contains information on security clearances, investigations, suitability, and credentialing determinations. It is intended for employees whose duties involve reciprocity determinations and reciprocity data sharing using CVS functions.

[25] Based on the date of final adoption of these measures, some fusion centers were unable to provide complete performance data for the entire period covered by the 2012 Assessment—August 1, 2011 through July 31, 2012. The performance data reported here, while not encompassing the entire National Network for the full reporting period, nevertheless provides a useful performance baseline to develop preliminary out-year performance targets.

[26] Since not all fusion centers were able to provide complete data, DHS and its interagency and fusion center partners analyzed the existing data to account for these gaps when determining targets.

[27] Global serves as a Federal Advisory Committee (FAC) and advises the U.S. Attorney General on justice information sharing and integration initiatives. Global was created to support the broadscale exchange of pertinent justice and public safety information. It promotes standards-based electronic information exchange to provide the justice community with timely, accurate, complete, and accessible information in a secure and trusted environment.

[28] The FBI JTTF initiates a JTTF investigation when it is able to demonstrate a nexus to terrorism.

[29] For a list of the primary and recognized fusion centers that currently make up the National Network, see http://www.dhs.gov/fusioncenters.

[30] Primary fusion centers serve as the focal points within the state and local environment for the receipt, analysis, gathering, and sharing of threat-related information. They have additional responsibilities related to the coordination of the Critical Operational Capabilities across the statewide fusion process with other recognized fusion centers.

[31] The federal government respects the authority of state governments to designate fusion centers. Any designated fusion center, including major urban area fusion centers, not designated as a primary fusion center is referred to as a recognized fusion center.

INDEX

D

E

F

G

H

I

J

L

M

Q

R

S

T

U

V

W

Y

ENVIRONMENTAL MICROBIOLOGY RESEARCH TRENDS

Environmental Microbiology Research Trends

George V. Kurladze
Editor

Nova Science Publishers, Inc.
New York

LIBRARY OF CONGRESS CATALOGING-IN-PUBLICATION DATA

Environmental microbiology research trends / George V. Kurladze (editor)
p. ;cm.
Includes bibliographical references and index.
ISBN 978-1-60021-939-9 (hardcover : alk paper)
ISBN: 1-60021-939-X (hardcover) alk paper)

1. Microbial ecology. I. Kurladze, George V.
2. [DNLM: Environmental Microbiology. 2. Environmental Monitoring. QW 55 E613 2008]

QR100.E586 2008
628 501'579--dc22

2007032724

Published by Nova Science Publishers, Inc. ✦ New York

CONTENTS

PREFACE

This new book presents the latest research in environmental microbiology which is area of interaction that studies the interaction of microorganisms with the environment. It includes the structure, activities and communal behaviour of microbial communities, microbial interactions and interactions with plants, animals and non-living environmental factors, population biology and clonal structure microbes and surfaces, adhesion and biofouling responses to environmental signals and stress factors growth and survival, modelling and theory development, microbial community genetics and evolutionary processes, microbial physiological, metabolic and structural diversity, pollution microbiology, extremophiles and life in extreme and unusual little-explored habitats, primary and secondary production, element cycles and biogeochemical processes and microbially-influenced global changes.

Chapter 1 - With the increasing number of innovative remediation technologies, the decision makers, the owners and other stakeholders should be guided by useful information ensured by a technology-assessment tool, which evaluates the technological, environmental, eco- and cost-efficiency of the technology. Especially the in situ technologies based on natural biological processes are mistrusted and suffer from lack of confidence, due to missing information, objective evaluation and transparent verification.

A complex evaluation/verification system was developed for soil remediation technologies, which can be applied generally both to bioremediation and in situ soil treatment. The multistage verification methodology includes 1. material balance, that is the mass flow balance of the soil phases and the modified or eliminated pollutant amount, 2. quantitative characterisation of the environmental risk before, during and after the remediation, 3. cost-efficiency or if necessary and possible, cost-benefit assessment and 4. SWOT analysis.

Both of the field applications introduced in this publication were the first demonstrations of the innovative technologies, developed in our laboratories in the frame of Hungarian R&D Projects. Main goals of the first field applications were to prove the findings of the laboratory experiments and to acquire data for the technology-verification, which has been developed and recommended for wider use by the authors.

This contribution introduces in detail the complex verification system developed and applied for the characterisation and evaluation of two very different in situ remediation technologies: 1. the cyclodextrin technology" (CDT), which is an innovative bioremediation developed and used for soil contaminated with hydrocarbons of low bioavailability; 2. the combined chemical and phytostabilisation (CCP) applied for point and diffuse sources contaminated by toxic metals.

The randomly methylated ß-cyclodextrin (RAMEB) was found to significantly enhance the bioremediation and detoxification of the transformer oil-contaminated soil increasing the bioavailability of the pollutants and the activity of indigenous microorganisms. The feasibility of the innovative cyclodextrin-enhanced bioremediation (CDT) was demonstrated in a field application. The verification of the CDT using the developed innovative tool-box proved the efficiency and the competitiveness of the CDT.

The combined chemical and phytostabilisation (CCP) is based on the concept of reducing risk making the metals irreversibly immobile, as well as stopping runoff and soil erosion. The results of the stabilisation microcosm experiments indicate that it is possible to reduce the mobility of toxic metals such as Cd, Zn, Pb, Cu and As by soil treatment with chemical stabilizers. The complex technology-monitoring of the CCP enabled differentiation between extractability, bioavailability and accessibility for plant uptake.

The development and application of a uniform remediation technology-verification system makes possible better understanding and evaluation of the remediation technologies and is able to increase trust in remediation, including in situ biotechnologies. The first demonstration of the technologies introduced here make possible the evaluation of the verification system itself and show the direction toward further development on the basis of the first experiences.

Chapter 2 - Disinfection of empty animal houses has routinely been incorporated in all-in all-out farm systems for decades. The scientific evidence for the efficacy of disinfecting farm buildings is sparse, both as regards general production parameters and the elimination of specific micro-organisms. Information on chemical disinfectants can often be obtained only from the companies that market or produce them.

Three aspects determine the outcome of disinfection: the detrimental factor (chemical and/or physical disinfection), the micro-organism, and the environment. The ideal farm disinfectant is unaffected by organic matter, it works at low temperatures, is non-corrosive to materials, and breaks down to harmless substances. Routine farm disinfection only involves chemical disinfectants, albeit these have been combined with heat to increase the effectiveness. Micro-organisms differ with regard to susceptibility to detrimental conditions, ranging from the very resistant prions to the relatively sensitive enveloped viruses. For bacteria, much is known about their phase and resistance, e.g., stationary vs. growth phase. This is closely interrelated with the environment in which factors such as the amount and type of organic matter, humidity, temperature, pH, and UV-light are important.

Most official disinfection tests, which have been implemented by only a few countries, are unrealistic suspension tests. These often yield best-case results because bacteria in suspensions are more susceptible to detrimental conditions than under real-life conditions on surfaces. With regard to viruses and fungi even less evidence on the effectiveness of disinfection exists.

This review outlines conditions that influence disinfection efficacy and elaborates on applied research which is useful for monitoring the disinfection of empty animal houses. Suggestions are given for future research areas which can generate scientific evidence for recommended procedures.

Chapter 3 - Bacteria are described as the smallest autonomous organism in the environment. Based on the data available on the complete genomes, the bacterial genome size varies from 0.27 Mb (*Bacillus anthracis* strain A2012) to 9.7 Mb (*Rhodococcus sp.* RHA1). This genome material allows the binary fission process which is the main way of reproduction of the bacteria. This mode of growth limits the genetic variations to sporadic mutations. However, the genetic potential of a bacterium is not limited to the genetic materials inherited from its parents. The bacteria have evolved mainly by exchanging genetic material from other bacteria via plasmids and DNA recombinations. This ability confers a large potential to the bacteria to adapt to the environment. Moreover, the bacterial cells are able to communicate to each other. This type of interaction offers facilities to coordinate some bacterial physiological processes such as the quorum sensing. The cell-to-cell communication exports the gene expression at the level of the bacterial population rendering the bacterial world more complex. This complexity is reinforced by the ability of the bacterial cells to form a well-structured cell cluster organization, namely biofilms. This dynamic bacterial structure ensures a bigger potential to survive to the environmental conditions by combining diverse phenotype responses. Through the biofilm formation, the bacteria developed new strategies to adapt and to survive to the environment. The aspects of the natural bacterial biofilms in the environment will be discussed in this chapter through the structure of the biofilms, the biofouling and the biocorrosion, and the biofilms in water.

Chapter 4 - In the last decade, the emphasis has shifted to the physical and microbiological quality of water sources as reports have shown that there are an increasing percentage of surface- and groundwater that are being contaminated with waterborne pathogens. Increased land use, rural development, informal settlements and inadequate infrastructure for water and sanitation have increased the risk of faecal contamination of these water sources. This is compounded by alterations in the hydrological cycle, associated with global climate change that increases the magnitude and frequency of run-off events. Waterborne diseases and epidemics result from the ingestion of faecally polluted water containing enteric bacterial pathogens, human-specific enteric viruses and protozoan parasites. Enteric bacteria have traditionally been used as indicators of faecal contamination of source, drinking and recreational water. However, research has demonstrated that these bacteria may not be appropriate indicators of pathogenic viruses and the need for reliable index or indicator organisms of these pathogens have been widely recognised. Studies conducted over the past couple of years have investigated, evaluated and compared bacteriophage and chemical assays as indicators of waterborne pathogens. In one study, the potential of F-RNA phage genotyping and chemical analysis of faecal sterols were evaluated to indicate if faecal pollution of water sources were of human or animal origin. When applied to environmental samples, F-RNA phage genotyping provided useful information in certain instances and confirmed the presence of either human or animal faecal pollution. Chemical assays yielded more conclusive results when F-RNA phage genotyping results obtained from river water samples were ambiguous. In another study F-RNA phage genotyping was used to determine the origin of faecal pollution in traditional and CDC safe storage containers in rural settlements. Results showed no difference between the different containers; both human and animal phage subtypes were detected. Although the detection of each specific pathogen seems to be the ideal, this is not always possible due to expensive analysis and the need of well-equipped laboratories and skilled personnel. It can be concluded that bacterial and bacteriophage indicators are still the best alternative and most cost-effective tools currently available and will continue to play a major role in the determination of the microbial quality of water.

Chapter 5 - Molecular and biochemical approaches have revealed that microbial communities in natural aquatic environments are more diverse than previously thought. However, few studies have examined how fine scale changes in environmental conditions can alter the structure, diversity, and function of aquatic microorganisms. The authors performed a number of studies that examined the influence of fine scale changes such as particle size or spatial location on microbial communities in freshwater systems. Bacterial communities associated with different sizes of particles in land sediment were characterized using 16S rRNA gene sequencing, which revealed fundamental differences in the structure of communities associated with very fine (0.063-0.25 mm diameter) and fine (0.25-1 mm) particles. Similarly, microbial activity was also influenced by particle size with different activities of lignin and cellulose degrading enzymes associated with different sized particles. Fine (cm) scale spatial variation in microbial activity was also seen on decomposing leaves in a stream, and spatial patterns in cellulose degrading enzymes suggest that the process of organic matter decomposition shows high spatial heterogeneity. Together, these findings demonstrate that aquatic microbial communities vary both structurally and functionally over finer scales than are usually considered in environmental microbiology. This variation should be considered in future surveys of microbial diversity and activity in environmental samples.

Chapter 7 - A major issue in microbial ecology is to identify the limits of life for growth and survival, and to understand the molecular mechanisms that define these limits. Thus, interest in the biodiversity and ecology of extreme environments has grown in recent years for several reasons. Some are basic and revolve around the idea that extreme environments are believed to reflect early Earth conditions. Other issues are related to the biotechnological potential of extremophiles, such as the use of the metabolic properties of some microorganisms for metal extraction.

In this regard, the study of extremely acidic environments ($pH<3$) has become increasingly important since environmental acidity is often caused by microbial activity. Highly acidic environments are relatively scarce worldwide and are generally associated with volcanic activity or mining operations. In addition to high acidity, these environments exhibit a range of chemical and physical conditions, depending on their origin and the geochemical nature of the site. For most acidic environments, low pH facilitates metal solubility, and therefore acidic waters tend to have high concentrations of heavy metals. Volcanic areas are even more inhospitable due to the exposure to toxic gases and elevated temperatures, and acidic lakes or rivers are sometimes deeply colored by humic acid or high concentrations of ferric iron, producing unfavorable conditions for photosynthetic organisms. However, highly acidic environments are usually inhabited by acidophilic and acidotolerant eukaryotic microorganisms such as algae, amoebas, ciliates, heliozoan and rotifers not to mention filamentous fungi and yeast. This chapter will review the general trends concerning the diversity and ecophysiology of eukaryotic acidophilic microorganims, as well as summarize our latest results on this topic in one of the largest extreme acidic rivers, Río Tinto (SW, Spain).

Chapter 8 - The widespread pollution of soils is an increasing urgent problem because of its contribution to environmental deterioration on a global basis. Several toxic compounds, such as heavy metals, often contaminate soils. The main sources of heavy metal pollution are mining, industries and application of metal-containing pesticides, fertilizers and sewage sludge. In recent decades there has been increasing concern with heavy metals, not only because of their toxicity to animals, plants and microorganisms, but also because they are highly toxic, mutagenic and/or carcinogenic to humans.

Due to their small size, which provides a large contact area that can interact with the surrounding environment, microorganisms are the first biota showing the impact of toxic compounds. Microorganisms being in intimate contact with the soil environment are considered to be the best indicators of soil pollution. In general, they are very sensitive to low concentrations of contaminants and provide a rapid response to soil perturbation.

Rhizobium spp. are ubiquitous gram-negative soil bacteria that have a profound scientific and agronomic significance due to their ability to establish nitrogen-fixing symbiosis with legumes, which is of major importance to the maintenance of soil fertility.

There is increasing evidence of the adverse effects of heavy metals on soil microbial processes, including on soil enzymatic activities. Soil enzymes are the driving force behind all the biochemical transformations occurring in the soil. Enzymes catalyse all biochemical reactions and are an integral part of nutrient cycling and soil fertility. Therefore, this chapter evaluated the impact of heavy metals on *Rhizobium* populations isolated from a lead mine which activity ceased 50 years ago. In order to reach this goal some physicochemical parameters that influence metal bioavailability was determined, as well as metal concentrations in soils. Soil enzyme activities are highly affected by soil conditions and their evaluation may provide useful information on soil microbial activity and survival. For this reason, soil enzyme activities have been proposed as biological indicators of pollution, specially organic, but information about the influence of heavy metal on soil enzyme activities is scarcer. Thus, it was determined the activity of enzymes such as dehydrogenases, hydrolases, phosphatases, catalase and lipase in heavy metal contaminated soils. Metal tolerance of *Rhizobium* isolates was also screened in artificial media supplemented with different metals (Pb, Cd, As, Ni, Cu and Co) and their tolerance related to soil contamination and enzyme activities.

This chapter can widen the knowledge about the pressure that soil microflora experience under the direct effect of different metals. *Rhizobium* and soil enzyme activities may be useful for the evaluation of agricultural soil pollution, which may be used on the improvement of soil productivity or on the reclaim of contaminated soils.

Chapter 9 - Virus-binding proteins (VBPs) are bacterial proteins to which human viruses preferentially adsorb in water environments. VBPs were discovered from a bacterial culture derived from activated sludge with affinity chromatography assay in which a viral capsid peptide was used as a ligand. As an example of the VBP isolation, the recovery and characterization of Adenovirus-binding proteins (AdVBPs) were introduced. The significant adsorption of infectious Adenovirus (AdV) particles to the isolated AdVBPs was confirmed with enzyme-linked immunosorbent assay (ELISA). A number of AdVBPs were successfully obtained from crude proteins extracted from activated sludge culture, which was revealed by two-dimensional electrophoresis. The determination of the N-terminal amino acid sequence of AdVBP indicates that some AdVBPs are derived from outer membrane proteins of bacteria, and exhibit virus-binding ability under conditions of water environments. The methodology for acquiring VBP gene from a genomic DNA library of activated sludge microorganisms was also described. The consensus-degenerate hybrid oligonucleotide primer (CODEHOP) method, touchdown PCR, seminested PCR and inosine-incorporated primers were employed to effectively screen the VBP gene from a genomic DNA library. Since VBPs are expected to be stable under conditions of water environments, VBPs might be utilized as feasible and inexpensive viral adsorbents in technologies for virus detection and enrichment from water specimens. In order to utilize VBPs as viral adsorbents in various technologies, it is desirable to prepare VBPs for key viruses responsible for waterborne infectious diseases, or to discover VBPs with a broad affinity to several species of pathogenic viruses, though significant research progress is required to find the VBPs with a broad affinity.

Chapter 10 - Coastal aquatic environments often suffer from anthropogenic pressure, posing severe threats to human health related to presence of pollutants in seawaters. Recent trends in environmental monitoring aiming at public health preservation highlight the need of a deep revision of the standards up to now used in the assessment of seawater quality, focusing the importance of new bacterial indicators, more reliable than those previously used, in the control of short and large scale-occurring pollution phenomena. Selected bacterial species (*Escherichia coli*) or related parameters are currently included in monitoring programs of marine environmental quality; they allow to track the occurrence and evolution of bacterial pollution events, and prevent human health risks related to the use of polluted waters. Moreover, several limitations intrinsic to culture methods traditionally used to detect bacterial pathogens (long response times, low specificity, high costs) confirm their inadequacy for coastal monitoring, stressing the need for updated standard analytical procedures. In response to this, several research efforts at the CNR - IAMC have recently been devoted to improve technical equipments and methodologies for the assessment of microbiological quality of seawater. The chapter reviews recent advances in coastal microbial pollution monitoring achieved in the framework of projects funded by the Italian Ministry for Scientific Research, addressing the detection and enumeration of *Escherichia coli* in seawater as an indicator of faecal pollution. A summary of the innovative methodologies (the fluorescent antibody method, the □-glucuronidase assay and Real time PCR) developed and optimised at the IAMC laboratory for monitoring bathing waters is reported, which allowed the high-resolution quantitative measurement of target bacterial molecules and accurate quantification of faecal pollution phenomena. These methods provided results significantly related to plate counts within a few hours from sampling, highlighting the main advantages (rapidity and specificity) related to the detection of bacterial antigens or molecules as markers of faecal pollution. New combined fluorescence-viability staining protocols were also set up, capable to detect bacteria which persist into seawater under different physiological states, maintaining intact living properties, and therefore have a pathogenic potential. The proposed methods proved to be rapid and specific analytic approaches for the screening of coastal areas with various degrees of pollution; therefore they offer new interesting perspectives to prevent outbreaks of waterborne diseases. Data obtained by these new analytical procedures encourage the use of *E. coli* or related parameters as successful tools for early warning of seawater bacterial pollution.

In: Environmental Microbiology Research Trends
Editor: G. V. Kurladze, pp. 1-57
ISBN: 978-1-60021-939-9

Chapter 1

EVALUATION AND VERIFICATION OF SOIL REMEDIATION

Katalin Gruiz[1], Mónika Molnár[1] and Éva Fenyvesi[2]
[1] Budapest University of Technology and Economics, Department of Applied Biotechnology and Food Science, Budapest, Hungary
[2] Cyclolab Cyclodextrin R&D Laboratory Ltd., Budapest, Hungary

ABSTRACT

With the increasing number of innovative remediation technologies, the decision makers, the owners and other stakeholders should be guided by useful information ensured by a technology-assessment tool, which evaluates the technological, environmental, eco- and cost-efficiency of the technology. Especially the in situ technologies based on natural biological processes are mistrusted and suffer from lack of confidence, due to missing information, objective evaluation and transparent verification.

A complex evaluation/verification system was developed for soil remediation technologies, which can be applied generally both to bioremediation and in situ soil treatment. The multistage verification methodology includes 1. material balance, that is the mass flow balance of the soil phases and the modified or eliminated pollutant amount, 2. quantitative characterisation of the environmental risk before, during and after the remediation, 3. cost-efficiency or if necessary and possible, cost-benefit assessment and 4. SWOT analysis.

Both of the field applications introduced in this publication were the first demonstrations of the innovative technologies, developed in our laboratories in the frame of Hungarian R&D Projects. Main goals of the first field applications were to prove the findings of the laboratory experiments and to acquire data for the technology-verification, which has been developed and recommended for wider use by the authors.

This contribution introduces in detail the complex verification system developed and applied for the characterisation and evaluation of two very different in situ remediation technologies: 1. the cyclodextrin technology" (CDT), which is an innovative bioremediation developed and used for soil contaminated with hydrocarbons of low bioavailability; 2. the combined chemical and phytostabilisation (CCP) applied for point and diffuse sources contaminated by toxic metals.

The randomly methylated ß-cyclodextrin (RAMEB) was found to significantly enhance the bioremediation and detoxification of the transformer oil-contaminated soil increasing the bioavailability of the pollutants and the activity of indigenous microorganisms. The feasibility of the innovative cyclodextrin-enhanced bioremediation (CDT) was demonstrated in a field application. The verification of the CDT using the developed innovative tool-box proved the efficiency and the competitiveness of the CDT.

The combined chemical and phytostabilisation (CCP) is based on the concept of reducing risk making the metals irreversibly immobile, as well as stopping runoff and soil erosion. The results of the stabilisation microcosm experiments indicate that it is possible to reduce the mobility of toxic metals such as Cd, Zn, Pb, Cu and As by soil treatment with chemical stabilizers. The complex technology-monitoring of the CCP enabled differentiation between extractability, bioavailability and accessibility for plant uptake.

The development and application of a uniform remediation technology-verification system makes possible better understanding and evaluation of the remediation technologies and is able to increase trust in remediation, including in situ biotechnologies. The first demonstration of the technologies introduced here make possible the evaluation of the verification system itself and show the direction toward further development on the basis of the first experiences.

1. INTRODUCTION

Many innovative soil and groundwater remediation technologies have been developed, are ready for application and some of them have proven their applicability and performance in demonstrations, but the market entry and widespread practical implementation of these innovative remediation technologies is very slow.

On the other hand environmental quality criteria and legal and social requirements are higher and higher. The association between the result (higher quality) and the effort (cost) in quality assurance shows a steep increase toward high quality standards after fulfilment of basic requirements. The relation between the higher quality and costs is true in case of the present risk management practice, including site assessment and remediation. With the application of innovative site assessment and remediation techniques, higher quality can be ensured at the same or lower costs (Figure 1).

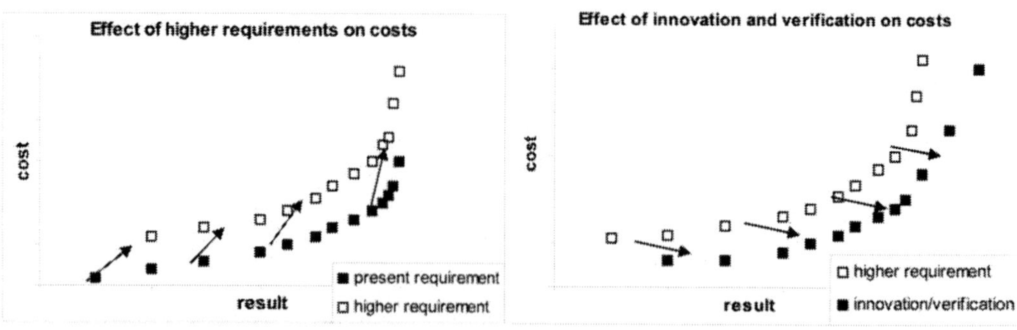

Figure 1. Relation between effort/costs and result in the environmental management

1.1. Environmental Technology Verification and Accreditation

Many European R & D projects are focussed on innovative technologies in the environmental field. Most of the expediently applicable methodologies as part of the latest environmental management approach have been developed and tested during the last years, part of them were verified and validated and only a few of them became standardized. Even the standardized new methods get only slowly commercialized due to the traditionally applied "chemical" environmental protection approach, to the lack of information and trust that hinders expansion of these efficient, mostly biological or ecological methods.

The practical, useful and uniform evaluation and characterisation of the innovative technologies are necessary to shorten the time between development and application of a new technology, to increase confidence and promote the commercialisation of the new remediation technologies.

Technology verification in the European wording means mainly the bureaucratic/administrative procedure, which leads to the accreditation of the technology or of the user/owner of the technology. The European Commission has decided to set up a European "*Environmental Technologies Verification*"(ETV) System in order to improve the competitiveness of European technologies on the Global market. Related to environmental technology verification a lot of information is available. The establishment of networks of testing centres, in order to develop common or co-ordinated protocols and practices of technology assessment in the water, soil or land use, is being promoted using Community research funding.

One of the aims of *Environmental Technologies Action Plan* (ETAP) is establishing a mechanism to validate objectively the performance of these products and to increase purchasers' confidence in new environmental technologies (http://ec.europa.eu/environment/etap/index_en.htm).

PROMOTE is integrated in a network of ETV related activities on European level, funded by the European Commission. PROMOTE develops prenormative protocols for credible environmental technology verification. The overall aim of the PROMOTE project is to set up an efficiency control and performance verification system for soil-groundwater protection and rehabilitation. The system will be based on a performance verification concept and generic testing as applied by a European network of testing centres (www.promote-etv.org).

TESTNET (*Towards a European verification system for Environmentally sound Technology*) launched by EU in this field is to design, develop and test an ETV system. Main objective of TESTNET is the development of a structure of organisations and of a system for the verification of ready-to-market innovative environmentally sound technologies (www.est-testnet.net).

The bureaucratic procedure of accreditation, however, should also be based on a technological / engineering tool, which measures the efficiency of the technology, the connected environmental risk compartments and the economical and social elements.

1.2. REMEDIATION TECHNOLOGY VERIFICATION

The Hungarian MOKKA (2005–2008) project (www.mokkka.hu) aims to develop a science-based technology-verification system harmonised with ETV. The MOKKA Verification System is restricted to the evaluation of the efficiency of the technology itself, and can be integrated into the administrative verification protocol with a wider scope. A complex assessment/verification tool for the evaluation of the innovative soil remediation technologies has been developed and applied with the aim to support decision-making, mainly in the selection of the suitable technology-alternatives, finding the best available technology (BAT) or – in case of innovative technologies, that have not entered the market yet, – a better technology, than the best available one.

The MOKKA verification system (Figure 2) includes quantitative and qualitative tools for the characterisation of the remediation technology. All the important, but not quantitative aspects are integrated in the SWOT tool, which is also part of the recommended methodology. If within the SWOT list there are quantifiable technology-specific elements (both positive and negative), they should be added to the quantitative characteristics and evaluated by objective (measured) values.

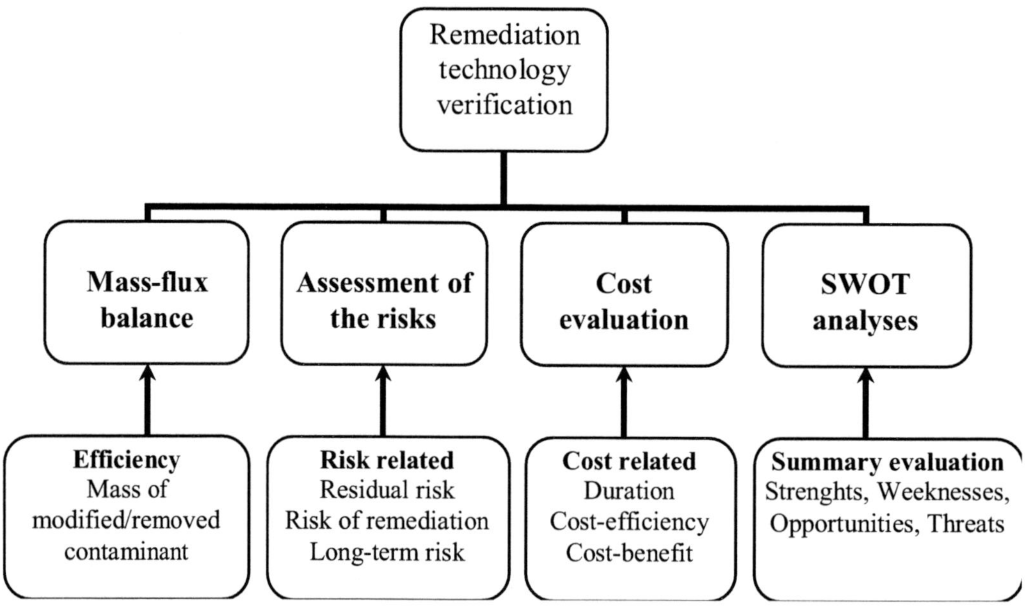

Figure 2. The MOKKA technology-verification system for the evaluation of soil remediation

The multistage MOKKA tool for the verification of the remediation includes at present:

- Material balance, including the eliminated or modified amount of pollutant
- The quantitative characterisation of the environmental risk of the site before and after remediation
- The assessment of the environmental risks of the technology due to emission during and after the technology application

- The assessment of the regional or global risk of the technology due to energy and water consumption and the load on global environment by greenhouse effect, ozone depletion, acid rains, the use of non-renewable and renewable resources, etc.
- Cost-efficiency or if necessary, cost-benefit assessment and
- SWOT analysis

The MOKKA verification tool is intended to be uniform, applicable for any remediation technology. As a part of the remediation strategy, together with the site assessment and technology-selection, the complex monitoring of the technology in aid of good quality verification should be planned. It has special importance in case of in situ remediation.

Technology-related information used for technology-selection and easy decision-making should be gathered already during the site assessment/monitoring (Figure 3). Site assessment, risk assessment and technology related assessment should be applied as an integrated tool. Risk assessment must not be considered as a separate tool, it should be planned and applied considering the possible risk reduction measures. The judgement of a contaminated site is much better, when we have got information on the possible solutions already during the site assessment, and instead of a simple risk value, which indicates only the necessity and the scale of the risk reduction, a certain solution can be predicted. The goal of site assessment should be the integrated assessment of the quantity of the risk and the technology-related characteristics of the site and the contaminant. The complex information on the contaminant and the site makes possible the stepwise technology selection for remediation.

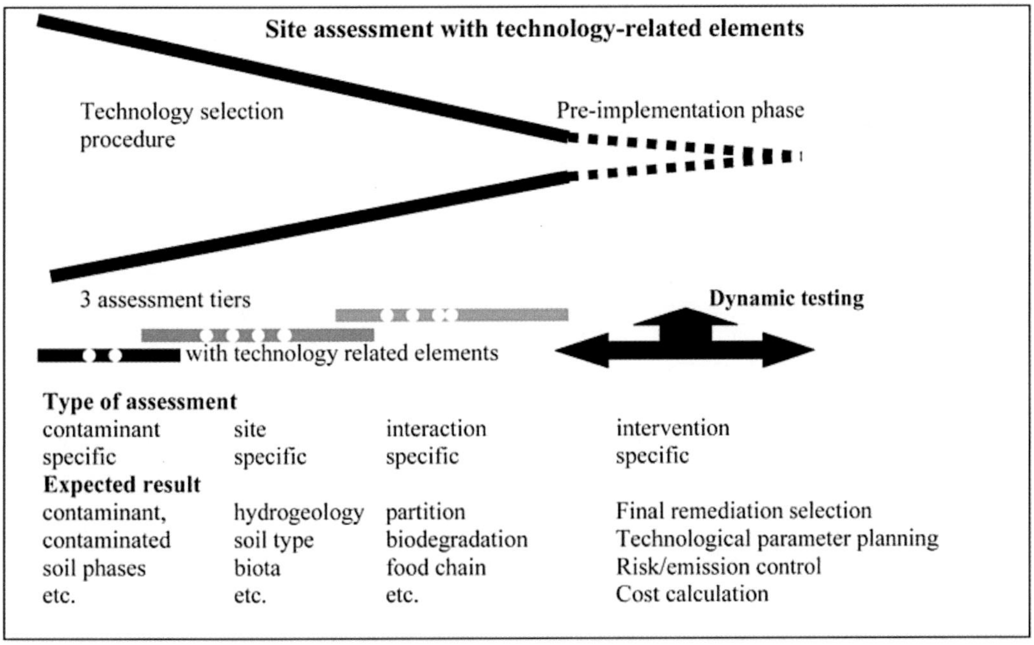

Figure 3. Collecting technology-related information during the tiered site assessment

During the application of the remediation, technology-monitoring should ensure not only the follow up of the history of the technology-application by measuring the technological parameters but also the evaluation of all the environmental and social (emissions, load on renewable resources, load on the society, etc.) as well as the economical aspects (costs and benefits) to evaluate. The technology verification considers the local, regional and global context in the risk, cost and benefit assessment (Figure 4).

The technology-monitoring has the following main goals:

1. To monitor technological parameters, like temperature, pH, redox-potential, aeration, water flow, flow of additives, products, etc. to control the efficient functioning of the technology.
2. To control possible emission from the technology to minimise local, regional or global environmental risk.
3. To measure energy and water consumption to characterise the eco-efficiency of the technology.
4. To measure (calculate from measured values) costs.
5. To assess social aspects.
6. To characterise the technology from any other, e.g. site specific, contaminant specific, country or vendor-specific point of views.

The data collected during technology monitoring will serve as the fundament of the technology-verification.

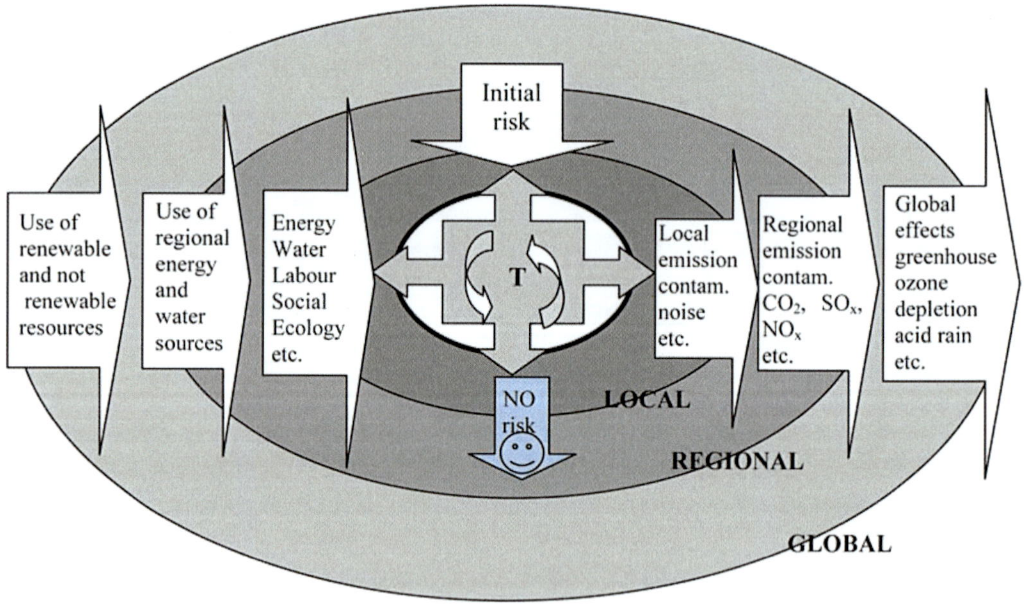

Figure 4. Local, regional and global context of a remediation technology (T)

The complex assessment tool developed and applied for the characterisation and evaluation of *in situ* remediation in the frame of the Hungarian MOKKA R&D project is introduced in this chapter. The feasibility of the MOKKA verification methodology is demonstrated on two complex *in situ* remediation cases, the first one for soil polluted by organic contaminant, the second for soil contaminated by toxic metals.

1. A combined biological and chemical soil treatment technology, used for transformer oil polluted soil and groundwater, based on in situ biodegradation, temporary in situ soil washing and ex situ physico-chemical groundwater-treatment, accelerated with cyclodextrin (CDT) (Molnár et al, 2003; Molnár et al, 2005).
2. A combined chemical and phytostabilisation (CCP), used for toxic metal contaminated mine-waste and polluted soil, based on the immobilisation of metals in the soil reducing their availablilty for water and plants (Gruiz and Feigl, 2006).

1.3. Characteristics and Monitoring of *In Situ* Soil Remediation

The control, regulation and monitoring of in situ technologies can be adequately handled by the "reactor approach". According to this approach the in situ soil remediation is considered as an engineering tool, executed in closed or partly closed reactor construction or isolated prisms.

In case of *in situ* technologies the material to be treated is not placed into a controlled reactor, equipped with operation-tools, but the operation-tools are put into the undisturbed soil.

With the reactor-approach one can well understand the in situ technologies and evaluate them similarly to the reactor-technologies, creating a gradual series of closed reactors, open-reactors and *in situ* quasi-reactors. The physical volume of an ex situ reactor can be substituted with the contaminated soil volume of the in situ quasi-reactor, the physical borders (walls) of the closed reactor, with the range of actions applied in situ (the scope of ventilation, or pumping).

The analyses and testing of soil in general, maybe a problem, starting from sampling, through physico-chemical analyses (extraction, digestion), to the testing of the biological state, the effects and risks of the contaminated soil, the physico-chemical and biological availability of the contaminant. The technology-related and pre-implementation testing is still at a developing stage (Figure 3).

In case of ex situ soil treatment one is faced with an easier situation – compared to the in situ cases – due to the relative homogeneity of the soil material to be treated and to the physical availability of the soil, to the relative easiness of sampling. It means that a well-established sampling strategy makes possible a good quality technology-monitoring. The follow-up of the processes is possible from soil gas, pore-water, leachate, or whole-soil samples, and the placement of sensors into the soil is also relatively easy. The data and their interpretation can result high quality information, supposing the application of modern environmental analytical as well as biological and toxicity test methods and their integrated evaluation and interpretation.

Applying an *in situ* remediation one is faced to two basic problems when sampling and analysing whole soil from the vadouse zone (three phase soil) or from the saturated zone (two phase soil). Core samples from boreholes give a false picture of the site. 1. Heterogeneity of both the soil and the contaminant. These heterogeneities may exceed the scale of changes in time, therefore to get an "average" sample or to take samples in different times from the same place is not possible. *In situ* measurements and sensors may help to a certain extent. 2. In case of sensitive hydrogeology or in case of a treatment applying water and soil gas circulation or directed flow, a borehole may cause disturbance and increase the risk of pollutant transport. To avoid these problems during the monitoring of *in situ* technologies it is recommended that the mobile soil phases, like soil gas and groundwater are sampled and analysed. It is advantageous also because these phases represent the quasi-average of the total treated volume. As they are circulated for technological reasons, sampling does not disturb the inner soil. From the data measured on soil-gas and soil-water it is possible to extrapolate to the whole soil, knowing the inner rules of the soil "black-box", like partition of the contaminant between soil phases, effects of soil pH and redox-potential on the chemical form and effects of the contaminant, mechanism of biodegradation, etc.

1.3.1. Technology Monitoring and the Mass-Balance of Bioremediation

To follow bioremediation, for example the biodegradation-based remediation, the microbial degradation activity has to be quantified. The biological processes in the soil, like biodegradation, bioleaching, biological stabilisation, bioaccumulation, can be described by the following general equation, where S = substrate, P = product of the microbial metabolic activity:

$$\mathbf{S + additive \xrightarrow{\text{soil microflora}} P + side\text{-}product}$$

The contaminant serves as substrate for the soil microbes, going through the microbial metabolic pathway producing harmless end-products (P) and side-products. Any element of this equation can be used for monitoring, to follow and control the biological process: the decrease of the substrate or of the additive, the increase of the product and of the side products, the quantitative and qualitative characteristics of the soil and of the soil microflora, like nutrient supply, pH, redox-potential of the soil and cell numbers, cell activities, enzyme activities, indicator species, etc. These elements can be measured in a direct or in an indirect way, e.g. instead of the concentration of the sorbed contaminant, the dissolved value is measured then the sorbed value is calculated by the partition coefficient (Kp), or instead of the concentration of the product, the pH is measured, if the product is an acid, or instead of the substrate decrease the CO_2 as product of aerobic biodegradation, etc. is measured.

Some often-applied measurement endpoints for the monitoring of bioremediation are given below. The end-points are grouped as relevant to soil, soil-microflora, substrate and to the product.

Soil-relevant monitoring-endpoints for bioremediation

- Soil or/and groundwater nutrient content (N- and P-source in case of biodegradation or plant activity, organic contents, microelement contents, etc.)
- Value and changes of pH of the soil, pore-water and groundwater
- Redox-potential or redox-indicators and their changes during the remediation in soil and groundwater
- Temperature
- Moisture content

Soil microflora- and plant-relevant monitoring-endpoints for bioremediation

- Whole soil, pore water and groundwater microbial cell concentration (total cell count, bacterial and fungal cell counts, aerobic, facultative anaerobic or anaerobic cell-concentrations, etc.)
- Microbial cell counts with specific biodegradative or other metabolic activities (hydrocarbon or PAH-degrading microbes, cometabolic strains, etc.)
- Cell count of microbes responsible for bioleaching, biological mobilisation and stabilisation, anaerobic digestion, rhyzosphere formation, etc. (sulphide oxidizing and sulphate-reducing bacteria, phosphate mobilising bacteria, metanogenic archea, etc.
- Plant biomass quantity and quality
- Microbes or plants with specific adaptation or resistance
- Genetic markers of total cell count or specific metabolic abilities or resistance
- Biochemical markers: total cell count and activity or specific metabolic abilities or resistance

Substrate(=contaminant)-relevant monitoring-endpoints for bioremediation

- Soil or/and groundwater: extractable organic or inorganic contaminant content
- Soil or/and groundwater total organic or inorganic contaminant content
- Soil gas O_2 content in case of aerobic biological processes
- Soil water electron-acceptor-concentration (NO_3^-, SO_4^{2-}, Fe^{3+}, acetate) for anaerobic biological processes
- Soil, pore water and groundwater toxicity in case of toxic contaminants

Product-relevant monitoring-endpoints for bioremediation

- Metabolic intermediers or end-products (NO_2, HCl, etc.) in soil phases
- The end products of the mineralization (CO_2, NH_4^+, etc.) in soil phases
- Effects of acidification or alkalisation in the soil
- Products of the changes of the redox-potential in the soil
- End-products and mobilised or accumulated contaminants in plants

The relatively homogeneous mobile soil phases, the soil gas and the groundwater are recommended for *in situ* technology monitoring and verification. Nevertheless the same matrix and measurement data can be used for the control and regulation of bioremediation to ensure optimal environment for the desired soil-microbial activity. The best technology-indicators are the volatile and water soluble little molecules, which get from the biofilm into the easy-to-sample mobile soil phases by partition. Substrates or products bound or strongly sorbed to the solid phase can be analysed only from the solid phase, which causes heterogeneity problems and high standard deviation in analytical results.

1.3.2. Environmental Monitoring

Besides technology monitoring, environmental monitoring of in situ remediation plays very important role in controlling emission and other risky processes to prevent nature and humans from adverse effects. The environmental monitoring data are necessary and used in the complex technology-verification, both on local and regional level risk assessments. Environmental monitoring plays extremely important role in the verification of in situ soil and groundwater remediation.

In situ and Ex situ

The detailed comparison of the consequences of in situ and ex situ soil bioremediation application clarifies that environmental risk due to emission from the soil treatment technology is primarily associated with the character of the pollutant (volatile, water-soluble, etc.) and secondarily with the ex situ or in situ application of the technology. Ex situ soil bioremediation takes place mainly in open reactors where the control of the emission or blocking the transport is always an additional measure.

As an example let us discuss the case of a biodegradable volatile soil-pollutant. The popular ex situ treatment in prisms results in a relatively large free surface with direct atmospheric contact making possible intensive volatilisation. Additional volatilisation risk is present during the excavation and transport of the contaminated soil. In situ bioventing applying gas exhaust and controlled soil-gas treatment at the same site, results in minimal emission of the volatile compound.

Ambivalent is the risk of water-soluble contaminants during in situ and ex situ soil treatments. The ex situ application should be completed with a leachate collecting and treating system, while *in situ* the emission of the water soluble compounds can be controlled by creating depression in the water pumping wells and treating contaminated groundwater ex situ. This is kind of source control, because by continuously lowering the water-table contaminated water emission from the *in situ* treated soil volume is completely restricted. The other possibility is blocking of the transport routes by permeable reactive barriers, and passive in situ treatment of the contaminated groundwater.

In case of sorbed contaminants with high Kp value (concentration in solid phase: concentration in water phase) the risk for uncontrolled mobilisation of the contaminant is low, that is the reason for the application of stabilisation technologies, which reduce the mobility of the contaminant irreversibly. The ex situ treatment of the soil polluted with the same sorbed pollutant increases the risk of dust and solid emission.

Integrated Monitoring

For a good quality environmental monitoring an integrated methodology is required in general: the physico-chemical analyses should be combined with environmental toxicity testing, ecological and biological assessments (Figure 5). It is extremely important when the polluted site is an old, inherited one with not completely identified mixture of contaminants. In such cases the assessment programme is not able to include all possible contaminants and intermediers, also the interactions between contaminants, contaminant and soil matrix and contaminant and soil microflora may result in endless risky effects, so the integration of toxicity and other effect-measuring methods is essential.

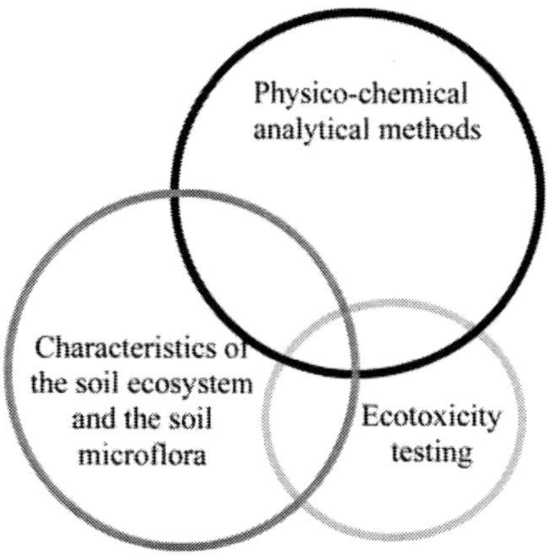

Soil Testing Triad (Gruiz, 2005)
During the monitoring of the bioremediation both the physico-chemical characteristics and the information about the state of the soil microflora are important. Part of the physico-chemical analyses serves the characterisation of the biological activity: respiration, metabolites, etc. Ecotoxicity testing serves the safety and gives information on bioavailability of the contaminant. In case of *in situ* remediation, ecotoxicity testing may play role in the monitoring of emission from the technology.
In the final phase of remediation it serves the qualification of the remedied soil.
The technology monitoring makes possible1. To run the technology on the optimum
2. To control and regulate the technology
3. To control the emission
4. To control and qualify the treated soil

Figure 5. Soil Testing Triad

Specific markers can be selected from the characterisation of the ecosystem (diversity, special species or variants with biodegrading abilities or resistance) and can be used in the follow up of environmental quality and of the short and long-term efficiency of remediation.

1.3.3. Post-Remediation Monitoring of Treated Sites

After-care of treated contaminated sites is always an important issue, because one can never be sure that the pollutant has been removed completely. More sensitive new land uses increase the risk and require higher precaution.

There are larger differences between the after-care of ex-situ and in-situ treatments, than in the technology monitoring itself, because excavation of the soil means not only removal of the risky pollution but also getting an open picture on the inside of the black-box which increases decision quality. Nevertheless after-monitoring of the ex situ soil remediation is also required, but the after care of the site and the treated soil are divided into two. Monitoring of the treated site should be confirmed by the final, cleaned-up state of the former contaminated soil-phases. Another part of the after-care is connected to the treatment, qualification and disposal or reuse of the ex situ treated soil. After-monitoring is necessary even in areas with less sensitive land uses.

The after-care of in situ treatment is more complex. It assumes monitoring not only of the treated soil, but of the whole site. After-monitoring of sites, where technology based on the mobilisation and removal of contaminants was applied, means the checking of the concentration and/or the effects of the residual contaminant. Once the contaminants' mobility is reduced by a stabilising technology, a long term integrated monitoring is needed to control the chemical forms and possible harmful effects of the contaminants.

Integrated monitoring is needed for the after-care of the remediated contaminated sites: an adequate combination of physico-chemical methods and toxicity-testing is to be applied. The evaluation and interpretation of the measured data should consider the future land use.

1.4. Two *in situ* Biotechnologies Evaluated by the MOKKA Verification System

1.4.1. *In situ* Cyclodextrin Technology (CDT)

CDT is an innovative bioremediation which applies cyclodextrin (CD) to further intensify a combined bioventing and bioflushing type remediation technology based on aerobic biodegradation eliminating the bottleneck caused by low availability of the contaminants in soil.

Low bioavailability of hydrophobic pollutants may limit their biodegradation by the "cell factory" in soils. Cyclodextrins are able to solubilise and mobilise high K_{ow} (octanol-water partition coefficient: the partition between soil water and solid phase is proportional with Kow) contaminants, and make them more available for the soil microflora. The use of CD may increase the bioavailability of poorly degradable pollutants and in turn intensify soil bioremediation (Gruiz et al, 1996; Fava et al, 1998; Wang et al, 1998, Bardi et al, 2003). It has been demonstrated that randomly methylated β-cyclodextrin (RAMEB) is able to decrease the toxic effects of contaminants on soil microbes, plants and animals (Gruiz et al., 1996). RAMEB was successfully used as bioavailability enhancing additive in soil bioremediation for diesel-oil in unsaturated soil by Molnár et al. (2003), for transformer oil both in saturated and unsaturated soil zones by Leitgib et al. (2003) and Molnár et al. (2005). It was found that RAMEB with one-year half-life time is slowly biodegradable in the three-phase soil (Fenyvesi et al, 2005).

The CDT was tested and demonstrated in several laboratory tests, microcosms and pilots, and – as the top of the increasing size of the experiments – on an inherited contaminated site with long-term pollution derived from a leaking spare-transformer of a transformer station in Budapest. A complex methodology was applied for the remediation of the soil and groundwater. The in situ bioventing of the unsaturated zone was combined with the *ex situ* physico-chemical treatment of the groundwater and the temporary flushing of the unsaturated soil. Randomly methylated ß-cyclodextrin (RAMEB) was applied to improve desorption, solubilisation and biological availability of hydrophobic contaminants. The field experiment has confirmed the laboratory findings. The calculated time requirement of the CDT from the results is considerably less, only 0.5–1.5 years compared to the 2.5 years needed by the next best technology-alternative.

1.4.2. Combined in situ Chemical- and Phytostabilisation (CCP)

CCP aims at immobilising the contaminants, in the contrary to CDT which is based on the mobilising effect of CD and biodegradation. Phytostabilisation can be combined with chemical stabilisation to lessen the leachability, mobility and bioavailability of toxic metals in the soil.

Heavy metal contamination at former mining sites is of global concern, because it poses a major threat to human and environmental health. Traditional and conventional engineering approaches rely on techniques possessing high cost, such as excavation and land filling, soil washing, thermal treatment (Vangronsveld and Cunningham, 1998). Phytoremediation may present a viable economical option (Raskin and Ensley, 2000). It has already received significant scientific and commercial attention (Salt et al, 1998; Meagher et al, 2000; Dietz and Schnoor, 2001; McGarth and Zhao, 2003).

Phytoremediation is a generic term for several ways in which plants can be used to clean up contaminated soils and water. Plants may remove or stabilize metal contaminants in soil. The most well known methods used to phytoremediate metal contaminated sites can be phytoextraction, rhizofiltration and phytostabilisation. Phytostabilisation is a relatively new and rapidly developing field in which heavy metal-tolerant plants are used to reduce the mobility of heavy metals by several mechanisms. The plant cover hinders leaching of metals, dusting and erosion, therefore reduces metal transport on all possible transport pathways. The revegetation and the activity of the rhizosphere increase the complexity and humus-content of the soil and result in a decrease in the metal-mobility. The amount of metal, which gets into the food chain, is diminished by the selection and application of plants, in which the translocation of the metals from the roots to the shoots is small. Phytostabilisation is an effective technology, proven by successful studies performed in both Europe and USA (van der Leile et al, 2001; Schwitzguebel et al, 2002; Vangronsveld et al, 1995).

Phytostabilisation is usually combined with chemical stabilisation applying chemical stabilisers added to the soil before settling of the plants. The mobility of bioavailable toxic metals in the soil will be lower on the effect of the chemical stabilizers, enabling the sprouting of seeds and growing of plants. Since the plant contains less metal, it becomes healthier and a higher biomass can be produced. On the effect of addition of certain chemical additives leaching of toxic metals from soils will be reduced and as a final result the environmental risk of the polluted soil and plants grown on the soil will decrease.

CCP was evaluated on the basis of microcosm and field experiments used for the planning of the *in situ* remediation of a former mining site in the Toka-valley in the Northern part of Hungary as part of a Hungarian R&D project, BÁNYAREM, 2004–2007 (www.ecorisc.hu). Fly ash was selected as the best chemical stabilizer and ray grace as plant not accumulating the toxic metals. Field demonstrations are still in progress. The first field-results validated the laboratory findings: the stabilising additives reduced toxic metal mobility, the leaching of the contaminant with water and plants were able to grow on completely non-vegetated, toxic mine waste after fly-ash treatment and were able to grow better on the contaminated garden soil. Also the metal accumulation of the vegetation was considerably reduced by the applied chemical stabilisation.

2. Materials and Methods

This chapter contains the description of the applied in situ biotechnologies (CDT and CCP), the characterisation of the contaminated sites, where the technologies have been applied and the technology-monitoring for data acquisition for the control and maintenance as well as for the verification of the two technologies.

2.1. CycloDextrin Enhanced Complex Technology (CDT)

Many small and large-scale laboratory experiments were performed and evaluated to find the optimal parameters of randomly methylated β-cyclodextrin (RAMEB) application that can be successfully used to enhance biodegradation of hydrocarbon pollutants in soil (Fenyvesi et al, 2003; Gruiz et al, 1996; Leitgib et al, 2003; Molnár et al, 2003). On the basis of the results acquired from laboratory studies a field demonstration on the remediation of an actual-site transformer oil-contaminated soil was designed and performed.

2.1.1. Description of the Transformer-Oil Contaminated Site

The selected site was an inherited contaminated site with a long-term pollution derived from a leaking spare-transformer of the Népliget Transformer Station in Hungary. The contaminated site for CDT demonstration was relatively small, 30 m^3 (50 t) of contaminated soil was treated.

The transformer oil (TO 40A) contamination has reached the groundwater. The chemical analyses of the environmental samples showed high level contamination (20 000–30 000 mg/kg extractable petroleum hydrocarbon (EPH) content and 20 000–44 000 mg/kg, extractable organic material (EOM) content in the soil at the upper 1–2 m, just under the transformer. The oil content of the subsurface water was: 0.99 mg/l. The concentration of the volatile fraction was under the detectable limit. Both the saturated and the unsaturated zones had to be decontaminated.

2.1.2. Laboratory Testing and Microcosm Experiments for the Development of CDT

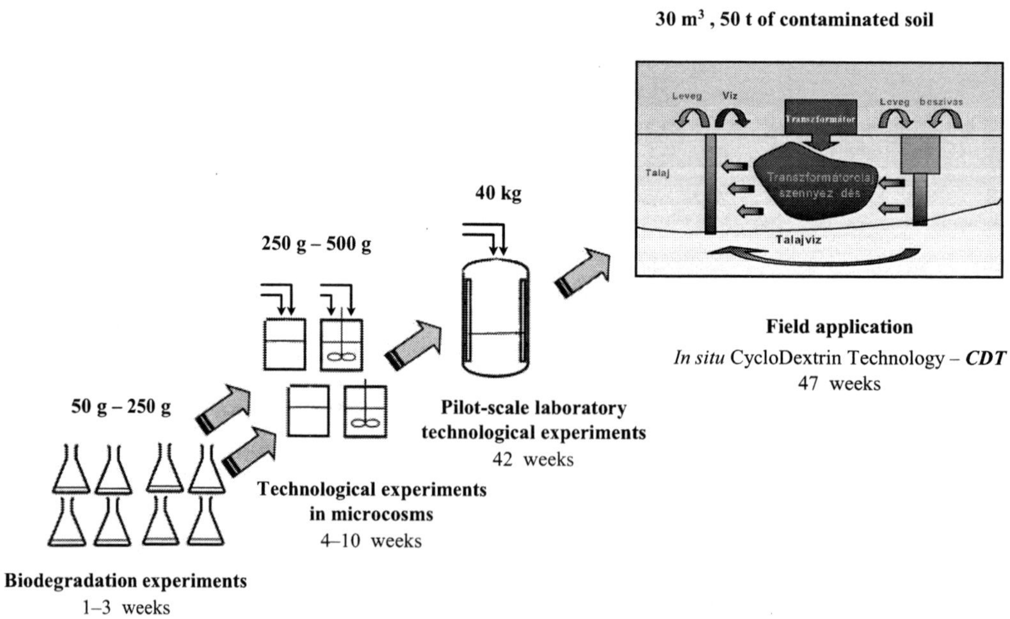

Figure 6. The scale-up from laboratory to the field: application of the cyclodextrin

The scale-up from the laboratory to the field included four steps during the development of the innovative CDT technology. Contaminants of different biodegradability and cyclodextrins of different mode of actions were tested in various combinations in small-scale biodegradation experiments. The influence of the soil type, cyclodextrin type, cyclodextrin concentration, aeration, pH, and moisture content on the biodegradation, the influence of other additives, nutrients and microbes on the technology was tested in soil microcosms, simulating real situations. Some parameters, like cyclodextrin type and concentration, necessary level of aeration and nutrients have been optimised for larger size application. To be able to follow the remediation on long term, larger amount of soil is needed. This was the main reason for the next scale-up step: pilot scale laboratory experiments (Figure 6). The methodology for the integrated technology-monitoring was worked out during these experiments.

2.1.3. Field Application of the Complex Cyclodextrin Technology

On the basis of the results and experiences of the stepwise growing size laboratory experiments, and the detailed assessment of the contaminated site the field experiment was designed.

Biological characterisation of the contaminated soil originated from the transformer station showed that the microflora has been adapted, able to biodegrade the contaminant, so the technology could be based upon the activity of the indigenous microflora. On a site, which is contaminated for long (3–4 years), a biotechnology able to utilise the activity of the cell factory is the most promising. The technological parameters found to be optimal in the laboratory experiments were assumed to provide optimal conditions for the transformer oil-degrading microbes. Based on the results of the site-assessment and the previous lab-scale technological experiments a site-specific combination of three technologies was selected and implemented:

- Treatment of the unsaturated zone by bioventing and intensification of the biodegradation with additives, like nutrients and cyclodextrin (RAMEB).
- *Ex situ* treatment of the groundwater after pumping it onto the surface
- Continuous moisture supply by slow infiltration of the treated water
- Temporary flushing the unsaturated and the saturated zones with part of the water treated on the surface.

Figure 7 shows the scheme of the complex technology, with the passive wells used for atmospheric air introduction and the active wells for water pumping and air exhaust (one well for the air and one combined well for air and water exhaust) and with the equipments on the surface for the water treatment and injection of the necessary additives.

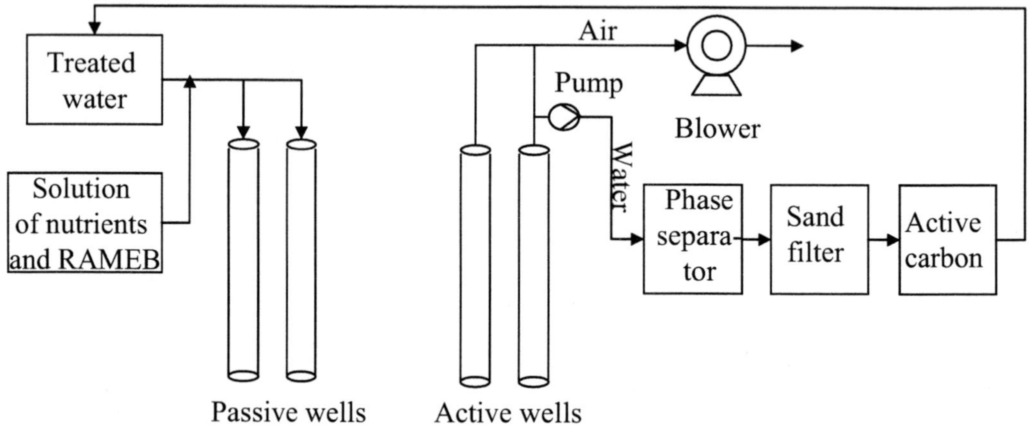

Figure 7. The scheme of the in situ CDT technology on the transformer station

Oxygen was supplied by bioventing for the biodegradation of hydrocarbons. Maximal air demand was calculated on the basis of the *McCarty's* equation (1988) of biodegradation of an average petroleum-hydrocarbon:

$$C_7H_{12} + 5\ O_2 + NH_3 = C_5H_7O_2N + 2\ CO_2 + 4\ H_2O \quad \textit{Eq. 1}$$

Molecular weights: 96 160 17 113 (biomass) 88 72

A slow air-flow was produced by a Siemens ELMO 2BH7-3G ventilator of low performance through aeration wells equipped with perforated casing. An air flow of 20–30 m^3/h was ensured.

Grundfos SP5 type plunger pump was applied for pumping of the ground-water, placed into the combined well. The treatment of the water happened in three steps: after phase separation thieving on sand filter and following adsorption on activated carbon was applied. The treated water was reserved in a closed tank and used in the technology for: 1. moistening of the treated soil volume by slow infiltration of part of the treated groundwater (15–16 m^3/day) through little ditches on the surface, 2. injection of nutrients, 3. temporary flushing of the contaminated soil volume by the RAMEB-solution.

Nutrients (40 kg chemical garden-fertilizer, containing 15% P_2O_5, 15% N and 15% K_2O (Pétisó, Agrolinz Chemikalien GmbH, Linz) were added 3 times, i.e., at the 9th, 13th and 21st week, along the 47-week experiment.

Randomly methylated ß-cyclodextrin (RAMEB) was applied to improve desorption of the contaminants strongly adsorbed on the surface of the soil particles and increase the contaminant concentration in the aqueous biofilms where the microbes work. Three times 10 kg aqueous RAMEB solution containing 50 % RAMEB (Cawasol W7 MTL, Wacker Chemie, Munich) was added together or separate with the nutrients dissolved in 1 or 2 m^3 water. Nutrients and additives have been supplied through the perforated casing of both the active and passive wells.

The injection of the additives was done after evolution of the steady-state of the soil system, while beside permanent water-pumping and air exhaust a constant O_2 and CO_2 value was measured in the exhaust gas and more-or-less constant oil-content in the ground-water.

The changes in the soil-gas and groundwater on the effect of nutrient supply and CD addition was measured and evaluated.

2.1.4. Integrated Assessment Tool for CDT Monitoring

Important part of a technology demonstration is the technology-monitoring. For the characterisation of processes in the contaminated soil a complex methodology should be used. (Gruiz, 2003; Molnár et al, 2003). The monitoring data reflect the processing of the technology, the activity of the soil microflora and the risks of the technology due to contaminant mobilisation. To evaluate the CDT an integrated tool-box including physico-chemical, biological and ecotoxicological methods was developed and applied.

Because the treated site was physically non-reachable from the surface, the technology monitoring was designed on the basis of analysing the exhausted soil gas and the ground water pumped out for treatment. The CO_2 and O_2 content of the soil gas is proportional with the microbiological activity, the oil content of the groundwater shows directly the biodegradation. The observed decrease in the oil content is the difference of the mobilised and the biodegraded amount.

Beside the frequent (at least once a week and after addition of the nutrients or RAMEB once a day) analysis of the gas (CO_2, O_2, volatile hydrocarbons) exhausted from the soil, and the water pumped out from the well, sampling and analyses of the whole soil were carried out at the start and end of the technology application.

Soil samples were analysed and characterized for the quality and quantity of the contaminant and of the microflora as well as for the toxicity of the soil using the integrated methodology by:

- physico-chemical characterisation of the soil and the groundwater: pH, redox-conditions, redox indicators, grain size distribution, air and water permeability, humus content, nutrient supply, microelement content,
- chemical methods for characterisation of the contaminants: oil content EOM and EPH content),
- biological methods: concentration of the aerobic heterotrophic cells, and that of the cells degrading transformer oil, the potential of the microflora to be activated, respiration, air demand,
- toxicity tests: using test organisms of three trophic levels, which together represent well the soil ecosystem and are sensitive to the contaminant.

Chemical Analyses

O_2 content and CO_2 content in soil gas: In the field experiments CO_2 and O_2 content in the air stream pumped out of the soil was measured by an Oldham Mx2Gas Analysator (Oldham Gas Detection Ltd. UK).

Volatile hydrocarbons in soil gas: The air stream pumped out of the soil was sampled by air-tight syringe (2 ml) and the needle of the syringe was sealed with a septum. The sample (1 ml) was injected into the gas chromatograph within 1 h after sampling. As the hydrocarbon content was negligible in the samples, this analysis was performed only at the start of the technology. These data showed that no treatment of the air was necessary.

TPH content in groundwater: The total petroleum hydrocarbon (TPH) content of the groundwater was analysed with gas chromatography after extraction with n-pentane (HS 1487–7, 1998).

Nutrients and redox-indicators in the groundwater: N, K, P, redox-potential, pH, conductivity, UV-absorbance, NO_2^-, NO_3^-, SO_4^{2+}, $Fe^{2+,}$ Fe^{3+}, etc. according to the need of biodegradation.

EOM content of the soil: Extractable organic material content was measured after hexane-acetone (2:1) extraction (HS 21470-94, 2001), by gravimetry.

EPH content of the soil: The Extractable Petroleum Hydrocarbon (EPH) content was analysed from the same hexane-acetone (2:1) extract by gas chromatography with flame ionisation detector (GC-FID) according to the Hungarian Standard (HS 21470-94, 2001).

Soil Toxicity

For direct contact ecotoxicity testing test-organisms of three different trophic levels were used. The interactive ecotoxicity tests ensure the contact between the soil and the test-organism, showing the actual toxicity and providing higher environmental reality than the tests with soil extract. These are self-developed tests based on similar Hungarian, German and European standard methods for wastewaters or hazardous waste materials. *Vibrio fischeri* bioluminescence test (DIN 38412, 1991; ISO 11348-1, 1998), *Sinapis alba* root and shoot elongation test (HS 21976-17, 1994) were modified for soil and together with *Folsomia candida* mortality test (ISO 11267, 1999) were used to follow-up the adverse effect of the soil during the laboratory and field experiments. *Vibrio fischeri* is a marine-living bacterium very commonly used for ecotoxicity testing. *Sinapis alba* is also widely used test plant, the white mustard. *Folsomia candida* also called Collembola and commonly known as springtail, is the most numerous and widely occurring insect in terrestrial ecosystems.

2.2. Combined Chemical and Phytostabilisation (CCP)

The combined chemical and phytostabilisation is being demonstrated on the field of a toxic metal polluted mining site in the Toka-valley, in Gyöngyösoroszi village in Hungary. Secondary diffuse pollution sources of mining origin were identified in the area and the residual pollution after removal of the point sources were subjected to combined chemical- and phytostabilisation (CCP).

The CCP for reducing the toxic metal emission and plant uptake from pollution sources was tested in laboratory microcosms. Field demonstration is still going on at two typical demonstration sites: the surface of an old mine waste dump, which is practically the mine yard, and the flooded hobby gardens. The complex evaluation of the CCP was completed on the basis of the microcosms and field experiments and the main results are presented here.

2.2.1. Description of the Toxic-Metal Contaminated Site

The site is a former lead-zinc sulphide ore mining-area in Hungary. Mining activity in the area has been suspended for 20 years, but final closure of the facility has not been done yet. The final mine closure is being planned and remediation scenarios are evaluated. Acidic-mine drainage has been continuously limed and the lime-precipitate has been settled and dumped in open reservoirs for 20 years, from 1985 to 2006. In 2006 a new mine-water treatment plant was established with a closed system and the open precipitate lagoons were emptied. Before the establishment of the neutralisation plant in 1985, the mine outflow entered directly the surface water system, where it was *in situ* neutralised. This lime precipitate is up to now part of the sediment of the surface water system.

Further contaminant source is the flotation tailings dump of 4 million tons of uncovered, highly contaminated waste material and the diffusely disposed, highly eroded mine waste heaps all over the area. Complex leaching, weathering, erosion and deflation are responsible for the emission and transport of the toxic metal containing waste material and its deposition in the sediments of the surface waters. The non-vegetated spots are long term sources of dissolved (ionic) toxic metals transported by runoff water and contaminated solid material transported by wind and water erosion (Gruiz and Feigl, 2006; Vaszita et al. 2006).

The sediment of the surface water system is deposited from year-to year on the regularly flooded gardens and by irrigation to the soil of many of the surrounding hobby gardens. Huge floods occur every 5 years, which mobilise and transport normally settled and stable sediment and affect the regularly not flooded area, depositing huge amount of toxic material, resulting in large scale diffuse pollution.

The pollution sources were identified and characterised between 1992 and 2005 by site assessment based on historical and field data. The results of the environmental survey indicated that toxic metal contamination of the Toka-valley area produced high ecological risk, therefore the remediation of the site became urgent. The main primary pollution sources are: mine wastes, flotation tailings, precipitate from acid mine water treatment by liming. The main pollutants, As, Cd, Pb and Zn, are transported by surface runoff and erosion. The runoff delivers only part of the emitted pollution into the surface water body, the rest is getting into the soil by sorption. Eroded solid materials pollute directly the soil and sediment causing long-term pollution of runoff and surface water.

2.2.2. Laboratory Testing and Microcosms Experiments

Prior to field experiments preliminary tests were performed in microcosm at laboratory scale to select the most suitable chemical stabilizer for the toxic-metal contaminated soil and mine-waste.

Before establishing full-scale demonstration of the combined chemical and phytostabilisation on the former mining site, the type of vegetation and the stabilising additives that fit to the local parameters (soil and waste type, slope, exposition, metal concentrations), had to be determined. Toxic-metal immobilising additives or mixture of additives are required to reduce the mobility and biological availability of the contaminants on long term, to reach an acceptable risk level according to the typical natural land use and hobby gardens.

The soil of the complex chemical and phytostabilisation experimental area was treated with three different types of fly ashes, two from the power plant in Oroszlány, Hungary (fly ash "A" and "B") in 1 w%, 2 w% and 5 w% and one from Tata, Hungary (fly ash "T"), which was added to the soil in 2 and 5 w%. Fly ash (also called cyclonic ash) was used successfully for full scale combined chemical and phytostabilisation in Belgium (Vangronsveld et al, 1995; Vangronsveld et al, 1996) and France (DIFPOLMINE, 2003–2006, www.difpolmine.org).

Besides commonly used soil amendments, like alginite (1.5 w%), hydrated lime (1 w%), raw phosphate (1 w%), lignite (10 w%), waste materials were also tested: two types of Fe-Mn-hydroxide precipitate from water treatment plant in Budapest (precipitate "R" and "C", in 2 and 5 w%), and red mud (2 and 5 w%) from bauxite processing.

The soil samples treated with different stabilising agents and the untreated control sample were placed in 2 kg pots each. Horse radish, ray grace and acacia were planted. They were incubated at 25 °C in a special thermostat, mixed and watered every two months. The water content of the soil was set to 60 % of the soil's water holding capacity. The duration of the experiments varied from 1 to 2 years.

Some other plants, like maize, energy grass and other grasses were tested for growth and metal uptake. To enhance the chance of the plants to survive in the contaminated waste soil nutrients were added and mycorrhiza fungi were tested, to prove their beneficial effect (Anton and Máthé-Gáspár, 2005; Takács et al, 2005; Anton and Murányi, 2007).

2.2.3. Field Experiments for the Combined Chemical and Phytostabilisation

Parallel to the laboratory experiments field experiments were implemented modelling two scenarios:

1. Flooded hobby garden along the Toka-creek.
2. Diffusely occurring eroded, weathered and leached acidic material deriving from sulphide mine waste (waste rock).

The first year of the field experiments was devoted to the characterisation of the plants cultivated in the hobby garden. The aim was to select plant species that do not accumulate metals to lower risk by plant uptake and food chain introduction. Horse-radish, rape, maize and grass species were planted and tested in the 45 x 20 m^2 area garden, close to the creek. Species with low BCF (Bioconcentration Factor = concentration in plant / concentration in soil) were identified and selected for further use.

The second year's experiments targeted testing of the effect of chemical stabilisation and measuring the water balance and contaminant transport on the field plots.

The flooded garden–soil was treated with 5% fly ash. Two different grasses and two different maize species were planted.

Three prisms of 0.6m height and 15 m x 6 m surface area, were constructed from spatially leached mine waste. Drainage pipes for collecting seepage were lain under the prism and runoff collection ditches were excavated around the prism.

After the addition of the chemical stabilisers, the field plots were revegetated with grass, ray grass, and maize.

2.2.4. Integrated Assessment Tools of CCP Monitoring

Due to the addition of stabilizers a complex process was initiated in the microcosms. Metal mobility, solubility and bioavailability are continuously changing until the new equilibrium has been reached. Long term monitoring of the processes is necessary to observe if a stabiliser is effective only on short term, or it is able to immobilize metals through a longer period. In our case–stabilisation and as a consequence the decreased mobility, solubility and bioavailability of toxic metals in the soil were monitored by an integrated methodology, which combined physico-chemical analyses with toxicity testing.

Chemical Analyses

Monitoring by chemical analysis included metal-analyses of the water-, ammonium-acetate- (pH=4.5) and ammonium-acetate + acetic acid + EDTA-extract as well as of the soil leachate, prepared by continuous leaching in mini-lysimeters. The total metal content was measured after aqua regia (with a 3:1 mixture of hydrochloric and nitric acids) digestion. The metal content of the various extracts and of the leachate was determined by ICP-AES: Inductively Coupled Plasma Atomic Emission Spectrometry.

The metal content of the different extracts was measured as a function of time, and the effects of the different stabilising agents was compared. The results were evaluated in accordance with the treatments and the time. The leaching-test was performed on the stabilised soil at the end of the experiments. The metal-content of the different extracts and the leachate were compared to the toxicity results, to find relation between extractable and effective metal-ratios in the soil.

Environmental Toxicity Testing

In order to assess the actual risk of the treated soils toxicity measurements were performed with the soil. The microcosm tests and filed experiments were monitored by bacterial and plant toxicity tests and plant bioaccumulation tests. The bacterial tests for predicting the risk of the soil were *Vibrio fisheri* luminescence inhibition test and *Azomonas agilis* dehydrogenase enzyme-activity inhibition test. Both tests are interactive tests, ensuring direct contact between soil and test-bacteria in a soil suspension, developed by the authors (Gruiz et al, 2001) on the basis of standardised methods for water-extracts of soil or waste (DIN 38412, 1991 and HS 21987/30, 1988)

Plant tests have increasing importance in the assessment of contaminated land and soils, their results play an important role in risk assessment and in the creation of quality criteria. Their response, as representatives of one of the most important trophic level (producers) in soil, is crucial. Also bioaccumulation and food chain effects are based on plant behaviour, so plant tests have growing importance in ecological and human risk assessment. The *Sinapis alba* (white mustard) was used in the root and shoot growth inhibition tests and in a self-developed five-days bioaccumulation test (Feigl, et al, 2007) for getting direct information on the suitability of the chemical stabilizer from the point of view of the following phytostabilisation process.

2.3. Technology-Verification Tools used for the Evaluation of the Field Demonstrations

Technological parameters, like air- and water-flows, contaminant fluxes and chemical forms, provide data for the mass-balance and cost-efficiency assessment, and ensure the emission-control data for the risk assessment of technology application. It means that technology-monitoring is the basis of technology verification.

The MOKKA verification tool-battery was worked out for soil remediation and was demonstrated on two innovative in situ soil bioremediation technologies, one is a biodegradation based technology for organic soil pollutants, the other is a phytostabilisation-based technology for inorganic ones. Both technologies were combined with physico-chemical technologies: ex situ groundwater treatment of the organic pollutant and chemical stabilisation of the inorganic one.

The MOKKA verification tool-battery has 4 elements as shown in Figure 2. The application and the detailed evaluation of the demonstrated technologies will be introduced hereunder.

2.3.1. Mass-Balance

The mass balance was calculated on the basis of the results of soil, soil-gas and groundwater monitoring. Soil-gas and groundwater were continuously analysed to characterise the CDT. In case of CCP soil leachate and the soil-growing plants were analysed.

The heterogeneity of the soil makes impossible following the slow and long-term processes, like biodegradation, because the spatial differences are usually larger than the changes in time. The mobile soil-phases, like soil gas and ground water, however, represent a quasi-average due to their cumulative nature. Plant biomass belongs to the averaging indicators, suitable for assessing toxicity and its metal content for bioaccumulation. Using data of soil gas, ground water and plant biomass will give more realistic results than the analyses of the soil-sample itself.

Calculation of the CDT mass balance was based on the equation *(Eq. 1)*, which was several times validated by the microcosms experiments (Gruiz and Kriston, 1995; Molnár et al, 2005). The residual amount was calculated from the difference of the original and calculated removed (biodegraded) values. Post-treatment soil sampling and analysis validated the calculated amount of residual contaminant.

The mass balance of CCP was produced on the basis of the mobile metal contents (separately for each metal). The comparison of the control and treated soil in respect of total (aqua-regia digestion) and mobile (extractable with diluted acids or water) metal content gives the total-mobile metal ratio. As a result of the stabilisation the mobile metal fraction decreases drastically, while the total is unchanged. The metal concentration in the leachate, in the runoff and in the plant is proportional with the mobile metal fraction. Not only the concentration is diminished in the leachate and runoff, but also the amount of the water fraction decreases on the effect of the chemical and phytostabilization.

2.3.2. Risk Assessment

The risk based monitoring of the technology is planned on the basis of the conceptual model (contaminants and their sources, transport routes, receptors), the sensitivity and land uses of the site, as well as on the basis of the processes and additives of the in situ technology.

Risk assessment studies deal with three types of risk.

1. The risk of the site to be reduced by the technology: the risk before and after technology application is the main positive element of the environmental-efficiency of the technology. The target risk can be determined on the basis of the land use specific *no effect* values.

The risk value before and after remediation is relevant to the environmental efficiency of the technology: the difference between the initial and the final risks can be expressed as $RQ_{initial}–RQ_{final}$ or $RQ_{initial}/RQ_{final}$, where RQ = Risk Quotient is the ratio of the Predicted Concentration in the Environment (PEC) and the Predicted No Effect (harmless) Concentration of the contaminant (PNEC) in case of natural land use. If human health risk is the dominant, due to human land use, the ratio of the Average Daily Intake (ADI) and the Tolerable Daily Intake (TDI) gives the quantity of the risk.

The risk is acceptable, if it is lower, than RQ = 1. RQ = 1–10 means high, over 10, very high risk. Negligible risk is under RQ = 0,001.

2. The risk of the remediation itself, is a site-specific element of the risk due to emissions from the technology. It has high importance in case of in situ technologies, when technology is applied directly in the environment. The emission can be inhibited by operations or by physical barriers. To reduce the emission from the technology, additional measures are necessary, similarly to ex situ or reactor-technologies. Similarly to any industrial technology the contaminant emission, the noise emission, odour, additives and the products of remediation have to be dealt with.

To quantify the risk of emission from the technology, direct measurements or transport modelling are the available alternatives.

3. The third type of remediation related risk is the regional or global risk of the technology, originated from water use and energy consumption as well as the load on the natural and social environment.

Energy and water consumption may be included into the cost assessment, but as a load on the resources, it is recommended to keep it in the verification system as a special item. This item is generally evaluated in comparison with the technology-alternatives. The predicted (planned) energy and water-consumption can be validated by the real measured value during remediation.

Amongst the global risk components of the technology application the use of water and energy, the production of CO_2, used materials or contaminants producing acid-rain and influencing ozone-depletion are the most important ones. These risk parameters can be evaluated in comparison with the same characteristics of the technology-alternatives, and help in prioritizing the eco-efficiency of the alternatives, on the basis of their contribution to the greenhouse-effect, to ozone-depletion, acid-rain production and to the consumption of non-renewable sources of the Earth. Global risk components can be calculated by one of the methodologies for life cycle assessment.

2.3.4. Cost Evaluation

Cost assessment and the comparative evaluation of the costs of the potential technology-alternatives maybe one of the basic arguments in the decision making process. The absolute cost is important for the owner of the problem, but the cost efficiency, and the relative assessment of the technology-alternatives is a good decision support tool and integrates not only economical aspects, but the used amount of water and energy with special ecological importance, and the necessary labour, which may have social aspects, are also included. Cost-benefit assessment is part of the spatial planning and complex land management and has economical and social aspect both for the owner and the local governments. Cost-benefit ratio is dependent on the future land use, in the selection of the most beneficial future land use, which does not agree always with the needs of the nature and humans. Cost-benefit assessment often brings contrary result to cost-efficiency or eco-efficiency evaluations.

Cost Assessment

Cost assessment is the planning and documentation of all monetary costs of the technology application from the pre-application assessment through the implementation to maintenance and after-care. The total costs include the equipment and operation costs, material costs, water and energy costs as well as labour. The costs dominantly depend on the duration of the remediation. The actual cost of the application validates the cost estimate.

Cost-Efficiency Assessment (CEA)

Cost-Efficiency Assessment is used to compare relative expenditure of technology-alternatives, which ensure the same target value and identical land uses. Specific cost indicators were created, like cost per surface-unit or volume-unit, cost per exposed population, etc. These indicators were then used for differentiation between remediation alternatives.

Cost-Benefit Assessment (CBA)

Cost-Benefit Assessment supports the decision-making procedure with the absolute cost estimates of the different technology-alternatives. Both the costs and the benefits are expressed in monetary value, if possible. The initial and ongoing expenses versus expected return are calculated. The revenues of the future land use, the suitable environmental target value and the technological alternatives, which ensure this target-value, are considered. Those aspects and indicators which cannot be quantified in money will give an additional, not monetary index, which can be taken into consideration during the decision making procedure.

2.3.5. SWOT Analysis

SWOT analysis, which is a descriptive, qualitative evaluation methodology, is also part of the MOKKA verification system, containing all those aspects, which were not quantified in the previous points. Using a uniform system of questions within Strengths, Weaknesses, Opportunities and Threats a relative point system can be coupled to the answers for further characterisation and comparison of remediation technologies.

3. Results and Discussion

The application of the MOKKA verification system in the CDT and CCP technologies is introduced in this chapter.

In the verification of a remediation technology a pre-implementation approach can be employed, considering a default scenario. The other type of verification is site specific and considers the site-specific values and the characteristics of the application. This is the post-application approach.

Both approaches of verification have strengths and weaknesses due to the site-specific nature of the contaminants and technology-applications. But the evaluation of technologies in general, or the comparative evaluation of technologies for the selection of the best possible one, cannot consider all site-specific parameters. This is the main reason for the frequent decision on the less site specific solution: “dig and dump”. Every polluted site is different, no identical cases exist! A technology can be excellent on one site, but absolutely not effective on an other, this is the reason why a site specific evaluation is so important. Nature-friendly, low cost and low risk-technologies can result an excellent certificate in a general evaluation, but may not be effective enough in an actual site-specific application, for example Enhanced

Natural Attenuation for chlorinated hydrocarbons contaminated site, where different chlorinated compounds are co-existing with different biodegradation pathways. On the other hand, a less nature-friendly, expensive and high-risk technology (in situ chemical oxidation, *in situ* vitrification) can be the best solution for not available, underground contaminants with high toxicity and risk. Instead of "dig and dump" the "dig and treat" on a proper treatment plant and reuse of the soil after treatment is a better solution but still not always efficient from the point of view of the environment and ecosystem.

Additionally to the verification we have to assess the suitability and applicability of the technology as well as its sustainability.

3.1. Verification of the CDT Technology

The site-specific evaluation of the CDT technology starts with the planning of the technology-monitoring and summarizing the result, required by the verification methodology. The calculation of the mass balance is based on the quantitative value of the removed contaminant, but characterizes the transparency of the technology at the same time: are quantitative parameters available, have they been measured proving the removal or decrease of the amount of the contaminant and its risk.

The reduction of the site-specific risk can be calculated from the decrease of the mass (concentration) of the contaminant. Site-specific risk values consider land-uses, therefore possible changes of the land use after remediation should be taken into consideration when calculating absolute risk values. In the case of transformer station the natural land use with no land-use change option was taken into account, because the station is integrated into a city-park and will remain there for a long time.

Water consumption and global risk were considered when comparing the technology-alternatives. For the transformer station the comparative cost-efficiency assessment was applied to support technology selection from the technology-alternatives. Changes in the land-use are not foreseen, so a simplified cost assessment could be applied.

The SWOT analyses include all the aspects, which were not assessed in the first three points and are good arguments pro or contra for the application of the technology. Some of the descriptive characters can also be quantified if necessary.

3.1.1. Summary Results of the Microcosm Tests and the In Situ Field Application

The soil of a transformer station was contaminated with transformer oil (not containing polychlorinated biphenyls). The microflora of the soil has already been adapted, but the biodegradation was slow, due to limited bioavailability of the contaminants. For the enhancement of bioavailability and as a consequence of biodegradation, cyclodextrin was applied in addition to the Enhanced Natural Attenuation and the ex situ groundwater treatment by phase separation and sorption on activated carbon. The results of the microcosms, pilot and field experiments are summarised below.

- Cyclodextrin was able to enhance both the water solubility and the bioavailability of the aged transformer oil.

- Biodegradation was more effective and the influence of CD was also much higher in the three-phase soil, compared to saturated and slurry phase soils. CD increased the transformer oil removal: from 40% measured in the untreated control, the removal of the transformer oil increased to 70% in the CD-treated soil.
- For the intensification of soil washing, a minimum of 5% CD is necessary in the water, which makes its application in such a way, too expensive.
- The extractable transformer-oil content in the soil first increased on the effect of CD, because the mobilisation of the contaminant precedes its biodegradation. Compared to the control (100%), the RAMEB treatment often caused 130–140% extractable contaminant concentration in the soil 1–2 weeks after the treatment: the "chemical availability" of the contaminant also increased on the effect of CD, similar to biological availability.
- For the intensification of the biodegradation of 10 000 mg/kg transformer oil in the unsaturated soil zone, 0.10-0.15% CD was enough. In case of higher contamination, e.g. 30 000 mg/kg, 0.5–0.7% CD was necessary.
- The CD was effective in different soil types: the low initial removal of the transformer oil in sandy soil was increased from 2% to 10%, in the humic and loamy soils from 10% to 30% in 1–2 weeks after treatment.
- Concentration of the oil-degrading cells increased to a 10–100 fold value after 2–4 weeks of CD-application.
- Different cyclodextrins show great differences in their effects: RAMEB was the most effective for transformer oil, compared to acetyl beta-cyclodextrin and beta-cyclodextrin
- An interesting and positive outcome of the microcosm tests was, that the increased bioavailability did not cause an increase in the toxicity of the contaminant. It is a general phenomenon: by closing the contaminant into the molecular CD-capsule, the CD-complex cannot realise its toxic effect, not being able to bound to the suitable receptor (Schwartz and Bar, 1995), while the biodegradability of the complexed contaminant increases, due to enhanced transport through the cell-membrane. The toxicity-lowering effect makes possible the biodegradation of highly toxic substances in the presence of CD.

In the field experiment we had no untreated control, but the strategy of the experiment, – the impulse-like treatment of the steady-state in situ soil-system with CD – showed clearly the effect of the treatments. We could differentiate between the non-treated and the CD-enhanced periods.

The combined technology (the bioventing of the unsaturated soil zone with temporary flushing and RAMEB and nutrients application combined with the *ex situ* physico-chemical treatment of the extracted groundwater) had a significant effect by causing a marked reduction of EPH-content of the groundwater and soil.

The initial TPH content of the ground water was 0.99 mg/dm^3, it decreased to 0.8 in the steady state after 40 days of aeration. After the first nutrient treatment it decreased to 0.6 mg/dm^3. The second treatment with RAMEB decreased the further to 0.4 mg/dm^3. After the third treatment of RAMEB + nutrients a small temporary decrease was measured, but then it remained at about 0.3–0.4 mg/dm^3 on long term, which was practically the background value of the site.

The CO_2 content of the soil gas increased to a large extent after the first nutrient and RAMEB addition, the third addition of both together caused smaller increase (Figure 8). The O_2 content of the soil gas shows the same trends but the relative value of the endpoint is smaller. The results of soil gas analyses indicated high activity of soil living microbes (validated by microbiological testing).

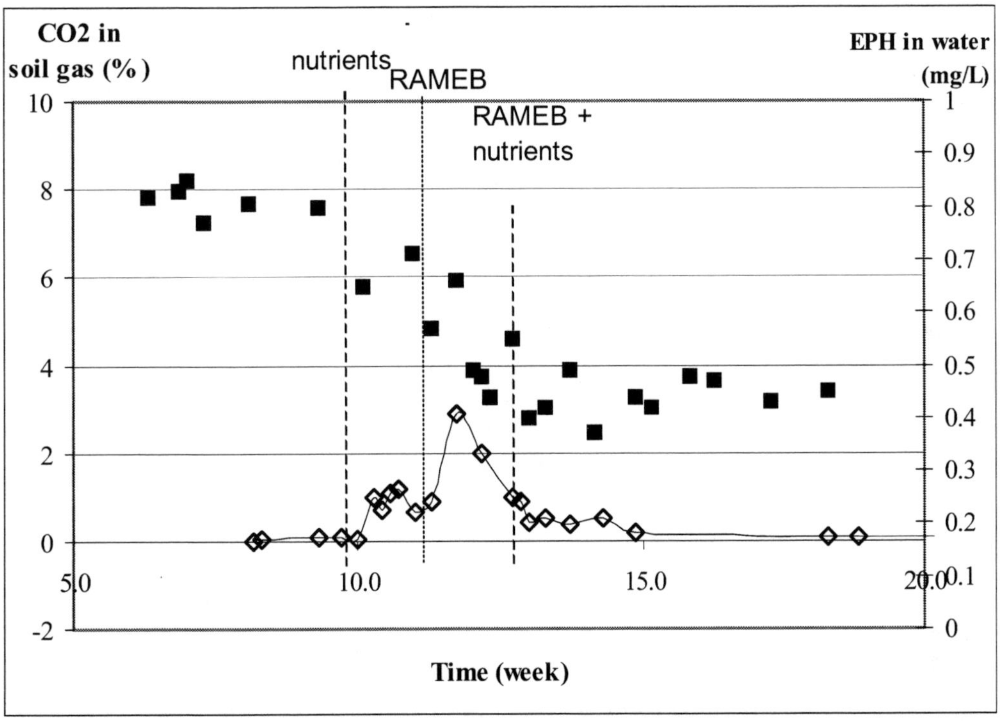

Figure 8. Changes in the CO_2 content in soil gas (◊) and in the EPH content in the groundwater (■) after treatment with CDT (RAMEB and nutrient additions are marked with dashed line)

The transformer oil removal in the soil was approximately 99 % after 47 weeks of *in situ* bioremediation (decreased from 20 000–30 000 mg/kg to 200–300 mg/kg).

The direct contact soil toxicity tests with bacterial (*Vibrio fischeri*), plant (*Sinapis alba*) and animal (*Folsomia candida*) testorganisms showed a decrease in toxicity, with an acceptable end-value after 24 weeks treatment, before the winter break. The *Vibrio fischeri* test indicated a mild toxicity in the upper 10–30 cm layer of the contaminated soil, but no toxicity in deeper levels, in accordance with the oil content, detected before the winter break. No toxicity was shown by the soil samples at the end of the *in situ* experiment (after 47 weeks of treatment).

3.1.2. Evaluation of the CDT Technology and the Validation of the Verification Tool

Mass Balance of the CDT Technology

The material balances indicate the efficiency of the technology; it lets us know what is the mass-flux in the different soil phases during remediation. With full knowledge of the numerical information about the mass (or element) fluxes the technologists design, perform, monitor and intervene in the applied technology to ensure optimal function.

Our technology monitoring was mainly based on the analyses of the *carbon content* of the mobile soil phases: carbon-dioxide in soil gas and total petroleum hydrocarbons in groundwater.

On the basis of the results of soil-gas and groundwater analyses, most part of the contaminating hydrocarbon has been biodegraded by microbes.

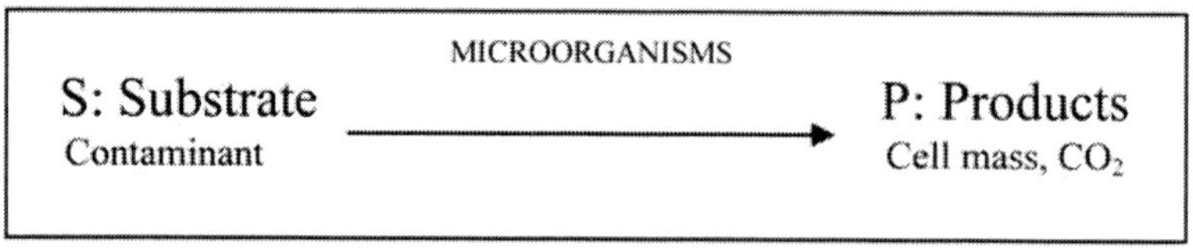

Calculation of the substrate's mass (S)

Treated soil-mass: 50 t; volume of contaminated water: 1000 m^3

Initial oil content of the soil: average concentration in the soil at start is 25 000 mg/kg, so 50 tons of soil contain 1 250 kg of hydrocarbons.

Initial oil in water: ~1 $mg/dm^3 \rightarrow$ 1000 g (1 kg) of hydrocarbon in the ground-water.

Total amount of hydrocarbons to be removed is **1 251 kg**.

Calculation of products' mass (P)

Contaminant removed by water:

Water extracted and treated: 0.7 m^3/h, 250 days of treatment, 4200 m^3 of water treated

Final concentration of oil in the groundwater: ~0.3 g hydrocarbon/m^3

The amount of hydrocarbons removed by water-treatment: 2 240 g

Biodegraded transformer oil calculated on the basis of the CO_2 production:

Volume of the produced CO_2 was 534 m^3, which is equivalent to 1 049 kg CO_2.

1 049 kg CO_2 has been produced from **1 144 kg** of hydrocarbon according to *Eq. 1*, which is the realistic estimate of the total amount in our case.

It means, that from the initial **1 251 kg** of transformer oil (in soil and water) ~ **1 146 kg** of hydrocarbon was removed by the complex cyclodextrin technology during 47 weeks of treatment.

At the end of the remediation the residual hydrocarbon content was about 12 kg (the average of the EPH content: 240 mg/kg^{-1} in the treated soil).

The mass balance accounts for 93% of the contaminants.

Risks of the Technology

The risk of the contaminant and of the contaminated soil and the site-specific risk of the applied technology in terms of the likely emission is separately discussed for each soil phase. The different soil phases pose different hazard to the environment.

The soil gas does not represent a risk, because the transformer oil does not contain volatile components (the gas chromatography of the soil pollution showed that the contamination is in the range of C15–C36), the gas-chromatographic analysis of the soil gas has confirmed this therefore in the field experiment there was no need for the soil-gas treatment.

The ground-water contains high level of petroleum hydrocarbons with continuous supply from the soil. The technology (continuous water extraction) helps to avoid the risk of spreading the contaminant through the natural movement of ground-water.

The results of ecotoxicity tests performed on test organisms of three trophic levels (microbes, plants, animals) show the risk of the contaminant sorbed on the solid particles.

Initial and Final Risk of the Contaminated Soil and Groundwater

The quantification of the initial and residual risk means, that the Predicted Environmental Concentration (PEC) of the site is compared to the Predicted No Effect Concentration (PNEC) at the beginning and at the end of remediation.

PEC is calculated as the average of the measured values at the transformer station. Applying a pessimistic model, the same concentration is supposed outside the fence of the station, which is the city parks' territory.

The applied PNEC value is a site-specific target value, – representing "no risk" situation for groundwater – it is 0.5 mg/dm^3 in the area of the transformer station, but 0.2 in the area of the city-park. "No risk" value for the soil of the transformer station is 300 mg/kg, the target value for multifunctional soil use is 100 mg/kg, which is not a realistic scenario, because the transformer station is completely isolated from the city-park.

Local risk of the groundwater within the transformer station:

RQinitial = 1.0 mg/dm^3 / 0.5 mg/dm^3 = 2
RQfinal = 0.3 mg/dm^3 / 0.5 mg/dm^3 = 0.6

Local risk of the groundwater out of the transformer station, within the city-park: based on conservative estimate, not considering dilution, sorption and biodegradation during transport by flow from the transformer station toward city-park:

RQinitial = 1.0 mg/dm^3 / 0.2 mg/dm^3 = 5
RQfinal = 0.3 mg/dm^3 / 0.2 mg/dm^3 = 1.5

Local risk of the groundwater out of the transformer station, within the city-park: based on a model considering dilution, sorption and biodegradation:

RQinitial = 1.0 mg/dm^3 / 0.2 mg/dm^3 = 5
RQfinal = 0.1 mg/dm^3 / 0.2 mg/dm^3 = 0.5

Local risk of the soil of the transformer station

RQinitial = 25 000 mg/kg / 300 mg/kg = 83
RQfinal = 250 mg/kg / 300 mg/kg = 0.8

The soil was tested by environmental toxicity tests, to control the real effect of the treated soil on soil living organisms: bacteria and plant. The soil samples proved to be very toxic at the beginning of the treatment and became non-toxic at the end (Table 1.; Molnár, 2005).

Table 1. Ecotoxicity of the contaminated soil before, on the 24th week and after the *CDT* application

Testorganisms and endpoints of the biotests	Depth of contaminated soil					
	10–30 cm			80–90 cm		
	Date of testing					
	Start	24. week	47. week	Start	24. week	47. week
Vibrio fischeri luminescence ED_{50} [g soil]	2	4	>5	1	>5	>5
ΣCu20 [mg Cu/kg sample]	320 toxic	230 slightly toxi	<80 non toxic	450 very toxic	<80 non toxic	<80 non toxic
Sinapis alba root / shoot elongation ED_{50} [g soil]	3 toxic	>5 non toxic	>5 non toxic	2 toxic	>5 non toxic	>5 non toxic
Folsomia candida mortality ED_{50} [g soil]	12 toxic	>20 non toxic	>20 non toxic	5 toxic	>20 non toxic	>20 non toxic

ED_{20} and ED_{50} = soil doses, which caused 20 % and 50 % inhibition in the endpoint value
$\Sigma Cu20 = ED_{20\,Cu} / ED_{20\,sample} * 10^6$; toxicity in Cu-equivalent: Cu-concentration, which would cause the same toxicity

After 47 weeks of treatment all of the soil samples were non-toxic for all of the applied test-organisms. This result is equivalent with the "no risk" situation. To find a better understandable interpretation, than the ED_{50} values, the *Vibrio fisheri* toxicity was expressed in copper-equivalent, which is a virtual concentration: the copper concentration, which would cause the same inhibition as the transformer-oil contaminated soil sample.

The CDT technology was able to reduce the risk of the soil to an acceptable value, it is proven both by the calculated PEC/PNEC value and the measured "no toxic effects".

The risk of the groundwater showed a value of 1.5, which is higher, than the acceptable RQ = 1 value. It is not the fault of the technology, but the influence of the background value of the site, which is much higher, than the treated part, so it is dominant in determining the concentration of transformer oil in the groundwater. The whole site is 50 times larger than the demonstration site, and includes many point and diffuse sources: it means that the experimental site was not completely independent from the whole.

Site Specific Environmental Risk of the Application of In Situ CDT

There was no need for the treatment of soil gas; we considered soil gas as a "no risk" element in the site-specific risk assessment. The emitted CO_2 will be evaluated as part of the regional and global risk components.

The risk of the contaminated soil moisture and groundwater is increased in the technology because of contaminant mobilisation. The treated soil volume is never isolated from the other parts of the soil (open reactor), therefore – if it is necessary – the transport of the eventually mobilised contaminant should be restricted by additional measures. This was not the case at the transformer station, because the availability of the contaminant was *ab ovo* limited, the fraction getting bioavailable was immediately biodegraded.

The risk of mobilisation is higher in case of cyclodextrin addition, increasing the mobility and the aqueous solubility of the transformer oil. On the other hand the transport with water is restricted in our case by the continuously ensured depression in the wells and pumping, followed by the treatment of the contaminated groundwater. With this technological step, the transport by the groundwater flow is blocked, and the level of the groundwater is lowered resulting in a deeper unsaturated zone favourable for the bioventing of the upper vadouse zone. The contaminant concentration in the saturated soil is low, its origin is not the vertical transport from the spare-transformer, but the slightly contaminated groundwater from the surroundings. The CDT was able to decontaminate this part of the subsurface area, too combining CD-flushing and activating the facultative anaerobic microflora.

The measures ensured and the monitoring proved that no volatile components and no contaminated water were emitted from the demonstration site.

Water was completely recycled; the only waste is the activated carbon filling the absorber used for water treatment. Less than 10% of the capacity of the absorber was used.

The nutrients, which were injected into the soil have some risk, when affecting drinking water wells, but it is not the case at the transformer station site and the surrounding city park. There are no wells for water extraction Ensuring depression in the treated area, the nutrient supply remained in place (within the quasi-reactor) and was utilised by the microbes within a short time.

RAMEB is a natural molecule, a starch-like organic substance, which is not toxic and has no other adverse effects. RAMEB injection into the soil could theoretically have some risk, but in the reality the transport of RAMEB within the soil is highly limited. Its introduction and distribution in the soil causes technological problems. The technology should optimise the concentration of the CD solution and mode of injection to ensure its distribution in the planned volume. The general depression further hinders its transport. RAMEB is biodegradable, its half-life-time is 1 year, an ideal life-span for the application in soil remediation.

In summary, the risks due to contaminant and additive-emission is low, there was no measurable emission at all. Emission of dust is not relevant, because the surface is vegetated and isolated by plants. Noise emission is not considerable, the pump and the ventilator are low performance ones, there is no residential area close to the station, background noise is stronger during the day.

Risk Reduction Alternatives of the CDT Technology

For comparative evaluation of CDT, various realistic alternative technologies were considered (Table 2.). The list includes the cyclodextrin-technology, which was demonstrated on the field.

A. "0" version: no remediation, risk changes due to the natural processes that are monitored for 15 years. After spending money for long-term monitoring, the contaminated site may still be present (Monitored Natural Attenuation, MNA).
B. "Dig & dump": excavation and transport to the disposal site or the off site treatment plant, soil replacement on site. Groundwater is treated for 1.5 year by "pump & treat", using activated carbon absorption. The excavation and transport is calculated for 0.2 year. In Table 2 the two activities' time requirement is given, as 0.2/1.5.
C. Ex situ, *on* site biological treatment, reuse of the treated soil on site. During the ex situ soil bioremediation (in prisms), the excavated hole is used for the treatment of the groundwater of free-surface. Water aeration and recirculation is done in the "pond".
D. "Pump & treat": in situ soil washing combined with ex situ water-treatment: the soil is continuously washed by infiltration and/or flushing the treated and recycled water. Depending on the partition of the contaminant between solid soil phase and groundwater, it can last longer. In our demonstration cca. 1.6 kg transformer oil was removed by the water, compared to the 1000 kg biodegraded amount, in spite of enhanced mobility. The disadvantage of this technology (very slow extraction of the contaminant and washing out the soil components) can be decreased by the addition of mobilising agents (surfactants or cyclodextrin), which can lower the time-requirement to the half.
E. In situ bioventing of the unsaturated zone combined with the ex situ physico-chemical treatment of the ground-water and the temporary flushing of the unsaturated soil (without additives).
F. CDT: in situ complex bioremediation using cyclodextrin: in situ bioventing of the unsaturated zone combined with the ex situ physico-chemical treatment of the ground-water and the temporary flushing of the unsaturated soil.

Time Requirement of the Alternatives

MNA is slow, sometimes an acceptable performance takes 15 years or more. Retrospective evaluation shows, that we have had this time in many cases.

Dig&dump procedure is relatively fast (0.2 year in our case), and sometimes economical for small volumes, but if contaminated groundwater treatment and soil replacement is needed, the time-benefit of fast removal is lost. Contaminated water treatment in pond takes 1.5 years for the transformer-oil polluted site. Vegetation of the new soil surface needs also time: depending on the vegetation cycle.

Ex situ bioremediation needs a little bit less time, but what is spared by the ex situ enhancement of biodegrading microbes is lost by the excavation-time, prisms forming, soil replacement and revegetation. In addition to these disadvantages, during the treatment of the excavated soil there is an excavated hole on the site: to compensate this, the hole can be utilised for ground-water treatment for 2.5 years. If a 2.5-year period is not enough, the total treatment time will be longer with consequences on land use or remaining water-contamination. Additional long-term measures could be necessary, when there is an intent to utilise the surface, e.g. implementation of an ex situ water-treatment-system (pump and treat).

In situ bioremediation needs about 2.5 years, the surface can be used in between. If the treatment time of the soil or the groundwater increases compared to the planned, due to unforeseen reasons, the loss from land use is lower, than in case of ex situ treatment and the technology should not be changed, but applied longer.

In situ treatment with CDT decreases the treatment time considerably, the results of CDT demonstration on the transformer station and former experiences prove, that from a 2.5-year period one can go down to 0.5–1.5 years, including one or two summer-periods.

Regional and Global Risk Elements in Comparison with the Technology-Alternatives

The technology-alternatives enlisted above are evaluated with the help of a score-system: the scores are partly based on quantitative parameters (like energy, water or fuel consumption), partly on the basis of relative marks (emissions from the technology or waste production). Permanent consumption was multiplied by the years of the treatment. The summary of the comparative evaluation of the technology-alternatives is shown in Table 2. Some items are discussed in details:

- CO_2 production and it's exhausting by ventilation: there is no difference between five of the six alternatives, which are based on biodegradation. The one, which applies soil washing by water, uses an activated carbon absorber for the water treatment, absorbing all of the contaminants on the sorbent. Burning of the oily absorber causes 40 times higher CO_2 production. If soil washing were combined with biological degradation, the CO_2 production value would be the same as for the others.
- Water consumption: no water use, no water discharge, complete recycling was the solution for CDT. The *in situ* alternatives can be combined with complete recycling, but the ex situ methods need some water for moistening the soil and dissolve the additives as well as for cleaning in connection with excavation and transportation.
- Energy consumption: CDT needed one pump of about 7 m^3/hour performance and a small "window-ventilator". The *in situ* biological alternatives do not differ from CDT, but the time of application differs a lot, e.g. soil washing uses energy for a long time, ex situ technologies require energy for excavation and transport. Ex situ treatment in prisms or by agrotechniques needs energy for the treatment.
- Material requirement: new soil, additives and cyclodextrin were taken into consideration.

Cost-efficiency of the CDT

Cost-efficiency Assessment was used for the comparison of technological alternatives, which ensure the same target value and identical land uses. Specific cost indicators were created, like cost per volume-unit. These indicators were then used for ranking the alternatives.

Table 2. Comparative risk assessment of the technology-alternatives

	"0" MNA	Dig & dump ex situ off site	Dig & treat ex situ on site	Pump & treat	*In situ* bio-venting	**CDT**
	A	***B***	***C***	***D***	***E***	***F***
Treatment duration (years)	***15***	***0.2/1.5***	***2.5***	***10***	***2.5***	***1.5***
Volatile	0	0	0	0	0	0
Water soluble with groundwater	2.5	1	1	2	2	2
Water soluble with leachate	0	3	3	0	0	0
Sorbed with erosion	0	3	3	0	0	0
Dust	0	4	4	0	0	0
Noise	0	3	3	3	2	2
By transport (0.2 year)		$10_{0.2}$				
Emission x years (score)	**37**	**23**	**35**	**50**	**10**	**6**
CO_2 by biodegradation (kg/ton)	20	20	20	0	20	20
Due to excavation, transport		20	20	0	0	0
Act. carbon regeneration/burning		2	2	80*	2	2
Water consumption (lit/ton)	0	50	25	0	0	0
Energy consumption (score)						
Pump (2 kWh)	0	5	5	20	5	3
Ventilator (0,5 kWh)	0	0	0		1	0.6
Machines (lit diesel/t)	0	50	50			
Transport (lit diesel/t)	0	50				
Waste (soil, activated carbon)	50	50	0	2	2	2

Table 2. Comparative risk assessment of the technology-alternatives (continued)

	"0" MNA	Dig & dump ex situ off site	Dig & treat ex situ on site	Pump & treat	In situ bio-venting	CDT
	A	**B**	**C**	**D**	**E**	**F**
Total regional items(score)	**70**	**247**	**122**	**102**	**30**	**27.6**
New soil		50	0	0	0	0
Nutrients (N,P,K)			2	2	2	2
Additives (CD)						2
Total material (score)	**0**	**50**	**2**	**2**	**2**	**4**
Total risk score	***107***	***320***	***159***	***154***	***42***	***37.6***

0.2/1.5: 0.2 year of soil excavation, and 1.5 year water treatment

The Népliget Transformer Station is an isolated site in the City Park of Budapest, the availability for ecosystem and humans is limited. The future land use of the site will be unchanged, so no benefit can be calculated. The model site is a little, separate volume, ideal for demonstration, but too small for cost estimation. The application of the same technology is more realistic for the whole transformer station; therefore the cost calculation was done both for 50 and 1 000 tons. The costs out of a mass-range are not proportional with the quantity. The detailed estimate is given for the 1 000 tons case, but the result for the small (50 tons) quantity is also given in the Table 3.

The operation sots increase on regular basis and include administrative costs, too. Investment is generally a one-off expenditure, but it can be given on yearly basis, considering the turnover of the capital. Costs estimation was prepared on the basis of bids or on the basis of references. Future costs (after-care, monitoring, etc.) were included, too.

According to the cost efficiency analysis of the 1 000 tons case we can see from Table 3, that the ex situ and *in situ* bioremediations have similar costs. The minor differences can be explained easily: the ex situ biological treatment in prisms (version ***C***) is combined with water-treatment in pond, which is much cheaper, than the reactor-treatment after pumping, but the surface area of the site cannot be used for a while. If the same water-treatment were used, the costs would be similar to ***E*** and ***F***. The "0" version has higher costs, than ***C*** or ***F***, equal with ***F***, in addition to that, the site cannot be utilised for minimum 15 years for other purposes. The selection of the "0" version can be acceptable, if 15 years pending of the site is scheduled, and the risk is restricted to the industrial area. An additional requirement to this case is the biodegradability of the contaminant and the definite existence of natural attenuation. Otherwise the "0" version has no right to come into existence, because after spending the money for remediation, one will still own contaminated land.

The application of RAMEB can be advantageous in those cases, when the saved time compensates higher costs. The enhancement with cyclodextrin can be economically beneficial, if some arguments and benefits originate from saving time, for example, the company can save the rental costs of buildings or costs of storage, or the change in land-use ensures a high benefit.

The duration of remediation has significant influence on the costs. The CDT cost in the comparative cost estimation was calculated with 1.5 year duration, compared to the 2.5 years of the not enhanced technology. In the demonstration case 24 weeks were enough for remediation, the continuation for another 23 weeks ensured the safety. 0.5 years instead of 2.5 is crucial, the time saving may lower the costs of CDT for the level of ***C*** and ***E***.

About one-third of the costs are spent for site assessment, planning and after-care, which are necessary expenditures even if remediation is not implemented.

When selecting and implementing CDT or any of the alternatives after decision-making of the environmental managers, in addition to the cost evaluation many other parameters, like environmental risks, eco-efficiency, and all aspects of the SWOT-analysis should be considered.

Table 3. Costs of the remediation alternatives for the transformer station (1000 tons soil)

	"0" MNA	Dig & dump GW: ex situ	*Dig&treat on site* GW: pond	*Pump & treat in situ soil wash* GW: ex situ	*In situ* bio-venting GW: ex situ	*CDT* GW: ex situ
	A	***B***	***C***	***D***	***E***	***F***
Treatment duration (years)	*15*	*0.2 soil 1.5 water*	*2.5*	*10*	*2.5 s*	*1.5*
Volume of soil (t)		*1 000*	*1 000*	*1 000*	*1 000*	*1 000*
Costs [EUR]						
Site assessment	1 200	1 200	1 200	1 200	1 200	1 200
Risk assessment	1 200	1 200	1 200	1 200	1 200	1 200
Design, planning of the technology and monitoring		1 000	4 000	4 000	4 000	4 000
Soil excavation	-	20 000	20 000	-	-	-
Transport with disposal	-	40 000	-	-	-	-
New soil (soil + transport)	-	40 000	-	-	-	-
Soil treatment – investment	-	-	6 000	12 000	10 000	10 000
Soil treatment – operation	-	-	20 000	80 000	10 000	7 200
Soil wash with surfactant*				*40 000		
Technology-monitoring	15 years monitor 72 000	3 600	6 000	24 000	6 000	3 600
Soil wash with surfactant*				*12 000		
After-monitoring		4 500	4 500	13 600	13 600	13 600
RAMEB/ (other additives)	-	-	-	*8 000	-	20 000

Table 3. Costs of the remediation alternatives for the transformer station (1000 tons soil) (continued)

	"0" MNA	Dig & dump GW: ex situ	Dig&treat on site GW: pond	Pump & treat in situ soil wash GW: ex situ	In situ bio-venting GW: ex situ	CDT GW: ex situ
	A	B	C	D	E	F
GW treatment – investment	-	12 000	-	12 000	12 000	12 000
GW treatment – operation With surfactant*	-	12 000	-	80 000 *40 000	20 000	12 000
GW treat. pond – investment	-	-	4 000			
GW treat. pond – operation	-	-	10 000			
Total cost for 1 000 t	**84 400**	**135 500**	**76 900**	**228 000/144 000**	**78 000**	**84 800**
Specific cost: 1 000 ton case	**84.4**	**135.5**	**76.9**	**228/144**	**78.0**	**84.8**
Total costs for 50 t (EUR)	10 900	13 400	9 750	27 700/19 200	11 300	11 000
Specific costs (EUR/t)	218	268	195	554/*384	226	220

*with the application of surfactants or other additives (the treatment time can be shortened to the half)
Monitoring of the 50 t site: with 1 monitoring well and 4 sampling/year
Monitoring after ex situ treatment: 1 year, after *in situ* treatment: 3 years

SWOT-analysis of the CDT

SWOT analysis was also performed to assist decision makers in evaluating CDT as an option for remediation of their sites. The main points are summarised below, in Table 4.

Table 4. SWOT analysis of the CDT

Strengths	***Weaknesses***
• CDT is an innovative technology-alternative, increasing the selection. • It is *an in situ* technology: no soil removal, excavation, transport is necessary. • It is remediation base on the beneficial utilisation of the soil microflora. • CDT is an environment-friendly technology. • Additives (RAMEB, nutrients) with defined technological parameters have no environmental risk. • RAMEB is moderately biodegradable natural compound. Biodegradation half-life time of RAMEB is 0.5–1.5 year, which is comparable with the duration of the technology. After fulfilling its role, it disappears from the soil. • CDT can be used for various types of contaminants (VOCs, SVOCs, PAHs, PCBs etc.) and to treat various types of environmental media. • CDs increase the bioavailability and are able to accelerate biodegradation of poorly degradable contaminants. • By encapsulation of the pollutants, their toxic effects can be decreased. • CDT is less time consuming than the alternative technologies; depending on the type of the contaminant, duration can be lowered to 40–70 % of the treatment without CD. Decreased treatment time results in sooner utilisation of the site and benefits from future land use.	• The price of RAMEB is relatively high, but comparable with other additives usually applied in remediation. • CDT is not a well-known technology, it has not entered to the market yet • Acceptance of CD as an additive can be problematic by the authorities. • Knowledge on the effect of the technology on the soil complex matrix and interactions is limited. • Emission from the technology should be controlled and monitoring is necessary. • There are only a few good references in the World and even fewer in Europe.
Opportunities	***Threats***
• After proving its effectiveness in soil bioremediation technologies CD application in other environmental biotechnologies is foreseen. • With the decreasing price of RAMEB the application can be widespread. • Applying the cost-efficiency and mainly the cost-benefit approach, its beneficial application may be recognised. • The "clean, environmentally benign" technologies can receive major role in the future parallel to widespread soil-protection. • The use of CD in eco-engineering and eco-technologies is recommended especially when the time available for treatment is limited.	• According to the common knowledge, *in situ* application of soil remediation has *in*creased environmental risk. Of course this is not true, a refined evaluation is necessary, by controlling the soil-moisture content and applying depression in the ground-water, the risk due to emission can be completely reduced.

Having collected data to the SWOT analysis it can be concluded that CDT is an advantageous alternative biotechnology for the reduction of the environmental risk of a site contaminated with poorly degradable hydrocarbons.

3.1.3. Summary of the Technology-Verification Applied for CDT

The complex verification tool can be applied for the CDT technology, and any other in situ bioremediation. The results can be utilised for decision making in environmental management.

- MOKKA verification-system is applicable for an in situ bioremediation based on biodegradation.
- Mass-balance can be calculated from the technology-monitoring data.
- The risk of the site before and after remediation can be calculated from the initial and final contaminant concentrations, and effect assessment data.
- The risk due to emission from the source and the technology can be easily monitored and reduced during the technology. In case of in situ technology-application better control of contaminant-transport can be reached than in case of ex situ technologies.
- The regional and global risk components can be evaluated in comparison with the other technology-alternatives. Some of the risk components can be quantified (CO_2-production, water and energy consumption), but some others can be characterised only by qualitative marks or scores, which also make possible the relative evaluation of alternative technologies.
- The majority of the cost elements can be quantified, cost-efficiency is an ideal tool for the comparison of remediation-alternatives and it supports technology-selection.

The CDT has proven its applicability, has been verified by the new verification tool. CDT can be characterised as a suitable technology for transformer oil and other moderately bioavailable contaminants, environment- and cost-efficient and sustainable technology.

3.2. Verification of the CCP-technology

The same tools were applied for the evaluation of CCP as for the verification of CDT to prove that these tools are generally applicable irrespective of contaminant type, and whether the technology is used for mobilisation or immobilisation of the contaminants.

Site-specific evaluation of the CCP starts with the planning of the technology, it's monitoring and summing up the results required by the verification methodology. The calculation of the mass balance is based on the quantitative value of the mobile metal fraction.

The site-specific risk reduction was calculated from the decrease of the mobile contaminant amount (concentration). Site-specific risk considers land-uses, in our case agricultural (hobby gardens) and natural land uses typical at the former mining-site.

Regional and Global risk components were evaluated and compared with technology-alternatives, and the same was applied in the cost-efficiency assessment. Changes in land-use are not foreseen, but it is not crucial, because the natural and the hobby uses of the soil are the most sensitive land uses, complying with the conservative risk-assessment approach.

SWOT analysis includes all the aspects, which have not been assessed previously and the arguments for and against the application of CCP.

3.2.1. Summary Results of the CCP in Lab-Microcosms and Field Experiments

The soil of the abandoned mining site is mainly contaminated with As, Cd, Cu, Hg, Pb and Zn, but out of these metals Cd (total content 4.2–23.3 mg/kg) and Zn (total content 926–4420 mg/kg) have the highest mobility and for that reason the availability of these two was more closely studied. According to the different extractions 26–34% of Cd and 23–24% of Zn are acetate extractable compared to the total metal content and 7–13% of Cd and 6–11% of Zn are water-soluble.

- Based on the chemical analytical, bacterial and plant toxicity test results, fly ash "A" from a power-plant in Hungary was the most effective: the mobile Cd and Zn concentration decreased by 50–99% in the fly ash-treated contaminated soil, the bacterial and plant toxicity and the bioaccumulated metal amount decreased by 30–70% and by 70%, respectively. The combination of lignite, alginite, lime and phosphate was also efficient.
- Fly ash "A" showed the best immobilising effect on long term (2 years). One single treatment with 5 w% fly ash "A" reduced by 45–49% and by more than 99% the acetate extractable and the water-soluble metal amount, respectively. It also reduced soil toxicity for both bacteria and plants and decreased the bioavailable metal amount by 70%.
- The rapid bioaccumulation test showed that the addition of 5 w% "A" fly ash to the soil diminished by 60–70% the Cd and Zn uptake of the 5 days old seedling used for testing.
- Amongst the other additives some decreased metal extractability (chemical availability), but were not able to reduce the toxicity of the soil.
- The stabilizers found to be promising in the microcosm experiments were applied in the field experiments: fly ash, fly ash with lime and other additives, which enhance microbial and plant activity in the soil.
- Fly ash and lime together increased soil pH from 2.4 to 6.8, metal content of the leachate decreased with 90% after one month.
- Spontaneously growing plants' number on the fly ash treated soil increased to 100 fold, on fly-ash and lime treated soil to 200 fold compared to untreated soil.
- Seeded plant size (average length) on fly ash treated soil was 500%, on fly ash + lime treated soil 800% compared to untreated soil after three weeks.
- Plant uptake of toxic metals was measured; horseradish, rape and grasses had low BCF in their leaves and stems and acceptable concentration in their roots (Anton and Murányi, 2007).
- Some BCF values are shown below:

BCF leaves/roots horse radish:	Cd: 0.2/0.2	Cu: 0.02/0.03	Zn: 0.06/0.14
BCF leaves/roots rape:	Cd: 0.07/0.6	Cu: 0.0/0.4	Zn: 0.5/1.4
	Pb: 0.4/0.7		
BCF leaves/roots maize:	Cd: 0.4/2.9	Cu: 0.07/1.0	Zn: 0.4/0.4

BCF leaves/roots sallow:	Cd: 3.1/3.4	Cu: 0.06/0.5	Zn: 1.0/1.2
	Pb: 0.0/0.2		

The basic difference between CDT and CCP is that bioremediation based on biodegradation decreases the environmental risk of the site and soil by eliminating the harmful contaminant, while toxic metals are not removed and eliminated by CCP. Their risk is reduced by making them unavailable for wind and water, diluted acids and plants. The risk of the stabilised toxic metals is lowered by stabilising agents and plants together, changing the physical and chemical form of the metals, blocking their transport by leaching, solution, partition, erosion, deflation and plant uptake, but they are still present in the environment. The aim of the technology is to ensure the irreversible effect of the stabilising agent and the long-term immobile, not available form of the contaminant. The conditions for low risk are: long-term stabilising effect, stable and balanced climatic and meteorological parameters.

This chapter shows a selection of the results, to demonstrate the changes in mobility further to the effect of the stabilising agent. One of the best results was shown by 5% fly-ash treatment, the total and mobile toxic metal contents of the soil of the hobby-garden was measured before and several times after the treatment. The tables below contain the final results of the long-term (2 years) stabilisation experiments and the stabilised amount is calculated for the whole hobby-garden.

The total and water-soluble metal contents of the soil and the mixture of soil and additive is compared and evaluated in time. The effect of the bioavailable fraction was measured by toxicity tests and the plant-uptake by a plant accumulation test. The toxicity tests (*Vibrio fisheri* luminescence, *Azomonas agilis* dehydrogenase activity and *Sinapis alba* root and shot-growth tests) and the rapid plant-accumulation test are self-developed environmental-toxicity tests (Gruiz, 2001).

3.2.2. Evaluation of the CPP Technology and Validation of the Verification Tool

Mass Balance of the CCP

The mass balance of CCP is determined and quantified considering the mobile fraction of the contaminants in the soil. The aim of the technology is to immobilise metals, to block the mobilisation and transport of the metal from the soil to the ground-water or pore water, to the surface waters and to the plants.

The mass balance was calculated on the basis of the long-term chemical-stabilisation experiments in microcosms and field, applying fly ash "A" as chemical stabilizer.

$$\textbf{Initial mobile metal content} \xrightarrow{\text{stabilising agent}} \textbf{Residual mobile metal content}$$

The difference was immobilised/stabilised by the chemical stabiliser. The role of plants is physical stabilisation of the surface and normalisation of the water-balance of the soil by plant uptake and evapo-transpiration and physical isolation of the soil from direct runoff and erosion.

Soil surface area: 500 m^2	Depth of treatment by fly-ash: 50 cm
Volume of the treated soil: 250 m^3	Mass of the treated soil: 450 tons

Amount of chemical amendments: 22 tons fly-ash

Table 5 and 6 show the total and mobile metal contents of the soil of the hobby-garden and the fly-ash. The fly ash has also some metal-content, but it is negligible compared to the soil.

Table 5. Metal content of the hobby garden soil before treatment

Untreated soil [450 t]	As mg/kg	Cd mg/kg	Cu mg/kg	Pb mg/kg	Zn mg/kg	As kg	Cd kg	Cu kg	Pb kg	Zn kg
Total metal	341	7.17	335	1571	1424	153	3.2	150	707	641
Mobile metal	<DL	1.00	0.66	<DL	171.00	<DL	0.45	0.297	<DL	76.95

Total metal content: ICP-AES after aqua regia digestion Mobile metal content: ICP-AES after water extraction

Table 6. Metal content of the fly-ash

Chemical amendment [22 t]	As mg/kg	Cd mg/kg	Cu mg/kg	Pb mg/kg	Zn mg/kg	As kg	Cd kg	Cu kg	Pb kg	Zn kg
Total metal	18.8	0.874	25.9	18.3	223	0.414	0.019	0.57	0.403	4.91
Mobile metal	<DL	<DL	<DL	0.09	0.43	<DL	<DL	<DL	0.002	0.009

Table 7. Metal content in of the treated soil after 25 months

Treated soil + fly-ash [472 t]	As mg/kg	Cd mg/kg	Cu mg/kg	Pb mg/kg	Zn mg/kg	As kg	Cd kg	Cu kg	Pb kg	Zn kg
Total metal	327	7.12	345	1540	1430	154.34	3.36	162.84	726.88	674.96
Mobile metal	<DL	0.01	0.41	<DL	0.55	<DL	0.005	0.193	<DL	0.259

Table 8. Results of the stabilisation experiment: immobilised metal amount: initial – final

	Immobilised mobile metal-doses				
Treated soil + fly-ash [472 t]	As kg	Cd kg	Cu kg	Pb kg	Zn kg
Immobilised metal	<DL	**0.443**	**0.103**	<DL	**76.42**

As a result of chemical stabilisation the mobile metal amount decreased (Table 8) with 0.4 kg of cadmium and 76 kg of Zn within the 500 m^2 treated surface of the hobby garden.

The mass balance of the CCP on the basis of the long-term stabilization experiments in microcosms referred to the Cd, Cu, Zn content, because arsenic and lead were in immobile form in the soil (Table 8). The stabilized metal-content is calculated as: Input – Output = Stabilized.

Stabilized **cadmium: 0.443 kg,** 98% of the initial mobile cadmium content
Stabilized **copper: 0.103 kg,** 35% of the initial mobile copper content
Stabilized **zinc: 76.42 kg,** >99% of the initial mobile zinc content.

The mass balance proves the efficiency of the stabilisation technology: the mobile metal content of Cd, Cu and Zn decreased to a high extent after chemical stabilisation. The emission and risks of the technology can be concluded also from the mass balance.

Risks Related to the CCP

Initial and Final Risk of the Contaminated Soil

The risk-reduction rate of stabilisation is calculated on the basis of the RQ = PEC/PNEC relation. The Cd and Zn contamination of the soil and soil-leachate was compared to the site-specific quality criteria, according to real water and land-uses. The estimates are highly conservative.

Risk of the water leachate of the soil, considering the leachate as groundwater for drinking water-base (highly conservative estimate, because there is no groundwater use for drinking water):

Cd: RQinitial = 1 000 μg/dm^3 / 5 μg/dm^3 = **200**
Cd: RQfinal = 10 μg/dm^3 / 5 μg/dm^3 = **2**
Zn: RQinitial = 171 000 μg/dm^3 / 200 μg/dm^3 = **855**
Zn: RQfinal = 550 μg/dm^3 / 200 μg/dm^3 = **2.75**

Risk of the water leachate of the soil, considering the leachate as groundwater in a less sensitive area (medium conservative estimate!):

Cd: RQinitial = 1 000 μg/dm^3 / 10 μg/dm^3 = **100**
Cd: RQfinal = 10 μg/dm^3 / 10 μg/dm^3 = **1.0**
Zn: RQinitial = 171 000 μg/dm^3 / 1 000 μg/dm^3 = **171**
Zn: RQfinal = 550 μg/dm^3 / 1 000 μg/dm^3 = **0.55**

Risk of the water leachate of the soil, as if flowing into a sensitive surface water system: a 100-fold dilution-rate is applied (highly conservative estimate!):

Cd: RQinitial = 1 000 μg/dm^3 / 1 μg/dm^3 = **1 000** →after dilution → **10**
Cd: RQfinal = 10 μg/dm^3 / 1 μg/dm^3 = **10** → after dilution → **0.1**
Zn: RQinitial = 171 000 μg/dm^3 / 100 μg/dm^3 = **1 710** → after dilution → **17.1**
Zn: RQfinal = 550 μg/dm^3 / 100 μg/dm^3 = **5.5** → after dilution → **0.055**

The Hungarian soil quality criteria are not effect-based values and are related to the total metal content. These values cannot be considered as "no effect" or "no risk" concentrations, therefore the final risk of the stabilised soil was characterised by toxicity testing. The soil proved to be very toxic at the beginning of the treatment and became non-toxic at the end (Table 9; Feigl, 2005).

Table 9. Toxicity of the soil treated by fly-ash, expressed in the % of the untreated

Toxicity test type	Treatment months	0% fly-ash	2% fly-ash	5% fly-ash
Vibrio fischeri luminescence [%]	25 months	100	91	66
Azomonas agile dehydrogenase [%]	25 months	100	136	43
Sinapis alba root growth [%]	2 months	100	93	60
	14 months		-7	-33
	25 months		-266	-400
Sinapis alba shoot growth [%]	2 months	100	100	71
	14 months		17	-50
	25 months		-266	-400

Marks: (-) toxicity means stimulation

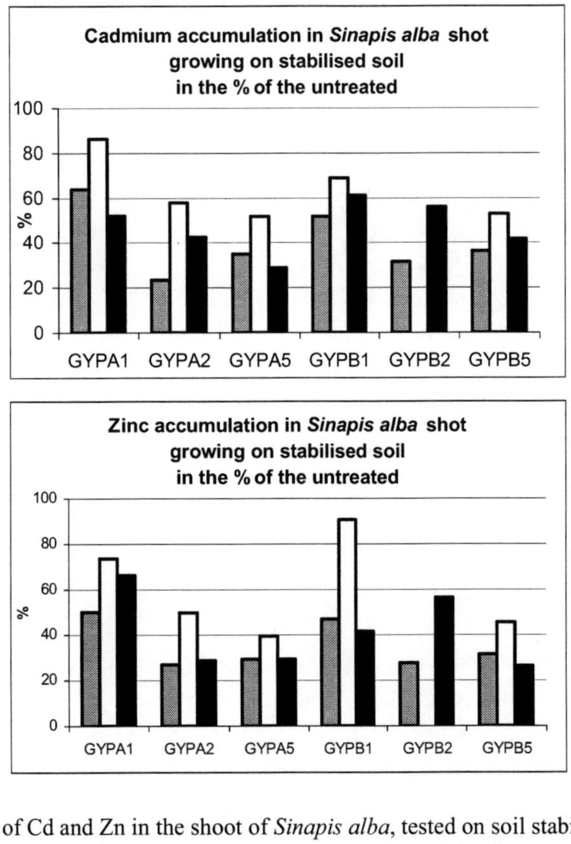

Figure 9. Accumulation of Cd and Zn in the shoot of *Sinapis alba*, tested on soil stabilised for 2, 14 and 25 months

Summarising the effect of fly-ash as stabilising agent, the most important is, that plant toxicity decreased drastically, and stimulation is efficient. The bacterial toxicity decreased to half (slightly toxic) of the initial (very toxic). Another important issue is the food-chain effect, namely the metal accumulation by plants. This kind of risk was followed by the rapid plant accumulation test. The fly-ash treatment resulted significant decrease in metal uptake (Figure 9). The graphs below show the effect of 1%, 2% and 5% fly-ash at three time intervals: the

2nd, the 14th and the 25th month. The best result was obtained by the 5% fly-ash "A" (GYPA5): 30% accumulation compared to the 100% of the untreated one.

To increase sensitivity of the test, the metal-uptake is provoked by the test circumstances using very young and well-bioaccumulating seedlings. In spite of all these, the Cd content of the test-seedlings was only 87% of the limit value for leafy-food-staffs, compared to the initial 260%.

Site Specific Environmental Risk of the Application of CCP

Surface water is the main endangered element of the site. Natural or agricultural water uses are typical. According to the GIS model of the site chemical stabilisation of the diffusely contaminated area is enough for diminishing risk to the target risk level in the surface water-system. To hinder erosion, leaching produced by heavy rains, strong runoffs and consequent floods and to increase aesthetic view additional vegetation is necessary.

The following site-specific risk elements are relevant to the area, and the CCP technology:

- The water-transport of contaminants before the settlement of a complete vegetative cover on the surface of the contaminated soil represents high risk in the upper flow of the creek, but low risk in the hobby-garden area.
- Fly-ash "A" is not toxic, its total and mobile metal-content is much lower, than that of the soil, posing very little hazard.
- Handling of the soil, mixing with amendment, preparation for plantation, and treatment of plants are very common agrotechnologies, with the same risk, as agriculture has in general, and in the neighbouring area.
- Transportation of the amendment to the site is a one-off event, with an acceptable risk, similar to the transportation of organic manure or other agricultural soil amendments.
- There is no risk and impact from special handling and disposal of plants with high toxic metal content; because the contaminants are retained in soil and, sometimes in the roots, no translocation to the leaves and other parts above the soil surface should be considered.
- Utilisation of a waste material is an additional benefit of the CCP technology.
- Other wastes can also be used; the research on it is still going on.
- In spite of the lowered mobile metal-content of the soil, – the total metal content remains and may serve as a standby supply ("chemical time bomb") for remobilising the toxic metals. Long term and irreversible effect should be ensured by environmental circumstances in favour of soil-formation (in contrary to soil destruction). The aim is to increase immobile metal forms including metals into the atomic and molecular grids of clay minerals and oxy-hydroxides, insuring high water-capacity (in contrary to leaching), high pH (in contrary to acidification), high biological activity and organic cycle to increase the biologically controlled element-ratio, etc.
- An integrated monitoring based on water and plant analyses ensures an effective control.

Risk Reduction Alternatives

A comparison between the risks and costs of several remediation alternatives considered for our model-site has been done to substantiate cost efficiency of the combined chemical and phytoremediation option (Table 10).

"0" alternative: there will be no remediation done, however monitoring and control is needed. In the best case a slow natural soil-formation and revegetation process will ensure the physical stabilisation of the surface, but spontaneous acidification and plant uptake will not be blocked. In a worse case scenario acidification and erosion hinder revegetation. Both of these spontaneous alternatives-result in high-risk situations.

D&D (Dig and Dump) alternative**:** removal and replacement of the polluted soil: excavation of the contaminated soil volume, transportation to the waste-disposal site and substitute of the removed soil with unpolluted borrow material, its transportation to the site, then revegetation. Soil replacement results in immediate risk reduction and makes possible more sensitive land use. A sub-version of this alternative is, when the contaminated soil is transported and disposed to the tailings-dump nearby, and then isolated and covered together with the 4 million tons mine-waste: **D&DTD**

Soil washing is an ex situ technology for the treatment of excavated, wetted soil. Toxic metal can be removed by the application of a strong water-jet, or high pressure cleaner, using the shear-force, when soil is wetted. When the shear force and hot water is not enough for the removal of mobile metals, further washing or extraction steps are needed. The wash-water should be treated separately. Wet soil should be desiccated, placed on the surface, revitalised and revegetated.

CCP alternative: Combined chemical and phytostabilisation: the application of the technology has been introduced in detail.

Time Requirement

The "0" version in case of toxic metal contaminated sites is very disadvantageous. "Natural attenuation" means dilution, extraction, deflation, erosion, etc. The dispersion of contamination increases risk by transport endangering sensitive areas and surface waters. The time requirement is "endless" or very long, depending on the mass of the source.

Soil washing takes 1–2 years in our case (50 000 tons) when the washing plant has 100 t/day capacity. An additional problem is the collection of diffusely polluted soil which takes time if it is possible at all.

Dig&dump needs a few months, but the new soil should be handled by agricultural methods and forming of the isolating vegetation takes some time. Some more time can be spared by the sub-version, placing contaminated soil on the flotation-tailings dump before its isolation.

CCP: Preparation of the soil by the addition of a stabilising agent and if necessary nutrients, takes a few days. The additional time comes from the application of agrotechnologies and general aftercare of the vegetation. This requirement is present in all cases, when revegetation is the task.

Phytoextraction was not included in the present comparative study, because the first assessment has proven, that it is not competitive with the stabilisation-technologies, its application is unrealistic at the model-site.

Regional and Global Risk Elements in Comparison with the Technology-Alternatives

The regional and global environmental load of CCP should be considered similarly to any agro-technology. The load on the environment, water and energy consumption can be calculated on the basis of agricultural experiences. We do not assess these risk elements in detail.

Risks of the alternatives are summarised in Table 10.

Table 10. Comparative risk assessment of the technology alternatives

	"0" MNA	D&D	D&DTD	Soil washing and aftercare	CCP *in situ* stab.
Treatment duration (years)	***30***	***0.5***	***0.3***	***2***	***2***
Water soluble with rain/runoff	10	10	10	2	2
Water soluble with leachate	10	10	10	2	2
Sorbable with erosion	10	10	10	3	5
Plant uptake	10	0	0	0	5
Dust	3	10	10	5	3
Noise	0	10	10	10	0
Emission x years (score)	**1290**	**25**	**15**	**44**	**34**
CO_2 due to excavation, transport	0	20	5	10	0
Water consumption	0	5	3	50	0
Energy consumption (score) Technology Transport Waste (soil, waste water)	1 0 0	20 20 50	20 5 10	20 0 20	3 0 0
Total regional items(score)	**1**	**115**	**43**	**100**	**3**
New soil Nutrients (N,P,K) Additives (fly-ash or amendment)	0 0 0	50 2 0	50 2 0	0 5 5	0 2 5
Total material (score)	**0**	**52**	**52**	**10**	**7**
Total risk score	***1291***	***192***	***110***	***149***	***44***

The risk scores of dig&dump are similar to soil washing, CCP has reached the lowest risk score. The “0” version, – contrary to the “0” alternative for transformer oil contaminated site– shows a very high risk, because the natural processes do not lower, but increase the risk, the contaminant is not degraded, but becomes more-and-more available for water (leaching, erosion) and plants, until the total metal content has not been mobilised.

Costs-Efficiency Assessment

Based on the currently available test results the most efficient alternative of chemical stabilisation is discussed for preliminary cost calculation: fly ash "A" additive in 3%. Grass species (*Poaceae*) were used for revegetation and phytostabilisation.

The total surface area that remains after removal of the mine wastes and soils of the contaminated gardens are considered for treatment. The surface area is 44 506 m^2, the average depths is 0.6 m, the contaminated soil volume is 50 000 tons. The summary of the calculated costs and unit costs/hectare is provided in Table 11. The cost details of the CCP technology are given in Table 12.

A comparison between the costs of five remediation alternatives considered for the mining-site has been done to substantiate cost efficiency of the combined chemical and phytostabilisation option (Table 11). The costs are based on the prices in 2006 in Hungary expressed in Euro.

Table 11. Comparison of the costs of some remediation alternatives

COSTS (EURO) of the treatment of 50 000 t	"0"	D&D	D&DTD	Soil washing	CCP
Duration (years)	30	0.5	0.3	2	2
Excavation of the polluted soil/mine waste		150 000	150 000	150 000	
Transport to the tailings dump			50 000		
Transport to a waste disposal facility		212 000			
Final disposal of the polluted material		3 840 000			
Preliminary experiments				5 000	5 000
Soil-washing and water treatment				2 400 000	
Soil desiccation and replacement				120 000	
Soil revitalisation and agrotechniques				12 000	
Agro-techniques and chemical stabilisation					13 884
Unpolluted borrow material and transport		324 000	324 000		
Management, organisation, safety	124 000	60 000	60 000		29 268
Monitoring	24 680				52 000
Risk communication	21 680				19 512
TOTAL (EURO)	**170 360**	**4 586 000**	**604 000**	**2 607 400**	**119 664**
Specific costs (Euro/tons)	**3.4**	**91.7**	**12.1**	**52.1**	**2.4**

The total costs of the CCP alternative is lower than the cost of the "0" version (no remediation), which still involves management, organisation, monitoring, protection and risk communication and highly endangers the area with its long-term risk.

The total cost of the CCP-option is 10-times lower, than the most frequently applied dig&dump method, with local disposal on the present tailings dump, waiting for isolation. Dig&dump on a remote waste dump-facility costs 40-times more, than the CCP.

In case of cost benefit analysis the following benefits can be taken into consideration:

- the hobby gardens at the mining area can not be used for production of plants either for human consumption or animal husbandry (the costs of the vegetables, fruits, meat, eggs etc. to be purchased for the families will be spared after remediation decreasing the costs of living for the inhabitants),
- vegetable production and animal husbandry can be a job for many people being unemployed since the mine has been abandoned,
- better health-conditions and reduced health-care costs, improved life quality in the area are further benefits to be expressed in monetary value.

Table 12. Detailed costs of CCP

Costs	Euro/ha	0. year	1. year	2. years	TOTAL costs (Euro)
Preliminary experiments	0	5 000	0	0	5 000
Treatment by fly ash	2 460	10 947	0	0	10 947
Autumn stripping	18	80	0	0	80
Autumn ploughing	25.2	112	0	0	112
Levelling	18	0	80	0	80
Spring fertilising	40	0	178	178	356
Preparation of the seed bed	16	0	71	0	71
Sowing	18	0	80	0	80
Spraying insecticides	8	0	35	35	70
Watering	0	0	902	902	1 804
Seeds 2 kg/hectar	32	0	142	0	142
Hoeing	16	0	71	71	142
Management, organisation, safety	0	9 756	9 756	9 756	29 268
Technology-monitoring	0	0	2 400	9 600	12 000
Risk communication	0	6 504	6 504	6 504	19 512
Long-term monitoring&aftercare		0	0	0	**40 000**
Total costs (EURO)	0	**32 399**	**20 219**	**27 046**	**119 664**

SWOT of the CCP

Tabe 13. SWOT analysis of in situ CCP technology

<table>
<tr><th>Strengths</th><th>Weakness</th></tr>
<tr><td>
• Applying this technology the mobility, and therefore the risk of inorganic contaminants is reduced without removing them from their location.
• Time requirement of CCP is less, than dig&dump considering consequent revegetation.
• Risk of transport of pollutants from soil can be blocked in more than 99%.
• The treated soil can be utilised for a broad range of agricultural production.
• The produced plant material does not need further treatment or safety measures.
• The risk of exposure (during remediation) is reduced by limiting direct contact with contaminated soils.
• Applicable to broad range of contaminants, including many metals with limited alternative options.
• CCP is a cost efficient method when compared to other technologies
• It requires minimal maintenance.
• The applied chemical additives in CCP pose no risks to the environment.
• The additive applied might be a waste in the energy sector (fly ash).
• At some appropriate sites CCP may completely replace traditional dig and dump systems.
• Compared to traditional remediation technologies it generates less secondary wastes.
• Associated environmental disturbance is minimal.
</td><td>
• Different toxic metal-types need different stabilisers.
• Metals that are readily transferred to leaves in plants may limit the applicability of phytostabilisation due to potential harm to the food chain, but CCP utilise plants, which do not accumulate the metals in their parts above the soil surface.
• The contaminants are left in place, so the site must be monitored continuously to make sure the stabilising conditions carry on.
• Sometimes stabilising agents should repeatedly be applied to maintain the effectiveness of the immobilisation.
</td></tr>
<tr><th>Opportunities</th><th>Threats</th></tr>
<tr><td>
• Land use after remediation of toxic metal contaminated mining sites may result in high benefit, instead of monetary, natural and social losses.
• To reduce costs further amendments can be selected and used to improve soil physical and chemical properties if they are compatible with the required functions.
</td><td>
• High water flow rates may erode applied amendments.
• Plant establishment must be carefully planned and executed: well growing, not accumulating species.
• Climatic factors may influence the effectiveness.
</td></tr>
</table>

3.2.3. Summary of the Verification Tool Applied for Combined Chemical and Phytostabilisation

The complex verification tool is applicable to the CCP technology, in spite of the fact, that toxic metals remain in the soil, however in a less risky form. The results of the verification can be utilised for decision making on technology selection.

- MOKKA verification-system is applicable for an in situ bioremediation based on stabilisation.
- Mass-balance can be calculated on the basis of the mobile metal fraction.
- The risk of the site before and after remediation can be calculated from the initial and final mobile contaminant concentrations, and effect assessment (toxicity) data.
- There is no additional local risk during the technology application, compared to the original situation: the emission from the treated site is decreasing.
- The regional and local risk elements of CCP are very similar to the agrotechnologies, the most widespread technology practice on land.
- The results of cost-efficiency assessment can be used in the comparative evaluation, but in case of CCP cost-benefit assessment is a better tool in aid of decision-making, because future land use, like production on the agricultural land or forestry are essential parts of the evaluation.

CCP has proven its applicability, has been verified by the new verification tool. CCP can be characterised as a suitable technology for toxic metal contaminated sites to reduce metal mobility and related risk. The verification-tool confirmed that compared to the existing alternatives CCP is the most realistic solution for diffusely polluted sites, where source treatment is not possible. The trust in CCP and in other technologies based on contaminant stabilisation can be increased with the help of the verification tool. The trusting and spreading of this technology is essential to support management of diffuse and residual pollution that cannot be removed or cleaned-up by traditional means due to the unrealistic volumes and costs.

4. CONCLUSION

The developed innovative tools for the verification of the technology proved the efficiency and the competitiveness of both technologies. The four-step complex evaluation – comprising mass balance, risk assessment, cost-efficiency (cost-benefit) assessment and SWOT analysis – gives a basis both for the characterisation of the innovative technologies and for the comparison of different technological alternatives. The methodology supports the technology-selection procedure including the comparative risk and cost assessments, preliminary mass-balance with the expected and planned efficiency. After implementation of the technology, measured data are collected and evaluated to validate the preliminary estimates. The mass-balance, the costs and the various risks are validated. The SWOT covers the whole process from the assessment of the site through the design and application, till the after-care. The SWOT serves also as a preliminary tool, mirroring the expectations towards the innovative technology. It is a real verification tool proving the expectations via a real-case experience.

Calculation of the hydrocarbon contaminants mass balance in the soil at the start, of the removed amount by the interventions, and of the remaining amount after finishing the remediation proves that the in situ remediation by CDT was suitable for cleaning up the site historically contaminated with transformer oil. Similarly, the calculation of the amount of the mobile fraction of toxic metals before and after the CCP treatment proves the successful immobilisation of the contaminants and risk reduction of polluted soil.

In the risk assessment procedure the risk of the contaminated sites as well as the risk of the technologies were considered. The risk of the sites can be effectively reduced both by the risk of the assessed technologies, as shown by the quantitative risk assessment and by toxicity testing. The Risk Quotient of the soil and ground-water calculated from measured contaminant concentrations before and after remediation gives the risk reduction rate. The effect assessment of the soil by soil-living organisms results in a direct, measured risk-related value, the "no adverse effect" value, which proves the "no risk" situation after treatment.

The technology-application has specific risks, resulted from the emissions (contaminants, additives, CO_2, NO_x and SO_x) and from the load on the environment due to water and energy use as well as the contribution to the global risk, like greenhouse effect, ozone depletion or the consumption of resources. The potential risk of the CDT due to increased contaminant-mobility requires special measures, e.g. depression of the groundwater level to avoid spreading of the contaminants. The potential risk of CCP includes the eventual re-mobilisation of toxic metals due to the environmental changes (acidification, soil degradation). To avoid these hazards continuous monitoring is necessary during and after technology-application.

According to the cost-efficiency assessment CDT is competitive with the alternative soil remediation technologies. It was found to have the potential to speed up and intensify the bioremediation by reducing the typical treatment time of a conventional biological soil treatment technology. The demonstration site was an industrial area where the land use was not changed after remediation, therefore the only quantifiable benefit was sparing of penalties for contamination of environment. On other contaminated sites shorter treatment-time and early utilisation of the land can make CDT cost-beneficial. The CCP technology proved to be much more cost-efficient than the "dig and dump", the removal and replacement of the polluted soil most often used for the risk reduction of such sites. The benefits of the CCP technology are coming from the agricultural use of the site and animal husbandry after remediation ensuring the living for the inhabitants mostly unemployed since the mining was stopped. The non-quantifiable benefits (effect on ecological environment and human health) of both technologies are beyond dispute. The no-remediation (monitoring the natural processes without any invasion) alternative can be a cheaper alternative for biodegradable pollutants in some cases (e.g. no utilisation of the site is planned for years) but it is not acceptable for toxic-metal contaminated sites, because risk increase is foreseen (secondary poisoning by food-chain transport and pollution of more sensitive area and waters) requiring high costs of the monitoring.

In the SWOT analysis the strengths, weaknesses, opportunities and threats were listed in a way to be understandable for the non-professionals, too.

The new approach of the *complex technology-verification* supports *decision-making* and the selection of the best possible technology or in case of verified innovative technologies, a better technology, than the former best one.

The verification of the remediation technologies will help in the decision-making, ensuring a better selection-procedure and higher quality in environmental management, increase the efficiency of remediation and of the utilisation of financial resources. This complex methodology is able to confirm the selection of environmental-friendly technologies based on natural processes (bioremediation and ecoremediation), enhanced natural attenuation and *in situ* biotechnologies.

A uniform verification would be necessary to make progress in the acceptance of innovative *in situ* technologies, to increase trust towards them and to support their market-entry.

5. REFERENCES

Anton, A. & Máthé-*Gáspár*, G. (2005). Factors affecting heavy metal uptake in plant selection for phytoremediation. *Zeitschrift für Naturforschung, 60*, 244–246.

Anton, A. & Murányi, A. (2007). Efficient Phytoremediation, In: Book of Abstracts of MOKKA Conference and EURODEMO Workshop, (Meeting date: 14–15 June 2007), p. 44, Budapest, Hungary, BME ABÉT and MOKKA Consortium

BANYAREM (2004–2007) Risk reduction of diffuse pollution from mining activities by integrated remediation technologies based on immobilisation, Hungarian GVOP 3.1.1-2004-05-0261/3.0-R&D Project http://www.ecorisc.hu

Bardi, L., Ricci, R. & Marzona, M. (2003). In situ bioremediation of a hydrocarbon-polluted site with cyclodextrin as a coadjuvant to increase bioavailability. *Water, Air, & Soil Pollution: Focus, 3(3),* 15–23.

Dietz, A.C. & Schnoor, J.L. (2001). Advances in Phytoremediation. *Environmental Health Perspectives, 109*, 163−168.

DIFPOLMINE (2002–2006) Diffuse pollution of mining activities, EU Life 02 ENV/F000291 Demonstration Project http://www.difpolmine.org

DIN 38412-L34 (1991) German standard methods for the examination of water, waste water and sludge; Bio-assays (group L); determination of the inhibitory effect of waste water on the light emission of Photobacterium phosphoreum – luminescent bacteria waste water test using conserved bacteria (L 34) German Standard

ETAP – Environmental Technologies Action Plan – http://ec.europa.eu/environment/etap

Fava, F., Di Gioia, D. & Marchetti, L. (1998). Cyclodextrin effects on the *ex-situ* bioremediation of a chronically polychlorobiphenyl-contaminated soil. *Biotechnology and Bioengineering, 58*, 345–355.

Feigl, V. (2005). Stabilisation of soils contaminated with toxic metals: Experiments for integrated phytostabilisation. *Diplomawork*, Budapest University of Technology and Economics, Hungary

Feigl, V., Atkári, Á., Anton, A. & Gruiz, K. (2007). Chemical stabilisation combined with phytostabilisation applied to mine waste contaminated soil in Hungary. In: Conference

Proceedings, 17th International Biohydrometallurgy Symposium 2–5 September 2007, Frankfurt am Main Germany, in press

Fenyvesi, É., Csabai, K., Molnár, M., Gruiz, K., Murányi, A. & Szejtli, J. (2003). Quantitative and Qualitative Analysis of RAMEB in Soil. *Journal of Inclusion Phenomena and Macrocyclic Chemistry, 44,* 413–416.

Fenyvesi, É., Gruiz, K., Verstichel, S., De Wilde, B., Leitgib, L. Csabai, K. & Szaniszló, N. (2005). Biodegradation of cyclodextrins in soil. *Chemosphere*, *60* , 1001–1008.

Gruiz, K. & Kriston, É. (1995). In situ Bioremediation of Hydrocarbon in Soil. *Journal of Soil Contamination, 4,* 163–173.

Gruiz, K., Fenyvesi, É., Kriston, É., Molnár, M. & Horváth, B. (1996). Potential use of cyclodextrins in soil bioremediation. *Journal of Inclusion Phenomena and Macrocyclic Chemistry*, *25,* 233–236.

Gruiz, K., Horváth, B. & Molnár, M. (2001). *Environmental Toxicology* (in Hungarian). Budapest, Hungary, BME Publisher.

Gruiz, K. (2003). Interactive Ecotoxicity Tests for Contaminated Soil. In: Annokkée, G.J., Arendt, F. & Uhlmann, O. (Eds.), *Wissenschaftliche Berichte* (FZKA 6943, pp. 267–275) Karlsruhe, Germany, Forschungszentrum Karlsruhe GmbH.

Gruiz, K. (2005). Biological tools for the soil ecotoxicity evaluation: Soil testing triad and the interactive ecotoxicity tests for contaminated soil. In: Fava, F. & Canepa, P. Ed(s), *Innovative approaches to the bioremediation of contaminated sites, Soil Remediation Series NO 6*, (pp. 45–70). Venice, Italy, INCA.

Gruiz, K., Vaszita, E. & Siki, Z. (2005). Environmental Risk Management of Mining Sites with Diffuse Pollution. In: Uhlmann, O., Annokkée, G.J. & F. Arendt, F. (Eds.), Conference Proceedings of 9th International FZK/TNO Conf.nce on Soil_Water Systems, (Meeting date: 3–7 October, 2005, Bordeaux) (pp.2568–2574) Karlsruhe, Germany, Forschungszentrum Karlsruhe GmbH.

Gruiz, K. & Feigl, V. (2006). Combined chemical and phytostabilisation of metal polluted soil. In: Book of Abstracts of the International Symposium on Environmental Biotechnology ISEB ESEB JSEB (Meeting date: 9–14 July, 2006). (p.312). Leipzig, Germany, UFZ Centre for Environmental Research Leipzig-Halle.

Gruiz, K. & Molnár, M. (2007). Monitoring and verification of remediation technologies. In: Book of Abstracts, Actual Issues in Soil Remediation, KSZGYSZ Conference, (Meeting date: 20–21 March 2007, Budapest). (pp. 7–8). Budapest, Hungary, KSZGYSZ.HS 21470-94, 2001 – Environmental protection. Testing of soils. Determination of extractable hydrocarbon content in a boiling point range from 160 °C to 520 °C. Gas chromatographic method. Hungarian Standard.

HS 1484-7 (1998) – Environmental protection. Testing of water. Determination of petroleum hydrocarbons in water. Hungarian Standard.

HS 21976-17 (1994) – Investigation of hard waste settlements. Seedling plant test (*Sinapis alba* root and shot growth inhibition test) Hungarian Standard.

HS 21978/30 (1988) – Investigation of hazardous waste. Microbiological test of soil (*Azotobacter agile* dehydrogenase enzyme activity test) Hungarian Standard.

ISO 11267 (1999) Inhibition of reproduction of Collembola (*Folsomia candida*) by soil pollutants, ISO Standard.

ISO 11348-1 (1998) Water quality. Determination of the inhibitory effect of water samples on the light emission of *Vibrio fischeri*. Part 1.Method using freshly prepared bacteria.

Leitgib, L., Gruiz, K., Molnár, M. & Fenyvesi, É. (2003). Bioremediation of Transformer Oil Contaminated Soil. In: Annokkée, G.J., Arendt, F. & Uhlmann, O. (Eds.), *Wissenschaftliche Berichte* (FZKA 6943, pp. 2762–2771) Karlsruhe, Germany, Forschungszentrum Karlsruhe GmbH Publisher.

McCarty, P.L. (1988). Bioengineering issues related to in situ remediation of contaminated soils and groundwater, *Basic Life Sciences, 45*, 143–162.

McGrath, S.P. & Zhao, F.J. (2003). Phytoextraction of metals and metalloids from contaminated soils, *Current Opinion in Biotechnology, 14*, 277–282.

Meagher, R.B. (2000). Phytoremediation of toxic elemental and organic pollutants. *Current Opinion in Plant Biology*, *3*, 153–162.

MOKKA (2005–2007) – Innovative decision support tools for risk based environmental management in Hungary, Hungarian Research and Development Grant NKFP-3-0020/2005 – www.mokkka.hu

Molnár, M., Fenyvesi, É., Gruiz, K., Leitgib, L., Balogh, G., Murányi, A. & Szejtli, J. (2003). Effects of RAMEB on Bioremediation of Different Soils Contaminated with Hydrocarbons. *Journal of Inclusion Phenomena and Macrocyclic Chemistry, 44*, 447–452.

Molnár, M., Leitgib, L., Gruiz, K., Fenyvesi, É., Szaniszló, N., Szejtli, J. & Fava, F. (2005). Enhanced biodegradation of transformer oil in soils with cyclodextrin – from the laboratory to the field, *Biodegradation, 16*, 159–168.

Molnár, M. (2007). Intensified bioremediation of contaminated soils with cyclodextrin – from the laboratory to the field, *PhD work*, Budapest University of Technology and Economics, Hungary.

Müller, D. (2007). EURODEMO and environmental efficiency. In: Book of Abstracts of MOKKA Conference and EURODEMO Workshop, (Meeting date: 14–15 June 2007), pp. 18–19, Budapest, Hungary, BME ABÉT and MOKKA Consortium.

PROMOTE – Environmental Technology Verification – http://www.promote-etv.org/

Raskin, I. & Ensley, B.D. (2000). *Phytoremediation of toxic metals; using plants to clean up the environment*. (Eds.: Raskin, I. & Ensley, B.D.). New York, US, John Wiley & Sons Inc.

Salt, D.E., Smith, R.D. & Raskin, I. (1998). Phytoremediation. *Annual Review of Plant Physiology and Plant Molecular Biology*, *49*, 643–668.

Schwartz, A. & Bar, R. (1995). Cyclodextrin-enhanced degradation of toluene and p-toluic acid by *Pseudomonas putida*. *Applied Environmental Microbiology, 61,* 2727-2731.

Schwitzguebel, J.P., van der Lelie, D., Baker, A., Glass, D.J. & Vangronsveld, J. (2002). Phytoremediation: European and American trends. *Journal of soils and sediments*, *2:2*, 91–99.

Takács, T., Vörös, I., Biró, I. & Anton, A. (2005). Application of AM fungi for promotion of phytostabilization in metal polluted soil. In: Proceedings of *International Scientific Conference Innovation and Utility in the Visegrád Fours*. (Meeting date: Oct 13–15, 2005), (pp. 115–121). Nyíregyháza, Hungary, Continent-Ph. Ltd.

TESTNET – Towards a European verification system for Environmentally sound Technology –http://www.est-testnet.net

van der Lelie D., Schwitzguebel J.P., Glass D., Vangronsveld J. & Baker A. (2001). Assessing phytoremediation's progress in the United States and Europe. *Environmental science and technology*, *35*, 446–452.

Vangronsveld, J., Streckx, J., Van Assche, F. & Clijsters, H. (1995). Rehabilitation studies on an old non-ferrous waste dumping ground: effects of revegetation and metal immobilization by beringite. *Journal of Geochemical Exploration*, *52*, 221–229.

Vangronsveld, J., Ruttens, A. & Clijsters, H. (1996). The use of cylonic ashes of fluidized bed burning of coal mine refuse for long-term immobilization of metals in soils. In: Sajwan, K.S., Alva, A.K., Keefer, R.F. (Eds.), *Biogeochemistry of Trace Elements in Coal and Coal Combustion Byproducts*. (pp. 223–233). New York, US, Plenum.

Vangronsveld, J. & Cunningham, S.D. (1998). Introduction to the concepts. In: Vangronsveld, J. & Cunningham, S.D. (Eds.), *Metal-contaminated soils: In situ inactivation and phytorestoration*, (pp.1–15). Georgetown, TX, R.G. Landes Co.

Vaszita, E. Gruiz, K. & Siki, Z. (2006). Quantitative Risk Assessment as part of the GIS based Environmental Risk Management of diffuse pollution of mining origin. In: Conference Proceedings, CD of the Difpolmine Conference. (Meeting date: 12–14 December, 2006) Montpellier, France.

Wang, J.-M., Marlowe, E. M., Miller-Maier, R. M. & Brusseau, M. L. (1998). Cyclodextrin-Enhanced Biodegradation of Phenanthrene. *Environmental Science and Technol*ogy, *32,* 1907–1912.

In: Environmental Microbiology Research Trends
Editor: G. V. Kurladze, pp. 59-98
ISBN: 978-1-60021-939-9

Chapter 2

DISINFECTION OF EMPTY ANIMAL HOUSES – SCIENTIFIC EVIDENCE FOR APPLIED PROCEDURES

Kim Oren Gradel *

Department of Infectious Diseases, Aalborg Hospital,
Århus University Hospital, Denmark

ABSTRACT

Disinfection of empty animal houses has routinely been incorporated in all-in all-out farm systems for decades. The scientific evidence for the efficacy of disinfecting farm buildings is sparse, both as regards general production parameters and the elimination of specific micro-organisms. Information on chemical disinfectants can often be obtained only from the companies that market or produce them.

Three aspects determine the outcome of disinfection: the detrimental factor (chemical and/or physical disinfection), the micro-organism, and the environment. The ideal farm disinfectant is unaffected by organic matter, it works at low temperatures, is non-corrosive to materials, and breaks down to harmless substances. Routine farm disinfection only involves chemical disinfectants, albeit these have been combined with heat to increase the effectiveness. Micro-organisms differ with regard to susceptibility to detrimental conditions, ranging from the very resistant prions to the relatively sensitive enveloped viruses. For bacteria, much is known about their phase and resistance, e.g., stationary vs. growth phase. This is closely interrelated with the environment in which factors such as the amount and type of organic matter, humidity, temperature, pH, and UV-light are important.

Most official disinfection tests, which have been implemented by only a few countries, are unrealistic suspension tests. These often yield best-case results because bacteria in suspensions are more susceptible to detrimental conditions than under real-life

* Correspondance should be addressed to Kim Oren Gradel, DVM, PhD. Department of Clinical Epidemiology, Forskningens Hus, Aalborg Hospital, Århus University Hospital, Sdr. Skovvej 15, 9100 Aalborg, Denmark. Phone: +45 99 32 69 02. Fax: +45 99 32 69 14. E-mail: kog@rn.dk

conditions on surfaces. With regard to viruses and fungi even less evidence on the effectiveness of disinfection exists.

This review outlines conditions that influence disinfection efficacy and elaborates on applied research which is useful for monitoring the disinfection of empty animal houses. Suggestions are given for future research areas which can generate scientific evidence for recommended procedures.

INTRODUCTION

Disinfection of empty animal houses has been incorporated in intensive all-in all-out farm systems, which are mainly found in the poultry and pig sectors [151]. It is used for the general reduction of micro-organisms before insertion of new animals. Moreover, with the implementation of control programs against specific zoonotic micro-organisms [8, 205] disinfection has gained in importance, which is paralleled by several farm disinfection guidelines compiled in recent years [11, 123, 137, 180, 186, 202].

General disinfection principles have been described comprehensively [25, 68]. Most studies have been conducted with conditions relevant to food premises, hospitals, and the pharmaceutical industry. Conditions in such premises, however, differ considerably from those encountered in animal houses; thus results are difficult to extrapolate. The scientific literature on disinfection of animal houses is sparse, in particular as regards realistic studies and evidence for recommended procedures [63, 123, 151]. Information on chemical disinfectants can often be obtained only from the companies that produce or market them.

This review summarizes theoretical aspects of disinfection, with emphasis on conditions prevailing in empty animal houses. This is followed by an overview of applied studies that may be used to assess the efficacy of disinfection programs in the field. Suggestions are given for future research areas which can generate scientific evidence for recommended procedures. Both theoretical aspects and applied research have mainly involved bacteria; hence they will constitute the main focus.

PROCEDURES FOR CLEANING AND DISINFECTION OF ANIMAL HOUSES

Detailed descriptions can be obtained from several sources [11, 123, 137, 180, 202] and only general principles will be outlined here. The following general cleaning and disinfection steps are described:

1. Manure and feed are removed and disposed of.
2. Any necessary repairs to the animal house and equipment are carried out.
3. As much equipment as possible is dismantled and, if possible, soaked in water, preferably with a detergent.
4. A dry cleaning step is described in some guidelines [137]. Removal of dust with an industrial vacuum cleaner will minimize the bacterial load in the aerosols formed during washing, but dry cleaning is probably rarely practiced.

5. The animal house is wetted with water, preferably with a detergent.
6. High pressure washing of the animal house, preferably using hot water at 40-50 °C [180] or 60 °C [137], as higher temperatures will denature proteins [137]. Often, an alkaline detergent is recommended [180, 202]. The washing is performed from the ceiling towards the floor and begins farthest from the drains. Ventilation systems should be washed from the outside of the house. Water systems are flushed with the highest possible pressure and a detergent or acidifier is often recommended. All washing should be continued until there is no visible organic matter.
7. Disinfection procedures as appropriate.

In 1987, Linton *et al.* stated that most of the experience in relation to cleaning is empirical [124] and this still applies. As a general rule of thumb ~99% of micro-organisms can be removed by cleaning under experimental conditions, but only a 90% reduction can be expected under more realistic conditions [124].

The utility of hot water and detergent vs. cold water only is mainly based on the easier dissolution of fats [70]. The few animal house studies, however, have not revealed any differences in microbial counts in relation to hot/cold water or detergents [13, 142, 187, 204]. In a questionnaire-based study comprising 78 broiler houses we found no associations between persistence of *Salmonella* (in 1 vs. >1 crop cycle) and the use of hot/cold water and/or detergents [82]. Even if differences exist it is doubtful whether fewer micro-organisms after cleaning will have a major impact on the microbial load after disinfection, given that all visible organic matter has been removed and the disinfection is effective.

Hence, the key message is that high pressure cleaning is a mechanical process that should remove as much organic matter as possible. Further, from a time perspective cleaning should be separated from the subsequent disinfection.

There are principally three chemical disinfection methods which can be applied in animal houses: surface disinfection, thermal fogging, and fumigation. Surface disinfection is performed manually, often with the use of a pressure cleaner. It has to cover all surfaces to be effective. In thermal fogging, a higher concentration of the disinfectant than used for surface disinfection is heated and dispersed in the air ('fogged') by a thermal fogger. Fumigation with formaldehyde (FOR) has been conducted in animal buildings, mainly in hatcheries [40, 151]. It can be generated by three methods, namely mixing FOR and potassium permanganate, heating the solid paraformaldehyde, or evaporating FOR by boiling [151]. As each of these methods requires a substantial number of units (e.g., paraformaldehyde boilers) dispersed in the house to achieve an even distribution, properly sealed buildings, rigid safety precautions, and experienced personnel its use is probably only feasible in small rooms, and not in larger animal houses normally encountered in intensive farming.

Factors that Influence the Effectiveness of Disinfection

General Principles

Three entities determine the outcome of disinfection: the micro-organism, its surroundings, and the disinfectant (Figure 1).

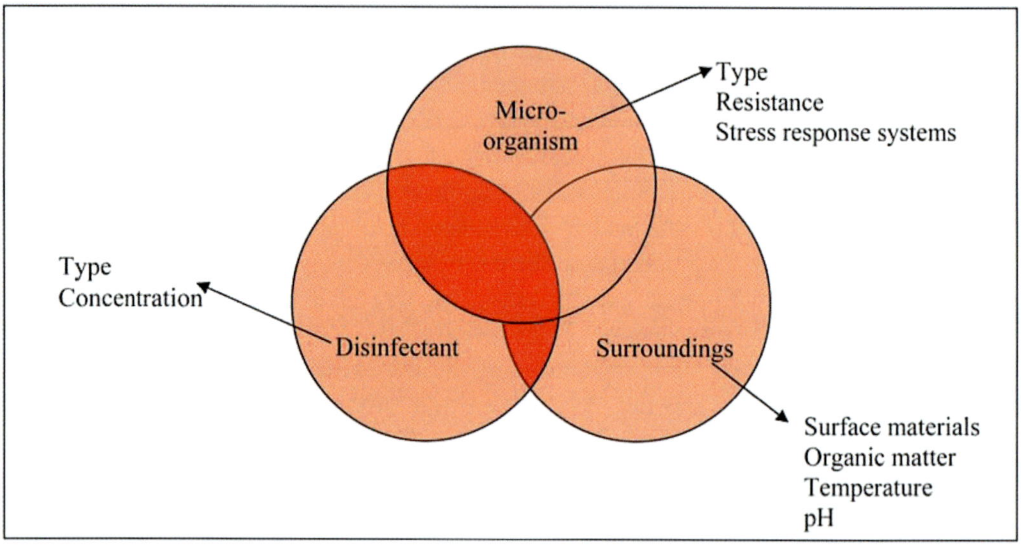

Figure 1. Schematic overview of the three entities involved in effectiveness of disinfection, with examples of relevant factors.

Importantly, several of these factors are closely interrelated. The abundance of such factors and their complicated interrelatedness explain the difficulties of extrapolating from well-controlled laboratory conditions to real-life situations. The surroundings are only pertinent with regard to their inherent role in the disinfectant/micro-organism interaction, hence they will be described under each of these entities.

For more detailed descriptions the reader is referred to text books [25, 68, 185] and review articles [60, 127, 128, 135, 162, 170, 171].

The Disinfectant

There are numerous chemicals which can be used for disinfection [140], but the number of relevant animal house disinfectants is more limited. The use of disinfectant types and their mode of application probably vary between countries and animal sectors, often determined by tradition or effective marketing rather than professional judgment.

In Denmark, FOR, a glutaraldehyde (GLA)/quaternary ammonium compound (QAC), or an oxidizing compound is mainly used on inanimate surfaces in the agricultural sector [117]. More detailed data are known for the Danish poultry sector. The disinfectants used in the previous downtime period have been recorded electronically for all broiler flocks until October 2001 (Table 1).

Table 1. Disinfectants used in downtime periods after 4,629 *Salmonella* positive Danish broiler flocks, 3 January 1992-3 October 2001 (Retrieved from the Poultry Database under the Danish Poultry Council).

Disinfectant type	Number (%)
Glutaraldehyde/quaternary ammonium compound[1]	1,785 (35.1)
Formaldehyde	1,491 (29.4)
Oxidizing disinfectant	685 (13.5)
Lime	251 (4.9)
Not recorded	240 (4.7)
Unknown	165 (3.2)
Quaternary ammonium compound[1]	137 (2.7)
Iodine disinfectant	95 (1.9)
Bases	79 (1.6)
Chlor disinfectants	74 (1.5)
Miscellaneous	67 (1.3)
Not disinfected	8 (0.2)
Acids	2 (0)
Total	5,079[2] (100.0)

[1] Mainly benzalkonium chloride.
[2] >4,629 as 1, 2, or 3 disinfectants could be recorded for each flock.

The disinfectants used for Danish *Salmonella* negative broiler flocks, including the few broiler houses that were not disinfected, do not deviate from Table 1 (data not shown). Thus, GLA/QACs, FOR, and oxidizing compounds comprise around 80% of the disinfectants used. However, these disinfectants are mainly used for the house itself whereas other disinfectant types more appropriate for biofilm are normally used for water systems. Such disinfectants comprise organic acids, silver salts, chlor compounds, or oxidizing disinfectants (pers. obs.), though there are no official records of this. Moreover, lime and other alkalines (mainly sodium hydroxide) are often applied on floors and walls in a second disinfection round (pers. obs.); hence they are probably also underrepresented in Table 1. The same disinfectants are also used mainly in non-broiler poultry houses (pers. obs.). There are no official records of the application mode, but surface disinfection or thermal fogging are used in the vast majority of animal houses, either separately or combined within the same downtime period.

There are no official records on the use of disinfectants in Danish pig houses, but oxidizing compounds are more popular in these, whilst FOR is rarely used.

Phenolic disinfectants are rarely, if at all, used in Denmark, because they do not break down into harmless compounds in the environment, but this differs from other countries, e.g., England [53, 55]. Several countries (e.g., the USA) have forbidden the use of FOR due to its alleged carcinogenic properties.

Here we will focus on the few main disinfectant groups commonly used for animal houses and their water systems.

Disinfectant Types and Factors that Influence their Efficacy

The ideal animal house disinfectant has the following characteristics:

- It eliminates the micro-organism rapidly
- It is unaffected by low temperatures
- It is unaffected by organic matter
- It is non-corrosive for the animal house and its equipment
- It is non-hazardous to the operator
- It breaks down into harmless components in the environment

Generally, highly reactive disinfectants (e.g., oxidizing, chlorine, and iodine compounds) eliminate micro-organisms rapidly, but they are also easily inactivated by organic matter because they react readily with proteins, whereas less reactive, and slower, compounds (e.g., strong bases) are less inactivated [169, 170]. One peculiar exception are the aldehydes which are relatively unaffected by organic matter in spite of their high reactivity with amino groups [75, 169].

Table 2 shows general properties for the commonly used animal house disinfectants.

Table 2. General properties for animal house disinfectants. Compiled from [12].

Disinfectant	Effective against			Rapid action	Susceptible to organic matter	Optimal pH/ temperapture (°C)	Corrosive	Detrimental to the environment
	Bacteria	Spores	Viruses					
Acids	+(+)[1]	-	+	++	++	< 2 / > 5	+++	No
Bases (strong)	++	(+)	+++	+	-	>11 / -	++	No
Formaldehyde	+++	+++	+++	-	-	- / ≥ 16	-	No
Glutaraldehyde	+++	+++	+++	+	-	≥ 7 / > 5	-	No
Chlorine[2]	+++	-	+++	++	+++/++[3]	< 7 / < 35 or -[4]	+++	No
Iodophors	+++	+	+	+++	++	≤ 6 / < 35	+	?
Oxidizing	+++	++[5]	+++	++	+	< 6 / ≥ 5	+[6]	No
Phenols[7]	++(+)	-	(+)	++	++	< 7 / < 40	-	Yes
QACs[8]	+(+)[9]	-	-	+++	+++	~8 / -	+	Yes

[1] -: none, +: low, ++: intermediate, +++: high. Brackets indicate in-betweens.
[2] Chlorine compounds are divided into hypochlorites and organic chlorine compounds.
[3] Hypochlorites: +++. Organic chlorine compounds: ++.
[4] Hypochlorites: < 35. Organic chlorine compounds: -.
[5] +++ for peracetic acid.
[6] ++ for peracetic acid.
[7] Two main groups: a) coal tar agents, b) synthetic phenols. There may be substantial variations in chemical properties between and within these two groups.
[8] Quaternary ammonium compounds.
[9] Mainly active against Gram-positive bacteria.

Because animal houses often remain empty for days before the insertion of animals the rapid action of disinfectants is less important than in other settings such as food premises or hospital wards. In contrast, the presence of organic matter constitutes one of the main problems in animal houses. These considerations advocate the use of aldehydes and strong bases, albeit the latter should not be used for equipment, due to their corrosive properties. There is a comprehensive literature on aldehydes as disinfectants [75, 140, 149] whilst research on strong bases is very limited [20]. The slow action of disinfectants could be disadvantageous on vertical surfaces (e.g., walls), due to the shorter contact time between the disinfectant and the micro-organism. This may also prompt the micro-organism to adapt more easily to the disinfectant because of its slower reaction (see Section 5.1). However, such speculations are theoretical, as nothing has been published on these aspects with regard to animal house disinfection.

Other factors that have a major impact on the effectiveness of disinfectants are temperature, pH, and concentration of the disinfectant.

Generally, the effectiveness of disinfectants increases with higher temperature [169] which is a basic concept of a chemical process. However, some disinfectants are more temperature dependent than others (cf. Table 2), but even less temperature dependent disinfectants gain considerably in activity at higher temperatures. The activity of GLA increases rapidly in the 20-40 °C temperature range [169]. GLA inactivated *Bacillus subtilis* spores within 5 minutes at 70 °C, whilst it took 180 minutes at 25 °C [75]. It has been stated that GLA is active down to 5 °C, but FOR needs at least 16 °C [12], but scientific documentation for this is difficult to find.

pH changes may influence both the micro-organism's cell surface and the disinfectant [18, 169]. Phenols, organic acids, and chlorine releasing compounds are most active in their unionized form and the degree of dissociation rises as pH increases, that is they are most active at low pH [18, 140, 169]. *Bacillus metiens* spores were killed by chlorine in 2.5 minutes at pH 6, whereas it took 2 hours at pH 10 [18]. QACs and GLA are examples of disinfectants that are most effective at alkaline pH [75, 105]. For GLA, the pH-dependent activity minimizes with increasing temperature, e.g., at 25 °C *B. subtilis* spores were killed in 180 minutes at pH 8.0, but they could not be inactivated at pH 4.0, whereas they were killed within 5 minutes at 70 °C regardless of pH (2.6, 3.7, 4.7, or 8.0) [75].

The concentration exponent, or dilution coefficient, (η) is a measure of the effect of change in concentration/dilution on death rate [18, 97, 169]. Reduction in activity, measured as the time to kill a population, is the dilution factor to the power η. For aldehydes and QACs, $\eta = 1$, the time to kill a microbial population is then increased by 2^1 or 3^1 if the concentration is reduced by a factor 2 or 3, respectively. For phenols, $\eta = 6$, then the parallel time increases are 2^6 (= 64) or 3^6 (= 729) [18, 169]. Thus, the disinfectant type can have an immense impact on the effectiveness if concentrations are more dilute than recommended. Little is known about dilution coefficients of other relevant animal house disinfectants.

To the knowledge of the author no study has evaluated the use of disinfectants for water systems in animal houses. The continuously low water pressure during the period in which animals are housed gives ample opportunities for biofilm to build up [134, 193]. Therefore, disinfectants that are effective against biofilm, such as oxidizing compounds [62, 189, 190] or certain chlorine compounds [118, 119], are recommended.

Heat

The killing of micro-organisms by heat is normally not described in relation to disinfection of animal houses, but steam and FOR treatment has been performed routinely in Danish poultry houses for years [150, 202]. As promising results have been observed (cf. Section 5.4) we will briefly describe principles involved in the killing of micro-organisms by heat.

Inactivation of micro-organisms by heat has been studied extensively in food microbiology. In general, the same factors which impede the effectiveness of disinfectants also render micro-organisms more heat resistant. Such factors comprise the presence of organic matter [4, 44, 88, 177], type of micro-organism [77] (similar to the range of micro-organisms depicted in Table 3 [see Section 3.5.1]), and stationary phase bacteria (in contrast to bacteria in the exponential growth phase) [103, 120, 200]. As for disinfectants, key events that lead to heat inactivation of micro-organisms are obscure [76].

In addition to temperature and time, one of the important factors to consider is moisture, because moist heat is more effective than dry heat [77, 88, 103]. A thermal sterilization is achieved with moist heat in 3 min at 134 °C, but dry heat requires 2 h at 160 °C [77]. A study involving *Salmonella* in milk chocolate (with a high content of sugar and fat and hence a low water activity) also showed the importance of moisture [15]. Initially, it took 20 h to achieve a 1-log reduction at 71 °C. This was reduced to 4 h by the addition of only 2% moisture, thus showing a high decline in heat resistance in spite of an insignificant change in relative sugar and fat content.

Most studies have dealt with water activity during heating, but equally important are studies showing that a decreased moisture before heating also renders micro-organisms more heat resistant [104, 133]. This advocates wet cleaning before heat disinfection.

The Micro-Organism

Though the relevant micro-organisms have their natural habitat in the living organism they will have to survive for long periods under detrimental conditions on inanimate surfaces until picked up by a new host. Throughout their long evolution micro-organisms have developed sophisticated adaptation mechanisms to enhance their survival abilities. Concerning mechanisms, much is known about bacteria, especially Gram-negatives, whilst less knowledge exists on other micro-organisms.

Type of Micro-Organism

Disinfectants constitute only one of several detrimental conditions that micro-organisms encounter in the extra-animal environment. Thus, micro-organisms that are generally resistant to detrimental factors (e.g., desiccation, heat, or, for bacteria, antibiotics) are also the ones most difficult to eliminate by disinfection (Table 3).

Table 3 should be used only as a general guideline, which is reflected in the different ranging of the most susceptible micro-organisms between the two references. Variations related to other conditions described in this chapter partly explain such differences [162], but many differences are also encountered within groups. Amongst Gram-negative bacteria *Pseudomonas* are relatively resistant [131, 162, 174, 183] and *Campylobacter* are generally susceptible [98]. Curiously, enterococci are more resistant than many Gram-negative species to both disinfectants [32, 83, 162] and heat [3, 32, 80].

Table 3. Relative susceptibility of groups of micro-organisms to disinfectants.

Range	Group of micro-organisms A[1]	Group of micro-organisms B[2]	Veterinary examples[3]
Resistant	Prions	Prions	BSE[4], scrapie
↓	Coccidia	Coccidia	*Eimeria*
	Spores	Spores	*Clostridium perfringens*
	Mycobacteria	Mycobacteria	*M. paratuberculosis*
	Cysts	Cysts	*Giardia*
	Small non-enveloped viruses	Small non-enveloped viruses	Foot and mouth disease
	Fungal spores	Gram-negative bacteria	*Salmonella*, *Campylobacter*
	Large non-enveloped viruses	Fungi	*Microsporum*, *Trichophyton*
	Gram-negative bacteria	Large non-enveloped viruses	Adenoviridae
	Enveloped viruses	Gram-positive bacteria[5]	*Staphylococcus*, *Streptococcus*
Susceptible	Gram-positive bacteria[5]	Enveloped viruses	Influenza

[1] Moderated from [63]. [2] Moderated from [162]. [3] Refers to the groups as ranged by [162]. [4] Bovine spongiform encephalopathy. [5] Other than Mycobacteria and spores.

General Aspects of Resistance in Micro-Organisms

In contrast to antibiotics, with their well-characterized impact on specific target sites, exact disinfection mechanisms are obscure, as there can be several target sites in the micro-organism and key events that cause microbial inactivation have not been elucidated [132, 162, 167]. Parallel to this, disinfectant resistance is also less well-defined than antibiotic resistance [183]. The somewhat vague definition of resistance to a disinfectant is that the strain is either insusceptible to a concentration of the disinfectant used in practice or it is not inhibited by a concentration that inhibits the majority of strains of that organism [162].

Disinfectant resistance is divided into the following categories [135]:

- Intrinsic resistance, which is due to inherent characteristics of the micro-organism. An inherent part are the membrane changes initiated by various conditions which also alter the resistance to disinfectants. Also, the phenotypic adaptation in biofilm is classified as intrinsic. Efflux pumps are activated by intrinsic resistance mechanisms in Gram-negative bacteria and fungi.
- Acquired resistance, which may arise by mutation, or the acquisition of plasmids or transposons. Acquired resistance to disinfectants is generally believed to be less important than intrinsic resistance [162]. Important efflux pumps in Gram-positive bacteria are plasmid-encoded.

Much is known about disinfectant resistance mechanisms in bacteria, less in fungi, and very little in other micro-organisms. Figure 2 gives a schematic overview of general resistance mechanisms in bacteria and fungi.

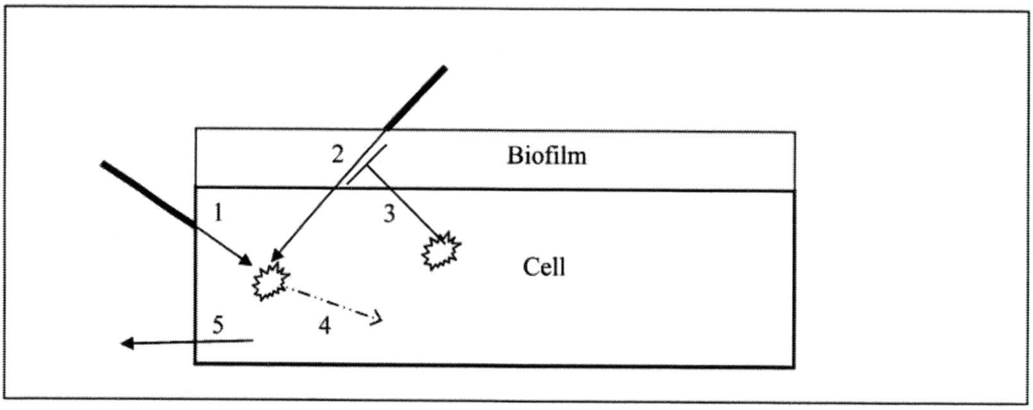

Figure 2. Schematic overview of main disinfectant resistance mechanisms in bacteria and fungi. 1: Cell membrane permeability barrier. 2: Biofilm permeability barrier. 3: Enzymatic breakdown of disinfectant in biofilm. 4: Enzymatic breakdown of disinfectant in cell. 5: Efflux pump.

Membrane-related mechanisms

The outer membrane is the main permeability barrier that the disinfectant has to cross to hit its targets, which are mainly found within the cell [128, 135, 162]. Viruses, however, differ from this general concept as their outer envelope renders them more, and not less, susceptible to disinfectants [127, 135]. Changes in the outer membrane composition are closely related to the conditions the micro-organisms encounter and several studies have shown that this can influence susceptibility to disinfectants [35, 36, 60, 85, 136] (also cf. Section 3.5.7). This is also an important aspect of adaptation studies (cf. Section 5.1). Table 4 gives a brief overview of membrane structures involved in resistance to disinfectants.

Table 4. Membrane structures in micro-organisms involved in resistance to disinfectants. Compiled from [60, 89, 110, 127, 135, 145, 171, 172, 183].

Group of micro-organisms	Membrane structures involved in resistance to disinfectants
Protozoa	Cyst wall?
Spores	Spore cortex, which consists largely of peptidoglycan.
	Spore coat, which consists largely of protein.
Mycobacteria	Mycoylarabinogalactan-peptidoglycan skeleton.
	Complex lipids, lipopolysaccharides, and proteins with porin channels.
Gram-negative bacteria	Lipopolysaccharides.
	Outer membrane proteins, which form porin channels.
Fungi	Cell wall glucan.
Viruses	Lipid envelope.

Vegetative forms of sporulating bacteria are not more resistant than non-sporulating Gram-positive species [135]. The increasing resistance to various detrimental conditions along the pathway from vegetative cells to spores has elucidated interesting aspects of the role of the spore cortex and coat [110, 135]. In one study with *B. subtilis*, FOR resistance developed at stage IV, phenol resistance between stages IV and V, moist heat resistance between stages V and VI, and GLA resistance just prior to stage VII (the final sporulation) [106].

The resistance of Mycobacteria is related to the high lipid content in their 'waxy' cell wall, which hampers the penetration of hydrophilic compounds [89, 135]. Differences in lipid composition explain differences in resistance between mycobacterial species [16, 49], but beyond this little is known about exact mechanisms or variations within species [16, 135].

The membrane structure in Gram-negative bacteria has been extensively studied and there are excellent reviews on this topic [60, 145, 172, 194]. Lipopolysaccharides (LPS) are unique components of the Gram-negative outer membrane. LPS-molecules are strongly linked together, among other things by the divalent cations Mg^{2+} and Ca^{2+} and these links form a strong permeability barrier, especially to hydrophobic disinfectants [145]. "Deep rough mutants", in which the LPS-layer is partly damaged, have been used extensively to study the role of LPS in permeability of many different compounds. Other studies have used agents that increase the permeability of the outer membrane (e.g., ethylendiamine tetraacetic acid [EDTA]) [194]. Outer membrane proteins (e.g., OmpC and OmpF) form porin channels, related to osmotic resistance, which allow only the passage of small hydrophilic molecules [60, 145, 194]. Studies of bacteria with defects in these outer membrane proteins have provided useful information on the role of porin channels in the uptake of many compounds.

Little is known about membrane resistance mechanisms in fungi [129, 135, 171]. It is not known if the higher resistance in molds compared to yeasts is related to cell membrane differences [135]. Studies with *Saccharomyces cerevisae* showed that increasing cell wall thickness and decreasing cell wall porosity, which was observed with increasing age of the cells, reduced the uptake of chlorhexidine (CHX) [91-95]. However, similar studies comprising 1, 2, or 6 day old *Candida albicans* and *C. glabrata* were inconsistent [91, 92].

Enveloped viruses are lipophilic and electronegatively charged, which render them more susceptible to most types of disinfectants than non-enveloped viruses [127, 130, 135].

Most of the membrane related resistance mechanisms are intrinsic, but plasmid-encoded resistance has been reported in bacteria. The R124 plasmid in *Escherichia coli* alters OmpF, thus rendering the cells less permeable to various agents [157]. Other plasmids may be involved in other outer membrane changes and this has been reported to confer increased resistance to FOR in *E. coli* [162], but exact mechanisms are not known [172].

Biofilm

A biofilm is defined as a population of cells growing on a surface and enclosed in an exopolysaccharide matrix (glycocalyx) [47, 122]. The formation of biofilm is influenced by several factors in micro-organisms and on surfaces which have been extensively described, such as hydrophobicity, electric charge, growth conditions, species, surface materials, and nutrients. Because biofilm formation depends on these and other unknown factors it is difficult to establish a model that will predict a specific biofilm formation. However, the two most important prerequisites are probably the presence of moisture and nutrients [7, 14, 108], though it has been stated that only low levels of nutrients favor biofilm formation [45]. Most laboratory experiments have involved only one species, but several types of micro-organisms (bacteria, protozoa, algae, and fungi) often form biofilm in the natural environment [37, 45, 101]. To the knowledge of the author there is no research on biofilm in animal houses, though there is every reason to believe that biofilm is formed in water lines [134, 193]. Microorganisms in biofilm are generally more resistant to antimicrobials and disinfectants than their planktonic counterparts [7, 46, 112, 182, 191]. However, this also illustrates the complexity of specific resistance mechanisms, as there are other differences between sessile and planktonic micro-organisms than the biofilm *per se*. Thus, the relative importance of different mechanisms in biofilm resistance are unknown [47, 73]. Generally, the biofilm resistance mechanisms to antimicrobials are summarized in three main hypotheses [71, 73, 182]:

- Slow or incomplete penetration of the disinfectant into the glycocalyx, either because of incomplete penetration or due to easy penetration accompanied by deactivation by enzymes in the glycocalyx.
- An altered chemical microenvironment in the biofilm, e.g., levels of nutrients and oxygen, pH, and osmolarity, which vary within the biofilm. Often, anaerobic conditions, which can minimize the efficacy of some disinfectants, are encountered in the deeper biofilm layers. Biofilm niches with low nutrient levels are also often found in the deeper biofilm layers, in which bacteria, and possibly other micro-organisms, enter a dormant/quiescent phase and become more resistant [34, 72].
- For bacteria, a subpopulation forms a special phenotypic biofilm state which is more resistant. This hypothesis is controversial, but it has been supported by the fact that ~1% of the bacteria often survive antimicrobial treatment, even in thin, newly formed biofilm. Lewis reviewed this phenomenon in depth [122].

Enzymatic Breakdown of Disinfectant in Cell

Plasmid-mediated breakdown of mercurials is well-described in bacteria, but there is probably no cross-resistance to unrelated compounds [160]. Breakdown of CHX has been studied in *Achromobacter xylosoxidans* [147], but it is not known if this is plasmid mediated [160]. Plasmid mediated FOR dehydrogenase has been reported in several bacterial species [102, 109, 148, 210]. Further studies are clearly needed to assess the importance of enzymatic breakdown of disinfectants.

Efflux Pumps

Research into efflux pumps has gained in importance in recent years after the finding by Moken *et al.* that pine oil could select *E. coli* that over-expressed the *mar* gene and had increased resistance to pine oil and several unrelated antibiotics [138]. Older studies unaware of the efflux pump mechanism may have interpreted efflux solely as a decreased outer membrane permeability [43, 161]. Efflux pumps have been described in bacteria and fungi.

In Gram-positive bacteria efflux pumps have mainly been related to the plasmid-encoded *qac* genes in *Staphylococcus aureus* [135, 148]. These confer increased resistance to a number of disinfectants, among which CHX and QACs are relevant for animal houses.

Efflux pumps in Gram-negative bacteria are related to multiple drug resistance (MDR) systems [121]. In contrast to the *qac* genes in *S. aureus*, MDR genes are activated by induction or mutation of genes that are part of the normal cell genome. In general, they are activated by stress factors [135, 152, 164], e.g., oxidative stress [5]. Activated MDR genes have conferred increased resistance to phenolics such as triclosan, but little is known about altered susceptibility to farm disinfectants.

Fungi possess two efflux pump systems, ATP binding cassette transporters and major facilitators, which confer resistance to specific antifungal drugs (e.g., azoles) [207]. There is little evidence of their role for disinfectants apart from their involvement in the efflux of weak organic acids [39, 129].

Stress Response Systems in Bacteria and Cross-Resistance

A detailed description of the various stress response systems is beyond the scope of this chapter and only main aspects will be outlined. Though stress response systems have been described in yeasts [167], much more is known about bacteria.

Genotypic aspects of stress response systems in bacteria have been excellently reviewed by Storz and Hengge-Aronis [185], but new findings are continuously added to this comprehensive topic.

The general stress response, regulated by RpoS in Gram-negatives and σ^B in Gram-positives, is probably the most important stress response system [185]. *Campylobacter* do not possess RpoS [143], which probably partly explains their high susceptibility to several detrimental conditions [98]. The general stress response is closely linked to the stationary/quiescent/dormant phase in which bacteria probably exist most of the time in the extra-animal environment due to nutrition limitation [107, 201]. Table 5 shows quiescent phase characteristics of the well-studied *E. coli* and *Salmonella*.

Table 5. Putative characteristic features in quiescent phase *E. coli* and *Salmonella*. Compiled from [2, 66, 90, 107, 158, 179].

Key area	Brief description	Possible impact on resistance
Morphology	Smaller, almost spherical, cells, thus the rod shape of the bacteria is lost. Cytoplasm is condensed and the volume of periplasm is increased. Changes in chromosome topology due to reduced gene expression.	Cell divisions without an increase in cell mass increase the number of bacteria which may improve survival for the clone.
Cell envelope changes	The surface is covered by more hydrophobic molecules which favor adhesion and aggregation.	Biofilm formation is favored.
	E. coli starved at low temperatures produce a fibronectin-binding element (curli).	May be involved in aggregation.
	Fatty acid composition in membranes changes, rendering them less permeable.	Less permeability to chemicals (e.g., disinfectants and antibiotics) increases the bacterial resistance to these. Protection from autolysis.

Table 5. (Continued)

Metabolism	The overall metabolic rate is reduced, but a low level of metabolism is maintained.	The low metabolic activity reduces susceptibility to detrimental conditions. Resumption of growth may occur if nutrients become available.
	Stability of RNA and proteins decreases, whereas DNA stability is maintained.	DNA stability is important for resumption of growth if conditions improve.
Protein synthesis	30-50 different proteins are synthesized under the general stress response, the number and kinds of proteins depending on the specific conditions.	Development of various protective mechanisms (e.g., involved in repair mechanisms and membrane stabilization).
Mutations	Mutation rates increase in starved bacteria.	Possible selection of strains with increased resistance to detrimental conditions.

Bacteria have adapted to the many different detrimental factors they encounter simultaneously by developing stress response systems that confer cross-protection (Table 6).

Table 6. Known cross-inductions by important detrimental factors and cross-protections by stress response systems considered to be important for the survival of Gram-negative (Gneg) and Gram-positive (Gpos) bacteria in the extra-animal environment. Compiled from [185]

Detrimental factor	Stress response system									
	General		Heat		Oxidation		Osmotic		Acid	
	Gneg	Gpos	Gneg	Gpos	Gneg	Gpos	Gneg	Gpos	Gneg	Gpos
pH↑		←								
Cold	→									
Starvation			→		→	→	←			
Heat	→←	→←					←		←	
Oxidation	←	←	→						←	
Osmosis	→←	→←							←	
pH↓	→	→←								

→: Cross-induction; ←: Cross-protection.

Some of the very basic mechanisms, however, are poorly understood, which is probably because the same applies to basic mechanisms of cell injury (e.g., related to disinfectants). Several of these cross-resistance phenomena have been elucidated in phenotypic studies [99, 125, 133, 173], also involving disinfectants [21].

DISINFECTION TESTS

General Principles

There is no general agreement on what disinfection really means, apart from "a reduction of microbes" [154]. Thus, there is no generally agreed success criterion for the efficacy of a disinfectant [48]. Moreover, only a few countries (France, Germany, Netherlands, UK, USA) have official disinfection test methods and even between these no harmonization exists [48, 154, 175].

In 1990, the European Committee for Standardization established Technical Committee 216 Chemical Disinfectants and Antiseptics (TC 216), the scope of which was [154]:

- "the standardisation of the terminology, requirements, test methods including potential efficacy under in-use conditions, recommendations for use and labelling in the whole field of chemical disinfection and antiseptics. Areas of activity include agriculture (but not crop protection chemicals), domestic service, food hygiene and other industrial fields, institutional, medical, and veterinary applications"

At present, only a few disinfection tests conform to this European standard and much work remains before all the above tasks are accomplished [154].

The lack of legislation and harmonization means that in most countries anybody can market a product as a disinfectant, without having to document its efficacy. Results from the European Suspension Test (cf. Section 4.3) are reported by many commercial companies, probably because suspension tests render impressive results of the elimination of micro-organisms [26].

A brief overview of disinfection test principles with their inherent strengths and limitations will be given. More detailed descriptions can be obtained from text books [48, 154].

Test Principles

In principle, disinfection tests do not differ from other laboratory tests in which rigidly standardized and controlled tests can be difficult to extrapolate to real-life conditions. However, disinfection tests differ from most other laboratory tests with regard to their two distinct phases. The first phase comprises contact between the micro-organism and the disinfectant and the second phase involves the optimized recovery of the micro-organism. The main challenge is the abrupt elimination of the detrimental first phase conditions by the initiation of the second phase, in which the disinfectant has to be neutralized. Three procedures exist for this neutralization of disinfectants [159, 188]:

1. Appropriate dilution in the enrichment broth
2. Treatment with a chemical neutralizer in the enrichment broth
3. Filtration, whereby the micro-organism stays at the filter while the disinfectant is washed away

The pros, cons and caveats of each of these methods have been reviewed [159, 188]. Of note, many published disinfection tests have not used or even considered using any of these methods [22, 126]. Results from such studies might have over-estimated the efficacy of chemical disinfectants because the putative inhibition by disinfectants in the recovery media was neglected.

For virus tests the involvement of organic matter constitutes an additional challenge, as this will often kill cell cultures or embryos and it is difficult to separate virus particles from the organic matter [42]. One of the main implications is that it is only possible to report on a virus reduction without concluding if a complete elimination has occurred because the amount of virus particles that stick to the organic matter cannot be determined [42].

Types of Disinfection Tests

Table 7 gives an overview of the main types of disinfection tests.

Table 7. Overview of the main types of disinfection tests. Compiled from [154].

Test	Comments	Standardization	Realistic
In vitro tests (MIC[1] tests)	Measure inhibition, but inactivation is the desirable endpoint.	Easy ↓	Low degree ↓
In vitro tests (suspension tests)	Widely used.		
In vitro tests (capacity tests)	The micro-organism encounters an increasing load of disinfectant, and sometimes organic matter, in a suspension.		
Carrier tests	Approach practical tests, but as carriers are standardized they often represent unrealistic surfaces.		
Practical tests	Mimic specific real-life conditions in the laboratory.		
In-use tests	Field studies.	Difficult	High degree

[1] Minimum inhibitory concentration.

Minimum inhibitory concentrations (MICs), which are determined in tests similar to those used for antibiotics, are mainly relevant for the preliminary selection of the most resistant strains.

In suspension tests, a volume of suspension with the micro-organism is added to the disinfectant in the concentration to be tested and after a predetermined exposure time an aliquot is examined, either qualitatively or quantitatively (standard dilutions and streaking on solid media) [154]. Various parameters can be compared, e.g., with or without an organic load, and suspension tests are supposedly easy to standardize. One study, however, found significant differences in lethal effect between laboratories that performed the European Suspension Test, which were mainly related to different pre-treatments of bacterial strains

[28]. A similar study with the Dutch 5-5-5 test, covering ten laboratories, seven disinfectants, four bacterial strains, and a time span of five weeks reached a similar conclusion [198]. The main disadvantage of suspension tests is that they are unrealistic and yield favorable results because micro-organisms in suspensions are more sensitive than micro-organisms attached to surfaces [61, 65, 69, 118]. Slow-reacting disinfectants (e.g., aldehydes) often perform worse than quick-reacting disinfectants, such as oxidizing compounds, within the 5 minutes often applied in suspension tests. However, as mentioned earlier (Section 3.3), the time aspect is less important in the disinfection of animal houses.

In capacity tests, the ability of a disinfectant to retain activity in the presence of an increasing load of bacteria, and often also of organic matter, is investigated [154]. It is considered to be more realistic than standard suspension tests as it mimics some real-life situations, e.g., for housekeeping and instrumental disinfection [50].

In a carrier test, a piece of solid material (e.g., a stainless steel coupon) is soaked in a bacterial suspension, after which it is dried and immersed in a disinfectant solution from which it is transferred to a nutrient broth for investigation [154, 197]. Carrier tests possess two main factors that are likely to increase the variability compared to suspension tests, namely the more inconsistent recovery of survivors from surfaces and the loss of viability due to desiccation on the surface [27, 197]. It was therefore surprising that one study group reported of less variability in a surface test [27] as compared to a suspension test [28]. Later, van Klingeren also found low variability between carrier tests performed at different laboratories [197].

The main purpose of practical tests is to mimic specific real-life conditions as closely as possible in the laboratory. It is difficult to determine factors that influence the resistance of test micro-organisms to disinfectants, which hampers the reproducibility between different laboratories [154]. German test methods (Deutsche Gesellschaft für Hygiene und Mikrobiologie [DGHM]) are probably the most comprehensive practical tests [154] and several evaluations have been published [19, 30, 206]. The results are useful for the specific conditions described, but they can rarely be extrapolated to other conditions.

The main principle in field (in-use) studies is that the in-use dilution of a disinfectant should not leave surviving naturally occurring target micro-organisms after use, even with an organic load [154]. Field studies have many unknown and uncontrollable factors and it is often difficult to include identical control units in which no disinfection is performed. Logically, a more extensive sampling will increase the likelihood of detecting micro-organisms. However, there are unfortunately numerous incidents of reappearance of persistent micro-organisms picked up by new animals after extensive negative post-disinfection sampling [79, 82]. Animals, with their access to all corners and crevices 24 h a day, are more effective 'sentinels' than the most effective human sampler. The detection of micro-organisms after disinfection yields interpretation problems because several other factors, such as rodent control or hygiene barriers, also influence the outcome. The only way to compensate for the many uncontrollable factors is probably to perform field tests under many different settings to deduce general tendencies.

APPLIED RESEARCH

Disinfectant Resistance Studies in which Laboratory Conditions were Regulated

Russell [162, 168] reviewed studies in which bacteria were exposed to gradually increasing disinfectant concentrations (i.e., adaptation studies), which most often involved QACs and CHX. Development of resistance is thought to be mainly due to outer membrane changes [136, 162], albeit the putative role of efflux pumps (cf. Section 3.5.6) has gained in importance in recent years [33, 116]. However, specific resistance mechanisms have rarely been investigated [135]. Russell stated that adaptation to QACs and CHX is normally lost when the bacteria are grown in broth without these disinfectants, but Norwegian studies involving adaptation to benzalkonium chloride (BC) followed by successive growth in BC-free broth showed the resistance to be stable [113, 178].

Pseudomonas, with their high intrinsic resistance, have been used in several adaptation studies. Langsrud and Sundheim reported that just an overnight incubation with a sublethal level of BC in the broth increased the BC resistance of two *Pseudomonas* strains [114]. Two other studies reported altered outer membrane fatty acid compositions in *Ps. aeruginosa* concomitantly with adaptation and increasing resistance to QACs [85, 136]. Cross-resistance to other disinfectants has been evaluated in some studies, including one in which *Pseudomonas* curiously became more susceptible to GLA after adaptation to QACs [115].

Two studies reported higher resistance to FOR in *E. coli* [208] and *Ps. aeruginosa* [181] after adaptation in broth. Interestingly, passage of *E. coli* in a medium with a phenolic compound (often involved in efflux pump resistance, cf. Section 3.5.6) did not alter the resistance to this disinfectant [208].

Few adaptation studies have involved other micro-organisms than bacteria, but one study found increasing resistance to chlorine in adapted Poliovirus [17].

To the knowledge of the author only one study has focused exclusively on adaptation to farm disinfectants [81]. MICs for six *Salmonella* isolates (three with high and three with low MICs) did not change in adaptation studies comprising five farm disinfectants (FOR, GLA/BC compound, oxidizing compound, tar oil phenol, iodophor). Moreover, isolates adapted to triclosan, to which MICs increased up to 500-fold, did not show changes in MICs to the five farm disinfectants, thus indicating that multidrug efflux pump mechanisms (cf. Section 3.5.6) were not involved in resistance to these.

Disinfection Resistance Studies Involving Field Strains

These studies have assessed susceptibility to disinfectants in relation to persistence of field isolates and/or the use of relevant disinfectants in the premises from which the micro-organisms were isolated. Table 8 summarizes studies that could be relevant for disinfection of animal houses.

Most of these screening studies used unrealistic MIC or suspension tests. Thus the results are mainly important for the impact of the micro-organisms *per se*. There were generally few variations in resistance in relation to persistence or the use of specific disinfectants. In studies that incorporated various bacterial species differences in resistance between these were generally larger than within species [1, 184], which corroborates the importance of intrinsic resistance. Only few of the studies evaluated in-use disinfectant concentrations [84, 199, 209].

In the food industry alternation between disinfectants is sometimes recommended to avoid development of disinfectant resistance [114]. The issue in health care settings was discussed in depth by Murtough *et al.* who did not find substantial evidence for this [144]. Neither was there any justification for such recommendations in a study involving farm disinfectants [81].

Table 8. Disinfectant resistance studies comprising field isolates, which may have implications for animal house disinfection

Bacteria	Disinfectant(s)	Setting	Main results	Ref.
Gram-negative bacteria, mainly *Escherichia coli*	CHX, GLA, phenol compound, antiseptic with BC	Urinary tract infections in humans	*E. coli* was equally susceptible to all disinfectants. *Proteus*, *Providencia*, and *Pseudomonas* exhibited higher resistance to cationic agents. Isolates from inpatients were more resistant to CHX than isolates from outpatients.	[184]
Gram-negative	CHX, QACs, other	Hospitals	*E. coli* from hospitals and standard laboratory strains were equally susceptible to all disinfectants.	[87]
Mycobacterium chelonae	GLA	Endoscope washers	Isolates resistant to 2% GLA, which also showed higher resistance to other disinfectants, were found in endoscope washers.	[199]
M. chelonae	GLA, other disinfectants	Endoscope washers	A field isolate from endoscope washers in which 2% GLA had been used was more resistant to GLA than laboratory strains of *M. chelonae*, which had not encountered GLA. There were no differences in resistance to the other disinfectants.	[84]
Various	QAC, phenolics, GLA	Hatcheries	From 2 of 3 hatcheries, ca. 8% of the bacteria were resistant to disinfection concentrations at or above recommended in-use concentrations. The highest level of resistance was seen for GLA and this was related to its common use in the hatcheries.	[209]

Table 8. (Continued)

Pseudomonas	BC	Poultry processing plant	Higher resistance to BC was found in isolates from a poultry processing plant using BC than in isolates from a plant that used chlorine.	[114]
Salmonella	Hypochlorous acid	Poultry abattoir	*Salmonella* isolated from steps before the abattoir's chlorine washing step was sensitive to hypochlorous acid. Some *Salmonella* isolated after the chlorine washing step was resistant to hypochlorous acid.	[139]
Listeria monocytogenes and *E. coli*	QAC, sodium hypochlorite	Food industry	Disinfectant resistance did not differ between persistent strains isolated from the food industry and laboratory strains of the same two species.	[96]
Salmonella Enteritidis	Phenolic compounds, QAC, FOR/QAC compound	Poultry houses	The susceptibility to all disinfectants was equal among all isolates regardless of whether these persisted in the poultry houses or not.	[59]
Salmonella	QACs, organic acids/FOR, other	Fish feed factory	*Salmonella* persisting in fish feed factories were not more resistant to nine disinfectants used in these than *Salmonella* from other sources.	[141]
Various	$CuSO_4$, $ZnCl_2$, BC, H_2O_2, CHX, FOR	Food animals	Bacteria had not or only to a limited degree developed resistance to disinfectants used in the agricultural sector.	[1]
Salmonella	GLA/BC, FOR, oxidizing compound, phenolic, iodophor	Mainly persistently infected broiler houses	The small variations in MICs could not be associated with *Salmonella* persistence in the broiler houses or previous use of relevant disinfectants (cf. Table 1).	[81]

BC = benzalkonium chloride; CHX = chlorhexidine; FOR = formaldehyde; GLA = glutaraldehyde; QAC = quaternary ammonia compound.

Other Laboratory Disinfectant Studies

Though suspension tests are the most commonly reported test methods they will only be briefly commented. Suspension tests confer valid information on specific micro-organism/disinfectant combination, thus giving general guidelines on the relative sensitivity of micro-organisms and efficacy of disinfectants. However, they rarely contribute to the explanation of mechanisms and they are unrealistic [38].

Most carrier tests have used stainless steel plates, often with biofilm models. This is highly relevant for the food industry [31, 70], but results are difficult to extrapolate to surface materials and disinfectants encountered in animal houses as realistic test results are generally valid only for the specific conditions they incorporate (cf. Section 4.3).

Only one practical test with specific relevance to the chemical disinfection of animal houses has been published [83]. The aim of this study was to mimic worst-case scenarios (low cleaning standard and temperature) in empty poultry houses. Table 9 shows the factors used in the study.

Table 9. Factors used in practical tests mimicking worst-case scenarios in empty poultry houses. For all factorial combinations tests were performed with formaldehyde, glutaraldehyde/benzalkonium chloride, an oxidizing compound, and water (control). Compiled from [83].

Animal house material	Organic matter	CFU	Disinfection time (minutes)					
			5	15	30			
			Temperature before/after disinfection (°C)[1]					
			6/6	6/6	6/6	11/11	20/11	30/30
Concrete paving stones	Feed10[2]	low					es[3]	
		high						
	Feed20[4]	low		es	es	es	es	
		high	es	es				
Feed chain	Fat	-			eE			eE
	Feed	-	es	es	es	es		
Wooden dowels	Fat	-			esE			esE
	Feed	-	esE	esE	esE	esE		
Jute egg belt	Yolk	low		es	es	es		
	Yolk	high	esE	es		esE		

[1] All animal house materials with organic matter dried 24 h before and 25 h after disinfection.
[2] Feed for layers, 10 g per concrete paving stone. [3] e = *Salmonella* Enteritidis;
s = *S.* Senftenberg; E = *Enterococcus faecalis*. [4] Feed for layers, 20 g per concrete paving stone.

For most of the factorial combinations the efficacy of the disinfectants was (in decreasing order): FOR > GLA/BC > oxidizing compound > water (Figure 3).

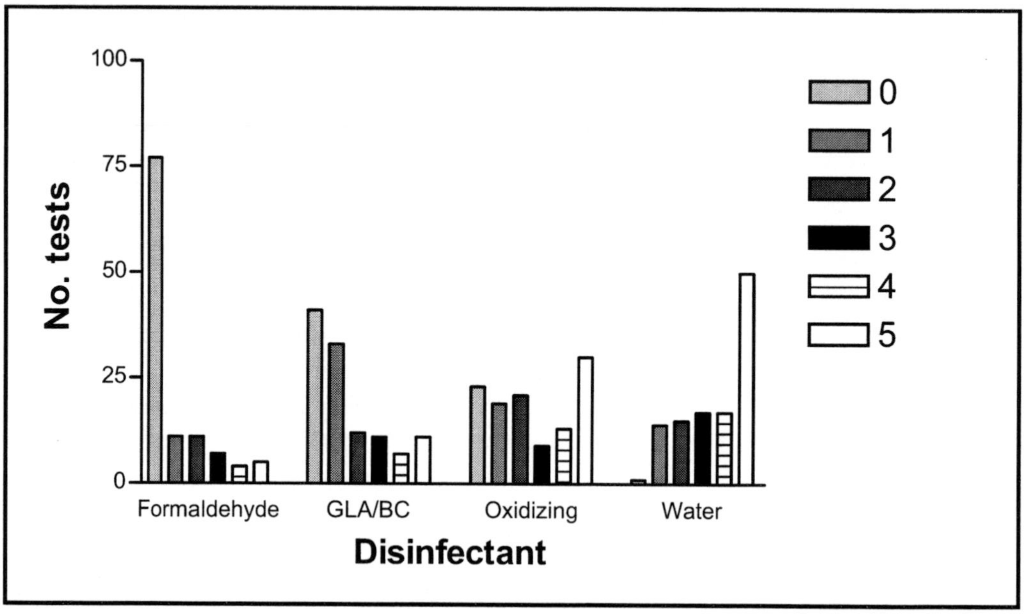

Figure 3. Results of practical disinfection tests mimicking worst-case scenarios in poultry houses. Legend (0-5) represents growth in dilutions ranging from 10^0 to 10^{-4} (0 = no growth in any dilution, 1 = growth in 10^0 only, 2 = growth in 10^0 and 10^{-1}, etc.). GLA/BC = glutaraldehyde/benzalkonium chloride. Compiled from [83].

The low efficacy of the oxidizing compound was not surprising, as these are susceptible to organic matter [9, 170]. Interestingly, FOR also performed better than GLA/BC at 6 °C, which contradicts the statement that FOR and GLA are active only above 16 and 5 °C, respectively, (cf. Table 2). GLA is believed to be more effective than FOR in some cases (e.g., against bacterial spores). However, this is based on much shorter disinfection times than the 25 h of this study. Shorter disinfection times are beneficial for GLA due to its quicker reaction compared to FOR [75, 140, 149]. The main exception to the overall results depicted in Figure 3 was for feed chain links with fats disinfected for 30 min at 30 °C before and after the disinfection, for which the oxidizing compound was the most effective. *Enterococcus faecalis* was found to be a putative indicator organism, as it was equally or less susceptible than the two *Salmonella* isolates. The consistent results in most tests could not be explained by standardization difficulties because deviations were not systemically related to specific disinfectants.

Another worst-case scenario laboratory test involved the heating of bacteria in organic matter to determine a gold-standard temperature-humidity-time treatment that could be applied subsequently in field studies [79]. Organic matter (poultry feces or feed) was inoculated with *Salmonella* and left to dry for 10 d after which heating was performed at 16-30 or 100% relative humidity (RH) to a final heating temperature of 50, 55, 60, 65, or 70 °C. The application of ≥60 °C and 100% RH during a 24-h period eliminated all *Salmonella* and naturally occurring *E. coli*. A high correlation between the inactivation of *Salmonella* and *E. coli* was observed, indicating the latter was a useful indicator organism for field studies.

Thermal fogging is often used to disinfect animal houses, either alone or in combination with surface disinfection. Fogging with a QAC in a 3 x 3 m room on bacteria inoculated on stainless steel coupons showed satisfactory results on upward-facing, but not on vertical or downward-facing, surfaces [41]. These common findings in thermal fogging are due to gravity forces that only allow the droplets to exert a long-time effect on upward-facing surfaces, the so-called 'shading' effect [10, 41]. Quinn concluded that trials with fogging have given variable results [151], which is also the experience of the author from numerous poultry houses being persistently *Salmonella* infected after thermal fogging.

Field Studies

The increase of human *Salmonella* Enteritidis infections in the Western Hemisphere [155] has resulted in control programs against zoonotic *Salmonella* in several countries [8, 205]. Parallel to this, field studies have assessed the impact of disinfection procedures on the persistence of *Salmonella*, mainly in poultry houses. Few, if any, other micro-organisms have been studied in disinfection field studies apart from putative indicator organisms. Further, only a few study groups have conducted disinfection field studies, thus the numbers of settings, countries, and observers are limited and the judgments of the latter may influence the immeasurable assessments.

One UK study group reported that FOR or synthetic phenols were more effective than other disinfectants such as GLA, tar oil phenols, or peroxygen compounds [52, 55, 64]. In another study conducted by the same study group both FOR and GLA appeared to be more effective than non-aldehyde disinfectants [203]. Moreover, a satisfactory *Salmonella* reduction could be achieved with FOR or a synthetic phenolic compound in spite of a relatively poor cleaning standard, whereas an equally effective disinfection with certain other disinfectants could only be achieved if the cleaning standard was very high [52, 55]. However, an objective assessment of the cleaning standard was not reported, probably because this is difficult. In several cases, in-use dilutions were only half of those recommended [55], which makes comparisons to Danish conditions, in which farmers tend to use higher concentrations than recommended (pers. obs.), difficult. Another study reported that surface disinfection with a phenolic disinfectant followed by FOR fogging was effective in broiler houses, as no *Salmonella* was detected in subsequent crops although it was found in post-disinfection samples [53]. In most of the UK studies *Salmonella* was detected in post-disinfection samples, often in 1/3 or more of the samples [51-58, 203].

French studies comprising layer houses generally showed better results than the UK studies, as *Salmonella* was not detected in six of 14 houses after cleaning and disinfection and it was not detected in more than 5% of the 100 post-disinfection samples taken in each of the remaining eight houses [67, 195]. Comparisons between disinfectant types was not possible because FOR disinfection was used in all 14 houses. *Salmonella* was generally detected in houses in which only surface disinfection was applied whilst surface disinfection followed by thermal fogging yielded *Salmonella* free post-disinfection samples. Similar findings were also reported in two questionnaire-based studies [82, 156]. However, the very different procedures applied in each of the layer houses, which were meticulously described, clearly illustrated the complexity of assessing the impact of individual factors.

The most satisfactory field study results have been obtained in Denmark by the use of 60 ^{o}C steam, with or without 30 ppm FOR, inserted during a 24-h period in six naturally *Salmonella* infected layer houses [80], which was performed after promising laboratory test results (cf. Section 5.3) [79]. No *Salmonella* was detected in the houses after this treatment, apart from six floor-related samples in one house, which may be related to the difficulty of reaching 60 °C at floor level and FOR was not used in that house. Results from beakers containing feed or feces with spiked or naturally occurring *E. faecalis* and *E. coli*, respectively, correlated well with the *Salmonella* results. In addition, these indicator bacteria results indicated that 30 ppm FOR in the steam lowered the lethal temperature by 2-5 °C.

The importance of moisture in heat treatment was indicated in a study comprising two identical layer houses situated on the same farm [78]. In one house (House A) treated with hot air (i.e., dry heat), a temperature in the range 61-70 °C (logged at 11 sites) was maintained for 8 days. In the other house (House B), which was treated with steam and 31 ppm FOR, the temperature ranged from 50 to 59 °C (logged at 10 sites) during a 6-day period. *Salmonella* was detected in 4/31 samples after the dry heat treatment, but in 0/68 samples after the moist heating ($p = 0.003$). However, other differences were also encountered between procedures in the two houses, such as dry cleaning and much organic matter in House A vs. wet cleaning, less organic matter, and the use of FOR in House B.

Scarlett and Mathewson, in an observational study conducted in 10 calf houses that were fumigated with FOR, concluded that proper cleaning and well-sealed houses were more important than temperature and relative humidity [176]. Interestingly, satisfactory results were achieved at 7-8 °C despite the alleged ineffectiveness of FOR at this temperature (cf. Table 2).

CONCLUSION

Disinfection of empty animal houses should be assessed as part of several appropriate measures applied on the farm (e.g., rodent control and bio-security). The routine use of disinfection in all-in all-out systems to minimize the general microbial load may improve the productivity of animals [6], though little is known about the separate impact of disinfection. Moreover, it has been used in the combat of specific diseases. Curiously, little research has focused on non-zoonotic non-statutory diseases [86]. Statutory diseases are under the auspices of the local veterinary services and disinfection procedures are regulated by law. Thus, the main focus in the few realistic disinfection tests has been on zoonotic diseases, in particular *Salmonella*, due to programs initiated in recent years [8, 205]. However, the importance of disinfection of animal houses was revealed in a WHO report, which mentioned nine key *Salmonella* research areas involved in the farm-to-fork chain, five of which related to the primary agricultural sector, but nothing on cleaning and disinfection on the farm [211].

A thorough cleaning is probably the most important prerequisite for an effective disinfection. Under ideal conditions, the equipment is accessible and there are no cracks or crevices in the inner building, which is made of hard, smooth, and impervious surfaces. All visible organic matter has been removed by cleaning and the subsequent disinfection covers all surfaces. The disinfectant is unaffected by organic matter, non-corrosive, breaks down to harmless components, and kills micro-organisms rapidly, even at low temperatures. However, the more realistic situation is less rose-colored. Manufacturers have not spent many resources on cleanable or accessible equipment, all animal houses have cracks and crevices, and surface materials (e.g., wood, plaster, concrete) are often porous, pervious and difficult to clean [29].

The job of cleaning and disinfecting is dirty, tedious, and hard, which could prompt the operator to be more lax at the end of the working day.

It is especially concerning such worst-case scenarios that very little research exists. Thus, an investigation into borderline conditions is needed, not in order to encourage poor disinfection procedures, but to obtain information on safety margins in the elimination of micro-organisms under sub-optimal conditions.

The issue is further complicated by the vague definition of disinfection as a reduction in micro-organisms, without any quantification or clear end-point [24, 111, 153]. With the implementation of the Danish *Salmonella* Control Program for Poultry in 1996 farmers were penalized economically in case they did not eliminate *Salmonella* from the empty poultry houses after the culling of *Salmonella* infected flocks. Thus, a *Salmonella* 'sterilization' was expected, but no specific guidance on how to accomplish this could be given. Persistently *Salmonella* infected poultry houses was a serious problem in many farms [79, 82] that caused severe economic problems, including bankruptcies, for several farmers.

In principle, the issues described in this chapter do not differ from microbiological research in general: the investigation of conditions and mechanisms in the laboratory are useful for the specific setting, but they are often difficult to extrapolate to other settings, in particular real-life situations [166]. The relevance of specific mechanisms has rarely been evaluated. Despite several papers on the function of *mar* (cf. Section 3.5.6) its natural inducer is unknown [152]. Plasmid-mediated FOR dehydrogenase could be highly relevant if micro-organisms were resistant to FOR, but nothing is known about the natural occurrence of this enzyme. Many disinfectant resistance studies have focused on putative cross-resistance to antibiotics [74, 165] or its impact on virulence [100], which has shed little light on the topics of this chapter. Adaptation to disinfectants has generally only resulted in a 2-8 fold MIC/MBC increase, which is still well below the 500-1000 times higher in-use concentrations [164].

Curiously, few studies have assessed if isolates with high and low MICs also had different susceptibilities in more realistic studies. In suspension and carrier tests, Thomas *et al.* found no differences between *Ps. aeruginosa* with high or low MICs [192]. We found that *Salmonella Senftenberg* had higher MICs than *S.* Enteritidis in MIC-tests [81], but the latter was more resistant in realistic surface disinfection tests [83].

Likewise, few studies have compared results between suspension and carrier tests. The classical thesis by Van Klingeren, in which he compared results between suspension and carrier tests, is worth mentioning [196]. As a very general rule of thumb he stated that a 5-log reduction in suspension tests was equal to a 3-log reduction in carrier tests, but it was emphasized that each unique situation should be assessed in separate tests. Griffiths *et al.* studied *M. chelonae* in both suspension and carrier tests and found comparable results between these [84].

Thus, the theoretical aspects outlined in this chapter corroborate that few of the conditions encountered in unrealistic MIC or suspension tests have much relevance to real-life conditions, inside or outside of animal houses [38]. Thus, one often has to rely on theoretical aspects related to the disinfectant (cf. Table 2), the micro-organism (cf. Table 3), the specific conditions prevailing in the animal house, and the few realistic studies. Such considerations indicate that surface disinfection with aldehydes, preferably FOR, combined with strong bases on floors and walls, are a good choice in badly cleaned animal houses, at least as regards vegetative bacteria. This may be supplemented with oxidizing compounds at high temperatures in feed troughs in which high fat contents are found [83], but care should be taken due to corrosion of materials (cf. Table 2). A supplementary thermal fogging with aldehydes is also beneficial. As stated earlier (cf. Section 3.3) oxidizing disinfectants [62, 189, 190] or certain chlorine compounds [118, 119] should be effective in water systems.

The first prerequisite for an effective disinfection in real-life situations, after the termination of cleaning, is contact between the disinfectant and the micro-organism. We suspect, albeit this is difficult to prove, that such a lack of contact at surface disinfection was responsible for many of the persistently *Salmonella* infected poultry houses in Denmark, which were especially encountered in battery cage houses with their inaccessible equipment. As stated earlier, thermal fogging did not show promising results either. Heat, rather than chemical disinfection, is generally recommended for contaminated items, whenever possible [163]. Moist heat at a temperature of 60 °C could be evenly distributed in tightly sealed layer houses without damaging equipment and the bacteriological results were promising, especially when FOR was added to the steam [78-80]. As the desired 60 °C was not accomplished until 10 cm above floor level additional chemical surface disinfection of the floor was recommended.

It is believed there is a need for more studies which mimic worst-case scenarios in the laboratory, followed by full-scale controlled field intervention studies. Various conditions, such as different types of organic matter, disinfectants, and micro-organisms, should be tested. Field studies are expensive, but the effect on a range of pathogens, indicator micro-organisms, and production parameters could be studied at the same time. Such studies are difficult to standardize and probably the main way of compensating for this is the repetition of tests to evaluate if results are consistent. A generally accepted standard monitoring system for disinfection in the field, preferably with the inclusion of relevant indicator micro-organisms, would be beneficial for farmers and contractors. Such monitoring systems, based on sound scientific studies, should be an inherent part of a certification system run by independent auditing bodies [23, 146], similar to the HACCP system implemented in food premises.

REFERENCES

[1] Aarestrup, F. M. & Hasman, H. (2004) Susceptibility of different bacterial species isolated from food animals to copper sulphate, zinc chloride and antimicrobial substances used for disinfection. *Vet. Microbiol., 100,* 83-89.

[2] Adams, J. L. & McLean, R. J. (1999) Impact of *rpoS* deletion on *Escherichia coli* biofilms. *Appl. Environ. Microbiol., 65,* 4285-4287.

[3] Adams, M. R. & Moss, M. O. (2000) The Microbiology of Food Preservation. In M. R. Adams & M. O. Moss (Eds.), *Food Microbiology* (2nd ed., pp. 65-120). Cambridge, UK: Royal Society of Chemistry.

[4] Ahmed, N. M.; Conner, D. E.; Huffman, D. L. (1995) Heat-resistance of *Escherichia coli* O157:H7 in meat and poultry as affected by product composition. *J. Food Sci., 60,* 606-610.

[5] Alekshun, M. N. & Levy, S. B. (1999) The *mar* regulon: multiple resistance to antibiotics and other toxic chemicals. *Trends Microbiol., 7,* 410-413.

[6] Allen, P. C. (1993) Effects of formaldehyde fumigation of housing on carotenoid pigmentation in three breeds of chickens. *Poult. Sci., 72,* 1040-1045.

[7] Allison, D. G. & Gilbert, P. (1995) Modification by surface association of antimicrobial susceptibility of bacterial populations. *J. Ind. Microbiol., 15,* 311-317.

[8] Altekruse, S. F.; Tollefson, L. K.; Bögel, K. (1993) Control strategies for *Salmonella* Enteritidis in five countries. *Food Control, 4,* 10-16.

[9] Amass, S. F.; Ragland, D.; Spicer, P. (2001) Evaluation of the efficacy of a peroxygen compound, Virkon S, as a boot bath disinfectant. *J. Swine Health Prod., 9,* 121-123.

[10] Anonymous (1998) *A Practical Guide to the Disinfection of Food Processing Factories and Equipment Using Fogging - Based on the Results of a Project Funded by MAFF and Industry Through the LINK Advanced and Hygienic Manufacturing Programme.* Ministry of Agriculture, Forestry and Fisheries, UK.

[11] Anonymous (2002) *Code of Practice for the Prevention and Control of Salmonella in Chickens Reared for Meat on Farm.* Department for Environment, Food & Rural Affairs, UK.

[12] Anonymous (2002) *Desinfektion i Husdyrbruget* (5th ed.). Landsudvalget for Svin - Danske Slagterier - Primærproduktion - Forsøg og udvikling, Denmark.

[13] Banhazi, T.; Murphy, T.; Hartung, J. (2003) Using 'Hygiene-pavers' to evaluate cleaning procedures used on pig farms. In *XI International Congress in Animal Hygiene, International Society for Animal Hygiene,* February 23-27, Mexico City, Mexico, pp. 353-362.

[14] Barker, J. & Bloomfield, S. F. (2000) Survival of *Salmonella* in bathrooms and toilets in domestic homes following salmonellosis. *J. Appl. Microbiol., 89,* 137-144.

[15] Barrile, J. C. & Cone, F. (1970) Effect of added moisture on the heat resistance of *Salmonella* Anatum in milk chocolate. *Appl. Microbiol., 19,* 177-178.

[16] Barry, C. E. III & Mdluli, K. (1996) Drug sensitivity and environmental adaptation of mycobacterial cell wall components. *Trends Microbiol., 4,* 275-281.

[17] Bates, R. C.; Shaffer, P. T.; Sutherland, S. M. (1977) Development of poliovirus having increased resistance to chlorine inactivation. *Appl. Environ. Microbiol., 34,* 849-853.

[18] Bean, H. S. (1967) Types and characteristics of disinfectants. *J. Appl. Bacteriol., 30,* 6-16.

[19] Beck, E. G.; Borneff, J.; Grün, L.; Gundermann, K. O.; Kanz, E.; Lammers, T. H.; Mühlens, K.; Primavesi, C. A.; Schmidt, B.; Schubert, R.; Weinhold, E.; Werner, H. P. (1977) Empfehlungen für die Prüfung und Bewertung der Wirksamkeit chemischer Desinfektionsverfahren. *Zbl. Bakt. Hyg. , I. Abt. Orig. B,* 335-380.

[20] Bennett, D. D.; Higgins, S. E.; Moore, R. W.; Beltran, R.; Caldwell, D. J.; Byrd II, J. A.; Hargis, B. M. (2003) Effects of lime on *Salmonella* Enteritidis survival in vitro. *Journal of Applied Poultry Research, 12,* 65-68.

[21] Berchieri, A. Jr. & Barrow, P. A. (1996) The antibacterial effects for *Salmonella* Enteritidis phage type 4 of different chemical disinfectants and cleaning agents tested under different conditions. *Avian Pathol., 25,* 663-673.

[22] Bergan, T. & Lystad, A. (1972) Evaluation of disinfectant inactivators. *Acta Pathol. Microbiol. Immunol. Scand [B], 80,* 507-510.

[23] Blaha, T. (1999) Epidemiology and quality assurance application to food safety. *Prev. Vet. Med., 39,* 81-92.

[24] Block, S. S. (1991) Definition of Terms. In S. S. Block (Ed.), *Disinfection, Sterilization and Preservation* (4th ed., pp. 18-25). London, UK: Lea & Fabiger.

[25] Block, S. S. (2000) *Disinfection, Sterilization and Preservation* (5th ed.). London, UK: Lippincott Williams & Wilkins.

[26] Bloomfield, S. F.; Arthur, M.; Looney, E.; Begun, K.; Patel, H. (1991) Comparative testing of disinfectant and antiseptic products using proposed European suspension testing methods. *Lett. Appl. Microbiol., 13,* 233-237.

[27] Bloomfield, S. F.; Arthur, M.; van Klingeren, B.; Pullen, W.; Holah, J. T.; Elton, R. (1994) An evaluation of the repeatability and reproducibility of a surface test for the activity of disinfectants. *J. Appl. Bacteriol., 76,* 86-94.

[28] Bloomfield, S. F. & Looney, E. (1992) Evaluation of the repeatability and reproducibility of European suspension test methods for antimicrobial activity of disinfectants and antiseptics. *J. Appl. Bacteriol., 73,* 87-93.

[29] Boon, C. R. & Wray, C. (1989) Building design in relation to the control of diseases of intensively housed livestock. *Journal of Agricultural Engineering Research, 43,* 149-161.

[30] Borneff, J. & Werner, H. P. (1977) Entwicklung einer neuen Prüfmethode für Flächendesinfektionsverfahren. *Zbl. Bakt. Hyg., I. Abt. Orig. B, 165,* 97-101.

[31] Boulange-Petermann, L. (1996) Process of bioadhesion on stainless steel surfaces and cleanability: a review with special reference to the food industry. *Biofouling, 10,* 275-300.

[32] Bradley, C. R. & Fraise, A. P. (1996) Heat and chemical resistance of enterococci. *J. Hosp. Infec., 34,* 191-196.

[33] Braoudaki, M. & Hilton, A. C. (2005) Mechanisms of resistance in *Salmonella enterica* adapted to erythromycin, benzalkonium chloride and triclosan. *Int. J. Antimicrob. Agents, 25,* 31-37.

[34] Brown, M. R.; Allison, D. G.; Gilbert, P. (1988) Resistance of bacterial biofilms to antibiotics: a growth-rate related effect? *J. Antimicrob. Chemother., 22,* 777-780.

[35] Brown, M. R.; Collier, P. J.; Gilbert, P. (1990) Influence of growth rate on susceptibility to antimicrobial agents: modification of the cell envelope and batch and continuous culture studies. *Antimicrob. Agents Chemother., 34,* 1623-1628.

[36] Brown, M. R.; Williams, P. (1985) Influence of substrate limitation and growth phase on sensitivity to antimicrobial agents. *J. Antimicrob. Chemother., 15 Suppl A,* 7-14.

[37] Brown, M. R. W. & Barker, J. (1999) Unexplored reservoirs of pathogenic bacteria: protozoa and biofilms. *Trends Microbiol., 7,* 46-50.

[38] Brown, M. R. W.; Costerton, J. W.; Gilbert, P. (1991) Leading article: extrapolating to bacterial life outside the test tube. *J. Antimicrob. Chemother., 27,* 565-567.

[39] Brul, S. & Klis, F. M. (1999) Mechanistic and mathematical inactivation studies of food spoilage fungi. *Fungal. Genet. Biol., 27,* 199-208.

[40] Buckle, A. E. (1981) Formaldehyde Fumigation in Animal Housing and Hatcheries. In C. H. Collins, M. C. Allwood, S. F. Bloomfield, A. Fox, (Eds.), *Disinfectants: Their Use and Evaluation of Effectiveness* (1st ed., pp. 213-222). London, UK: Academic Press Inc. Ltd.

[41] Burfoot, D.; Hall, K.; Brown, K.; Xu, Y. (1999) Fogging for the disinfection of food processing factories and equipment. *Trends in Food Science & Technology, 10,* 205-210.

[42] Chen, J. H. S. (1991) Methods of Testing Virucides. In S. S. Block, (Ed.), *Disinfection, Sterilization, and Preservation* (4th ed., pp. 1076-1093). London, UK: Lea & Fabiger.

[43] Chuanchuen, R.; Karkhoff-Schweizer, R. R.; Schweizer, H. P. (2003) High-level triclosan resistance in *Pseudomonas aeruginosa* is solely a result of efflux. *Am. J. Infect. Control, 31,* 124-127.

[44] Corry, J. E. L. (1974) The effect of sugars and polyols on the heat resistance of salmonellae. *J. Appl. Bacteriol., 37,* 31-43.

[45] Corry, J. E. L. & Allen, V. M. (2000) Biofilm formation and machine cleaning. *International Food Safety News, 9,* 2-6.

[46] Costerton, J. W.; Cheng, K. J.; Geesey, G. G.; Ladd, T. I.; Nickel, J. C.; Dasgupta, M.; Marrie, T. J. (1987) Bacterial biofilms in nature and disease. *Annu. Rev. Microbiol., 41,* 435-464.

[47] Costerton, J. W.; Lewandowski, Z.; Caldwell, D. E.; Korber, D. R.; Laapin-Scott, H. M. (1995) Microbial biofilms. *Annu. Rev. Microbiol., 49,* 711-745.

[48] Cremieux, A. & Fleurette, J. (1991) Methods of Testing Disinfectants. In S. S. Block, (Ed.), *Disinfection, Sterilization and Preservation* (3rd ed., pp. 1009-1027). London, UK: Lea & Febiger.

[49] Croshaw, B. (1971) The Destruction of Mycobacteria. In W. B. Hugo, (Ed.), *Inhibition and Destruction of the Microbial Cell* (1st ed., pp. 429-449). London, UK: Academic Press.

[50] Croshaw, B. (1981) Disinfectant Testing - With Particular Reference to the Rideal-Walker and Kelsey-Sykes Tests. In C. H. Collins, M. C. Allwood, S. F. Bloomfield, A. Fox, (Eds.), *Disinfectants: Their Use and Evaluation of Effectiveness* (1st ed., pp. 1-15). London, UK: Academic Press Inc. Ltd.

[51] Davies, R. H. & Breslin, M. (2003) Observations on *Salmonella* contamination of commercial laying farms before and after cleaning and disinfection. *Vet. Rec., 152,* 283-287.

[52] Davies, R. H.; Breslin, M.; Bedford, S.; Wray, C. (1998) Observations on *Salmonella* contamination of turkey farms. In *1st International Symposium on Turkey Diseases, German Branch of the World Veterinary Poultry Association and Institute of Poultry Diseases*, 19-21 February, Berlin, Germany, pp. 274-290.

[53] Davies, R. H.; Breslin, M.; Corry, J. E. L.; Hudson, W.; Allen, V. M. (2001) Observations on the distribution and control of *Salmonella* species in two integrated broiler companies. *Vet. Rec., 149,* 227-232.

[54] Davies, R. H.; Liebana, E.; Breslin, M. (2003) Investigation of the distribution and control of *Salmonella* enterica serovar Enteritidis PT6 in layer breeding and egg production. *Avian Pathol., 32,* 225-237.

[55] Davies, R. H. & Wray, C. (1995) Observations on disinfection regimens used on *Salmonella* Enteritidis infected poultry units. *Poult. Sci., 74,* 638-647.

[56] Davies, R. H. & Wray, C. (1996) Determination of an effective sampling regime to detect *Salmonella* Enteritidis in the environment of poultry units. *Vet. Microbiol., 50,* 117-127.

[57] Davies, R. H. & Wray, C. (1996) Persistence of *Salmonella* Enteritidis in poultry units and poultry food. *Br. Poult. Sci., 37,* 589-596.

[58] Davies, R. H. & Wray, C. (1996) Studies of contamination of three broiler breeder houses with *Salmonella* Enteritidis before and after cleansing and disinfection. *Avian Dis.*, *40,* 626-633.

[59] Davison, S.; Benson, C. E.; Munro, D. S.; Rankin, S. C.; Ziegler, A. E.; Eckroade, R. J. (2003) The role of disinfectant resistance of *Salmonella enterica* serotype Enteritidis in recurring infections in Pennsylvania egg quality assurance program monitored flocks. *Avian Dis.*, *47,* 143-148.

[60] Denyer, S. P. & Maillard, J. Y. (2002) Cellular impermeability and uptake of biocides and antibiotics in Gram-negative bacteria. *J. Appl. Microbiol.*, *92 Suppl,* 35S-45S.

[61] Dhir, V. K. & Dodd, C. E. (1995) Susceptibility of suspended and surface-attached *Salmonella* Enteritidis to biocides and elevated temperatures. *Appl. Environ. Microbiol.*, *61,* 1731-1738.

[62] Eginton, P. J.; Holah, J.; Allison, D. G.; Handley, P. S.; Gilbert, P. (1998) Changes in the strength of attachment of micro-organisms to surfaces following treatment with disinfectants and cleansing agents. *Lett. Appl. Microbiol.*, *27,* 101-105.

[63] Engvall, A. & Sternberg, S. (2004) Veterinary Practice. In A. P. Fraise, P. A. Lambert, J. Y. Maillard, (Eds.), *Russell, Hugo & Ayliffe's Principles and Practice of Disinfection Preservation & Sterilization* (4th ed., pp. 604-613). London, UK: Blackwell Publishing.

[64] Evans, S. J.; Davies, R. H.; Wray, C. (1999) Epidemiology of *Salmonella Enterica* Serovar Enteritidis Infection in British Poultry Flocks. In A. M. Saeed, R. K. Gast, M. E. Potter, P. G. Wall, (Eds.), *Salmonella Enterica Serovar Enteritidis in Humans and Animals - Epidemiology, Pathogenesis, and Control* (1st ed., pp. 313-323). Ames, USA: Iowa State University Press.

[65] Foschino, R.; Nervegna, I.; Motta, A.; Galli, A. (1998) Bactericidal activity of chlorine dioxide against *Escherichia coli* in water and on hard surfaces. *J. Food Prot.*, *61,* 668-672.

[66] Foster, J. W. & Spector, M. P. (1995) How *Salmonella* survive against the odds. *Annu. Rev. Microbiol.*, *49,* 145-174.

[67] Fournier, G.; Drouin, P.; Valancony, H.; Toux, J. Y. (2001) *Etude de la Decontamination des Batiments de Poules Pondeuses en Cages - Rapport Final.* AFSSA, Unité de Recherche en Epidémiologie et Qualité en Aviculture, Ploufragan, France.

[68] Fraise, A. P.; Lambert, P. A.; Maillard, J. Y. (2004) *Russell, Hugo & Ayliffe's Principles and Practice of Disinfection Preservation & Sterilization* (4th ed.). London, UK: Blackwell Publishing.

[69] Gawande, P. V. & Bhagwat, A. A. (2002) Inoculation onto solid surfaces protects *Salmonella* spp. during acid challenge: a model study using polyethersulfone membranes. *Appl. Environ. Microbiol.*, *68,* 86-92.

[70] Gibson, H.; Taylor, J. H.; Hall, K. E.; Holah, J. T. (1999) Effectiveness of cleaning techniques used in the food industry in terms of the removal of bacterial biofilms. *J. Appl. Microbiol.*, *87,* 41-48.

[71] Gilbert, P.; Allison, D. G.; McBain, A. J. (2002) Biofilms in vitro and in vivo: do singular mechanisms imply cross-resistance? *J. Appl. Microbiol.*, *87,* 98S-110S.

[72] Gilbert, P.; Collier, P. J.; Brown, M. R. (1990) Influence of growth rate on susceptibility to antimicrobial agents: biofilms, cell cycle, dormancy, and stringent response. *Antimicrob. Agents Chemother.*, *34,* 1865-1868.

[73] Gilbert, P.; Das, J.; Foley, I. (1997) Biofilm susceptibility to antimicrobials. *Adv. Dent. Res.*, *11,* 160-167.

[74] Gilbert, P. & McBain, A. (2004) Live and let die. *Microbiology Today*, *31,* 62-63.

[75] Gorman, S. P.; Scott, E. M.; Russell, A. D. (1980) A review - antimicrobial activity, uses and mechanism of action of glutaraldehyde. *J. Appl. Bacteriol.*, *48,* 161-190.

[76] Gould, G. W. (1989) Heat-Induced Injury and Inactivation. In G. W. Gould, (Ed.), *Mechanisms of Action of Food Preservation Procedures* (1st ed., pp. 11-42). London, UK: Elsevier Applied Science.

[77] Gould, G. W. (2004) Sterilization - Heat Sterilization. In A. P. Fraise, P. A. Lambert, J. Y. Maillard, (Eds.), *Russell, Hugo & Ayliffe's Principles and Practice of Disinfection Preservation & Sterilization* (4th ed., pp. 361-383). London, UK: Blackwell Publishing.

[78] Battery Cage Houses. In *Disinfection of Salmonella in Poultry Houses*, Thesis, University of Bristol, UK. ISBN 87-988795-3-7 (pp. 141-154) (http://www.kimorengradel.com/Disinfection%20of%20Salmonella%20in%20poultry%20houses_27-4.pdf, accessed 6 May 2007).

[79] Gradel, K. O.; Jørgensen, J. C.; Andersen, J. S.; Corry, J. E. (2003) Laboratory heating studies with *Salmonella* spp. and *Escherichia coli* in organic matter, with a view to decontamination of poultry houses. *J. Appl. Microbiol.*, *94,* 919-928.

[80] Gradel, K. O.; Jørgensen, J. C.; Andersen, J. S.; Corry, J. E. (2004) Monitoring the efficacy of steam and formaldehyde treatment of naturally *Salmonella*-infected layer houses. *J. Appl. Microbiol.*, *96,* 613-622.

[81] Gradel, K. O.; Randall, L. P.; Sayers, A. R.; Davies, R. H. (2005) Possible associations between *Salmonella* persistence in poultry houses and resistance to commonly used disinfectants and a putative role of *mar*. *Vet. Microbiol.*, *107,* 127-138.

[82] Gradel, K. O. & Rattenborg, E. (2003) A questionnaire-based, retrospective field study of persistence of *Salmonella* Enteritidis and *Salmonella* Typhimurium in Danish broiler houses. *Prev. Vet. Med.*, *56,* 267-284.

[83] Gradel, K. O.; Sayers, A. R.; Davies, R. H. (2004) Surface disinfection tests with *Salmonella* and a putative indicator bacterium, mimicking worst-case scenarios in poultry houses. *Poult. Sci.*, *83,* 1636-1643.

[84] Griffiths, P. A.; Babb, J. R.; Bradley, C. R.; Fraise, A. P. (1997) Glutaraldehyde-resistant *Mycobacterium chelonae* from endoscope washer disinfectors. *J. Appl. Microbiol.*, *82,* 519-526.

[85] Guerin-Mechin, L.; Dubois-Brissonnet, F.; Heyd, B.; Leveau, J. Y. (1999) Specific variations of fatty acid composition of *Pseudomonas aeruginosa* ATCC 15442 induced by quaternary ammonium compounds and relation with resistance to bactericidal activity. *J. Appl. Microbiol.*, *87,* 735-742.

[86] Gutiérrez, C. B.; Barbosa, J. I. R.; Suárez, J.; González, O. R.; Tascón, R. I.; Ferri, E. F. R. (1995) Efficacy of a variety of disinfectants against *Actinobacillus pleuropneumoniae* serotype 1. *Am. J. Vet. Res.*, *56,* 1025-1029.

[87] Hammond, S. A.; Morgan, J. R.; Russell, A. D. (1987) Comparative susceptibility of hospital isolates of Gram-negative bacteria to antiseptics and disinfectants. *J. Hosp. Infec.*, *9,* 255-264.

[88] Hansen, N. H. & Riemann, H. (1963) Factors affecting the heat resistance of nonsporing organisms. *J. Appl. Bacteriol.*, *26,* 314-333.

[89] Hawkey, P. M. (2004) Bacterial Resistance - Mycobactericidal Agents. In A. P. Fraise, P. A. Lambert, J. Y. Maillard, (Eds.), *Russell, Hugo & Ayliffe's Principles and Practice of Disinfection Preservation & Sterilization* (4th ed., pp. 191-204). London, UK: Blackwell Publishing.

[90] Hengge-Aronis, R. (2000) The General Stress Response in *Escherichia Coli*. In G. Storz & R. Hengge-Aronis, (Eds.), *Bacterial Stress Responses* (1st ed., pp. 161-178). Washington DC, USA: ASM Press.

[91] Hiom, S. J.; Furr, J. R.; Russell, A. D. (1995) Uptake of 14C-chlorhexidine gluconate by *Saccharomyces cerevisiae, Candida albicans* and *Candida glabrata. Lett. Appl. Microbiol., 21,* 20-22.

[92] Hiom, S. J.; Furr, J. R.; Russell, A. D.; Dickinson, J. R. (1992) Effects of chlorhexidine diacetate on *Candida albicans, C. glabrata* and *Saccharomyces cerevisiae. J. Appl. Bacteriol., 72,* 335-340.

[93] Hiom, S. J.; Furr, J. R.; Russell, A. D.; Dickinson, J. R. (1993) Effects of chlorhexidine diacetate and cetylpyridinium chloride on whole cells and protoplasts of *Saccharomyces cerevisiae. Microbios, 74,* 111-120.

[94] Hiom, S. J.; Furr, J. R.; Russell, A. D.; Hann, A. C. (1996) The possible role of yeast cell walls in modifying cellular response to chlorhexidine diacetate. *Cytobios, 86,* 123-135.

[95] Hiom, S. J.; Hann, A. C.; Furr, J. R.; Russell, A. D. (1995) X-ray microanalysis of chlorhexidine-treated cells of *Saccharomyces cerevisiae. Lett. Appl. Microbiol., 20,* 353-356.

[96] Holah, J. T.; Taylor, J. H.; Dawson, D. J.; Hall, K. E. (2002) Biocide use in the food industry and the disinfectant resistance of persistent strains of *Listeria monocytogenes* and *Escherichia coli. J. Appl. Microbiol., 92 Suppl,* 111S-120S.

[97] Hugo, W. B. & Denyer, S. P. (1987) The Concentration Exponent of Disinfectants and Preservatives (Biocides). In R. G. Board, M. C. Allwood, J. G. Banks, (Eds.), *Preservatives in the Food, Pharmaceutical and Environmental Industries* (1st ed., pp. 281-291). Oxford, UK: Blackwell Scientific Publications.

[98] Humphrey, T.; O'Brien, S.; Madsen, M. (2007) Campylobacters as zoonotic pathogens: A food production perspective. *Int. J. Food Microbiol.*, in press.

[99] Humphrey, T. J.; Slater, E.; McAlpine, K.; Rowbury, R.; Gilbert, R. J. (1995) *Salmonella* Enteritidis Phage type 4 isolates more tolerant of heat, acid and hydrogen peroxide also survive longer on surfaces. *Appl. Environ. Microbiol., 61,* 3161-3164.

[100] Humphrey, T. J.; Williams, A.; McAlpine, K.; Lever, M. S.; Guard-Petter, J.; Cox, J. M. (1996) Isolates of *Salmonella enterica* Enteritidis PT4 with enhanced heat and acid tolerance are more virulent in mice and more invasive in chickens. *Epidemiol. Infect., 117,* 79-88.

[101] James, G. A.; Beaudette, L.; Costerton, J. W. (1995) Interspecies bacterial interactions in biofilms. *J. Ind. Microbiol., 15,* 257-262.

[102] Kaulfers, P. M. & Marquardt, A. (1991) Demonstration of formaldehyde dehydrogenase activity in formaldehyde-resistant Enterobacteriaceae. *FEMS Microbiol. Lett., 63,* 335-338.

[103] Kaur, J.; Ledward, D. A.; Park, R. W. A.; Robson, R. L. (1998) Factors affecting the heat resistance of *Escherichia coli* O157:H7. *J. Appl. Microbiol., 26,* 325-330.

[104] Kirby, R. M. & Davies, R. (1990) Survival of dehydrated cells of *Salmonella* Typhimurium LT2 at high temperatures. *J. Appl. Bacteriol., 68,* 241-246.

[105] Klimek, J. W. & Bailey, J. H. (1956) Factors influencing the rate of killing of *Escherichia coli* exposed to benzalkonium chloride. *Appl. Microbiol., 4,* 53-59.

[106] Knott, A. G.; Russell, A. D.; Dancer, B. N. (1995) Development of resistance to biocides during sporulation of *Bacillus subtilis. J. Appl. Bacteriol., 79,* 492-498.

[107] Kolter, R.; Siegele, D. A.; Tormo, A. (1993) The stationary phase of the ife cycle. *Annu. Rev. Microbiol., 47,* 855-874.

[108] Kumar, C. G. & Anand, S. K. (1998) Significance of microbial biofilms in food industry: a review. *Int. J. Food Microbiol., 42,* 9-27.

[109] Kummerle, N.; Feucht, H. H.; Kaulfers, P. M. (1996) Plasmid-mediated formaldehyde resistance in *Escherichia coli*: characterization of resistance gene. *Antimicrob. Agents Chemother., 40,* 2276-2279.

[110] Lambert, P. A. (2004) Bacterial Resistance - Resistance of Bacterial Spores to Chemical Agents. In A. P. Fraise, P. A. Lambert, J. Y. Maillard, (Eds.), *Russell, Hugo & Ayliffe's Principles and Practice of Disinfection Preservation & Sterilization* (4th ed., pp. 184-190). London, UK: Blackwell Publishing.

[111] Lambert, R. J. W. (2004) Evaluation of Antimicrobial Efficacy. In A. P. Fraise, P. A. Lambert, J. Y. Maillard, (Eds.), *Russell, Hugo & Ayliffe's Principles and Practice of Disinfection Preservation & Sterilization* (4th ed., pp. 345-360). London, UK: Blackwell Publishing.

[112] Lamfon, H.; Porter, S. R.; McCullough, M.; Pratten, J. (2004) Susceptibility of *Candida albicans* biofilms grown in a constant depth film fermentor to chlorhexidine, fluconazole and miconazole: a longitudinal study. *J. Antimicrob. Chemother., 53,* 383-385.

[113] Langsrud, S. (1998) *Resistance to Disinfectants used in the Food Processing Industry, with Emphasis on Resistance to Benzalkonium Chloride.* Thesis, Department of Biotechnological Sciences, Agricultural University of Norway.

[114] Langsrud, S. & Sundheim, G. (1997) Factors contributing to the survival of poultry associated *Pseudomonas* spp. exposed to a quaternary ammonium compound. *J. Appl. Microbiol., 82,* 705-712.

[115] Langsrud, S.; Sundheim, G.; Borgmann-Strahsen, R. (2003) Intrinsic and acquired resistance to quaternary ammonium compounds in food-related *Pseudomonas* spp. *J. Appl. Microbiol., 95,* 874-882.

[116] Langsrud, S.; Sundheim, G.; Holck, A. L. (2004) Cross-resistance to antibiotics of *Escherichia coli* adapted to benzalkonium chloride or exposed to stress-inducers. *J. Appl. Microbiol., 96,* 201-208.

[117] Lassen, C.; Skårup, S.; Hagen Mikkelsen, S.; Kjølholt, J. (2001) Inventory of Biocides used in Denmark - Environmental Project No. 585 2001. The Danish Environmental Protection Agency (http://www2.mst.dk/udgiv/Publications/2001/87-7944-383-4/pdf/87-7944-384-2.PDF, accessed 6 May 2007).

[118] LeChevallier, M. W.; Cawthon, C. D.; Lee, R. G. (1988) Factors promoting survival of bacteria in chlorinated water supplies. *Appl. Environ. Microbiol., 54,* 649-654.

[119] LeChevallier, M. W.; Cawthon, C. D.; Lee, R. G. (1988) Inactivation of biofilm bacteria. *Appl. Environ. Microbiol., 54,* 2492-2499.

[120] Lemcke, R. M. & White, H. R. (1959) The heat resistance of *Escherichia coli* cells from cultures of different ages. *J. Appl. Bacteriol., 22,* 193-201.

[121] Levy, S. B. (2002) Active efflux, a common mechanism for biocide and antibiotic resistance. *J. Appl. Microbiol., 92 Suppl,* 65S-71S.

[122] Lewis, K. (2001) Riddle of biofilm resistance. *Antimicrob. Agents Chemother., 45,* 999-1007.

[123] Linton, A. H.; Hugo, W. B.; Russell, A. D. (1987) *Disinfection in Veterinary and Farm Animal Practice* (1st ed.). London, UK: Blackwell Scientific Publications.

[124] Linton, A. H.; Hugo, W. B.; Russell, A. D. (1987) Practical Aspects of Disinfection and Infection Control. In A. H. Linton, W. B. Hugo, A. D. Russell, (Eds.), *Disinfection in Veterinary and Farm Animal Practice* (1st ed., pp. 144-167). London: Blackwell Scientific Publications.

[125] Lou, Y. & Yousef, A. E. (1996) Resistance of *Listeria monocytogenes* to heat after adaptation to environmental stresses. *J. Food Prot., 59,* 465-471.

[126] MacKinnon, I. H. (1974) The use of inactivators in the evaluation of disinfectants. *J. Hyg. (London), 73,* 189-195.

[127] Maillard, J. Y. (2001) Virus susceptibility to biocides: an understanding. *Reviews in Medical Microbiology, 12,* 63-74.

[128] Maillard, J. Y. (2002) Bacterial target sites for biocide action. *J. Appl. Microbiol., 92 Suppl,* 16S-27S.

[129] Maillard, J. Y. (2004) Antifungal Activity of Disinfectants. In A. P. Fraise, P. A. Lambert, J. Y. Maillard, (Eds.), *Russell, Hugo & Ayliffe's Principles and Practice of Disinfection Preservation & Sterilization* (4th ed., pp. 205-219). London, UK: Blackwell Publishing.

[130] Maillard, J. Y. (2004) Viricidal Activity of Biocides. In A. P. Fraise, P. A. Lambert, J. Y. Maillard, (Eds.), *Russell, Hugo & Ayliffe's Principles and Practice of Disinfection Preservation & Sterilization* (4th ed., pp. 272-323). London, UK: Blackwell Publishing.

[131] Majtan, V. & Majtanova, L. (2002) Antibacterial efficacy of disinfectants against some gramnegative bacteria. *Cent. Eur. J. Public Health, 10,* 104-106.

[132] Maris, P. (1995) Modes of action of disinfectants. *Rev. sci. tech. Off. int. Epiz., 14,* 47-55.

[133] Mattick, K. L.; Jørgensen, F.; Legan, J. D.; Lappin-Scott, H. M.; Humphrey, T. J. (2000) Habituation of *Salmonella* spp. at reduced water activity and its effect on heat tolerance. *Appl. Environ. Microbiol., 66,* 4921-4925.

[134] Mattila-Sandholm, T. & Wirtanen, G. (1992) Biofilm formation in the food industry: a review. *Food Reviews International, 8,* 573-603.

[135] McDonnell, G.; Russell, A. D. (1999) Antiseptics and disinfectants: activity, action, and resistance. *Clin. Microbiol. Rev., 12,* 147-179.

[136] Mechin, L.; Dubois-Brissonnet, F.; Heyd, B.; Leveau, J. Y. (1999) Adaptation of *Pseudomonas aeruginosa* ATCC 15442 to didecyldimethylammonium bromide induces changes in membrane fatty acid composition and in resistance of cells. *J. Appl. Microbiol., 86,* 859-866.

[137] Meroz, M. & Samberg, Y. (1995) Disinfecting poultry production premises. *Rev. sci. tech. Off. int. Epiz., 14,* 273-291.

[138] Moken, M. C.; McMurry, L. M.; Levy, S. B. (1997) Selection of multiple-antibiotic-resistant (*mar*) mutants of *Escherichia coli* by using the disinfectant pine oil: roles of the *mar* and *acrAB* loci. *Antimicrob. Agents Chemother.*, *41,* 2770-2772.

[139] Mokgatla, R. M.; Brozel, V. S.; Gouws, P. A. (1998) Isolation of Salmonella resistant to hypochlorous acid from a poultry abattoir. *Lett. Appl. Microbiol.*, *27,* 379-382.

[140] Moore, S. L. & Payne, D. N. (2004) Types of Antimicrobial Agents. In A. P. Fraise, P. A. Lambert, J. Y. Maillard, (Eds.), *Russell, Hugo & Ayliffe's Principles and Practice of Disinfection Preservation & Sterilization* (4th ed., pp. 8-97). London, UK: Blackwell Publishing.

[141] Møretrø, T.; Midtgaard, E. S.; Nesse, L. L.; Langsrud, S. (2003) Susceptibility of *Salmonella* isolated from fish feed factories to disinfectants and air-drying at surfaces. *Vet. Microbiol.*, *94,* 207-217.

[142] Morgan-Jones, S. C. (1981) Cleansing and Disinfection of Farm Buildings. In C. H. Collins, M. C. Allwood, S. F. Bloomfield, A. Fox, (Eds.), *Disinfectants: Their Use and Evaluation of* Effectiveness (1st ed., pp. 199-212). London, UK: Academic Press.

[143] Murphy, C.; Carroll, C.; Jordan, K. N. (2006) Environmental survival mechanisms of the foodborne pathogen *Campylobacter jejuni*. *J. Appl. Microbiol.*, *100,* 623-632.

[144] Murtough, S. M.; Hiom, S. J.; Palmer, M.; Russell, A. D. (2001) Biocide rotation in the healthcare setting: is there a case for policy implementation? *J. Hosp. Infec.*, *48,* 1-6.

[145] Nikaido, H. & Vaara, M. (1987) Outer Membrane. In F. C. Neidhardt, J. L. Ingraham, K. B. Low, B. Magasanik, M. Schaechter, H. E. Umbarger, (Eds.), *Escherichia Coli and Salmonella Typhimurium - Cellular and Molecular Biology* (1st ed., pp. 7-22). Washington DC, USA: ASM Press.

[146] Noordhuizen, J. P. &; Frankena, K. (1999) Epidemiology and quality assurance: applications at farm level. *Prev. Vet. Med.*, *39,* 93-110.

[147] Ogase, H.; Nagai, I.; Kameda, K.; Kume, S.; Ono, S. (1992) Identification and quantitative analysis of degradation products of chlorhexidine with chlorhexidine-resistant bacteria with three-dimensional high performance liquid chromatography. *J. Appl. Bacteriol.*, *73,* 71-78.

[148] Poole, K. (2004) Bacterial Resistance - Acquired Resistance. In A. P. Fraise, P. A. Lambert, J. Y. Maillard, (Eds.), *Russell, Hugo & Ayliffe's Principles and Practice of Disinfection Preservation & Sterilization* (4th ed., pp. 170-183). London, UK: Blackwell Publishing.

[149] Power, E. G. M. (1997) Aldehydes as biocides. *Prog. Med. Chem.*, *34,* 149-201.

[150] Profe, D. & Trenner, P. (1994) Experimental Investigations on Nebulizing Disinfectants in Large Poultry Houses. Environmental and Management Systems for Total Animal Health Care in Agriculture. In *8th International Congress on Animal Hygiene, International Society for Animal Hygiene*, 12-16 September, St. Paul, Minnesota, USA.

[151] Quinn, P. J. (1991) Disinfection and Disease Prevention in Veterinary Medicine. In S. S. Block, (Ed.), *Disinfection, Sterilization, and Preservation* (4th ed., pp. 846-868). London, UK: Lea & Fabiger.

[152] Randall, L. P. & Woodward, M. J. (2002) The multiple antibiotic resistance (mar) locus and its significance. *Res. Vet. Sci.*, *72,* 87-93.

[153] Reybrouck, G. (1999) Evaluation of the Antibacterial and Antifungal Activity of Disinfectants. In A. D. Russell, W. B. Hugo, G. A. J. Ayliffe, (Eds.), *Principles and*

Practice of Disinfection, Preservation and Sterilization (3rd ed., pp. 124-144). London, UK: Blackwell Science, Inc.

[154] Reybrouck, G. (2004) Antifungal Activity of Disinfectants. Evaluation of the Antibacterial and Antifungal Activity of Disinfectants. In A. P. Fraise, P. A. Lambert, J. Y. Maillard, (Eds.), *Russell, Hugo & Ayliffe's Principles and Practice of Disinfection Preservation & Sterilization* (4th ed., pp. 220-240). London, UK: Blackwell Publishing.

[155] Rodrigue, D. C.; Tauxe, R. V.; Rowe, B. (1990) International increase in *Salmonella* Enteritidis: a new pandemic? *Epidemiol. Infect., 105,* 21-27.

[156] Rose, N.; Beaudeau, F.; Drouin, P.; Toux, J. Y.; Rose, V.; Colin, P. (2000) Risk factors for *Salmonella* persistence after cleansing and disinfection in French broiler-chicken houses. *Prev. Vet. Med., 44,* 9-20.

[157] Rossouw, F. T. & Rowbury, R. J. (1984) Effects of the resistance plasmid R124 on the level of the OmpF outer membrane protein and on the response of *Escherichia coli* to environmental agents. *J. Appl. Bacteriol., 56,* 63-79.

[158] Roszak, D. B. & Colwell, R. R. (1987) Survival strategies of bacteria in the natural environment. *Microbiol. Rev., 51,* 365-379.

[159] Russell, A. D. (1981) Neutralization Procedures in the Evaluation of Bactericidal Activity. In C. H. Collins, M. C. Allwood, S. F. Bloomfield, A. Fox, (Eds.), *Disinfectants: Their Use and Evaluation of Effectiveness* (1st ed., pp. 45-59). London, UK: Academic Press Inc. Ltd.

[160] Russell, A. D. (1997) Plasmids and bacterial resistance to biocides. *J. Appl. Microbiol., 82,* 155-165.

[161] Russell, A. D. (1998) Mechanisms of bacterial resistance to antibiotics and biocides. *Prog. Med. Chem., 35,* 133-197.

[162] Russell, A. D. (1999) Bacterial resistance to disinfectants: present knowledge and future problems. *J. Hosp. Infec., 43 (Supplement),* S57-S68.

[163] Russell, A. D. (1999) Heat Sterilization - Sterilization and Disinfection by Heat Methods. In A. D. Russell, W. B. Hugo, G. A. J. Ayliffe, (Eds.), *Principles and Practice of Disinfection, Preservation and Sterilization* (3rd ed., pp. 629-639). London, UK: Blackwell Science Inc.

[164] Russell, A. D. (2000) Do biocides select for antibiotic resistance? *J. Pharm. Pharmacol., 52,* 227-233.

[165] Russell, A. D. (2002) Antibiotic and biocide resistance in bacteria: comments and conclusions. *J. Appl. Microbiol., 92 Suppl,* 171S-173S.

[166] Russell, A. D. (2003) Biocide use and antibiotic resistance: the relevance of laboratory findings to clinical and environmental situations. *Lancet Infect. Dis., 3,* 794-803.

[167] Russell, A. D. (2003) Similarities and differences in the responses of microorganisms to biocides. *J. Antimicrob. Chemother., 52,* 750-763.

[168] Russell, A. D. (2004) Bacterial adaptation and resistance to antiseptics, disinfectants and preservatives is not a new phenomenon. *J. Hosp. Infect., 57,* 97-104.

[169] Russell, A. D. (2004) Factors Influencing the Efficacy of Antimicrobial Agents. In A. P. Fraise, P. A. Lambert, J. Y. Maillard, (Eds.), *Russell, Hugo & Ayliffe's Principles and Practice of Disinfection Preservation & Sterilization* (4th ed., pp. 98-127). London, UK: Blackwell Publishing.

[170] Russell, A. D. & Chopra, I. (1996) Antiseptics, Disinfectants and Preservatives: Their Properties, Mechanisms of Action and Uptake into Bacteria. In A. D. Russell & I.

Chopra, (Eds.), *Understanding Antibacterial Action and Resistance* (2nd ed., pp. 96-149). London, UK: Ellis Horwood.

[171] Russell, A. D. & Furr, J. R. (1996) Biocides: mechanisms of antifungal action and fungal resistance. *Sci. Prog., 79 (Pt. 1),* 27-48.

[172] Russell, A. D. & Gould, G. W. (1988) Resistance of Enterobacteriaceae to preservatives and disinfectants. *J. Appl. Bacteriol. - Symposium supplement,* 167S-195S.

[173] Ryu, J. H. & Beuchat, L. R. (1999) Changes in heat tolerance of *Escherichia coli* O157:H7 after exposure to acidic environments. *Food Microbiol., 16,* 317-324.

[174] Sagripanti, J. L.; Eklund, C. A.; Trost, P. A.; Jinneman, K. C.; Abeyta, C., Jr.; Kaysner, C. A.; Hill, W. E. (1997) Comparative sensitivity of 13 species of pathogenic bacteria to seven chemical germicides. *Am. J. Infect. Control, 25,* 335-339.

[175] Sattar, S. A. (2006) Allen Denver Russell Memorial Lecture, 2006 - The use of microbiocides in infection control: a critical look at safety, testing and applications. *J. Appl. Microbiol., 101,* 743-753.

[176] Scarlett, C. M. & Mathewson, G. K. (1977) Terminal disinfection of calf houses by formaldehyde fumigation. *Vet. Rec., 101,* 7-10.

[177] Senhaji, A. F. (1977) The protective effect of fat on the heat resistance of bacteria (II). *J. Food Technol., 12,* 217-230.

[178] Sidhu, M. S. (2001) *Disinfectant- and Antibiotic Resistant Bacteria from Food and Clinical Environments.* Thesis, Department of Chemistry and Biotechnology, Agricultural University of Norway.

[179] Siegele, D. A. & Kolter, R. (1992) Life after log. *J. Bacteriol., 174,* 345-348.

[180] Søeberg, H. P. & Pedersen, N. (1998) *Rengøring og Desinfektion af Fjerkræstalde.* Landskontoret for Fjerkrærådgivning, Denmark.

[181] Sondossi, M.; Roosmoore, H. W.; Wireman, J. W. (1985) Observations of resistance and cross-resistance to formaldehyde and a formaldehyde condensate biocide in *Pseudomonas aeruginosa. Int. Biodeterior., 21,* 105-106.

[182] Stewart, P. S. & Costerton, J. W. (2001) Antibiotic resistance of bacteria in biofilms. *Lancet, 358,* 135-138.

[183] Stickler, D. J. (2004) Bacterial Resistance - Intrinsic Resistance of Gram-Negative Bacteria. In A. P. Fraise, P. A. Lambert, J. Y. Maillard, (Eds.), *Russell, Hugo & Ayliffe's Principles and Practice of Disinfection Preservation & Sterilization* (4th ed., pp. 154-169). London, UK: Blackwell Publishing.

[184] Stickler, D. J. & Thomas, B. (1980) Antiseptic and antibiotic resistance in Gram-negative bacteria causing urinary tract infection. *J. Clin. Path., 33,* 288-296.

[185] Storz, G. & Hengge-Aronis, R. (2000) *Bacterial Stress Responses* (1st ed.). Washington DC, USA: ASM Press.

[186] Strauch, D. & Böhm, R. (2002) *Reinigung Und Desinfektion in Der Nutztierhaltung Und Veredelungswirtschaft* (2nd ed.). Stuttgart, Germany: Enke Verlag.

[187] Sundahl, A. M. (1975) Cleanability of building materials. *Farm Building Progress, 40,* 19-21.

[188] Sutton, S. V.; Proud, D. W.; Rachui, S.; Brannan, D. K. (2002) Validation of microbial recovery from disinfectants. *PDA J. Pharm. Sci. Technol., 56,* 255-266.

[189] Takeo, Y.; Oie, S.; Kamiya, A.; Konishi, H.; Nakazawa, T. (1994) Efficacy of disinfectants against biofilm cells of *Pseudomonas aeruginosa. Microbios, 79,* 19-26.

[190] Tanner, R. S. (1989) Comparative testing and evaluation of hard-surface disinfectants. *J. Ind. Microbiol.*, *4,* 145-154.

[191] Theraud, M.; Bedouin, Y.; Guiguen, C.; Gangneux, J. P. (2004) Efficacy of antiseptics and disinfectants on clinical and environmental yeast isolates in planktonic and biofilm conditions. *J. Med. Microbiol.*, *53,* 1013-1018.

[192] Thomas, L.; Russell, A. D.; Maillard, J. Y. (2005) Antimicrobial activity of chlorhexidine diacetate and benzalkonium chloride against *Pseudomonas aeruginosa* and its response to biocide residues. *J. Appl. Microbiol.*, *98,* 533-543.

[193] Tuschewitzki, G. J.; Exner, M.; Thofern, E. (1983) Induktion einer mikrobiellen Wandbesiedlung in Kunststoffschläuchen durch Trinkwasser. *Zentralblatt für Bakteriologie, Mikrobiologie und Hygiene [B]*, *178,* 380-388.

[194] Vaara, M. (1992) Agents that increase the permeability of the outer membrane. *Microbiol. Rev.*, *56,* 395-411.

[195] Valancony, H.; Fournier, G.; Drouin, P.; Danguy, R.; Toux, J. Y.; Balaine, L. (2001) Le nettoyage et la désinfection des bâtiments de poules pondeuses en cages vis à vis de *Salmonella* Enteritidis: 2e partie/bilan des pratiques. *Sciences et Techniques Avicoles*, *36,* 16-25.

[196] van Klingeren, B. (1983) *A Two-tier System for the Evaluation of Disinfectants*. Thesis, University of Utrecht, Netherlands.

[197] van Klingeren, B. (1995) Disinfectant testing on surfaces. *J. Hosp. Infec.*, *30 Suppl,* 397-408.

[198] van Klingeren, B.; Leussink, A. B.; van Wijngaarden, L. J. (1977) A collaborative study on the repeatability and the reproducibility of the Dutch Standard-suspension-test for the evaluation of disinfectants. *Zbl. Bakt. Hyg. , I. Abt. Orig. B*, *164,* 521-548.

[199] van Klingeren, B. & Pullen, W. (1993) Glutaraldehyde resistant mycobacteria from endoscope washers. *J. Hosp. Infec.*, *25,* 147-149.

[200] Verrips, C. T.; Kwast, R. H.; de Vries, W. (1980) Growth conditions and heat resistance of *Citrobacter freundii*. *Antonie Van Leeuwenhoek*, *46,* 551-563.

[201] Völker, U.; Maul, B.; Hecker, M. (1999) Expression of the sigmaB-dependent general stress regulon confers multiple stress resistance in *Bacillus subtilis*. *J. Bacteriol.*, *181,* 3942-3948.

[202] von Löhren, U. (1994) Maßnahmen zur Desinfektion und Entwesung von Geflügelstallen nach dem Auftreten von S. Enteritidis. *Dtsch. Tierärztl. Wochenschr.*, *101,* 290-292.

[203] Wales, A.; Breslin, M.; Davies, R. (2006) Assessment of cleaning and disinfection in *Salmonella*-contaminated poultry layer houses using qualitative and semi-quantitative culture techniques. *Vet. Microbiol.*, *116,* 283-293.

[204] Walters, A. H. (1967) Hard surface disinfection and its evaluation. *J. Appl. Bacteriol.*, *30,* 56-65.

[205] Wegener, H. C.; Hald, T.; Wong, D. L.; Madsen, M.; Korsgaard, H.; Bager, F.; Gerner-Smidt, P.; Mølbak, K. (2003) *Salmonella* control programs in Denmark. *Emerg. Infect. Dis.*, *9,* 774-780.

[206] Werner, H. P. (1975) Investigations on the efficacy of surface disinfection and surface cleaning procedures. 2. Laboratory testing of the efficacy under conditions simulating those of real-life. *Zbl. Bakt. Hyg. , I. Abt. Orig. B*, *B 160,* 568-578.

[207] White, T. C.; Marr, K. A.; Bowden, R. A. (1998) Clinical, cellular, and molecular factors that contribute to antifungal drug resistance. *Clin. Microbiol. Rev.*, *11,* 382-402.

[208] Wille, B. (1976) Möglichkeiten einer Resistenzentwicklung von Mikroorganismen gegen Desinfektionsmittel. *Zentralblatt für Bakteriologie [Originale B]*, *162,* 217-220.

[209] Willinghan, E. M.; Sander, J. E.; Thayer, S. G.; Wilson, J. L. (1996) Investigation of bacterial resistance to hatchery disinfectants. *Avian Dis.*, *40,* 510-515.

[210] Wollmann, A. & Kaulfers, P. M. (1991) Formaldehyde-resistance in Enterobacteriaceae and *Pseudomonas aeruginosa*: identification of resistance genes by DNA-hybridization. *Zentralblatt für Hygiene und Umweltmedizin*, *191,* 449-456.

[211] World Health Organization (1988) *Salmonellosis Control: the Role of Animal and Product Hygiene*. WHO Expert Committee on Salmonellosis Control. Technical Report Series, report no. 774, Geneva, Switzerland.

In: Environmental Microbiology Research Trends
Editor: G. V. Kurladze, pp. 99-135
ISBN: 978-1-60021-939-9

Chapter 3

NATURAL BACTERIAL BIOFILMS IN THE ENVIRONMENT

***Odile Tresse*[1*]*, Rutger de Wit*[2]*, Viviane Cassisa*[3]*, Gaël Le Pennec*[3]*, Dominique Haras*[3] *and Michel Federighi*[1]**

[1] UMR-INRA 1014 SECALIM ENVN/ENITIAA, Ecole Nationale Vétérinaire de Nantes, France

[2] UMR-CNRS 5119, Université Montpellier II, Ifremer, Montpellier, France

[3] LBCM EA 3884, Université de Bretagne-Sud, LORIENT, France

ABSTRACT

Bacteria are described as the smallest autonomous organism in the environment. Based on the data available on the complete genomes, the bacterial genome size varies from 0.27 Mb (*Bacillus anthracis* strain A2012) to 9.7 Mb (*Rhodococcus sp.* RHA1). This genome material allows the binary fission process which is the main way of reproduction of the bacteria. This mode of growth limits the genetic variations to sporadic mutations. However, the genetic potential of a bacterium is not limited to the genetic materials inherited from its parents. The bacteria have evolved mainly by exchanging genetic material from other bacteria via plasmids and DNA recombinations. This ability confers a large potential to the bacteria to adapt to the environment. Moreover, the bacterial cells are able to communicate to each other. This type of interaction offers facilities to coordinate some bacterial physiological processes such as the quorum sensing. The cell-to-cell communication exports the gene expression at the level of the bacterial population rendering the bacterial world more complex. This complexity is reinforced by the ability of the bacterial cells to form a well-structured cell cluster organization, namely biofilms. This dynamic bacterial structure ensures a bigger potential

* Corresponding Author: Odile Tresse, UMR-SECALIM 10174 ENVN-ENITIAA, Ecole Nationale Vétérinaire de Nantes, Route de Gachet BP 40706, F-44307 Nantes, France Cedex 03, tel.: +(33) 240 687 811, fax: +(33) 240 687 762, e-mail: tresse@vet-nantes.fr

to survive to the environmental conditions by combining diverse phenotype responses. Through the biofilm formation, the bacteria developed new strategies to adapt and to survive to the environment. The aspects of the natural bacterial biofilms in the environment will be discussed in this chapter through the structure of the biofilms, the biofouling and the biocorrosion, and the biofilms in water.

I. STRUCTURE AND FUNCTIONS OF NATURAL BIOFILMS

I.1. Biofilm Bibliometry

The theory of bacterial biofilms was stated for the first time by Costerton et al. in 1978 [17]. Consequently, the word biofilm appeared in the literature in the early 80's of last century (Figure 1). The occurrence of the word 'biofilm' found in the title or in the abstract of the scientific publications was observed in two publication databases. A total of 7,141 publications on biofilms were found in PubMed database (from 1980 to 2006) and 12,398 publications were found in Web of Science (WOS) database (from 1991 to 2006). The database analysis on the word 'biofilm' indicated a lag of publications on biofilms during the first decade followed by an exponential interest until today with more than 1600 publications in 2006 listed on WOS database. The same trend was observed with publications from PubMed database with fewer publications listed on biofilms than on WOS database. PubMed database is less complete than WOS database because it covers journals (about 5,000 with more than 15 million records from mid 1950's) essentially related to medicine areas including nursing, dentistry, veterinary medicine, health care, and preclinical sciences whereas WOS covers over 8,000 journals (more than 37 million records from 1945) in scientific areas including science, technology, medicine, psychology, sociology, and economics. With these data, a deeper bibliometric analysis was conducted. The publications on biofilms come mostly from USA, England, Germany, Canada, and France representing 63% of the total publications on biofilms listed in WOS (Figure 2). The fifteen countries listed on Figure 2 represent 93% of the publications on biofilms listed in WOS. Over 3% (370) of the publications on biofilms come from Montana State University (MSU) (Figure 3). Montana State University is the world's premiere biofilm research facility with its Center for Biofilm Engineering (CBE), Bozeman, MT, USA, founded by William G. Characklis in 1990. Today, the CBE directed by Philip S. Stewart is composed of more than 30 faculty researchers. The BioCentrum Department (BIC) at the Technical University of Denmark (DTU), Denmark and the Department of Microbiology and Molecular Genetics at the Harvard Medical School, Cambridge, MA, USA are the two institutes that have published the most on biofilms after the CBE (1.57% and 1.17%, respectively, of the total publications on biofilms listed on WOS). However, only 16.46% of the publications on biofilms are published by the 15 first biofilm-publishing institutes indicating that research areas on biofilms are not reduced to very specialized institutes of research but are spread out in research institutes in the 15 countries represented on figure 2.

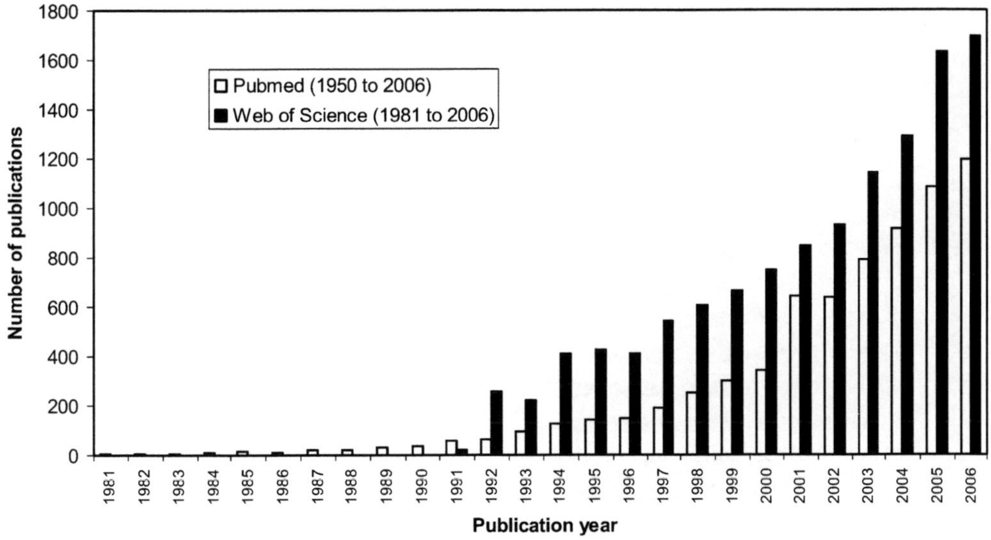

Figure 1. Occurrence of the word 'biofilm*' in the title or in the abstract [Ti/AB] of the scientific publications listed in PubMed and in Web of Science (WOS) databases.

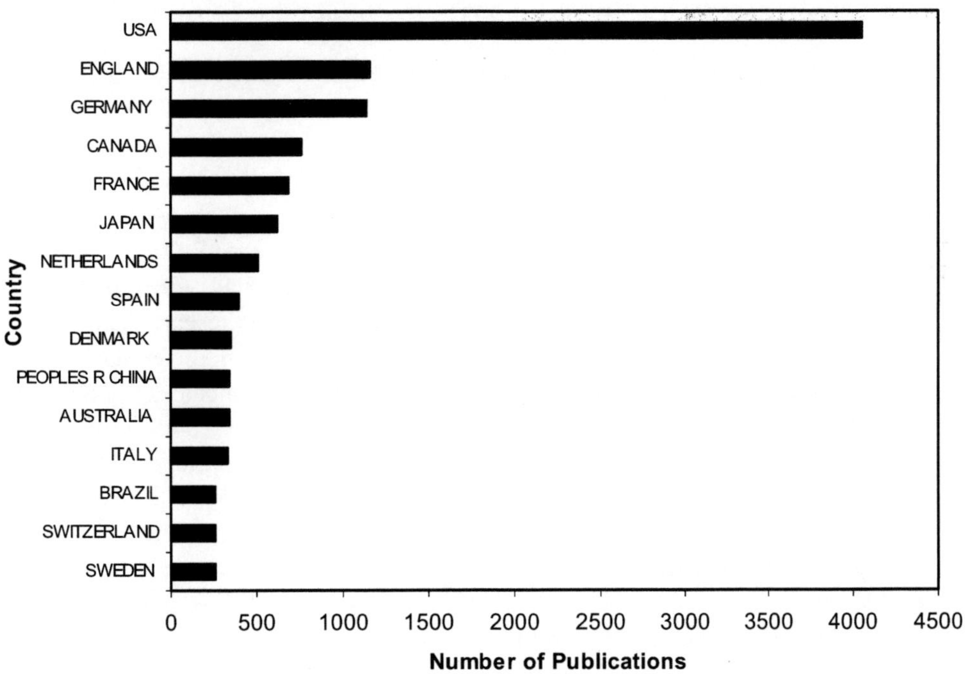

Figure 2. The fifteen first Countries over the world among the 12,338 publications containing the word "biofilm*" [Ti/AB] listed by WOS from 1981 to June 2007.

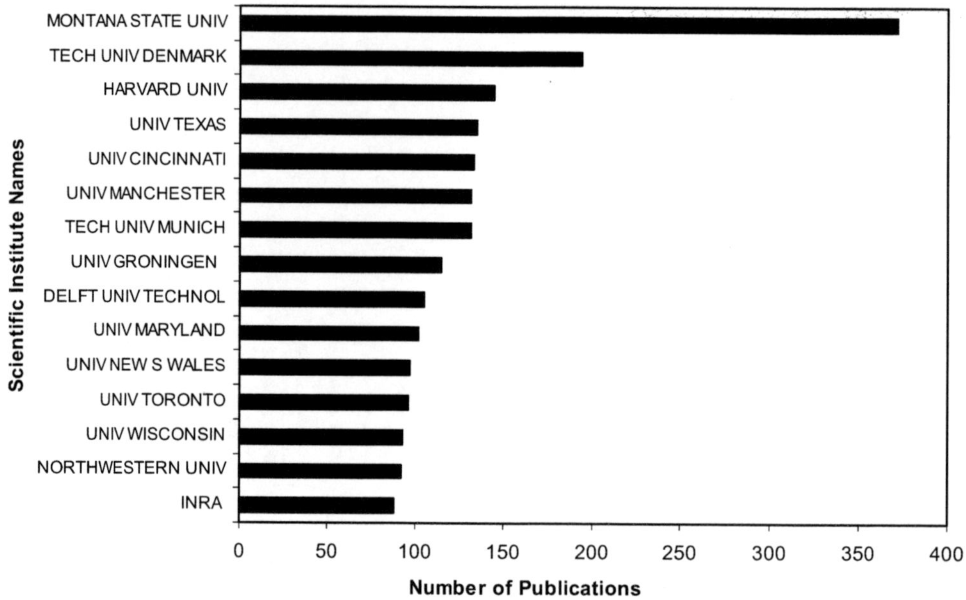

Figure 3. The fifteen first Institutes over the world among the 12,338 publications containing the word "biofilm*" [Ti /AB] listed by WOS from 1981 to June 2007.

Most of the publications on biofilms listed in WOS are represented by Research Articles (85%) followed by Reviews (7%) (Figure 4A). These data are biased by WOS because this database was designed to record mostly research articles. Noteworthy, the publications could have been grouped into four categories (Figure 4B). Most of the publications were grouped in the General category (44%) because the subject dealt with general knowledge on biofilms or because it was not possible to distinguish the category from the WOS classification. However, from the publications that could be grouped in specific fields (56% of the total), 70% belonged to the Environment category indicating that the biofilm research is more spred in the environment than in the medicine or the in food areas. This could be explained by the broad range of biofilms that could be found in the environment which includes biofilms found in the seawater, drinking water, biofilms associated with plants and biofilms grown for industrial biotechnologies. The interest on biofilms in the Environment category is confirmed by the scientific journals targeted for publications on biofilms (Figure 5). The Water Science and Technology, the Applied and Environmental Microbiology and Water Research represented 33% where the articles on biofilms are published. Up to now, only one scientific journal is dedicated to biofilm. The journal 'Biofilms' is edited by Mickael Wilson and published by Cambridge Journals of Cambridge University Press.

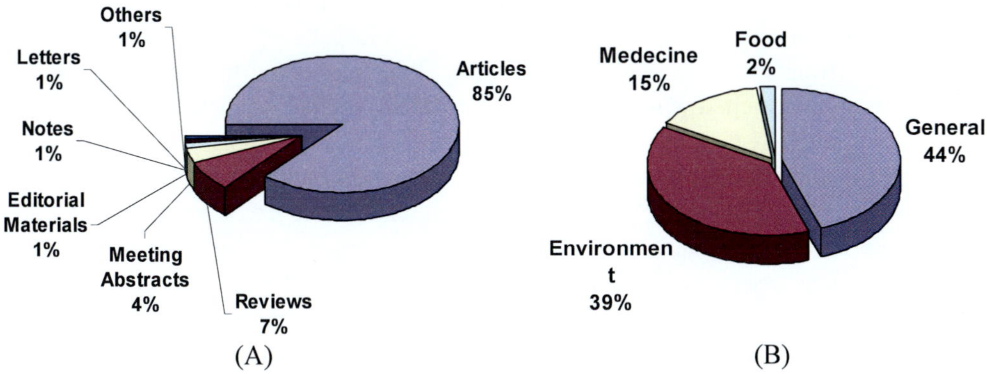

Figure 4. Distribution of the Type (A) and the Category (B) of the references about biofilms [Ti /AB] listed in WOS from 1981 to June 2007.

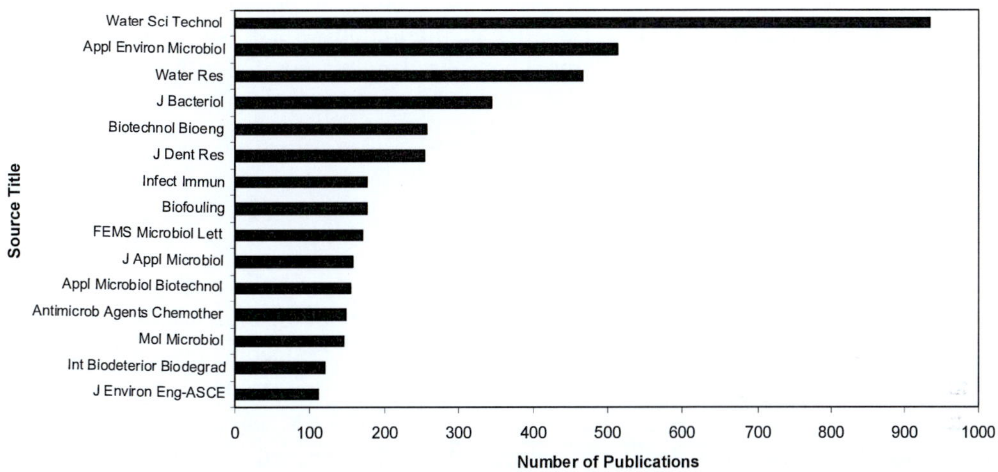

Figure 5. The fifteen first Scientific Journals where the publications on biofilms are published among the 12,338 publications containing the word "biofilm*" [Ti /AB] listed by WOS from 1981 to June 2007.

I.2. Biofilm History

Claude Ephraim Zobell (1904-1989, USA) is recognized as the pioneer of the modern marine microbiology. Not only known for his work on the microbiological processes in the ocean including microbial corrosion, petroleum microbiology, bacteriology of deeps and trenches (discovery of the barophile microorganisms), Zobell gave the first description of the adhesion of the bacteria to surfaces in 1943 [111]. Before 1943, scientists have noticed that many water bacteria grow attached to solid surfaces [39, 42, 102]. In 1937, Zobell [110] suggested that nutrients might be concentrated on solids surfaces as food available for bacterial cells. In 1940, Heukelekian and Heller [41] confirmed the presence of organic compounds accumulated at the solid surfaces by increasing the specific solid surface using smaller flasks or adding glass beads to the culture. The authors suggested that the concentration of food at the surface would attract the bacteria especially when the culture is deficient in nutrients such as water from sea, lakes and oceans. If the authors observed the presence of bacteria at the solid surfaces, they postulated that the bacterial attachment was superficial as shaking readily detached the cells. In 1943, Zobell [111] tested 96 bacterial species isolated from marine materials using glass slides immerged in wide mouth bottles containing seawater enriched with peptone. After different periods of incubation at 25°C, 29 bacterial species exhibited a larger number of firmly attached cells, 20 had variable number of attached cells, and 47 did not adhere to glass slides. The author concluded that many bacteria found in seawater are growing exclusively or preferentially attached to a solid surface. Zobell qualified them as 'sessile bacteria' referring to not motile organisms found on the sediments in the ocean, namely sessile organisms in marine biology. Likewise motile organisms living in the plankton, the viable bacteria in suspension in liquids were named 'planktonic microorganisms' later on. Moreover, Zobell observed an exuding mucilaginous holdfast surrounded the sessile cells. The author was not able to determine the nature of this cementing substance. Because dilute HCL or H_2SO_4 had no effect on the holdfasts, Zobell noted that the adhesive material was not calcareous.

From these observations, Zobell concluded that solid surfaces accumulated nutrients and bacteria and hypothesized that this bacterial configuration would delay the diffusion of exoenzymes and hydrolyzates away from the cells thereby promoting the assimilation of nutrients in deficient media.

I.3. Biofilm Definition

The definition of microbial biofilms evolved over the two last decades along with the knowledge accumulated on the structure and the function of natural biofilms. The word 'biofilm' appeared in the literature for the first time in 1978 defined as glycocalyx-enclosed cells adherent to available surfaces [17]. Before, the resulting phenomenon of attached cells was qualified as microbial mats, bacterial adherence or bacterial adhesion [6] without considering these microbial mat as an entity. The first proposed definitions on biofilms focused on the adhesion capability of the cells to a surface and the presence of a gelatinous matrix surrounding the microbial cells. Later on, it was stipulated that biofilms could be composed of multiple bacterial species or multiple microorganisms other than bacteria including fungi, algae, protozoa and small invertebrates. The microbial diversity of the biofilms depends on the ecological niches where the biofilm grows. The most diverse biofilms (multispecies biofilms) are usually described whilst fouling of underwater structures such as ship hulls, pipelines, and reservoirs and the least diverse biofilms, reduced to one microbial species (monospecies biofilms), are usually described in highly restrictive environment such as harsh environments or antimicrobial well-equipped environments like the human body. With the traditional light microscopy, the biofilm was described as a two-dimensional planar structure which was composed of monolayers of cells attached to a surface. This point of view evolved with the growing development of microscopic techniques such as scanning electron microscopy (SEM) and the transmission electron microscopy (TEM). These techniques rose off the biofilm analyse to a three-dimensional point of view. The first observations were performed on biofilms growing upon medical devices dedicated to the human body including intravenous and intraarterial catheters, pacemakers, coils, and nasogastric tubes [59-61, 58]. The observations of biofilm complex shapes overwrote the schematic planar representation of biofilms. Futhermore, these studies confirmed that the mucous matrix was synthesized by the bacteria and was composed of exopolymeric substances as proved by using specific exopolymer dyes like the ruthenium red. Consequently, it was suggested that biofilm is a collection of microorganisms, predominantly bacteria, enmeshed within a three-dimensional gelatinous matrix of extracellular polymers secreted by the microorganisms. In 1989, Costerton and Lappin-Scott [18] defined the biofilm as aggregates of microcolonies attached to a surface and embedded in exopolymeric substances. Electron microscopy techniques had some limitations since dehydration steps were necessary to the biofilm preparation resulting in artefacts on the mucilaginous matrix that was reduced to filamentous structures between the cells. The three-dimensional structure was also more compact under the electron microscopy than in real. The confocal laser scanning microscopy (CLSM) had probably revolutionized the way of analyzing the structure of the biofilms. The optical laser slices of the biofilms obtained with CLSM informed the researchers about the real biofilm thickness and its shape but also allowed them to explore the ultrastructure of the biofilm by pointing out the distribution of the cells within the biofilms (Figure 4). This new technique using specific fluorochromes avoided any dehydration steps destructing the three-dimensional aspect of the sample and allowed to picture the heterogeneity of the biofilm resulting in a representation of biofilms closer to the reality. Moreover, the flow of water of substances through the biofilm could be analysed using specifically stained microbeads [84]. These analyses indicated that biofilms were structured from cell clusters embedded in their exopolymeric substances that could trap substances from the liquid or detritus from the immobilized or dead cells which led to a new definition of biofilms: complex associations of cells, extracellular products and detritus either trapped within the biofilm or released from cells which have lysed as the biofilm ages [15]. By examining biofilms from different bacterial species, it was noticed that the exopolymeric substances could be very different from one species to another and in some cases they could not be detected. Therefore, Characklis and Marshall [14] corrected their first definition of biofilm by cells immobilized at a substratum and frequently embedded in an organic polymer matrix of microbial origin. Later on, the adhesion to a surface was less important in the definition of a biofilm than the complexity and the well-structured organization of the cells in the biofilms. Bacterial complexes such as pellicle growing at the liquid/air interface like those performed by *Bacillus cereus* [106], *Bacillus subtilis* [50], and *Campylobacter jejuni* [46] were also considered as biofilms. By extention, the flocs in granular sludge were also named as biofilms or sessile bacteria in suspension in a liquid [8, 88]. Consequently, the biofilm definition had evolved in matrix-enclosed bacterial populations adherent to each other and/or to surfaces or interfaces [20]. The dynamics studies conducted on biofilms using CLSM and flow cells indicated that the shape and the structure of the biofilm was not uniform in time and space. From these data, Bryers [12] suggested that a biofilm is a surface accumulation, which is not necessary uniform in time or space that comprises cells immobilized at a substratum and frequently embedded in an organic polymer matrix of microbial origin. From the previous observations, Branda et al. [10] proposed more recently a new definition of biofilm: Bacterial cells often found in close association with surfaces and interfaces in the form of multicellular aggregates. The heterogeneity and the complexity of the biofilm are not described and understood enough today to be able to give a final definition. However, it is well admitted that the biofilm forms an entity and could be defined as an ecosystem *per se*.

I.4. Biofilm Formation and Structure

Formation of bacterial biofilms on a solid submerged surface is a complex phenomenon which involves several parameters. The setting up of a mature biofilm needs three main stages: (i) bacterial adhesion to the surface, (ii) biofilm growth and matrix production, and (iii) biofilm maturation (Figure 6).

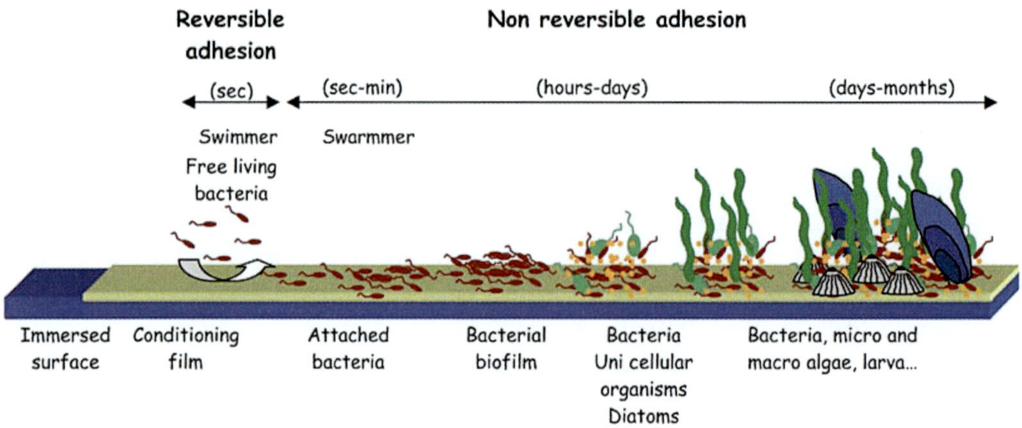

Figure 6. Schematic representation of the different steps involved in a marine biofilm formation.

I.4.1. Bacterial Adhesion

Approach of bacteria to surface is conditioned by sedimentation, convective forces, Brownian motions, or bacterial motility. The bacterial attachment to the surface is performed in two steps: a reversible adhesion and a non reversible adhesion. The former one depends on the physicochemical properties of the cell surface and the substratum and the effect of the environment (conditioned substratum by nutrients, influence of the environment on the cell adhesion capability, medium hydrodynamics). The material surface is the place for adsorption of medium components as well as organic molecules and ions, leading to the formation of a conditioning film. This organic film becomes able to partially neutralize the whole charge and the surface free energy, a phenomenon being able to modify bacteria's interactions with the surface. This could lead to two opposite phenomenon: promotion or inhibition of bacterial adhesion. The physicochemical properties of the cells surface and the substratum determine the cell adhesion capability. Furthermore, nature and strength of involved interactions vary, depending on distance between the bacterium and the surface: (i) long distance forces (> 50 nm, Lifshitz-van der Waals forces), (ii) intermediate distance forces (between 20 nm and 50 nm, Lifshitz-van der Waals forces and electrostatic interactions) and (iii) short distance forces (< 20 nm, Lifshitz-van der Waals forces, electrostatic interactions, hydrophobic/hydrophilic interactions, and Lewis acid-base interactions) [100] (Figure 7). When distance is higher than 10 nm, bacterium can be considered as a particle carrying a uniform net charge. So, week interactions, van der Waals-like and repulsive electrostatic, are involved if net charges are the same on both surfaces. When distance is lower than 10 nm, bacterium structure must be taken into account. Indeed, macro molecular composition and its surface visco-elasticity will contribute to charge distribution heterogeneity (macro molecules differential ionization, medium ion adsorption in bacterial glycocalyx), allowing attractive electrostatic interactions. Final bacterium adhesion needs flow conditions close to zero (condition met at the extreme surface of submerged materials) and specific interactions between surface and macro molecules expressed on the bacterium surface. As long as those specific interactions are not established, the cell can further detach from the surface and return to its planktonic lifestyle. This adhesion step is reversible. At this stage, contact between surface and bacterium is carried out on a cellular pole.

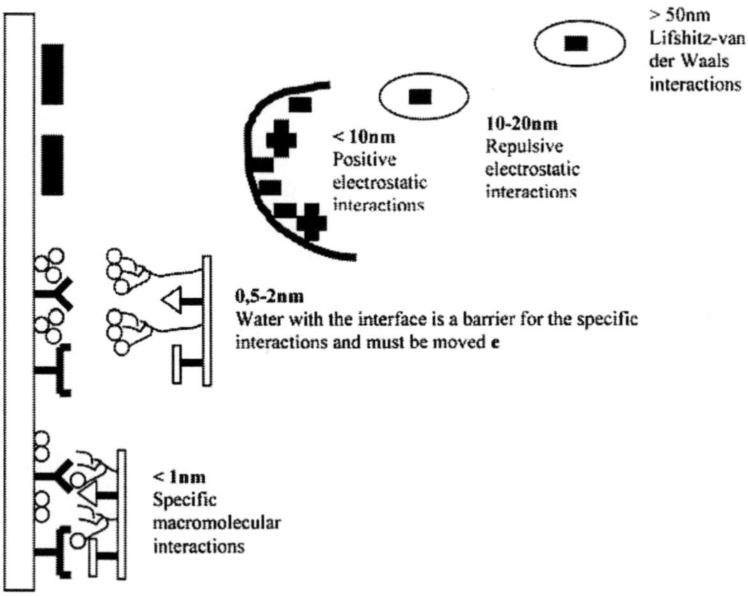

Figure 7. Summary of strengths involved in bacterial adhesion.

Non reversible bacterial adhesion is characterized by reorientation of the cells on the surface. Contact is established according to cell longitudinal axis. Non reversible adhesion implies that bacterium moves to the surface (swarming), towards place(s) where it will be able to start strong interactions with the surface through its surface macro molecules [21]. Different bacterial appendixes are useful to promote bacteria adhesion without being really essential to biofilm maintenance. Cellular appendages including flagella, curli, fimbriae, type I pili and type IV pili were shown to contribute to the early biofilm formation during the first stage [5, 62, 67, 66, 75, 97, 98, 103]. The non reversible adhesion is stated when hydrogen and covalent bonds are present between cells through the extracellular polymeric substances synthesized during the second stage.

I.4.2. Biofilm Growth and Matrix Production

Once bacterial adhesion is non reversible, the biofilm become organized with the formation of cell clusters that resulted of sessile cell multiplication, planktonic cell recruiting and matrix synthesis. The colony formation will cover all or a part of the surface. This differential colonization is in part linked to material and bacterium surface properties (Figure 8). The biofilm formed by a surface hydrophilic bacterium onto a hydrophilic surface as glass coverslip is characterized by the whole surface covering, whereas the biofilm formed by a moderate hydrophobic bacterium is made of differentiated piles. Laser confocal microscopy indicated that the biofilm forms a heterogeneous tridimensional film (Figure 9). The matrix might account for 50% to 90% of the total organic carbon [65], it is hydrated up to 97% or 99% [45, 109] and it can occupy up to 75-95% of a mature biofilm volume [101]. Matrix synthesis constitutes a metabolic and an energetic burden for the sessile bacteria. Different expressions were used to qualify the matter surrounding the sessile cells within biofilms. Some expressions were used as for comparison of the texture and the aspect to other known biological secreted matters surrounding eukaryotic or prokaryotic cells (e.g.: mucous, glycocalyx [11], gelatinous matrix, slime [44]) and other expressions relied on the nature of the matter (e.g.: organic polymer matrix, exopolymeric substances (EPS), extracellular polymeric substances (EPS) [12], exopolysaccharides (EPS) [89], mucoïd exopolysaccharides (MEP) [43], capsular polysaccharide adhesins (CPA) [31], polysaccharide intercellular adhesion (PIA) [56]). The acronym EPS is frequently used although the definition varies according to the authors as mentioned before. The composition of the polymers synthesized by sessile bacteria in biofilms varies with the bacterial species and the environment. They are usually composed of polysaccharides [89] and/or proteins [52] which contribute to the spatial limits of the biofilm unit. The *Pseudomonas aeruginosa* example, an opportunist and pathogen bacterium, illustrates the phenomenon. Davies and Geesey [22] have shown that the *alg*C gene encoding for a phosphomannomutase, involved in alginates synthesis (exopolysaccharides), is over-expressed few minutes after adhesion onto a solid surface. The use of a transcriptional fusion between the gene promoter and a reporter gene showed that gene expression is more strongly induced in sessile *P. aeruginosa* cells than in planktonic counterparts [23]. The EPS could be reinforced by molecules recruiting from the liquid medium or cell detritus including lipids, DNA, ions which could alter the physicochemical properties of the exopolymers [87]. The position of the microcolonies enmeshed in the EPS will determine the hydrodynamic routes (namely voids, pores, and channels) within the biofilm necessary for cell survival through molecules exchanges (oxygen, detritus, nutrients) from the bulk liquid and the sessile cells. The frequent shapes described in biofilms correspond to mushroom-like, finger-like, and honeycomb-like structures.

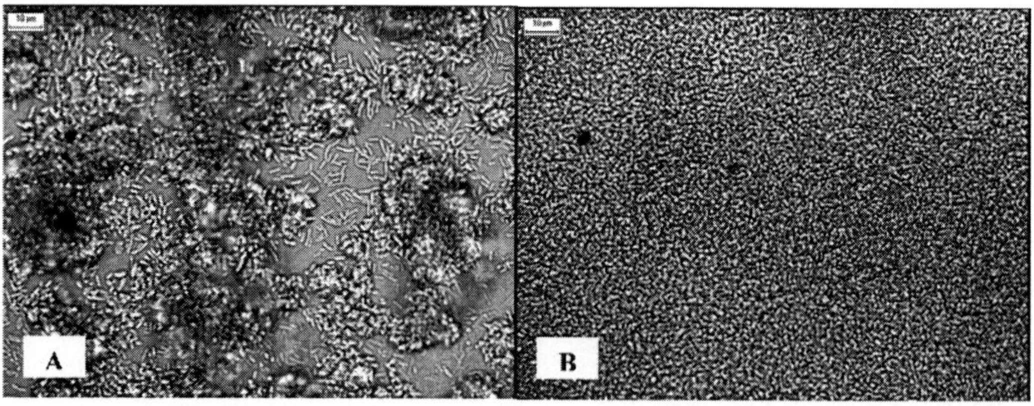

Figure 8. Phase-contrast microscopy images of bacterial biofilm after 48 h of flow cell culture. A: Moderate hydrophobic strain, *Pseudoalteromoras* sp. (water contact angle, 64°±2). B: Hydrophilic strain, *Vibrio* sp. (water contact angle, 29°±7).

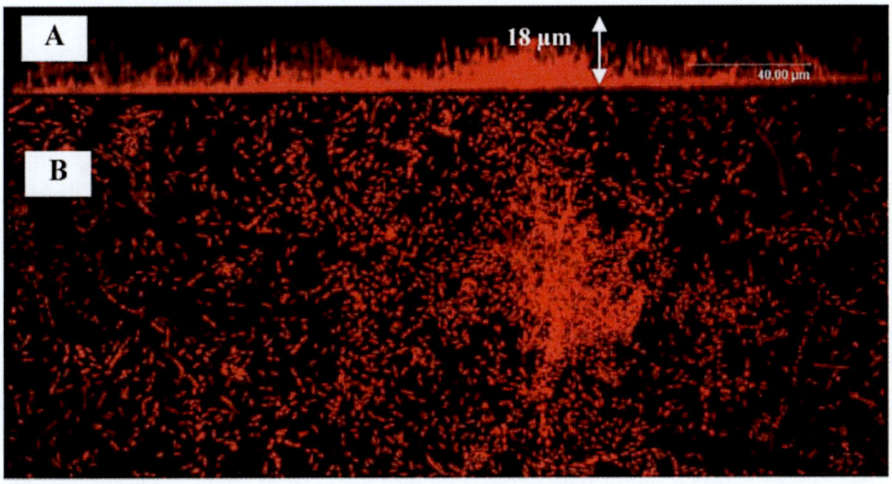

Figure 9. Laser confocal microscopy observation of bacterial biofilm.
A: (x, y) observation. B: (x, z) observation.

I.4.3. Biofilm Maturation

The biofilm thickness and development will result of a net accumulation between cell growth and cell detachment which is determined by the nutrient and gas availability, the adaptation capability of the bacterial species and the hydrodynamic flows of the liquid. Under low laminar flow conditions, the biofilm growth is isotropic while under higher laminar flows, the cell clusters in biofilms are elongated and formed streamers [86]. Under turbulent flows, Stoodley et al. [85] described some migratory ripples at the surface of the biofilms. Regularly, the biofilm releases cells in different ways [9]. It can take place either by cellular lysis or by viable cells departure, during the biofilm maturation and also as an answer to environment changes (e.g.: hydrodynamic flow, carbon source type). Biofilm biomass diminution can also be due to chemical agents like tensioactive molecules, enzymes, chlorine derivatives, chelators or pH modifications. According to the considered agent, a cellular death or a bacterium detachment with a low death rate can also occur. Single sessile cells could be released from the biofilm and become planktonic cells. The abrasion process due to the physical forces of the liquid could also extract cells from the biofilm: this is the natural erosion of the biofilm. Another process, named sloughing, consists on the detachment of portions of the biofilms that might initiate other sporadic biofilms on the surface. Many passive mechanisms leading to the lost of intact cells have been described: limitation of oxygen availability in thick biofilms [93], detachment due to hydrodynamic conditions and available nutrients diminution and modification of their composition [79, 80]. A cell death mechanism was also described in biofilms. In *Pseudomonas aeruginosa* biofilms, the death of the cells seems to be programmed by mutations occurring in Pf1-like phage in specific regions of microcolonies in biofilms which initiate the superinfection and the killing of the cells [104].

Mass transport of oxygen was studied in biofilms using microelectrodes to analyse local mass transfer in different areas of the biofilms. The results indicated that the oxygen concentration decreases with the distance from the surface of a cell aggregate due to the rapid oxygen consumption by cells at the surface of the aggregate while no gradient of oxygen was demonstrated in channels, voids or pores [27]. The same trend was described for the nutrients with an increase of nutrient rarefaction with the distance from the cell aggregate surface. Consequently, the oxygen and nutrient gradients in the cell aggregates were correlated with a cell metabolic gradient. Highly metabolic cells, dormant cells, and dead cells were found in biofilms [3, 53, 96]. It was suggested that metabolic active cells would be located at the cell aggregate surface whereas dormant cells will be located in the centre of the aggregate. In that concept, different bacterial subpopulations should coexist in a monospecies biofilm and these populations may include the different states of cell adaptation to various environmental conditions described on planktonic cells. Moreover, the sessile cells in the biofilm are directed by signalling molecules that play an important role in the structure of the biofilm. Davies *et al.* have shown that a *P. aeruginosa* mutant, unable to synthesize inter bacterial communication molecules, N-acyl-homoserine lactones (HSL), was forming a radically different biofilm than the one formed by the wild strain. The biofilm obtained with the mutant was like packed cell layers whereas the biofilm obtained with the parental strain was aerated with channels and pores. Culture complementation with exogenous HSL restored wild phenotype [24]. This suggests that these interbacterial communications, also called quorum sensing molecules (QS), are essential to the establishment of cellular community organization in the biofilm. HSL, produced by Gram negative bacteria, are not the only communication molecules identified. Gram positive bacteria, as *Bacillus subtilis* and *Staphylococcus spp*., secrete modified oligopeptides. A third type of communication molecule, furanosyl borate diester (AI2), has been highlighted in Gram positive and Gram negative bacteria [38]. Although these molecules are involved in bacterium-bacterium relationship and in multispecies biofilms, their role in biofilm formation is unknown. Studies conducted on mutant strains for QS regulators reveal that communication molecules can affect all the steps of biofilm formation: adhesion, growth and maturation [71].

Although the biofilm formation could be separated into three main phases, the evolution of the biofilm has to be seen as a continuous phenomenon with an overlapping of these different phases. Planktonic cells could be also part of the biofilm, floating between the cell aggregates in the voids and the channels.

I.5. Biofilm Phenotype?

An important point in biofilm maturation is in relationship between its structure and its genetic expressions. Many bacteria organized in biofilms have different susceptibilities to environmental aggressions, disinfecting agents or antibiotics. Most of the time, the sessile cells were shown to be less susceptible than the planktonic counterparts (e.g.: [28, 48, 70, 72]). It was suggested that the presence of different subpopulations due to multiple gradients (nutrient, oxygen, metabolic, phenotypic) in cell aggregates would favor the emergence of multiple cells equipped to resist at many aggressions via cross protection. In this case, the more susceptible subpopulations are firstly killed whereas other subpopulations could resist and survive inside the biofilm. This was well illustrated by the presence of cells with different growth rates in biofilms and their correlative decrease of susceptibility to β–lactam antibiotics. As β–lactams are efficient only on growing cells, the decrease of susceptibility of sessile cells was explained by the decrease of the cell growth rate due to the oxygen depletion in the microcolonies [2, 1, 93]. Other antibiotic mechanisms independent to the cell growth rate could be dependent on the presence of the oxygen, like the aminoglycosides (e.g. tobramycine) which enter the cells only if the respiratory chain is active. This was shown with the partially restoration of the aminoside activity on sessile cells by adding a final electron acceptor other that the oxygen [95]. The phenotypic shifts due to the specific conditions in the biofilms were demonstrated by proteomic and transcriptomic studies performed on planktonic and sessile cells. The first description of the genetic implication in biofilm formation was illustrated by the alteration of initial attachment in a genome-wide screen using random chromosomal insertions of a *lac*Z reporter gene fusion construction [73]. More recently, proteomic studies conducted on *P. aeruginosa* have highlighted that 35% (or 525 proteins) have a modified production during biofilm formation and more than 800 proteins (or more than 50% of proteome) have a different expression level of at least six times in a mature biofilm comparing to the planktonic state [79]. Among those 800 proteins, 300 have only been observed in biofilms. They are divided into five categories: metabolism, phospholipids, lipopolysaccharides biosynthesis, transport and membrane secretion proteins and protection mechanisms. These results are in agreement with *P. aeruginosa* transcriptomic analysis [105], although only 70 genes have been considered. Proteomic and transcriptomic comparative analyses highlighted 427 protein spots that revealed a significant difference in expression between sessile and planktonic cells of *Staphyloccus aureus* [76]. The identification of the specific non-redondant proteins indicated that these proteins were mainly involved in the attachment, the peptidoglycan synthesis, and in particular fibrinogen-binding proteins. The protein SarA associated with the expression of the operon *ica* was also upregulated in sessile cells. The expression of the *ica* locus was previously demonstrated to be necessary to *S. epidermidis* biofilm accumulation to produce some polysaccharide intercellular adhesins (PIA) [37, 56]. Proteins contributing to the survival of the cells to adverse conditions were also upregulated in biofilms of *Campylobacter jejuni*. Among them, the alkyl hydroperoxide reductase (AhpC), required in the oxidative defence process was induced in both immobilized cells on agar and biofilms [47, 78], heat shock proteins (GroEL, GroES, ClpP, and EF-G) are also overexpressed as compared to planktonic counterparts. Proteins involved in the phosphate and molybdate-transport systems, in the iron uptake, in the scaffolding protein requested in the synthesis of Fe-S proteins, and in the ferritin transportation exhibited also enhanced expression in immobilized cells or biofilms [47, 78]. An experiment conducted on the mutation of the gene encoding the putative phosphate acetyltransferase (*Cj*0688) affected the cell attachment meaning that this enzyme is important in the biofilm formation. The biofilm formation was also affected in the *Escherichi coli* counterpart muted on the gene encoding a phosphate transferase (Acp) involved in the maintenance of the acetyl phosphate pool in the cell [107]. Ribosomal synthesis (ribosomal release factor and 50S ribosomal protein L7/L12), proteins involved in the energy pathway (Succinyl-CoA synthetase α and β chains) and proteins that could contribute to synthesis of the efflux system (possible membrane fusion component of efflux system, putative ABC transport system ATP-binding protein) were also upregulated in both immobilized cells and biofilms of *C. jejuni* [47, 78]. This would indicate that the biofilm formation comes with induced systems that would protect the cells against adverse conditions.

Other genes encoding biofilm phenotype were discovered. In *Streptococcus gordonii*, nine mutants that were not able to form biofilms displayed some alterations in the quorum sensing, the osmoadaptation and signal transduction mechanisms [55]. Studies conducted on membrane protein indicated that the porine OmpF was underexpressed in sessile cells of *E.*

coli as compared to planktonic counterparts. This modification which is usually the signature of the response to an osmotic stress could contribute to the antibioresistance of sessile cells as some antibiotic enter the cells through these non-specific porins [94]. Another study conducted on *E. coli* indicated that the outer membrane protein OmpA was upregulated in biofilms as compared to planktonic cells [69].

All these phenotype studies conducted on sessile cells revealed that the sessile cells have a phenotype different from the one observed in planktonic counterparts. It is not known whether those systems are induced by the nutrient depletion in the spent medium, which could initiate the biofilm formation or whether the specific biofilm environment is responsible for the induction of these regulations. Although some gene expressions were specifically identified in biofilms, no consensus gene was detected among the bacterial species, indicating that the biofilm process is different according to the genetic potential of the bacterial species. The biofilm process is undoubtedly idiosyncratic, however, no elegant demonstration has been settled up already to answer to the question of the biofilm structure origin: stochastic or genetic?

II. Biofouling and Biocorrosion

II.1. Biofilm Context and Concept in Biofouling and Biocorrosion

As mentioned before, the formation of a bacterial biofilm is a complex phenomenon involving the medium, the bacteria, and the colonized surfaces. It results from energetic interactions between the surfaces of the material and the micro-organisms, and from their response to the adhesion and to the increase of their cellular density. The formation of an extracellular polymeric matrix is at the origin of the biofilm resistance to biocides and is involved in the acceleration of the biocorrosion by creating an anoxic zone in which anaerobic bacteria grow, and by trapping anodic breakdown products of metal surfaces. The prevention of biofouling and biocorrosion in marine environments can be ensured by antifouling coatings. Prohibition to use organostanic paintings in 2008 led to the development of self-polishing paints able to release biocides other than tributyltin (TBT). The evolution of these antifouling paints by taking into account the latest discoveries on cell-to-cell communication molecules and the use of new polymers is discussed.

From now onwards, it is clearly recognized that the main living style of most bacteria is in association within a sessile biofilm. When environmental factors are favorable microorganisms adhesion to materials is a phenomenon that leads firstly to their multiplication and then to biofilm formation. Economic and sanitary consequences are numerous: biocorrosion of submerged metal surfaces, pipes and filtration systems, making opaque optical glasses, increasing boat fuel consumption, presence and maintenance of pathogenic flora and/or food deterioration… Whatever the medium is, it is now recognized that a multispecies biofilm is preceded by the formation of a bacterial biofilm. This preliminary step is required for the adhesion of eukaryotic organisms. This is particularly the case in marine environment.

For many years, bacterial biofilms were subjected to intense researches, mainly in the marine, medical, and food fields. Our actual knowledge has been obtained from the following models: *Vibrio fischeri, Vibrio harveyi, Pseudomonas aeruginosa, Agrobacterium tumefaciens, Staphylococcus aureus, Escherichia coli,* and *Serratia liquefaciens.* An essential point is underlined: during bacterial growth in the biofilm, metabolic modifications occur because of coordination between bacteria, which is a consequence of synthesis and secretion of interbacterial communication molecules. Among these induced modifications, the synthesis and secretion of polymeric substances contribute to the biofilm structure and confer a particular environment to the microcolony, delimiting a zone with reduced oxygenation. In such zones, bacteria using other molecules than oxygen for respiration will be promoted. For example, sulfate-reducing and methanogenous bacteria are favored mainly due to their use of sulfate and methane, respectively, for respiration. Upon contact with metal surfaces, these bacteria accelerate the electrochemical corrosion processes. Prevention strategies are mainly based on material choice, surface treatment, and their protection systems (electrochemical, surface…) [101]. Important progress have been made in marine paint field to reduce their toxicity by integrating organic and mineral biocides in different erasable/and biodegradable polymers.

After reminding biofilm formation conditions and properties, we will illustrate their effect on metal made material surfaces. Then, we will develop some biofouling prevention ways and strategies based on bacterial genetics, some mechanisms governing antifouling paint activity and new polymers allowing the development of surface erosion and biocide release control.

II.2. Biofouling and Biocorrosion Processes

II.2.1. Interface Bacterial Metabolism

One of the consequences of bacterial biofilm developed on a submerged surface is biocorrosion, or microbiologically induced corrosion (MIC). Biocorrosion include all phenomena of corrosion where bacteria act directly or indirectly onto electronic transfer through their metabolism. They can either create favorable conditions to corrosion development or accelerate existing processes. Nevertheless, corrosion is not always associated to the presence of a biofilm and all bacteria can not induce a MIC. Bacteria influencing corrosion have different metabolic properties including reduction of oxygen, sulfates, thiosulfates and iron (III), oxidation of sulfides and ferrous ions, fermentation and/or acid production.

II.2.2. Bacteria Respiration and Biocorrosion

The formation of dissipate colonies onto a material leads to the formation of differential ventilation zones: the open spaces on the metal surface between colonies are oxygenated whereas the central zones of the colonies in contact with the metal surface are strongly oxygen depleted. This difference of oxygenation at two metal places induces a difference of electric potential and consequently a current of corrosion. This phenomenon is not as so simple. The nature of the bacteria, the ability of exopolymer secretion, and the respiration mode have to be taken into consideration. If, in bacteria, the final electron acceptor respiration metabolism is oxygen, biofilm formed will be able to prevent the surface from corrosion as long as oxygen diffusion rate into biofilm is lower than bacteria oxygen consumption rate [54].

The example on the figure 5 shows how oxygen conditions of a *Shewanella oneidensis* culture, a facultative aerobic bacterium reducing Fe (III), may influence biocorrosion. As we saw before, non reversible bacteria adhesion and growth in biofilm create anaerobic zones while non colonized surfaces stay in contact with oxygenated medium. So, an oxygen gradient sets up, inducing an electric potential difference between cathode and anode, Fe (O) and cathode O_2, and as a consequence, a corrosion current (Figure 10A). If biofilm maturation conditions are in such a way that flow rate is below bacterial doubling time, metallic surface will be covered by a biofilm and some bacteria will be in suspension in the liquid. Dissolved oxygen is consumed both by sessile and planktonic bacteria. This results in an oxygen gradient decreasing oxygen concentration at the metal surface and therefore the disappearance of local anodes and cathodes. Cell respiration metabolism is therefore reoriented towards Fe (III) reduction, used as an electron primary acceptor. Accumulated Fe (II) ions in the liquid are oxydized in the presence of oxygen traces (Figure 10B, C), thus decreasing in corrosion. Fe (III) can be reduced again by bacteria. If biofilm forms itself under high hydrodynamic flows, Fe (II) is taken along by the liquid and oxygen diffuses into the biofilm: the corrosion is enhanced (Figure 10D).

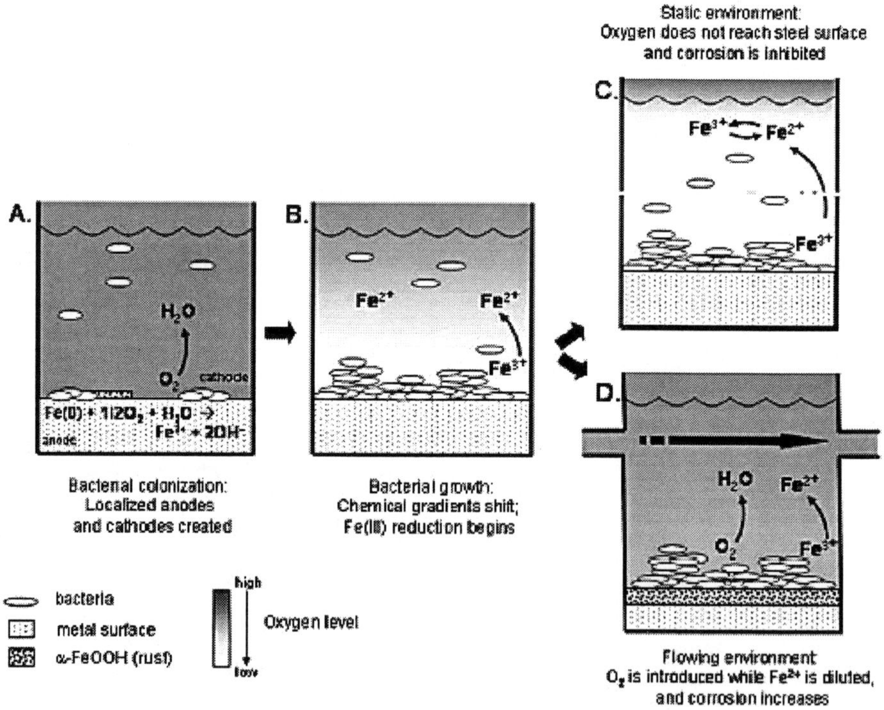

Figure 10. Schematic representation of developmental process of corrosion, or corrosion inhibition with facultative iron-respiring bacteria.

II.2.3. Sulfate-Reducing Bacteria (SRB)

The SRB taxonomic group is composed of more than 40 genera and 150 species distributed in the two bacterial domains: i.e. the *Archea* and *Bacteria*. These are strictly anaerobic bacteria that reduce sulfur compounds as sulfate, thiosulfate, and sulfur to sulfide.

Many species of the *Desulfovibrio* genus are able to grow using nitrate or fumarate as an alternative final electron acceptor. More generally, SRB use, in the presence of sulfate as an electron acceptor, many substrates as electron donors and/or carbon sources: hydrogen, organic acids (e.g.: lactate, fumarate, acetate), alcohols (e.g.: methanol, ethanol, propanol), high molecular weight fatty acids, saturated hydrocarbons, ordinary aromatic compounds (e.g.: phenol, benzene) and sugars (e.g.: fructose, glucose).

SRB are currently isolated from biofilm oxygen free or well aerated environments. The presence of biofilm extracellular matrix and hydrogen sulfide production (H_2S) contribute to the formation of an anoxic niche. Some tolerance towards oxygen is noted among some species, suggesting defense mechanisms against free radicals. For example, in *D. gigas*, catalysis and superoxyde dismutase are expressed in a constitutive way during anaerobic bacterial growth. SRB are involved in ferrous materials and their alloys wells-corrosion, and that either in marine (rich in sulfates) or land environment. To illustrate this phenomenon, we can consider an associated mechanism example: cathodic depolarization coupled with sulfide production. An essential point is hydrogen elimination (cathodic depolarization) by a bacterial hydrogenase. This hydrogenase catalyses hydrogen reversible oxidation following the relation $H_2 \leftrightarrow 2H^+ + 2e^-$. During bacterial growth, carbonate metabolism generates electrons allowing hydrogen formation by a cytoplasmic hydrogenase. Hydrogen diffuses in bacterial periplasm where it is oxidized again by a hydrogenase. Protons activate an ATP synthetase, allowing an energy production for the cell and electrons crossing the membrane in order to participate to sulfate into sulfide reduction.

In the presence of SRB, the main corrosion products are ferric sulfides (FeS). The sulfide (S^{2-}) comes from bacterial metabolism and the Fe (II) is released through the anodic reaction on the metal surface. FeS presence at the metal surface creates a galvanic cell, FeS/Fe, where Fe is anode and FeS is cathode. Cathode efficiency decreases progressively, probably because of the atomic hydrogen binding into FeS crystalline network. FeS film can also play a protector role. Nevertheless, bacterial hydrogenases can erase hydrogen and so restore FeS activity. Consequently, SRB can maintain a high corrosion rate [32].

II.2.4. Biofilm EPS Presence is also a Promoting Biocorrosion Factor

The research conducted on pyrite degradation in biofilms of by *Thiobacillus ferrooxidans*, an acidophilic Fe (II) oxidizing species, is very illustrative. Electrochemical corrosion potential on pyrite surface (work electrode) has been measured to be around +690 mV compared to a Kelvin micro probe. This value is stable when dead bacteria and EPS are added. In the presence of an EPS-producing biofilm, this potential strongly increases during biofilm maturation, reaching a + 990 mV value after 18 h of culture. In the same conditions, but with a mutant that does not produce EPS, the corrosion potential does not exceed + 880 mV [15]. Besides the fact that cellular viability is necessary to biocorrosion, EPS are an aggravating factor, chelating Fe (III), leading to electrochemical interaction with negatively charged surface.

Two models are proposed to display this phenomenon. Considering a ferric metal, Fe (II) produced at the anode is oxidized in Fe (III) in the presence of oxygen. EPS trap Fe (III). And, the EPS-Fe (III) complexes settle at the metal surface where Fe (III) is subjected to a cathodic reduction. In the second model, electrons are directly transferred from Fe (0) to EPS-Fe (III) complex's Fe (III) where it is reduced into Fe (II). In the presence of oxygen, Fe (II) is oxidized again in Fe (III). The presence of the EPS makes electron transfer from metal to nearby available acceptor more easily.

II.3. Targets and Biofilm Prevention Strategies

It is not possible herein to develop all the strategies described in different fields (health, industry and sea) to prevent biofilm formation, rather we will concentrate on preventing biofouling in marine environments. Overall, it is possible to target the environment where the biofilm and/or micro-organisms themselves get formed. Briefly, the targets for prevention of biofilm formation are:

- Environment by modifying flow rate. Only some situations allow modifying temperature, pH, or its composition (biocides adding and/or detergent);
- Material by modifying its nature, its manufacturing and its physicochemical properties;
- Micro-organisms by inhibiting their growth and/or their metabolic activity.

Bacterial biofilms are subjected of two complementary approaches, i.e. (i) how to limit or to prevent bioadhesion and (ii) how to eliminate biofilm maturation?

At the material level, it is possible to modify different surface properties, as roughness, visco-elasticity, hydrophilic/hydrophobic character and electron donor/acceptor property.

The elaboration of functional surfaces is a promising research axis. Two strategies can be considered: (i) a surface modification by the addition of bacteriostatic or bacteriolytic molecules and (ii) the application of these molecules onto material surface. It is obvious that in the case of metallic materials, it can only be considered by an adapted surface coating addition, therefore the application is limited. These different strategies can be considered in food and sea industries, but come up against a medium biodiversity problem. Bacteria potentially adhering to a surface have surface physicochemical properties and different metabolisms.

Viable and culturable bacteria have been isolated and their phylogenetic affiliation have been determined as well as their hydrophilic/hydrophobic and electrons donor/acceptor characteristics [36]. Results in table 1 show that the surface is colonized by different phylogenetically bacteria and that they have different surface physicochemical properties. They also suggest that a microbial biofouling prevention strategy in marine environment can not be based only on surface properties.

Another observation partially contradicts this result. Two antifouling coatings with radically different surface properties, one silicone coating and a commercial erosive lactic polyacid (PLA) based paint, have been submerged into natural environment during 42 days. Biodiversity analysis highlights more different bacteria on the silicone than on PLA paint. At first sight this is surprising because low surface energy of silicone should prevent adhesion, but all the bacteria isolated from this support secrete tensioactive molecules (Figure 11): this could explain their adhesion by modifying properties at the bacterium-silicone interface. Only two bacteria have been found on both supports. Silicone coating low surface energy is favorable to bacteria detachment by a simple increase of the water flow, however silicone coatings are too fragile to be massively used.

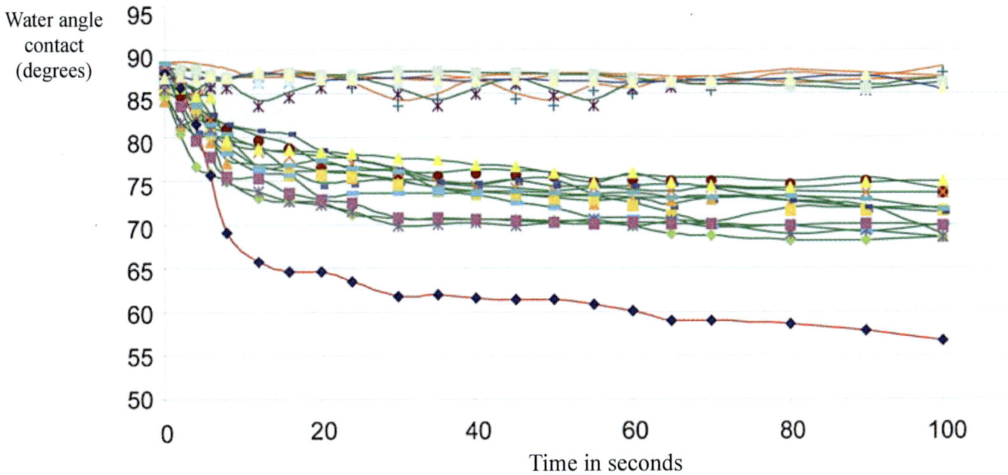

Figure 11. Water contact angle evolution after addition of marine bacteria culture supernatants. Upper and median groups of curves correspond to the addition of culture supernatants of bacteria isolated from PLA paints and silicon coatings, respectively. The lower curve corresponds to a positive control obtain with *P. aeruginosa* culture supernatant.

As seen before, genetic regulations depending on inter-bacterial communication molecules have a strong effect on biofilm maturation and structure. Using the original method for HSL detection [64], we looked for their production among marine bacteria forming biofilms. Among Gram-negative bacteria introduced in table 1, not all of them produce HSL, leading to the following questions: How are genetic responses coordinated within a multi-species marine biofilm? Can HSL produced by resident bacteria influence bacterial adhesion? In order to answer the first question, we have noted, among the bacteria listed in table 1, that some of them produce HSLs and/or AI2, or any identifiable communication molecule. Further researches should focus on the bacterial phenotypes possibly induced by cross communications due to HSLs and AI2. To answer the second question, adhesion and growth into biofilm of bacteria producing or not HSL have been studied, either on HSL conditioned surface, or in presence of a culture medium containing those HSL during bacteria adhesion step. On one hand, whatever HSL presentation mode is, productive bacteria are not affected by their presence during adhesion period. On the other hand, bacteria which do not produce HSL showed an adhesion defect and a decrease of the capacity to grow into biofilm (Figure 12). This suggested that inter-bacterial communications can play a role in biofilm biodiversity and that bacterial adhesion and biofilm maturation can be modified by targeting communication molecules and quorum sensing. Several data complete this comment. The work of Kjelleberg's group have shown that a bromated furanone, isolated from a red seaweed, *Delicea pulcha*, was able to inhibit phenomenon depending on QS by entering in competition with their targets [40, 57].

Table 1. Physicochemical properties of biofilm-forming marine bacteria.

Taxonomic affiliation	Water contact angle (deg)	Hydrophily	Electron accepting (A) or donating (D) character	Isoelectric point (IEP)
Rhodospirillum	23±3	+	A=D	3.05
Colwellia	30±3	+	None	2.8
Pseudoalteromonas	33±2	+	A<D	2.75
Pracoccus	47±5	+	A=D	2.9
Micrococcus	51±2	+	None	3.1
Roseobacter	51±6	+	D	2.7
Bacillus	51±4	+	D	3.2
Cytophaga	53±4	+	D	2.5
Paracoccus	53±6	+	D	2.2
Alteromonas	54±2	+	A<D	2.9
Pseudoalteromonas	55±4	+	A<D	2.75
Pseudoalteromonas	64±2	-	A<D	3.15
Cytophaga	64±6	-	D	2.4
Micrococcus	77±10	-	None	3.4
Sulfitobacter	90±4	-	D	3.15
Paracoccus	101±6	-	D	3.1

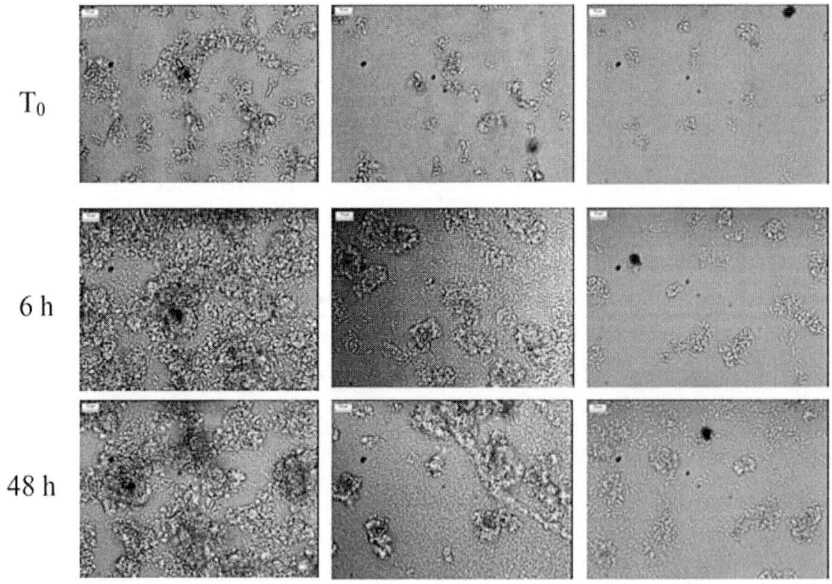

Figure 12. Homoserine Lactone (HSL) influence on biofilm formation with a marine strain deficient for HSL biosynthesis. Images were recorded after 2 h of static adhesion and after 6 and 48 h under laminar flow in flow cell containing HSL-free medium. The left, central, and right panels correspond to the adhesion without HSL, to a HSL conditioned layer, and to the adhesion in a HSL conditioned medium, respectively.

Within mixed biofilms composed of *Pseudomonas aeruginosa* and *Burkholderia cepacia*, Gram negative bacteria producing HSL, *B. cepacia* was able to detect HSL produced by *P. aeruginosa*, when the latter did not answer to molecules produced by *B. cepacia* [77].

Recently, Qazy *et al.* [74] have shown that HSLs having an acyl chain superior or equal to 10 carbons were unable to inhibit virulence gene expression in *Staphylococcus aureus*, a Gram-positive bacterium forming biofilms, by getting fixed on membrane receptors. It was the first demonstration that a communication between Gram-negative and Gram-positive bacteria could be due to HSLs.

Data introduced above suggest that a prevention strategy for multispecies biofilm, as encountered in marine environments could be developed by considering the bacterial differential answer to communication molecules (AI2, HSL) and on antagonist molecules used (halogenated furanones). This strategy can not be developed without the evolution of anti-biofilm surface coating formulations.

In the marine environment, biofouling prevention has been based mainly on the use of antifouling paints. Their composition of the paints is often complex: polymers, solvents, biocides, Cu_2O, additives and pigments. It is supposed that the mode of action of these biocide paints depends on their more or less controlled release from the polymer matrix progressively degrading itself. Hard matrix for which diffusion predominates is distinguished from erasable matrix. Erasable reference paints are organostanic. Discovered in the seventies, their efficiency lays on the presence of TBT (highly active against marine organisms), linked by an ester function on a polyacrilic skeleton. Progressive hydrolysis of the polymer allows TBT molecules activation and erosion of superficial layers allows the surface activity revival. These paints are described to be auto polishing and hold a plurality of chemical prevention and mechanic cleaning. TBT toxicity on coastal ecosystems and its stability lead to progressively reduce its use and a European directive advocates its total prohibition for 2008.

So, it has been proved to be necessary to develop new antifouling paints. Their development necessitates (i) research of discriminative erasable antifouling paint activity, (ii) molecules able to substitute for TBT, and (iii) research of bacterial parameters involved in biofouling.

Among activity discriminative factors, we are interested in surface roughness, biocide release (minerals and organics), erosion, and paint surface energy. Paints have been formulated with copolymers associating hydrophilic, hydrophobic and hydrolysable units. Biocides used were of minerals, zinc oxide or covered copper oxide, or organics algicide and/or fungicide type.

Results have been surprising. Briefly, biocide quantity really released, either in static or dynamic conditions, is much below the currently admitted one and in insufficient quantity to have a bacterial effect. Copper, usually active on microfouling is nevertheless necessary to paint activity against microfouling (bacteria) [51, 91]. Concerning surface properties, only a relationship between the antifouling activity and erosion has been statistically highlighted [92]. Within erosive polymers, paints components, it has not been highlighted any relationship between polymer hydration and erosion, unlike the principle that chemists have assumed: erosion is the consequence of a hydration followed hydrolysis [90].

So it is necessary to understand how the copolymer evolves within its thickness in presence of biocide. By coupling scanning electronic microscopy and ED analysis (energy-dispersive X-ray analysis) it has been possible to follow the distribution evolution of organic and mineral biocides within paint thickness function of submerging time. Results show that depending on polymer and biocides considered (biocide solubility is an essential point for its implementation), distribution of the latter evolves differently. For example, a diffusion front is remarkable in the case of an organic biocide unlike a mineral biocide (Figure 13). In addition, organic biocide diffusion is reduced in the absence of copper inducing modifications in interactions between biocides and paint components [29].

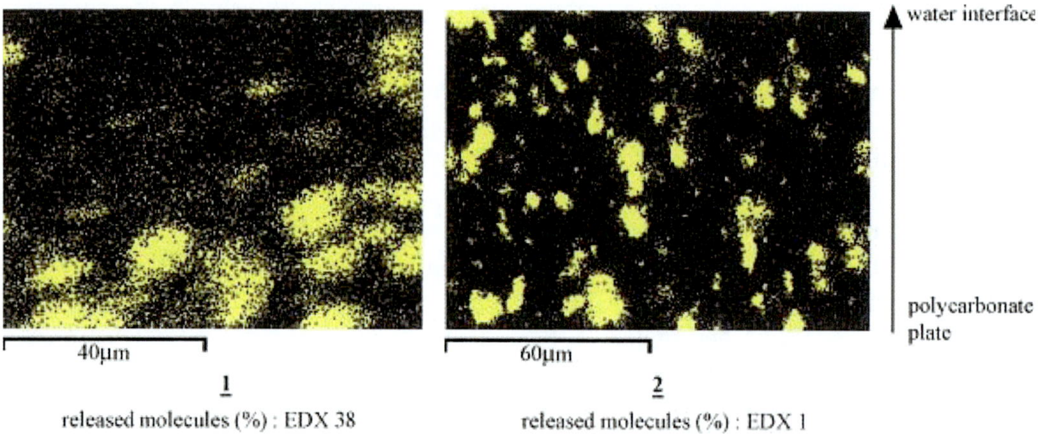

Figure 13. Biocide distribution in the cross-section of paint, after 36 weeks of immersion. The biocides used are Tolyfluanid (1) and (2) copper.

II.4. Prospect

The control and of the prevention of the biofouling in marine environment will rest on the summation of the obtained knowledge as well as on the colonizing organizations and the characteristics of material and surface coatings. Nevertheless, of new tracks are now possible.

II.4.1. Use of Natural Molecules with Antifouling Activity

This issue is promising and many active molecules have already been identified [30]. They are of particular interest when they lack the toxicity and the problems of solubility characteristics of most organic biocides. However, their implementation is related to their availability and their possibility of being built-in. Furthermore, it is possible to supplement natural molecules with molecules agonists and antagonists of the bacterial QS. The potential antifouling activity could result from the summation of their respective effects.

II.4.2. Development of New Polymers for the Formulation of Paintings

An orientation towards biodegradable paintings is an issue. These paintings combine the advantages of being more erasable, respecting the environment (their products of hydrolysis are not toxic) and facilitating the incorporation of biocides. Such paintings were formulated in the laboratory and showed their effectiveness over several months.

II.4.3. Capping Way

This strategy consists into capping molecules having an antifouling activity within a hydrolysable polymer included into erasable and biodegradable paint formulation. It allows to solve the problem of biocide solubility and to control in lasting quality at the extreme paint surface. Finally, this antifouling coating type would have no incidence on marine ecosystems [30].

III. Photosynthetic Biofilms in the Environment

III.1 Similarities and Differences between Phototrophic and Chemotrophic Biofilms

In the natural environment many biofilms are directly or indirectly exposed to sunlight. This favors the establishment of eukaryotic microalgae and prokaryotic cyanobacteria in these biofilms. These organisms are photoautotrophic and as a result such photosynthetic biofilms can grow at the expense of inorganic nutrients (N, P) and inorganic carbon (CO_2 and HCO_3^-) present in the water column and do not rely on organic carbon. Among the eukaryotic micro-algae, the pennate diatoms with a raphe (Bacillariophyceae) are particularly common in the photosynthetic biofilms. These pennate diatoms are single cells encased within an elongated silicate frustule that comprises of two parts which fit into each other like a Petri-dish. The raphe is a linear structure located in the center of the frustule running parallel to its long sides that is involved in gliding movement. Pennate diatoms produce copious amounts of EPS, as is characteristic for biofilm organisms and this EPS can be involved both in providing gliding motility as well as a cementing compound be involved in attachment. Diatoms often occur as single cells, while some species may form microcolonies. Among the photosynthetic prokaryotes, the filamentous cyanobacteria are particularly well adapted for growth in photosynthetic biofilms. These cyanobacteria also produce large amounts of EPS. A part of this cyanobacterial EPS occurs as slime or mucilage. In addition, several filamentous cyanobacteria produce sheaths which are tubular structures made of EPS that are clearly visible by optical microscopy. Some species of diatoms also produce sheaths. Many cyanobacteria species occur as a single filament within their sheath. However, in some species a large number of filaments form a bundle within a single sheath. In the genus *Microcoleus*, originally described according morphological criteria, these filaments are clearly intertwined as in a rope which gives strength to these structures. *Microcoleus chthonoplastes* is a cosmopolitan marine cyanobacterium that forms such conspicuous high density and cohesive biofilms, which resemble to carpets and are often referred to as microbial mats. In addition to these major players, photosynthetic biofilms may also comprise other oxygenic phototrophs like single cell cyanobacteria and other eukaryotes like Chlorophycaea. The photosynthetic community is always accompanied by heterotrophic bacteria and often by yeasts and fungi.

III.2. Structure and Composition of Phosynthetic Biofilms

Photosynthetic biofilms develop very strongly at the surface of peddles and stones in rivers and streams. In flowing water, the phenotypic mode of living adhered to a surface in a biofilm has clear advantages with respect to the planktonic mode where the organisms are subjected to passive transport. Hence it has been calculated that more than 90 % of the microbial biomass in rivers occurs as attached in biofilms and only less than 10 % occurs as planktonic forms [19]. Photosynthetic biofilms also develop on the surface of soft sediments like sand and mud, on ice and on biological surfaces like submerged plant tissues. Figure 14 gives a schematic representation of the different photosynthetic biofilms compared to the more commonly studied bacterial biofilms. Obviously light is an important structuring factor for the photosynthetic biofilms. The photon flux density as well as the spectral composition of the light may strongly change with depth in the biofilm.

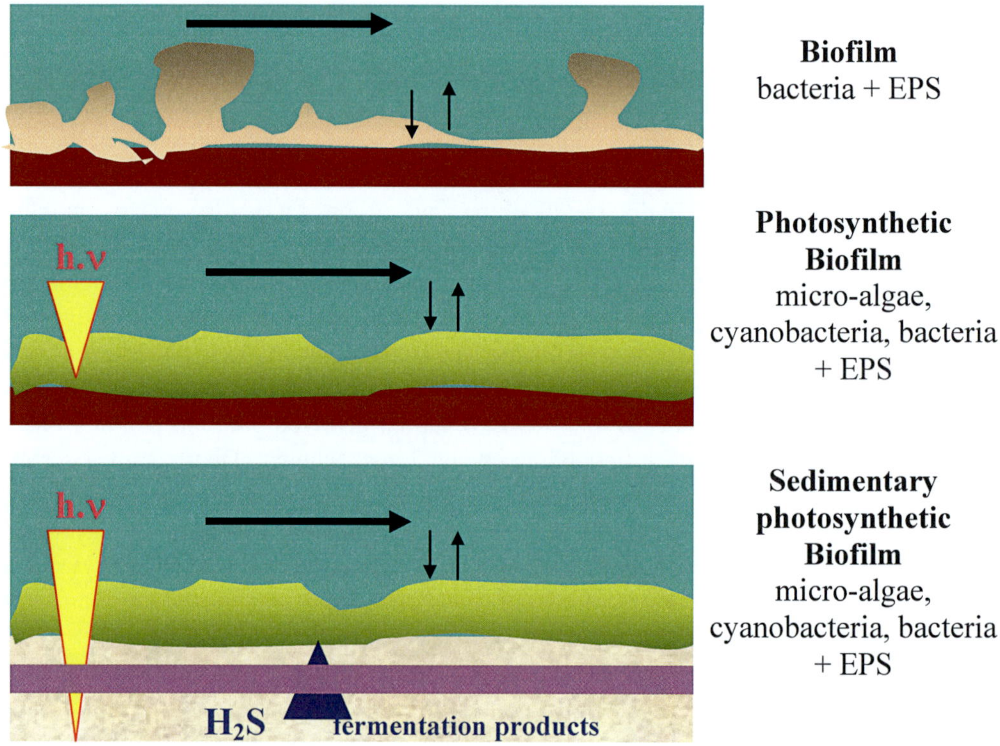

Figure 14. Photosynthetic biofilms growing on hard substrates (middle panel) and on soft sediments (lower panel) compared to bacterial biofilms as e.g. in potable water tubings and involved in biofouling and corrosion of metal surfaces.

The photosynthetic biofilms growing on the soft sediments are different from most of the commonly studied biofilms that grow on solid surfaces immerged in a flowing liquid. The sediment comprises two physical phases i.e., the solid (particles) and the liquid phases. The spaces between the particles are called the interstices and are filled with water. This has two important consequences. First, the organisms may migrate into the sediment through the interstitial spaces and some biofilms even develop below the sediment surface. Second, nutrients and growth substrates within the sediment diffuse upward and can be used by the biofilm organisms for growth.

III.2.1. Adaptations to High Light Intensities

For biofilms that are exposed to full sunlight, the algae and cyanobacteria at the surface of the biofilm may be inhibited by the high light intensity, i.e. suffer from photoinhibition; while the growth of the algae and cyanobacteria at the bottom of the biofilm may be limited by the low light intensities due to shading. Hence, within a well developed thick photosynthetic biofilm, different ecophysiological strategies to cope with different light climates may be found. Thus, the surface of the biofilms that are exposed to full sunlight are often more orange colored reflecting that the phototrophs are rich in carotenoids and have low levels of chlorophylls which are efficient adaptations to high light intensities. More deeply green layers can often be found at the bottom of the biofilm. The presence of Ultraviolet radiation at the surface of the biofilm is particularly hazardous for photosynthesis and cell integrity. Mycosporine like amino acids (MAA) are water soluble compounds that accumulate in the cytoplasm of several species of micro-algae, cyanobacteria and also non-photrophs like yeasts and fungi, which have absorption maxima ranging from 310-360 nm and serve as sun-screen pigments [35, 68]. In addition, some cyanobacteria accumulate scytonemin [34] in their sheaths, which gives these biofilms a brownish or blackish color. Scytonemin is a dimeric indole alkaloid and has an absorption maximum of around 380 nm, which is thus nicely complementary to the absorption maximum of the MAA. The high light intensities only occur around zenith, and therefore, some cyanobacteria and diatoms have developed strategies to migrate up and down during a diel cycle. Thus, in the early morning and late afternoon these species occur on the surface of the biofilm, while around zenith they retrieve below the surface to hide away from the high inhibitory light intensities.

The migration of phototrophic micro-organisms down into the sediment has been mentioned before as a strategy to hide from inhibitory and damaging high light intensities. In addition, this migration may be an efficient strategy to prevent erosion of the biofilm. This is a particularly common phenomenon in diatom biofilms in the intertidal flats where the migration cycles are often synchronized to the tidal cycle. This way, the diatoms benefit from light at the surface when the shear-stress at the surface is relatively low and occur in the sediments when the tidal currents exert a particularly strong shear stress. This migration appears to be regulated by an endogenous clock that is synchronized to the tidal cycle but also influenced by the diel light variations [63].

III.2.2. Stratified Sedimentary Biofilms and Microbial Mats

The sedimentary biofilms are open to mass transfer of solutes both at the top and at the bottom and the microorganisms interact therefore both with the overflowing water as well as with the deeper sedimentary layers. Below the surface at one to several millimeter depth, anoxic conditions occur and these sediment layers may harbor important microbial activities like fermentation and anaerobic respiration including nitrate, metal and sulfate-reduction. The end products of these processes can be used as substrates by the biofilm. Thus, the fermentation products and the hydrogen sulfide provide substrates for anoxygenic phototrophic bacteria that may develop beautifully colored layers below the oxygenic phototrophs (Figs. 14 and 15).

Purple sulfur bacteria (Chromatiaceae and Ectothiorhodospiraceae) are pink to reddish colored due to their carotenoids and use Bacteriochlorophylls *a* or *b* in photosynthesis, with absorption maxima in the Near Infrared (NIR) between 800 and 900, and at 1030 nm, respectively. The non-motile coccoid purple sulfur bacterium *Thiocapsa roseopersicina* is very commonly present in many marine biofilms and microbial mats and often accompanied by the motile *Marichromatium* species. Both *Thiocapsa* and *Marichromatium* species are very versatile since these are facultative anaerobes both capable of chemoautotrophic growth at the expense of oxygen respiration and of photolithoautotroph and photoheterotropic growth. This is an advantage in biofilms where they live in close proximity to cyanobacteria and micro-algae that produce oxygen during day-time and organic excretion products during the entire diel cycle. These biofilms are thus characterized by diel shifting of the oxygen and sulfide profiles. The immobile *Thiocapsa roseopersicina* is thus exposed to oxygen during daytime and to anoxic conditions at night. It has been shown that while oxygen inhibits photosynthetic pigments synthesis in this species, it is capable to synthesize the photosynthetic pigments during the anoxic night periods and thus continue anoxygenic photosynthesis in the presence of oxygen during the day periods [25]. During daytime they produce polyglucose as a storage product, which is degraded to acetate and CO_2 under anaerobic dark conditions a process which is coupled to the reduction of sulfur into hydrogensulfide. In contrast, the mobile *Marichromatium* species are capable to track the shifting oxygen- sulfide interface and have been observed at the surface of the biofilm at night where it can perform aerobic chemosynthesis. During daytime they migrate deeper into the sediment where they can perform pigment synthesis and anoxygenic photosynthesis in the anoxic parts. Some marine photosynthetic biofilms and microbial mats also comprise strictly anaerobic species in deeper layers as the purple sulfur bacterium *Thiococcus pfennigii*, which contains BChl*b* and the green sulfur bacteria as *Prosthecochloris* sp., which contains BChlc as the major light-harvesting pigment (absorption maximum at 760 nm). A beautiful example where these organisms form clearly visible layers is found in Sippewisset salt marsh on the USA east coast. These biofilms are up to 7 mm depth and represent up to five different colored laminations (Figure 15).

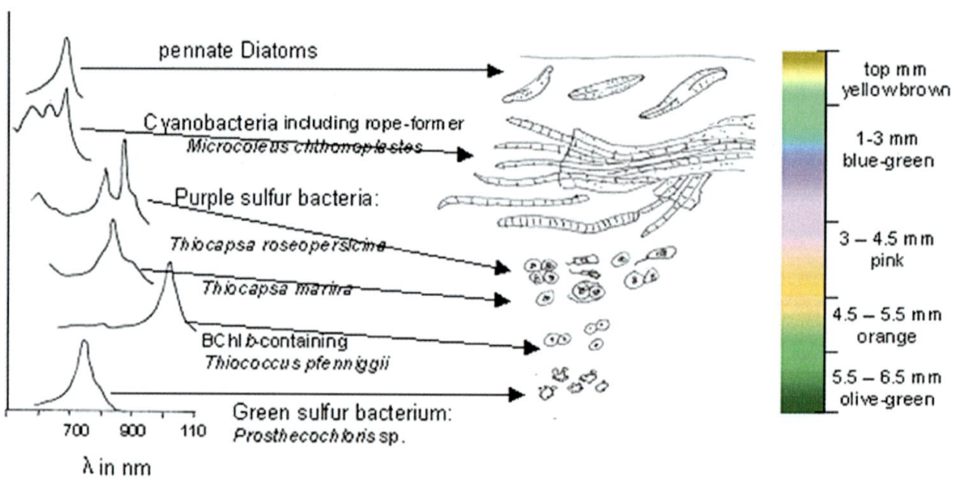

Figure 15. Scheme of a stratified photosynthetic biofilm or microbial mat that has been found in Sippewisset Salt Marsh (MA, USA, Eastern coast). This mat is up to 7 mm thick and shows five different beautiful coloured layers (see right-hand side). The absorption spectra in the red and near infrared part of the spectrum are shown for the different organisms from the mat on the left hand-side. Note that light-absorption spectra are complementary among the different taxa, which allows them to co-occur in the mat. The drawing of the different organisms is not to scale.

Some photosynthetic biofilms comprise photosynthetic Chloroflexi that were previously called green non-sulfur bacteria. Within the Chloroflexi phylum the known photosynthetic members form a clade described as the family Chloroflexaceae. The Chloroflexi are a deep-branching phylum that apart from the photosynthetic Chloroflexaceae also accommodates non-phototrophic taxa like *Herpetosiphon*, *Thermomicrobium* and *Dehalococcoides*. *Chloroflexus aurantiacus* was the first species isolated and fully described since the early

1970's and is the most studied organism within the Chloroflexaceae. *C. aurantiacus* occurs in biofilms at high temperatures along the outflow of thermal springs, where it often occurs in association with thermophilic cyanobacteria i.e. often with *Synechococcus* species [13]. This species has a versatile metabolism as it can grow photohetero- and photoautotrophically, as well as chemoautotrophically at the expense of oxygen respiration. Some deep-green colored eco-types have been described that grow mainly as a photoautroph at the expense of sulfide oxidation along the outflow of hydrogen sulfide containing springs. Bacteria resembling *Chloroflexus* are also commonly observed in hypersaline microbial mats at salinities ranging from 40 to 90 g/kg, where they often occur in association with the cyanobacterium *Microcoleus chthonoplastes.* The presence of these halophilic *Chloroflexus* like species in these systems is also reflected by BChl*c* and BChl*d* which are their main light-harvesting pigments. However, much less is known about these species and only one has been recently obtained in culture and characterized as Candidatus *Chlorothrix halophila* [49]. The diversity and function of the *Chloroflexus*-like bacteria in the hypersaline biofilms has been recently studied by using PCR and primers targeting the Chloroflexi and by using micro-electrodes [4]. The clone library comprised 49 clones that grouped into 16 different phylotypes (96 % sequence similarity for 400 bp). Among these, 10 clones corresponding to 4 different phylotypes clustered within the Chloroflexaceae family. This shows that the biofilms comprised both photosynthetic and non-photosynthetic Chloroflexi. The photosynthetic Chloroflexi are also capable of chemoheterotrophic growth under aerobic conditions and were found to switch rapidly from anoxygenic photosynthesis to aerobic respiration when NIR light illumination was turned off.

The presence and activity of anoxygenic phototrophic bacteria in photosynthetic biofilms is an advantage for the cyanobacteria and the diatoms in the top layers, because the former oxidize the hydrogen sulfide that is very toxic and may limit growth of the latter. Furthermore, the different groups use different parts of the solar spectrum, which is a nice example of niche differentiation that prevents competition for light between the different major groups in the biofilm. In addition, the diatom and cyanobacterial species in sedimentary photosynthetic biofilms have a certain capability to resist to low hydrogen sulfide concentrations that are clearly toxic for most planktonic species; moreover some species of cyanobacteria are capable of anoxygenic photosynthesis [16].

III.3. Wax and Wane of Photosynthetic Biofilms

III.3.1. Photosynthetic Biofilm Development and Succession Phenomena

Photosynthetic biofilms often undergo succession phenomena. For the biofilms that occur on hard substrates in rivers (peddles and stones) it has been described that the nude surface is first colonized by heterotrophic bacteria in a way that is very similar to the classical formation of a bacterial biofilm (Figure 6). After adsorption, attachment, growth and EPS formation by bacteria happened, oxygenic phototrophs colonize the biofilm and start growing. After a lag-phase the growth of the phototrophs becomes exponential and the specific growth rates are both dependent on species as well as on the environmental conditions. This represents the start of the accretion phase. As the biofilm attains a certain thickness, the mass transfer of substrates from the water column to the biofilm may become limiting and phototrophs in the lower part may become light limited due to shading. During this phase of the biofilm development, specific growth rates slow down and net biomass increase becomes linear and finally levels off to zero. A stationary phase will be achieved, when biomass density is at its maximum which can be considered as the carrying capacity for the biofilm in that environment. Finally the biofilm enters in a loss phase, where biomass death and removal exceeds growth. These losses can be due to predation and senescence; biomass removal by sloughing can be auto induced by senescence of the lower parts of the biofilm loosening the attachment of the biofilm [7]. During this whole process, the species compositions of the phototrophic and of the heterotrophic communities change with time. The lower parts of the biofilm may become anoxic temporarily or permanently, which favors the establishment of anaerobic bacteria in the biofilm.

In marine environments, it has been described that bare nutrient-poor sandy sediments can be colonized by filamentous cyanobacteria belonging to the genera *Oscillatoria* and *Lyngbya*. These cyanobacteria do not possess heterocysts but are nonetheless capable of fixing nitrogen. The nitrogen fixation rate is often not constant in time but subject to diel fluctuations that are determined by a circadian rhythm. By maximizing nitrogen fixation during early morning and late afternoon, *Oscillatoria limosa* has a strategy to separate this process from the periods of highest oxygen production [82]. These early colonizers thus develop a biofilm and by their EPS production and senescence enrich the sediment with organic matter that is remineralized by heterotrophic bacteria, which results in increasing availabilities of inorganic N and P. In a later stage of the biofilm development, the rope-forming cyanobacteria *Microcoleus chthonoplastes* colonizes the biofilm, which process converts the biofilm in a cohesive microbial mat. *M. chthonoplastes* does not posses the *nif* genes implied in nitrogen fixation and pure cultures of this species are indeed incapable to fix nitrogen [82]. Nevertheless, mats of *M. chthonoplastes* often fix nitrogen by the accompanying heterotrophic bacterial flora [26, 83]. This may explain the fact that a large part of the accompanying heterotrophic bacterial community in the mat relies on EPS as the substrate which has a very low N-content. The organic matter is degraded in the lower parts of the mat by sulfate-reducers and the hydrogen sulfide is used as an electron donor by the anoxygenic phototrophic bacteria and particularly *Thiocapsa roseopersicina* often forms a nicely colored band below the layer of *M. chthonoplastes*.

Some microbial mats accumulate large amounts of organic matter over time because degradation is not complete. The system may accrete with about 0.5-1 mm per year and remnants of the biofilm forming organisms can thus be found in the deeper layers. Because growth and degradation rates of the mat vary on seasonal time scales, these microbial mat constructed sediments may show annual laminations very similar to the growth rings observed in the trunk of a tree. This phenomenon is particularly pronounced in hypersaline environments and a spectacular example are 1 m long cores in the hypersaline Solar Lake (Egypt), which represents a history of 2000 years of biofilm accretion.

III.3.2. Role of Predation in Photosynthetic Biofilms

In photosynthetic biofilms, the phototrophic organisms live together with heterotrophic bacteria and fungi, and often with small animals as well. However, these small animals including ciliates, copepods, nematodes, and sometimes gastropods feed on the micro-organisms in the biofilm. In some cases, the predation pressure may exceed the growth rates and the biofilm will fully disappear. On the island of Schiermonnikoog, I have observed that the cyanobacterial biofilms were predated by mullets (fish), and occasionally by flies

(Diptera) and springtails (Colembola). At present, the occurrence of viruses has not been well studied in photosynthetic biofilms. However, some observations in sediment environments are surprising because very high number of virus-like particles have been observed together with a low number of infected prokaryotic cells. This phenomenon has been described as the paradox of viruses in sediments [33]. An explanation could be that the viruses in the sediments are incorporated by sedimentation and do not result from viral cell burst in the sediment itself. The occurrence and role of viruses in biofilms need further study.

In temperate environments, the biofilms are always susceptible to grazing and erosion and may completely disappear. Conspicuous biofilms are therefore characteristic of habitats where grazing is continuously or temporarily reduced. This is the case for the pebblestone river bed in a fast-flowing river and in the marine environment in the higher part of the tidal range. Another environment is presented by the floodplains. Immediately after flooding the conditions are appropriate for biofilm development and predators are still low in density. The biofilms develop during stagnant water but simultaneously the predators increase in density as well. The persistency of the photosynthetic biofilms in these environments is thus determined by the immersion submersion cycles. In the marine environment, it has been shown that the diatom biofilm and the bare sediment state present alternative attractors on the intertidal flats, which gives rise to a mosaic landscape composed of diatom biofilms patches interspersed with bare sediment patches [99]. Regularly when the grazing pressure exceeds the growth of the biofilm or when there is excessive erosion, the biofilm will flip over to the bare sediment state. The persistency of the biofilm in the landscape thus depends on the continuous recolonization of sediments by the diatoms and the spatial distribution of the biofilm and bare sediment patches various continuously. Hence, in many temperate environments the occurrence of biofilms is a temporal phenomenon at the local scale and the persistency of the biofilms in the landscape depends on disturbance patterns and recolonization processes. Well-developed persistent photosynthetic biofilms seem to be restricted to so-called extreme environments, including high and low temperatures, acidic environments and hypersaline environments.

III.4. Photosynthetic Biofilms and the Geological History of Life on Earth

Photosynthetic biofilms have an extremely long history in the geology of the earth as these have given rise to laminated rocks known as stromatalites. The established fossil record starts with two rock-sequences consisting of stromatolites, the Warrawona Group of West Australia and the Onverwacht Group of South Africa, which are about 3,500 million years old. The microfossils in these rocks show some resemblance to present day cyanobacteria and it has been claimed that these fossils indeed were cyanobacteria [81]. This is very controversial and has been criticized by various researchers. It is highly questionable that oxygen producing organisms were present as early as 3,500 million years BP, because several geochemical data indicate that the atmosphere remained fully anoxic until 2,800 million and because it seems unlikely that such a complicated process as oxygenic photosynthesis evolved so early during the evolution of life on earth. A comparative analysis of the genes involved in photosynthesis has indicated that two anoxygenic phototrophic groups preceded oxygenic photosynthesis which appears to have evolved by lateral gene transfer and the heterologous fusion of photosystems I and II [108]. This has probably occurred some 3,000 million years

BP and there is quite good consensus that bona-fide cyanobacterial fossils occur in fossil records since 2,800 million years BP. We suggest that the filamentous microfossils in the older strata may correspond to anoxygenic photosynthetic bacteria that were perhaps similar to the current Chloroflexaceae. Photosynthetic biofilms had their golden age during the Precambrium. After the evolution of eukaryote animals their distribution became more restricted in space due to the grazing pressure exerted by the animals. Hence, photosynthetic biofilms have played a major role in the evolution of micro-organisms on earth. It has been suggested that we can study the persistent microbial mats in present-day extreme environments, like the high and low temperature and high salinity environments, and consider them as the analogues of the Precambian photosynthetic biofilms.

Conclusion

As seen along this chapter, the definition of biofilms was in constant evolution with the knowledge accumulation along the two last decades. The interest on biofilms in the different scientific categories is in its exponential phase. The appearance in the literature of the new world (biofilm) defining the complex microbial aggregates frequently attached to a surface signified the importance of considering the biofilm as a unit. The description of the biofilm evolved from an amount of juxtaposed cells accumulated at a surface to a real micro-ecosystem created by the cells to constitute a well-organized structure with sessile cell interrelations resulting in an entity able to behave differently from the planktonic cells. From a reductionist point of view in 1943 by Zobell, the biofilm structure is observed nowadays from a holistic point of view. The basic molecular mechanisms underlying the initiation, the formation, and the life of the biofilm entity are not yet fully described. Much more has to be discovered from this bacterial heterogen unit.

Acknowledgments

This work was supported by the program CYANOCARBO of the Agence Nationale de la Recherche, France and by the regional program AISQAL of Pays de la Loire, France.

References

[1] Anwar, H., van Biesen, T., Dasgupta, M., Lam, K. & Costerton, J.W. (1989) Interaction of biofilm bacteria with antibiotics in a novel in vitro chemostat system. *Antimicrob. Agents Chemother.*, *33*, 1824-6.

[2] Anwar, H., Dasgupta, M.K. & Costerton, J.W. (1990) Testing the susceptibility of bacteria in biofilms to antibacterial agents. *Antimicrob. Agents Chemother.*, *34*, 2043-6.

[3] Anwar, H., Strapp, J. & Costerton, J. (1992) Establishment of aging biofilms: possible mechanism of bacterial resistance to antimicrobial therapy. *Antimicrob. Agents Chemother.*, *36*, 1347-1351.

[4] Bachar, A., Omoregie, E., de Wit, R. & Jonkers, H.M. (2007) Diversity and function of *Chloroflexus*-like bacteria in a hypersaline microbial mat: phylogenetic characterization and impact on aerobic respiration. *Appl. Environ. Microbiol.*, *73*, 3975-83.

[5] Barnhart, B. & Chapman, M. (2006) Curli Biogenesis and Function. *Annu. Rev. Microbiol.*, *60*, 131-147.

[6] Beachey, E. (1980) *Bacterial adherence* London and New York: Chapman and Hall.

[7] Biggs, B.F. (1996) *Patterns in benthic algae of streams. In: Algal ecology : freshwater benthic ecosystems.* San Diego: Academic Press.

[8] Blackall, L. & Per Halkjaer, N. (2000) *Biofilms without a substratum: Flocs and Microbial Communities.* In: L. Evans (Eds.). *Biofilms: Recent advances in their study and control.* Amsterdam: Harwood Academic Publishers; 435-454.

[9] Brading, M., Jass, J. & Lappin-Scott, H. (1995) *Dynamics of bacterial biofilm formation.* In: H. Lappin-Scott & J. Costerton (Eds.). *Microbial Biofilms.* Cambridge: Cambridge University Presse; 46-63.

[10] Branda, S.S., Vik, S., Friedman, L. & Kolter, R. (2005) Biofilms: the matrix revisited. *Trends Microbiol.*, *13*, 20-6.

[11] Brown, M.L., Aldrich, H.C. & Gauthier, J.J. (1995) Relationship between glycocalyx and povidone-iodine resistance in *Pseudomonas aeruginosa* (ATCC 27853) biofilms. *Appl. Environ. Microbiol.*, *61*, 187-93.

[12] Bryers. (2000) *Biofilm II. Process Analysis and Applications.* New York: Wiley-Liss.

[13] Castenholz, R. & Pierson, B. (2006) *Ecology of Thermophilic Anoxygenic Phototrophs.* In: R. Blankenship, M. MT & C. Bauer (Eds.). *Advances in Photosynthesis and Respiration* Dordrecht Springer Netherlands

[14] Characklis, W. & Marshall, K. (1990) *Biofilms: a basis for an interdisciplinary approach.* In: W. Characklis & K. Marshall (Eds.). *Biofilms.* New York: Wiley; 3-15.

[15] Christensen, B. (1989) The role of extracellular polysaccharides in biofilms. *J. Biotechnol.*, *10*, 171-202.

[16] Cohen, Y., Jørgensen, B., Revsbech, N. & Poplawski , R. (1986) Adaptation to Hydrogen Sulfide of Oxygenic and Anoxygenic Photosynthesis among Cyanobacteria. *Appl. Environ. Microbiol.*, *51*, 398-407.

[17] Costerton, J., Geesey, C. & KJ, C. (1978) How bacteria stick. *Scientific American*, *238*, 86-95.

[18] Costerton, J. & Lappin-Scott, H. (1989) Behavior of bacteria in biofilms. *Amer. Soc. Microbiol. News*, *55*, 650-654.

[19] Costerton, J.W., Lewandowski, Z., DeBeer, D., Caldwell, D., Korber, D. & James, G. (1994) Biofilms, the customized microniche. *J. Bacteriol.*, *176*, 2137-42.

[20] Costerton, J.W. (1995) Overview of microbial biofilms. *J Ind Microbiol*, *15*, 137-40.

[21] Davey, M.E. & O'Toole G, A. (2000) Microbial biofilms: from ecology to molecular genetics. *Microbiol. Mol. Biol. Rev.*, *64*, 847-67.

[22] Davies, D.G., Chakrabarty, A.M. & Geesey, G.G. (1993) Exopolysaccharide production in biofilms: substratum activation of alginate gene expression by Pseudomonas aeruginosa. *Appl. Environ. Microbiol.*, *59*, 1181-6.

[23] Davies, D.G. & Geesey, G.G. (1995) Regulation of the alginate biosynthesis gene algC in *Pseudomonas aeruginosa* during biofilm development in continuous culture. *Appl. Environ. Microbiol.*, *61*, 860-7.

[24] Davies, D.G., Parsek, M.R., Pearson, J.P., Iglewski, B.H., Costerton, J.W. & Greenberg, E.P. (1998) The involvement of cell-to-cell signals in the development of a bacterial biofilm. *Science*, *280*, 295-8.

[25] de Wit, R. & van Gemerden, H. (1990) Growth and metabolism of the purple sulfur bacterium *Thiocapsa roseopersicina* under combined light/dark and oxic/anoxic regimens. *Arch. Microbiol.*, *154*, 459-464.

[26] de Wit, R., Falcón, L. & Charpy-Roubaud, C. (2005) Heterotrophic dinitrogen fixation (acetylene reduction) in phosphate-fertilised *Microcoleus chthonoplastes* microbial mat from the hypersaline inland lake "la Salada de Chiprana" (NE Spain). *Hydrobiologia*, *534*,, 245 - 253.

[27] DeBeer, D., Stoodley, P., Roe, F. & Lewandowski, Z. (1994) Effects of biofilm structures on xoygen distribution and mass transport. *Biotechnol. Bioeng.*, *43*, 1131-1138.

[28] Donlan, R.M. (2000) Role of biofilms in antimicrobial resistance. *Asaio J*, *46*, S47-52.

[29] Faÿ, F., Linossier, I., Langlois, V., Haras, D. & Vallée-Réhel, K. (2005) SEM and EDX microanalysis: Two powerful techniques for the study of antifouling paints. *Progress in Organic Coatings*, *54*, 216-223.

[30] Faÿ, F., Linossier, I., Langlois, V., Renard, E. & Vallée-Réhel, K. (2006) Degradation and controlled release behaviour of ♏-caprolactone copolymers in biodegradable antifouling coatings. . *Biomacromolecules*, *7*, 851-857.

[31] Farber, B., Hsieh, H., Donnenfeld, E., Perry, H., Epstein, A. & Wolff, A. (1995) A novel antibiofilm technology for contact lens solutions. *Ophtalmology*, *102*, 831-836.

[32] Feugeas, F., Magnin, J., Cornet, A. & Rameau, J. (1997) Corrosion influence par les micro-organismes : influence du biofilm sur la corrosion des aciers, techniques et résultats récents. *Journal of Physique III France*, *7*, 631-663.

[33] Filippini, F., Buesing, N., Bettarel, Y., Sime-Ngando, T. & Gessner, M. (2006) Infection paradox: high abundance but low impact of freshwater benthic viruses. *Appl. Environ. Microbiol.*, *72*, 4893-4898.

[34] Garcia-Pichel, F., Sherry, N. & Castenholz, R. (1992) Evidence for an ultraviolet sunscreen role of the extracellular pigment scytonemin in the terrestrial cyanobacterium *Chlorogloeopsis sp.* . *Photochemistry and Photobiolology*, *56*, 17–23.

[35] Garcia-Pichel, F. & Castenholz, R.W. (1993) Occurrence of UV-Absorbing, Mycosporine-Like Compounds among Cyanobacterial Isolates and an Estimate of Their Screening Capacity. *Appl. Environ. Microbiol.*, *59*, 163-169.

[36] Grasland, B., Mitalane, Briandet, J., Quemener, E., Meylheuc, T., Vallée-Réhel, K., Linossier, I. & Haras, D. (2003) Bacterial biofilm in seawater: cell surface properties of early-attached marine bacteria. *Biofouling*, *19*, 307-313.

[37] Heilmann, C., Schweitzer, O., Gerke, C., Vanittanakom, N., Mack, D. & Gotz, F. (1996) Molecular basis of intercellular adhesion in the biofilm-forming Staphylococcus epidermidis. *Mol. Microbiol.*, *20*, 1083-91.

[38] Henke, J.M. & Bassler, B.L. (2004) Bacterial social engagements. *Trends Cell Biol.*, *14*, 648-56.

[39] Henrici, A. (1936) Studies of freshwter bacteria. III. Quantitative aspects of the direct microscopic method. *J. Bacteriol.*, *32*, 265-280.

[40] Hentzer, M., Riedel, K., Rasmussen, T.B., Heydorn, A., Andersen, J.B., Parsek, M.R., Rice, S.A., Eberl, L., Molin, S., Hoiby, N., Kjelleberg, S. & Givskov, M. (2002)

Inhibition of quorum sensing in *Pseudomonas aeruginosa* biofilm bacteria by a halogenated furanone compound. *Microbiology*, *148*, 87-102.

[41] Heukelekian, H. & Heller, A. (1940) Relation between food concentration and surface for bacterial growth. *J. Bacteriol.*, *40*, 547-558.

[42] Hotchkiss, M. & Waskman, S. (1936) Correlative studies of microscopic and plate methods for evaluating the bacterial population of the sea. *J. Bacteriol.*, *32*, 423-432.

[43] Hoyle, B.D., Alcantara, J. & Costerton, J.W. (1992) *Pseudomonas aeruginosa* biofilm as a diffusion barrier to piperacillin. *Antimicrob. Agents Chemother.*, *36*, 2054-6.

[44] Hussain, M., Wilcox, M. & White, P. (1993) The slime of coagulase-negative staphylococci: biochemistry and relation to adherence. *FEMS Microbiolological Reviews*, *104*, 191-208.

[45] Ichimiya, T., Yamasaki, T. & Nasu, M. (1994) In-vitro effects of antimicrobial agents on *Pseudomonas aeruginosa* biofilm formation. *J. Antimicrob. Chemother.*, *34*, 331-41.

[46] Joshua, G., Guthri-Irons, C., Karlyshev, A. & Wren, B. (2006) Biofilm formation in *Campylobacter jejuni*. *Microbiology*, *152*, 387-386.

[47] Kalmokoff, M., Lanthier, P., Tremblay, T., Foss, M., Lau, P., Sanders, G., Austin, J., Kelly, J. & Szymanski, C. (2006) Proteomic analysis of *Campylobacter jejuni* 11168 biofilms reveals a role for the motility complex in biofilm formation. *J. Bacteriol.*, *188*, 4312-4320.

[48] Kim, H., Ryu, J.H. & Beuchat, L.R. (2007) Effectiveness of disinfectants in killing *Enterobacter sakazakii* in suspension, dried on the surface of stainless steel, and in a biofilm. *Appl. Environ. Microbiol.*, *73*, 1256-65.

[49] Klappenbach, J. & Pierson, B. (2004) Phylogenetic and physiological characterization of a filamentous anoxygenic photoautotrophic bacterium '*Candidatus Chlorothrix halophila*' gen. nov., sp. nov. recovered from hypersaline microbial mats. *Arch. Microbiol.*, *181*, 17-25.

[50] Kobayashi, K. (2007) Bacillus subtilis Pellicle Formation Proceeds through Genetically Defined Morphological Changes. *J. Bacteriol.*, *189*, 4920-31.

[51] Langlois, V., Vallée-Réhel, K., Péron, J., Le Borgne, A., Walls, M. & Guérin, P. (2002) Synthesis and hydrolytic degradation of graft copolymers containing poly(lactic acid) side chains : in vitro release studies of bioactive molecules. *Polymer Degradation and Stability*, *76*, 411-417.

[52] Latasa, C., Solano, C., Penades, J.R. & Lasa, I. (2006) Biofilm-associated proteins. *C. R. Biol.*, *329*, 849-57.

[53] Lewandowski, Z. (2000) *Structure and function of biofilms*. In: L. Evans (Eds.). *Biofilms: Recent advances in their study and control*. Amsterdam: Harwood Academic Publishers; 1-17.

[54] Little, B. & Ray, R. (2002) A perspective on corrosion inhibition by biofilms. *Corrosion*, *58*, 424-428.

[55] Loo, C.Y., Corliss, D.A. & Ganeshkumar, N. (2000) *Streptococcus gordonii* biofilm formation: identification of genes that code for biofilm phenotypes. *J. Bacteriol.*, *182*, 1374-82.

[56] Mack, D., Fischer, W., Krokotsch, A., Leopold, K., Hartmann, R., Egge, H. & Laufs, R. (1996) The intercellular adhesin involved in biofilm accumulation of *Staphylococcus epidermidis* is a linear beta-1,6-linked glucosaminoglycan: purification and structural analysis. *J. Bacteriol.*, *178*, 175-83.

[57] Manefield, M., de Nys, R., Kumar, N., Read, R., Givskov, M., Steinberg, P. & Kjelleberg, S. (1999) Evidence that halogenated furanones from *Delisea pulchra* inhibit acylated homoserine lactone (AHL)-mediated gene expression by displacing the AHL signal from its receptor protein. *Microbiology, 145 (Pt 2)*, 283-91.

[58] Marrie, T.J., Nelligan, J. & Costerton, J.W. (1982) A scanning and transmission electron microscopic study of an infected endocardial pacemaker lead. *Circulation, 66*, 1339-41.

[59] Marrie, T.J. & Costerton, J.W. (1983) A scanning and transmission electron microscopic study of the surfaces of intrauterine contraceptive devices. *Am. J. Obstet. Gynecol., 146*, 384-94.

[60] Marrie, T.J. & Costerton, J.W. (1984) Morphology of bacterial attachment to cardiac pacemaker leads and power packs. *J. Clin. Microbiol., 19*, 911-4.

[61] Marrie, T.J. & Costerton, J.W. (1984) Scanning and transmission electron microscopy of in situ bacterial colonization of intravenous and intraarterial catheters. *J. Clin. Microbiol., 19*, 687-93.

[62] Mireles, J.R., 2nd, Toguchi, A. & Harshey, R.M. (2001) Salmonella enterica serovar typhimurium swarming mutants with altered biofilm-forming abilities: surfactin inhibits biofilm formation. *J. Bacteriol., 183*, 5848-54.

[63] Mitbavkar, S. & Anil, A. (2004) Vertical migratory rhythms of benthic diatoms in a tropical intertidal sand flat: influence of irradiance and tides. *Mar. Biol. (Berl.), 145*, 9-20.

[64] Morin, D., Grasland, B., Vallée-Réhel, K., Dufau, C. & Haras, D. (2003) On line high performance liquid chromatography mass spectrometric detection and quantification of N-acylhomoserine lactone, quorum sensing signal molecules, in presence of biological matrixes. *J. Chromatogr. A, 1002*, 79-92.

[65] Nielsen, P., Jahn, A. & Palmgren, R. (1997) Conceptual model for production and composition of exopolymers in biofilms. *Water Sci. Technol., 36*, 11-19.

[66] O'Toole, G.A. & Kolter, R. (1998) Initiation of biofilm formation in Pseudomonas fluorescens WCS365 proceeds via multiple, convergent signalling pathways: a genetic analysis. *Mol. Microbiol., 28*, 449-61.

[67] O'Toole, G.A. & Kolter, R. (1998) Flagellar and twitching motility are necessary for *Pseudomonas aeruginosa* biofilm development. *Mol. Microbiol., 30*, 295-304.

[68] Oren, A. & Gunde-Cimerman, N. (2007) Mycosporines and mycosporine-like amino acids: UV protectants or multipurpose secondary metabolites? *FEMS Microbiol. Lett., 269*, 1-10.

[69] Orme, R., Douglas, C.W., Rimmer, S. & Webb, M. (2006) Proteomic analysis of Escherichia coli biofilms reveals the overexpression of the outer membrane protein OmpA. *Proteomics, 6*, 4269-77.

[70] Pan, Y., Breidt, F., Jr. & Kathariou, S. (2006) Resistance *of Listeria monocytogenes* biofilms to sanitizing agents in a simulated food processing environment. *Appl. Environ. Microbiol., 72*, 7711-7.

[71] Parsek, M.R. & Greenberg, E.P. (2005) Sociomicrobiology: the connections between quorum sensing and biofilms. *Trends Microbiol., 13*, 27-33.

[72] Perumal, P., Mekala, S. & Chaffin, W.L. (2007) Antifungal drug resistance in Candida albicans biofilms: a role for cell density. *Antimicrob. Agents Chemother.*

[73] Prigent-Combaret, C., Vidal, O., Dorel, C. & Lejeune, P. (1999) Abiotic surface sensing and biofilm-dependent regulation of gene expression in *Escherichia coli. J. Bacteriol.*, *181*, 5993-6002.

[74] Qazi, S., Middleton, B., Muharram, S.H., Cockayne, A., Hill, P., O'Shea, P., Chhabra, S.R., Camara, M. & Williams, P. (2006) N-acylhomoserine lactones antagonize virulence gene expression and quorum sensing in *Staphylococcus aureus*. *Infect. Immun.*, *74*, 910-9.

[75] Reisner, A., Haagensen, J.A., Schembri, M.A., Zechner, E.L. & Molin, S. (2003) Development and maturation of Escherichia coli K-12 biofilms. *Mol. Microbiol.*, *48*, 933-46.

[76] Resch, A., Leicht, S., Saric, M., Pasztor, L., Jakob, A., Gotz, F. & Nordheim, A. (2006) Comparative proteome analysis of *Staphylococcus aureus* biofilm and planktonic cells and correlation with transcriptome profiling. *Proteomics*, *6*, 1867-77.

[77] Riedel, K., Hentzer, M., Geisenberger, O., Huber, B., Steidle, A., Wu, H., Hoiby, N., Givskov, M., Molin, S. & Eberl, L. (2001) N-acylhomoserine-lactone-mediated communication between *Pseudomonas aeruginosa* and Burkholderia cepacia in mixed biofilms. *Microbiology*, *147*, 3249-62.

[78] Sampathkumar, B., Napper, S., Carillo, C., Willson, P., Taboada, E., Nash, J., Potter, A., Babiuk, L. & Allan, B. (2006) Transcriptional and translational expression patterns associated with immobilized growth of *Campylobacter jejuni*. *Microbiology*, *152*, 567-577.

[79] Sauer, K., Camper, A.K., Ehrlich, G.D., Costerton, J.W. & Davies, D.G. (2002) *Pseudomonas aeruginosa* displays multiple phenotypes during development as a biofilm. *J. Bacteriol.*, *184*, 1140-54.

[80] Sauer, K., Cullen, M.C., Rickard, A.H., Zeef, L.A., Davies, D.G. & Gilbert, P. (2004) Characterization of nutrient-induced dispersion in *Pseudomonas aeruginosa* PAO1 biofilm. *J. Bacteriol.*, *186*, 7312-26.

[81] Schopf, J.W., Kudryavtsev, A.B., Agresti, D.G., Wdowiak, T.J. & Czaja, A.D. (2002) Laser--Raman imagery of Earth's earliest fossils. *Nature*, *416*, 73-6.

[82] Stal, L.J. (2000) *Cyanobacterial mats and stromatolites*. In: B. Whitton & M. Potts (Eds.). *The ecology of cyanobacteria.* Dordrecht: Kluwer Academic Publisher,;

[83] Steppe, T., Olson, J., Paerl, H., Litaker, R. & Belnap, J. (1996) Consortial N_2 fixation: a strategy for meeting nitrogen requirements of marine and terrestrial cyanobacterial mats. *FEMS Microbiology Ecology*, *21*, 149-156.

[84] Stoodley, P., Debeer, D. & Lewandowski, Z. (1994) Liquid Flow in Biofilm Systems. *Appl. Environ. Microbiol.*, *60*, 2711-2716.

[85] Stoodley, P., Lewandowski, Z., Boyle, J.D. & Lappin-Scott, H.M. (1999) The formation of migratory ripples in a mixed species bacterial biofilm growing in turbulent flow. *Environ. Microbiol.*, *1*, 447-55.

[86] Stoodley, P., Lewandowski, Z., Boyle, J.D. & Lappin-Scott, H.M. (1999) Structural deformation of bacterial biofilms caused by short-term fluctuations in fluid shear: an in situ investigation of biofilm rheology. *Biotechnol. Bioeng.*, *65*, 83-92.

[87] Sutherland, I. (2001) Biofilm exopolysaccharides: a strong and sticky framework. *Microbiology*, *147*, 3-9.

[88] Sutherland, I.W. (2001) Exopolysaccharides in biofilms, flocs and related structures. *Water Sci. Technol.*, *43*, 77-86.

[89] Sutherland, I.W. (2001) The biofilm matrix--an immobilized but dynamic microbial environment. *Trends Microbiol.*, *9*, 222-7.

[90] Thouvenin, M., Linossier, I., Sire, O., Peron, J. & Vallée-Rehel, K. (2002) Structural and dynamic approach of early hydration steps in erodable polymers by ATR-FTIR and fluorescence spectroscopies. *Macromolecules*, *35*, 489-498.

[91] Thouvenin, M., Peron, J., Langlois, V., Guerin, P. & Vallée-Rehel, K. (2002) Formulation and antifouling activity of marine paints: a study by a statistically based experiment plan. *Progress in Organic Coatings 44*, 85-92.

[92] Thouvenin, M., Langlois, V., Briandet, R., Langlois, J., Guerin, P., Péron, J., Haras, D. & Vallée-Réhel, K. (2003) Study of erodable paint properties involved in antifouling activity. *Biofouling 19*, 177-186.

[93] Tresse, O., Jouenne, T. & Junter, G.A. (1995) The role of oxygen limitation in the resistance of agar-entrapped, sessile-like *Escherichia coli* to aminoglycoside and beta-lactam antibiotics. *J. Antimicrob. Chemother.*, *36*, 521-6.

[94] Tresse, O., Jouenne, T. & Junter, G.A. (1997) Underexpression of porin protein OmpF in agar-entrapped, sessile-like *Escherichia coli*. *Antonie Leeuwenhoek*, *72*, 271-4.

[95] Tresse, O., Jouenne, T. & Junter, G.A. (1997) Antibacterial efficacy of tobramycin against anaerobic *Escherichia coli* cultures in the presence of electron acceptors. *J. Antimicrob. Chemother.*, *40*, 419-21.

[96] Tresse, O., Lescob, S. & Rho, D. (2003) Dynamics of living and dead bacterial cells within a mixed-species biofilm during toluene degradation in a biotrickling filter. *J. Appl. Microbiol.*, *94*, 849-54.

[97] Tresse, O., Lebret, V., Benezech, T. & Faille, C. (2006) Comparative evaluation of adhesion, surface properties, and surface protein composition of *Listeria monocytogenes* strains after cultivation at constant pH of 5 and 7. *J. Appl. Microbiol.*, *101*, 53-62.

[98] Vallet, I., Olson, J.W., Lory, S., Lazdunski, A. & Filloux, A. (2001) The chaperone/usher pathways of *Pseudomonas aeruginosa*: identification of fimbrial gene clusters (cup) and their involvement in biofilm formation. *Proc. Natl. Acad. Sci. U. S. A.*, *98*, 6911-6.

[99] van de Koppel, J., Herman, P., Thoolen, P. & Heip, C. (2001) Do alternate multiple stable states occur in natural ecosystems? Evidence from tidal flat. *Ecology (N. Y.)*, *82*, 3449 - 3461.

[100] van Oss, C. (1994) *Interfacial forces in aqueous media* New-York: Masson.

[101] Videla. (2002) Prevention and control biocorrosion. *Int. Biodeterior. Biodegrad.*, *49*, 259-270.

[102] Waskman, S. & Vartiovaara, U. (1938) The adsorption of bacteria by marine bottom. *Biol. Bull. (Woods Hole)*, *74*, 56-63.

[103] Watnick, P.I. & Kolter, R. (1999) Steps in the development of a *Vibrio cholerae* El Tor biofilm. *Mol. Microbiol.*, *34*, 586-95.

[104] Webb, J.S., Thompson, L.S., James, S., Charlton, T., Tolker-Nielsen, T., Koch, B., Givskov, M. & Kjelleberg, S. (2003) Cell death in *Pseudomonas aeruginosa* biofilm development. *J. Bacteriol.*, *185*, 4585-92.

[105] Whiteley, M., Bangera, M.G., Bumgarner, R.E., Parsek, M.R., Teitzel, G.M., Lory, S. & Greenberg, E.P. (2001) Gene expression in *Pseudomonas aeruginosa* biofilms. *Nature*, *413*, 860-4.

[106] Wijman, J.G., de Leeuw, P.P., Moezelaar, R., Zwietering, M.H. & Abee, T. (2007) Air-liquid interface biofilms of Bacillus cereus: formation, sporulation, and dispersion. *Appl. Environ. Microbiol.*, *73*, 1481-8.
[107] Wolfe, A., Chang, D., Walker, J., Seitz-Partridge, J., Vidaurri, M., Lange, C., Prüss, B., Henk, M., Larkin, J. & Conway, T. (2003) Evidence that acetyl phosphate functions as a global signal during biofilm development. *Mol. Microbiol.*, *48*, 977-988.
[108] Xiong, J. & Bauer, C. (2002) Complex evolution of photosynthesis. *Ann. Rev. Plant Physiol.*, *53*, 503-521.
[109] Zhang, X., Bishop, P. & Kupferle, M. (1998) Measurement of polysaccharides and proteins in biofilms extracellular polymers. *Water Sci. Technol.*, *37*, 345-348.
[110] Zobell, C. (1937) The influence of solid surface upon the physiological activities of bacteria in sea water. *Journal of Bacteriology*, *33*, 86.
[111] Zobell, C. (1943) The effect of solid surfaces upon bacterial activity. *J. Bacteriol.*, *46*, 39-56.

In: Environmental Microbiology Research Trends
Editor: G. V. Kurladze, pp. 137-166
ISBN: 978-1-60021-939-9

Chapter 4

MICROBIAL AND CHEMICAL ASSAYS TO DETERMINE THE ORIGIN OF FAECAL POLLUTION AND THE PRESENCE OF WATERBORNE PATHOGENS

M. M. Ehlers[1], A. Sundram[*], M. M. Kock[1] and N. Potgieter[#]
[1] Department of Medical Microbiology, University of Pretoria/National Health Laboratory Services, South Africa
[*] Umgeni Water, Kwazula Natal, South Africa
[#] Department of Microbiology, University of Venda, South Africa

ABSTRACT

In the last decade, the emphasis has shifted to the physical and microbiological quality of water sources as reports have shown that there are an increasing percentage of surface- and groundwater that are being contaminated with waterborne pathogens. Increased land use, rural development, informal settlements and inadequate infrastructure for water and sanitation have increased the risk of faecal contamination of these water sources. This is compounded by alterations in the hydrological cycle, associated with global climate change that increases the magnitude and frequency of run-off events. Waterborne diseases and epidemics result from the ingestion of faecally polluted water containing enteric bacterial pathogens, human-specific enteric viruses and protozoan parasites. Enteric bacteria have traditionally been used as indicators of faecal contamination of source, drinking and recreational water. However, research has demonstrated that these bacteria may not be appropriate indicators of pathogenic viruses and the need for reliable index or indicator organisms of these pathogens have been widely recognised. Studies conducted over the past couple of years have investigated, evaluated and compared bacteriophage and chemical assays as indicators of waterborne pathogens. In one study, the potential of F-RNA phage genotyping and chemical analysis of faecal sterols were evaluated to indicate if faecal pollution of water sources were of human or animal origin. When applied to environmental samples, F-RNA phage genotyping provided useful information in certain instances and confirmed the presence of either human or animal faecal pollution. Chemical assays yielded more conclusive results when F-RNA phage genotyping results obtained from river water samples were ambiguous. In another study F-RNA phage genotyping was used to determine the origin of faecal pollution in traditional and CDC safe storage containers in rural settlements. Results showed no difference between the different containers; both human and animal phage subtypes were detected. Although the detection of each specific pathogen seems to be the ideal, this is not always possible due to expensive analysis and the need of well-equipped laboratories and skilled personnel. It can be concluded that bacterial and bacteriophage indicators are still the best alternative and most cost-effective tools currently available and will continue to play a major role in the determination of the microbial quality of water.

INTRODUCTION

Diarrhoeal diseases are responsible for approximately 2.5 million deaths annually in developing countries, mostly affecting children younger than five years, especially those in areas devoid of access to potable water supply and sanitation (Kosek *et al.,* 2003; Obi *et al.*, 2003; Lin *et al.*, 2004; Obi *et al.*, 2004). One of the Millennium Declaration goals was to reduce the amount of people without safe drinking water by half in the year 2015 (UN, 2000). Safe drinking water for human consumption should be free from pathogens such as bacteria, viruses and protozoan parasites; meet the standard guidelines for taste, odour, appearance and chemical concentrations and must be available in adequate quantities for domestic purposes (Kirkwood, 1998). However, inadequate sanitation and persistent faecal contamination of water sources is responsible for a large percentage of people in both developed and developing countries not having access to microbiologically safe drinking water and suffering from diarrhoeal diseases (WHO, 2002a; WHO, 2002b).

Political upheaval, high numbers of refugees in some developing countries and the global appearances of squatter camps and shanty rural towns, which lack proper sanitation and water connections have contributed to conditions under which disease causing microorganisms can survice (Leclerc *et al.*, 2002; Sobsey, 2002; Theron and Cloete, 2002). The people most susceptible to waterborne diseases include young children, the elderly, people suffering from malnutrition, pregnant woman, immunocompromised individuals, people suffering from chemical dependencies and persons predisposed to other illnesses like diabetes (Sobsey *et al.*, 1993; Gerba *et al.*, 1996; Grabow, 1996; Leclerc *et al.*, 2002; Theron and Cloete, 2002). Furthermore, an increasing number of people are becoming susceptible to infections with specific pathogens due to the indiscriminate use of antimicrobial drugs, which have lead to the selection of antibiotic resistant bacteria and drug resistant protozoa (WHO, 2002c; NRC, 2004).

In developing countries, many people are living in rural communities and have to collect their drinking water some distances away from the household and transport it back in various types of containers (Sobsey, 2002). Microbiological contamination of the water may occur between the collection point and the point-of-use in the household due to unhygienic practices causing the water to become a health risk (Sobsey, 2002; Gundry *et al.*, 2004; Moyo *et al.*, 2004).

Waterborne diseases and epidemics have been associated with water supplies polluted by faecal matter containing a range of human-specific bacterial, viral and protozoan pathogens

(Jagals *et al.*, 1995; Sinton *et al.*, 1998; Scott *et al.*, 2002). Research has indicated that more than 100 types of pathogenic human viruses may be present in faecally polluted water (Havelaar *et al.*, 1993; Scott *et al.*, 2002). It must be noted that some waterborne pathogens such as *Cryptosporidium* spp. and a limited number of bacteria and viruses may be of animal origin (Sinton *et al.*, 1998). Information on the human or animal origin of faecal pollution is therefore important because it gives an indication of the possible risk of infection and the treatment that might be needed to control the transmission of waterborne diseases (Jagals *et al.*, 1995).

The major causes of faecal contamination of water sources such as rivers, dams, groundwater as well as drinking water are: i) release of partially treated sewage or sewage leakage, ii) leaching of poorly maintained septic tanks, iii) improper management of farm waste and iv) run-off of faecal matter during rainy periods (Isobe *et al.*, 2004). The management of faecal contamination of water can only improve if the sources of pollution are identified. Water analysis and detection tools to distinguish between human and animal faecal sources are therefore needed (Schaper *et al.*, 2002a).

Waterborne enteric viruses can reach large human populations and cause diseases such as gastroenteritis and hepatitis (Beekwilder *et al.*, 1996). Human enteric viral diseases are considered to be predominantly associated with the ingestion of human-derived wastes because of the host-specific nature of enteric viruses (Calci *et al.*, 1998; Sinton *et al.*, 1998). Studies conducted by Havelaar and colleagues (1993) showed that viruses are more persistent than bacteria in water environments and are not readily removed by water treatment processes. Water treatment and catchment management strategies based on bacteriological indicators seems inadequate tools to be used to assess the virological safety of water (Havelaar *et al.*, 1993; Cole *et al.*, 2003; Skraber *et al.*, 2004).

Bacteriophages have the closest correlation with enteric viruses making them invaluable indicators of the possible presence and behaviour of enteric viruses (Geldenhys and Pretorius, 1989; Brion *et al.*, 2002; Skraber *et al.*, 2004). Although enteric viruses are the ultimate viral indicator, analyses for coliphages (phages) such as somatic and male specific F-RNA phages are easier and more rapid to enumerate and less expensive compared to the detection of specific enteric viruses (Rhodes and Kator, 1991). The International Association for Water Pollution Research and Control (IAWPRC) (1991) as well as Donnison and Ross (1995) reported that phages have similar behaviour patterns to enteric viruses in the environment. Phages are found in abundance in wastewater, since they are excreted in human and animal faeces (Armon, 1993). Depending on the conditions prevailing, it was found that phages outnumbered enteric viruses by a factor of at least a 1 000 or more (Grabow *et al.*, 1984). In addition, phages are more resistant than enteric viruses to water treatment and disinfection processes as well as to unfavourable environmental conditions shown by studies conducted at pH 4 and pH 10 and temperatures ranging from 4°C to 37°C (Grabow *et al.*, 1984; Schaper *et al.*, 2002a; Allwood *et al.*, 2003; Cole *et al.*, 2003).

The male specific F-RNA phages have been associated exclusively with animal or human faecal contamination and have been classified into four groups (also referred to as serological groups or subgroups) (Havelaar *et al.*, 1990). Two groups have been reported to originate from animal sources and the other two groups originating from human sources (Osawa *et al.*, 1981; Furuse, 1987; Havelaar *et al.*, 1990; Hsu *et al.*, 1995; Schaper and Jofre, 2000; Schaper *et al.*, 2002b). Researchers have successfully developed and exploited genotyping techniques to group F-RNA phage isolates into these four respective groups (Hsu *et al.*, 1995; Beekwilder *et al.*, 1996; Griffin *et al.*, 2000).

In addition to F-RNA phage typing to distinguish between faecal pollution of humans and animals, the chemical analysis of faecal sterols such as cholesterol and coprostanol have yielded valuable results in attempts to distinguish between faecal pollution of human and animal origin (Nguyen *et al.*, 1995; Leeming and Nichols, 1996). The profiles of faecal sterols such as cholesterol and coprostanol differ in different warm-blooded animals and are gaining wide use as biomarkers indicating faecal pollution (Nguyen *et* al., 1995; Leeming *et al.*, 1996). The addition of a silylating agent converts these compounds into trimethylsilyl (TMS) ethers, which are more stable for gas chromatographic assays (Elhmmali *et al.*, 2000). The coupling of a mass spectrometer to a gas chromatograph proved suitable for the separation and identification of the spectrum of compounds belonging to faecal sterols and TMS ethers to distinguish between human and animal excreta (Pool, 1978; Nguyen *et al.*, 1995; Leeming and Nichols, 1996). The aim of this first study was to use genotyping of F-RNA phages and chemical assays for the faecal sterols, cholesterol and coprostanol, to track faecal pollution to human or animal sources in different wastewater and environmental samples.

Poor sanitation, unhygienic practices and close living associations between people and animals in rural communities increase the risk of zoonoses and add to faecal contamination of stored drinking water. Point-of-use interventions can improve the microbiological quality of household drinking water and a combination of microbial and chemical indicator tests could identify the origin of faecal pollution. Following the first study, a second study was conducted to evaluate the improvement of the microbiological quality of drinking water in rural households. The implementation of intervention strategies, which included the use of traditional storage containers as well as an improved safe storage container (CDC, USA), with or without the addition of a sodium hypochlorite solution as well as the origin of faecal pollution were investigated. However, for the purpose of this chapter we only focused on the origin of faecal contamination in the water sources and household stored water using male specific F-RNA group genotyping.

METHODOLOGY FOR THE IDENTIFICATION OF THE ORIGIN OF FAECAL POLLUTION IN WATER SOURCES

Genotyping of F-RNA Phages

The F-RNA phages have been classified into 4 groups based on their phylogenetic diversity, eg. MS-2 in group 1, GA in group 2, Qβ in group 3 and SP in group 4 (Havelaar and Hogeboom, 1984; Furuse, 1987). Serotyping of F-RNA phages has been suggested as a method to determine the origin of faecal pollution (Schaper and Jofre, 2000). However, serotyping was found to be laborious and required antiserum reagents that were scarce and not readily available (Havelaar *et al.*, 1990; Hsu *et al.*, 1995). Genotyping was suggested as the better alternative to serotyping because several F-RNA phages were reported as serological intermediates between group 1 and 2 and between groups 3 and 4, possibly resulting in ambiguous serotyping results (Hsu *et al.*, 1995). Hsu and co-workers (1995) researched highly specific nucleic acid probes for the four groups of F-RNA phages that were successfully used for genotyping F-RNA phages. The presence of F-RNA phages in a water sample generally indicates pollution by wastewater, which contains human and/or animal faeces (DWAF, 1996). The F-RNA phage serogroups 1 and 4 occurred in wastewater from animal sources while serogroups 2 and 3 were found in wastewater from human sources such as hospital wastewater (Osawa *et al.*, 1981; Havelaar *et al.*, 1986; Havelaar *et al.*, 1990; Hsu *et al.*, 1995; Schaper *et al.*, 2002b).

Schaper and Jofre (2000) confirmed that groups 2 and 3 predominated in municipal sewage illustrating that these genotypes were of human origin. Research conducted by Schaper *et al.* (2002b) found the association of groups 2 and 3 to human excreta and groups 1 and 4 to animal excreta significant. Other research conducted by Griffin *et al.* (2000) found that genotyping of F-RNA phages could be used successfully to help distinguish between faecal pollution of animal or human origin.

It is noteworthy that all isolates from animal faecal sources were grouped as groups 1 and 4 with the exception of isolates from pig and piglet faeces, which often contained groups 2 or 3 F-RNA phages (Hsu *et al.*, 1995; Cole *et al.*, 2003). This suggests that group classification will not always distinguish between human and porcine faecal contamination (Osawa *et al.*, 1981; Furuse, 1987; Havelaar *et al.*, 1990; Hsu *et al.*, 1995). This occurrence could be explained by the dietary and living conditions of pigs that have historically involved exposure to human faecal wastes and thus human-specific F-RNA phages (Hsu *et al.*, 1995). Once introduced into pig populations, these F-RNA phages could persist because the gastrointestinal physiology and flora of pigs are similar to those of humans (Hsu *et al.*, 1995).

Gene Probes used for F-RNA Phage Genotyping

Gene probes are homologous nucleic acid material that could bind with or hybridise to specific target nucleic acids and facilitate the detection of specific target nucleic acids (Hurst *et al.*, 1989). The development of F-RNA phages probes involved searching for stretches of 20 to 30 nucleotides which showed complete conservation within one subgroup, while being absent from other subgroups (Table 1) (Hsu *et al.*, 1995; Beekwilder *et al.*, 1996).

Table 1. Nucleotide sequences of oligomers used for probing F-RNA phages (Beekwilder *et al.*, 1996)

Group	Probe Sequence	Locus
1	CGCATCTAAGGTATGGACCATCGAGA	Maturation protein
2	AATCGTTCAGGAAGTGAGATTCAAAACC	Maturation protein
3	AGCCAGAGATTACCAGCAGTAGC	5' Non-translated region
4	GGCATAGATTCTCCTCTGTAGTGCG	5' Non-translated region

Various computer software gene analysis and alignment programmes were used to select oligonucleotide sequences having the least sequence homology with phages of heterologous groups (Hsu *et al.*, 1995; Beekwilder *et al.*, 1996). These oligoprobes, which were end-labeled with digoxigenin, were applied in DNA-RNA hybridisations and hybrids were observed for colorimetric or chemiluminescent detection (Hsu *et al.*, 1995; Beekwilder *et al.*, 1996; Griffin *et al.*, 2000).

Gene Hybridisation of F-RNA Isolates

Nucleic acid hybridisation involves the use of nucleic acid probes for detecting viral nucleic acid that has been trapped on filter material or membranes (Hurst *et al.*, 1989). The method for transfer of phages from zones of lysis (plaques) on a host cell lawn to candidate membrane filters and fixation on the membranes were optimised to yield the best possible detection following hybridisation (Hsu *et al.*, 1995; Beekwilder *et al.*, 1996; Griffin *et al.*, 2000). Many types of filters including nitrocellulose, non-charged and charged nylon Hybond N filters were tested for their ability to retain and expose phage RNA from plaques (Hsu *et al.*, 1995; Beekwilder *et al.*, 1996). The Hybond N+ nylon membranes were most satisfactory and reproducibly yielded sharp plaque signals, contrasting clearly to a low background, even when plaques had a small diameter (Hsu *et al.*, 1995; Beekwilder *et al.*, 1996; Griffin *et al.*, 2000; Schaper and Jofre, 2000).

Following fixation of phages onto membranes, the phage RNA would have to be released and denatured, thereby exposing its bases to the complementary oligonucleotides (Beekwilder *et al.*, 1996; Schaper and Jofre, 2000). This was achieved by alkaline treatment with NaOH followed by neutralisation with sodium acetate (Hsu *et al.*, 1995; Beekwilder *et al.*, 1996; Griffin *et al.*, 2000; Schaper and Jofre, 2000). Although alkaline treatment could lead to hydrolysis of the RNA chain, studies have found that 1 minute exposure to 0.05 M NaOH leaves the RNA sufficiently intact to serve as a target for the oligonucleotide probes (Beekwilder *et al.*, 1996; Uys, 1999).

Following fixation and denaturation, the membranes need to undergo a pre-hybridisation step in preparation for the binding of the probes (Hsu *et al.*, 1995). Research done by Uys (1999) found that a modified pre-hybridisation step used by Beekwilder *et al.* (1996) was more efficient than the method used by Hsu *et al.* (1995). This modification included increasing the pre-hybridisation time to 1 hour, which resulted in the least background colour development when chemiluminescent detection was performed (Uys, 1999).

Various studies used probe concentrations ranging from 2.5 – 5 pmol.mL^{-1} with hybridisation conditions ranging from 37°C – 45°C for 1 hour to overnight (Hsu *et al.*, 1995; Beekwilder *et al.*, 1996; Griffin *et al.*, 2000; Schaper and Jofre, 2000). Studies conducted by Uys (1999) found that overnight incubation of the viral nucleic acids with 2.5 pmol.mL^{-1} of labeled probe at 37°C allowed maximum probe-target interaction. This lower probe concentration that was used, yielded better results when chemiluminescent detection was performed (Uys, 1999).

Detection of DNA:RNA Hybrids of F-RNA Phages

Colorimetric and radioactive detection techniques used by Hsu and co-workers (1995) and Beekwilder and colleagues (1996) have been superceded by chemiluminescent detection techniques used by researchers such as Griffin and colleagues (2000) as well as Schaper and

Jofre (2000). The colorimetric detection technique with the DIG Nucleic Acid Detection Kit showed hybrids to appear as dark-blue circular spots on membranes (Hsu *et al.*, 1995; Uys, 1999). Research conducted by Uys (1999) found that colorimetric detection was time consuming and some hybrids tended to appear as light to dark blue spots resulting in subjective assigning of probes to subgroups. Chemiluminescent detection is performed with Lumigen-CSPD and hybridised plaques appeared as dark-black circular spots on the X-Ray film (Schaper and Jofre, 2000).

Faecal Sterols Used as a Tool to Trace the Origins of Faecal Pollution in Water

There are at least seventeen sterols found in the faeces of humans and animals including sterols such as; cholesterol and campesterol and stanols such as coprostanol and cholestanol (Leeming *et al.*, 1996). Leeming and colleagues (1996) discussed that bacterial indicators are unable to distinguish between animal and human pollution whereas the use of biomarkers, in particular faecal sterols such as cholesterol and coprostanol are advantageous as they can distinguish between the origins of faecal pollution. Biomarkers are organic compounds (Writer *et al.*, 1995) that have maintained their structural integrity for their source to be recognised (Leeming *et al.,* 1996). These chemical signatures overcome many of the shortcomings (e.g. die-off, lack of correlation with faecal pathogens) of classical microbiological indicators of sewage pollution (Nichols *et al.*, 1996; Elhmmali *et al.*, 2000). Pollution from animal and human wastes is a cause of deteriorating water quality and the management of the problem could depend on tracing the source of pollution using the sterol profiles of human and animal faeces (Leeming *et al.,* 1996; Sinton *et al.*, 1998).

The sterol profiles from various animal faeces showed that there are differences in both the content and composition of faecal sterols between warm-blooded animals (Leeming *et al.*, 1996; Leeming *et al.*, 1998). The source-specificity of faecal sterols is caused by a combination of three main factors (Leeming *et al.*, 1996). The first is the animal's diet that has a different sterol profile so the proportions of sterol precursors entering the digestive tract are different (Leeming *et al.*, 1996; Nichols *et al.*, 1996). Secondly, even with low dietary intake of sterols, endogenous sterols are biosynthesised by mammalian animals and discharged to the digestive tract for example, humans on low cholesterol diets will still synthesise cholesterol (Leeming *et al.*, 1996). Thirdly, and most importantly, anaerobic bacteria in the digestive tract of some animals biohydrogenate sterols to stanols of various isomeric configurations (Leeming *et al.*, 1996). The combination of these three factors determines "the sterol fingerprint" of the faeces for any animal (Nichols *et al.*, 1996).

Studies conducted by Nichols *et al.* (1996) found that the total sterol content in human faeces was 3 000 – 8 800 $\mu g.g^{-1}$, being five times higher than the concentrations detected from other animal samples. Human faeces contained as much as ten times more coprostanol on a dry weight basis than faeces analysed from animals (Leeming *et al.*, 1996; Scott *et al.*, 2002). The sterol profile of pigs was found to be similar to that of humans, although the absolute concentrations were about 10 fold lower (Leeming *et al.*, 1996; Nichols *et al.*, 1996; Scott *et al.*, 2002). Murtuagh and Bunch (1967) found that the concentration of coprostanol excreted by humans was at least seventeen times higher than that excreted in pigs and cows.

Later research found that coprostanol concentrations in human faeces were one to three orders of magnitude greater than that found in other animals (Nichols *et al.*, 1996).

Research conducted by Leeming and colleagues (1996) indicated that the ratios of coprostanol:cholesterol in humans were as high as 10:1. This was opposed to certain animals that had relatively similar coprostanol:cholesterol ratios and others that had cholesterol concentrations that were more than two orders of magnitude higher than coprostanol concentrations (Leeming *et al.*, 1996). Nguyen and co-workers (1995) cited that these two major sterols: cholesterol and coprostanol are poorly soluble in water and have been detected in wastewater in concentrations exceeding 1 000 $ng.L^{-1}$ (Leeming and Nichols, 1996). Assays for the sterols coprostanol and cholesterol could prove to be better than traditional microbiological techniques for detecting human sewage pollution versus faecal contamination from animal sources (Leeming and Nichols, 1996).

Cholesterol Used as a Faecal Indicator

Cholesterol originates from the diet, liver, intestinal epithelium and other tissues in the body (Macdonald *et al.*, 1983). Cholesterol occurs widely in the human body, but not all of the biological functions of cholesterol are known (Graham Solomons, 1980). This widely occurring steroid is known to serve as an intermediate in the biosynthesis of steroid hormones and of bile acids (Graham Solomons, 1980). However, it is reported that more cholesterol is present in the human body than is needed for the biosynthesis of steroid hormones (Graham Solomons, 1980). As cholesterol is also found in eggs, milk, lard and wool grease, it is not as specific an indicator of faecal pollution as coprostanol (Dutka *et al.*, 1974; Dutka and El-Shaarawi, 1975).

Coprostanol Used as a Faecal Indicator

According to Martin and co-workers (1973), coprostanol in human faeces resulted from the biohydrogenation of cholesterol by the intestinal microflora. The biohydrogenation of the unsaturated sterol cholesterol to coprostanol in the small intestine of mammalian animals is carried out by a mixed population of faecal bacteria such as *Bifidobacterium* spp., *Clostridium* spp., *Bacteroides* spp. and *Eubacterium* spp. (Dutka *et al.*, 1974; Macdonald *et al.*, 1983; Vivian, 1986; Venkatesan and Santiago, 1989; Nichols *et al.*, 1996; Elhmmali *et al.*, 2000). In the metabolic formation of coprostanol, the double bonds between carbon atoms 5 and 6 in the B ring of cholesterol are enzymatically hydrogenated resulting in the formation of three stereo-isomers; coprostanol (5β-coprostanol), epicoprostanol (5β-epicoprostanol) and dihydrocholesterol (5α-cholestanol) (Matusik *et al.*, 1988).

Coprostanol is a major sterol found in human faeces (24% - 89% of total steroids) and has been proven to be a promising indicator of faecal pollution by various studies of coprostanol concentrations in the water and sediments of rivers, lakes and estuaries (Macdonald *et al.*, 1983; Scott *et al.*, 2002; Isobe *et al.*, 2004). The intestinal tract of adults contains approximately 1 kg of bacteria (10^{14} organisms), the bulk of which is in the colon and both dietary and endogenous substances are destined to come into intimate contact with this population of more than 400 species in the lower gut (Macdonald *et al.*, 1983). As a result, human faeces and municipal wastewater sludge contain a high concentration of coprostanol (Chan *et al.*, 1998).

Coprostanol is aerobically degraded by natural bacteria and thus the presence of coprostanol in an aerobic environment would indicate recent sewage contamination (Vivian, 1986). The reported half-life of coprostanol in aerobic conditions are generally <10 days at 20°C, thus the presence of coprostanol in an aerobic environment can be considered to be of recent faecal input to the water (Isobe *et al.*, 2004). Coprostanol has been suggested to be useful in tracing sewage effluents disinfected by chlorination since it is unaffected by the process unlike faecal bacteria (McCalley *et al.*, 1981; Vivian, 1986). Another attribute that makes coprostanol a good chemical indicator of human pollution is that it is a primary sterol in domestic wastes and it is unaffected by physical factors like temperature and salinity (Brown and Wade, 1984; Writer *et al.*, 1995). However, humans may vary as to the amount of coprostanol they excrete (Leeming and Nichols, 1996).

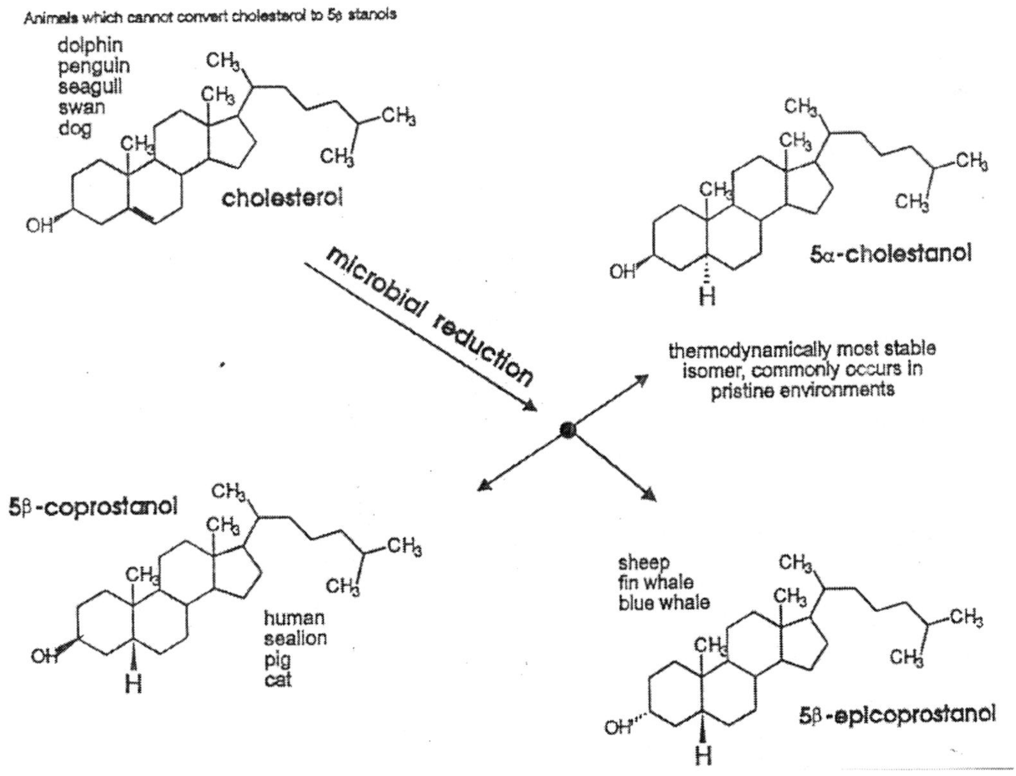

Figure 1. Sterol structures (C_{27} sterols and stanols), biotransformation pathways and indication of the major sterols/stanols in human and animal faeces (Leeming *et al.*, 1996)

Faecal Sterol Formation and Structure

The structural differences between cholesterol and the three common saturated isomeric (stanol) products are shown in Figure 1. The seemingly small changes in orientation of the hydrogen atom at the carbon-5 position and the hydroxyl group at the carbon-3 position result in different compounds which can be used as biomarkers (Leeming *et al.*, 1996; Nichols *et al.*, 1996). The 5α configuration of the C_{27} stanol, 5α-cholestanol, is the thermodynamically stable isomer, whereas 5β-coprostanol and 5β-epicoprostanol are produced only through the mediation of anaerobic bacteria (Leeming *et al.*, 1996; Nichols *et al.*, 1996).

Anaerobic bacteria preferentially biohydrogenate Δ^5-sterols to their corresponding 5β(H), 3β(OH)-stanols (Leeming *et al.*, 1996). Matusik and co-workers (1988) reported that coprostanol, cholesterol and 5α-cholestanol are the principal faecal sterols found in human faeces. Anaerobic bacteria in the guts of other animals either preferentially biohydrogenate Δ^5-sterols to one or more corresponding stanols (Figure 1), or lack the ability to biohydrogenate Δ^5-sterols at all (Leeming *et al.*, 1996).

Extraction of Faecal Sterols from Water

The ideal solvent or solvent mixture for extracting lipids should be sufficiently polar to remove all lipids from the mixture but should not chemically react with the lipid itself (Christie, 1982). Lipids, which contain no markedly polar groups, for example cholesterol, are highly soluble in hydrocarbon solvents such as hexane, benzene or cyclohexane as well as in slightly more polar solvents like chloroform but are rather insoluble in polar solvents such as methanol (Bligh and Dyer, 1959; Christie, 1982). The solubility of faecal sterols in alcoholic solvents increases with the chain length of the hydrocarbon moiety of the alcohol so these compounds become more soluble in ethanol and completely soluble in n-butanol (Christie, 1982).

During the formation of silyl ethers, the character of the sterol molecule is changed from polar and active to non-polar and inert, which is generally coupled with an increase in volatility and thermal stability, which are the properties most desirable for gas chromatography (Pool, 1978). A powerful silyl donor such as bis(trimethylsilyl)trifluoroacetamide (BSTFA) is widely used to form silyl derivatives of organic compounds such as faecal sterols (Pool, 1978; Writer *et al.*, 1995; Leeming *et al.*, 1996; Nichols *et al.*, 1996; Elhmmali *et al.*, 2000). Thus the addition of the silylating agent converts these organic compounds into TMS ethers (Elhmmali *et al.*, 2000). The coupling of a mass spectrometer to a gas chromatograph has proved to be a good method of separating and identifying the components of a complex organic mixture in a simple yet highly diagnostic manner (Pool, 1978).

Gas Chromatography-Mass Spectrometry used for the Detection of Faecal Sterols

Gas chromatography (GC) is the physical separation of two or more compounds based on their differential distribution between a stationary phase and a gaseous mobile phase (Fowles, 1998). Compounds to be analysed must be volatile to be present in the gas phase under experimental conditions so that it can be transported through the fused silica capillary columns where compounds are separated (Fowles, 1998). Gas chromatographs require a supply of carrier gas, such as nitrogen, helium or hydrogen, of sufficient quality and pressure to achieve the desired separations (Fowles, 1998). Therefore, the basic principle of GC is that the greater the affinity of the compound for the stationary phase, the more the compound will be retained by the column and the longer it will take before it is eluted and detected (Fowles, 1998). A detector converts the column eluent to an electrical signal that is measured and recorded (Watson, 1985; Furniss *et al.*, 1989).

Mass Spectrometry (MS) is one kind of GC detector (Watson, 1985). As the separated sample component molecules elute form the column to the inside of the MS they are bombarded with energy causing them to loose an electron and form ions with a positive charge (Watson, 1985). Some of the bonds holding the molecule together are broken in the process and the resulting fragments may rearrange or break up further to form stable fragments (Watson, 1985; Furniss *et al.*, 1989). Due to the natural laws that govern the relative strengths of chemical bonds, a given compound will ionise, fragment and rearrange reproducibly under a given set of conditions (Watson, 1985). A mass spectrum is a recording of the mass of each of the ionised fragments, representing a unique fingerprint of a molecule that can be used in identification (Watson, 1985; Furniss *et al.*, 1989). Molecular fragments appear in a mass spectrum and provide clues to the identity and molecular structure of the parent molecule similar to the way pieces of a jigsaw puzzle provide clues to the structure of the intact puzzle (Watson, 1985; Furniss *et al.*, 1989). A mass spectrum can be described as a molecular fingerprint consisting of a graph showing the mass:charge ratio (in Daltons or atomic mass units) versus abundance data for ions in the sample molecule and its fragments where the largest peak in the spectrum is called the base peak (Watson, 1985; Furniss *et al.*, 1989). The mass:charge ratio of any fragment therefore is normally equal to the mass of that fragment (Watson, 1985).

Mass spectrometers have been used to detect and quantify compounds at concentrations as low as only a few parts per billion (Watson, 1985). Gas chromatographic data is two dimensional, i.e. a plot of signal versus time (Fowles, 1998). A mass spectrometer adds another dimension to GC data, i.e. abundance and mass versus time (Watson, 1985; Furniss *et al.*, 1989). The GC-MS chromatogram represents the sum of all ions detected (Watson, 1985; Furniss *et al.*, 1989). Quantification with GC-MS can be accomplished by using calibration curves obtained from injecting known amounts of standards and recording the responses of the MS for each amount injected making up these curves (Watson, 1985; Furniss *et al.*, 1989; Fowles, 1998). As the compound is injected at an unknown concentration, the amount of the unknown can be calculated by relating the response to the amount on the curve (Watson, 1985; Furniss *et al.*, 1989).

Sample Collection for F-RNA Genotyping and Chemical Assays (Study 1)

Wastewater samples (500 mL) representative of human faecal pollution were collected from two local hospitals in Pietermaritzburg, Kwa-Zulu Natal, South Africa. Wastewater (500 mL) from a cattle feedlot in the Umgeni River catchment and wastewater from a piggery in the Pietermaritzburg midlands were collected as being representative of cattle and pig faecal pollution. Chicken wash and wastewater (500 mL) from a poultry farm and an abattoir in the Cato Ridge area was collected as representative chicken faecal pollution. River water samples (500 mL) were collected from the Slangspuit, Baynespruit, uMsunduze and

Dorpspruit rivers. River water samples analysed for faecal sterols were collected in 2 L pyrex glass bottles.

Sample Collection for F-RNA Genotyping During an Intervention Study (Study 2)

The second study focused on rural communities in the Vhembe region of the Limpopo Province, South Africa and investigated the microbiological quality of drinking water in rural households, evaluated the implementation, compliance and sustainability of intervention strategies such as the CDC safe storage container and chlorine practices, assessed the survival of selected pathogens and investigated sources of faecal contamination in household stored water. However, in this chapter we will just focus on the genotyping of F-RNA phages in the determination of the origin of faecal pollution.

Forty households were randomly selected in two rural villages (Vembe region, Limpopo province, South Africa). Two rounds of water collection from the households and the water sources were carried out over a period of 5 months. Water samples (2 L) were collected aseptically in sterile Nalgene water collection bottles (Merck, Darmstadt, Germany) from 7 communal taps in village 1 and from 4 points on the Sambandou River in village 2.

Two water storage containers in each household were randomly selected and vigorously shaken before water samples were collected. Water samples (1 L each) were collected aseptically in sterile Nalgene water collection bottles (Merck, Darmstadt, Germany) from each of the two selected storage containers in each household on both rounds of water collection. The two water samples from each household were pooled into one sample (2 L) representative of the household container water, placed on ice and transported to the laboratory for further analyses within 8 hours. After the first round of water sampling, 20 households in each village were randomly selected and provided with two CDC safe storage containers each. These households were requested to use the CDC safe storage containers instead of the traditional household storage containers. The water samples obtained from the households using the CDC safe storage containers were compared with water samples obtained from the households in the same village using traditional storage containers in order to determine the impact of an improved storage container on the origin of faecal pollution.

Water contaminated with human faeces is regarded as a greater risk to human health as there is a more likely chance that it would contain human-specific enteric pathogens (Scott *et al.*, 2002). It has become increasingly important to distinguish between faecal pollution of human or animal origin. Various microbiological and chemical methods have been demonstrated to help identify the source of faecal pollution, thereby assisting in establishing the associated risks (Hsu *et al.*, 1995; Beekwilder *et al.*, 1996; Leeming and Nichols, 1996; Griffin *et al.*, 2000; Schaper *et al.*, 2002a; Isobe *et al.*, 2004).

Results and Discussion

In the first study the isolation of F-RNA phages, following the standard ISO-10705–1 (1995) double-layer agar technique, was found to be simple and easy once established in the laboratory. Plaques that developed were opaque and not as clear as those formed by typical somatic phages. Due to the nature of some of the environmental samples, a fair amount of background bacterial growth did occur. The identification of F-RNA phages by nucleic acid hybridisation has clear advantages over other techniques since it is genome-based and very specific.

Evaluation of DNA:RNA Hybridisation Techniques Using Control Phages

The hybridisation protocols established by Hsu *et al.* (1995) and Beekwilder *et al.* (1996) and optimised by Uys (1999) were carefully followed. The Hybond N+ nylon membranes were most satisfactory and reproducibly yielded sharp plaque signals, contrasting clearly to a low background, even when plaques had a small diameter (Hsu *et al.*, 1995; Beekwilder *et al.*, 1996; Griffin *et al.*, 2000; Schaper and Jofre, 2000). Overnight incubation of the viral nucleic acids with 2.5 $pmol.mL^{-1}$ of labeled probe at 37°C allowed maximum probe-target interaction and yielded good results when chemiluminescent detection was performed. Initial experiments to fix phage RNA onto the membranes using a standard UV lamp (365 nm), in the absence of a UV Transilluminator, placed over the membranes in a dark box proved to be unsuccessful. This was substituted with baking the membranes in a hot air oven at 80°C for 2 hours. The DNA:RNA hybrids appeared as dark spots on the X-Ray film. Spots that developed were clearly visible and exposure time of 3.5 – 4 minutes was adequate in generating enough signal to allow detection on the film. Some background colour development did occur on some films whenever F-RNA phage plates were left in the cold room for longer periods, usually more than a week, allowing bacterial re-growth to occur.

Researchers such as Hsu *et al.* (1995) and Beekwilder *et al.* (1996) developed probes for the four different subgroups of F-RNA phages by searching for stretches of 20 to 30 nucleotides, which showed complete conservation within one subgroup, while being absent from other subgroups. The F-RNA phages GA, SP, MS2 and Qβ representative of each of the four F-RNA phage groups were used as controls for the DNA:RNA hybridisation. These control phages confirmed that there was no cross reactivity between probes of the different F-RNA phage genotypes.

Genotyping of F-RNA Phages from Wastewater and River Samples

Although both the Cabelli *E. coli* and Havelaar *S. typhimurium* WG 49 hosts detected other phages such as somatic and F-DNA phages, it was reported that more than 90% – 95% of phages detected from sewage and environmental samples using *S. typhimurium* WG 49 as the host, were F-RNA phages (Havelaar and Hogeboom, 1984; Debartolomeis and Cabelli, 1991; Hsu *et al.*, 1995; Grabow *et al.*, 1997). With this in mind it would be safe to assume that most of the phages isolated from the environmental samples using *S. typhimurium* WG 49 as the host, were F-RNA phages, confirmed by the positive genotyping results obtained.

Sample sites representative of the predominant animal sources in the catchment such as; cattle, chicken and pigs, were selected from accessible sites at abattoirs, feedlots and piggeries. Wastewater samples obtained from two private hospitals in Pietermaritzburg were selected as representative human faecal input. Samples were collected from these different sites and F-RNA phages were isolated following the standard ISO-10705–1 (1995) methodology. These phages were hybridised with probes specific for each of the F-RNA phage groups and detected using chemiluminescent detection techniques as described earlier.

The results showed that F-RNA groups 3 and 4 were the only two groups detected in pig wastewater. Unlike previous studies conducted by Hsu *et al.* (1995), F-RNA phage group 2 was not detected in the pig wastewater tested. Another interesting finding was that F-RNA phage groups 1 and 4 were detected along with group 3 in the chicken wastewater. Previously, groups 2 and 3 was found to be more specific to humans and by exception in pigs that were considered to have a similar gastrointestinal physiology and flora to humans partly because of the close living conditions (Hsu *et al.*, 1995; Schaper *et al.*, 2002; Cole *et al.*, 2003). It was therefore, unusual that F-RNA phage group 3 was detected in chicken wastewater on two separate occasions. It is likely that farming activities on the chicken farms could have contributed to human input in the chicken wastewater that was possibly not exclusively chicken waste. The results indicated the specificity of groups 2 and 3 for humans, as these were the only two F-RNA phage groups detected in all four of the hospital wastewater samples.

River sites in the Pietermaritzburg catchment were selected on historical *E. coli* data indicating faecal pollution. Samples from the Baynspruit, Dorpspruit, Slangspruit and uMsunduze rivers were taken between the summer periods of October 2002 and February 2003. The F-RNA analyses were conducted on samples when *E. coli* counts exceeded 10 000.100 mL^{-1} resulting from various faecal inputs. These faecal inputs ranged from the faeces of grazing animals to broken and overflowing blocked sewers and informal sanitation often reaching water sources following heavy rainfall events.

All four F-RNA phage genotypes were detected in the river samples analysed. The plaques were detected as dark circular spots on the X-ray Lumi film and varied in size from small to large. The background colour development was possibly due to a combination of background bacterial growth, inadequate washing, poor handling of the Lumi film and over-exposure. There were instances where poor development of the DNA:RNA hybrids occurred on the film and these membranes were subsequently exposed to the Lumi film for longer periods and this over-exposure was sometimes unavoidable.

In addition, plaques were obtained from selected river water samples, harvested and spotted onto specific areas of Tryptone Yeast Extract Glucose Agar plates to determine the F-RNA phage genotypes present. Up to five environmental samples could be analysed per Tryptone Yeast Extract Glucose Agar plate, saving time and making the genotyping assay for multiple environmental samples more cost effective.

The Slangspruit River situated close to an informal settlement in Pietermaritzburg often receives faecal input from run-off and poor sanitation infrastructure unable to contain human sewage. The human faecal input is evident by the detection of F-RNA phage groups 2 and 3 in all samples. Groups 1 and 4 were also detected indicating the presence of animal faecal excrement. Groups 1 and 3 were the only F-RNA phage groups present in samples from 3 different sites on the Baynesspruit River sampled on the 23/1/03, whilst all 4 groups were detected from samples taken from the Baynespruit River on other days. This river runs through an industrial area with some cattle grazing and domesticated animals including chickens present in informal settlements. This river often receives faecal input from these sources and the results suggested that both human and animal sources were responsible for the faecal pollution. A similar picture presented in the Dorpspruit River that meanders along the city of Pietermaritzburg, even passing horse stables before confluence with the uMsunduze River. The uMsunduze River that flows through the upper Pietermaritzburg catchment, eventually joins the Umgeni River, receives faecal input from run-off of various animals ranging from cattle and chickens to human faecal matter originating from broken and blocked sewers and informal settlements. Samples taken from various points along the uMsunduze River indicated that there were instances (n=6) that only groups 2 and 3 were detected suggesting that the main source of faecal pollution in these samples were of human origin. Despite being time consuming and expensive, this technique could be used to help distinguish between human and animal faecal pollution in environmental samples.

The quantification of the sterols detected was done using the gas chromatography results (from HP Chemstation). These results were obtained for the calibration standards that were plotted using Microsoft Excel and calculated from the calibration curve obtained for each batch of samples.

Faecal Sterol Assays on Wastewater Samples

After careful preparation of the 40 ppm, 80 ppm and 160 ppm coprostanol and cholesterol standards, it was injected into the GC. The peaks obtained after approximately 22 minutes were identified by the mass spectrometer as coprostanol, followed shortly afterwards by the cholesterol peak. The mass spectra of these compounds detected after 22.71 minutes and 24.33 minutes were matched to the reference library in the mass spectrometer and confirmed as coprostanol and cholesterol respectively.

The wastewater samples were very turbid and each extraction did not separate as clear chloroform/water phases. All three extracts had to be combined into a separate flask before a proper phase separation could be seen. This additional step was successful in obtaining sterol extracts with minimal trapped water remaining. Following extraction and derivatisation of extracts from the different wastewater samples, samples were injected into the GC as described above and the mass spectra of peaks obtained after 22 minutes where identified as coprostanol and cholesterol. These peak areas were quantified once the calibration standards were plotted and the area of abundance under each peak could be converted to the corresponding concentrations. The results indicated that there were instances when higher faecal sterol concentrations were detected (as high as 4 208 $\mu g.L^{-1}$ cholesterol in chicken wastewater) as opposed to instances where relatively low concentrations of 56.3 $\mu g.L^{-1}$ cholesterol was detected in chicken wastewater. These trends of varying low or high concentrations of either cholesterol or coprostanol were found in all of the wastewater samples analysed. It could be attributed to a number of factors including; samples taken over different flows, different diets, microflora in the gut and general health of the individuals.

Coprostanol was generally detected in higher concentrations (23.1 – 1 441 $\mu g.L^{-1}$) than cholesterol (28.2 – 555 $\mu g.L^{-1}$) in both the local hospital and pig wastewater samples. This is possibly due to the gastrointestinal physiology of pigs that have been reported to be similar to that of humans (Scott *et al.*, 2002). The first sample analysed from the local hospital was the only exception where 23.1 $\mu g.L^{-1}$ of coprostanol was detected in the presence of 28.2 $\mu g.L^{-1}$ of cholesterol. Cholesterol was consistently detected at much higher concentrations (181 – 4 208 $\mu g.L^{-1}$) than coprostanol (22.6 – 142.3 $\mu g.L^{-1}$) in both cattle and chicken wastewater.

This is in keeping with literature that highlighted that most animals are unable to biohydrogenate cholesterol to coprostanol due to the physiology of the animal gut including the microflora present (Elhmmali *et al.*, 2000).

It is clear that the average concentrations of coprostanol:cholesterol were greater than 2:1 in both human and pig wastewater. The reverse was found with cattle and chicken wastewater where the average cholesterol concentrations were higher (158 – 1 542 $\mu g.L^{-1}$) than the average coprostanol concentrations (49 – 58 $\mu g.L^{-1}$).

Faecal Sterol and F-RNA Phage Genotyping Assays on Environmental Samples

Faecal sterols were generally below the detection limit when 500 mL sample volumes were used. After numerous attempts it was found that better cholesterol and coprostanol recoveries in environmental samples were obtained using 2 L sample volumes. The results indicated that this method was not sensitive in detecting faecal sterol concentrations below 318 x $10^{-3} \mu g.L^{-1}$. While in general, all four genotypes of F-RNA phages were detected in the Msunduze River (site 2), which is downstream of a wastewater treatment plant. The coprostanol concentrations were higher (ranging from 2 424 – 7 107 $\mu g.L^{-1}$) than the cholesterol concentrations (1 592 – 5 670 $\mu g.L^{-1}$). However, the opposite was found in the Dorpspruit River sampled during an agricultural show where the coprostanol concentrations were either below the detection limit or very low while the cholesterol concentrations were as high as 8 014 $\mu g.L^{-1}$. The impact of animal faecal material in the Dorpspruit River was clearly detected by the respective coprostanol:cholesterol ratios and further confirmed by the detection of only group 1 F-RNA phages, known to be of animal origin. The Slangspruit River known to have faecal input from informal settlements in the catchment, contained groups 2 and 3 F-RNA phages known to be mainly of human origin. Apart from confirming the presence of faecal matter in the Slangspruit River, the coprostanol and cholesterol concentrations could not be used to determine if the pollution was of human origin as the coprostanol (17 – 412 $\mu g.L^{-1}$) concentrations detected were lower than the cholesterol concentrations (55 – 1 243 $\mu g.L^{-1}$). The Baynespruit River contained all four groups of F-RNA phages suggesting that the faecal pollution was of human and animal origin but there was 19.1 $\mu g.L^{-1}$ of coprostanol opposed to 9.3 $\mu g.L^{-1}$ of cholesterol suggesting that the faecal matter was predominantly of human origin. This site is known to have faecal pollution resulting from overflowing broken and blocked sewers in the area and would confirm the presumptions made from the faecal sterol assays that the faecal input was predominantly of human origin. Despite the shortcomings in both the F-RNA phage genotyping and faecal sterol assays, both methods could be used to determine the origin of faecal pollution. This could assist with the assessment of associated health risks in the event of faecal contamination of water sources.

Origin of Male Specific F-RNA Bacteriophage Groups in the Primary Water Sources

In the second study genotyping of F-RNA isolates from the communal tap and river water sources for both the villages identified group 1 male specific F-RNA bacteriophages as the predominant bacteriophage group present (Table 2). Group 1 male specific F-RNA bacteriophages are indicative of animal faecal pollutions, specifically cattle, sheep and pig faeces (Hsu *et al.*, 1995; Beekwilder *et al.*, 1996; Uys, 1999). In village 1 using communal tap water sources it was observed that faeces of animals such as pigs, goats and cattle were lying next to the taps. The water reservoir in village 1 was also exposed to small animals, bird droppings and dust particles which might have contained faeces from animals grazing in the vicinity of the reservoir.

The Sambandou River used by households in village 2 was frequently used by domestic animals and cattle for drinking purposes and it was common to find animal faeces in the vicinity of the drinking water sources or close to the areas where people collect their drinking water or even in the water source (Table 2). All these animal activities in the vicinity of the water sources contributed to the presence of group 1 male specific F-RNA bacteriophage contamination that was identified in the water sources. The National Research Council (NRC, 2004) has reported that group 1 male specific F-RNA bacteriophages are found in both human and animals faeces and sewage. Therefore, it could be possible that the predominance of group 1 male specific F-RNA bacteriophages in both the water sources and especially in high concentrations in the river source could be due to both animal and human activities in and near the river source.

No male specific F-RNA bacteriophages belonging to groups 2 and 3 (associated mainly with human faecal pollution) and group 4 (associated mainly with animal faecal pollution) have been isolated from the communal tap water source samples. These bacteriophage groups may have had a fast die-off curve or were just not present at all. A study carried out by Schaper and co-workers (2002b) have shown that group 1 male specific F-RNA isolates were more resistant than group 2 F-RNA isolates followed by group 3 male specific F-RNA isolates and lastly group 4 male specific F-RNA isolates to chlorine, temperature, pH and salt concentrations in water samples. The absence of groups 2, 3 and 4 in the tap water sources could therefore give a false indication that the group 1 isolates were primarily of animal faecal origin and not from human origin (Hsu *et al.*, 1995; Beekwilder *et al.*, 1996; Uys, 1999).

However, male specific F-RNA bacteriophages belonging to group 2 were found in the river water samples (50%), which could indicate possible human pollution of the source water (Hsu *et al.*, 1995; Beekwilder *et al.*, 1996; Uys, 1999; Brion *et al.*, 2002). Group 4 bacteriophages have been shown to be associated with bird faeces (Brion *et al.*, 2002; Schaper *et al.*, 2002a) and even though no group 4 male specific F-RNA bacteriophages were identified during this study, both the river and communal tap reservoirs were exposed to faecal contamination from small animals and birds (Table 2).

Table 2. Prevalence of male specific F-RNA bacteriophages in river and communal tap water sources in two rural villages in the Vhembe region of the Limpopo Province, South Africa

Village 1 using communal tap water Male specific F-RNA bacteriophages genotype isolated (percentage %)					Village 2 using Sambandou River water Male specific F-RNA bacteriophages genotype isolated (percentage %)				
Number of water samples tested	Group 1 (MS2)	Group 2 (GA)	Group 3 (QB)	Group 4 (F1)	Number of water samples tested	Group 1 (MS2)	Group 2 (GA)	Group 3 (QB)	Group 4 (F1)
14*	14 (100%)	0 (0%)	0 (0%)	0 (0%)	8*	8 (100%)	4 (50%)	0 (0%)	0 (0%)

* Water samples collected for round 1 and round 2

Origin of Male Specific F-RNA Bacteriophage Subgroups in the Stored Household Water at the Point-of-Use in the Traditional and CDC Safe Water Storage Containers in Rural Households

A total of four (7%) male specific F-RNA bacteriophages belonging to group 1 male specific F-RNA bacteriophages (associated with animal faecal pollution) was identified in the traditional storage containers in the study households using the tap water source (Table 3). Similarly only one (5%) of the CDC safe storage containers in the households using tap water sources tested positive for the presence of group 1 male specific F-RNA bacteriophages (associated with animal faecal pollution) (Table 3).

In the study households using the river water source, a total of 37 (62%) of the traditional storage containers contained group 1 male specific F-RNA bacteriophages (associated with animal faecal pollution) (Table 3). Similarly, nine (45%) of the CDC safe storage containers tested positive for the presence of group 1 male specific F-RNA bacteriophages (associated with animal faecal pollution) (Table 3). Since animals were observed during this study to lick the communal taps in village 1 and defaecate in the vicinity of the taps and river water area where people collect their domestic water from, the presence of group 1 male specific F-RNA bacteriophages (associated with animal faecal pollution) was similar to the results obtained for the two water sources analysed (Table 2). This is in agreement with similar studies, which found that the presence of group 1 male specific F-RNA bacteriophages in water samples primarily indicated animal faecal pollution (Hsu *et al.*, 1995; Beekwilder *et al.*, 1996; Uys, 1999).

Since it was observed that the storage containers were left out in the yard or stored inside a traditional hut in many instances without a cover, the exposure to dust and faecal contamination from domestic animals, insects and poultry could have introduced group 1 male specific F-RNA bacteriophages to the containers (Rosas *et al.*, 2006). Many of these households also used fresh cow dung to smear the floors of their huts. The dust that originates from the dried cow dung could have contributed to the contamination of the open water storage containers (Benenson, 1995; Rosas *et al.*, 2006).

No group 2 male specific F-RNA bacteriophages (associated with human faecal pollution) were isolated from the tap water sources (Table 2), or in any of the storage containers in village 1 households (Table 3). However, group 2 male specific F-RNA bacteriophages (associated with human faecal pollution) were isolated in both the traditional and the CDC safe storage containers in households from village 2 (Table 3). Nine (15%) of the sixty households (40 households from round 1 water collection and 20 households from round 2 water collections) using the traditional water storage containers and nine (45%) of the twenty households (from second water collection trip) using the CDC safe storage containers contained group 2 male specific F-RNA bacteriophages associated with human pollution (Table 3).

Table 3. Prevalence of male specific F-RNA bacteriophages in stored drinking water containers from rural households in two villages in the Vhembe region of the Limpopo Province, South Africa

Household storage container	Village 1 using communal tap water Male specific F-RNA genotypes isolated (percentage %)				Village 2 using Sambandou River water Male specific F-RNA genotypes isolated (percentage %)			
	Group 1 (MS2)	Group 2 (GA)	Group 3 (QB)	Group 4 (F1)	Group 1 (MS2)	Group 2 (GA)	Group 3 (QB)	Group 4 (F1)
Traditional storage containers (n = 60)*	4 (7%)	0 (0%)	0 (0%)	0 (0%)	37 (62%)	9 (15%)	0 (0%)	0 (0%)
CDC safe storage containers (n = 20)**	1 (5%)	0 (0%)	0 (0%)	0 (0%)	9 (45%)	9 (45%)	0 (0%)	0 (0%)

*40 households selected in each village (first water collection round) using traditional storage containers + 20 households (second water collection round) used as control group in each village using traditional storage containers
**20 households selected in each village (second water collection round) using CDC safe storage containers

Brion and co-workers (2002) have stated that the presence of group 2 male specific F-RNA bacteriophages was an indication of distant or sporadic faecal pollution of human origin. Previous studies have confirmed that group 2 male specific F-RNA bacteriophages are predominantly found in human faeces and sewage (Hsu *et al.*, 1995; Beekwilder *et al.*, 1996; Uys, 1999). Consequently, contamination of the stored water in this study by humans might have occurred when members of the households used dirty utensils to transfer the stored water from these large open storage containers to a smaller storage container or directly through faecally contaminated hands – especially by small children touching the storage containers and utensils (Jagals *et al.*, 1999). In addition, a study conducted in South Africa and Spain (Schaper *et al.*, 2002a) analysed various sewage and faecal samples and showed that faeces from poultry, cattle and pigs could also contribute to the presence of group 2 male specific F-RNA bacteriophages.

A close human to animal association were observed in these rural communities and domestic animals and poultry were frequently seen walking into the household area where the water containers were stored. Consequently, the presence of the group 2 male specific F-RNA bacteriophages in the traditional and especially in the CDC safe storage containers suggested that faecal contamination could also have originated from these domestic animals and cattle at the households as well as from the primary water sources (Jagals *et al.*, 1999; Schaper *et al.*, 2002a). No group 2 (associated mainly with human faecal pollution) or group 4 (associated mainly with animal faecal pollution such as poultry and pig faeces) (Schaper *et al.*, 2002a) were detected in any of the traditional or CDC safe storage containers during the study period (Table 3). These results were similar to the results obtained for the primary water sources (Table 3). However, according to a 2004 review on *Indicators for Waterborne Pathogens* by the National Research Council of the National Academies of Science (NRC, 2004), group 1 was found in both human and animals faeces and sewage. Therefore, the absence of group 3 and 4 from the water samples tested during this study, might mean that isolates belonging to these two groups might not persist in water as long as groups 1 and 2 (Schaper *et al.*, 2002b). Consequently, groups 1 and 2 isolates present in these water samples might have been introduced into the water due to both human and animal contamination (NRC, 2004).

Summary of the Use of Male Specific F-RNA Bacteriophages Group Typing to Determine the Faecal Source Origin in Primary Water Sources and Drinking Water Stored in Traditional and CDC Safe Storage Containers in Rural Households

This is the first study to use male specific F-RNA bacteriophages to determine the origin of faecal pollution in household storage containers in rural households without adequate water and sanitation infrastructures. The results demonstrated that water from the water sources and the household storage containers were primarily contaminated by animal faecal matter because mainly group 1 F-RNA bacteriophages (associated with animal faecal pollution) were isolated. In addition, households using an unprotected water source also had group 2 male specific F-RNA bacteriophages present in the household stored water, which could have been either due to poor sanitation and hygienic conditions during storage and handling or due to contamination by animal faeces (Rosas *et al.*, 2006). It was difficult to determine the reason for the human faecal contamination because this study did not focus on household hygiene practices. It was however, observed that people removed the taps and the caps of the containers because they were afraid the children would break them. This happened in spite of the educational intervention on the proper use of the CDC safe storage container. In addition a recent study suggests that group 2 male specific F-RNA bacteriophages could have been from faecal samples of poultry and cattle (Schaper *et al.*, 2002a). Consequently, it could be speculated that both groups 1 and 2 isolates could have been introduced to the stored drinking water from both human and animal origin (NRC, 2004). However, it is important to note that Schaper and co-workers (2002a) concluded that the association between the specific groups cannot be used for absolute distinction between human and animal faecal pollution. Genotyping, therefore, seems not to be such an accurate tool to determine the origin of faecal pollution due to the potential for cross-reactions between some human and animal groups (NRC, 2004). This indicated the need for more intensive studies to confirm the specificity of the four groups of male specific F-RNA bacteriophages.

The absence of groups 3 and 4 male specific F-RNA bacteriophage isolates in both the sources and storage containers indicated (i) no human contamination of the household stored water, (ii) isolates from these subgroups does not survive for long periods in the environment and (iii) temperature, pH and turbidity of the water could affect the survival of this specific group isolates (Schaper *et al.*, 2002b). More studies are therefore needed to investigate the prevalence of male specific F-RNA groups in human and animal faeces especially in rural communities where a close living relationship exists between humans and animals.

Although the CDC safe storage container was specifically designed to reduce external microbial pollution of stored drinking water, it was observed that the households did not, at all times put the caps and/or the taps/spigot on the CDC safe storage containers exposing the water in these containers to potential faecal pollution. Possible reasons were that the parents were scared that the children would break the tap or throw away the cap, which could have increased the risk of faecal contamination of the water. Although this study reported on a small study group, the results clearly illustrated the need to provide these households with proper water and sanitation infrastructures to reduce the storage period of household drinking water and in the process try to prevent the possible faecal contamination of the stored water. In general this study has found that the use of male specific F-RNA bacteriophage genotyping could be used to some extend to distinguish between human and animal faecal pollution. However, this is an expensive technique, which requires skilled personnel and more studies in rural settings are needed. This was, however, the first study according to the literature to describe the origin of faecal pollution in household stored drinking water in a rural setting.

CONCLUSION

The first study was conclusive in proving that genotyping of F-RNA phages using chemiluminescent detection techniques was easy to perform producing results that were easy to interpret. The use of a hot air oven held at 80°C was successful in fixing the viral RNA onto the positively charged membranes due to a lack of a UV Transilluminator. The lowest background development on the X-ray film was achieved if plaques were transferred before any re-growth of bacteria occurred on plates stored in the cold room (4°C – 10°C). The probes selected for the hydridisation were sensitive and no cross-reactivity between the four F-RNA phages groups occurred.

The results confirmed earlier reports on the specificity of F-RNA phage genotypes 1 and 4 for animal wastes, and genotypes 2 and 3 for human excreta, in a part of the world where not much research has been done (Havelaar *et al.*, 1986). Male specific F-RNA phage group 3 was detected in both chicken and pig wastewater indicating that this group may not be specific to humans. There is a possibility that the chicken wastewater could have been contaminated with human faecal input due to farming activities. The major sources of faecal contamination in river water samples were not established in most instances as all four groups were detected in river water samples. The rivers that were surveyed were influenced by human and animal activities and genotyping used in isolation was not sufficient in determining which of these sources had more impact. There would appear to be an abundance of F-RNA phage genotypes 1 and 2 in the environmental samples, possibly due to their resistance to the prevailing environmental conditions. This research suggested that the results of F-RNA phage genotyping of F-RNA phages isolated from river water samples needs to be used together with other discriminating microbiological or chemical analyses to be more conclusive in establishing whether faecal input was of human or animal origin. Information on the human or animal origin of faecal pollution is important because it gives an indication of the possible risk of infection and the possible water treatment that may be needed to control the transmission of potential waterborne diseases.

The GC-MS method used for the detection of cholesterol and coprostanol was successful and most positive results were obtained when faecal sterol extractions from samples were done as soon as possible after sampling. The average concentrations of coprostanol detected in human (299 $\mu g.L^{-1}$) and pig (623 $\mu g.L^{-1}$) wastewater was higher than their respective average cholesterol concentrations (148 $\mu g.L^{-1}$ and 276 $\mu g.L^{-1}$). The opposite was found with chicken and cattle wastewater where the average cholesterol concentrations (1 542 $\mu g.L^{-1}$ and 158 $\mu g.L^{-1}$ respectively) were higher than the coprostanol concentrations (58 $\mu g.L^{-1}$ and 49 $\mu g.L^{-1}$respectively). The results for coprostanol and cholesterol are in keeping with other research findings where animals in general, apart from pigs, have higher cholesterol than coprostanol concentrations because of the limitations in the gut where the flora present in most animals are unable to biohydrogenate cholesterol to coprostanol (Elhmmali *et al.*, 2000). The analyses were unable to discriminate between human and pig faecal pollution although it has been reported that pigs would have lower concentrations of coprostanol than humans but it would be difficult to discriminate between human and pig faecal pollution in water. When these analyses were applied to environmental samples, larger sample volumes of up to 2 L were used and sterol concentrations as low as 318 x 10^{-3} $\mu g.L^{-1}$ was detected.

Genotyping of F-RNA phages isolated in these environmental samples could sometimes be used to source track faecal pollution, especially when groups associated with either animal or human were identified. Only group 1 F-RNA phages, known to be of animal origin was detected in samples taken from the Dorpspruit during an agricultural show and the specificity of these phages for animal faecal pollution was confirmed by the higher cholesterol:coprostanol ratios obtained. Genotyping results were not useful when all four groups of F-RNA phages were detected but the coprostanol and cholesterol concentrations obtained for these sites were more discriminatory in tracking the faecal pollution to be of human or animal origin depending on the respective coprostanol and cholesterol concentrations.

Both these chemical and microbiological methods could be used to determine if pollution was of human or animal origin but more conclusive and reliable discriminatory results were obtained if used together. This was because faecal sterol assays could be used in situations when F-RNA phage genotypes could not be used to distinguish faecal pollution. Only two faecal sterols, predominant in faeces, were selected for the investigation in this study due to the cost implications and specialised chemical methods required for assays of all the sterol assays present in faeces. Analysing for all of the faecal sterols and stanols may provide more useful and conclusive data when the sensitivity of using copostanol and cholesterol alone fails. These chemical and microbial assays are difficult, expensive and time-consuming. Despite having these shortcomings, important and useful data were obtained by applying both chemical and F-RNA phage genotyping assays.

The second study emphasizes the importance to determine the pathways of faecal contamination within the domestic household to decide on an effective point-of-use treatment system. Male specific F-RNA bacteriophage groups were used in this study to determine the origin of faecal pollution. The study was carried out specifically in rural households with a close living association with domestic animals and cattle. Differences in male specific F-RNA bacteriophages prevalence in the storage containers of households using different water sources were seen in this study. The prevalence of male specific F-RNA bacteriophages ranged between 30% and 65% for households using tap water and between 85% and 90% for households using river water. The higher prevalence of phages in the river water could have been due to animal and human activities in or near the river source. In addition, no difference between the traditional and CDC safe storage container water samples were seen with regard to the prevalence of male specific F-RNA bacteriophages. This is in agreement with the results from the formal intervention study (results not included here) indicating that the container without a sodium hypochlorite treatment is not improving the microbiological quality of the stored drinking water.

The results further demonstrated that water from the communal tap water and the household storage containers in village 1 were primarily contaminated by animal faecal matter because the majority of samples contained group 1 male specific F-RNA bacteriophages (associated with animal faecal pollution). However, water from the river water sources and the household storage containers in village 2 were primarily contaminated by animal and human faecal matter because the samples contained group 1 male specific F-RNA bacteriophages (associated with animal faecal pollution) and group 2 male specific F-RNA bacteriophages (associated with human faecal pollution). The results furthermore confirmed that storage containers do not prevent faecal contamination of stored drinking water in the absence of improved hygiene and sanitation behavior practices by the household members.

Since this was the first study to use male specific F-RNA bacteriophages to determine the origin of faecal pollution in household storage containers in rural households; the following aspects were identified for further research:

1. Survival of male specific F-RNA subgroups in household water storage containers. It would be important to investigate factors such as container type, storage conditions, role of temperature, pH and turbidity, water source, prevalence and role of biofilm in container and the survival period of different male specific F-RNA subgroups
2. Compare male specific F-RNA subgroups genotyping with new molecular PCR technique (Ogorzaly and Zantzer, 2006) to compare effectivity and costs

3. Determine the male specific F-RNA subtypes present in different animals from these rural communities to assess the specificity of male specific F-RNA subtyping as a source tracking technique.

Consequently the results of the two studies did give some indication of the origin of faecal pollution. Research has shown that there is no single method that could be used with absolute certainty and therefore, a combination of detection and identification methods could contribute to a better understanding in an attempt to obtain more useful and meaningful data regarding the origin of faecal pollution. Additional studies may be needed to confirm and develop these methodologies.

Although people know that the water can be contaminated, they are often ignorant of their contribution to faecal pollution at the resource as well as point-of use level. Educational aspects need to be addressed focusing on health issues, which will include training on basic hygiene and sanitation practices at the household level. Research on all the various levels will be of extreme importance in water quality studies and will provide valuable data to improve the microbial quality of water both at the source and at the point-of use. New data will assist various role players and decision makers at government level in the formulation of policies regarding water, sanitation and hygiene aspects and changes in countries such as South Africa to improve the general well-being of its people.

Acknowledgements

The authors would like to thank the Department of Medical Virology, University of Pretoria/NHLS and Umgeni Water for analyses conducted.

References

Allwood PB, Malik YS, Hedberg CW, Goyal SM. Survival of F-specific coliphage, feline calicivirus, and *Escherichia coli* in water: a comparative study. Applied and Environmental Microbiology 2003;69:5707-5710.

Armon R. Bacteriophage monitoring in drinking water: do they fulfil the index or indicator function? *Water Science and Technology* 1993;27:463-470.

Beekwilder J, Nieuwenhuizen R, Havelaar AH, Van Duin J. An oligonucleotide hybridization assay for the identification and enumeration of F-specific RNA bacteriophages in surface water. Journal of Applied Bacteriology 1996;80:179-86.

Benenson AS. *Control of communicable diseases in man.* 16th ed. Washington: American Public Health Association; 1995. p 530.

Bligh EG, Dyer WJ. A rapid method of total lipid extraction and purification. Canadian *Journal of Biochemistry and Physiology* 1959;37:911–917.

Brion GM, Meschke JS, Sobsey MD. F-specific RNA coliphages: Occurrence, types, and survival in natural waters. *Water Research* 2002;36:2419-2425.

Brown RC, Wade TL. Sedimentary coprostanol and hydrocarbon distribution adjacent to a sewage outfall. *Water Research* 1984;18:621–632.

Calci KR, Burkhardt 3rd W, Watkins WD, Rippey SR. Occurrence of male - specific bacteriophage in feral and domestic animal wastes, human faeces, and human - associated wastewaters. *Applied and Environmental Microbiology* 1998;64:5027-5029.

Chan KH, Lam MHW, Poon KF, Yeung HY, Chiu TKT. Application of sedimentary fecal stanols and sterols in tracing sewage pollution in coastal waters. *Water Research* 1998;32:225–235.

Christie WW. *Lipid Analysis: Isolation, Separation, Identification and Structural Analysis of Lipids*. 2nd ed. Oxford: Pergamon Press; 1982.

Cole D, Long SC, Sobsey MD. Evaluation of F+RNA and DNA coliphages as source-specific indicators of fecal contamination in surface waters. *Applied and Environmental Microbiology* 2003;69:6507–6514.

Debartolomeis J, Cabelli VJ. Evaluation of an *Escherichia coli* host strain for enumeration of F male - specific bacteriophages. *Applied and Environmental Microbiology* 1991;57:1301–1305.

Donnison AM, Ross CM. Somatic and F - specific coliphages in New Zealand waste treatment lagoons. *Water Research* 1995;29:1105–1110.

Department of Water Affairs and Forestry (DWAF). Holmes ed. *South African Water Quality Guidelines : Domestic Use*. 1996;1:89–90.

Dutka BJ, Chau ASY, Coburn J. Relationship between bacterial indicators of water pollution and faecal sterols. *Water Research* 1974;8:1047–1055.

Elhmmali MM, Roberts DJ, Evershed RP. Combined analysis of bile acids and sterols/stanols from riverine particulates to assess sewage discharges and other fecal sources. *Environmental Science and Technology* 2000;34:39–46.

Fowles IA. *Gas Chromatography*. 2nd ed. Chichester: John Wiley and Sons; 1998.

Furniss BS, Hannaford AJ, Smith PWG, Tatchell AR. Vogels. *Textbook of Practical Organic Chemistry*. 5th ed. New York: John Wiley and Sons, Inc; 1989.

Furuse K. Distribution of coliphages in the environment: general considerations. In: Goyal SM, Gerba CP, Bitton, G, editors. *Phage Ecology*. New York: Wiley – Interscience; 1987. p. 87–124.

Geldenhys JC, Pretorius PD. The occurrence of enteric viruses in polluted water, correlation to indicator organisms and factors influencing their numbers. *Water Science and Technology* 1989;21:105–109.

Gerba CP, Rose JB, Haas CN, Crabtree KD. Waterborne rotavirus: A risk assessment. *Water, Science and Technology* 1996;30:2929-2940.

Grabow WOK, Coubrough P, Nupen EM, Bateman BW. Evaluation of coliphages as indicators of the virological quality of sewage - polluted water. *Water SA* 1984;10:7–14.

Grabow WOK. Waterborne diseases: Update on water quality assessment and control. *Water SA* 1996;22:193-202.

Grabow WOK, Very A, Uys M, de Villiers JC. Evaluation of the application of bcateriophages as indicators of water quality. *South African Water Research Commission Final Report* 540/1/98. 1997.

Graham Solomons TW. *Organic Chemistry*. 2nd ed. USA: John Wiley and Sons, Inc: 1980.

Griffin DW, Stokes R, Rose JB, Paul JH. Bacterial indicator occurrence and the use of an F^+ specific RNA coliphage assay to identify fecal sources in Homosassa Springs, Florida. *Microbial Ecology* 2000;39:56–64.

Gundry S, Wright J, Conroy R. A systematic review of the health outcomes related to household water quality in developing countries. *Journal of Water and Health* 2004;2:1-13.

Havelaar AH, Hogeboom WM. A method for enumeration of male -specific bacteriophages in sewage. *Journal of Applied Bacteriology* 1984;56:439–447.

Havelaar AH, Furuse K, Hogeboom WM. Bacteriophages and indicator bacteria in human and animal faeces. *Journal of Applied Bacteriology* 1986;60:255–262.

Havelaar AH, Pot-Hogeboom WM, Furuse K, Pot R, Hormann MP. F - Specific RNA bacteriophages and sensitive host strains in faeces and wastewater of human and animal origin. *Journal of Applied Bacteriology* 1990;69:30–37.

Havelaar AH, Van Olphen M, Drost YC. F-specific RNA bacteriophages are adequate model organisms for enteric viruses in fresh water. *Applied and Environmental Microbiology* 1993;59:2956-2962.

Hsu FC, Shieh YSC, Van Duin J, Beekwilder MJ, Sobsey MD. Genotyping male - specific RNA coliphages by hybridisation with oligonucleotide probes. *Applied and Environmental Microbiology* 1995;61:3960–3966.

Hurst CJ, Benton WH, Stetler RE. Detecting viruses in water. *Journal of the American Water Works Association: Research and Technology* 1989;9:71–80.

International Association for Water Pollution Research and Control (IAWPRC). Study group on Health related Water Microbiology. AH Havelaar ed. Bacteriophages as model viruses in water quality control. *Water Research* 1991;25:529–545.

ISO 10705–1. *Water quality: Detection and enumeration of bacteriophages. Part 1: Enumeration of F-specific RNA bacteriophages*, International Organisation for Standardisation. 1995.

Isobe KO, Tarao M, Chiem NH, Minh LY, Takada H. Effect of environmental factors on the relationship between concentrations of coprostanol and fecal indicator bacteria in tropical (Mekong Delta) and temperate (Tokyo) freshwaters. *Applied and Environmental Microbiology* 2004;70:814–821.

Jagals P, Grabow WOK, De Villiers JC. Evaluation of indicators for assessment of human and animal faecal pollution of surface run-off. *Water, Science and Technology* 1995;31:235-241.

Jagals P, Bokato TC, Grabow WOK. Changing consumer water-use patterns and their effect on microbiological water quality as a result of an engineering intervention. *Water SA* 1999;25:297-300.

Kirkwood A. Safe water for Africa. DFID Conference Features. *Africa Health* 1998:9-11.

Kosek M, Bern C, Guerrant RL. The global burden of diarrhoeal disease, as estimated from studies published between 1992 and 2000. *Bulletin of the World Health Organization* 2003;81:197-204.

Leclerc H, Schwartzbrod L, Dei-Cas E. Microbial agents associated with waterborne diseases. *Critical Reviews in Microbiolog* 2002;28:371-409.

Leeming R, Ball A, Ashbolt N, Nichols P. Using faecal sterols from humans and animals to distinguish faecal pollution in receiving waters. *Water Research* 1996;30:2893–2900.

Leeming R, Nichols PD. Concentrations of coprostanol to existing bacterial indicator guideline limits. *Water Research* 1996;30:2997–3006.

Leeming R, Bate N, Hewlett R, Nichols PD. Discriminating faecal pollution : a case study of stormwater entering Port Phillip Bay, Australia. *Water Science and Technology* 1998;38:15–22.

Lin J, Biyda PT, Puckree T, Bezuidenhout CFC. Antibiotic resistance profiles and environmental isolates from Mhlathuze River, KwaZulu-Natal (RSA). *Water SA* 2004;30:23-28.

Macdonald IA, Bokkenheuser JW, McLernon AM, Mosbach EH. Degradation of steroids in the human gut. *Journal of Lipid Research* 1983;24:675–694.

Martin WJ, Ravi Subbiah MT, Kottke BA, Birk CC, Taylor M C. Nature of faecal sterols and intestinal bacterial flora. *Lipids* 1973;8:208–215.

Matusik JE, Hoskin GP, Sphon JA. Gas Chromatography/Mass Spectrometric confirmation of identity of coprostanol in Mercenaria mercenaria (Bivalvia) taken from sewage-polluted water. *Journal of the Association of Official Analytical Chemists* 1988;71:994–999.

McCalley DV, Cooke M, Nickless G. Effect of sewage treatment on faecal sterols. *Water Research* 1981;15:1019–1025.

Moyo S, Wright J, Ndamba J, Gundr S. Realising the maximum health benefit from water quality improvements in the home: A case study from Zaka District, Zimbabwe. *Physics and Chemistry of the Earth* 2004;29:1295-1299.

Murtaugh JJ, Bunch RL. Sterols as a measure of fecal pollution. *Journal Water Pollution Control Federation* 1967;39:404–409.

Nguyen DK, Bruchet A, Arpino P. Determination of sterols in sewage sludge by combined *in situ* trimethylsilylation/supercritical fluid extraction and GC-MS. *Environmental Science and Technology* 1995;29:1686–1690.

Nichols PD, Leeming R, Rayner MS, Latham V. Use of capillary gas chromatography for measuring fecal - derived sterols. Application to stormwater, the sea - surface microlayer, beach greases, regional studies, and distinguishing algal blooms and human and non - human sources of sewage pollution. *Journal of Chromatography* 1996;733:497–509.

NRC. Indicators for waterborne pathogens. Committee on Indicators for Waterborne Pathogens, National Research Council. Internet URL: *http://www.nap.edu/catalog/11010.html.* 2004.

Obi CL, Potgieter N, Bessong PO, Matsuang G. Scope of potential bacterial agents of diarrhoea and microbial assessment of quality of river water sources in rural Venda communities in South Africa. *Water, Science and Technology* 2003;47:59-64.

Obi CL, Green E, Bessong PO, De Villiers B, Hoosen AA, Igumbor EO, Potgieter N. Gene encoding virulence markers among *Escherichia coli* isolates from diarrhoic stool samples and river sources in rural Venda communities of South Africa. *Water SA* 2004;30:37-42.

Ogorzaly L, Zanther C. The development of real time RT-PCR for specific detection of F-specific RNA bacteriophage genotypes. *Journal of Virological Methods* 2006;138:131-139.

Osawa S, Furuse K, Watanabe I. Distribution of ribonucleic acid coliphages in animals. *Applied and Environmental Microbiology* 1981;41:64–168.

Pool FP. Recent advances in the Silylation of organic compounds for gas chromatography. In: Blau K, King GS editors. *Handbook of Derivatives for Chromatography*. London: Heydon;1978. p. 152–200.

Rhodes MW, Kator HI. Use of *Salmonella typhimurium* WG 49 to enumerate male - specific coliphages in an estuary and watershed subject to non - point pollution. *Water Research* 1991;25:1315–1323.

Rosas I, Salinas E, Martinez L, Calva E, Cravioto A, Eslava C, Amabile-Cuevas CF. Urban dust fecal pollution in Mexico City: Antibiotic resitance and virulence factors of *Escherichia coli. International Journal of Hygiene and Environmental Health* 2006;209:461-470.

Schaper M, Jofre J. Comparison of methods for detecting genotypes of F - specific RNA bacteriophages and fingerprinting the origin of faecal pollution in Water Samples. *Journal of Virological Methods* 2000;89:1–10.

Schaper M, Jofre J, Uys M, Grabow WOK. Distribution of genotypes of F-specific RNA bacteriophages in human and non-human sources of faecal pollution in South Africa and Spain. *Journal of Applied Microbiology* 2002a;92:657-667.

Schaper M, Duran AE, Jofre J. Comparative resistance of phage isolates of four genotypes of F-specific RNA bacteriophages to various inactivation processes. *Applied and Environmental Microbiology* 2002b;68:3702-3707.

Scott TM, Rose JB, Jenkins TM, Farrah SR, Lukasik J. Microbial source tracking: current methodology and future directions. *Applied and Environmental Microbiology* 2002;68:5796–5803.

Sinton LW, Finley RK, Hannah DJ. Distinguishing human from animal faecal contamination in water: A review. *New Zealand Journal of Marine and Fresh Water Research* 1998;32:323-348.

Skraber S, Gassilloud B, Schwartzbrod L, Gantzer C. Survival of infectious poliovirus-1 in river water compared to the persistence of somatic coliphages, thermotolerant coliforms and poliovirus-1 genome. *Water Research* 2004;38:2927-2933.

Sobsey MD, Dufour AP, Gerba CP, LeChavallier MW, Payment P. Using a conceptual framework for assessing risks to health from microbes in drinking water. *Journal of the American Water Works Association* 1993;85:44-48.

Sobsey MD. *Managing water in the home: Accelerated health gains from improved water supply*. World Health Organization Sustainable Development and Healthy Environments. World Health Organization, Geneva. WHO/SDE/WSH/02.07. 2002.

Theron J, Cloete TE. Emerging waterborne infections: contributing factors, agents and detection tools. *Critical Reviews in Microbiology* 2002;28:1-26.

UN. *United Nations Millennium Declaration.* General Assembly Res. 55/2. 18 September 2000.

Uys M. MSc Dissertation: *Molecular characterisation of F-specific RNA phages in South Africa*. Department of Medical Virology, University of Pretoria, South Africa. 1999.

Venkatesan MI, Santiago CA. Sterols in ocean sediments : novel tracers to examine habitats of cetaceans, pinnipeds, penguins and humans. *Marine Biology* 1989;102:431–437.

Vivian CMG. Tracers of sewage sludge in the marine environment: a review. *The Science of the Total Environment* 1986;53:5–40.

Watson JT. *Introduction to mass spectrometry*. 2nd ed. New York: Raven Press; 1985.

WHO. The world health report: Reducing risks, promoting healthy life. World Health Organization, Geneva. Internet URL: *http://www.who.int/whr/en. 2002a.*

WHO. Water for Development: A practical advocacy guide for World Water Day 2002. Internet URL: *http://www.worldwaterday.org/advocacy/adv.html*. 2002b.

WHO. *Heterotrophic plate count measurement in drinking water safety management, Protection of the Human environment.* Water, Sanitation and Health. World Health Organization, Geneva. WHO/SDE/WSH/02.10. 2002c.

Writer JH, Leenheer JA, Barber LB, Amy GL, Chapra SC. Sewage contamination in the upper Mississippi river as measured by the fecal sterol, coprostanol. *Water Research* 1995;29:1427–1436.

In: Environmental Microbiology Research Trends
Editor: G. V. Kurladze, pp. 167-190
ISBN: 978-1-60021-939-9

Chapter 5

The Effects of Fine Scale Environmental Variation on Microbial Community Structure and Function in Aquatic Environments

Kurt A. Smart[1], Hsuanhua L. Smart[#] and Colin R. Jackson[1*]
[1]The University of Mississippi, Department of Biology, Shoemaker Hall, MS, USA
[#]The University of Mississippi, Department of Mathematics, Hume Hall, MS, USA

Abstract

Molecular and biochemical approaches have revealed that microbial communities in natural aquatic environments are more diverse than previously thought. However, few studies have examined how fine scale changes in environmental conditions can alter the structure, diversity, and function of aquatic microorganisms. We performed a number of studies that examined the influence of fine scale changes such as particle size or spatial location on microbial communities in freshwater systems. Bacterial communities associated with different sizes of particles in wetland sediment were characterized using 16S rRNA gene sequencing, which revealed fundamental differences in the structure of communities associated with very fine (0.063-0.25 mm diameter) and fine (0.25-1 mm) particles. Similarly, microbial activity was also influenced by particle size with different activities of lignin and cellulose degrading enzymes associated with different sized particles. Fine (cm) scale spatial variation in microbial activity was also seen on decomposing leaves in a stream, and spatial patterns in cellulose degrading enzymes suggest that the process of organic matter decomposition shows high spatial heterogeneity. Together, these findings demonstrate that aquatic microbial communities vary both structurally and functionally over finer scales than are usually considered in environmental microbiology. This variation should be considered in future surveys of microbial diversity and activity in environmental samples.

---

* Send correspondence to Dr. Colin R. Jackson.

INTRODUCTION

Interest in microbial community structure and function in aquatic ecosystems has been increasing dramatically. The significance of microorganisms in biogeochemical cycles and ecosystem function has been noted since Lindeman [1] placed the bacterial 'ooze' at the center of his trophic cycle, but until the last few decades bacteria were often regarded as a single entity in aquatic environments as studying them in any detail was difficult. Recent developments in molecular and biochemical techniques are helping to overcome that difficulty and are beginning to shed some light on microbial processes at very fine scales [2]. These new methods and techniques are allowing more accurate, detailed descriptions of microbial communities and their activities, and are revealing how diverse these communities are, both in structure and function.

To understand how microorganisms interact with each other and with their environment, it is important to consider the scale at which the interactions occur. Microorganisms respond to localized, fine-scale changes in their environment, both spatially and temporally, and it is important that these responses and interactions be understood more thoroughly [3]. On a hierarchal scale, where organizational levels are created from lower levels but also act to create higher levels of organization, it is important to consider multiple levels as the relationships between levels are what provide the insights into the function of the system [4]. Lower levels of hierarchal organization (i.e. fine scales) are highly variable and operate at high rates, but those rates can be averaged out when looking at the system from higher levels [5]. By overlooking processes and patterns at fine scales, any variability that may be present is missed, making it impossible to know what is actually occurring to create the larger scale system and its function. Looking at patchiness in planktonic organisms, Krembs *et al.* [6] argue that concentration dependent rate processes may be underestimated by failing to take into account fine-scale spatial variability. Knowledge of such fine-scale processes are critical in understanding larger scale phenomenon, such as ecosystem or global level cycles, as fine-scale interactions and activities of microorganisms combine together to form these larger scale processes. Until recently, the ability to observe and measure fine-scale microbial processes was very limited.

Early studies of environmental microbiology relied upon culture-based methods for describing microbial communities. However, the vast majority of prokaryotic species could not be cultured, and most still have yet to be cultured using current culturing techniques. Culture-based methods greatly underestimate the diversity of natural microbial communities, and may select for organisms which either do not make up a significant portion of the community or do not contribute a great deal to the activity of the community, providing a skewed representation of what is actually present. Rapid advances in molecular and biochemical methods have allowed microbial communities to be described without the bias involved in culturing techniques [2]. They have also become increasingly sensitive, enhancing the ability for measurement on finer and finer scales. The application of the polymerase chain reaction (PCR) has been the most significant development for dealing with environmental microorganisms, allowing replication of minute amounts of environmental DNA into quantities large enough to be analyzed. The use of fluorescently labeled compounds has also greatly benefited environmental microbiology, detecting organisms and measuring a wide range of enzymatic or metabolic processes at very high sensitivities.

Fluorescent *in-situ* hybridization (FISH) combined with confocal laser microscopy has enabled direct observations of microbial community structure [7]. Along with molecular tools and advances in microscopy, the development of new biochemical assays and instruments have proved helpful in measuring fine-scale activities and function [8]. Microsensors have also been widely implemented in determining microenvironmental conditions and processes, measuring chemical concentrations and gradients over very fine scales [9]. The use of such methods and several more are discussed in this chapter, primarily focusing on the effects of fine-scale environmental variation on aquatic microbial communities. We follow the discussion by presenting two examples of studies that we performed examining fine scale patterns in the structure and function of microbial communities in aquatic environments.

Microorganisms do not show homogeneous distribution patterns in any aquatic environment. Microbial species composition and abundance in lakes are known to vary with depth, depending upon physical (e.g. light availability, temperature), chemical (e.g. O_2, CO_2), and biological (e.g. symbiotic or predator-prey relationships) characteristics [10]. They are also known to vary between littoral and pelagic habitats, and seasonally [10]. In lotic systems the distribution varies more with horizontal rather than vertical profiles because of differences in hydrological conditions [11]. However, our knowledge of that variability is based upon observations at spatial scales of meters or tens of meters, and temporal scales of weeks to months. Microorganisms have more recently been shown to be heterogeneously distributed throughout the water column, on submerged surfaces, and in aquatic sediments over much finer spatial and temporal scales.

Fine Scale Variation in Microbial Communities in the Water Column of Aquatic Environments

Microorganisms are found to be very heterogeneously distributed in the water column of aquatic environments. Bacterioplankton abundance has been shown to vary in pelagic marine environments on a scale of several millimeters [12], and at even finer scales bacteria have been shown to form aggregates or associations on or near suspended organic particles [13] and phytoplankton [14], or with other microorganisms [15]. Microbial communities have even been observed to be patchily distributed on the surfaces of particulate matter, demonstrating how small the microenvironments that they inhabit are [16]. There appear to be several reasons for this non-uniform distribution.

The most obvious reason is the availability of nutrients. Live phytoplankton release photosynthetic byproducts that attract high concentrations of bacteria [14]. Phytoplankton are not distributed evenly throughout the water column, and may be more heterogeneously distributed than previously thought, forming thin layers or concentrated sheets that may be only centimeters thick [17]. These concentrated layers of phytoplankton are also highly concentrated with bacteria. Particulate organic matter (POM) is also a prime source of nutrients and energy, and is the remains of larger organic matter which has been partially degraded by bacteria and fungi. In comparison to the surrounding water column, POM is rich in nutrients, and microorganisms aggregate around POM, increasing overall spatial heterogeneity [18]. Over fine scales the distribution of detrital particles is not uniform, which further increases the heterogeneous distribution of microorganisms [18]. Detrital particles vary greatly in size, shape, and nutrient composition, but in all cases it is a much more plentiful source of nutrients and carbon for bacteria and fungi than scavenging in the surrounding water.

The majority of particulate matter-microbial community research has focused on particulate matter towards the larger end of the size scale. These large particles, or macroaggregates, dubbed 'marine snow', 'lake snow', and more recently 'river snow', were the first to be studied in detail as they are easily visible with the naked eye (typically ≥0.5 mm in diameter). However, macroaggregates are formed from finer particles which are bound together with transparent exopolymer particles produced by algae, diatoms, and bacteria [19]. These aggregates are composed of a wide variety of smaller particles, such as diatom frustules, dead phytoplankton cells, fecal matter, or decomposing plant matter, and are highly variable in both nutrient content and availability. Nutrients in POM are not homogenously distributed, and not all particles are equal in nutritional quality or availability; fine-scale heterogeneity of attached microorganisms may therefore be increased by the surfaces of the particles they are attached to.

A variety of forces, both physical and biological, act to create very steep physical and chemical gradients associated with POM. Respiration of heterotrophic bacteria colonizing both the interior and surface of particles can create an oxygen gradient [20] and the diffusion of gases and dissolved nutrients is constrained within the inner core of aggregates [21]. Smith *et al.* [22] measured the activity of a wide range of hydrolytic enzymes on individual aggregates of marine snow collected off the California coast and found high variability in all of the enzymes tested, suggesting their are major differences between particles. The surface area of POM is more variable than is normally considered, which may explain some of the variability in activity and chemical and physical gradients. Over very fine scales the surface of detritus can be very fractal in nature, which would mean that the microbial communities are not spread evenly across a perfect sphere as is often assumed [23]. Interstitial spaces may also be highly variable between particles [24]. These gradients may lead to differences in community structure as they create a wide range of microenvironments with dramatically different physical conditions.

Not all of the microenvironments occur on or in the particle itself, however, such as the formation of nutrient plumes released from sinking POM. On the surface of POM, heterotrophic bacteria and fungi attached to the surface produce extracellular enzymes, hydrolyzing the POM and releasing nutrients which are then free to be taken up by the colonizing microbes. Not all of the nutrients released by this enzymatic degradation are taken up by the colonizing microorganisms, and some may leak into the surrounding water column [13]. As a particle sinks the fluid flow past the particle creates a trail, or plume, of released nutrients in the wake of the particle. These plumes have been observed to be several meters in length and remain intact for several minutes [25]. Plumes of this nature attract chemotactic bacteria, zooplankton, and protists which are thought to be well-adapted to life unattached to particles and may also play a role in attracting new inhabitants to particles [25].

All of the particles examined to date have been found to support highly abundant and diverse microbial communities, with the species composition of suspended particles being shown to be different from that of free-living microbial populations. In a study of the Columbia River estuary, Crump *et al.* [26] compared the 16S rRNA gene sequences of aggregate-associated bacteria with those of free-living bacteria and observed major differences in freshwater, saltwater, and brackish environments. DeLong *et al.* [27] compared the 16S rRNA gene sequences of aggregate-associated bacteria with those of free-living bacteria in marine waters and found they were also very distinct: aggregate-associated species were typically members of the Cytophagales, Planctomycetes, and gamma-Proteobacteria, while the free-living species were all alpha-Proteobacteria. In a similar analysis in Lake Constance, alpha-Proteobacteria were found to be the dominant members of the macroaggregate-associated community along with the beta-Proteobacteria, although alpha-Proteobacteria were not detected on finer microaggregates [28]. This suggests that bacterial communities may be adapted to the microenvironments of particulate matter and possibly to specific niches within those microenvironments. 'River snow' also appears to have different aggregate-associated microbial communities [16] and the structure of microbial communities appears to differ between these environments, but the reasons for this are still unknown. We describe differences in bacterial community structure associated with different sizes of particles later in this chapter.

As well as supporting diverse communities of microorganisms, detrital particles are also described as 'hot-spots' of microbial activity, supporting microbial populations several orders of magnitude greater than the surrounding environment, with larger, more active individual cells [29]. Growth rates are much greater for attached bacteria because of their elevated activity and the greater availability of nutrients [30]. Upon attaching to surfaces, planktonic bacteria up-regulate their activity and increase production of extracellular enzymes; enzymatic activity of attached bacteria can be orders of magnitude greater than planktonic bacteria [31]. Up-regulation occurs very suddenly, within minutes, and leads to rapid decomposition of the detritus and remineralization of nutrients [25]. There is a very dynamic structure to the fine-scale formation and degradation of macroaggregates, which has significance at larger scales. Macroaggregates are degraded by highly active bacteria and smaller particles are released; the degradation of aggregates effect the rate at which they sink, with larger particles sinking at a greater rate [32]. As particles are degraded and reformed rather rapidly, it may reduce the overall sinking rate and allow more time for microbial remineralization of nutrients, which has major implications for carbon cycling and sedimentation in aquatic environments.

Microorganisms are closely associated on POM and it is likely that competition for resources is high. There is some evidence that suggests microbial communities are functioning as consortia with interspecific interactions that enhance the ability of other microorganisms to colonize the substrate and take up nutrients at a greater rate, as Grossart *et al.* [33] found that the presence of certain bacterial species on aggregates enhanced the ability of other species to colonize the substrate while reducing the ability of others. It is also likely there are fine spatial and temporal scale successional patterns occurring in these microenvironments [34]. Very little is known about competition, succession, or mutualistic relationships on aggregates, but it seems likely considering the interactions in other closely associated microbial communities, such as biofilms.

A possible advantage to the patchy distribution of microorganisms may be defense against predation. Predation by protists can significantly control bacterial populations, and grazing pressure from protists has been shown to alter the dominant cell morphology within bacterial communities [35]. Other species may form large colonies to avoid predation [15]. Residing on large particles may provide similar benefits, although other studies have found that protists are also closely associated with aggregates and that grazing pressure on aggregates is quite high [13]. Higher bacterial growth rates on POM may be able to overcome grazing effects, or may be a response to them. It is also possible that particle-associated bacterial communities may form biofilms, producing extracellular polymeric substances (EPS) which may offer some grazing protection. More attention is being given to understanding such interactions, but it is highly speculative and too early to draw any general conclusions.

FINE SCALE VARIATION IN BIOFILMS

Microorganisms colonize every available submerged surface in aquatic environments, and attached microorganisms are often present in much higher numbers than microorganisms unattached to surfaces [36]. Microorganisms inhabiting surfaces form densely packed, complex, interactive communities (biofilms) composed of living cells and both organic and inorganic matter heterogeneously distributed in both horizontal and vertical directions and encased in EPS. Biofilms provide an advantage for microorganisms in stressful environments, such as those exposed to extreme temperatures or pH, and almost function as multicellular organisms [37]. Very fine-scale interactions and dynamics, both temporal and spatial, occur within biofilms, between biofilms and the colonized substratum, and between biofilms and the surrounding environment, which exhibit a wide array of functions and metabolic processes and which play a significant role in nutrient and energy cycling in aquatic ecosystems [38].

Bacteria that come into contact with and attach to surfaces form microcolonies which spread both across the surface and upwards above the surface in a three-dimensional manner. This colonization and growth leads to spatial heterogeneity of biofilms as microcolonies approach each other and as microenvironments are formed in both the horizontal and vertical planes. Across the substratum heterogeneity in biofilm structure is caused by both the presence of other inhabitants and by the surface to which the biofilm is attached. Surfaces vary greatly in chemical and physical characteristics, and microbial communities respond to those differences. Jones *et al.* [39] found that the microbial communities on different artificial substrata in an estuary were similar in species composition during the early stages of biofilm formation but were different after a week of incubation. Their results suggest that attachment is at first random, but that characteristics of the substratum favor certain microbial inhabitants over others. At very fine scales surfaces can be highly heterogeneous and fractal in nature, which affects not only the surface area available for colonization but also environmental conditions, such as flow, which can affect pH, nutrient availability, waste removal, and oxygen availability, among others [40, 41]. Fine-scale surface characteristics can have large-scale impacts, such as significant alterations in microbial productivity and respiration in stream ecosystems [42].

Other forces also act to create heterogeneity in both microbial community structure and activity within biofilms. Communication between microbial populations is a dominant factor, responsible for coordinating the activity of the tightly connected communities, as biofilms contain structures not seen in other microbial communities and are very detailed at fine scales [43]. Channels are also formed throughout the biofilm, allowing water to flow through the film, transporting nutrients and wastes. The flow is often less than that at the surface of the biofilm and has been observed to flow both with and against the surface current [44], demonstrating the differences in physical forces acting upon organisms within biofilms compared to the surface.

A large portion of the biofilm may consist of inactive or dormant cells that are not contributing to the activity measured at larger scales. Francoeur *et al.* [45] demonstrated this heterogeneity using fluorescently-labeled substrate to detect extracellular protease activity, observing a few highly active cells surrounded by a void of inactive, or 'dead', cells. Analysis of a biofilm in drinking water that received an addition of several substrates demonstrated similar spatial heterogeneity in microbial activity [46].

As mentioned previously, communication between microbial populations in biofilms is an important factor that operates at very fine spatial and temporal scales. Chemical signals within biofilm matrices are more concentrated than signals outside of biofilms, likely because of decreased flow rates in biofilms and the high density of extracellular polymeric substances that encapsulate them, reducing the diffusion rate of the signal and localizing its effects [47]. The hydrophobic properties of many of the signal molecules may also allow the signal to remain localized [43]. Other gradients within the biofilm, such as pH gradients, also restrict the dispersion of signals by affecting the degradation rate of the chemical [43]. Restricted diffusion of signals in biofilms is another example of an extremely fine-scale process that could have a tremendous impact on larger scale functions.

In addition to the patterns already noted regarding heterogeneity across surfaces, the vertical dimension of biofilms also creates diverse microenvironments as biofilms are often several hundred micrometers thick and support a wide range of metabolic activities [48]. Diffusion of gases or nutrients through the biofilm matrix is often restricted, and microsensor measurements show that anoxic conditions can occur within 30 micrometers of the surface even if the surface is saturated with oxygen [49]. At different levels within the vertical profile of biofilms there are distinct functional processes occurring and often specific community compositions. Even in single-species biofilms grown under laboratory conditions there can be differentiation of cells and a non-uniform distribution of function [50]. Biofilms contain niches and microenvironments which allow important processes to occur that would otherwise not be possible in the particular environment. Okabe *et al.* [51] found that sulfate-reducing bacteria were dominant at the oxic-anoxic chemocline in activated sludge biofilms and formed a thin, highly active sulfate-reducing layer in the film. Microenvironments within biofilms enable sulfate-reducing bacteria to be active in an otherwise aerobic environment [52], and other metabolic processes can show similar patterns in biofilms [53, 54].

Protozoan grazing of biofilms also affects the structure and function of biofilm bacterial communities and plays a major role in influencing fine-scale interactions within biofilms. Biofilms might be thought to offer protection against predation by protists, but protozoan grazing can dramatically affect biofilm population dynamics [55]. Grazing has been shown to increase heterogeneity of biofilms as protists preferentially graze on small patches in the biofilm, significantly reducing the local microbial populations [56]. Protists also appear to target areas that others have already grazed, emphasizing local grazing patterns [56]. The cause of this selective grazing is not yet known, but it is likely to have an effect on larger-scale processes.

Temporal scales are also important to consider, as microorganisms present in younger, newly developing biofilms, appear to be much more active than those in mature biofilms [46]. Conditioning of the substratum and the subsequent attachment of microbes occur at very fine temporal scales and growth and spread of colonies over the surface is rapid, with surfaces introduced to aquatic environments being densely covered in a few days. Over longer time intervals biofilm communities undergo successional changes as the biofilm develops and matures [57]. These changes in community composition are a result of fine-scale interactions and changes in microenvironmental conditions which enable a more diverse set of metabolic activities [58]. Microbial inhabitants of biofilms are closely linked to each other, often forming a consortium of interacting organisms, benefiting one another by co-metabolizing substrates or metabolizing each others waste products. They are very intricately detailed communities which appear to function almost as multicellular organisms.

Fine Scale Variation in Microbial Communities in Sediments

Aquatic sediments share many of the characteristics of biofilms and suspended POM, and fine-scale heterogeneity of microbial community structure and function are similar. Sediments consist of a wide range of particles that are diverse in both physical and chemical characteristics, varying greatly in size, shape, density, organic and inorganic nutrient composition, and surface features [18]. The environment in which the sediment particles are located are also highly diverse and significantly impact the structure and activity of the microbial biota inhabiting them; river and stream sediments are markedly different than their lake and ocean counterparts, and tidal sediments have their own distinct properties due to the very different physical forces acting upon them [59 - 61]. River and stream sediments are constantly changing as sediments are pushed downstream and resuspended from the benthos. Lake sediments fluctuate because of suspended particles settling out, and tidal sediments fluctuate in response to tidal currents at fine temporal scales.

Sediments are similar to biofilms in regard to their vertical profiles, where different processes occur at different depths and where microenvironmental variations support a diverse range of activities. The inability of nutrients and gases to diffuse evenly through sediments creates layers which are significantly different in composition of nutrients and energy [62]. In lotic systems, turbulent flow that disrupts sediments can greatly increase bacterial density and activity on fine-scales, especially at the sediment surface [63]. Fine-scale fluctuations in pore size and sediment topography also lead to highly diverse patterns in biogeochemical cycles at fine temporal (seconds) and spatial (cm) scales, increasing or decreasing the flow of water through sediments and altering the physical and chemical microenvironment [64].

Dynamics on the surface of particles in sediments are similar to the dynamics on suspended particles, with differences in activity having been measured between different size fractions of particles in sediments in a wide range of aquatic habitats. Finer particles in wetland and river sediments have greater bacterial biomass and productivity compared with coarser particles [65]. Particle size also influences extracellular enzyme activity and bacterial community structure, as we describe later in this chapter.

Uneven distribution of nutrients and energy also results in fine scale heterogeneity in sediments. Particulate matter is not distributed homogeneously in sediments and is not distributed evenly over time. In aquatic systems organic matter is distributed in patches, as in the case of allocthonous plant matter [66] or decaying fish and plankton carcasses [67].

Uneven distribution of organic nutrients in wetland sediments has been shown to be correlated with spatial heterogeneity in methane production [68], suggesting spatial patterns in methanogen communities. Fine-scale spatial heterogeneity may also arise due to metal contamination, as pollutants such as lead and mercury are often patchily distributed [69]. A study of heavy metal contaminated soils revealed that the composition and activity of microbial communities varied dramatically over fine scales, with the potential metabolic activity varying up to 10,000 fold over a single centimeter [70].

Invertebrate burrowing can also increase the heterogeneity of microenvironments in aquatic sediments, creating oxic conditions in layers of sediment that would otherwise be anaerobic [71]. Invertebrates, fish, and other macrofauna are also responsible for disturbing sediments and altering microenvironments, altering fine-scale distributions of nutrients and microorganisms while feeding or traveling along the benthos [72]. Variability at fine scales may also arise because of aquatic plants and their root structure, with bacterial populations in the rhizosphere differing from those in the surrounding sediment [73]. Fine-scale interactions are common within the rhizosphere as a variety of factors influence nutrient availability and environmental conditions over small areas [74].

The Effects of Particle Size on Bacterial Community Structure and Activity in Wetland Sediments

As stated previously, particle size influences bacterial biomass and productivity in aquatic sediments [65]. At relatively coarse scales, sediment particle size also influences the structure of the associated microbial community. Particles in aquatic environments can be designated as either coarse particulate organic matter (CPOM, >1 mm diameter) or fine particulate organic matter (FPOM, <1 mm diameter) based upon size [75], and there are differences in the microorganisms associated with these classes of particles. Fungi are thought to dominate the decomposition of CPOM, whereas the smaller size of FPOM limits the growth of fungal hyphae and bacteria tend to be more abundant [76]. However, fewer studies have examined how bacterial community structure changes with decreasing size of FPOM, i.e. how fine scale changes in particle size might influence the attached bacterial community. While FPOM refers to all particles below 1 mm in diameter, it essentially consists of particles that are the remains of decomposing CPOM, and smaller (generally <100-200 μm diameter) particles that may come from a variety of sources, such as the precipitation and flocculation of dissolved material [77]. Given these differences, it seems reasonable to hypothesize that there may be differences in the bacterial communities associated with different sizes of FPOM, and basic DNA-DNA dot blot hybridizations have suggested that this is indeed the case [78]. The DNA-DNA hybridization technique does not directly assess community structure or diversity, however, and interpretation of patterns can be problematic [79]. Thus, we used 16S rRNA sequencing techniques to investigate the structure and diversity of the bacterial community present on different sizes of particles in wetland sediments. A companion study examined microbial extracellular enzyme activity associated with the different sizes of particles.

Sediment samples were collected from a cypress-tupelo swamp in southeastern Louisiana, USA, and sieved into two size ranges of particles (38-250 and 250-1000 μm diameter). DNA was extracted from each size range of particles using a modified version of a protocol originally designed for soil [80] but also used for geothermal spring sediment [81]. Residual humic contamination was subsequently removed from extractions using Sepharose 4B spin columns [82]. DNA extracted from both sizes of particles was used as the template in PCR amplifications [81] using primers specific for Domain Bacteria. These primers (Bac8f and Univ1492r) amplify positions 8-1492 of the 16S rRNA gene in Bacteria [83]. PCR products were purified, cloned into artificial plasmid vectors, and clone libraries (one for each size of particles) generated following procedures described previously [84]. The inserts from the first 96 clones obtained in each library were amplified and digested with three separate restriction enzymes (EcoRI, RsaI, HaeIII; 2 h digest at 37°C). After each digest the resulting restriction patterns were visualized on agarose gels. Clones in the same library that showed the same restriction patterns for all three restriction enzymes were assumed to have similar 16S rRNA genes inserted and were grouped together as a single phylotype [81, 84].

The frequency of each phylotype in each clone library was used to estimate the total bacterial richness present on particles of each size range using the non-parametric abundance-based estimator (S_{Chao1}) of Chao [85]. Calculations were performed using a web interface [86]. For each dominant phylotype, a portion of the 16S rRNA gene insert in one representative clone was sequenced, using the original Bac8f primer. This sequencing protocol yielded approximately 600 bp of sequence information, corresponding to roughly the 50-650 bp region of the 16S rRNA gene. The partial 16S rRNA sequences obtained were compared to those in GenBank to identify closest relatives and subsequently imported into the ARB software package [87]. Sequences were aligned automatically (FastAligner) and alignments checked manually. Because the partial 16S rRNA gene sequences obtained in this study represented a number of diverse lineages, novel phylogenetic trees were not constructed as this might produce erroneous results compared to existing relationships for major bacterial taxa. Rather, ARB's "Quick add by parsimony" function was used to incorporate the sequences into existing phylogenetic trees in the ARB database. 16S rRNA sequences in the existing trees that were unrelated to those obtained in this study were subsequently removed without altering tree topology, so that phylogenetic trees showing only the lineages specific to this study were obtained. This treeing procedure has been used previously to minimize distortions to established tree topologies that might arise from a phylogenetic analysis of short, highly divergent sequences [84].

When S_{Chao1} was calculated by repeated random sampling from each library, estimates of the total bacterial phylotype richness in the original community were 177 phylotypes associated with larger particles and 288 phylotypes associated with the finer particles. In each case, S_{Chao1} began to approach a stable asymptotic value although this was not pronounced for the clone library derived from the finer sediment particles (Figure 1). This suggests that while the estimated richness for the community associated with primary particles is a reasonable approximation, the value of S_{Chao1} determined for the community associated with the finer, secondary particles is probably an underestimate. Thus, not only does the structure of the bacterial community differ between sediment particles of different size ranges, but overall community properties such as species diversity appear to differ also, with finer particles harboring substantially more diverse bacterial communities. This supports previous observations of increased bacterial community heterogeneity with decreasing FPOM particle size in aquatic sediments, and may be the result of increasing surface area/volume ratios on finer particles, which would result in greater relative habitat area and more available ecological niches [78]. The greater chemical complexity of secondary particles could also account for increased bacterial diversity on those particles.

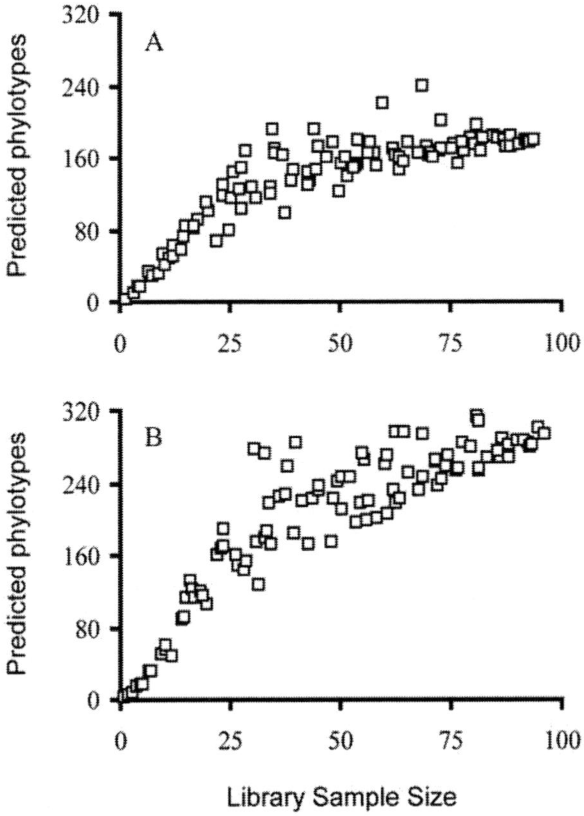

Figure 1. Predicted species (phylotype) richness as determined from analyses of 16S rRNA clone libraries generated from bacterial communities associated with two different sizes of particles (A: 250-1000 μm diameter; B: 38-250 μm diameter) in wetland sediments. Finer particles (B) harbor substantially more diverse bacterial communities than coarser particles (A).

Most 16S rRNA sequences showed low (<97 %) similarity to those already in the GenBank/EMBL/DDBJ databases. The majority of phylotypes occurred just once in each library, and repeated phylotypes were relatively rare. Across both sizes of particles, the sequenced phylotypes represented thirteen major bacterial lineages as well as a number of other taxa that have only been described from molecular studies. Sequences affiliated with the delta- and beta-Proteobacteria were the most abundant sequences found in the clone libraries for both sizes of particles, although the delta-Proteobacteria were more dominant in the library generated from 250-1000 μm particles (Figure 2). Both of these groups, along with the alpha-Proteobacteria are typically dominant in freshwater sediment communities [88]. Sequences affiliated with the alpha-Proteobacteria were abundant in the clone library derived from the larger particles but were comparatively rare in the finer particle library (Figure 2). Similar differences between the two clone libraries were also seen for the Chlorobi (green sulfur bacteria), Nitrospira, and Spirochaetes, the latter being undetected in the clone library derived from 38-250 μm particles. In contrast, the library derived from these finer particles contained more 16S rRNA sequences affiliated with the Verrucomicrobia, Chloroflexi (green non-sulfur bacteria), and various uncultured bacterial lineages (Figure 2). Thus, the 16S rRNA sequences derived from the different size ranges of particles showed appreciable differences in their phylogenetic affiliation at broad taxonomic levels.

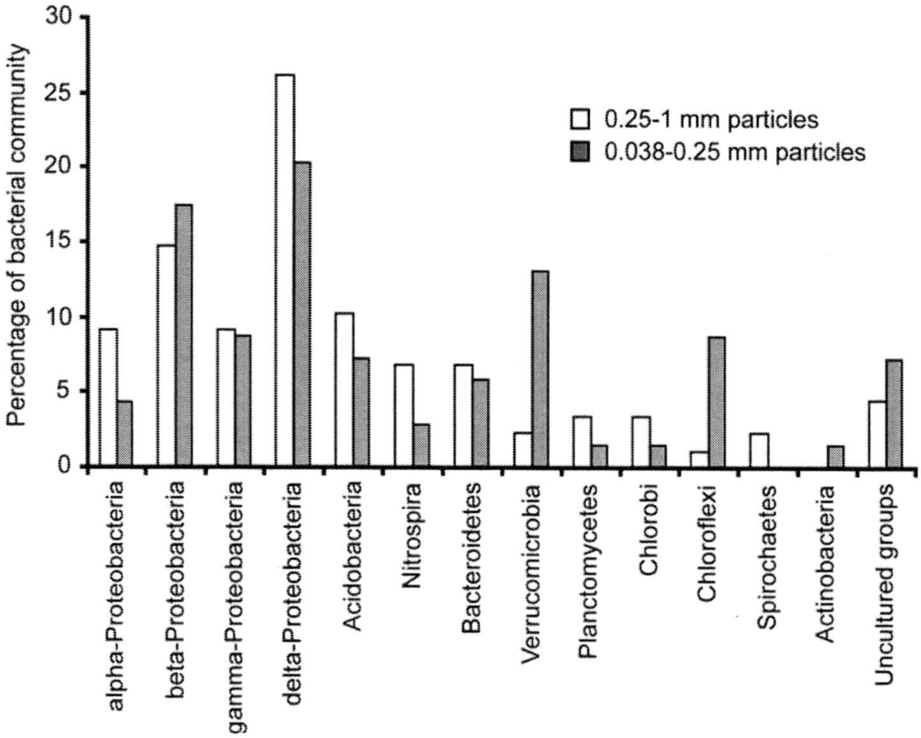

Figure 2. Frequency of major bacterial lineages in 16S rRNA clone libraries generated from PCR-amplified DNA extracted from two different sizes of fine particles (0.25-1mm diameter and 0.038-0.25 mm diameter) in wetland sediments. Representative of some bacterial lineages were found associated with both sizes of particles, but other groups are specific to just one type of particle, suggesting variation in bacterial community structure at fine scales.

The identity of the dominant phylotypes in each clone library also differed substantially. 16S rRNA sequences affiliated with members of the Bacteroides and the Methylococcales (gamma-Proteobacteria), a group of methanotrophic Bacteria, were the most abundant individual phylotypes in the clone library derived from larger particles, and these phylotypes each accounted for 5% of the clones sequenced. Other specific phylotypes that were abundant in this clone library were affiliated with the Rhodocyclales (beta-Proteobacteria), Pseudomonadales (gamma-Proteobacteria), and Myxococcales (delta-Proteobacteria). None of these orders of Bacteria were represented by abundant phylotypes in the clone library derived from finer particles. As might be expected from its higher diversity, the distribution of cloned sequences in this library was more even, with no individual phylotypes accounting for more than 3% of the community composition. Thus, as well as the two clone libraries differing in overall phylotype diversity and in general phylogenetic composition, they also differed in the specific groups of Bacteria that were most abundant within each.

Only one phylotype was found in both libraries. This is despite sequences being grouped into phylotypes by a fairly liberal 97% sequence similarity criterion, which would have led to increased overlap. This phylotype was affiliated with the Nitrosomonadales (beta-Proteobacteria) and was represented by just a single clone sampled in each library. Other than that phylotype, the two libraries contained no overlapping 16S rRNA genes, at least as apparent from sampling 96 clones within each. While it's possible that this may represent inadequate sampling, it strongly suggests that the different size ranges of particles harbor very different bacterial communities.

Differences between bacterioplankton and particle- or sediment-associated bacterial communities have been previously reported for aquatic environments [27, 89], but the influence of particle size on aquatic bacterial community structure or function has rarely been specifically addressed. This is in contrast to terrestrial ecosystems where soil particle size distributions (e.g. sand, silt, and clay) and their associations with organic matter are known to result in spatially heterogeneous environments [90]. This heterogeneity can result in differences in the bacterial populations associated with the different soil particle size fractions, and the influence of particle size on the structure of the bacterial community can be greater than that of larger scale treatments [91]. The results from this study clearly show differences in the bacterial phylotypes present in 16S rRNA clone libraries derived from DNA associated with 250-1000 μm and 38-250 μm diameter FPOM in wetland sediments. Sediment was separated into the two different size ranges by a wet sieving procedure, and because this involves washing the sediment with running water, unattached cells are likely to be removed. Thus, the differences in the bacterial phylotypes present in each size range are likely to reflect actual differences in the microbial communities attached to these types of particles.

Functional differences in the microbial communities associated with different sizes of sediment particles were examined by assaying microbial extracellular enzyme activity. Enzymes such as cellobiohydrolase, beta-glucosidase, and beta-xylosidase are involved in the microbial degradation of lignocellulose and the activity of these enzymes has been linked to rates of POM decomposition [8, 92]. Sediment was collected from the same wetland site and sieved into five different sizes of particles of diameters 1000-2000 μm, 500-1000 μm, 250-500 μm, 125-250 μm, and 63-125 μm. Material in each size range was assayed for the activity of four extracellular enzymes (beta-glucosidase, cellobiohydrolase, beta-xylosidase, and beta-n-acetylglucosaminidase) using artificial p-nitrophenol linked substrates [84, 92]. Absorbance of the resulting end product was determined at 410 nm and converted to micromoles of substrate consumed using standard values [84].

Activity of all four enzymes was correlated (R values > 0.90 for each pair wise comparison) and declined on particles below 500 μm (Figure 3). This decline was consistent as particle size was further reduced, with the lowest activity of all enzymes being found associated with particles collected on the 63 μm sieve. The decline in activity on particles finer than 500 μm strongly suggests functional differences in the attached microbial community, and supports the differences in bacterial community structure reported above. Given that extracellular enzyme activity is related to rates of organic matter decomposition and nutrient cycling, these fine scale differences in microbial activity with particle size suggest that rates of lignocellulose degradation and other aspects of ecosystem function also differ over fine spatial scales.

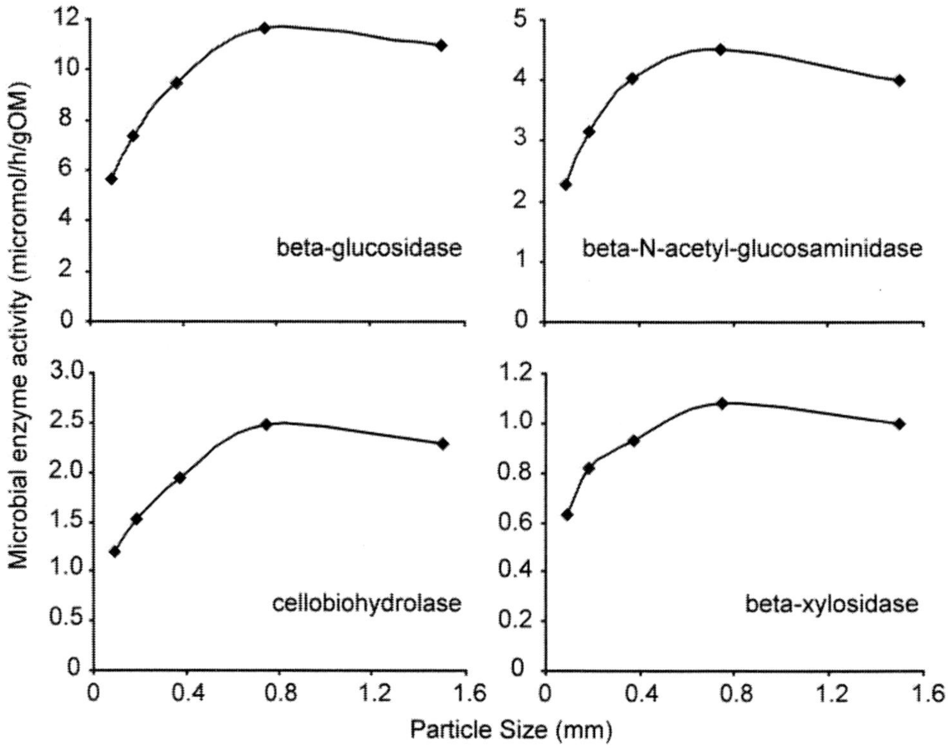

Figure 3. Changes in the activity of microbial extracellular enzymes associated with decreasing particle size in wetland sediments. Each point represents the mean of three sediment samples collected concurrently.

FINE SCALE SPATIAL VARIATION IN MICROBIAL ACTIVITY ACROSS THE SURFACE OF DECOMPOSING LEAVES

Variation in microbial enzyme activity and community structure with different sizes of fine particulate organic matter is one example of how fine scale environmental variation affects aquatic microbial communities. A more direct measurement of spatial variation in microbial activity could be made by examining distribution patterns of enzyme activity across the surface of larger particles, such as decomposing leaves in aquatic systems. The surface of living leaves, or phyllosphere, supports variable microbial populations of bacteria and fungi and colonization of the phyllosphere is random and patchy [93]. However, no studies have looked at spatial variation in microbial activity on decomposing leaf-litter at fine scales. In this study we examined the fine-scale variation in microbial extracellular enzyme activity across the surface of decomposing leaves in a small stream. As we stated previously in this chapter, the activities of lignocellulose-degrading enzymes are a reliable measure of rates of cellulose and lignin decomposition, as leaf-litter is composed primarily of lignin and cellulose, both of which require enzymatic degradation to be metabolized [8]. Here we measure the activities of two extracellular enzymes involved in cellulose decomposition (beta-glucosidase and cellobiohydrolase), and a combination of peroxidase and phenol oxidase activity as a broad measurement of enzymes involved in lignin decomposition.

Freshly fallen leaves of sycamore (*Platanus occidentalis*), northern red oak (*Quercus rubra*), scarlet oak (*Quercus coccinea*), and wild black cherry (*Prunus serotina*) were collected from Cypress Creek, a third order stream which flows through Holly Springs National Forest in northern Mississippi. Leaves were collected in the early winter, the period of greatest leaf fall at this site. Five replicate leaves of each species were collected from the surface of the streambed and refrigerated in water collected from the site until processing (1-3 days). On each day of processing, random leaves were chosen for assays of extracellular enzyme activity. Small circular discs (5 mm diameter) were bored at different points across each leaf (typically 15-35 points per leaf) and each disc was subsequently assayed for the activity of one microbial enzyme. Digital images of the remaining leaf (minus discs) were taken to identify the location of sample points for use in the subsequent spatial analysis.

Discs were assayed for enzymes using chromogenic artificial substrates. Beta-glucosidase and cellobiohydrolase activities were determined using the same p-nitrophenol linked substrates as for the wetland sediments study. Leaf discs were incubated with 300 μl substrate at room temperature for 2-4 hours, whereupon the reaction mixture was diluted with NaOH as described previously [84, 92]. Absorbance of the end product was determined at 405 nm [94] and converted to activity on an areal basis of leaf surface (i.e. activity as μmoles of substrate consumed per hour per area). Activities of phenol oxidase and peroxidase were combined into one measurement of overall oxidative enzyme activity using the artificial substrate L-3,4-dihydroxyphenylalanine (L-DOPA) and 0.015% hydrogen peroxide. Leaf discs were incubated in 300 μl of 5 mM L-DOPA with hydrogen peroxide for 2-4 hours and the absorbance of the diluted reaction mixture determined at 450 nm [95]. As with beta-glucosidase and cellobiohydrolase, oxidative enzyme activity was expressed as μmoles of substrate consumed per hour per area of leaf surface for each disc.

Activities of the microbial enzymes on the different discs taken from each leaf were used to calculate mean and standard deviation of activity for each enzyme and leaf species. These values were used to calculate the coefficient of variation (CV), a basic measurement of spatial variability [96, 97]. Spatial patterns in enzyme activity across the leaf surface were visualized by interpolation using the geostatistical software package SADA v.4.1.50 (Spatial Analysis and Decision Assistance, University of Tennessee).

In general, beta-glucosidase showed the highest activity of the three enzymes examined and cellobiohydrolase activity the lowest, regardless of leaf species (Figure 4). Oxidative enzyme activity and beta-glucosidase activity were similar on cherry and scarlet oak leaves (median oxidative activities of 0.04 and 0.05 $\mu mol/h/cm^2$, respectively, and median beta-glucosidase activities of 0.13 and 0.10 $\mu mol/h/cm^2$, respectively). These values were almost twice those seen on the other two leaf types (median oxidative activity was 0.03 $\mu mol/h/cm^2$ on both northern red oak and sycamore leaves, whereas median beta-glucosidase activity was 0.06 $\mu mol/h/cm^2$ for both). Median cellobiohydrolase activity was also similar for northern red oak and sycamore (0.01 $\mu mol/h/cm^2$) but differed substantially between scarlet oak (0.015 $\mu mol/h/cm^2$) and cherry (0.03 $\mu mol/h/cm^2$). These differences are likely because of a wide range of physical and chemical characteristics that differ between decomposing leaf types [98]. As would be expected based on their roles in cellulose degradation [99, 100], activities of beta-glucosidase and cellobiohydrolase were correlated, but this correlation ranged from weak ($R = 0.32$) on scarlet oak to moderately strong ($R = 0.79$) on cherry.

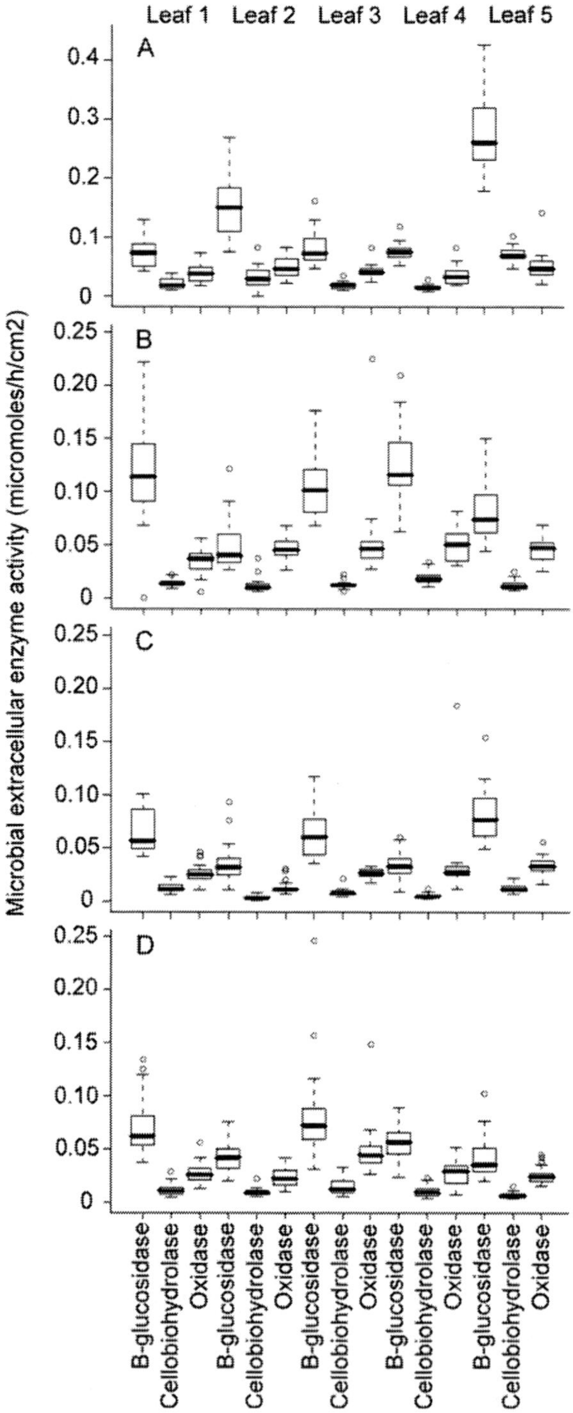

Figure 4. Statistical distributions for microbial extracellular enzyme activity sampled across of decomposing leaves. Five leaves of each species (A: cherry, B: scarlet oak, C: northern red oak, D: sycamore) were sampled for beta-glucosidase, cellobiohydrolase, and a combination of phenol oxidase and peroxidase activity. Solid lines for each leaf-enzyme combination indicate median values, with boxes indicating 25th and 75th quartiles, and whiskers representing 1.5x interquartile range. Most leaves showed high spatial variability in microbial activity even when outlying samples (open circles) were excluded.

Variability in microbial activity across the surface of each leaf type was determined using a linear model fitted to the data comparing each sample point to the mean. Results of this model yielded significance values of $p < 0.001$ for all three enzymes on each leaf type, confirming a significant degree of spatial variability. CV values ranged from 29.5 to 43.8 for the different leaf types, and on any particular leaf were similar for the three different enzymes. Several-fold variation in activity between sample points across the surface of individual leaves was common for all three enzymes, and the range of activities reported for a given leaf was substantial (Figure 4).

Because the median enzyme activity and the range of activities were similar between replicates, a single northern red oak leaf was chosen for a more detailed representation of the variability in activity of each of the three microbial enzymes across the leaf surface (Figure 5). All three enzyme measurements showed fine scale variability with individual sample points differing in activity even over distances of a few centimeters. This variability was typical of that seen in other leaves of northern red oak and in the other leaf types. Different spatial distributions of activity were visible for the three enzymes. Both beta-glucosidase and the combined oxidative enzymes showed distributions characterized by low background levels of activity with isolated "hot spots" of much higher enzyme activity. In contrast, cellobiohydrolase activity was intermediate on most of the discs sampled with intermittent points of both high and low activity. This finding is somewhat unusual given that activities of cellobiohydrolase and beta-glucosidase are more typically correlated [92], and the oxidative enzymes tend to show distributions different from those of the cellulases [92, 101]. However, most studies of microbial enzymatic activity sample at much larger scales than those examined here, and fine scale differences in environmental conditions across the leaf surface may be more important in influencing the distribution of some enzymes over others. Regardless, all three enzymes showed appreciable fine scale spatial heterogeneity in activity, even across the surface of a single leaf.

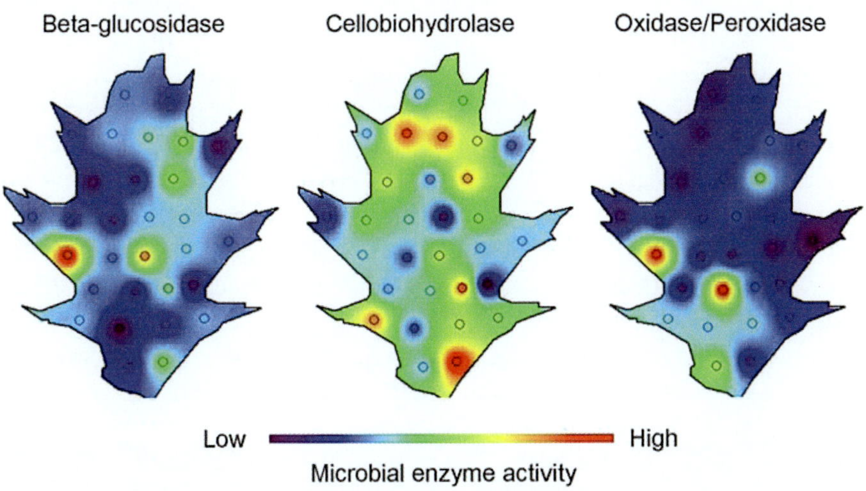

Figure 5. Spatial patterns of microbial extracellular enzyme activity across the surface of a northern red oak leaf. The images show the fine scale spatial distribution of beta-glucosidase, cellobiohydrolase and combined phenol oxidase/peroxidase activity measured across the surface of the same leaf. Sample points are represented by an open circle and enzyme activity is interpolated between them.

CONCLUSION

Aquatic microbial communities clearly function at fine scales and studies suggest that environmental heterogeneity at a level finer than that commonly examined in environmental microbiology can influence microbial community structure and function. This is apparent from planktonic communities, where differences in bacterial community composition and activity can occur between free-living cells and those associated with particles. Microorganisms in biofilms show clear spatial structure, largely because of environmental gradients that form within the biofilm matrix. Similar gradients occur with depth in sediments, although other fine scale environmental variation in sediment is also apparent. A survey of microbial activity and community structure in wetland sediment showed that particle size plays an important role in determining the microorganisms present, with substantially different bacterial communities being found on fine particles less than 250 μm compared to those greater than that diameter. These structural changes are also reflected in changes in microbial enzyme activity as particle size decreases. Microbial enzyme activity itself can be used to assess fine scale spatial patterns, such as those that occur on the surface of decomposing leaves. Activities of enzymes involved in lignocellulose degradation show high spatial variability over individual leaves, again demonstrating that microbial communities vary both structurally and functionally over finer scales than are usually considered in environmental microbiology. The impact of this variation on broader processes is unknown, but fine scale environmental variation should be considered in future surveys of microbial diversity and activity in aquatic environments.

REFERENCES

[1] Lindeman, R. (1942). The trophic-dynamic aspect of ecology. *Ecology, 23,* 399-417.

[2] Amann, R. & Kühl, M. (1998). *In situ* methods for assessment of microorganisms and their activities. *Current Opinion in Microbiology, 1,* 352-358.

[3] Paerl, H. W. & Pinckney, J. L. (1996). A mini-review of microbial consortia: their roles in aquatic production and biogeochemical cycling. *Microbial Ecology, 31,* 225-247.

[4] Allen, T. F. H. & Hoekstra, T. W. (1992). *Toward a Unified Ecology*. New York, NY: Columbia University Press.

[5] O'Neill, R. V. (1989). Perspectives in Hierarchy and Scale. In J. Roughgarden, R. M. May, & S. A. Levin (Eds.), *Perspectives in Ecological Theory* (140-156). Princeton NJ: Princeton University Press.

[6] Krembs, C., Juhl, A. R., Long, R. A. & Azam, F. (1998). Nanoscale patchiness of bacteria in lake water studied with the Spatial Information Preservation method. *Limnology and Oceanography, 43,* 307-314.

[7] Moter, A. & Gobel, U. B. (2000). Fluorescence in situ hybridization (FISH) for direct visualization of microorganisms. *Journal of Microbiological Methods, 41,* 85-112.

[8] Sinsabaugh, R. L. (1994). Enzymic analysis of microbial pattern and process. *Biology and Fertility of Soils, 17,* 69-74.

[9] Santegoeds, C. M., Schramm, A. & de Beer, D. (1998). Microsensors as a tool to determine chemical microgradients and bacterial activity in wastewater biofilms and flocs. *Biodegradation, 9,* 159-167.

[10] Riemann, B. & Christofferson, K. (1993). Microbial trophodynamics in temperate lakes. *Aquatic Microbial Ecology, 7,* 69-100.

[11] Vannote, R. L., Minshall, G. W., Cummins, K. W., Sedell, J. R. & Cushing, C. E. (1980). The river continuum concept. *Canadian Journal of Fisheries and Aquatic Sciences, 37,* 130-137.

[12] Seymour, J. R., Mitchell, J. G., Pearson, L. & Waters, R. L. (2000). Heterogeneity in bacterioplankton abundance from 4.5 millimetre resolution sampling. *Aquatic Microbial Ecology, 22,* 143-153.

[13] Simon, M., Grossart, H. P., Schweitzer, B. & Ploug, H. (2002). Microbial ecology of organic aggregates in aquatic ecosystems. *Aquatic Microbial Ecology, 28,* 175-211.

[14] Cole, J. J. (1982). Interactions between bacteria and algae in aquatic ecosystems. *Annual Review of Ecology and Systematics, 13,* 291-314.

[15] Hahn, M. W., Moore, E. R. B. & Höfle, M. G. (2000). Role of microcolony formation in the protistan grazing defense of the aquatic bacterium *Pseudomonas* sp. MWH1. *Microbial Ecology, 39,* 175-185.

[16] Böckelmann, U., Manz, W., Neu, T. & Szewyzk, U. (2000). Characterization of the microbial community of lotic aggregates ('river snow') in the Elbe River of Germany by cultivation and molecular methods. *FEMS Microbiology Ecology, 33,* 157-170.

[17] Holliday, D. V., Donaghy, P. L., Greenlaw, C. F., McGehee, D. E., McManus, M. M., Sullivan, J. M. & Miksis, J. L. (2003). Advances in defining fine- and micro-scale pattern in marine plankton. *Aquatic Living Resources, 16,* 131-136.

[18] Moore, J. C., Berlow, E. L., Coleman, D. C., de Ruiter, P. C., Dong, Q., Hastings, A., Johnson, N. C., McMann, K. S., Melville, K., Morin, P. J., Nadelhoffer, K. Rosemond, A. D., Post, D. M., Sabo, J. L., Scow, K. M., Vanni, M. J. & Wall, D. H. (2004). Detritus, trophic dynamics and biodiversity. *Ecology Letters, 7,* 584-600.

[19] Alldredge, A. L., Passow, U. & Logan, B. E. (1993). The abundance and significance of a class of large, transparent organic particles in the ocean. *Deep Sea Research I, 40,* 1131-1140.

[20] Ploug, H. (2001). Small-scale oxygen fluxes and remineralization in sinking aggregates. *Limnology and Oceanography, 46,* 1624-1631.

[21] Ploug, H. & Passow, U. (2007). Direct measurement of diffusivity within diatom aggregates containing transparent exopolymer particles. *Limnology and Oceanography, 52,* 1-6.

[22] Smith, D. C., Simon, M., Alldredge, A. L. & Azam, F. (1992). Intense hydrolytic enzyme activity on marine aggregates and implications for rapid particle dissolution. *Nature, 359,* 139-141.

[23] Logan, B. & Wilkinson, D. B. (1990). Fractal geometry of marine snow and other biological aggregates. *Limnology and Oceanography, 35,* 130-136.

[24] Alldredge, A. L. (2000). Interstitial dissolved organic carbon (DOC) concentrations within sinking marine aggregates and their potential contribution to carbon flow. *Limnology and Oceanography, 45,* 1245-1253.

[25] Kiørbee, T., Ploug, H. & Thygesen, U. H. (2001). Fluid motion and solute distribution around sinking aggregates. I. Small-scale fluxes and heterogeneity of nutrients in the pelagic environment. *Marine Ecology Progress Series, 211,* 1-13.
[26] Crump, B. C., Baross, J. A. & Simenstad C. A. (1998). Dominance of particle-attached bacteria in the Columbia River estuary, USA. *Aquatic Microbial Ecology, 14,* 7-18.
[27] DeLong, E. F., Franks, D. G. & Alldredge, A. L. (1993). Phylogenetic diversity of aggregate-attached vs. free-living marine bacterial assemblages. *Limnology and Oceanography, 38,* 924-934.
[28] Schweitzer, B., Huber, I., Amann, R., Ludwig, W. & Simon, M. (2001). α- and β-*Proteobacteria* control the consumption and release of amino acids on lake snow aggregates. *Applied and Environmental Microbiology, 67,* 632-645.
[29] Grossart, H. P., Tang, K. W., Kiørbee, T. & Ploug, H. (2007). Comparison of cell-specific activity between free-living and attached bacteria using isolates and natural assemblages. *FEMS Microbiology Letters, 266,* 194-200.
[30] Grossart, H. P. & Ploug, H. (2000). Bacterial production and growth efficiencies: direct measurements on riverine aggregates. *Limnology and Oceanography, 45,* 436-445.
[31] Tang, K. W., Hutalle., K. M. L. & Grossart, H. P. (2006). Microbial abundance, composition and enzymatic activity during decomposition of copepod carcasses. *Aquatic Microbial Ecology, 45,* 219-227.
[32] Grossart, H. P., Kiørbee, T., Tang, K. W., Allgaier, M., Yam, E. M. & Ploug, H. (2006). Interactions between marine snow and heterotrophic bacteria: aggregate formation and microbial dynamics. *Aquatic Microbial Ecology, 42,* 19-26.
[33] Grossart, H. P., Kiørbee, T., Tang, K. & Ploug, H. (2003). Bacterial colonization of particles: growth and interactions. *Applied and Environmental Microbiology, 69,* 3500-3509.
[34] Miki, T. & Yamamura, N. (2005). Theoretical model of interactions between particle-associated and free-living bacteria to predict functional composition and succession in bacterial communities. *Aquatic Microbial Ecology, 39*, 35-46.
[35] Sherr, B. F., Sherr, E. B. & Hopkinson, C. S. (1988). Trophic interactions within pelagic microbial communities: indications of feedback regulation of carbon flow. *Hydrobiologia, 159,* 19-26.
[36] Branda, S. S., Vik, A., Friedman, L. & Kolter, R. (2005). Biofilms: the matrix revisited. *Trends in Microbiology, 13,* 20-26.
[37] Palková, Z. (2004). Multicellular microorganisms: laboratory versus nature. *EMBO Reports, 5,* 470-476.
[38] Donlan, R. M. (2002). Biofilms: microbial life on surfaces. *Emerging Infectious Diseases, 8,* 881-890.
[39] Jones, P. R., Cottrell, M. T., Kirchman, D. L. & Dexter, S. C. (2007). Bacterial community structure of biofilms on artificial surfaces in an estuary. *Microbial Ecology, 53,* 153-162.
[40] Bergey, E. A. (2006). Measuring the surface roughness of stream stones. *Hydrobiologia, 563,* 247-252.
[41] Purevdorj, B., Costerton, J. W. & Stoodley, P. (2002). Influence of hydrodynamics and cell signaling on the structure and behavior of *Psuedomonas aeruginosa* biofilms. *Applied and Environmental Microbiology, 68,* 4457-4464.

[42] Cardinale, B. J., Palmer, M. A., Swan, C. M., Brooks, S. & Poff, L. (2002). The influence of substrate heterogeneity on biofilm metabolism in a stream ecosystem. *Ecology, 83,* 412-422.

[43] Horswill, A. R., Stoodley, P., Stewart, P. S. & Parsek, M. R. (2007). The effect of the chemical, biological, and physical environment on quorum sensing in structured microbial communities. *Analytical and Bioanalytical Chemistry, 387,* 371-380.

[44] Stoodley, P., deBeer, D. & Lewandowski, Z. (1994). Liquid flow in biofilm systems. *Applied and Environmental Microbiology, 60,* 2711-2716.

[45] Francoeur, S. N., Wetzel, R. G. & Neely, R. K. (2001). New spatially explicit method for detecting extracellular protease activity in biofilms. *Applied and Environmental Microbiology, 67,* 4329-4334.

[46] Kalmbach, S., Manz, W. & Szewyk, U. (1997). Dynamics of biofilm formation in drinking water: phylogenetic affiliation and metabolic potential of single cells assessed by formazan reduction and in situ hybridization. *FEMS Microbiology Ecology, 22,* 265-279.

[47] Stewart, P. S. (2003). Diffusion in biofilms. *Journal of Bacteriology, 185,* 1485-1491.

[48] Wimpenny, J., Manz, W. & Szewyzk, U. (2000). Heterogeneity in biofilms. *FEMS Microbiology Reviews, 24,* 661-671.

[49] Xu. K. D., Stewart, P. S., Xia, F., Huang, C. & McFeters, G. A. (1998). Spatial physiological heterogeneity in *Pseudomonas aeruginosa* biofilm is determined by oxygen availability. *Applied and Environmental Microbiology, 64,* 4035-4039.

[50] Whiteley, M., Bangera, M. G., Bumgarner, R. E., Parsek, M. R., Teitzel, G. M., Lory, S. & Greenberg, E. P. (2001). Gene expression in *Pseudomonas aeruginosa* biofilms. *Nature, 413,* 860-864.

[51] Okabe, S., Santegoeds, C. M., Watanabe, Y. & deBeer, D. (2002). Successional development of sulfate-reducing bacterial populations and their activities in a wastewater biofilm growing under microaerophilic conditions. *Applied and Environmental Microbiology, 68,* 1392-1402.

[52] Santegoeds, C. M., Ferdelman, T. G., Muyzer, G. & deBeer, D. (1998). Structural and functional dynamics of sulfate-reducing populations in bacterial biofilms. *Applied and Environmental Microbiology, 64,* 3731-3739.

[53] Schramm, A. (2003). In situ analysis of structure and activity of the nitrifying community in biofilms, aggregates, and sediments. *Geomicrobiology Journal, 20,* 313-333.

[54] Newman, D. K. & Banfield, J. F. (2002). Geomicrobiology: how molecular-scale interactions underpin biogeochemical systems. *Science, 296,* 1071-1077.

[55] Huws, S. A., McBain, A. J. & Gilbert, P. (2005). Protozoan grazing and its impact upon population dynamics in biofilm communities. *Journal of Applied Microbiology, 98,* 238-244.

[56] Lawrence, J. R. & Snyder, R. A. (1998). Feeding behaviour and grazing impacts of a *Euplotes* sp. on attached bacteria. *Canadian Journal of Microbiology, 44,* 623-629.

[57] Jackson, C. R., Churchill, P. F. & Roden, E. E. (2001). Successional changes in bacterial assemblage structure during epilithic biofilm development. *Ecology, 82,* 555-566.

[58] Jackson, C. R. (2003). Changes in community properties during microbial succession. *Oikos, 101,* 444-448.

[59] Hedin, L. O. (1990). Factors controlling sediment community respiration in woodland stream ecosystems. *Oikos, 57,* 94-105.

[60] Capone, D. G. & Kiene, R. P. (1988). Comparison of microbial dynamics in marine and freshwater sediments: Contrasts in anaerobic carbon catabolism. *Limnology and Oceanography, 33,* 725-749.

[61] Hutchison, N., Nagarkar, S., Aitchison, J. C. & Williams, G. A. (2006). Microspatial variation in marine biofilm abundance on intertidal rock surfaces. *Aquatic Microbial Ecology, 42,* 187-197.

[62] Lavilla, I., Filgueiras, A. V., Valverde, F., Millos, J., Palanca, A. & Bendicho, C. (2006). Depth profile of trace elements in a sediment core of a high-altitude lake deposit at the Pyrenees, Spain. *Water, Air, & Soil Pollution, 172,* 273-293.

[63] Fischer, H., Sukhodolov, A., Wilczek, S. & Engelhardt, C. (2003). Effects of flow dynamics and sediment movement on microbial activity in a lowland river. *River Research and Applications, 19,* 473-482.

[64] Huettel, M., Røy, H., Precht, E. & Ehrenhauss, S. (2003). Hydrodynamical impact on biogeochemical processes in aquatic sediments. *Hydrobiologia, 494,* 231-236.

[65] Sinsabaugh, R. L. & Findlay, S. (1995). Microbial production, enzyme activity, and carbon turnover in surface sediments of the Hudson River estuary. *Microbial Ecology, 30,* 127-141.

[66] Webster, J. R. & Benfield, E.F. (1986). Vascular plant breakdown in freshwater ecosystems. *Annual Review of Ecology and Systematics, 17,* 567-594.

[67] Gooday, A. J., Turley, C. M. & Allen, J. A. (1990). Responses by benthic organisms to inputs of organic material to the ocean floor: A review (and discussion). *Philosophical Transactions of the Royal Society of London. Series A, Mathematical and Physical Sciences, 331,* 119-138.

[68] Wachinger, G., Fiedler, S., Zepp, K., Gattinger, A., Sommer, M. & Roth, K. (2000). Variability of soil methane production on the micro-scale: spatial association with hot spots of organic material and Archaeal populations. *Soil Biology and Biochemistry, 32,* 1121-1130.

[69] Bringmark, L. & Bringmark, E. (2001). Soil respiration in relation to small-scale patterns of lead and mercury in mor layers of southern Swedish forest sites. *Water, Air, & Soil Pollution: Focus, 1,* 395-408.

[70] Becker, J. M., Parkin, T., Nakatsu, C. H., Wilbur, J. D. & Konopka, A. (2006). Bacterial activity, community structure, and centimeter-scale spatial heterogeneity in contaminated soil. *Microbial Ecology, 51,* 220-231.

[71] Zorn, M. E., Lalonde, S. V., Gingras, M. K., Pemberton, S. G. & Konhauser, K. O. (2006). Microscale oxygen distribution in various invertebrate burrow walls. *Geobiology, 4,* 137-145.

[72] Stief, P. & de Beer, D. (2006). Probing the microenvironment of freshwater sediment macrofauna: Implications of deposit-feeding and bioirrigation for nitrogen cycling. *Limnology and Oceanography, 51,* 2538-2548.

[73] Singh, B. K., Millard, P., Whiteley, A. S. & Murrell, J. C. (2004). Unraveling rhizosphere-microbial interactions: opportunities and limitations. *Trends in Microbiology, 12,* 386-393.

[74] Hinsinger, P., Gobran, G. R., Gregory, P. J. & Wenzel, W. W. (2005). Rhizosphere geometry and heterogeneity arising from root-mediated physical and chemical processes. *New Phytologist, 168,* 293-303.

[75] Wotton, R. S. (1994). The classification of particulate and dissolved matter. In R. S. Wotton (Ed.), *The biology of particles in aquatic systems* (1-6). New York, NY: Lewis Publishers.

[76] Sinsabaugh, R. L. & Linkins, A. E. (1990). Enzymic and chemical analysis of particulate organic matter from a boreal river. *Freshwater Biology, 23*, 301-309.

[77] Ward, G. M., Ward, A, K., Dahm, C. N. & Aumen, N. G. (1994). Origin and formation of organic and inorganic particles in aquatic systems. In R. S. Wotton (Ed.), *The biology of particles in aquatic systems* (45-73). New York, NY: Lewis Publishers.

[78] Yeager, P. E. & Sinsabaugh, R. L. (1998). Microbial diversity along a sediment detrital particle size gradient. *Aquatic Ecology, 32*, 281-289.

[79] Lee, S. & Fuhrman, J. A. (1991). Spatial and temporal variation of natural bacterioplankton assemblages studies by total genomic DNA cross-hybridization. *Limnology and Oceanography, 36*, 1277-1287.

[80] Zhou, J., Bruns, M. A. & Tiedje, J. M. (1996). DNA recovery from soils of diverse composition. *Applied and Environmental Microbiology*, 62, 316-322.

[81] Jackson, C. R., Langner, H. W., Donahoe-Christiansen, J., Inskeep, W. P. & McDermott, T. R. (2001). Molecular analysis of microbial community structure in an arsenite-oxidizing acidic thermal spring. *Environmental Microbiology, 3*, 532-542.

[82] Jackson, C. R., Harper, J. P., Willoughby, D., Roden, E. E. & Churchill, P. F. (1997). A simple, efficient method for the separation of humic substances and DNA from environmental samples. *Applied and Environmental Microbiology, 63*, 4993-4995.

[83] Amann, R. I., Ludwig, W. & Schleifer, K. H. (1995). Phylogenetic identification and in situ detection of individual microbial cells without cultivation. *Microbiology Reviews, 59*, 143-169.

[84] Jackson, E. F., Echlin, H. L. & Jackson, C. R. (2006). Changes in the phyllosphere community of the resurrection fern, *Polypodium polypodioides*, associated with rainfall and wetting. *FEMS Microbiology Ecology, 58*, 236-246.

[85] Chao, A. (1987). Estimating the population size for capture-recapture data with unequal catchability. *Biometrics, 43*, 783-791.

[86] Kemp, P. F. & Aller, J. Y. (2004). Estimating prokaryotic diversity: When are 16S rDNA libraries large enough? *Limnology and Oceanography: Methods, 2*, 114-125.

[87] Ludwig, W., Strunk, O., Westram, R., Richter, L., Meier, H., Yadhukumar, Buchner, A., Lai, T., Steppi, S., Jobb, G., Förster, W., Brettske, I., Gerber,S., Ginhart, A. W., Gross, O., Grumann, S., Hermann, S., Jost, R., König, A., Liss, T., Lüßmann, R., May, M., Nonhoff, B., Reichel, B., Strehlow, R., Stamatakis, A., Stuckmann, N., Vilbig, A., Lenke, M., Ludwig, T., Bode, A. & Schleifer, K. H. (2004). ARB: a software environment for sequence data. *Nucleic Acids Research, 32*, 1363-1371.

[88] Nold, S. C. & Zwart, G. (1998). Patterns and governing forces in aquatic microbial communities. *Aquatic Ecology, 32*, 17-35.

[89] Besemer, K., Moeseneder, M. M., Arrieta, J. M., Herndl, G. J. & Peduzzi, P. (2005). Complexity of bacterial communities in a river-floodplain system (Danube, Austria). *Applied and Environmental Microbiology, 71*, 609-620.

[90] Tisdall, J. M. & Oades, J. M. (1982). Organic matter and water stable aggregates in soils. *Journal of Soil Science, 33*, 141-163.

[91] Sessitsch, A., Weilharter, A., Gerzabek, M. H., Kirchmann, H. & Kandeler, E. (2001). Microbial population structures in soil particle size fractions of a long-term fertilizer field experiment. *Applied and Environmental Microbiology, 67*, 4215-4224.

[92] Jackson, C. R., Foreman, C. M. & Sinsabaugh, R. L. (1995). Microbial enzyme activities as indicators of organic matter processing rates in a Lake Erie coastal wetland. *Freshwater Biology, 34*, 329-342.

[93] Lindow, S. E. & Brandl, M. T. (2003). Microbiology of the phyllosphere. *Applied and Environmental Microbiology, 69,* 1875-1883.

[94] Blum, D. L., Kataeva, I. A., Li, X. L & Ljungdahl, L. G. (2000). Feruloyl esterase activity of the *Clostridium thermocellum* cellulosome can be attributed to previously unknown domains of XynY and XynZ. *Journal of Bacteriology, 182,* 1346-1351.

[95] Larson, J. L., Zak, D. R. & Sinsabaugh, R. L. (2002). Extracellular enzyme activity beneath temperate trees growing under elevated carbon dioxide and ozone. *Soil Science Society of America Journal, 66,* 1848-1856.

[96] Rossi, R. E., Mulla D. J., Journel, A. G. & Franz, E. H. (1992). Geostatistical tools for modelling and interpreting ecological spatial dependence. *Ecological Monographs, 62*, 277-314.

[97] Ettema, C. H. & Wardle, D. A. (2002). Spatial soil ecology. *Trends in Ecology and Evolution, 17*, 177-183.

[98] Cornelissen, J. H. C. (1996). An experimental comparison of leaf decomposition rates in a wide range of temperate plant species and types. *Journal of Ecology, 84,* 573-582.

[99] Divne, C., Stahlberg, J., Teeri, T. T. & Jones, T. A. (1998). High-resolution cryst structures reveal how a cellulose chain is bound in the 50 angstrom long tunnel of cellobiohydrolase I from *Trichoderma reesei*. *Journal of Molecular Biology, 275,* 309-325.

[100] Peshin, A. & Mathur, J. M. S. (1999). Purification and characterization of β-glucosidase from *Aspergillus niger* strain 322. *Letters in Applied Microbiology, 28,* 401-404.

[101] Alvarez, S. & Guerrero, M. C. (2000). Enzymatic activities associated with decomposition of particulate organic matter in two shallow ponds. *Soil Biology & Biochemistry, 32*, 1941-1951.

In: Environmental Microbiology Research Trends
Editor: G. V. Kurladze, pp. 191-212
ISBN: 978-1-60021-939-9

Chapter 6

CHANGES OF MARINE BACTERIAL POPULATIONS IN A SHIP'S BALLAST WATER AND SEDIMENT, AND APPLICATION OF SHOCK PRESSURES TO COMPLETE KILLING OF *VIBRIO* SP. CELLS ISOLATED FROM BALLAST WATER

Haruo Mimura, Akihisa Abe and Hiroshi Ishida
Faculty of Maritime Sciences, Kobe University, 5-1-1, Fukae, Higashinada, Kobe, Japan

1. INTRODUCTION

A ships' ballast water is used to ensure stability, strength, and proper draft of the hull since the 19th century. Before the century, solid ballast had mainly been used. The use of seawater as ships' ballast seems to be consistent with containerization, which contributed to the reduction of operation time of loading, or unloading, cargos at a port. Ballast water, in general, is pumped in during the unloading operation of cargos, while it is pumped out during the loading operation of them. Consequently, ballast water is transported from one port to another port by ships. Especially, huge overseas vessels such as crude oil carriers and liquefied natural gas (LNG) carriers transport large amounts of ballast water to a loading place of call.

Marine living things invaded in ballast water are transported and spread into a new environment. Some of the non-native species transported in the ballast water have already become major species in a local marine environment and disrupting the ecosystem. Infectious disease caused by pathogenic *Vibrio cholerae* is also a major concern for the people who live near the coastal area. As for another impact of ballast water, economical damage is pointed out. When marine resources are infested with invasive species, the estimated cost is predicted to be exceeded 138 billion US dollars per year in the United States alone (Pimentel, 2000). Therefore, ballast water management is very important to ensure marine ecosystems, human health, and profit.

The International Maritime Organization (IMO) has estimated that approximately 3 to 5 billion tons of ballast water are transported around the world each year and showed ten of the most unwanted marine invasive species, in which pathogenic *V. cholerae*, cladoceran water flea, mitten crab, toxic algae, North American comb jelly, North Pacific seastar, zebra mussel, and Asian kelp are included (IMO, available to see in web site). Pathogenic *V. cholerae* distributed with broad ranges has been introduced to South America, Gulf of Mexico, and other areas. Asian kelp, which is native to northern Asia, has been widely introduced to southern Australia, New Zealand, west coast of the United States, Europe, and Argentina. The European zebra mussel is the one which has spread most successfully in the United States (Ambros,1996).

Historically, great pandemics of cholera had occurred along coastlines of the world oceans. Fishermen and boatmen were primarily infected, and outbreaks were commonly ascribed to ships arrived from the areas of epidemics of cholera. Recently, it is well known that outbreaks of cholera are closely related to ships' ballast water taken aboard from rivers, swamps and marshes, where flow of streams is much reduced, in the warm countries (Colwell, 1996; Louis, 2003).

In section 2, we mainly explained the population changes in the number of colony-forming marine bacterial cells in the ballast *Water SA*mples taken aboard of a LNG carrier sailing for Qatar from Japan. I think that the bacterial colony-forming ability is primarily important to become dominant in the new environment when nutritional condition becomes well. In section 3, complete killing of *Vibrio* sp. by the exposure to shock pressures was explained in relation to the ballast water management. Conclusions are shown in section 4.

2. Changes of Marine Bacterial Populations in Ballast Water and Sediment of LNG Carrier Bound from Japan to Qatar for Loading LNG

2.1. Navigation Route and a Ship Used for Sampling Ballast Water and Sediment

An ocean going LNG carrier sailing in the Akashi Channel located in the Inland Sea is shown in Figure 1. The amounts of LNG transported to Japan increase continuously sine 1970th.

We investigated the changes of marine bacterial populations in ballast water and sediment loaded on a large LNG carrier, ZEKREET (110,000 tons gross), KAWASAKI KISEN KAISHA, LTD., at ports in Japan. The navigation route of the ship is shown in Figure 2. It takes approximately two weeks to go from Japan to the Ras Laffan port in Qatar. The ship has one forward- and one after-peak ballast tanks as well as ten side ballast tanks located tandem on the starboard and port sides. The total capacity of the tanks is 55,000 m^3.

Figure 1. A LNG carrier (approximately 110,000 tons gross) sailing at the Straits of Akashi in the Inland Sea, Japan

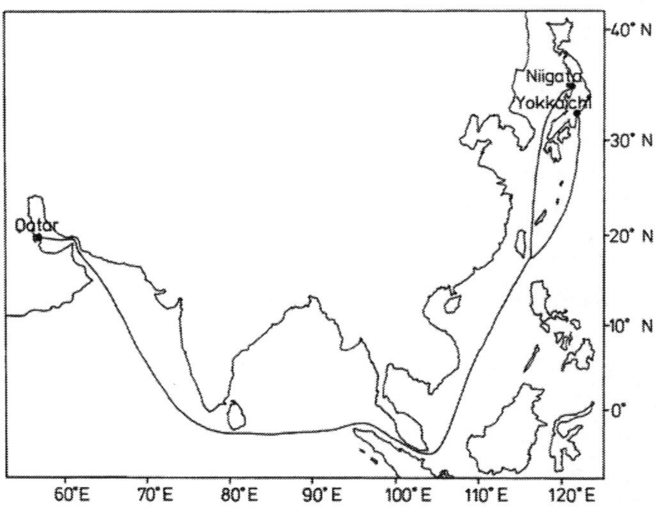

Figure 2. Outline of the navigation route bound for Qatar from Japan. The solid line shows the navigation route between the Niigata port or the Yokkaichi port in Japan and the Ras Laffan port in Qatar.

2.2. Changes in the Number of Viable Marine Bacterial Populations in Ballast Water and Sediment

Yokkaichi port and Niigata port (see Figure 2) are included in the nine major bases for reserves of LNG in Japan, as of 2006. LNG carriers, in general, take ballast water on board at the port of Japan to maintain the strength of the hull while LNG is unloading from the ship. While, on the voyage, ballast water is necessary to maintain the draft in a certain depth. On the way to Qatar, the exchange of ballast water is performed every time; new ballast water is reloaded on board in the high seas located in the Indian Ocean after the ballast water transported from Japan was discharged in there. The ballast water exchange sites for all the six voyages from May 2002 to July 2003 are shown in Figure 3. Finally the new ballast water taken in the high seas was transported to the Ras Laffan port in Qatar.

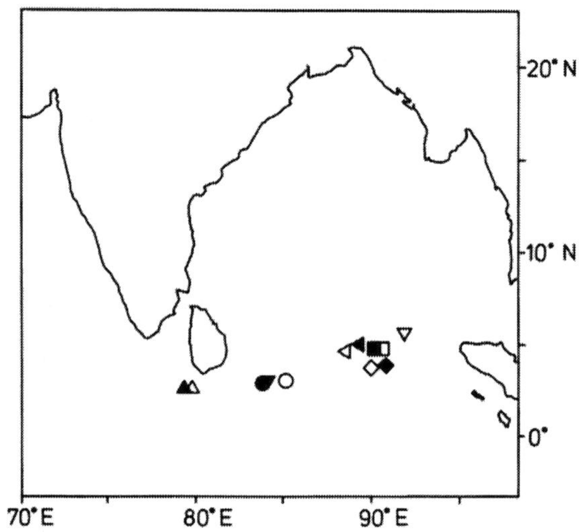

Figure 3. Ballast water exchange sites on the way to Qatar from Japan. Ballast water exchange sites for the voyage to Qatar from Japan in May 2002 (circles), September 2002 (triangles), December 2002 (squares), February 2003 (triangles, upside down), April 2003 (lozenges), and August 2003 (triangles, sideward) are shown. Open and closed symbols mean that sampling was carried out while discharging ballast water from the ship and reloading ballast water onto the ship, respectively.

Changes in the number of colony-forming marine bacterial cells in ballast *Water SA*mples are shown in Figure 4 (Mimura et al. 2005). Counting the total number of colony-forming cells of eutrophic marine microorganisms was carried out by the use of agar plates filled in aseptically with a sterile medium containing 5 g Bacto peptone (Difco, Michigan, USA), 1 g yeast extract (Difco, Michigan, USA), and 15 g agar per liter of natural seawater. After serial dilution with autoclaved natural seawater, the samples, 0.1 ml, were spread onto the agar plates, and incubation was carried out for two days at 30°C.

As shown in Figure 4, variable viable cell numbers were observed regardless of the sampling time and season: $10^{2.3}$ - $10^{4.8}$ colony-forming units (CFU) ml^{-1} in May 2002, $10^{4.2}$ - $10^{4.9}$ CFU ml^{-1} in September 2002, $10^{3.9}$ - $10^{5.0}$ CFU ml^{-1} in December, $10^{3.1}$ - $10^{4.8}$ CFU ml^{-1} in February 2003, $10^{1.8}$ - $10^{3.4}$ CFU ml^{-1} in April 2003, and $10^{2.7}$ - $10^{3.8}$ CFU ml^{-1} in August 2003.

When ballast water taken aboard in Japan was discharged in the high seas, which is generally located in the area of more than 200 nautical miles offshore, it was sampled, and the number of viable cells was counted (Figure 4). Again, variable viable cell numbers were observed: $10^{3.5}$ - $10^{3.8}$ CFU ml^{-1} in May 2002, $10^{4.3}$ - $10^{4.9}$ CFU ml^{-1} in September 2002, $10^{4.0}$

- $10^{4.8}$ CFU ml^{-1} in December 2002, $10^{1.6}$ - $10^{4.3}$ CFU ml^{-1} in February 2003, $10^{2.8}$ - $10^{3.2}$ CFU ml^{-1} in April 2003, and $10^{4.4}$ - $10^{4.8}$ CFU ml^{-1} in August 2003.

Until the ship arrived in the high seas in the Indian Ocean, the ballast water was continuously stirred in the tanks as a result of wave action. Nevertheless, the number of viable cells in the samples taken at any given time was variable. Since the port of the ballast water outlet pipes is located near the bottom of the ballast tanks, some sediment samples containing microbial populations that were approximately 10 times higher than those in the ballast water (Table 1) appeared to be mixed in with the discharged ballast water.

Samples were also taken each time when new ballast water was reloaded. With the exception of February 2003, there were no obvious reductions in the number of viable cells in samples taken in the high seas in comparison with samples taken from ballast water loaded in Japan. No colonies were detected from the samples taken in February 2003 (Figure 4).

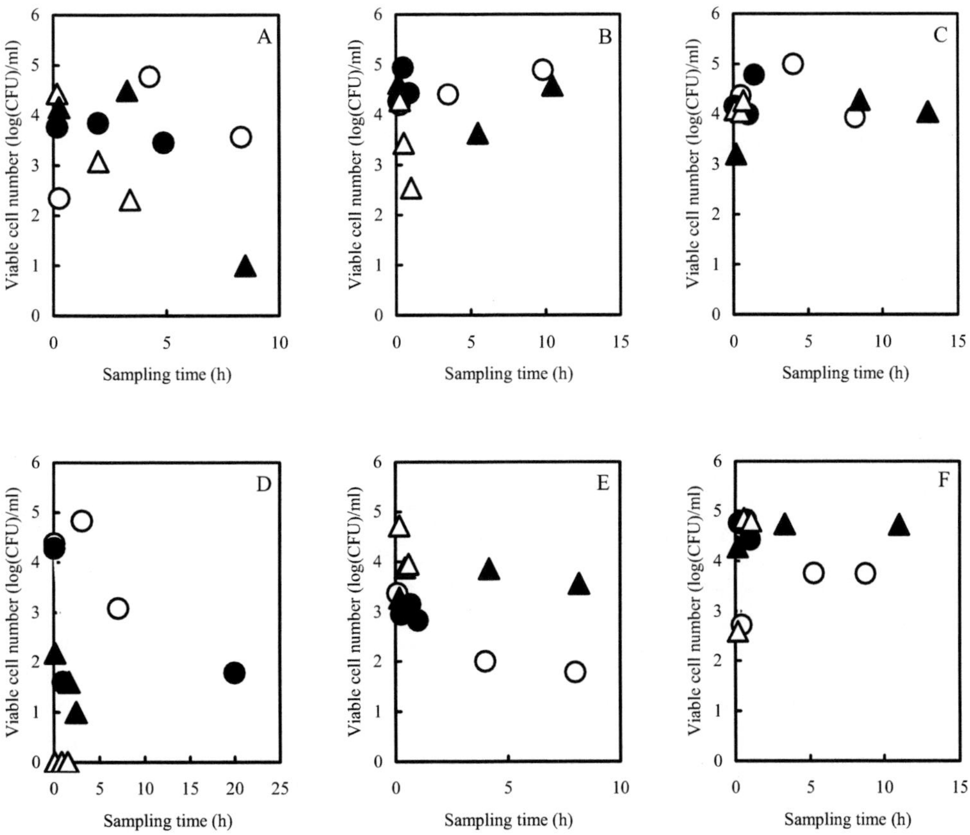

Figure 4. Changes in the number of viable cells in ballast water while loading and discharging from the ship. Ballast water was loaded at the Niigata port in May 2002 (A). Except for that, it was loaded at the Yokkaichi port in September 2002 (B), December 2002 (C), February 2003 (D), April 2003 (E), and July 2003 (F). Ballast water was sampled when it was loaded at a port in Japan (open circle), discharged (closed circle) and reloaded (open triangle) in the high seas, and discharged from the ship at the Ras Laffan port in Qatar (closed triangle). The experiment was carried out twice for each sample, and the averaged value is shown here. The difference between the individual and the averaged values was less than 0.2 log cycle for all the samples. This figure is reprinted from Marine Pollution Bulletin, 50, H. Mimura, et al., Changes of microbial populations in a ship's ballast water and sediments on a voyage from Japan to Qatar, 751-757, 2005, with permission from Elsevier.

At the Ras Laffan port, ballast water, which had already been exchanged in the high seas, was discharged prior to loading LNG (Figure 4). In the ballast water discharged at the port, the number of viable cells in the samples varied from $10^{1.0}$ - $10^{4.5}$ CFU ml^{-1} in May 2002, $10^{3.6}$ - $10^{4.6}$ CFU ml^{-1} in September 2002, $10^{3.2}$ - $10^{4.3}$ CFU ml^{-1} in December 2002, $10^{1.0}$ - $10^{2.2}$ CFU ml^{-1} in February 2003, $10^{3.3}$ - $10^{3.9}$ CFU ml^{-1} in April 2003, and $10^{4.3}$ - $10^{4.7}$ CFU ml^{-1} in August 2003. An obvious reduction in the number of viable cells was observed in the samples from ballast water discharged at the Ras Laffan port in February 2003 in comparison with that in the samples taken before departing Japan. The effectiveness of exchanging the ballast water in the high seas was only confirmed for the trip in February 2003.

Table 1. Total number of viable cells in the sediments of ballast tanks.

Sampling date	Viable number of cells (log (CFU) ml^{-1})[a]
June 17 (2002)	5.6
September 16 (2002)	5.8 – 5.9
December 20 (2002)	5.5 – 5.8
February 24 (2003)	5.2 – 5.3
May 3 (2003)	5.9 – 6.0
August 10 (2003)	5.7 – 5.9

[a]Sediments were taken from two different ballast tanks, except for June 2002. The sediment (1 g) was diluted with distilled seawater (9 ml). Serial dilution, when necessary, was carried out, and the sample (0.1 ml) was spread onto non-selective agar plates. The viable cells were calculated on the basis of the water content of each sample. For example, the viable number of cells, 5.6 log (CFU) ml^{-1}, obtained from the sample in June 2002 was calculated by the following equation: 180 (colony numbers on the plate) x (9.4/0.4) x (10/1) x (1/0.1) = 4.2 x 10^5 CFU ml^{-1}, where 0.4 ml was the water content in 1 g of the sample.

Experiments were carried out twice for each sample by taking sediments from different sites, and the averaged value is shown here. The difference between the individual and the averaged values was less than 0.2 log cycle for all the samples.

Reprinted from Marine Pollution Bulletin, 50, H. Mimura, et al., Changes of microbial populations in a ship's ballast water and sediments on a voyage from Japan to Qatar, 751-757, 2005, with permission from Elsevier.

Regardless of the exchange sites for ballast water in the high seas (see Figure 3) and the season in which the samples were taken (Figure 4), the total number of viable cells in ballast water reloaded in the high seas varied considerably, and remained nearly identical to that in the samples from seawater taken aboard in Japan, except for the values obtained in February 2003. The effectiveness of ballast water exchange in the high seas was hardly confirmed in relation to the number of viable marine bacterial populations.

On the same voyages, changes in the surface color of seawater were monitored at the wave length of 490 nm along the sailing route of the ship using a man-made satellite (Kozai et al., 2006). The remote sensing images obtained showed the good correlation with the number of *in site* plankton counted directly. The exchange of the ballast water in the high seas resulted in the obvious reduction of the number of plankton in ballast tanks.

There were seasonal variations in the number of viable cells in the samples obtained from the pools of ballast water in the tanks (Figure 5). The maximum and minimum values on the surface of the body of water were $10^{4.9}$ in September 2002 and $10^{2.7}$ CFU ml^{-1} in May 2002, respectively. At the middle depth of about 10 m from the surface, the maximum and minimum values were $10^{4.5}$ in September 2002 and $10^{2.6}$ CFU ml^{-1} in April 2003, respectively. The difference in the values obtained from the samples taken at the same time from the surface and a 10m depth was within a 0.5 log cycle, except for that in May 2002, indicating that the invading microorganisms might have been diffused within the ballast tanks during the voyage.

As for the number of viable cells in sediments in the ballast tanks, a 5 log cycle of the number was estimated on the basis of the water content in the sample regardless of the season in which the voyage took place (Table 1). All the values estimated from the sediment samples were higher than those obtained from the ballast water. These results indicate the importance of sediment management as well as that of ballast water.

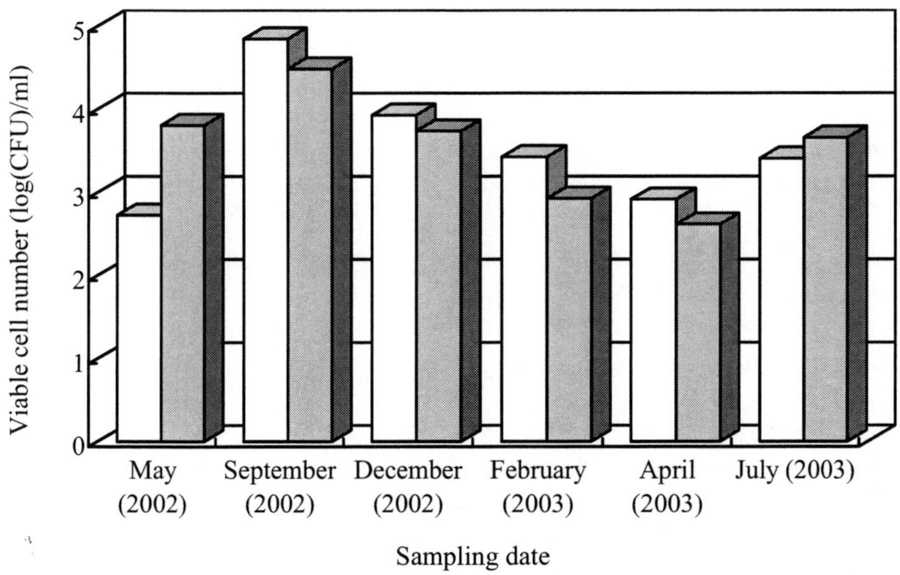

Figure 5. Seasonal variations in the number of viable cells in the ballast water stored in a ballast tank. The ballast water stored in a ballast tank was taken from the surface (open column) and at a 10m depth of the body of water (closed column). Experiments were carried out twice for each sample, and the averaged value is shown here. The difference between the individual and the averaged values was less than 0.2 log cycle for all the samples. This figure is reprinted from Marine Pollution Bulletin, 50, H. Mimura, et al., Changes of microbial populations in a ship's ballast water and sediments on a voyage from Japan to Qatar, 751-757, 2005, with permission from Elsevier.

2.3. *Vibrio* Species Isolated from Ballast Water and Sediment

A thiosulphate-citrate-bile salts-sucrose (TCBS) selective medium was used for the isolation of an estuarine *Vibrio* species in the sampled ballast water and sediment in ballast tanks. The medium contains 10 g peptone, 5 g yeast extract, 20 g sucrose, 5 g bile powder, 3 g sodium cholate, 10 g NaCl, 10 g sodium citrate, 7 g sodium thiosulfate, 1 g iron (III) citrate, 0.04 g bromothymol blue, 0.04 g thymol blue, and 15 g agar per liter of distilled water, pH 8.2 (Pearlcore TCBS Agar "Eiken," Eiken Chemical Co., Ltd.). The medium boiled at the atmosphere was filled in aseptically to the plates. After serial dilution with autoclaved natural seawater, if necessary, the samples, 0.5 ml, were spread onto TCBS selective agar plates, and incubation was carried out for one day at 30°C.

Viable cell numbers on the TCBS selective plates are shown in Table 2. In five of the six voyages, except for that in February 2003, colonies were detected from the ballast water and sediment samples. No colonies were detected in any of the samples taken from the ballast water loaded in Japan. Several colonies, however, were detected when the samples taken from the pooled ballast water in September and December 2002 and April and July 2003 were examined. Moreover, one colony was obtained from each sample taken as ballast water was discharged in the high seas in May 2002 and July 2003. No colonies were observed on the plates for the samples taken from ballast water reloaded in the high seas and discharged at the Ras Laffan port in Qatar.

Although the *Vibrio* species can be effectively detected by the use of the TCBS selective plate, selectivity is not quite complete (Pfeffer and Oliver, 2003). Therefore, we examined all the isolates that had been picked up from the individual colonies on the TCBS selective plates. As for the isolates obtained from ballast *Water SA*mples, not from the sediment samples, every isolate was Gram-negative, rod-shaped, motile, and not spore-forming. The isolates had catalase, oxidase, and glucose fermentation activities. The zone of inhibition was confirmed on the plate for each isolate by exposure to a paper disc containing an antibacterial agent, 2,4-diamino-6,7-di-isopropyl pteridine phosphate. These results indicate that the isolates belong to the genus *Vibrio* (Krieg, 1984). On the TCBS selective plates, *Vibrio cholerae* was a yellow colony. Only two isolates, September 1 and December 1, taken in September and December 2002 (see Table 2), resulted in yellow colonies. Consequently, these two colonies were used for further identification. The remaining colonies were dark green. As for the isolates obtained from the sediment samples, spore formation was observed in cells for all isolates with a phase-contrast microscope, indicating that the isolates are not a *Vibrio* species but a *Bacillus* species.

For isolates September 1 and December 1, further identification was carried out. Although we did not obtain 100% homologous sequences in the database (Applied Biosystems, CA, USA), the isolate September 1 was related to several species of the genus *Vibrio*, such as *V. campbellii* [99.26%], *V. alginolyticus* [97.03%], *V. mediterranei* [94.42%], and *V. tubiashii* [93.49%]. As for the isolate December 1, the related species of the genus *Vibrio* were *V. campbellii* [92.19%], *V. alginolyticus* [92.01%], *V. mediterranei* [91.45%], *and V. furnissii* [89.96%]. These results indicate that those isolates differ from the type cultures of the *Vibrio* species listed in the database. The partial rRNA sequences of the isolates September 1 and December 1 were deposited in the DDBJ/GenBank/EMBL under the accession numbers AB195981 and AB195982, respectively.

V. cholerae can survive in seawater as well as in fresh water for more than 50 days regardless of being in a viable and colony-forming stage or entered in a viable but non-colony-forming stage (Roszak and Colwell, 1987; Colwell, 1996; Munro and Colwell, 1996). Therefore, development of complete killing of *V. cholerae* in ships' ballast water is one of the most important things to get progressed internationally.

Table 2. Viable number of cells on the TCBS selective plates

Voyage date	Viable number of cells (CFU ml^{-1})	Sampling time and site
May 19 (2002)	0	while loading at the Niigata port in Japan
May 27	0	surface of ballast water
May 27	0	10m depth of ballast water
May 30	2	while discharging in the high seas
May 30	0	while reloading in the high seas
June 5	0	while discharging at the Ras Laffan port in Qatar
June 17	47[a, c]	sediment in a ballast tank
August 26 (2002)	0	while loading at the Yokkaichi port in Japan
September 5	2[b]	surface of ballast water
September 5	0	10m depth of ballast water
September 6	0	while discharging in the high seas
September 6	0	while reloading in the high seas
September 10	0	while discharging at the Ras Laffan port in Qatar
September 16	0[a]	sediments in ballast tanks
November 28 (2002)	0	while loading at the Yokkaichi port in Japan
December 5	4[b]	surface of ballast water
December 5	0	10m depth of ballast water
December 7	0	while discharging in the high seas
December 7	0	while reloading in the high seas
December 13	0	while discharging at the Ras Laffan port in Qatar
December 20	0 - 124[a, c]	sediments in ballast tanks
January 31 (2003)	0	while loading at the Yokkaichi port in Japan
February 8	0	surface of ballast water
February 8	0	10m depth of ballast water
February 8	0	while discharging in the high seas
February 9	0	while reloading in the high seas
February 15	0	while discharging at the Ras Laffan port in Qatar
February 24	0[a]	sediments in ballast tanks
April 6 (2003)	0	while loading at the Yokkaichi port in Japan
April 14	0	surface of ballast water

Table 2. Viable number of cells on the TCBS selective plates (cont.)

Voyage date	Viable number of cells (CFU ml^{-1})	Sampling time and site
April 14	2	10m depth of ballast water
April 16	0	while discharging in the high seas
April 16	0	while reloading in the high seas
April 22	0	while discharging at the Ras Laffan port in Qatar
May 3	0[a]	sediments in ballast tanks
July 14 (2003)	0	while loading at the Yokkaichi port in Japan
July 21	0	surface of ballast water
July 21	110	10m depth of ballast water
July 23	2	while discharging in the high seas
July 23	0	while reloading in the high seas
July 30	0	while discharging at the Ras Laffan port in Qatar
August 10	48 - 144[a, c]	sediments in ballast tanks

[a]Sediments were taken from two different ballast tanks except in June 2002. After dilution of the sediment (1 g) with distilled seawater (9 ml), the sample (0.5 ml) was spread onto TCBS selective plates. The number of viable cells was calculated on the basis of the water content of each sample. For example, the number of viable cells, 47 CFU/ml, obtained from the sample in June 2002 was calculated by the following equation: 1 (colony numbers on the plate) x (9.4/0.4) x (1/0.5) = 47 CFU ml^{-1}, where 0.4 ml was the water content in 1 g of the sample.

[b]Yellow colonies were named as Sep1 and Dec1.

[c]All the colonies were disc-shaped and dark green, and spore-forming in the cells was observed with a phase-contrast microscopic.

Experiments were carried out three times for each sample, and the maximum value is shown here.

Reprinted from Marine Pollution Bulletin, 50, H. Mimura, et al., Changes of microbial populations in a ship's ballast water and sediments on a voyage from Japan to Qatar, 751-757, 2005, with permission from Elsevier.

Japan imports large amounts of crude oils and LNG from the Middle East and other countries, indicating almost the same amounts of ballast water are exported from Japan to the foreign countries described above with very large crude oil carriers and LNG carriers. Therefore, investigation for detecting pathogenic *V. cholerae* in the ports and along the coastal area of Japan is very important. Fifty-one *V. cholerae* O1 strains, which were identified to be El Tor biotype, Ogawa serotype, have been isolated in a port of Osaka, Japan in 1987 to 2001 (Miyagi et al., 2003). All of the isolates were cholera toxin (CT) negative and CT gene negative. Continuous investigations should be carried out to ensure that coastal seawater is not polluted by pathogenic *V. cholerae.*

The detection of hazardous *Vibrio* species by the use of the plate-counting method is time consuming; therefore, the development of an on-time detection system is required for the effective management of ballast water. Polymerase chain reaction (PCR) to amplify *rfb* gene which is specific for the O1 and the O139 serogroups of *V. cholerae* was applied to the rapid detection of pathogenic *V. cholerae* O1 and O139 (Hoshino et al., 1998). The PCR technique has been developed to detect *V. cholerae* more reliable and rapid (Gubala, 2006). Colony hybridization assay is a potent technique to detect environmental *V. cholerae* (Robert-Pillot et al., 2002).

3. Ballast Water Management in Order to Prevent Diffusion of Non-Native Species

3. 1. Treatment of Ballast Water by Chemical and Physical Approaches

Complete killing of all the living things, e.g., invertebrates and their eggs, dinoflagellate cysts, and marine bacteria, in ships' ballast water is the final goal of the ballast water management. The sophisticated technology of the ballast water treatment, however, has not been developed yet.

Chemical treatment of ballast water and sediment were proposed. Successful results were obtained by the addition of sodium hypochlorite (NaOCl) to residual ballast sediment including diapausing invertebrate eggs (Gray, et al., 2006). Neutralization of NaOCl, however, is not negligible before the discharge of treated residuals with sodium bisulfite. Naphthoquinones, which are the broad spectrum biocides, showed effectiveness to phytoplankton and marine bacteria (Wright, et al., 2007). Resting eggs of invertebrates were sensitive to menadione (Raikow, et al., 2006) which is in the group of naphthoquinones. Ozonation of seawater is an option to treat ballast water (Perrins et al., 2006). Ozone dose not persist in seawater. Toxicity of seawater ozonation is likely resulted from the oxidation of bromide ion in seawater to bromine species such as HOBr and OBr^- (Jones, et al., 2006). These compounds persist more than 2 days in seawater; therefore, addition of sodium thiosulfate ($Na_2S_2O_3$) was necessary to eliminate total residual oxidant. The residual chemicals in the treated ballast water and sediment might affect on the local marine environment where the ballast water is discharged. Further study is required in order to apply any chemicals to the treatment of real ships' ballast water and sediment.

Oxygen limitation for two to three days by purging with nitrogen gas in a real ship's ballast tank was effective for larvae of green crab and zebra mussel (Tamburri, et al., 2002). Oxygen limitation also contributed for reducing corrosion of ballast tanks.

Physical treatment of ballast water and sediment seem to be environmentally friendly methods although, at present, it is difficult to treat huge amounts of ballast water loaded on board within a given time. Pulsed electric field of up to 25 KV/cm^2 was applied to the inactivation of Gram negative *Escherichia coli*, Gram positive *Staphylococcus aureus*, and spore-forming *Bacillus cereus* cells suspended in glycerol solution in combination with 20 MPa of CO_2 (Spilimbergo et al., 2003). Reciprocal hydrostatic pressures under 200 – 400 MPa enhanced the damage of *Bacillus subtilis* spores morphologically and structurally in comparison with those treated by continuous hydrostatic pressures (Furukawa et al., 2003). These results indicate that high pressure variations cause mechanical stress to the cells. Actually, dynamic shock pressures inactivated marine *Vibrio* sp. cells (Abe et al., 2005; Mimura et al., 2006; Abe et al., 2007; Mimura et al., 2007) (see chapters below).

As for the mechanical treatment of ballast water, filtration of seawater using crumb rubber is a good option as a primary treatment process (Tang, et al., 2006). A substantial reduction of phytoplankton and zooplankton in seawater has been achieved by this method.

3.2. *Vibrio* sp. September 1 and Properties of Shock Pressures

We examined the lethality of shock pressures to the *Vibrio* sp. September 1 cells. This strain was isolated from a ship's ballast water and identified as genus *Vibrio* based on the biochemical, physiological, and the partial 16S ribosomal DNA sequences. The sequences have been deposited in the DDBJ/EMBL/GenBank under the accession number AB195981 (Mimura et al., 2005).

Microbial control of ships' ballast water is mainly to prevent the outbreak of infectious dieses caused by pathogenic *V. cholerae*. Since it is hazardous to experiment on pathogenic *V. cholerae* in the laboratory with no specific equipment to prevent infection, we used non-toxic *Vibrio* sp. September 1. In general, most of marine *Vibrio* sp. show temperature sensitivity for growth at more than 20°C. The isolate, however, could grow even at 37°C. As the energy source, the isolate metabolized sucrose. These properties are similar to those of *V. cholerae*.

The schematic of the single-stage gas gun is shown in Figure 6. Shock pressures can be generated by hitting a projectile (Figure 6, circle 3) to the aluminum container (Figure 6, circle 6), where cell suspension was maintained tightly. The diameter and the length of the launch tube for hitting a projectile directly upon the aluminum container were 40 mm and 2 m, respectively. Total length of the mechanism from the high pressure gas reservoir to the vacuum chamber was 4.25 m. In this experiment, pressurized helium gas was used to shoot a projectile, where the value of the maximum gas pressure was 2 MPa in that reservoir. The projectile was shot when the valve opened (Figure 6, circle 13). The velocity of the projectile just before hitting the aluminum container was measured by the magnet-flyer method. Briefly, the velocity of a projectile containing a magnet (Figure 6, circle 3) was calculated from the time, which was measured when the projectile passed through two of the magnetic coils located at the guide pipe, and the distance between them (60 mm). The velocity of a projectile adjusted to 56 g was roughly regulated by the high pressure gas charged into the reservoir (Figure 6, circle 1 and 11). After the experiment, the cell suspension was recovered and the number of colony-forming cells was counted by the plate counting method.

A pressure gauge (Piezofilm PVF_2, 11-.125-EK, Dynasen, CA, USA), which had 9 mm^2 of detectable area and 28 μm of thickness, was used to measure the changes in shock pressures propagated in the cell suspension. The average value for the response period to the changes in shock pressures was 10 ns, and the detectable maximum pressure was 10 GPa. This pressure gauge was placed in the aluminum container.

Just after the projectile hit the aluminum container, shock pressures (σ, MPa) were generated, and their values were calculated by the following equation listed in the instruction manual of the pressure gauge:

$$\sigma = \left\{ 5.8 \cdot \left(\frac{Q}{A} \right) + 3.8 \cdot \left(\frac{Q}{A} \right)^{1.6} + 0.55 \cdot \left(\frac{Q}{A} \right)^{3.5} \right\} \times 10^2 \text{ (MPa)} \tag{1}$$

where $$\frac{Q}{A}=\frac{0.0198\cdot V_m}{C_s}\cdot\frac{0.9955}{1+0.01\cdot(20-T_c)} \qquad (2).$$

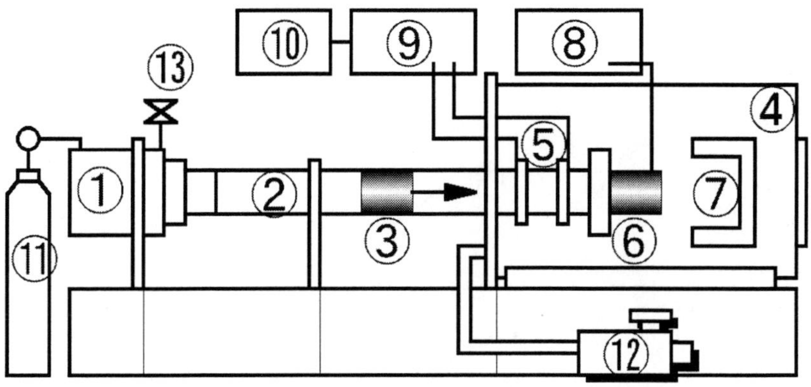

Figure 6. Schematic of the single-stage gas gun. The single-stage gas gun is composed of some main parts as follows: a high pressure gas reservoir (1), launch tube (2), projectile (3), vacuum chamber (4), magnet coils (5), aluminum container (6), receiver (7), oscilloscope for the pressure gauge (8), oscilloscope for the magnet coils (9), x-y plotter (10), high pressure He gas cylinder (11), vacuum pump (12), and valve (13). This figure is reprinted from Biocontrol Science, 11, H. Mimura, et al., Lethality of shock pressures to a marine *Vibrio* sp. isolated from a ship's ballast water, 159-166, 2006, with permission from the society for antibacterial and antifungal agents, Japan.

The value of Q/A means the electric charge (μC cm^{-2}) per the active area of pressure gauge (cm^2). The pressure gauge converts the strain, which was caused by shock pressures, into the voltage (V). The values of the integrated voltages (V_m) with the charge integrator (CI-50-0.1, Dynasen, CA, USA) were used in equation (2), where the quasi calibration value of C_s (μC cm^{-2}) and the calibration temperature of T_c (°C) are individual for each pressure gauge.

Changes in shock pressures propagated and reflected in the cell suspension were measured as a function of time just after the projectile hit the aluminum container (Figure 7). It took 3 - 4 μs for the front waves to reach the bottom of the cylindrical well, regardless of the impact speeds of projectiles. The maximum value in shock pressures increased in response to the impact speed of a projectile; 114 MPa at 56 m s^{-1} (Figure 7A), 239 MPa at 96 m s^{-1} (Figure7B), and 282 MPa at 168 m s^{-1} (Figure 7C). Negative pressures were observed in a narrow range just behind the peak pressure, and a wide range of them appeared after about 26 μs and 15 μs for the impact velocities of 96 m s^{-1} and 168 m s^{-1}, respectively (Figure 7B and 7C). The reflection of shock waves resulted in the complicated pressure changes behind the front wave.

Changes in the maximum shock pressures were closely related to those in the impact velocities against the aluminum container (y = 2.15x) (Figure 8), indicating the lethality of shock pressures can be discussed in terms of either of them.

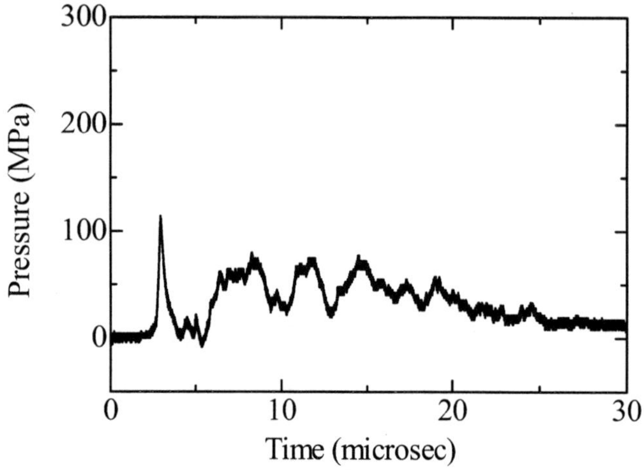

(A)

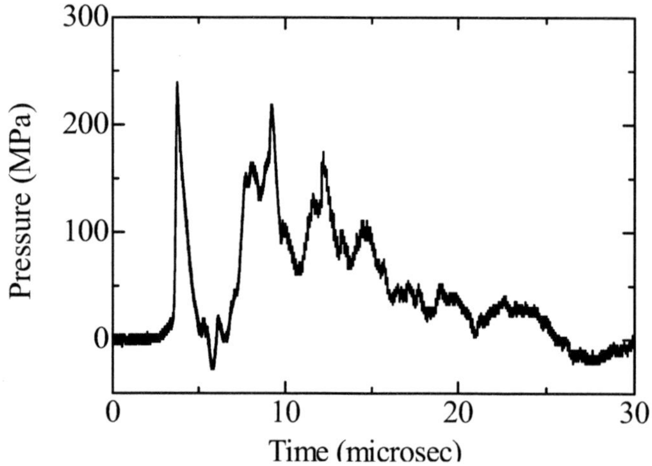

(B)

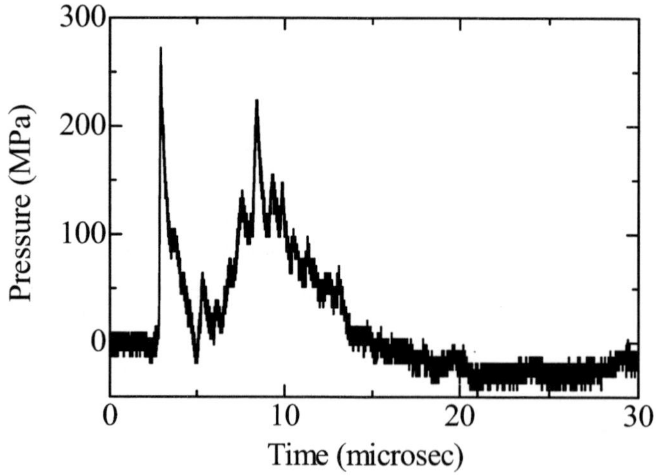

(C)

Figure 7. Changes in shock pressures detected at the bottom of a cylindrical well. Changes of shock pressures in the cell suspension are shown in response to the time (μs) just after the projectile hit the aluminum container at the velocities of 56 (A), 96 (B), and 168 m/s (C). This figure is reprinted from Biocontrol Science, 11, H. Mimura, et al., Lethality of shock pressures to a marine *Vibrio* sp. isolated from a ship's ballast water, 159-166, 2006, with permission from the society for antibacterial and antifungal agents, Japan.

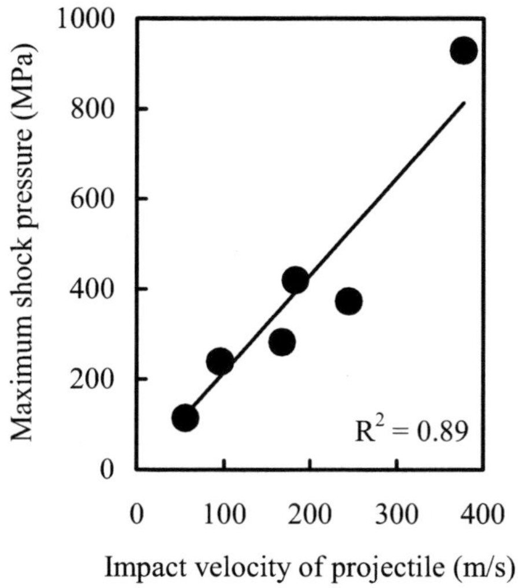

Figure 8. Correlation between the maximum shock pressure generated and the impact velocity of a projectile against the aluminum container. This figure is reprinted from Biocontrol Science, 11, H. Mimura, et al., Lethality of shock pressures to a marine *Vibrio* sp. isolated from a ship's ballast water, 159-166, 2006, with permission from the society for antibacterial and antifungal agents, Japan.

3.3. Inactivation of *Vibrio* sp. September 1 by Exposure to Shock Pressures

Cells at the early stationary phase of growth were suspended in the solution containing 0.4 M NaCl, 10 mM KCl, 10 mM $CaCl_2 \cdot 2H_2O$, 53 mM $MgCl_2$, and 28 mM Na_2SO_4, where pH was adjusted to 7.8 by 10 mM 2-[4-(2-hydroxyethyl)-1-piperazinyl]ethanesulfonic acid - tetramethylammonium hydroxide. After the cells were exposed to shock pressures, the number of colony-forming cells was counted using the plate counting method (Figure 9). There was a correlation between the increase in the impact velocity of a projectile and the reduction of the number of colony-forming cells (y = -0.076x + 8.13). The initial number of colony-forming cells was $10^{8.5\pm0.1}$ CFU ml^{-1}. When the velocities of the projectiles were increased 56 - 64 m s^{-1}, total numbers of colony-forming cells reduced to $10^{3.3}$ - $10^{3.4}$ CFU ml^{-1}. The reduction of $10^{7.0}$ CFU ml^{-1} was observed when the impact velocity of a projectile was 96 m s^{-1}. Complete loss of colony-forming ability was seen at the impact velocity of more than 115 m s^{-1} against the aluminum container. These results indicate that the reduction of colony-forming cells is primarily related to the maximum value of shock pressures.

As for *E. coli* cells, they became inactivated by a high hydrostatic pressure of around 200 MPa (Aertsen et al., 2005). Inactivation, however, was incomplete even at 400 MPa. When shock pressures were employed, the peak value of 282 MPa was enough to obtain the complete inactivation of the *Vibrio* sp. cells. In the process of propagation and reflection of shock pressures, negative shock pressures as well as high positive ones occurred within microsecond order. Drastic changes in shock pressures including negative ones might play an important role in the complete inactivation efficiency.

3.4. Additional Effect of Sodium Ascorbate on the Number of Colony-Forming *Vibrio* sp. September 1 Cells After Exposure to Shock Pressures

Sodium ascorbate (VitC-Na) has a potent radical-scavenging ability (Sawai et al., 2005). When the cells were exposed to shock pressures generated by hitting a projectile against the aluminum container at the velocity of 84 m/s in the presence of VitC-Na at a final concentration of 2%, the total number of colony-forming cells was scarcely changed in comparison to the initial number of $10^{8.5\pm0.1}$ CFU/ml. Slight reduction, 0.6-log cycle, was obtained at the projectile velocity of 91 m/s. In the absence of VitC-Na, the total numbers of colony-forming cells were estimated to be $10^{1.2}$ - $10^{1.7}$ CFU ml^{-1} at the impact velocities of 84 to 91 m s^{-1} on the basis of the regression curve shown in Figure 9. These results indicate the possibility that radicals are generated in the process of the propagation of shock pressures in the cell suspension, and the generated radicals contribute to the loss of the colony-forming ability of the cells directly or indirectly.

A high hydrostatic pressure around 300 to 400 MPa gave endogenous oxidative stress to *E. coli* cells (Aertsen et al., 2005). Therefore, it could be thought that the lethality of shock pressures is closely related to the generation of radicals in the cell suspension.

As shown in Figure 7 (B) and 7 (C), negative pressures had been detected during the propagation of shock pressures in the solution. These negative pressures can induce cavitations in the solution, and radical species such as hydroxyl radicals (Clarke and Hill, 1970) and chloride radicals seem to be generated when cavitations are disrupted by drastic changes in shock pressures. Those radicals generated might contribute the synthesis of a toxic compound such as sodium hypochlorite (NaOCl) in the solution during the propagation of shock pressures.

The samples obtained in the presence and absence of VitC-Na were also spread onto the agar plates containing 0.8% sodium cholate (Figure 9). When the impact velocities were 84 and 91 m s^{-1}, total numbers of colony-forming cells in the samples obtained in the presence of VitC-Na were reduced to $10^{4.9}$ and $10^{4.6}$ CFU ml^{-1} from $10^{8.5}$ and $10^{7.9}$ CFU ml^{-1}, respectively. The reduction of the number of colony-forming cells was also confirmed in the absence of VitC-Na at the impact velocity of 45 m s^{-1}. The intact cells showed the ability to make colonies on the agar plate containing 0.8% of sodium cholate, and the number of colony-forming cells was consistent with that on the agar plate without sodium cholate. The cells surviving the exposure to shock pressures in the absence and presence of VitC-Na showed sensitivity to sodium cholate, indicating that the surviving cells had been given sub-lethal damage by shock pressures.

In general, gram-negative bacteria show the resistance to high levels of bile salts including sodium cholate, which are powerful detergents that disrupt biological membranes. The outer membrane barrier plays an important role in the cell survival in the presence of bile salts. However, bile salts should be able to pass through the OmpF porin in *E. coli* cells (Plésiat and Nikaido, 1992) and enter into the cytoplasm. The bile salts in the cytoplasm are pumped out by an energy-dependent efflux mechanism (Thanassi et al., 1997; Yokota et al., 2000). Consequently, the increased sensitivity of the isolate to sodium cholate by the exposure to lethal shock pressures including the maximum value of around 239 MPa closely depends on damage of the outer membrane structure and/or the inactivation of membrane-bound proteins, which can pump sodium cholate out into the periplasm.

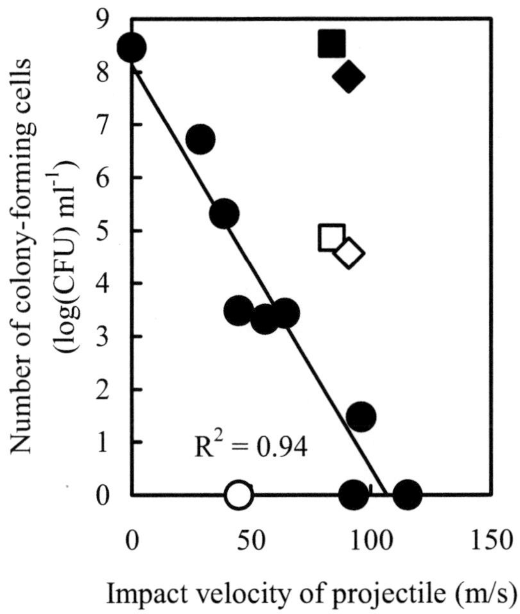

Figure 9. Changes in the number of colony-forming cells after the exposure to shock pressures in the absence and presence of sodium ascorbate. Colony-forming cells were counted after the cells were exposed to shock pressures in the absence (closed circles) and presence (a closed square and a closed lozenge) of sodium ascorbate (VitC-Na) at a final concentration of 2%. The samples obtained in the absence (an open circle) and the presence (an open square and an open lozenge) of 2% VitC-Na were also spread onto the agar plates containing 0.8% sodium cholate. This figure is reprinted from Biocontrol Science, 11, H. Mimura, et al., Lethality of shock pressures to a marine *Vibrio* sp. isolated from a ship's ballast water, 159-166, 2006, with permission from the society for antibacterial and antifungal agents, Japan.

Proteins in both the supernatant and cell pellet were measured after the cells were exposed to lethal shock pressures which were generated by hitting projectiles at the velocities of 120-150 m s^{-1} in the absence of VitC-Na. The initial value of the cell-associated protein content was 0.70 ± 0.01 mg ml^{-1} (n=3) in the cell suspension. After the exposure to lethal shock pressures, the protein content in the supernatant was increased to 0.07 mg ml^{-1}, while the cell-associated protein content was decreased to 0.62 ± 0.02 mg ml^{-1} (n=3). The exposure to lethal shock pressures resulted in the reduction of about 11% of the cell-associated proteins, indicating that shock pressures give damage to the outer membrane structure.

As for gram-negative bacteria, channel proteins called porins are localized in the outer membrane, and the periplasm contains hydrolytic enzymes, substrate binding proteins, and chemoreceptors. If the cytoplasmic membrane was burst by the exposure to shock pressures, the protein content measured in the supernatant should be higher than 11% of total cell-associated proteins. It seems likely that the loss of colony-forming ability caused by the exposure to lethal shock pressures mainly depends on the structural changes of the outer membrane rather than the damage to the cytoplasmic membrane.

3.5. Observation of Morphological Changes of Cells Exposed by Shock Pressures with a Scanning Electron Microscope

Complete killing of the cells were obtained when the projectile velocities were more than 196 m/s even in the presence of 2% sodium ascorbate (Figure 10), where the maximum shock pressure estimated was 421 MPa.

Morphological changes of the cells were observed with a scanning electron microscope before (Figure 11A) and after the exposure to lethal shock pressures (Figure 11B and 11C). The rod shape was maintained, where the impact velocity of a projectile was 168 m/s against the aluminum container (Figure 11B). The center of all the cells, however, was caved in like erythrocytes. Although it seems hard to conclude that lethal shock pressures caused the cave-in on the center of each cell, it is possible to think that the cave-in was created after the cells were dead. Morphological changes after the exposure to lethal shock pressures in the presence of 2% sodium ascorbate are shown in Figure 11C. Burst cells were seen at the projectile velocity of 267 m/s, where the maximum shock pressure estimated was 574 MPa. These results strongly indicate that the lethal shock pressures are able to cause structural damage to the bacterial cell wall.

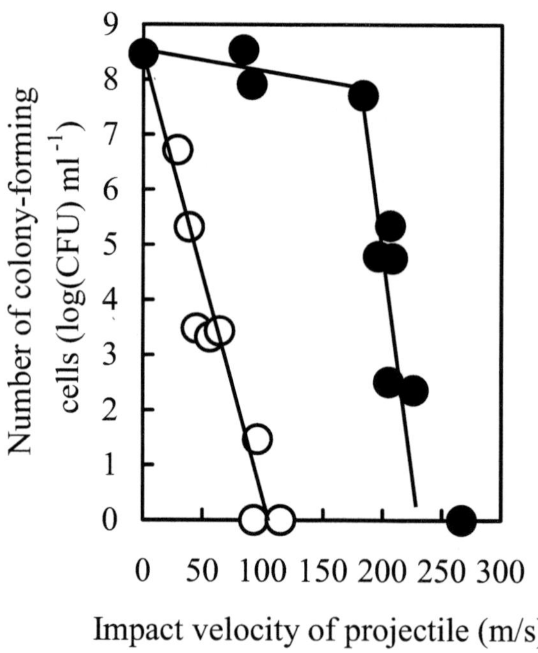

Figure 10. Changes in the number of colony-forming cells after exposure to high shock pressures. Cells were exposed to various values of shock pressures, where the peak value varied up to 574 MPa, in the absence (open circles) and presence of 2% sodium ascorbate (closed circles). This figure is reprinted from bulletin of the society of sea water science, Japan, 61, H. Mimura, et al., Changes in the number of colony-forming marine *Vibrio* sp. cells after exposure to shock pressures in the presence of sodium ascorbate, in press, 2007, with permission from the society of sea water science, Japan.

(A) (B) (C)

Figure 11. Morphological changes of the *Vibrio* sp. September 1 cells after exposure to shock pressures. Before (A) and after the exposure to shock pressures generated at the projectile velocities of 168 m/s (B) and 267 m/s (C), morphological changes of the cells were observed with a scanning electron microscope. Sample preparation for scanning electron microscopy is shown below. Cells at the early stationary phase of growth (10 ml) were filtrated with a membrane filter (pore size, 0.45 μm) and washed with 50 ml of the solution. Then cells on the membrane filter were resuspended in 50 ml of the same solution. Cells were fixed in 1% (vol/vol) glutaraldehyde for 1 h at 4°C after the exposure to shock pressures; dehydrated once for 1 h in 50, 70, 90, 95, and 100% of ethanol; and suspended in 100% of *t*-butyl alcohol. After being freeze-dried, they were pasted on a carbon tape and coated with Pt-Pd particles under vacuum. The samples thus obtained were observed with a scanning electron microscope (XL30 CP, FEI Company, Eindhoven, the Netherlands). The figures, (A) and (C), are reprinted from bulletin of the society of sea water science, Japan, 61, H. Mimura, et al., Changes in the number of colony-forming marine *Vibrio* sp. cells after exposure to shock pressures in the presence of sodium ascorbate, in press, 2007, with permission from the society of sea water science, Japan. The figure (B) is reprinted from Biocontrol Science, 11, H. Mimura, et al., Lethality of shock pressures to a marine *Vibrio* sp. isolated from a ship's ballast water, 159-166, 2006, with permission from the society for antibacterial and antifungal agents, Japan.

CONCLUSION

Recently, the consumption of LNG is increasing in the world. Japan is not exceptional. Therefore, the export of ballast water from Japan to the port of call increases with an increase in the demand of LNG in Japan. The unloading time of the cargo is about 1 day at a port in Japan as for a LNG carrier (110,000 tons gross). It seems difficult to use solid ballast mainly for LNG ships because of the short stay at the port, indicating the importance of the efficient management of ballast water and sediment.

Microbial control of ships' ballast water is very important to maintain human health because pathogenic *V. cholerae* has been detected from ballast water and sediment in some overseas vessels. Throughout the experiment, we could confirm that shock pressures have great potential to kill marine *Vibrio* sp. However, the technical problem still remains regarding the volume treated in one batch. Precise analyses for the lethality of shock pressures to the bacterial cells are necessary in order to develop an efficient system for the treatment of ballast water by the use of shock pressures.

REFERENCES

Abe, A., Mimura, H., Ikeda, T., and Katakura, R. 2005. Shock compression of marine bacterial cells enclosed in aluminum container (in Japanese). *J. Jpn. Inst. Mar. Eng.*, 40, pp. 260-265.

Abe, A., Mimura, H., Ishida, H., and Yoshida, K. 2007. The effect of shock pressures on the inactivation of a marine *Vibrio* sp. Shock Waves, in press.

Aertsen, A, Spiegeleer, P. D., Vanoirbeek, K., Lavilla, M., and Michiels, C. W. 2005. Induction of oxidative stress by high hydrostatic pressure in *Escherichia coli. Appl. Environ. Microbiol.*, 71, pp. 2226-2231.

Ambros, P. 1996. US legislate to prevent zebra mussel spread. *Mar. Pollut. Bull.,* 32, pp. 765-766.

Clarke, P. R. and Hill, C. R. 1970. Physical and chemical aspects of ultrasonic disruption of cells. *J. Acoust. Soc. Amer.*, 47, pp. 649-653.

Colwell, R. R. 1996. Global climate and infectious disease: The Cholera paradigm. *Science*, 274, pp. 2025-2031.

Furukawa, S., Shimoda, M., and Hayakawa, I. 2003. Mechanism of the inactivation of bacterial spores by reciprocal pressurization treatment. *J. Appl. Microbiol.*, 94, pp. 836-841.

Gray, D. K., Duggan, I. C., and Macisaac, H. J. 2006. Can sodium hypochlorite reduce the risk of species introductions from diapausing invertebrate eggs in non-ballasted ships? *Mar. Pollut. Bull.*, 52, pp. 689-695.

Gubala, A. J. 2006. Multiplex real-time PCR detection of Vibrio cholerae. *J. Microbiol. Methods*, 65, pp. 278-293.

Hoshino, K., Yamasaki, S., Mukhopadhyay, A. K., Chakraborty, S., Basu, A., Bhattacharya S. K., Nair, G. B., Shimada, T., and Takeda, Y. 1998. Development and evaluation of a multiplex PCR assay for rapid detection of toxigenic *Vibrio cholerae* O1 and O139. *FEMS Immunol. Med. Microbiol.,* 20, pp. 201-207.

International Maritime Organization, Global ballast water management program. available from the web site *<http://globallast.imo.org/index.asp?page=AwarenessMaterials.htm&menu=true>*.

Jones, A. C., Gensemer, R. W., Stubblefield, W. A., van Genderen, E., Dethloff, G. M., and Cooper, W. J. 2006. Toxicity of ozonated seawater to marine organisms. *Environ. Toxicol. Chem.*, 25, pp. 2683-2691.

Kozai, K., Ishida, H., Okamoto, K., and Fukuyo, Y. 2006. Feasibility study of ocean color remote sensing for detecting ballast water. *Adv. Space Res.*, pp. 787-792.

Krieg, N. R. 1984. *Bergey's manual of systematic bacteriology*. Vol. 1, Williams and Wilkins, Baltimore, MD.

Louis, V. R., R-Cohen, E., Choopun, N., Rivera, I. N. G., Gangle, B., Jiang, S. C., Rubin, A., Patz, J. A., Huq, A., and Colwell, R. R. 2003. Predictability of *Vibrio cholerae* in Chesapeake Bay. *Appl. Environ. Microbiol.,* 69, pp. 2773-2785.

Mimura, H., Katakura, R., and Ishida, H. 2005. Changes of microbial populations in a ship's ballast water and sediments on a voyage from Japan to Qatar. *Mar. Pollut. Bull.*, 50, pp. 751-757.

Mimura, H., Abe, A., Katakura, R., Kawasaki, H., Yoshida, K., and Ishida, H. 2006. Lethality of shock pressures to a marine *Vibrio* sp. isolated from a ship's ballast water. *Biocont. Sci.*, 11, pp. 159-166.

Mimura, H., Abe, A., Yoshida, K., and Ishida, H. 2007. Changes in the number of colony-forming marine *Vibrio* sp. cells after exposure to shock pressures in the presence of sodium ascorbate. *Bull. Soc. Sea Water Sci.*, Jpn., in press.

Miyagi, K., Nakano, T., Yagi, T., Hanafusa, M., Imura, S., Honda, T., Nakano, Y., and Sano, K. 2003. Survey of *Vibrio cholerae* O1 and its survival over the winter in marine water of Port of Osaka. *Epidemiol. Infect.*, 131, pp. 613-619.

Munro, P. M. and Colwell, R. R. 1996. Fate of *Vibrio cholerae* O1 in seawater microcosms. *Water Res.*, 30, pp. 47-50.

Perrins, J. C., Cooper, W. J., van Leeuwen, J., and Herwig, R. P. 2006. Ozonation of seawater from different locations: formation and decay of total residual oxidant-implications for ballast water treatment. *Mar. Pollut. Bull.*, 52, 1023-1033.

Pfeffer, C. and Oliver, J. D. 2003. A comparison of thiosulphate-citrate-bile salts-sucrose (TCBS) agar and thiosulphate-chloride-iodide (TCI) agar for the isolation of *Vibrio* species from estuarine environments. *Lett. Appl. Microbiol.*, 36, pp. 150-151.

Pimentel, D., Lach, L., Zuniga, R., Morrison, D., 2000. Environmental and economic costs of nonindigenous species in the United States. *BioScience*, 50. pp. 53-65.

Plésiat, P. and Nikaido, H. 1992. Outer membranes of gram-negative bacteria are permeable to steroid probes. *Mol. Microbiol.*, 6, pp. 1323-1333.

Raikow, D. E., Reid, D. E., Maynard, E. E., and Landrum, P. E. 2006. Sensitivity of aquatic invertebrate resting eggs to SeaKleen (Menadione): a test of potential ballast tank treatment options. *Environ. Toxicol. Chem.*, 25. pp. 552-559.

Robert-Pillot, A., Baron, S., Lesne, J., Fournier, J. M., and Quilici, M. L. 2002. Improved specific detection of *Vibrio cholerae* in environmental *Water SA*mples by culture on selective medium and colony hybridization assay with an oligonucleotide probe. *FEMS Microbiol. Ecol.*, 40, pp. 39-46.

Roszak, D. B. and Colwell, R. R. 1987. Survival Strategies of bacteria in the natural environment. *Microbiol. Rev.,* 51, pp. 365-379.

Sawai, Y., Moon, J-H., Sakata, K., and Watanabe, N. 2005. Effects of structure on radical-scavenging abilities and antioxidative activities of tea polyphenols: NMR analytical approach using 1,1-diphenyl-2-picrylhydrazyl radicals. *J. Agric. Food Chem.*, 53, pp. 3598-3604.

Spilimbergo, S., Dehghani, F., Bertucco, A., and Foster, N. R. 2003. Inactivation of bacteria and spores by pulse electric field and high pressure CO_2 at low temperature. *Biotechnol. Bioeng.*, 82, pp. 118-125.

Tamburri, M. N., Wasson, K., and Matsuda, M. 2002. Ballast water deoxygenation can prevent aquatic introductions while reducing ship corrosion. *Biol. Conservation*, 103, pp. 331-341.

Tang, Z., Butkus, M. A., and Xie, Y. F. 2006. Crumb rubber filtration: a potential technology for ballast water treatment. *Mar. Environ. Res.*, 61, pp. 410-423.

Thanassi, D., Cheng, L. W., and Nikaido, H. 1997. Active efflux of bile salts by *Escherichia coli*. *J. Bacteriol.*, 179, pp. 2512-2518.

Yokota, A., Veenstra, M., Kurdi, P., Veen, H. W., and Konings, W. N. 2000. Cholate resistance in *Lactococcus lactis* is mediated by an ATP-dependent multispecific organic anion transporter. *J. Bacteriol.*, 182, pp. 5196-5201.

Wright, D. A., Dawson, R., Cutler, S. J., Cutler, H. G., Orano-Dawson, C. E., and Graneli, E. 2007. Naphthoquinones as broad spectrum biocides for treatment of ship's ballast water: Toxicity to phytoplankton and bacteria. *Water Res.*, 41, pp. 1294-1302.

In: Environmental Microbiology Research Trends
Editor: G. V. Kurladze, pp. 213-235
ISBN: 978-1-60021-939-9

Chapter 7

Biodiversity and Ecology of Eukaryotic Organisms in Extreme Acidic Environments, the Río Tinto Case

***Angeles Aguilera*[1]*, *Virginia Souza-Egipsy*[1] *and Ricardo Amils* [1,2]**

[1] Centro de Astrobiología, Instituto Nacional de Técnica Aeroespacial, Carretera de Ajalvir, Torrejón de Ardoz, Madrid, Spain

[2] Centro de Biología Molecular (UAM-CSIC). Universidad Autónoma de Madrid. Canto Blanco, Madrid, Spain.

Abstract

A major issue in microbial ecology is to identify the limits of life for growth and survival, and to understand the molecular mechanisms that define these limits. Thus, interest in the biodiversity and ecology of extreme environments has grown in recent years for several reasons. Some are basic and revolve around the idea that extreme environments are believed to reflect early Earth conditions. Other issues are related to the biotechnological potential of extremophiles, such as the use of the metabolic properties of some microorganisms for metal extraction.

In this regard, the study of extremely acidic environments (pH<3) has become increasingly important since environmental acidity is often caused by microbial activity. Highly acidic environments are relatively scarce worldwide and are generally associated with volcanic activity or mining operations. In addition to high acidity, these environments exhibit a range of chemical and physical conditions, depending on their origin and the geochemical nature of the site. For most acidic environments, low pH facilitates metal solubility, and therefore acidic waters tend to have high concentrations of heavy metals. Volcanic areas are even more inhospitable due to the exposure to toxic gases and elevated temperatures, and acidic lakes or rivers are sometimes deeply colored

* Corresponding author: Angeles Aguilera. Mailing address: Centro de Astrobiología (INTA-CSIC). Instituto Nacional de Técnica Aeroespacial. Carretera de Ajalvir Km4, 28850 Torrejón de Ardoz. Madrid. Spain. Phone:+34-915206461. Fax: +34-915201074. Email: aaguilera@cbm.uam.es

by humic acid or high concentrations of ferric iron, producing unfavorable conditions for photosynthetic organisms. However, highly acidic environments are usually inhabited by acidophilic and acidotolerant eukaryotic microorganisms such as algae, amoebas, ciliates, heliozoan and rotifers not to mention filamentous fungi and yeast. This chapter will review the general trends concerning the diversity and ecophysiology of eukaryotic acidophilic microorganims, as well as summarize our latest results on this topic in one of the largest extreme acidic rivers, Río Tinto (SW, Spain).

1. INTRODUCTION

Extreme Environments and Extremophiles

Exploration of the Biosphere has led to continued discoveries of life in environments that were previously considered uninhabitable. Thus, life can survive and sometimes thrive under what seem to be harsh environmental conditions. Extreme environments (defined from our anthropocentric view) usually possess various factors incompatible with most life forms. However, in spite of the apparent hostility of such habitats, they may contain a higher level of biodiversity than expected. The environment that we are familiar with is full of oxygen, never too cold nor too hot (most of the visible organisms live in a relatively limited range of temperatures from 5°C to 40°C), and is protected from most damaging atmospheric radiation. This familiar world defines what we consider normal, and the organisms that live at the edges of this world or beyond it are the 'extremophiles.'

The number of different organisms known to reside and thrive in these environmentally extreme conditions has grown rapidly in recent years (Table 1). For example, we find robust microbial communities at high temperature ranges, i.e. the hot springs acidophilic algae (Cyanidiaceae) grow at 45-56ºC, while the hyperthermophilic archaea tolerate a temperature range above the boiling point (>100ºC) [93]. Other organisms live in cold polar zones, such as the psychrophiles of the Antarctica, which are able to live in briny waters, with several times the salinity of seawater and temperatures below -10ºC, beneath 20 m thick ice [81]. Similarly, there are microbes living in very alkaline environments (as high as pH 12) like the rose chafer larvae host [26]. On the other end of the pH scale there are the acidophilic archaea (i.e. *Thermoplasma acidophilum*), or the unicellular alga *Cyanidium caldarium* thriving in very acidic habitats (pH ranges from 0-4) [93]. Some microbial communities have been isolated from hypersaline areas, lakes or mines containing saturated salt solutions such as those present in the Dead Sea, or are able to grow under potent ionizing radiation fields in nuclear reactors. We can also find some microbes that grow under extremely dry conditions and we find others that grow in the deepest parts of the oceans and require 500 to 1000 bars of hydrostatic pressure. To survive, organisms can assume forms that enable them to withstand freezing, complete desiccation, starvation, high-levels of radiation exposure, and other physical or chemical challenges. Furthermore, they can survive exposure to such conditions for weeks, months, years, or even centuries [88].

Interest in discovering extreme environments and the organisms that inhabit them has grown over the past years due to both basic, the idea that extreme environments are believed to reflect early Earth conditions in which prokaryotes originally evolved and adapted, and applied aspects, i.e. extremophiles as sources of enzymes and other cell products.

Table 1. Definitions of the main extremophile groups and their environmental conditions

Extreme	Name	Minimum	Optimum	Maximum
Temperature	Thermophiles		> 50ºC	> 60ºC
	Hyperthermophiles	> 60ºC	> 65ºC	> 70ºC
	Psycrophiles	0ºC	< 25-30ºC	
pH	Alkaliphiles		< 8.5	> 10.0
	Acidophiles	> 0	< 3.0	
Salt	Halophiles	> 2 %	5- 20 % 30 %	
Pressure	Barophiles	> 0.1 MPa	10 - 50 MPa	< 100 MPa

From Olliver et al. (2000)

Microbial life probably began about 3.5 billion years ago, and the first evolutionary steps occurred in a world without oxygen, with an atmosphere unable to provide protection from ultraviolet radiation, and with water bodies which were hot and probably acidic. The diversity of life on Earth today is the result of the dynamic interplay between genetic opportunity, metabolic capability and environmental challenges. For most of its existence, our habitable environment has been dominated by microorganisms and subjected to their metabolisms. As a consequence of such microbial activities, the physico-chemical conditions on Earth has been constantly changing, determining the path of evolution. For example, the release of molecular oxygen by cyanobacteria as a by-product of photosynthesis had to have an effect on organisms not prepared to deal with the negative aspects of an oxidant atmosphere, leading them to migrate to less stressful anoxic micro-environments. Life has evolved strategies that allow it to survive even the daunting physical and chemical limits to which it has adapted. The altered environment, in turn, posed novel evolutionary challenges to the organisms present, which ultimately resulted in the formation of complex cell systems. Therefore this 'co-evolution' between organisms and their environment is apparently an inherent feature of living systems.

Although originally considered to be nothing more than 'scientific curiosities', the biotechnological potential of these microorganisms and their cellular products is now a major impetus driving research on extremophiles. The fields of biotechnology that could benefit from mining the extremophiles are numerous and include the search for new bioactive compounds for industrial, agricultural, environmental and pharmaceutical uses (Table 2). Many biologists are dependent for their molecular biology work on an extremozyme, the *Taq* polymerase. Isolated in 1965 from a microbe that lives in a bubbling thermal pool in Yellowstone National Park, *Taq* is the heart of the polymerase chain reaction, and companies are still fighting over its patent with annual sales of $80 million [90]. New research initiatives, new companies, even a new journal (*Extremophiles*) are melding basic biology with commercial development. Other examples of extremozymes that are presently used commercially include alkaline proteases for detergents. This is a huge market which is taking up 30% of the total world wide enzyme production. β-carotene, a product used in the food industry is commercially produced from the halophilic green algae, *Dunaliella bardawil.*

Although applications of extremozymes or cell products from extremophiles in industry are still limited, potential applications are extensive [28, 77].

Table 2. Extremophiles and their uses in biotechnology.

Source	Enzymes and biomolecules	Applications
Hyperthermophiles	DNA polymerases	DNA amplification by PCR
50-110ºC	Alkaline phosphatase	Diagnostics
	Proteases and Lipases	Dairy products
	Xylanases	Paper bleaching
	Alcohol dehydrogenase	Chemical synthesis
Psychrophiles	Cellulases and amylases	Detergents
0-15ºC	β-galactosidase	Lactose hydrolysis in milk products
	Ice nucleating proteins	Artificial snow, ice cream
	Polyunsaturated fatty acids	Food additives, dietary supplements
Halophiles	Bacteriorhodopsin	Optical switches in bioelectronics
3-20% salts	γ-linoleic acid, β-carotene	Health foods, food colouring
	Membranas	Surfactants for pharmaceuticals
	Lipids	Liposomes for drug delivery
	Rheological polymers	Oil recovery
Alkaliphiles	Cellulases, xylanases, lipases	Detergents
pH>9	Proteases	Gelatin removal on X-ray film
	Amylases, lipases	Polymer degrading in detergents
Acidophiles	Sulfide oxidizing microorganisms	Recovery of metals
pH 1-5	Microorganisms	Organic acids and solvents

Since the cultured strains already available probably account for less than 1% of the total number of species in most environments, a new approach named *ecogenomics*, based on the complete sequencing of clones containing cosmids or artificial bacterial chromosomes with inserts from extremophiles, has considerably extended the possibility of finding new genes leading to products suitable for industry [21]. However conventional screening methods to seek for novel products and applications are still effective. For example, sampling of deep-sea hydrothermal vents using selective substrates for enrichment cultures has led to the discovery of new thermostable enzymes (esterases, lipases, proteases, xylanases, etc.) [102].

The biotechnology potential of extremophiles is increasing exponentially with the isolation of new organisms, the identification of novel compounds and pathways, and through molecular and biochemical characterization of cellular components. Major advances are likely in the area of protein engineering. For example, the identification of structural properties important for thermal activity and stability will enable the construction of proteins with required catalytic and thermal properties [102].

Advances are also likely to arise from the construction of recombinant microorganisms for specific purposes. A recombinant strain of *Deinococcus radiodurans* has been engineered to degrade organopollutants in radioactive, mixed waste environments [9]. Considering the high number of waste sites contaminated with organopollutants, radionuclides and heavy metals around the world, and the safety hazards and cost involved in physico-chemical clean-up methodologies, the potential use of genetically engineered extremophilic microorganisms, is an important and exciting prospect.

Eukaryotes in Extreme Environments

When we think of extremophiles, prokaryotes come to mind first. Thomas Brock's pioneering studies of extremophiles carried out in Yellowstone's hydrothermal environments, set the focus of life in extreme environments on prokaryotes and their metabolisms [19]. However, eukaryotic microbial life may be found actively growing in almost any extreme condition where there is a source of energy to sustain it, with the only exception of high temperature (>70ºC) [86] and the deep subsurface biosphere. The development of molecular technologies and their application to microbial ecology has increased our knowledge of eukaryotic diversity in many different environments [23]. This is particularly relevant in extreme environments, generally more difficult to replicate in the laboratory.

Recent studies based on molecular ecology have demonstrated that eukaryotic organisms are exceedingly adaptable and not notably less so than the prokaryotes, although most habitats have not been sufficiently well explored for sound generalizations to be made. In fact, molecular analysis has also revealed novel protist genetic diversity in different extreme environments [86] (Figure 1).

Temperature is one of the main factors determining the distribution and abundance of species due to its effects on enzymatic activities [6]. Most extremophiles that survive at high temperatures (95-115ºC) are microorganisms from the archaeal or bacterial domains. On the contrary, for eukaryotic microorganisms, the highest temperature reported is 62ºC, and most of the metazoans are unable to grow above 50ºC [88]. Surprisingly, photosynthetic prokaryotes, such as cyanobacteria, have never been found in hot acidic aquatic systems [18]. Instead, these ecological niches are usually profusely colonized by species of the order Cyanidiales, red unicellular algae [18]. Thus, species from the genera *Galdieria* and *Cyanidium* have been isolated from hot sulfur springs, showing an optimal growth temperature of 45ºC and a maximum growth temperature of 57ºC [93, 104]. These extreme hot springs are usually acidic (pH 0.05-4) and frequently characterized by high concentrations of metals such as cadmium, nickel, iron or arsenic, that are highly toxic to almost all known organisms.

Additionally, eukaryotic microorganisms have colonized environments characterized by temperatures at or below 0ºC. Some algal species bloom at the snow surface during spring [66], and complex microbial communities have been found on glaciers, probably the most widely studies environments after marine ice habitats. Aplanospores of *Chlamydomonas nivalis* are frequently found in high-altitude, persistent snowfields where they are photosynthetically active despite cold temperatures and high levels of ultraviolet radiation [95]. Distinct microbial communities composed of psychrophilic bacteria, microalgae and protozoa colonize and grow in melt pools on the ice surface, or in brine channels in the sub-ice platelet in the Arctic even during winter, at extremely low temperatures of -20ºC [49].

Eukayotes are also frequently found in anaerobic habitats. These environments can be found throughout the Earth, from waste management plants to deep hydrothermal vents on the ocean floor. Important clues about the evolutionary origins of eukaryotes resulted from studies of protists from anoxic, extreme environments. Of particular interest are warm anoxic sediments associated with hydrothermal vents and iron-rich environments that might be analogues for early life [30]. Ciliates are the most common eukaryotes present in anoxic habitats. Free-living ciliates are usually aerobic and they need mitochondrial respiration for energy production. However in anaerobic ciliates mitochondria has been replaced by hydrogenosomes [33]. These anaerobic ciliates are not phylogenetically related, implying that the processes allowing their adaptation developed several times along their evolution, and they have strong morphological similarities to their aerobic relatives, implying that these adaptive processes were rather recent. In addition to the ciliates there is a large number of anaerobic eukaryotes, some of them belonging to the protists, and many of them to the yeasts.

Non aquatic environments, where desiccation is common and water is a scarce resource, are also colonized by eukaryotes. In these ecosystems, open spaces are usually covered by biological soil crusts, a highly specialized community of cyanobacteria, mosses and lichens. Without a doubt, the most colorful coatings on rocks are produced by lichens, a remarkable symbiotic relationship between microscopic algal cells and fungal filaments. Although lichens can also withstand extreme environmental conditions, they generally cannot survive as well in the dry, sun-baked deserts [50].

The most recurrent species of lichens found in deserts are the large colonies of the lime-green map lichen *Rhizocarpon geographicum*, the ashy-gray *Aspicilia cinerea* and the orange *Caloplaca saxicola.* They might be thousands of years old. In fact, the colorful chartreuse rock lichen *Acarospora chlorophana* may grow only a few millimeters per century.

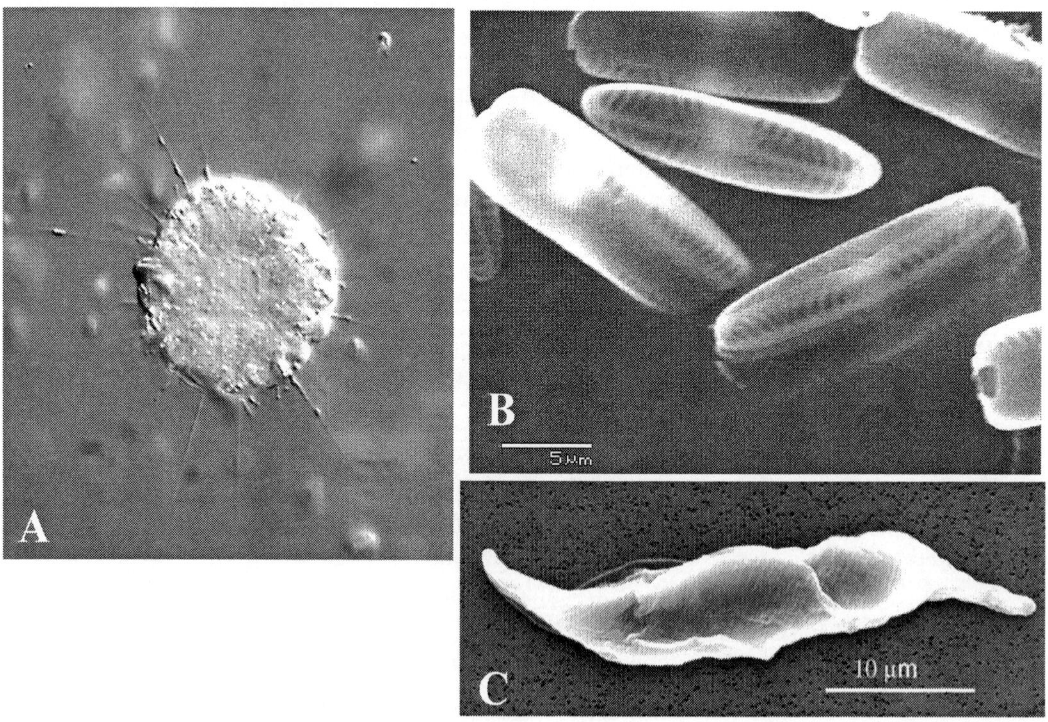

Figure 1. Some examples of eukaryotic acidophiles. A.- The heliozoo *Actinophyris* sp. B.- The diatom *Pinnularia* sp. C.- *Euglena mutabilis*.

Besides deserts, the Antarctic Dry Valleys are some of the driest and most extreme ecosystems on Earth. In these regions there is no ice present and periodically there is very little free water. Mean annual temperatures rarely reach above -30ºC, and annual rainfall of less than 10 mm makes these glacial conditions approach desertification. However, there are microbes and multi-cellular organisms that can survive in this periodically extremely cold and dry ecosystem The top of the food chain is occupied by microscopic nematode worms, In winter, when the weather is too cold and dry, nematodes enter a state of suspended animation, called anhydrobiosis, in which they lose up to 99 percent of the water in their bodies.

In the same manner, a considerable number of eukaryotes can be found in hypersaline environments, such as the Dead Sea, one of the largest and saltiest lakes in the world (close to 34% total dissolved salts) [108]. The unicellular green algae *Dunaliella salina* is able to grow under these high concentrations of salt exposed to intense solar irradiation. This algae can be also found in a wide range of marine habitats such oceans, brine lakes and salt bodies containing more than 2M salt and high levels of magnesium. *Dunaliella* produces and accumulates large amounts of intracellular glycerol as a compatible solute to prevent the high osmotic pressure produce by the ionic concentrations of the surrounding medium, and a high concentration of β-carotene to protect the cell from the damaging effect of solar radiation [14].

Deep-sea hydrothermal vents are also extreme environments in which eukaryotes are widely distributed. These habitats are hot undersea volcanic vents belching sulphur, typically found in the peaks of the midoceanic ridges, where the continental plates are spreading apart. Deep-sea hydrothermal vents support extraordinary *ecosystems* deep beneath the surface of the oceans. These ecosystems are the only communities on Earth whose immediate energy source is not sunlight. Tubeworms (i.e. *Alvinella pompejana)* and clams are the most distinctive inhabitants of Pacific Ocean vent sites, while eyeless shrimp are found only at vents in the Atlantic Ocean. These organisms are capable of surviving sustained, long-term exposure to temperatures up to 80° [24].

Most eukaryotes found in extreme environments are unicellular and the main obstacle to their study is the lack of reliable cultivation methods. Recent advances in DNA technology and statistical analyses have revolutionized the way we make inferences about the biodiversity and biology of organisms. Molecular ecology is an exciting and expanding area that poses a wide array of questions on biodiversity, ecology, physiology, evolution, conservation and management that molecular biology approaches can address. Although these techniques have revealed an unexpectedly high eukaryotic phylogenetic diversity in all kinds of environments, their impact is even more evident in the field of extreme environments, usually more difficult to reproduce in the laboratory. Researchers are now capable of dealing with important questions about microbial diversity that could not be realistically formulated a few years ago.

2. Acidic Environments

One group of extremophiles that is becoming increasingly important, both ecologically and economically, corresponds to acidophilic organisms that live in low pH environments (pH <3). Aquatic extreme acidic systems are in general highly toxic environments because of the high concentrations of protons and metals. Until recently only four eukaryotic organisms were known to grow near pH 0: one algae, *Cyanidium caldarium*, and three fungi, *Acontium cylatium*, *Cephalosporium* spp., and *Trichosporon cerebriae* [91].

Most aquatic acidic habitats have two major origins, one associated to volcanic activities and the other to metal and coal mining [62, 69]. In the first case, acidity is mainly generated by the biological oxidation of elemental sulfur produced as a result of the condensation reactions among sulfur containing volcanic gases. In the second case, metal and coal mining expose sulfidic minerals to the combined action of water and oxygen, which facilitate microbial attack. The most abundant sulfidic mineral, pyrite, is of particular interest in this context. Both habitats vary greatly in their physico-chemical characteristics, and as a consequence, in their microbial ecology. Acidic environments associated to mining operations are very recent on the geological and evolutionary scale, although some metal mining activities have a relatively long history [32].

In the acidic habitats related to mining activity, the extreme conditions found in the environment are the product of the metabolic activity of chemolithotrophic microorganisms, mostly iron- and sulfur-oxidizing bacteria, that can be found in high numbers in their waters. Their iron-oxidizing microorganisms are responsible for the solubilization of sulfidic minerals, mainly pyrite, and the correspondent high concentration of ferric iron, sulphate and protons in the water column [36, 53]. Most of these chemolithotrophic prokaryotes are autotrophic, thus, in addition to promoting the extreme conditions of the habitat they are primary producers [53, 70]. Acidophilic chemolithotrophs, especially *Acidithiobacillus ferrooxidans* and *Leptospirillum* spp. accelerate the rate of pyrite oxidation [31, 53]. At the same time, low pH facilitates metal solubility, therefore acidic water tends to have high concentrations of heavy metals [62].

In this regard, Río Tinto (SW, Spain), a 92-km long acidic river (mean pH 2.3), is one of the most extensive examples of a natural extreme acidic environment. The river springs up in the core of the Iberian Pyritic Belt, one of the largest bodies of iron and copper sulfide deposits in the world [17]. These ores have been mined since 3000 BC, making it one of the oldest mining areas known. Ferric iron and sulfuric acid are the most common components found in this acidic environment, establishing a buffer system at pH values of approximately 2.3. Ferric iron is produced by the metabolism of iron oxidizing microorganisms, which are very active in the aerobic part of the river, Sulfuric acid originates from sulfides through chemical oxidation or the activity of sulfur-oxidizing microorganisms, depending on the sulfide mineral substrate [53]. The result is a strongly acidic solution of ferric iron which brings into solution other heavy metals, increasing their concentrations in relation to neighboring rivers with neutral pH [36]. Fe concentrations of ca. 22 g L^{-1}, Zn ca. 0.5 g L^{-1} or Cd ca. 70 mg L^{-1}, have been reported in the river [2, 4]. Comparison of physical conditions and concentrations of heavy metals ions throughout the year denotes a clear bimodality in their annual distribution. Oxygen and pH generally show higher values in winter, while heavy metals reach their peaks in summer and late summer.

Recent microbial ecology studies in the Tinto basin have shown that ca. 80% of the prokaryotic diversity in the water column corresponded to three chemolithotrophic bacteria, *Acidithiobacillus ferrooxidans*, *Leptospirillum ferrooxidans* and *Acidiphilium* spp., all of them involved in the iron cycle [53].

Río Tinto has gained recent astrobiological interest since the extreme conditions in the river may be analogous to other locations in the solar system thought to contain liquid water, such as the subsurface of Mars. The chemistry of the water in which the sedimentary rocks of *Meridiani Planum* were deposited on Mars has been compared to Río Tinto [37] Likewise Jupiter's moon Europa is theorized to contain an acidic ocean of water underneath its icy surface.

3. Eukaryotic Diversity and Ecology in Rio Tinto

It is usually assumed that high metal concentrations in acidic habitats limit eukaryotic growth and diversity due to their toxicity. However, what makes Río Tinto a unique acidic extreme environment is the unexpectedly high degree of eukaryotic diversity found in its waters and that these eukaryotic organisms are the principal contributors to the biomass in the river [4, 7, 70]. Over 65% of the total biomass is due to photosynthetic protists. Members of the phylum Chlorophyta such as *Chlamydomonas*, *Chlorella*, and *Euglena*, are the most frequent species found followed by two filamentous algae belonging to the genera *Klebsormidium* and *Zygnemopsis*. The most acidic part of the river is inhabited by a eukaryotic community dominated by two species related to the genera *Dunaliella* and *Cyanidium* (Rhodophyta), well known for their metal and acid tolerance [103]. Molecular ecology techniques have identified algae closely related to those characterized phenotypically, emphazising the high degree of eukaryotic diversity existing in the extreme acidic conditions of the Tinto Basin [3, 4, 7].

Within the decomposers, fungi are very abundant and exhibit great diversity, including yeast and filamentous forms. Near hundred strains of yeast have been isolated from the Río Tinto Basin. Fifty-two percent are able to grow in media amended with river water (pH 2.3). They belong to six genera of basidiomycetes (*Rhodotorula*, *Cryptococcus*, *Tremella*, *Holtermannia* and *Mrakia)* and two ascomycetes (*Candida* and *Williopsis*). In addition, over thousand strains of hyphomycetes have been isolated from the Tinto ecosystem and most of them characterized phenotypically. Around fifty percent of the isolated filamentous fungi are able to grow in the extreme acidic conditions of the river. Of this nineteen percent belong to the genus *Penicillium* and the rest have been identified as members of the *Scytalidium*, *Bahusakala*, *Phoma* and *Heteroconium* genera or showed dark sterile mycelia (probably dematiaceous hyphomycetes). In addition, some isolates have been identified as strains of the ascomycete genera *Lecythophora* and *Acremonium* and the zygomycete genus *Mortierella* [70, 71]. Many of the fungi detected using molecular techniques have sequences that probably correspond to novel genera [7, 53, 54].

The mixotrophic community is dominated by cercomonads and stramenopiles related to the genera *Bodo*, *Ochromonas*, *Labyrinthula* and *Cercomonas*. The protistan consumer community is characterized by two different species of ciliates tentatively assigned to the genera *Oxytrichia* and *Euplotes*. Amoebas related to the genera *Valhkampfia* and *Naegleria* can be found frequently even in the most acidic parts of the river (pH<1) and one species of heliozoan belonging to the genus *Actinophyris* seems to be the characteristic top predator of the benthic food chain of the river [2]. We know from microscopy observations that rotifers also inhabit the river [7].

But not only unicellular eukaryotic systems develop in the extreme conditions of the Tinto Basin. Different plants can be found growing in the acidic soils of the river banks. The strategies used by these plants to overcome the physiological problems associated to the extreme conditions of the habitat are diverse. Some are resistant to the heavy metals concentrated in the soils in which they grow [8, 87]. Others specifically concentrate metals in different plant tissues. Recent analysis by XRD and Mössbauer spectroscopy of the iron minerals found in the rizhomes and leaves of *Imperata cylindrica*, an iron hyperaccumulator perennial grass growing in the Río Tinto banks, showed significant concentrations of jarosite and iron oxyhydroxides [8, 87].

This fact demonstrates that complex eukaryotic systems can thrive and dominate extremely acidic, heavy, metal-laden environments. Since some of these acidophiles are closely related to cultured neutrophiles, we have to conclude that eukaryotes must have the ability to adapt from neutral to acidic environments over relatively short geological time-scales. Thus, eukaryotic extremophiles are more widely distributed and phylogenetically diverse than previously thought.

4. Extreme Acidic Photosynthetic Biofilms

Most of the eukaryotic microbial communities found in acidic environments are distributed in extensive biofilms. Although the development of biofilms in aquatic and terrestrial extreme environments has been documented [38, 48, 57], the distribution pattern and factors controlling their development in acidic extreme environments are not yet well understood. In the case of Río Tinto the distribution of these photosynthetic communities seems to be more influenced by the presence of heavy metals than low pH [4]. Metal toxicity depends on their bioavailability, and this accessibility depends mainly on physico-chemical factors, on the presence of chelators and on the concentration of free ions in the water [98]. In general, at acidic pH most heavy metals are in a soluble cationic form, thus more easily available to microorganisms [34].

Little is know about biofilms formed mainly by eukaryotic organisms, not to mention eukaryotic biofilms from extreme acidic environments, where studies are even more scarce. The biofilm matrix is a dynamic environment in which the microbial cells are organized [101, 106]. The major components, besides water, are extracellular polymeric substances (EPS). The production of EPS is a general property of microorganisms in natural environments. EPS are mainly responsible for the structural and functional integrity of biofilms, and are considered the key components that determine their physico-chemical and biological properties [25]. The EPS are formed by a complex mixture of carbohydrates, proteins, lipids, DNA and humic acid substances, although, given the wide range of environments in which biofilms are found, it is extremely difficult to generalize about their structure and physiological activities [60]. Early reports have proposed EPS matrix as a sink or reservoir of available carbon for the community [45]. An important function of the EPS is to give cohesive strength to natural biofilms [5]. Understanding the cohesive interactions in the biofilm matrix could lead to the identification of the factors controlling biofilm development in extreme acidic environments.

Previous studies have shown that biosorption of heavy metals in biopolymers [67] has many advantages for the microbial community [96]. The extracellular matrix could be partly responsible for an increase in biofilm tolerance, particularly to heavy metals [12, 40]. The role of EPSs in relation to potentially toxic metals is even more important in acidic environments, usually characterized by high concentrations of metals as well as high bioavailibilty. Although there are numerous reports documenting these topics in several aquatic and terrestrial environments [57], there is little information about this aspect of photosynthetic biofilms from acidic environments. In addition, since most of these studies have focused exclusively on prokaryotes [39], references to the contribution of biofilm-forming eukaryotic microorganisms to the increase of solid phase partitioning of dissolved metals are even more scarce.

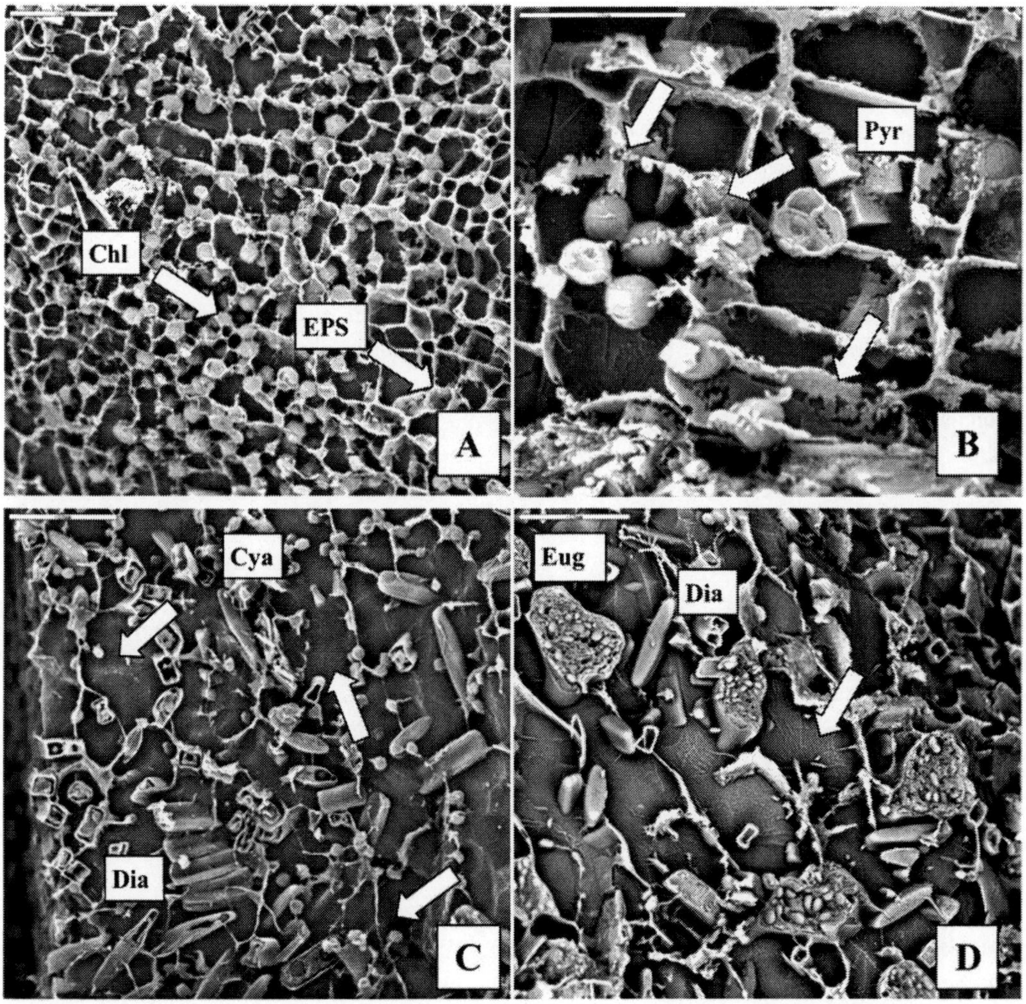

Figure 2. Low Temperature Scanning Electron Microscopy images (LTSEM) of different photosynthetic eukaryotic biofilms. This samples allowed to visualized fresh frozen biofilms. **A**. *Chlorella* biofilm. Notice the amount of extracellular polymeric substances (EPS) around the cells (Chl) . Bar= 20 μm. **B**. Detail image of a *Chlorella* biofilm. Notice the mineralized aspect of the EPS around the cells (arrows) and the presence of iron minerals (Pyr) embedded in the matrix. Bar= 10 μm. **C.** A mix biofilm with diatoms (Dia) and *Cyanidium* (Cya) cells. Notice that the EPS seems to be less mineralized and the water filled spaces (arrows). Bar= 20 μm. **D.** A mix biofilm with *Euglena* (Eug) and diatoms (Dia). Notice the amount of space filled with water around the cells (arrows). Bar= 20 μm

5. Structure of Extreme Acidic Photosynthetic Biofilms

There are striking similarities in the morphology of biofilms growing in widely different environments, suggesting an adaptative convergence of forms. In high shear flows, biofilms tend to form filamentous streamers, whether in acid mine drainage [16], hydrothermal vents [85] or surface hot springs [84]. In low flow water bodies biofilms seem to form, in general, surface attached structures. There is a general consensus among researchers that these elaborate structures are a consequence of the adaptation to specific environmental conditions. The regulation of surface attachment, surface binding, biofilm maturation and detachment is affected by the physiology and by the physico-chemical parameters of the solid surface and the environment [27]. An essential question is whether attached cells use this physical contact for structural, nutritional or protective purpose or whether these intercellular interactions are a consequence of having developed a resistance mechanism [61].

As mentioned most of the eukaryotic microbial communities found in Rio Tinto are distributed in biofilms. The macroscopic shape and species composition of the biofilms vary greatly throughout the river [2]. Some of them adopt filamentous morphologies while others form thick colorful patches firmly attached to the mineral substrates. Río Tinto microbial biofilms are tridimensional structures that show a spectrum of structurally heterogeneous forms determined by the dominating photosynthetic organisms in which fungal hyphae and prokaryotic microorganisms are also included [4]. The ultrastructure of the photosynthetic acidic eukaryotic biofilms has been described using scanning electron microscopy in back-scattered electron mode [4] and with low-temperature scanning electron microscopy (LTSEM) in order to preserve the ultrastructure of hydrated samples (Figure 2).

These ultrastructural observations indicate a close link between the photosynthetic communities and other components of the trophic web. Some studies support a possible role for the large biomass of photosynthetic organisms as primary producers for the prokaryotic-fungal consuming communities [54, 89]. Previous studies focused on the diversity of chemolithotrophic bacteria and archaeae in relation to the iron cycle in the water column [10, 53] and on bacterial biofilms and streamers [31]. The diversity of fungi associated with harsh water conditions has also been described [11, 46, 71] but little is known about the fungal communities associated with photosynthetic biofilms. Preliminary results using fluorescence in situ hybridization (FISH and CARD-FISH) have shown that in some areas of the river the chemolithotrophic prokaryotic communities are important structural components of photosynthetic biofilms.

In addition, heterotrophic prokaryotes and fungi have been found associated with photosynthetic biofilms (Figure 3). It has also been shown that the interaction between yeast and chemolithotrophic bacteria stimulate ferrous iron oxidation [44, 107]. These interactions may be of crucial importance in extreme oxidative environments were Fe (III) reduction to Fe(II) is rapid and strongly coupled to oxidation of organics in water and sediments [72]. In the case of the acidic photosynthetic biofilms we can think of an association between prokaryotic microorganisms and fungi interacting synergistically to stimulate photosynthetic biofilm formation through mechanisms that could include improved nutrient acquisition. Future mesocosms experiments will therefore strive to improve understanding of the functional mechanisms behind such microbial interactions.

6. Extracellular Matrix Assembly Extreme Acidic Eukaryotic Biofilms

The EPS content of a biofilm can differ in quantity and characteristics as a result of environmental factors. The application of lectin-binding analysis in microcosm experiments using natural biofilm communities indicated changes in EPS abundance and a shift in the glycoconjugates after Ni treatments [65]. Other authors demonstrated increased production of exopolymers [35] and changes in EPS composition in response to metals [58], also linked with changes in community structure [65]. These changes may be associated with increased resistance to metal toxicity. In acidic environments with stable communities such as the ones in Rio Tinto those changes may occur by the induction of specific resistance mechanisms in the community members [1, 13, 22].

In general, studies from neutral microphytobenthic communities have reported EPS reaching only $\mu g\ gr^{-1}$ of biofilm dry weight [56, 80]. The Río Tinto photosynthetic biofilms produce high amounts of EPS that always reach concentrations in the order of $mg\ gr^{-1}$ of biofilm dry weight, which agrees with the fact that high production of EPS has been always associated to extreme environments, such as arctic sea ice or deep-sea hydrothermal vents [64, 74].

We have found in the Tinto basin that the total amount of EPS showed positive correlation with the total concentration of heavy metals present in the different sampling locations. In addition, the total amount of EPS correlated negatively with the increase in pH. These results are comparable to those measured in other environments [55] and with the observations made by García-Meza et al. (2005) using photosynthetic biofilms from mine tailings. These correlations are due to the well documented fact that at low pH the availability of negatively charged sites is greatly reduced [38]. Thus, higher EPS amounts are necessary to chelate the larger amount of metals present in more acidic environments.

Carbohydrates are the main constituent of the EPS for most environments and cultures [42, 100, 101]. In the biofilms studied, carbohydrates reach values between 15% and 85% of the total EPS amounts. The second most important component of the EPS are metals, reaching values up to 10% of the EPS weight. Humic acids made up 4% of the EPS, a concentration much lower than reported previously [68]. Humic substances are thought to be formed during the microbial degradation of organic matter and they have been related to nutrient depletion and heavy metal complexation [99]. Our results on the characterization of acidic eukaryotic biofilms are supported by previous studies on acidic environments in which the total concentration of humic substances in the water was also scarce, probably influenced by the low pH [94]. The total amount of proteins in the EPS reached only 2%, whereas in nutrient-rich environments it can contribute up to 60% of algal biofilms biomass [23, 41].

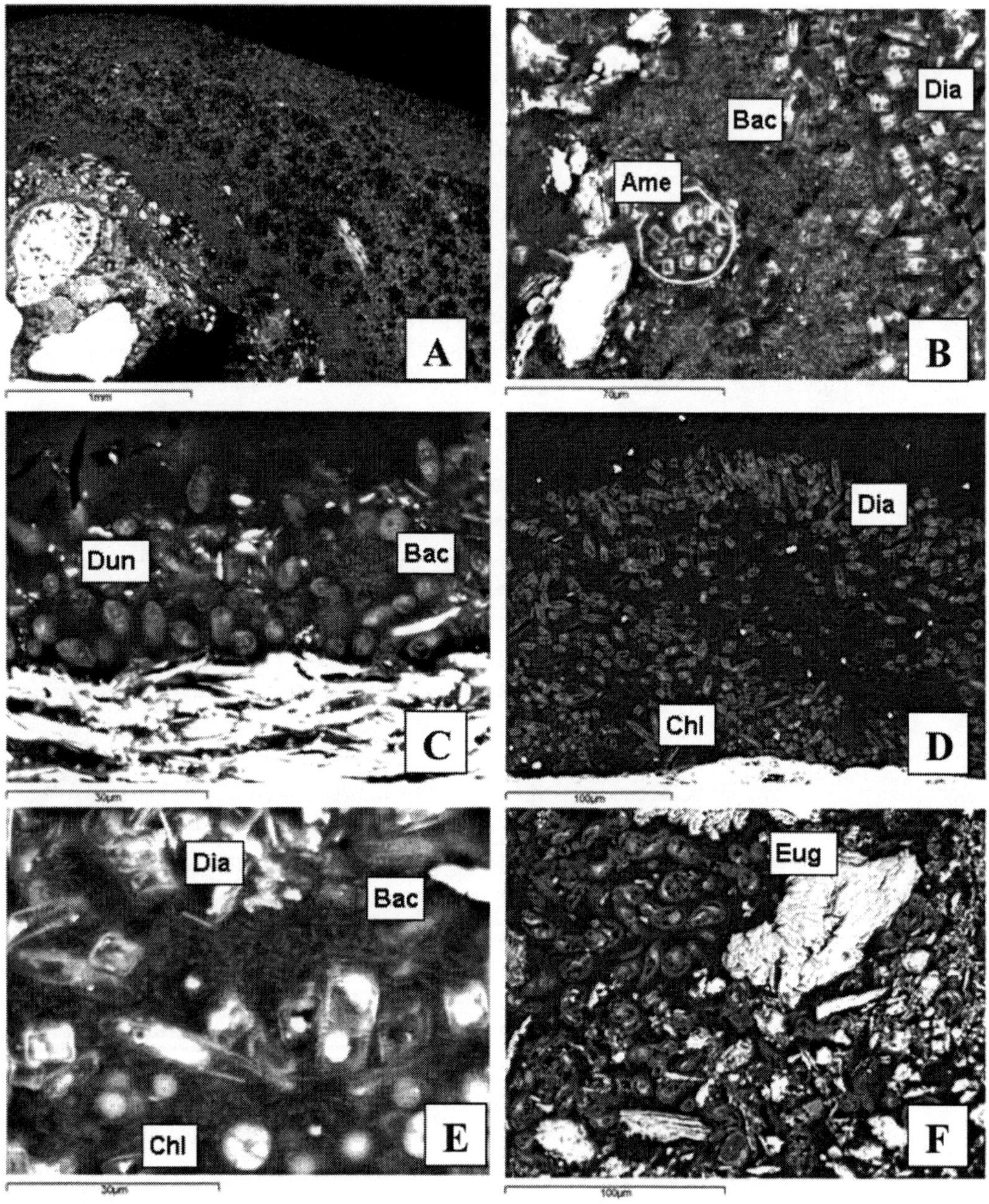

Figure 3. Scanning Electron Microscopy by Backscattered Electron Detection (SEM-BSE). These samples allowed to visualized transversal sections of the biofilms. **A.** The biofilms from CEM locality are the thickest studied along the river. They reach millimeter thickness above the sediments. **B**. Most of the lower part in contact with the substrate is formed by filaments of bacteria (Bac). Some protozoa are also visualized (Ame) with diatom frustules inside (Dia). **C.** *Dunaliela* biofilm (Dun) with bacteria colonies (Bac). The biofilms from RI locality are the thinner ones, with only tens of microns. **D.** In general biofilms are of hundreds of microns thick clearly distributed above the sediments. In this case made of diatoms (Dia) and *Chlorella* (Chl). **E.** In areas in contact with the substrate there is always a higher abundance of bacteria (Bac) between the photosynthetic eukaryots, diatoms (Dia) and *Chlorella* (Chl). **F.** In the case of the *Euglena* (Eug) biofilms it seems that they are able to penetrated inside the sediment particles.

Nevertheless, EPSs extracted from natural environments are generally believed to contain few or no proteins [56]. Previous studies carried out in prokaryots from other extreme environments showed similar low amounts of proteins in their EPSs [73, 82]. The presence of extracellular DNA in biofilms has been recently described as being involved in the flocculating ability of photosynthetic marine bacterium [78], and in some cases, seems to be necessary for bacterial biofilm formation [105]. The eukaryotic or prokaryotic origin of extracellular DNA from Rio Tinto photosynthetic biofilms has not yet been analyzed. The role of extracellular DNA in the microbial ecology of diverse environments and its importance in biofilms of mixed eukaryotic and bacterial populations still remains unclear.

7. Implication of the Extracellular Matrix in Heavy Metal Absorptions

Biofilm sorption and desorption of metals play an important role in metal distribution in aquatic systems [92]. Since the EPS of different biofilms can vary in their components, some may interact more strongly with some metals than with others. We have also examined the distribution of the metals in the extracted EPS. In general, metal distribution in EPS correlates well with the metal composition of the water where biofilms were collected, except for Al, Cu, Zn and Pb. The biofilms collected from different sampling sites with the highest concentrations of Cu and Zn in the waters were able to accumulate only half the Cu and Zn that in biofilms from other areas with lower concentrations of these metals. This suggests a competitive threshold in the binding of metallic ions, which agrees with the results reported by García-Meza et al. (2005) in biofilm mesocosms studies with these two metals. These results support the idea suggested by Aguilera et al. (2006) that, based on PCA analysis, these two particular metals play a substantial role in controlling the epiphytic eukaryotic diversity and distribution in the river and is probably the reason why not all the biofilms are equally distributed along the river. Some studies have reported that metals such us Zn and Cd cause changes in the diatom species composition of the periphyton in streams [51, 52, 76]. The relationship between heavy metals and the distribution of eukaryotic benthic communities is an important question yet to be answered.

The adsorption of heavy metals by EPSs is attributed to their large number of negatively charged functional groups such as carboxyl, phosphate and sulfate at neutral pH [15, 20, 63]. However, interactions between metallic ions and polymeric organic substances are strongly influenced by pH [97]. It is well known that pH is an important physico-chemical property that determines metal solubility and also the organic ligand adsorption capacities [96]. In general, at acidic pH most heavy metals are in free cationic form, and more available to microorganisms, whereas at higher pH they tend to precipitate as insoluble compounds [43, 83]. Low pH modifies the ionic status of the different EPSs functional groups changing their characteristics [38].

The EPS structure of different photosynthetic biofilms differed markedly, even though they were isolated from close sampling locations. Some biofilms revealed the presence of mineral deposits on the walls of the cells surrounded by a fibrillated texture identified as the exopolymer matrix, where mineral precipitates were also forming. However, other biofilms showed no mineral precipitation around the living active parts of the structure. These observations strongly suggest that biofilms are possible locations for metal and mineral precipitation, and that EPS composition and physiology have a significant impact on the assemblage and architecture of biofilms in extreme acidic environments.

The reduction of surface charge density with decreasing pH also serves to weaken electrostatic free energy contributions to metallic ion adsorption [59]. However a possible mechanism that could explain metal accumulation in the biofilms might be the precipitation of metal oxides in the extracellular matrix which might favor the adsorption of other metals. This process was also noted in lake biofilms adsorption studies, that showed that Pb binding to metal oxides was greater than the estimate for organic phases [75]. Fe and Mn oxides can have an important effect on the adsorption of heavy metals in natural environments [29]. The precipitation of iron oxyhydroxides and hydroxysulfates is a common process in acid mine waters and they likely contribute to increase solid phase partitioning of dissolved metals in the Río Tinto system [39].

8. Conclusion

Extremophiles are not only important resources for developing novel biotechnological processes, but also ideal models for research in the ecological and molecular fields. An understanding of the versatility of life on Earth, as well as the mechanisms that allow some organisms to survive or develop in extreme conditions, will help to gain more insights into the evolution of life, the development of special ecosystems and in the search for life beyond Earth. Although most habitats have not been sufficiently well explored, colonization of extreme habitats is not usually limited to a unique taxonomic domain, and eukaryotic species are exceptionally adaptable comparable in this aspect to the prokaryotes. Of the different extreme environments, acidic habitats are rather peculiar because in most cases they are the product of metabolism of active chemolithotrophic microorganisms. The microbial diversity characterization of Río Tinto allowed to detect a high level of eukaryotic diversity, which contrasts with the rather low level of prokaryotic diversity found in the system. The highest concentration of biomass of the ecosystem corresponds to photosynthetic algae, although other protists, yeast and filamentous fungi have been isolated along the river. Most the photosynthetic eukaryotes in the Tinto ecosystem are forming biofilms. In this case the distribution of these photosynthetic communities seems to be more influenced by the presence of heavy metals, than low pH. The high level of eukaryotic diversity found in the Tinto basin demonstrates that complex eukaryotic systems can thrive and dominate extremely acidic, heavy, metal-laden environments. Since some of these acidophiles are closely related to cultured neutrophiles, we can conclude that eukaryotes must have the ability to adapt from neutral to acidic environments over relatively short periods of time. Thus, eukaryotic extremophiles are more widely distributed and phylogenetically diverse than previously thought.

Acknowledgements

A.A and V.S-E have been supported by the Spanish Ministry of Education and Science through the Ramón y Cajal program. This work has been supported by grant CGL2005-05470/BOS and grants to the Centro de Astrobiología at the Instituto National de Técnica Aeroespacial.

References

[1] Aguilera, A. & Amils, R. (2005). Tolerance to cadmium in *Chlamydomonas* sp. (Chlorophyta) strains isolated from an extreme acidic environment, the Tinto River (SW, Spain). *Aquatic Toxicol.* 75, 316-329.

[2] Aguilera, A., Souza-Egipsy, V., Gómez, F. & Amils, R. (2006). Development and structure of eukaryotic biofilms in an extreme acidic environment, Río Tinto (SW, Spain). *Microb. Ecol.* 53, 294-305.

[3] Aguilera, A., Gómez, F., Lospitao, E. & Amils, R. (2006). A molecular approach to the characterization of the eukaryotic communities of an extreme acidic environment: methods for DNA extraction and denaturing gradient electrophoresis analysis. *Syst. Appl. Microbiol.* 29, 593-605.

[4] Aguilera, A., Manrubia, S.C., Gómez, F., Rodríguez, N. & Amils, R. (2006). Eukaryotic community distribution and their relationship to water physicochemical parameters in an extreme acidic environment, Río Tinto (SW, Spain). *App. Environ. Microbiol.* 72, 5325-5330.

[5] Ahimou, F., Semmens, M.J., Haugstad, G., & Novak, P.J. (2007). Effect of protein, polysaccharide, and oxygen concentration profiles on biofilm cohesiveness. *App. Environ. Microbiol.* 73, 2905-2910.

[6] Alexandrof, V.Y. (1977). *Cells, molecules and temperature. Conformational flexibility of macromolecules and ecological adaptations.* Springer-Verlag, Berlin.

[7] Amaral, L. A., Gómez, F., Zettler, E., Keenan, B.G., Amils, R. & Sogin, M.L. (2002). Eukaryotic diversity in Spain's river of fire. *Nature* 417, 137.

[8] Amils, R., de la Fuente, V., Rodriguez, N., Zuluaga, J., Menendez, N., & Tornero, J. (2007). Composition, speciation and distribution of iron minerals in *Imperata cylindrica. Plant Physiol. Biochem.* 45: 335-340.

[9] Appukuttan, D., Rao, A.S., & Apte, S.K. (2006). Engineering of *Deinococcus radiodurans* R1 for Bioprecipitation of Uranium from Dilute Nuclear Waste. *Appl. Environ. Microbiol.* 72(12), 7873–7878.

[10] Baker, B.J. & Banfield, J.F. (2003). Microbial communities in acid mine drainage. *FEMS Microbiol. Ecol.* 44, 139-152.

[11] Baker, B.J., Lutz, M.A., Dawson, S.C., Bond, P.L. & Banfield, J.F. (2004). Metabolically active eukaryotic communities in extremely acidic mine drainage. *App. Environ. Microbiol.* 70, 6264-6271.

[12] Barranguet, C., Charantoni, E., Plans, M. & Admiraal, W. (2000). Short-term response of monospecific and natural algal biofilms to copper exposure. *Eur. J. Phycol.* 35, 397-406.

[13] Barreto, M., Jedlicki, E. & Holmes, D.S. (2005). Identification of a gene cluster for the formation of extracellular polysaccharide precursors in the chemolithoautotroph *Acidithiobacillus ferrooxidans*. *App. Environ. Microbiol.* 71, 2902-2909.
[14] Ben-Amotz, A. (1999). Dunaliella β-carotene. In: Seckbach J, editor. *Enigmatic microorganisms and life in extreme environments*. Kluwer Academic Publishers; pp. 401-410.
[15] Bitton, G. & Friehofer, V. (1978). Influence of extracellular polysaccharide on the toxicity of copper and cadmium toward *Klebsiella aerogenes*. *Microb. Ecol.* 4, 119-125.
[16] Bond, P.L., Smriga, S.P. & Banfield, J.F. (2000). Phylogeny of microorganisms populating a thick, subaerial, predominantly lithotrophic biofilm at an extreme acid mine drainage site. *App. Environ. Microbiol.* 66, 3842-3849.
[17] Boulter, C. A. (1996). Did both extensional tectonics and magmas act as major driver of convection cell during the formation of the Iberian Pyrite Belt massive sulfide deposits?. *J. Geol. Soc. London* 153, 181-184.
[18] Brock, T. (1973). Lower pH limit for the existence of blue-green algae: Evolutionary and ecological implications. *Science* 179, 480-483.
[19] Brock, T. (1978). *Thermophilic Microorganisms and Life at High Temperatures*. Springer-Verlag, New York.
[20] Brown, M.J. & Lester, J.N. (1979). Metal removal in activated sludge: the role of bacterial extracellular polymers. *Water Res.* 13, 817-837.
[21] Bull, A.T., Ward, A.T., & Goodfellow, M. (2000). Search and Discovery Strategies for Biotechnology: the Paradigm Shift. *Microbiol. Mol. Biol. Rev.* 64, 573–606.
[22] Cánovas, D., Mukhopadhyay, R., Rosen, B. P. & de Lorenzo, V. (2003). Arsenate transport and reduction in the hyper-tolerant fungus *Aspergillus* sp. P37. *Environ. Microbiol.* 5, 1087-1093.
[23] Caron, D.A., Countway, P.D. & Brown, M.V. (2004) The growing contributions of molecular biology and immunology to protistan ecology: molecular signatures as ecological tools. *J. Eukaryot. Microbiol.* 51, 38-48.
[24] Cary, S.C., Shank T. & Stein J. (1998). Worms bask in extreme temperatues. *Nature* 391, 545-546.
[25] Christensen, B. E. &Characklis, W.G. (1990). Physical and chemical properties of biofilms, In: Characklis WG, & Marshall KC, editors. *Biofilms*. John Wiley; NY; pp. 93-130.
[26] Curds, C.R., Bamforth, S.S. & Finlay, B.J. (1986). Report on the fresh-water workshop in Kisumu, Kenya. *Insect Sci. Applicat.* 7, 447-449.
[27] Davis, D.G. (2000). Physiological events in biofilm formation. In: Allison DG, Gilbert P, Lappin-Scott HM, Wilson M, editors. *Community structure and co-operation in biofilms.* Cambridge University Press; Cambridge; pp. 37-52.
[28] Demirgian, D.C., Moris-Vara, F. & Cssidy, C.S. (2001). Enzymes from extremophiles. *Curr. Opin. Chem. Biol.* 5, 144-151.
[29] Dong, D., Nelson, Y.M., Lion, L.W., Shuler, M.L. & Ghiorse, W.C. (2000). Adsorption of Pb and Cd onto metal oxides and organic material in natural surface coatings as determined by selective extractions: new evidence for the importance of Mn and Fe oxides. *Water Res.* 34(2), 427-436.

[30] Edgcomb, V.P., Kysela, D.T., Teske, A., Gomez, A.D.V. & Sogin, M. L. (2002). Benthic eukaryotic diversity in the Guaymas Basin hydrothermal vent environment. *Proc. Nat. Acad. Sci.* 99(11), 7663-7668.

[31] Edwards, K.J., Gihring, T.M. & Banfield, J.F. (1999). Seasonal variations in microbial populations and environmental conditions in an extreme acidic mine drainage environment. *Appl. Environ. Microbiol.* 65, 3627-3632.

[32] Edwards, K.J., Bond, P.I., Gihrin, T.M. & Banfield, J. F. (2000) An archaeal iron oxidizing extreme acidophile important in acid mine drainage. *Science* 287, 1796-1798.

[33] Embley, T. M., Finlay, B. J., Dyal, P. L., Hirt, R. P., Wilkinson, M. & Williams, A. G. (1995). Multiple origins of anaerobic ciliates with hydrogenosomes within the radiation of aerobic ciliates. *Proc.Royal Soc. London Ser B-Biol. Sci.* 262, 87-93.

[34] Ernst, W. H. O. (1998). Effects of heavy metals in plants at cellular and organismic level, In: Schürmann G, Marker B, editors. *Ecotoxicology*. John Wiley & Sons Inc; NY; pp. 587-620.

[35] Fang, H.H.P., Xu, L.-C. & Chan, K.Y. (2002). Effects of toxic metals and chemicals on biofilm and biocorrosion. *Water Res.* 36, 4709-4716.

[36] Fernández-Remolar, D.C., Rodríguez, N., Gómez, F. & Amils, R. (2003). Geological record of an acidic environment driven by the iron hydrochemistry: the Tinto river system. *J. Geophys. Res.* 108, 5080-5095.

[37] Fernández-Remolar, D. C., Gómez-Elvira, J., Gómez, F., Sebastián, E., Martín, J., Manfredi, J.A., Torres, J., González-Kesler, C. & Amils, R. (2004). The Tinto river, an extreme acidic environment under control of iron, as an analog of the *Terra Meridiani* hematite site of Mars. *Planet. Space Sci.* 52, 239-248.

[38] Ferris, F. G., Schultze, S., Witten, T.C.,Fyfe, W.S. & Beveridge, T.J. (1989). Metal interactions with microbial biofilms in acidic and neutral pH environments. *Appl. Environ. Microbiol.* 55, 1249-1257.

[39] Ferris, F., Hallbeck, L., Kennedy, C.B. & Pedersen, K. (2004). Geochemistry of acidic Rio Tinto headwaters and role of bacteria in solid phase metal partitioning. *Chem. Geol.* 212, 291-300.

[40] Fleming, H. (1993). Biofilms and environmental protection. *Water Sci. Technol.* 27, 1-10.

[41] Flemming H. C., Wingender, J., Moritz, R., Borchard, W. & Mayer, C. (1999). Physico-chemical properties of biofilms- a short review. In: Keevil CW, Goodfree A, Holt D, Dow C, editors. Biofilms in the aquatic environment, *Royal Society of Chemistry, Special Publication* N° 242; Cambridge; pp. 1-12.

[42] Flemming H. C. & Wingender, J. (2001). Relevance of extracellular polymeric substances (EPSs)- Part I: Structural and ecological aspects. *Water Sci. Technol.* 43, 1-8.

[43] Förstener, U. & Prosi, F. (1979). Heavy metal pollution in freshwater ecosystem. In: Ravera O, editor. *Biological Aspects of Freshwater Pollution*. Pergamon Press; NY; pp. 129-161.

[44] Fournier, D., Lemieux, R. and Couillard, D. (1998). Essential interactions between Thiobacillus ferrooxidans and heterotrophic microorganisms during a wasterwater sludge biolecheaing process. *Environ. Pol.* 101, 303-309.

[45] Freeman, C. & Lock, M.A. (1995). The biofilm polysaccharide matrix: a buffer against changing organic substrate supply. *Limnol. Oceanogr.* 40, 273-278.

[46] Gadanho, M., Libkind, D. & Sampaio, J. (2006). Yeast diversity in the extreme acidic environments of the Iberian Pyrite Belt. *Microb. Ecol.* 52, 552-563.

[47] Gadanho, M. & Sampaio, J. (2006). Microeukaryotic diversity in the extreme environments of the Iberian Pyrite Belt: a comparison between universal and fungi-specific primer sets, temperature gradient gel electrophoresis and cloning. *FEMS Microb. Ecol.* 57, 139-148.

[48] García-Meza, J. V., Barrangue, C. & Admiraal, W. (2005). Biofilm formation by algae as a mechanism for surviving on mine tailings. *Environ. Toxicol. Chem.* 24, 573581.

[49] Garrison, D.L. & Close, A.R. (1993). Winter ecology of the sea ice biota in Weddel Sea pack ice. *Mar. Ecol. Prog. Ser.* 96, 17-31.

[50] Garthy, J. (1999). Lithobionts in the eastern mediterranean. In: Seckbach. J. editor. *Enigmatic Microorganisms and Life in Extreme Environments*, Kluwer Academic Publ. London; pp. 257-276.

[51] Genter, R.B., Cherry, D.S., Smith, E.P. & Cairns Jr, J. (1987). Algal periphyton population and community changes from Zn in stream mesocosms. *Hydrobiologia* 153, 261-328.

[52] Gold, C., Feurtet-Mazel, A., Coste, M. & Boudou, A. (2003). effects of Cad stress on periphytic diatom communities in indoor artificial streams. *Freshwater Biol.* 48, 316-328.

[53] González-Toril, E., Llobet-Brossa, E., Casamayor, E.O., Amann, R. & Amils R. (2003). Microbial ecology of an extreme acidic environment. The Tinto River. *Appl. Environ. Microbiol.* 69, 4853-4865.

[54] Gross, W. & Robbins, E.I. (2000). Acidophilic and acid-tolerant fungi and yeast. *Hydrobiologia* 433, 91-109

[55] Hill, W.R. & Larsen, I.L. (2005). Growth dilution of metals in microalgal biofilms. *Environ. Sci. Technol.* 39(6), 1513-1518.

[56] Hirst, C.N. & Jordan, I.A. (2003). Distribution of exopolymeric substances in the littoral sediments of an oligotrophic lake. *Microb. Ecol.* 46, 22-32.

[57] Hughes, N. M. & Poole, R.K. (1989). *Metals and Microorganisms.* Chapman and Hall, N.Y. USA.

[58] Jang, A., Kim, S.M., Kim, S.Y. & Kim, I.S. (2001). Effect of heavy metals (Cu, Pb, Ni) on the compositions of EPS in biofilms. *Water Sci. Technol.* 43, 41-48.

[59] Jefree, C.E. & Read, N.D. (1991). Ambient and low-temperature scanning electron microscopy. In: Hall JL, Hawes C, editors. *Electron microscopy of plant cells.* Academic Press; London; pp. 313-413.

[60] Jenkinson H.F. & Lappin-Scott, H.M. (2001). Biofilms adhere to stay. *TRENDS Microbiol.* 9, 9-10

[61] Jirku, V., Masak, J. & Cejkova, A. (2001). Significance of physical attachment of fungi for bio-treatment of water. *Microbiol. Res.* 156, 383-386.

[62] Johnson, D.B. (1998). Biodiversity and ecology of acidophilic microorganisms. *FEMS Microbial. Ecol.* 27, 307-317.

[63] Kaplan, D., Christiaen, D. & Arad, S. (1987). Binding of heavy metals by algal polysaccharides. In: Stadler T, Mollion J, Verdus MC, Karamanos Y, Moran H, Christiaen D, editors. *Algal Biotechnology.* Elsevier Applied Sciences; London UK.; pp. 179-187.

[64] Krembs, C., Eicken, H., Junge, K. & Deming, J.W. (2002). High concentrations of exopolymeric substances in Arctic winter sea ice: implications fro the polar ocean carbon cycle and cryoprotection of diatoms. *Deep-Sea Res.* 49, 2163-2181.

[65] Lawrence, J.R. Chenier, M.R., Roy, R., Beaumier, D., Fortin, N., Swerhone, G.D.W., Neu, T.R. & Gree, C. (2004). Microscale and molecular assessment of impacts of nickel, nutrients, and oxygen level on structure and function of river biofilm communities. *Appl. Environ. Microbiol.* 70, 4326-4339.

[66] Ling, H.U. (2001). Snow algae of the windmill islands, continental antarctica: *Desmotetra aureospora*, sp. nov. and *D. antarctica*, comb. nov. (chlorophyta). *J. Phycol* 37, 160-174.

[67] Lion, L.W., Shuler, M.L., Hsieh, K.M. & Ghiorse, W.C. (1987). Trace-metal interactions with microbial biofilms in natural and engineered systems. *CRC Critical Rev. Environ. Contr.* 17, 273-306.

[68] Liu, H. & Fang, H.P. (2002). Extraction of extracellular polymeric substances (EPS) of sludges. *J. Biotechnol.* 95, 249-256.

[69] Löhr, A.J., Laverman, A.M., Braster, M., Straalen, N.M. & Röling, F.M. (2006). Microbial communities in the world's largest acidic volcanic lake, Kawah Ijen in Indonesia, and in the Banyupahit River originating from it. *Microb. Ecol.* 52, 609-618.

[70] López-Archilla, A.I., Marín, I. & Amils, R. (2001). Microbial community composition and ecology of an acidic aquatic environment: the Tinto river, Spain. *Microbial. Ecol.* 41, 20-35.

[71] López-Archilla, A.I., Gonzalez, A., Terron, M. & Amils, R. (2004). Ecological study of the fungal populations of the acidic Tinto River in southwestern Spain. *Can. J. Microbiol.* 50, 923-934.

[72] Lovley, D.R., Phillips, E.J.P. & Lonergan, D.J. (1991). Enzymatic versus noenzymatic mechanisms for Fe(III) reduction acuatic sediments. *Environ. Sci. Technol.* 25, 1062-1067.

[73] Mancuso-Nichols, C.A., Garon, S., Bowman, J.P., Raguenes, G. & Guezennec, J. (2004). Production of exopolysaccharides by Antartic marine bacterial isolates. *J. Appl. Microbiol.* 96, 1057-1066.

[74] Mancuso-Nichols, C.A., Guezennec, J. & Bowman, J.P. (2005). Bacterial exopolysaccharides from extreme marine environments with special consideration of the Southern Ocean, Sea Ice, and Deep-Sea hydrothermal vents: A review. *Mar. Biotechnol.* 7, 253-271.

[75] Nelson, Y.M., Lion, L.W., Shuler, M.L. & Ghiorse, W.C. (1999). Lead binding to metal oxide and organic phases of natural aquatic biofilms. *Limnol. Oceanogr.* 44, 1715-1729.

[76] Niederlehner, B.R. & Cairns Jr, J. (1992). Community response to cumulative toxic impact: effects of acclimatation on zinc tolerance of Aufwuchs. *Can. J. Fish. Aquat. Sci.* 49, 2155-2163.

[77] Niehaus, F., Bertoldo, C., Kähler, M. & Antranikian, G. (1999). Extremophiles as a source of novel enzymes fro industrial application. *Appl. Microb. Biotechnol.* 51, 711-729.

[78] Nishimura, S., Tanaka, T., Fujita, K., Itaya, M. & Hiraishi, A. (2003). Extracellular DNA and RNA produced by a marine photosynthetic bacterium *Rhodovulum sulfidophilum*. *Nucl. Ac. Res. Supp.* 3, 279-280.

[79] Olliver, B., Patel B.K.C. & García, J.L. (2000). Anaerobes from extreme environments. In: Seckbach J, editor. *Journey to Diverse Microbial Worlds*. Kluwer Academic Publ.; London; pp. 75- 90.

[80] Orvain, F., Galois, R., Barnard, C., Sylvestre, A., Blanchard, G. & Sauriau, P.G. (2003). Carbohydrate production in relation to microphytobenthos biofilm development: An integrated approach in a tidal mesocosm. *Microb. Ecol.* 45, 237-251.

[81] Price, P.B. (2000) A habitat for psychrophiles in deep Antarctic ice. *Proc. Natl. Acad. Sci. USA* 97, 1247–1251.

[82] Raguenes, G., Cambon-Bonavita, M.A., Lohier, J.F., Boisset, C. & Guezennec, J. (2003). A novel, highly viscous polysaccharide excreted by an *Alteromonas* isolated from a deep-sea hydrothermal vent shrimp. *Current Microbiol.* 46, 448-452.

[83] Rai, L.C., Gaur, J.P. & Kumar, H.D. (1981). Phycology and heavy metal pollution. *Biol. Rev.* 56, 99-151.

[84] Reysenbach, A.L. & Cady, S. (2001). Microbiology of ancient and modern hydrothermal systems. *Trends Microbiol.* 9(2), 79-86.

[85] Reysenbach, A.L.· & Shock, E. (2002). Merging genomes with geochemistry in hydrothermal ecosystems. *Science* 296(5570), 1077-1082.

[86] Roberts, D.M.L. (1999). Eukaryotic cells under extreme conditions. In: Seckbach J, editor. *Enigmatic Microorganisms and Life in Extreme Environments.* Kluwer Academic Publ.; London; pp. 165-173.

[87] Rodriguez, N., Menendez, N., Tornero, J., Amils, R., & de la Fuente, V. (2005). Internal iron biomineralization in *Imperata cylindrica*, a perennial grass: chemical composition, speciation and plant localization. *New Phytol.* 165(3), 781-789.

[88] Rothschild, L.J. & Mancinelli, R.L. (2001). Life in extreme environments. *Nature*, 409, 1092-1101.

[89] Sabater, S., Buchaca, T., Cambra, J., Catalan, J., Guasch, H., Ivorra, N., Muñoz, I., Navarro, E., Real, M. & Romani, A. (2003). Structure and function of benthic algal communities in an extremely acid river. *Phycology*, 39, 481-489.

[90] Schiraldi, C. & DeRosa, M. (2002). The production of biocatalysts and biomolecules from extremophiles. *TRENDS Biotechnol.* 20, 515-521.

[91] Schleper, C., Pühler, G., Kühlmorgen, B. & Zillig, W. (1995). Life at extremely low pH. *Nature* 375, 741-742.

[92] Schorer, M. & Eisele, M. (1997). Accumulation of inorganic and organica pollutants by biofilms in aquatic environment. *Water Air Soil Poll.* 99, 651-659.

[93] Seckbach, J. (editor) (1994). Evolutionary pathways and enigmatic algae: *Cyanidium caldarium* (*Rhodophyta*) and related cells. In: *Developments in Hydrobiology*, 91. Dordrecht, Kluwer Academic Publ.; pp. 349.

[94] Stevenson, F.J. (1994). *Humus chemistry. Genesis, composition, reactions.* Wiley; New York; pp. 231.

[95] Stibal, M., Elster, J., Šabacká, M. & Kaštovská, K. (2006). Seasonal and diel changes in photosynthetic activity of the snow alga *Chlamydomonas nivalis* (*Chlorophyceae*) from Svalbard determined by pulse amplitude modulation fluorometry. *FEMS Microbiol. Ecol.* 59, 265-273.

[96] Stone, A.T. 1997. Reactions of extracellular organic ligands with dissolved metal ions and mineral surfaces. In: Banfield JF, Nealson KH, editors. Geomicrobiology:

Interactions Between Microbes and Minerals. *Reviews in Mineralogy*, 35. Mineralogical Society of America; Washington; pp. 309-334,

[97] Stumm, W. & Morgan, J.J. (1985). *Aquatic Chemistry*. John Wiley & Sons, Inc. New York.

[98] Sunda, W.G. & Huntsman, S.A. (1998). Processes regulating cellular metal accumulation and physiological effects: phytoplankton as model systems. *Sci. Total. Environ.* 219, 165-181.

[99] Suteerapataranon, S., Bouby, M., Geckeis, H., Fanghanel, T. & Grudpan, K. (2006). Interaction of trace elements in acid mine drainage solution with humic acid. *Water Res.* 40(10), 2044-2054.

[100] Sutherland, I.W. (1999). Biofilm exopolysaccharides. In: Wingender J, editor. *Microbial Extracellular Polymeric Substances*. Springer ; pp. 73-92.

[101] Sutherland, I.W. (2001). The biofilm matrix- an immobilized but dynamic microbial environment. *TRENDS Microbiol.* 9(5), 222-227.

[102] Vieille, C., & Zeikus, G.J. (2001).Hyperthermophilic Enzymes: Sources, Uses, and Molecular Mechanisms for Thermostability. *Microbiol. Mol. Biol. Rev.* 65, 1-43.

[103] Visviki, I., & Santikul, D.(2000). The pH tolerance of *Chlamydomonas applanata* (Volvocales, Chlorophyta). *Arch. Environ. Contam. Toxicol.* 38, 147-151.

[104] Weber, A.P.M., Oesterhelt, C., Gross, W., Brautigam, L.A.I., Krassovskaya, I., Linka, N., Truchina, J., Schneidereit, J., Voll, H., Voll, L.M., Zimmerman, M., Jamai, A., Riekhof, W., Yu, B., Garavito, R.M. & Benning, C. (2004). EST-analysis of the thermo-acidophilic red microalga Galdieria sulphuraria reveals a potential for lipid A biosynthesis and unveils the pathway of carbon export from rhodoplasts. *Plant Mol. Biol.* 55, 17-32.

[105] Whitchurch, C.B., Tolker-Nielsen, T., Ragas, P.C. & Mattick, J.S. (2002). Extracellular DNA required for bacterial biofilm formation. *Science* 295, 1487.

[106] Wingender, J., Neu, T.R. & Flemming, H.C. (1999). *Microbial Extracellular Polymeric Substances. Characterization, Structure and Function*. Springer; Heidelberg ; pp. 259.

[107] Wong, J.W.C. & Gu, X.Y. (2004). Enhanced heavy metal bioleaching efficiencies from anaerobically digested sewage sludge with coinoculation of Acidithiobacillus ferrooxidans ANYL-1 and Blastoschizomyces capitatus Y5. *Water Sci. Technol.* 50(9), 83-89.

[108] Yechieli, Y., Ronen, D., Berkowitz, B., Dershowitz, W.S. & Hadad, A. (1995). Aquifer characteristics derived from the interaction between water levels of a terminal lake (Dead Sea) and an adjacent aquifer. *Water Resour. Res.* 31, 893-902.

In: Environmental Microbiology Research Trends
Editor: G. V. Kurladze, pp. 237-255

ISBN: 978-1-60021-939-9

Chapter 8

ARE RHIZOBIUM AND SOIL ENZYME ACTIVITIES GOOD INDICATORS OF HEAVY METAL SOIL CONTAMINATION?

S. I. A. Pereira[1]*, I. V. Castro[2] and E. Figueira[1]

[1] Centre for Cell Biology, Department of Biology, Campus Santiago, 3810-193 Aveiro, Portugal

[2] Departamento de Ecologia, Recursos Naturais e Ambiente, EFN-INRB, Av. da República 2780-159 Oeiras, Portugal

ABSTRACT

The widespread pollution of soils is an increasing urgent problem because of its contribution to environmental deterioration on a global basis. Several toxic compounds, such as heavy metals, often contaminate soils. The main sources of heavy metal pollution are mining, industries and application of metal-containing pesticides, fertilizers and sewage sludge. In recent decades there has been increasing concern with heavy metals, not only because of their toxicity to animals, plants and microorganisms, but also because they are highly toxic, mutagenic and/or carcinogenic to humans.

Due to their small size, which provides a large contact area that can interact with the surrounding environment, microorganisms are the first biota showing the impact of toxic compounds. Microorganisms being in intimate contact with the soil environment are considered to be the best indicators of soil pollution. In general, they are very sensitive to low concentrations of contaminants and provide a rapid response to soil perturbation.

Rhizobium spp. are ubiquitous gram-negative soil bacteria that have a profound scientific and agronomic significance due to their ability to establish nitrogen-fixing symbiosis with legumes, which is of major importance to the maintenance of soil fertility.

There is increasing evidence of the adverse effects of heavy metals on soil microbial processes, including on soil enzymatic activities. Soil enzymes are the driving force

* Send correspondence to Dr. Sofia Isabel Almeida Pereira, Centro de Biologia Celular, Departamento de Biologia, Campus de Santiago, Universidade de Aveiro, 3810-193 Aveiro, Portugal; E-mail: siapereira@portugalmail.com; Phone: 00351 234 370 782; Fax: 00351 234 865 008

behind all the biochemical transformations occurring in the soil. Enzymes catalyse all biochemical reactions and are an integral part of nutrient cycling and soil fertility. Therefore, this chapter evaluated the impact of heavy metals on *Rhizobium* populations isolated from a lead mine which activity ceased 50 years ago. In order to reach this goal some physicochemical parameters that influence metal bioavailability was determined, as well as metal concentrations in soils. Soil enzyme activities are highly affected by soil conditions and their evaluation may provide useful information on soil microbial activity and survival. For this reason, soil enzyme activities have been proposed as biological indicators of pollution, specially organic, but information about the influence of heavy metal on soil enzyme activities is scarcer. Thus, it was determined the activity of enzymes such as dehydrogenases, hydrolases, phosphatases, catalase and lipase in heavy metal contaminated soils. Metal tolerance of *Rhizobium* isolates was also screened in artificial media supplemented with different metals (Pb, Cd, As, Ni, Cu and Co) and their tolerance related to soil contamination and enzyme activities.

This chapter can widen the knowledge about the pressure that soil microflora experience under the direct effect of different metals. *Rhizobium* and soil enzyme activities may be useful for the evaluation of agricultural soil pollution, which may be used on the improvement of soil productivity or on the reclaim of contaminated soils.

1. Introduction

Soil is an important natural resource that needs to be preserved and, if possible, its quality and productive ability improved. Doran and Parkin (1994) defined soil quality as the capacity to function within an ecosystem and sustain biological productivity, maintain environmental quality and promote plant, animal and human health. Soil biological and biochemical properties are responsive for small changes that occur in soil properties, thereby providing immediate and accurate information on changes in soil quality. For this reason, soil microbial activity has a direct influence in the ecosystem stability and in soil fertility (Smith and Papendick, 1993). Microorganisms play a fundamental role on the biogeochemical cycles and are involved in forming the structure of a soil (Harris and Birch, 1989). The physical, chemical, and biological properties of the soil are all important for its behaviour (Arshad and Coen, 1992; Parr et al., 1992). Characterization of this behaviour should focus on the properties that are most sensitive to environmental stress (Dick and Gupta, 1994; Elliott, 1997; Pankhurst et al., 1995; Vanhala and Ahtiainen, 1994).

Soil equilibrium can easily be disturbed, especially by human intervention. Heavy metal contamination in soils is of major environmental concern on a world scale. Beside their natural occurrence, heavy metals may enter the ecological environment through anthropogenic activities, such as mining, smelting, sewage sludge disposal, application of pesticides and inorganic fertilizers and atmospheric deposition (Alloway, 1995a; Carrasco et al., 2005; Giller et al., 1989; Malik, 2004; McGrath et al., 1995; Robinson et al. 2001; Shen et al. 2005).

Since microorganisms are the most abundant and most genetically diverse living organisms adapted to almost all environments that exist on the Earth, they have been object of study in numerous works on environmental stress. Several authors have shown that metals adversely influence microorganisms (Shi et al., 2002), affecting their growth, morphology and activities (Bååth et al., 1998; Lakzian et al., 2002; Pereira et al., 2006;), including symbiotic N_2 fixation (Castro et al., 1997; Chaudhary et al., 2004). It is well known that metals are direct and/or indirectly involved in all aspects of microbial growth, metabolism and differentiation. Some metals such as Zn, Cu, Ni and Cr are essential or beneficial micronutrients for plants, animals and microorganisms, whereas others such as Cd, Hg and Pb have no known biological and/or physiological functions being toxic even at very low concentrations (Gadd, 1992).

The increasing occurrence of heavy metal-contaminated areas and the consciousness of their highly toxic effects to humans, as well as to animals, plants and microorganisms explain the growing concern about heavy metal pollution. Hence, the pressure to decontaminate heavy metal polluted soils has increased recently, however concern with the cost of soil remediation lead to explore not only cost effective technologies but also alternative monitoring tools. The immediate concern of rehabilitation practitioners is the availability and capacity or degradative potential of the autochthonous microbial communities. The adverse effects of heavy metals can lead to a reduction in biodiversity and resultant functions in the soil, for this reason it is deem necessary to use more relevant ecological test species.

Rhizobium are ubiquitous bacteria that have a profound agronomic importance, since the symbiotic association between legumes and rhizobia is by far the most important contributor to the world's supply of biologically fixed N_2 (Somasegaran and Hoben, 1994). For this reason and taking into consideration the importance of legumes in animal and human consumption, some attention has been given to the effects that these elements exert on *Rhizobium* (Ibekwe et al., 1995). Several authors reported that leguminous species grown on contaminated soils, exhibited reduced yields and N content (Chaudhary et al., 2004), since rhizobia isolated from host plants root nodules were completely ineffective to fix N_2 (Giller et al., 1989; Hernandez et al., 2002). In others studies (Pereira et al., 2006) *Rhizobium* has shown to be a genus very sensitive to environmental stresses, evidencing to be a good indicator of soil contamination.

Contradictions on heavy metal ecotoxicity can be attributed to overgeneralization of the outcomes from short-term laboratory studies that focus on a single soil type under controlled conditions. Field data on the effects of heavy metal are limited, and most of the information has become from experiments using sludge containing several metals. However, heavy metal toxicity requires assays with sensitive, reliable and ecologically relevant biological tools. Parameters involving species abundance and diversity along with functional parameters can give a better understanding of heavy metal toxicity.

The presence of heavy metals in the soil may influence the biochemical process by affecting both microbial proliferation and enzyme activities (Gianfreda et al., 2005). Visser and Parkinson (1992) have suggested that the biological and biochemical properties that are most useful for detecting the deterioration of soil quality are those that are most closely related to nutrient cycles, including the activities of soil enzymes. Soil enzyme activities are the driving force behind all the biochemical transformations occurring in the soil since they catalyse all biochemical reactions and are an integral part of nutrient cycling and soil fertility (Bandick et al., 1999). Soil enzymes are believed to be primarily of microbial origin but also originate from plants and animals (Tabatabai, 1994). They are usually associated with viable proliferating cells, but enzymes can be either excreted from a living cell or released into soil solution from dead cells (Tabatabai, 1994). Soil heavy metal contamination exerts an influence on the microbiota, which manifests itself in changes in the enzyme activity (Baran et al., 2004; Gianfreda et al., 2005). There is growing evidence that soil biological parameters may have a potential as early and sensitive indicators of soil ecological stress and restoration (Dick and Tabatabai, 1992).

For this reason, one of the objectives of this chapter was to evaluate the impact of heavy metals on *Rhizobium* populations isolated from a real world pollution site in an abandoned mine deactivated 50 years ago. In order to reach this goal some physicochemical parameters that influence metal bioavailability were determined, as well as total heavy metal concentrations in soils. Metal tolerance of *Rhizobium* isolates was screened in artificial media supplemented with different metals (Pb, Cd, As, Ni, Cu and Co) and their tolerance related to soil contamination. Since soil enzymes are very sensitive to soil contaminants, such as heavy metals, soil enzyme activities have been proposed as biological indicators of pollution (Dick and Tabatabai, 1992; Nannipieri, 1994). Therefore, this chapter also aimed to determine the activity of soil enzymes such as dehydrogenases, hydrolases, phosphatases, catalase and lipase in order to evaluate the degree of soil contamination.

2. Heavy Metal Tolerance of *Rhizobium* Strains Isolated from Braçal Mine

The soil is a dynamic, multi-component system, whose properties are continually modified by microbial, chemical, geological and anthropogenic processes (Saeki et al., 2002). In addition, soil undergoes short-term fluctuations, such as variations in moisture, pH and redox conditions. These changes in soil properties may affect the form and bioavailability of metals. So, the amounts of metals accumulated in soils are dependent on the emission levels, the transport of the metal from the source to the accumulation site and the retention of the metal once it has reached the soil (Alloway, 1995b).

Three composite soils were obtained from a lead mine (Braçal) in Portugal (Aveiro region), deactivated 50 years ago. BA and BD soils were collected in the most contaminated area of the mine, while BC soil was collected in the periphery. This soil was used as control, since its contamination is lower (Figure 1).

Table 1 summarizes the physical and chemical properties of investigated soils. The pH values determined varied significantly ($P< 0.05$) between locations, being in most soils below the optimal pH (6.8) for rhizobia growth. BC and BA soils showed a quite acid pH (4.5 and 4.15 respectively), while the BD soil has a pH of 5.2. According to Ibekwe et al. (1997, 1998), soil pH has a significant effect on rhizobia survival. These authors reported that in the more acid soils clover nodules were ineffective for N_2 fixation irrespective of soil metal content. Under lower pH conditions, rhizobia numbers and nodule number *per* plant were both significantly reduced. Broos et al. (2005) also reported that *Rhizobium leguminosarum* bv. *trifolii* survival was reduced at pH <5.5 and can be completely inhibited at pH < 4.5.

Table 1. Physicochemical analysis of the soils from different locations. Data are the mean ± SE from three replicate measurements. Different superscripts letters (a-c) represent significant differences (P < 0.05) between values at same column.

Soil	Physicochemical analysis			
	Water content (%)	pH	Redox potential (Eh)	Organic matter (%)
BC	16.4 ± 0.26^{a}	4.50 ± 0.08^{a}	127.7 ± 40.38^{a}	9.35 ± 0.35^{a}
BA	7.8 ± 0.18^{b}	4.15 ± 0.13^{b}	123.3 ± 4.04^{a}	4.72 ± 0.53^{b}
BD	24.1 ± 1.20^{c}	5.21 ± 0.005^{c}	121.7 ± 2.89^{a}	10.81 ± 1.06^{a}

Total heavy metal concentrations (Pb, As, Cd, Zn, Ni, Cu, Cr and Co), measured after extraction with *aqua regia*, varied significantly between locations (P< 0.05) as shown in Figure 1. Generally, contaminated soils (BA and BD) presented higher concentrations of metals than the control soil (BC). However, Cr concentrations were higher in BC soil than in the other soils, but were below the higher EC limits permitted for heavy metals (CEC, 1986) The concentrations of non-essential metals (Pb and As) were higher in BA soil, while BD soil showed higher levels of essential metals (Ni, Co and Cu). Cadmium concentrations were similar in both soils (Figure 1). Maximum permitted levels imposed by the CEC (1986) were exceed for almost metals in BA and BD soils. (Figure 1). As shown in Figure 1 BA and BD soils are extremely contaminated with Pb and As, imposing a enormous degree of stress in these soils.

Several authors reported that long-term metal deposition into soils results in high metal concentrations, which affects negatively soil microflora (Smith and Giller, 1992; Matsuda et al., 2002). In this work, we were able to isolate rhizobia from all soils, indicating that these bacteria were capable to survive under the metal concentrations determined. According to Ibekwe et al. (1997) survival can be related to the physical protection of clay minerals and organic matter or to the existence of microsites where metal contamination may be minimal. These "niches" may harbour rhizobia that are not resistant to heavy metals and may explain the presence of sensitive genotypes in contaminated soils.

Gross measurements of microbial diversity have been used to assess environmental stress (Atlas, 1984), but such studies are hampered by problems of sampling, extraction and culturing leading to bias towards certain groups within microbial communities. Pollution may lead to a decrease in microbial diversity due to the extinction of species which lack sufficient tolerance to the stress imposed, and enhanced population of other species which thrive under stress (Atlas, 1984). Microorganisms within species of the same genus or within strains of the same species can differ in their sensitivity to metals. Giller et al. (1993) demonstrated that *Sinorhizobium meliloti* was less sensitive, in terms of growth, to Cd than *R. leguminosarum* and *R. loti.* Therefore, the use of microbial populations which are easily culturable, ubiquitous, sensitive to several contaminants, and whose intraspecific diversity is enough to point out tolerance differences to contaminated soils, can be a way to overcome the problems enumerated above.

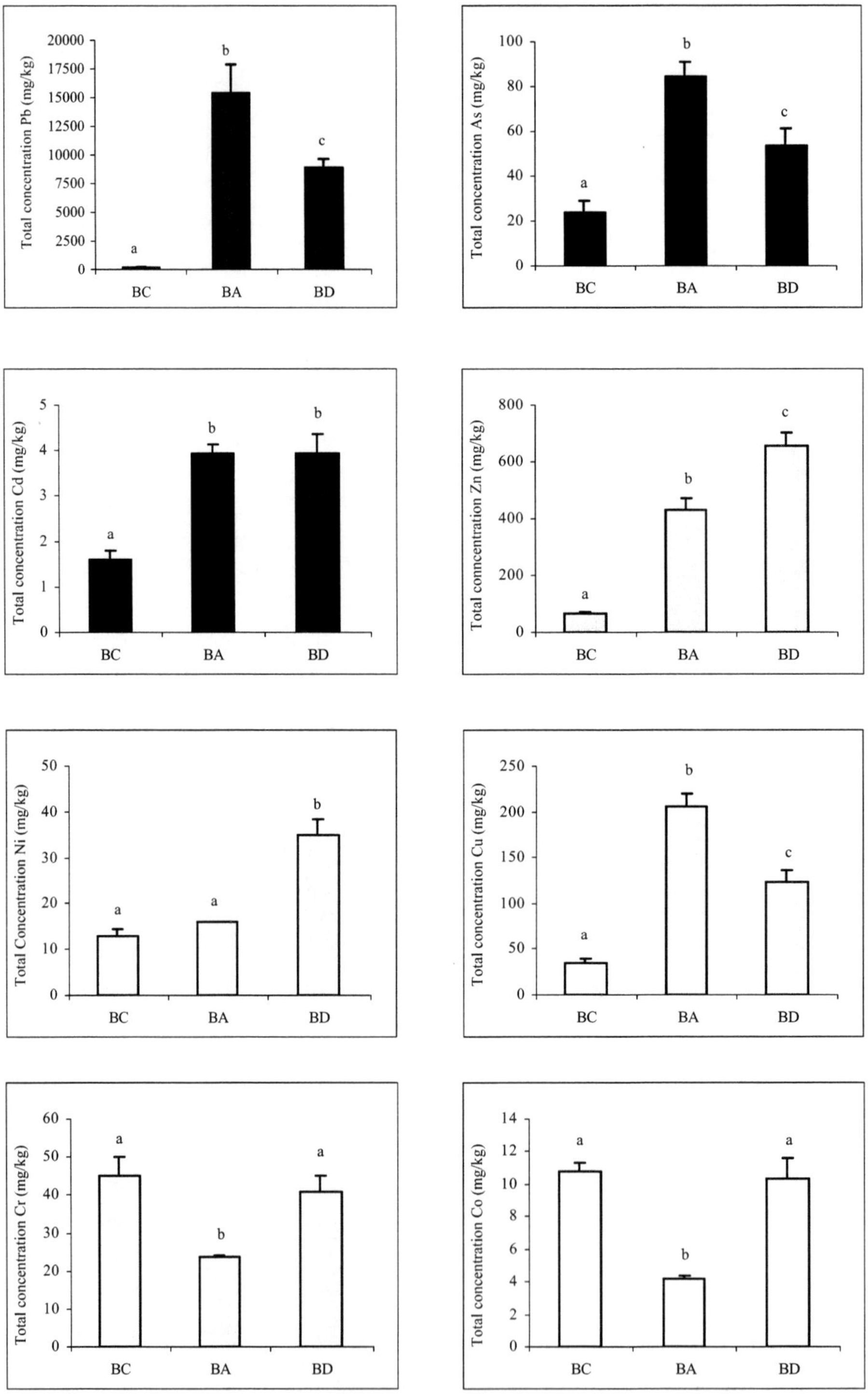

Figure 1. Total heavy metal concentration (Pb, As, Cd, Zn, Ni, Cu, Cr and Co) in the different soils. Data are mean ± SE of three replicate measurements. Different letters indicate means that are significantly different ($P< 0.05$) from each other.

Ubiquitous species, such as rhizobia, allow a wider comparison of heavy metal effects between different environments. *Rhizobium* can probably be used as an effective tool in ecotoxicity assays since these bacteria are known to be sensitive to a wide variety of pollutants and are very important to soil fertility in a wide range of environments (Figueira, 2000; Figueira et al., 2005; Pereira et al., 2006; Vig et al., 2003).

In order to evaluate the influence of heavy metal contamination by a lead abandoned mine in the soil microflora, forty-one isolates of *Rhizobium leguminosarum* bv. *trifolii* were obtained from nodules of white clover (*Trifolium repens*, L.) plants grown in BA and BD contaminated soils and also in control soil (BC).

Based on the percentage of growth inhibition, the 41 isolates obtained were classified as: sensitive (growth inhibition – 80-100%), moderately tolerant (growth inhibition - 60-80%) and tolerant (growth inhibition - <60%).

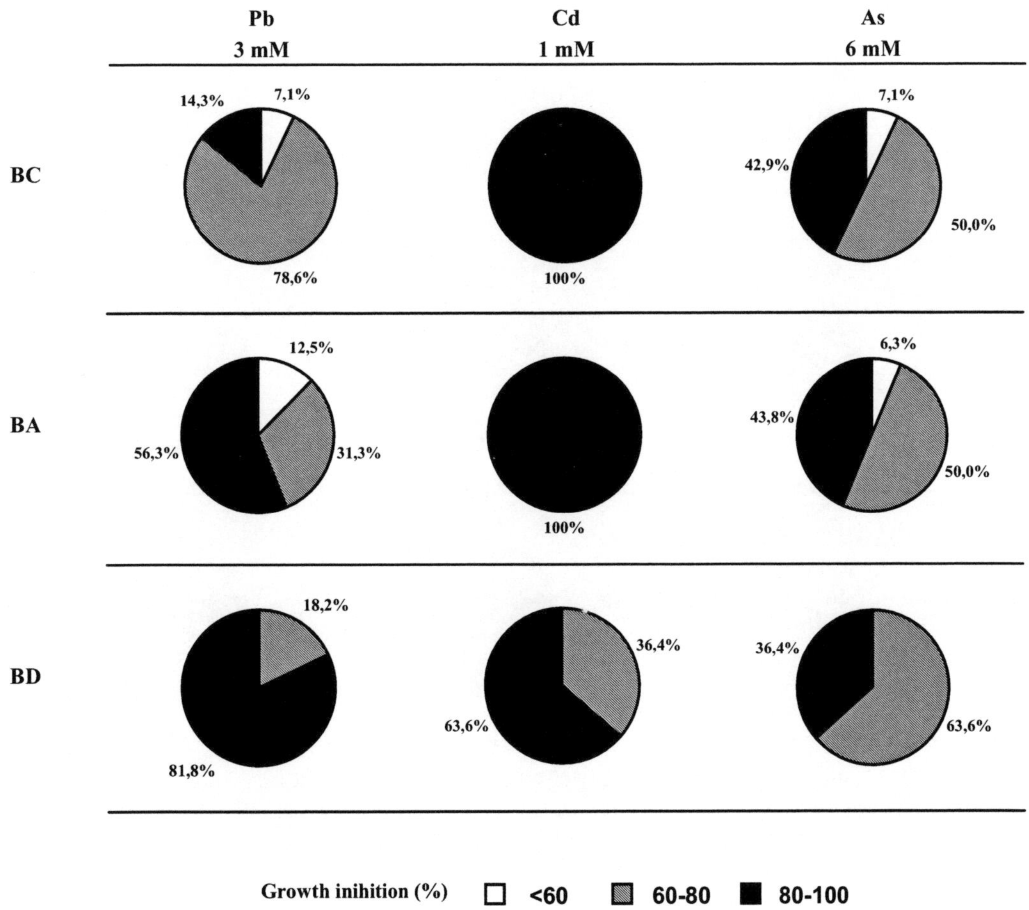

Figure 2. Percentage of isolates exhibiting a growth inhibition <60% - tolerant, 60-80% - moderately tolerant and 80-100% - sensitive in the different locations, for non-essential metals: Pb, Cd and As.

Figure 2 shows the percentage of sensitive, moderately tolerant and tolerant isolates in each location, for the concentration where all isolates still showed growth, to non-essential metals (Pb – 3 mM, Cd – 1 mM and As – 6 mM). Generally, isolates showed high sensitivity to Cd, since growth was severely inhibited at 1 mM for all isolates of BC and BA soils and to 2/3 of BD soil, and moderately tolerance to As, since in the three soils the percentage of sensitive isolates to 6 mM As was similar (between 36.4% and 43.8%). Pb was the metal where tolerance differences between soils were more marked. BC isolates showed the highest tolerance, since only 14.3% of them were sensitive to Pb. *Rhizobium* BD population showed the lowest tolerance, being more than 80% of the isolates sensitive to 3 mM Pb.

Figure 3 shows the percentage of sensitive, moderately tolerant and tolerant isolates in each location for the essential metals (Ni – 0.5 mM, Cu – 0.5 mM and Co – 0.5 mM). Once again, BC isolates showed a moderately tolerance to all essential metals tested. On the other hand, BA isolates showed high sensitivity to all metals.

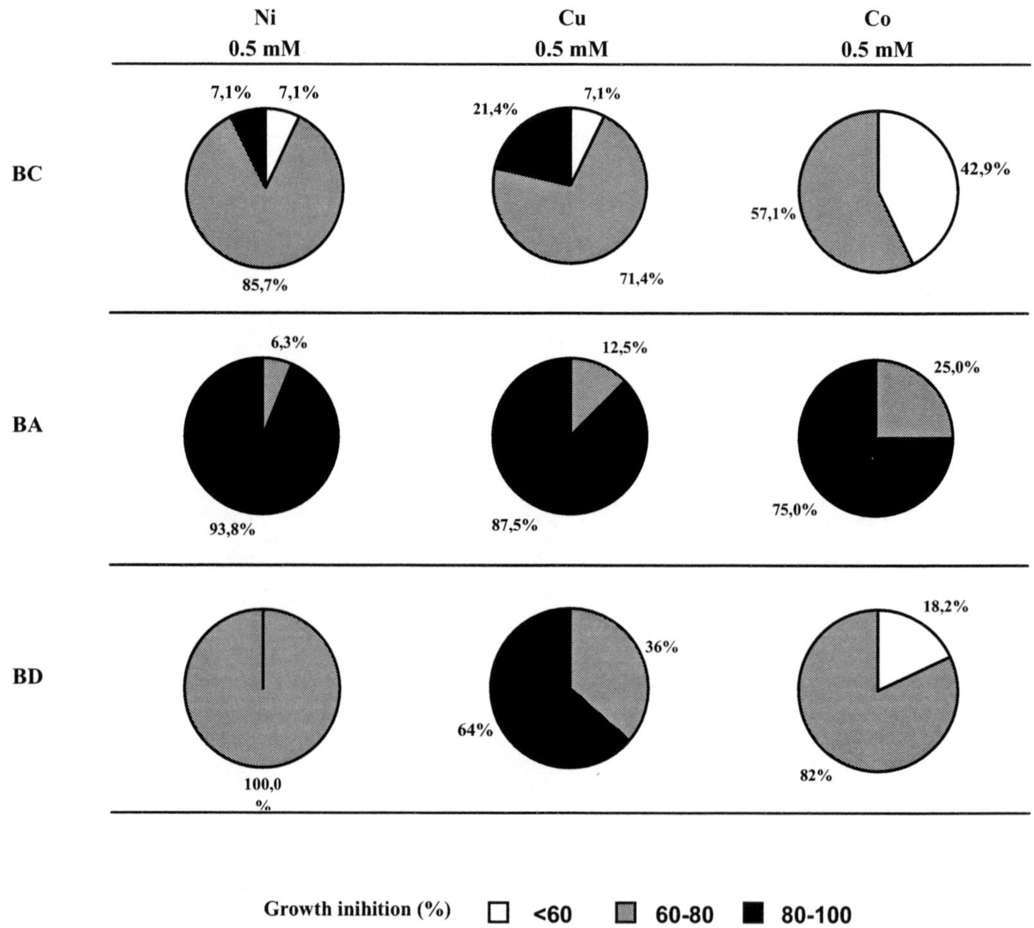

Figure 3. Percentage of isolates exhibiting a growth inhibition <60% - tolerant, 60-80% - moderately tolerant and 80-100% - sensitive in the different locations, for essential metals: Ni, Cu and Co.

Pb concentrations were extremely high in BA and BD soils, while in control soil the level of this metal was 50 times lower. The activity of the mine ceased 50 years ago, however the inputs of metals resulting from the old smelter and from the tunnels that access to the mine continue to happen. Due to their localization towards the tunnels accessing to the mine and the old smelter, BA and BD soils are easily waterlogged with water from the smelter and the tunnels, which easily became inundated when there is heavy rainfall or floods from a nearby river. These events take place frequently during winter, inputting heavy metals, even now, 50 years after the mine deactivation. BC soil was collected from the periphery of the mine, where the inputs of metals at the present are low.

Nevertheless, *Rhizobium* population from BC soil shows higher tolerance to Pb and As than the populations from BA and BD soils. Probably when the mine was laborating, BC isolates suffered the influence of higher heavy metal concentrations, which originate a selective pressure leading, at that time, to the appearance of genotypes with high lead tolerance, fact already described by Bååth (1992) and Bååth et al. (1998) who considered the possibility of heavy metals to exert a selective pressure in bacteria of contaminated soils, resulting in the presence of more tolerant organisms. These tolerant genotypes persisted until now in the population, evidencing an overlap of time between actual heavy metal concentrations and *Rhizobium* tolerance, probably due to the time needed for the population to adapt to the new conditions.

Interestingly, results show that *Rhizobium* population with higher resistance to Pb (BC isolates) also have tolerance to other metals such as As, Cu, Ni ad Co. This fact suggests that the selective pressure induced by Pb allowed the development of resistance mechanisms that bestow tolerance to different metal stresses, which is corroborated by Díaz-Raviña et al. (1994) and Nies (1992), who reported the existence of heavy metal multiple tolerance patterns in soil microorganisms.

3. Soil Enzyme Activities

Soil enzymes are important to several crucial functions. They are intimately involved in the cycling of nutrients, they affect the efficiency of fertilization, reflect the microbiological activity in soil and act as indicators of soil change (Gianfreda et al., 2005; Giller et al., 1998). Soil enzymes are the catalysts of important metabolic process functions including the decomposition of organic inputs and the detoxification of xenobiotics (Gianfreda et al., 2005).

Soil enzymes activity is used as a sensitive indicator of the effect of pollutants, including metals in soils (Bayer et al., 1982; Dick, 1997; Giller et al., 1998; Top et al., 1999). As previously pointed out (Brookes, 1995), applications of European Community standards for heavy metal concentrations result in significant negative impacts on microbial biomass and activity, indicating the greater sensitivity of the soil to these impacts in comparison with plants or animals. Important questions are what constitutes a significant environmental impact on soils and when is reclamation complete. Indicators are needed, not only as surrogates for reflecting the functionality of soils, but also to guide reclamation. The soil microbial component and soil enzyme activities are attractive as indicators for monitoring disturbance or pollution of soils because of their central and crucial role in the functions of the soil ecosystem.

Enzymes may rapidly respond to the changes caused by both natural and anthropogenic factors (Gianfreda et al., 2005). The strong inhibition of the activities of a variety of enzymes has been reported in metal polluted soils over the past years (Doelman and Haanstra, 1986;

Marzadori et al., 1996; Mathur et al., 1980; Tyler, 1974; Tabatabai, 1977) and these effects vary considerably.

Heavy metals may inhibit enzyme activities by masking catalytically active groups, having denaturing effects on the conformation of proteins, competing with the natural ions involved in the formation of enzyme-substract complexes (Gianfreda et al., 2005; Hinojosa et al., 2004; Nannipieri, 1994), or by affecting the synthesis of the enzymes within the microbial cells. For these reasons soil enzymes activities have been suggested as suitable indicators of soil quality since they have been considered sensitive indicators to measure the degree of soil degradation in both natural and agro-ecosystems, being thus well suited to measure the impact of pollution on the quality of soil (Dick, 1997; Giller et al., 1998; Trasar-Cepeda et al., 2000).

Dehydrogenase (DHA) activity typically occurs in all viable microbial cells (Gianfreda et al., 2005). Thus, its measurement is usually related to the presence of viable microorganisms and their oxidative ability has been often used as a functional indicator of soil health. DHA is related to a group of intracellular enzymes that are present in active soil microorganisms. This enzyme is found in all living organisms and takes part in many metabolic reactions involved in oxidative energy transfer in microbes. As dehydrogenases are not active as extracellular enzymes in the soil, the management of DHA has been used as a good overall indicator of microbial activity and of the capacity of microbes to oxidize soil organic matter (Bolton et al., 1985; Dick, 1997). Several studies have demonstrated that dehydrogenase enzyme activity of microorganisms is among the most sensitive parameters for the evaluation of toxicity (Shen et al., 2005).

In this chapter, dehydrogenase activity was determined using a method developed by Casida et al. (1964) using as subtract triphenyltetrazolium chloride (TTC) and glucose. After 24 hours of incubation triphenylformazan formed (TPF) from TTC was extracted with methanol. According to Obbard et al. (2001) substrate-induced DHA was found to be a sensitive assay for determining metal effects on the physiologically active soil microbial biomass. The precision of the assay allows evaluating, separately, effects due to pH, contaminant concentration and other soil properties.

DHA activity varied significantly ($P< 0.05$) between control soil and BA and BD soils (Figure 4), being the DHA activity in BC soil 2 times higher. This finding is in agreement with Trasar-Cepeda et al. (2000) who reported less dehydrogenase activity in metal-contaminated soil than in a similar uncontaminated soil, and with Marzadori et al. (1996) who stated that dehydrogenase activity was inhibited by the toxic effects of heavy metals, particularly Pb. Dar (1996) also reported a decrease in dehydrogenase activity at 50 mg Cd kg^{-1} in a laboratory study.

DHA activity appears to depend on the type of pollutant; for example, it is high in soils polluted with pulp and paper mill effluents and low in soils polluted with fly ash (Trasar-Cepeda et al., 2000). Nevertheless, several studies have demonstrated that dehydrogenase enzymatic activity of microorganisms is among the most sensitive parameters for evaluation of toxicity (Shen et al., 2005), which may be the reason why dehydrogenase activity is a frequently used test for determining the influence of various pollutants (heavy metals, pesticide, crude oil, etc.) on the microbiological quality of soil (Margesin et al., 2002).

The fluorescein diacetate hydrolysis (FDAH) assay measures the hydrolytic enzyme activities of microbial populations and can provide an estimate of overall microbial activity in an environmental sample (Adam and Duncan, 2001; Bandick et al., 1999; Burns, 1982). The assay is considered non-specific because it is sensitive to the activity of several enzyme classes including urease, lipases, phosphatases, glucosidase, esterases and proteases (Bandick et al, 1999; Hayano and Tubakai, 1985). The enzymes responsible for Fluorescein diacetate (FDA) hydrolysis are plentiful in the soil environment, and are involved in the decomposition of many types of tissues (Adam and Duncan, 2001). The ability to hydrolyse FDA thus seems widespread, especially among the major decomposers, bacteria and fungi. Generally more tan 90% of the energy flow in a soil system passes through microbial decomposers, therefore an assay which measures microbial decomposing activity will provide a good estimation of total microbial activity (Adam and Duncan, 2001).

In our study FDA assay was performed according to Adam and Duncan (2001). However, no relationship was detected between soil contamination and FDA assay, since all soils presented similar activities of these enzymes (Figure 4).

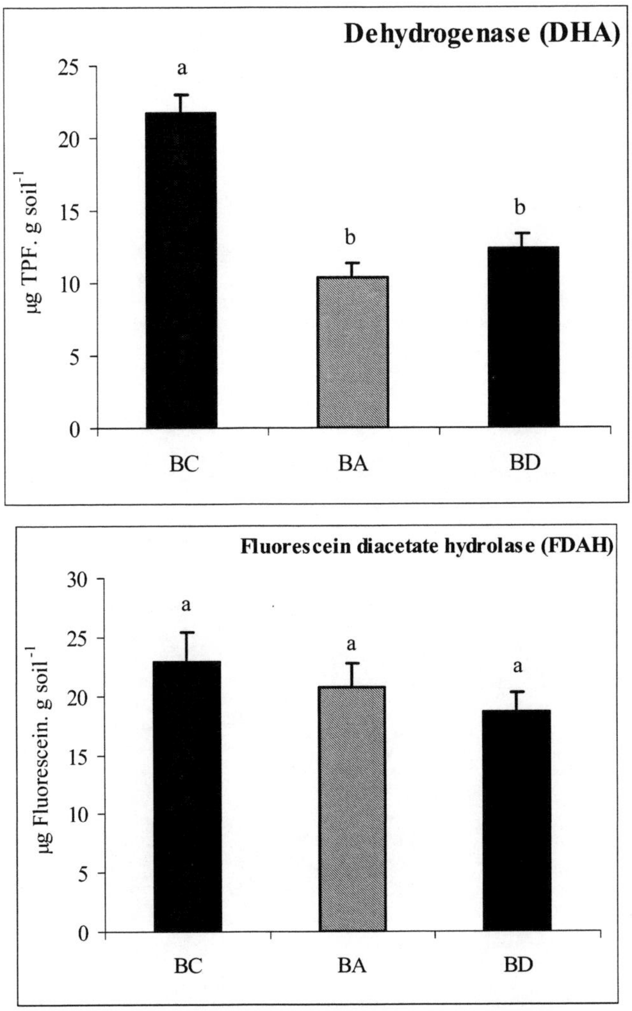

Figure 4. Dehydrogenase activity (µg TPF g soil^{-1}) determined over a period of 24 hours; and FDA activity (µg Fluorescein g soil^{-1}) determined over a period of 20 minutes, in BC, BA and BD soils. Data are mean ± SE of 30-40 replicate measurements. Different letters indicate means that are significantly different ($P < 0.05$) from each other.

Catalase is an intracellular enzyme found in all aerobic bacteria and in most facultative anaerobes. Catalase activity in soils is considered an indicator of aerobic microbial activity and has been related to both the number of aerobic microorganisms and to soil fertility (Garcia and Hernández, 1997).

In this work catalase activity varied significantly (P<0.05) between control soil (BC) and BA and BD soils. The soil with higher organic matter content (BD) was the same where catalase activity was lower (Figure 5). This is in disagreement with Kizilkaya et al. (2004) who related increases of catalase activity to the higher soil organic matter content. Heavy metal contamination negatively influences catalase activity, since catalase is a metaloenzyme, and the presence of heavy metals such as Ni and Cu inhibits its activity (White and White, 1997). Kizilkaya et al. (2004) reported that catalase activity is reduced by heavy metal contamination in agricultural soils. On the other hand, under heavy metal stress catalase activity of microorganisms, such as *Rhizobium* (Corticeiro et al., 2006), increases markedly. Thus, catalyse activity appears to be influenced in different ways by heavy metals, explaining why the results between BA and BD soils are difficult to interpret.

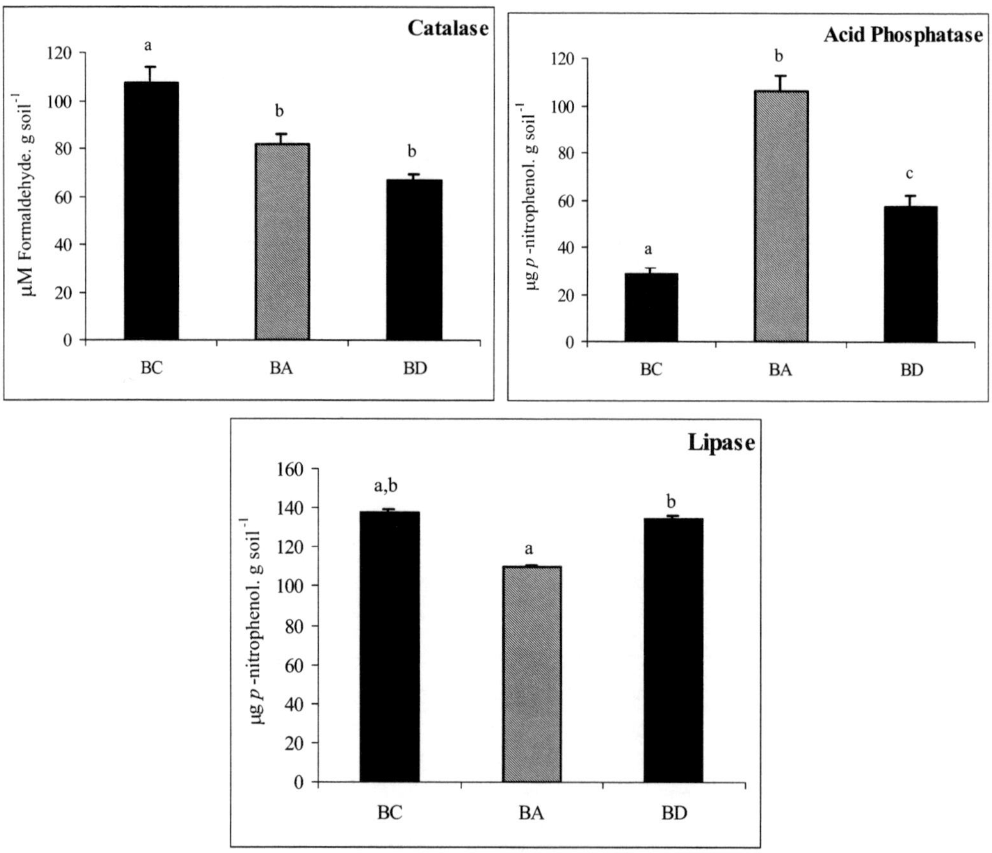

Figure 5. Catalase activity (μM Formaldehyde g soil^{-1}) determined over a period of 1 hour; Acid phosphate activity (μg *p*-nitrophenol g soil^{-1}) determined over a period of 40 minutes; and Lipase activity (μg *p*-nitrophenol g soil^{-1}) determined over a period of 10 minutes, in BC, BA and BD soils. Data are mean ± SE of 30-40 replicate measurements. Different letters indicate means that are significantly different (P< 0.05) from each other.

Phosphatases are broad enzymes that catalyze the hydrolysis of both esters and anhydrides of H_3PO_4 (Eivazi and Tabatabai, 1977). These enzymes are responsible for soil organic phosphorous mineralization and the release of inorganic phosphorous needed by microorganism and plants. The enzymes are classified as acid and alkaline phosphatases due to their optimal activities at (< 6.5) and (11) pH ranges, respectively. Phosphatases activities have been described as a good indicator for heavy metal contamination (Wyszkowska, 2002). However, Al-Khafaji and Tabatabai (1979), Bardgett et al. (1994) and Yeates et al. (1994) described that acid phosphatase activity was less affected by heavy metals than arylsulphatase. Acid and alkaline phosphatase activities were determined according to Eivazi and Tabatabai (1977). Results showed in Figure 5 indicate that acid phosphatase activity varied significantly ($P<0.05$) between locations. However, it was not detected activity of alkaline phosphatase in all of the tested soils. According to Gianfreda et al. (2005) soil enzyme activities are usually significantly correlated to soil pH. The investigated soils showed low pH values (Table 1), which could affect the activity of alkaline phosphatase. Arguably, the field soil pH would not directly affect the enzyme assay as the assays are run using buffers at their optimal pH. However, the long-term effect of low pH would probably cause shifts in microbial community composition and size and this, in turn, would affect enzyme dynamics at the time of sampling (Hinojosa et al., 2004). Furthermore, according to Eivazi and Tabatabai (1977) acid phosphates are predominant in acid soils and alkaline phosphatase is predominant in alkaline soils. Acid phosphate activity was higher in the most contaminated soils. However, according to Wyszkowska (2002) the activity of acid and alkaline phosphatases decreased in soils contaminated with Cr (IV), and in fact our work shows that acid phosphatase activity is negatively correlated with Cr levels. On the other hand, phosphatases can be inhibited not only by heavy metals (Tyler, 1974), but also by inorganic phosphate, which produces a feedback inhibition of this enzyme (Nannipieri et al., 1979). Actually, in this study acid phosphatase activity is higher in the BA soil with the lower level of phosphorus (7 mg kg^{-1}) and lower in BC, which has a higher level of phosphorus (131 mg kg^{-1}).

Lipase activity was determined according to Margesin et al. (2002). Lipase activity is often associated to oil degradation; however information about its behaviour in the presence of metals is limited. In this work, lipase activity was similar in all soils (Figure 5), showing that its activity is not differentially influenced by heavy metals concentrations present in the three soils.

4. Conclusion

Due to their small size, which provides a large contact area that can interact with the surrounding environment, microorganisms are the first biota showing the impact of toxic compounds. For this reason they are considered to be the best indicators of soil pollution. Metals exert a selective pressure on organisms, resulting in microbial populations with higher tolerance, but with lower diversity, when compared to unpolluted neighbouring areas (Bååth, 1992; Bååth et al., 1998). The soil microbial population presents variability, which, in a non-stressed environment, would not bring any advantage. However, when the conditions are changed and this population is submitted to a selective pressure, the genotypes presenting tolerance ability can survive, hence yielding a tolerant population, with lower genetic variability. Hinojosa et al. (2004) referred that indicators of soil quality and health, to be useful and practical, must meet certain criteria. These include: sensitivity to perturbation or contamination; a relationship to soil function; reproducibility; low temporal and spatial variability; and have simple sampling and analytical methods. Both enzymes activity and *Rhizobium* tolerance showed to meet some of these criteria. Our results evidenced that dehydrogenases and catalase, which are intracellular oxirreductases, showed a good correlation with the heavy metal contamination of soils. Nevertheless, there are several works (Gianfreda et al., 2005; Kizilkaya et al., 2004) alerting to several factors (pH, organic matter, clay etc.) that affect soil enzymatic activity, and they should be taken into consideration, if we want to extrapolate or compare values from environments with distinct edaphic, climatic or contamination features. *Rhizobium* isolates showed a wide range of heavy metals tolerance, confirming the responses showed to lower levels of heavy metal contamination (Pereira et al, 2006) and other environmental stresses (Figueira, 2000), which indicates that, in addition to their ubiquity, culturability, and involvement in the N cycle, *Rhizobium* populations are a good indicator of soil quality and health. However, it should be taken in consideration that rhizobia populations take some time to adapt to the habitat conditions, which can limit their ability as immediate indicators of the soil's health. Even so, this feature presents the advantage of reflecting the circumstances that conditioned the population's evolution in the past.

A study, like this chapter, that simultaneously determine the soil enzyme activity and the tolerance *Rhizobium* populations towards the heavy metal contamination, will provide an indication of not only the perturbations that a specific pollutant is causing in the present, but also the effects induced in the past, which is of extreme importance in long-term contaminations or with pollutants that are recalcitrant like heavy metals, and may be useful for the evaluation of natural and agricultural soils pollution, and for the improvement of soil productivity or the reclaim of contaminated soils.

6. References

Adam, G; Duncan, H. Development of sensitive and rapid method for the measurement of total microbial activity using fluorescein diacetate (FDA) in a range of soils. *Soil Biology and Biochemistry*, 2001 33, 943-951.

Al -Khafaji, AA; Tabatabai, MA. Effects of trace elements on arylsulfatase activity in soils. *Soil Science*, 1979 127, 129–133.

Alloway, BJ. Introduction. In: Alloway BJ editor. *Heavy Metals in Soils*. New York: Blackie Academic and Professional; 1995a. 3-9.

Alloway, BJ. Soil processes and the behaviour of metals. In: *Heavy Metals in Soils*. New York: Blackie Academic and Professional; 1995b. 11-37.

Arshad, MA; Coen, GM. Characterization of soil quality: physical and chemical criteria. *American Journal of Alternative Agriculture*, 1992 7, 25–33.

Atlas, RM. Use of microbial diversity measurements to assess environmental stress. In: Klug MJ, Reddy CA editors. *Current Perspectives in Microbial Ecology*. Washington: American Society for Microbiology; 1984; 540–545.

Bååth, E. Measurement of heavy metal tolerance of soil bacteria using thymidine incorporation into bacteria extracted after homogenization-centrifugation. *Soil Biology and Biochemistry*, 1992 24, 1167-1172.

Bååth, E; Díaz-Ravina, M; Frostegård, Å; Campbell, CD. Effect of metal-rich sludge amendments on the soil microbial community. *Applied and Environmental Microbiology*, 1998 64, 238-245.

Bandick, AK; Dick, RP. Field management effects on soil enzyme activities. *Soil Biology and Biochemistry*, 1999 31, 1471-1479.

Baran, S; Bielinska, JE; Oleszczuk, P. Enzymatic activity in an air.eld soil polluted with polycyclic aromatic hydrocarbons. *Geoderma*, 2004 118, 221–232.

Bardgett, RD; Speir, TW; Ross, DJ; Yeates, GW; Kettles, HA. Impact of pasture contamination by copper, chromium, and arsenic timber preservative on soil microbial properties and nematodes. *Biology and Fertility of Soils*, 1994 18, 71–79.

Bayer, H; Mitterer, M; Schinner, F. Der Ein.uss von Insektiziden auf mikrobiogene Prozesse in Ah-Materialien eines landwirtschaftlich genutzten Bodens. *Pedobiologia*, 1982 23, 311–319.

Bolton Jr, H; Elliot, LF; Papendick, RI; Berdicek, DF. Soil microbial biomass and selected soil enzyme activities: effects of fertilization and cropping practices. *Soil Biology and Biochemistry*, 1985 14, 423-427.

Brookes, PC. The use of microbial parameters in monitoring soil pollution by heavy metals. *Biology and Fertility of* Soils, 1995 19, 269-275.

Broos, K; Bryens, H; Smolders, E. Survival of rhizobia in soil is sensitive to elevated zinc in the absence of the host plant. *Soil Biology and Biochemistry*, 2005 37, 573-579.

Burns, RG. Enzyme activity in soil: location and a possible role in microbial ecology. *Soil Biology and Biochemistry*, 1982 34, 121-125.

Carrasco, JA; Armario, P; Pajuelo, E; Burgos, A; Caviedes, MA; López, R; Chamber, MA; Palomares AJ. Isolation and characterisation of symbiotically effective *Rhizobium* resistant to arsenic and heavy metals after the toxic spill at the Aznalcóllar pyrete mine. *Soil Biology and Biochemistry*, 2005 37,1131-1140.

Casida, LE; Klein, DA; Santaro, T. Soil desidrogenase activity. *Soil Science*, 1964 96, 371-376.

Castro IV; Ferreira EM; McGrath, SP. Effectiveness and genetic diversity of *Rhizobium leguminosarum* bv. *trifolii* isolates in Portuguese soils polluted by industrial effluents. *Soil Biology and Biochemistry*, 1997 29, 1209-1213.

Chaudhary, P; Dudeja, SS; Kappor, KK. Effectivity of host *Rhizobium leguminosarum* symbiosis in soils receiving sewage water containing heavy metals. *Microbiology Research*, 2004 159, 121-127.

CEC - Commission of the European Communities. Council Directive on the protection of the environment, and in particular of the soil, when sewage sludge is used in agriculture. *Official Journal of European Community*, 1986 L181. Annex 1A, 10.

Corticeiro, S; Lima, A; Figueira, E. The importance of glutathione in oxidative status of *Rhizobium leguminosarum* bv. *viciae* under Cd exposure. *Enzyme and Microbial Technology*, 2006 40, 132-137.

Dar, GH. Effects of cadmium and sewage-sludge on soil microbial biomass and enzyme activities. *Bioresource Technology*, 1996 56, 141-145.

Díaz-Raviña, M; Bååth, M; Frostegård, A. Multiple heavy metal tolerance of soil bacterial communities and its measurement by thymidine incorporation technique. *Applied and Environmental Microbiology*, 1994 60, 2238-2247.

Dick, WA; Tabatabai, MA. Potential uses of soil enzymes. In: Metting B editor. *Soil Microbial Ecology*. New York: Marcel Dekker; 1992; 95–127.

Dick, RP; Gupta, VVSR. A conceptual model for the role of abiotic soil enzymes in a microbial ecology: A potential analogue for soil quality. In: Pankhurst CE, Doube BM, Gupta VVSR, Grace PR editors. *Soil Biota: Management in Sustainable Farming Systems*. Adelaide: Commonwealth Scientific and Industrial Research Organization Information. 1994. 167–168.

Dick, RP. Soil enzyme activities as integrative indicators of soil health. In: Pankhurst CE, Doube BM, Gupta VVSR editors. *Biological indicators of soil health*. Wallingford, USA: CAB International; 1997; 121-156.

Doelman, P; Haanstra, L. Short- and long –term effects of heavy metals on urease activity in soils. *Biology and Fertlity of Soils*, 1986 2, 213-218.

Doran, JW; Parkin, TB. Defining and assessing soil quality. In: Doran JW editor. *Defining Soil Quality for Sustainable Environment*. Madison: SSSA Special Publication; 1994; 3-23.

Eivazi, F; Tabatabai, MA. Phosphatases in soils. *Soil Biology and Biochemistry*, 1977 9, 167-172.

Elliott, ET. 1997. Rationale for developing bioindicators of soil health. In: Pankhurst CE, Doube BM, Gupta, VVSR editors. *Biological Indicators of Soil Health*. Wellington: CAB International; 1997;. 49–78.

Figueira, E. Aspectos da tolerância salina em *Pisum sativum* L.: influência da nutrição azotada. PhD Thesis. Aveiro University. 2000.

Figueira, EMAP; Lima, AIG; Pereira, SIA. Cadmium tolerance plasticity in *Rhizobium leguminosarum* bv. *viciae*: glutathione as a detoxifying agent. *Canadian Journal of Microbiology*, 2005 51: 7–14

Gadd, GM. Metals and microorganisms: A problem of definition. *FEMS Microbiology Letters*, 1992 100, 197-204.

García, C; Hernández, T. Biological and biochemical indicators in derelict soils subjected to erosion. *Soil Biology and Biochemistry*, 1997 29, 171-177.

Gianfreda, L; Rao, MA; Piotrowska, A; Palumbo, G; Colombo, C. Soil enzyme activities as affected by anthropogenic alterations: intensive agricultural practices and organic pollution. *Science of Total Environment*. 2005 341, 265-279.

Giller, KE; McGrath, SP; Hirsch, PR. Absence of nitrogen fixation in clover grown on soil subject to long-term contamination with heavy metals is due to survival of only ineffective *Rhizobium*. *Soil Biology and Biochemistry*, 1989 21, 841-848.

Giller, KE; Nussbaum, R; Chaudri, AM; McGrath, SP. *Rhizobium meliloti* is less sensitive to heavy-metal contamination in soil than *R. leguminosarum* bv. *trifolii* or *R. loti*. *Soil Biology and Biochemistry*, 1993 25, 273-278.

Giller, KE; Witter, E; McGrath, SP. Toxicity of heavy metals to microorganisms and microbial process in agricultural soils: a review. *Soil Biology and Biochemistry*, 1998 300, 1389-1414.

Harris, JA; Birch, P. Soil microbial activity in opencast coal mine restoration. *Soil Use and Management*, 1989 5, 155-160.

Hayano, K; Tubaki, K. Origin and properties of b-glucosidase activity of tomato field soil. *Soil Biology & Biochemistry*, 1985 17, 53-557.

Hernandez, T; Moral, R; Perez-Espinosa, A; Moreno-Caselles, J; Perez-Murcia, MD; Garcia, C. Nitrogen mineralization potential in calcerous soils amended with sewage sludge. *Bioresource Technology*, 2002 83, 213-219.

Hinojosa, MB; Carreira, JA; García-Ruíz, R; Dick, RP. Soil moisture pre-treatment effects on enzyme activities as indicators of heavy metal-contaminated and reclaim soils. *Soil Biology and Biochemistry*, 2004 1559-1568.

Ibekwe, AM; Angle, JS; Chaney, RL; van Berkum, P. Sewage sludge and heavy metal effects on nodulation and nitrogen fixation of legumes. *Journal of Environmental Quality*, 1995 24, 1199-1204.

Ibekwe, AM; Angle, JS; Chaney, RL; van Berkum, P. Differentiation of clover *Rhizobium* isolated from biosolids-amended soils with varying pH. *Soil Science Society American Journal*, 1997 61, 1679-1685.

Ibekwe, AM; Angle, JS; Chaney, RL; van Berkum, P. Zinc and cadmium effects on Rhizobia and white clover using chelator-buffered nutrient solution. *Soil Science Society American Journal*, 1998 62, 204-211.

Kizilkaya, R; Askin, T; Bayrakli, B; Saglam, M. Microbiological characteristics of soils contaminated with heavy metals, *European Journal of Soil Science*, 2004 40, 95-102.

Lakzian, A; Murphy, P; Turner, A; Beynon, JL; Giller, KE. *Rhizobium leguminosarum* bv. *viciae* populations in soils with increasing heavy metal contamination: abundance, plasmid profiles, diversity and metal tolerance. *Soil Biology and Biochemistry*, 2002 34, 519-529.

Malik, A. Metal bioremediation through growing cells. *Environmental International*, 2004 30, 261-278.

Margesin, R; Zimmerbauer, A; Schinner, F. Monitoring of bioremediation by soil biological activities. *Chemosphere*, 2002 40, 339-346.

Mathur, SP; MacDougall, JI; McGrath, M. Levels of activities of some carbohydrates, protease, lipase and phosphates in organic soils of differing copper content. *Soil Science*, 1980 129, 376-385.

Marzadori, C; Ciavatta, C; Montecchio, D; Gessa, C. Effetcs of lead pollution on different soil enzyme activities. *Biology and Fertility of Soils*, 1996 22, 53-58.

Matsuda A; Moreira, FMS; Siqueira, JO. Tolerância de rizóbios de diferentes procedências ao zinco, cobre e cádmio. *Pesquisa Agropecuaria Brasileira*, 2002 37, 343-355.

McGrath, SP; Chaudri, AM; Giller, KE. Long-term effects of metals in sewage sludge on soils, microorganisms and plants. *Journal of Industrial Microbiology* 1995 14, 94-104.

Nannipieri, P; Pechozzini, F; Arcada, PG; Pioranelli, C. Changes in amino acids, enzyme activities and biomass during soil microbial growth. *Soil Science*, 1979 127, 26–34.

Nannipieri, P. The potential use of soil enzymes as indicators of productivity, sustainability and pollution. In: Pankhurst CE, Doube BM, Gupta VVSR, Grace PR editors. *Soil Biota, Management in Sustainable Farming Systems*. Australia: CSIRO Publication; 1994; 238–244.

Obbard, JP. Ecotoxicological assessment of heavy metals in sewage sludge amended soils. *Applied Geochemistry*, 2001 16, 1405-1411.

Pankhurst, CE; Hawke, BG; McDonal, HJ; Kirkby, CA; Buckerfield, JC; Michelsen, P ; O'Brien, KA; Gupta, VVSR; Doube, BM. Evaluation of soil biological properties as potential bioindicators of soil health. *Australian Journal of Experimental Agriculture*, 1995 35, 1015–1028.

Parr, JF; Papendick, RI; Hornick, SB; Meyer, RE. Soil quality: attributes and relationship to alternative and sustainable agriculture. *American Journal of Alternative Agriculture*, 1992 7, 5–11.

Pereira, SIA; Lima, AIG; Figueira, EMAP. Screening possible mechanisms mediating cadmium resistance in *Rhizobium leguminosarum* bv. *viciae* isolated from contaminated portuguese soils. *Microbial Ecology*, 2006 52, 176-186.

Robinson, B; Russell, C; Hedley, M; Clothier, B. Cadmium adsorption by rhizobacteria: implications for New Zealand pastureland. *Agriculture Ecomical Environmental*, 2001 87, 315-321.

Saeki, K; Kunito, T; Oyaizu, H; Matsumoto, S. Relationships between bacterial tolerance levels and forms of copper and zinc in soils. *Journal of Environmental Quality*, 2002 31, 1570-1575.

Shen, G; Lu, Y; Zhou, Q; Hong, J. Interaction of polycyclic aromatic hydrocarbons and heavy metals on soil enzyme. *Chemosphere*, 2005 61. 1175-1182.

Shi, W; Bischoff, M; Turco, R; Konopka, A. Long-term effects of chromium and lead upon the activity of soil microbial communities. *Applied and Soil Ecology*, 2002 21, 169-177.

Smith, SR; Giller, KE. Effective *Rhizobium leguminosarum* biovar *trifolii* present in five soils contaminated with heavy metals from long-term applications of sewage sludge or metal mine spoil. *Soil Biology and Biochemistry*, 1992 24, 781-788.

Smith, LJ; Papendick, RI. Soil organic matter dynamics and crop residue management. In: Metting B editor. *Soil Microbial Ecology*. New York: Marcel Dekker; 1993

Somasegaran, P; Hoben, HJ. *Handbook for Rhizobia*. Berlin: Springer-Verlag; 1994.

Tabatabai, MA. Effects of trace elements on urease activity. *Soil Biology and Biochemistry*, 1977 9, 9-13.

Tabatabai, MA. Soil enzymes. In: Weaver RW, Angle JS, Bottomly PS editors. *Methods of Soil Analyses, Part 2, Microbiological and Biochemical Properties*. USA: Soil Science Society of America; 1994; 775–833.

Top, EM; Maila, MP; Clerinx, M; Goris, J; De Vos, P; Verstraete, W. Methane oxidation as method to evaluate the removal of 2,4-D from soil by plasmid-mediated bioaugumentation. *FEMS Microbiology Ecology*, 1999 28, 203–213.

Trasar-Cepeda, C; Leirós, MC; Seoane, S; Gil-Sotres, F. Limitations of soil enzymes as indicators of soil pollution. *Soil Biology and Biochemistry*, 2000 32, 1867-1875.

Tyler, G. Heavy metal pollution and soil enzyme activity. *Plant and Soil*, 1974 41, 303-311.

Vanhala, PT; Ahtiainen, JH. Soil respiration, ATP content and photobacterium toxicity test as indicators of metal pollution in soil. *Environmental Toxicology and Water Quality: An International Journal*, 1994 9, 115–121.

Vig, K; Megharaj, M; Sethunathan, N; Naidu, R. Bioavailability and toxicity of cadmium to microorganisms and their activities in soil: a review. *Advances in Environmental Research*, 2003 121–135.

Visser, S; Parkinson, D. Soil biological criteria as indicators of soil quality: soil microorganisms. *American Journal of Alternative Agriculture*, 1992 7, 33-37.

White, JS; White, DC. *Source book of enzymes*. Boca Raton- Florida: CRC Press LC; 1997

Wyszkowska, J. Soil contamination by chromium and its enzymatic activity and yielding. *Polish Journal of Environmental Studies*, 2002 11, 79-84.

Yeates, GW; Orchard, VA; Speir, TW; Hunt, JL; Hermans, MCC. Reduction in soil biological activity following pasture contamination by copper, chromium, arsenic timber preservative. *Biology and Fertility of Soils*, 1994 18, 200–208.

In: Environmental Microbiology Research Trends
Editor: G. V. Kurladze, pp. 257-272
ISBN: 978-1-60021-939-9

Chapter 9

VIRUS-BINDING PROTEINS IN WATER ENVIRONMENTS: NATURAL LIGANDS FOR HUMAN VIRUSES

***Daisuke Sano*[1,2,*] *and Tatsuo Omura*[1]**

[1]Department of Civil and Environmental Engineering, Graduate School of Engineering, Tohoku University, Aoba 6-6-06, Sendai, 980-8579, Japan

[2]Department of Microbiology, School of Biology, University of Barcelona, Av. Diagonal 645, 08026, Barcelona, Spain.

ABSTRACT

Virus-binding proteins (VBPs) are bacterial proteins to which human viruses preferentially adsorb in water environments. VBPs were discovered from a bacterial culture derived from activated sludge with affinity chromatography assay in which a viral capsid peptide was used as a ligand. As an example of the VBP isolation, the recovery and characterization of Adenovirus-binding proteins (AdVBPs) were introduced. The significant adsorption of infectious Adenovirus (AdV) particles to the isolated AdVBPs was confirmed with enzyme-linked immunosorbent assay (ELISA). A number of AdVBPs were successfully obtained from crude proteins extracted from activated sludge culture, which was revealed by two-dimensional electrophoresis. The determination of the N-terminal amino acid sequence of AdVBP indicates that some AdVBPs are derived from outer membrane proteins of bacteria, and exhibit virus-binding ability under conditions of water environments. The methodology for acquiring VBP gene from a genomic DNA library of activated sludge microorganisms was also described. The consensus-degenerate hybrid oligonucleotide primer (CODEHOP) method, touchdown PCR, seminested PCR and inosine-incorporated primers were employed to effectively screen the VBP gene from a genomic DNA library. Since VBPs are expected to be stable

* Mailing address of the corresponding author: Department of Microbiology, School of Biology, University of Barcelona, Av. Diagonal 645, 08026, Barcelona, Spain. Phone: +34-93-403-46-20. Fax: +34-93-403-46-29. Electronic mail address: dsano@ub.edu

under conditions of water environments, VBPs might be utilized as feasible and inexpensive viral adsorbents in technologies for virus detection and enrichment from water specimens. In order to utilize VBPs as viral adsorbents in various technologies, it is desirable to prepare VBPs for key viruses responsible for waterborne infectious diseases, or to discover VBPs with a broad affinity to several species of pathogenic viruses, though significant research progress is required to find the VBPs with a broad affinity.

INTRODUCTION

Water pollution with pathogenic viruses such as Enteroviruses and Noroviruses has been reported frequently even in industrialized countries where hygiene conditions are considerably improved [Haramoto et al., 2005; He and Jiang, 2005; Sano et al., 2006b]. The contamination of these pathogenic viruses in water environments is primarily attributed to insufficient removal of viruses in wastewater treatment, because a number of infectious viruses are included in the feces of patients with viral diseases. The linkage of virus occurrence in water environments and the proliferation of viral infectious diseases in geographically close areas was elucidated with a molecular epidemiological method [Ueki et al., 2005], but details of the pathway of pathogenic viruses in water environments have not been fully elucidated so far.

Adsorption phenomena of pathogenic viruses to various materials would have an important role in the transport and survival of viruses in water environments. Pathogenic viruses in water are well captured by several substances such as membrane filters [Sobsey et al., 1980; Shields et al., 1985; Guttman-Bass et al., 1985] and organic polymers [Biziagos et al., 1987], and it is not troublesome work to elute viruses from these substances. Therefore, these substances have been utilized for recovering viruses from water [Wyn-Jones and Sellwood, 2001]. In contrast, seeded viruses to sewage sludge easily adhere to sludge flocs, whereas the recovery efficiency of the seeded viruses from sewage sludge is generally poor [Pancorbo 1981]. There are two main reasons why seeded viruses in sewage sludge are not well recovered, one being an inactivation of the seeded viruses. Several proteases produced by bacteria can degrade proteins including viral surface proteins [Nasser et al., 2002]. Since the viral infection of human cells is initiated by binding viral surface proteins to specific receptors on human cells [Bewley et al., 1999; Forrest and Dermody, 2003; Zarate et al., 2004; Makino et al., 2006], the degradation of virus surface proteins by proteases causes the inactivation of viruses. The other reason is the irreversible adsorption of viruses to sludge polymers. The recovery of adhered viruses from sludge flocs is almost impossible if virus particles are irreversibly captured by specific substances in sewage sludge. Of these two reasons, irreversible adsorption is more appropriate than the inactivation of viruses, because prolonged infectious activity of viruses in sewage sludge also has been reported [Damgaard-Larsen 1977]. It can be hypothesized that there are virus-binding polymers in sewage sludge, which can tightly bind viruses.

Virus-binding proteins (VBPs) are found in a bacterial culture derived from activated sludge, based on the hypothesis that there might be virus-binding polymers [Sano et al., 2004]. Since viruses adsorbed to suspended solids in water can survive for a longer period than freely suspended viruses [Foster et al., 1980], VBPs could contribute to subsistence of pathogenic viruses in an aquatic environment where several factors such as sunlight influence the inactivation of infectious viruses [Schaper et al., 2002; Sinton et al., 1999] in a way that viruses adsorb to bacteria harboring VBPs. Furthermore, VBPs exhibiting the stable binding ability to viruses under the conditions of water environments might be utilized as viral adsorbents in VBP-based technologies for virus removal, enrichment and detection. In this chapter, several features of VBPs including occurrence, functions and properties are described. Then, the recovery and characterization of adenovirus-binding proteins (AdVBPs) is explained as an example of the VBP isolation from activated sludge microorganisms. Finally, strategies for acquiring the VBP gene from activated sludge microorganisms are introduced, and the future applications and perspectives of VBPs in a variety of fields are discussed.

Occurence, Functions and Properties of VBP

Many pathogenic viruses, especially enteroviruses, have been observed to preferentially adhere sewage sludge, and these viruses adsorbing to sludge flocs are hardly recovered. As described above, the main reason is a virtually irreversible adsorption of viruses to sludge polymers. Microorganisms in sewage sludge yield various polymeric substances including polysaccharides, lipopolysaccharides, proteins and nucleic acids, and these substances play an important role in the virus adsorption. In our previous study, bacterial proteins were regarded as the most probable candidates of virus-binding biopolymer in sewage sludge because proteins have a conformational diversity, which makes it possible to specifically adsorb to various substances. Since a particle surface of waterborne pathogenic viruses mainly consists of proteins [Block, 1989], there might be specific proteins that could attract virus particles by a specific interaction.

The finding of VBPs was achieved by applying crude proteins to the affinity column in which a custom-made capsid peptide of PV1 Mahoney was immobilized as a ligand (Figure 1). The peptide used in this assay is the protruding part of the capsid protein and is a part of the major neutralization antigenic site of the PV1 particle [Fiore et al., 1997; Hogle et al., 1985]. As shown in Figurel, VBPs having affinity with the Poliovirus capsid peptide (i.e., Poliovirus-binding proteins: PoVBPs) are trapped in the affinity column, but the other proteins without affinity to the PV1 capsid peptide pass through the column at the washing step. PoVBPs in the affinity column are recovered by introducing an elution buffer including 6M urea. The ionic strength and flow rate of the start buffer significantly affect the yield of PoVBPs, so it was necessary to optimize the buffer conditions for the affinity isolation of PoVBPs from crude proteins of an activated sludge culture.

Although the isolated VBPs had an affinity with the poliovirus capsid peptide, it is unclear whether they can bind intact virions (virus particles). Therefore, the virus-binding ability of the isolated VBPs was evaluated with ELISA using PV1 Sabin 1, an attenuated strain of PV1 Mahoney. There are two different amino acids between PV1 Mahoney and Sabin 1 in the ligand region of capsid peptide (12 residues) used in the affinity chromatography, but it was clearly elucidated by ELISA that the isolated VBPs have the ability of adsorbing PV1 Sabin strain [Sano et al., 2004]. The differences of amino acids (2 out of 12 residues) did not affect the ability of VBPs to bind Poliovirus particles.

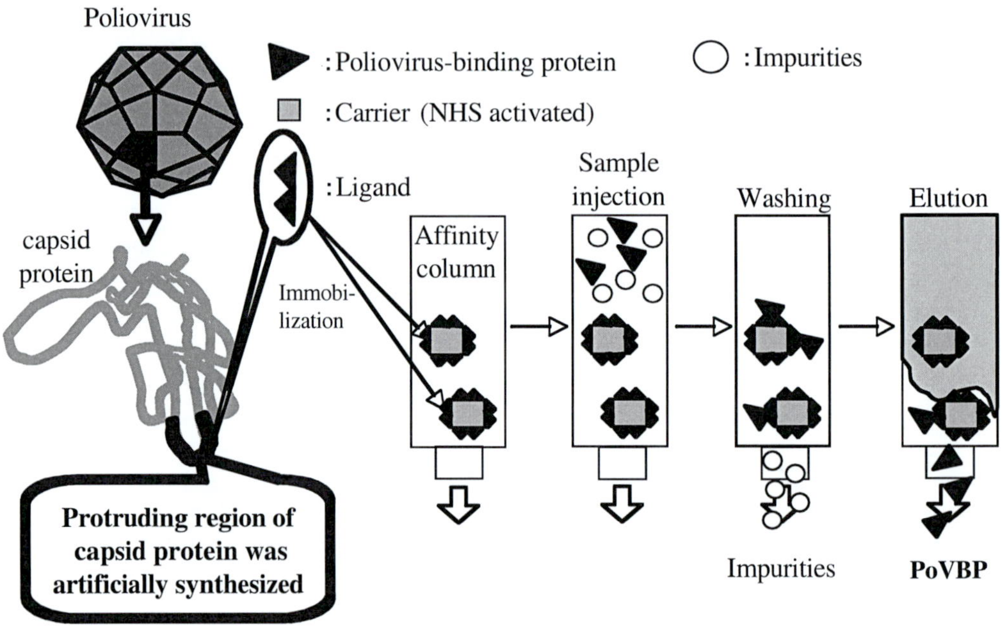

Figure 1. Schematic representation of the isolation of Poliovirus-binding proteins (PoVBPs) with the affinity column in which the viral capsid peptide was immobilized as a ligand.

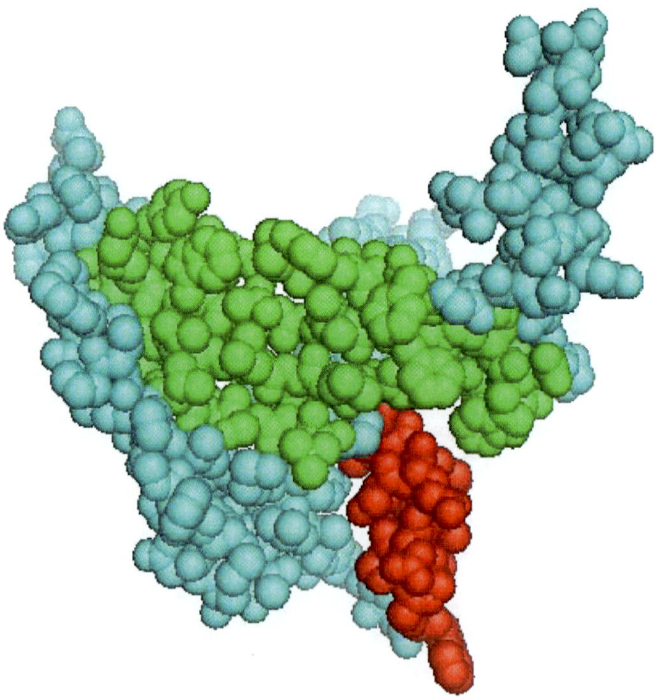

Figure 2. Tertiary structure of Poliovirus-binding protein (PoVBP) estimated by SWISS-MODEL (http://swissmodel.expasy.org//SWISS-MODEL.html). The estimated structure was visualized with PyMol (http://pymol.sourceforge.net/). Residues forming alpha-helix and beta-sheet are colored in red and green, respectively.

The gene of PoVBP was acquired from a genomic DNA library of activated sludge bacteria based on N-terminal amino acid sequences of the isolated VBPs with a colony hybridization technique [Sano et al., 2005]. The result of the homology search against all protein sequences in the databases of National Center for Biotechnology Information (NCBI) implies that PoVBP is categorized to the membrane protein located on the outer membrane of gram-negative bacteria, and the three-dimensional structural model of PoVBP was estimated by the SWISS model [Schwede et al., 2003] with the sequence analogy to OmpK from vibrio species (Figure 2). Some researchers reported that no proteolysis was observed after intact bacteria were subjected to the protease digestion [Worobec et al., 1988; Siehnel et al., 1990], which means that some outer membrane proteins of bacteria are protease-resistant and environmentally stable. VBPs originated from the outer membrane protein of bacteria in activated sludge are also expected to be stable under the conditions of water and wastewater treatments, and this is one of major reasons we sought VBPs from activated sludge bacteria in order to utilize them as viral adsorbents in VBP-based technology.

The Isolation of Adenovirus-Binding Protein

Not only PoVBP but also VBPs for the other pathogenic viruses such as Adenoviruses (AdVs) and Noroviruses (NoVs) could exist in water environments. In this section, the recovery and characterization of VBPs for AdVs (AdVBPs) from activated sludge bacteria are described. AdVs are composed of at least 51 serotypes and are associated with various infections of the eyes and the respiratory and gastrointestinal systems [Jalal et al., 2005]. The number of isolated strains of AdVs from humans is larger than 2,000 per year in Japan, and the most frequently isolated serotype is AdV type 3 (AdV3; 1,003 isolates in 2006). Other serotypes such as AdV types 31 (AdV31), 40 (AdV40) and 41 (AdV41) also have been linked to acute gastroenteritis in infants [Adrian and Wigand, 1989; Brown, 1990]. These facts mean that AdVs are important etiological agents, and attention should be paid to the proliferation of AdVs in human society including water environments.

AdVBPs were recovered with the affinity chromatography assay using surface-exposed peptide composing a fiber head protein of AdV. The amino acid sequences of the ligands used in the affinity chromatographic assay are indicated in Table 1. The fiber head peptides of AdV3 and AdV40 were artificially synthesized and immobilized in the affinity column. The peptide sequence of AdV40 was the same as that of AdV41, so the peptide code was named AdV40/41FiberHead (FH). These peptides are located on the terminal end of the fiber head and are exposed to the outside of the AdV capsid protein (Figure 3). Crude proteins from activated sludge culture were prepared as described elsewhere [Sano et al., 2004]. The ionic strength and flow rate of the affinity chromatography assay were optimized for the isolation of AdVBPs, and a start buffer of 0.01M NaCl in 20mM Tris-HCl (pH: 8.0) and a flow rate of 1ml/min were employed.

Table 1. Amino acid sequence of peptide ligand used for the isolation of adenovirus-binding proteins with affinity chromatography assay

Peptide code	amino acid sequence
AdV3FH*	1 N C Y Y K A S D G A L F 12
AdV40/41FH	1 M A L T Y T F L Q G D P 12

* fiber head.

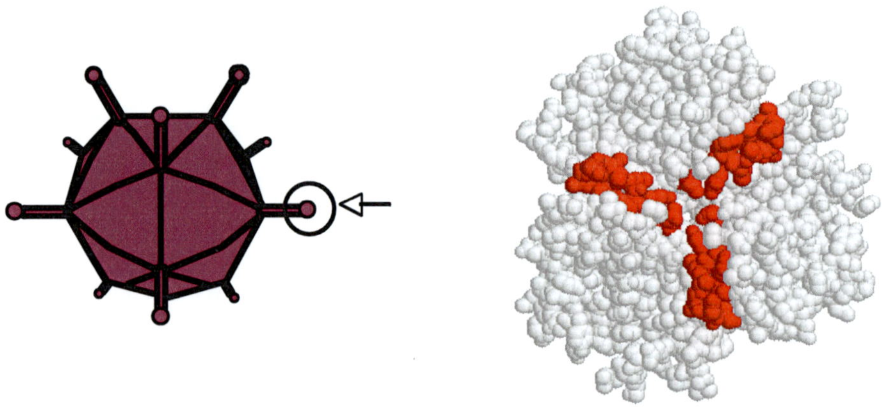

(a) (b)

Figure 3. Schematic representation of Adenovirus (AdV) particle (a) and tertiary structure of fiber head protein of adenovirus. The fiber head protein in AdV is indicated by the arrow. The red region in (b) was artificially synthesized and utilized as a ligand in the affinity chromatography assay in order to isolate AdV-binding proteins. The structure of the fiber head protein was visualized with PyMol (http://pymol.sourceforge.net/).

Figure 4 shows affinity chromatographic profiles of AdVBPs for AdV3 and AdV40/41. Three peaks were observed after the injection of the elution buffer, which indicates that AdVBPs were successfully recovered from the crude proteins of activated sludge microorganisms. The chromatography assay was repeated 80 times for each AdV serotype in order to obtain a significant amount of AdVBPs for subsequent experiments, but the number, height and appearance position of these peaks were reproducible. The relative molecular weight of AdVBPs in these peaks was analyzed by SDS-PAGE (Figure 5). The isolated AdVBPs in the first peak (peaks A and D) include a number of proteins, and their molecular weights were widely distributed, whereas those in the second and third peaks (peaks B, C, E and F) were composed of a lower number of AdVBPs, as reflected by the peak height in Figure 4.

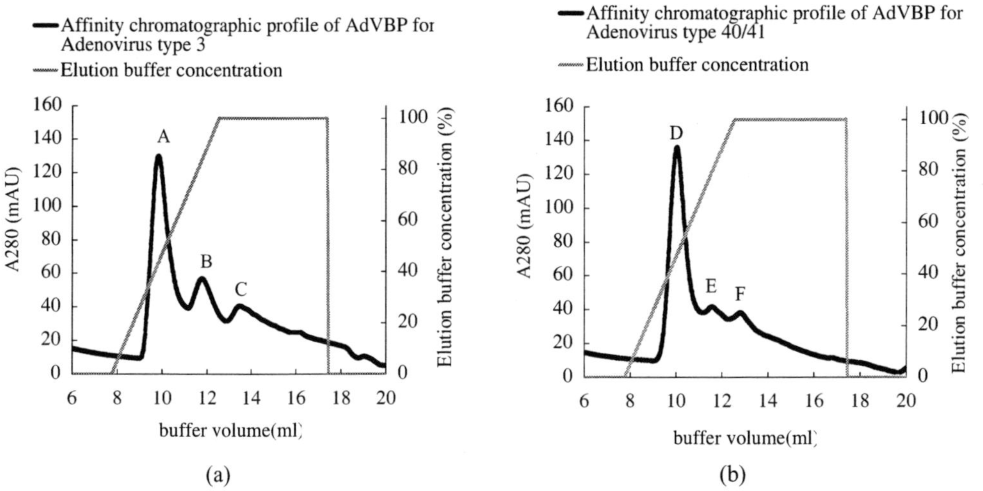

Figure 4. Affinity chromatographic profiles of Adenovirus-binding proteins (AdVBPs). (a) Affinity chromatographic profile of AdVBPs for Adenovirus type 3, (b) Affinity chromatographic profile of AdVBPs for Adenovirus types 40 and 41.

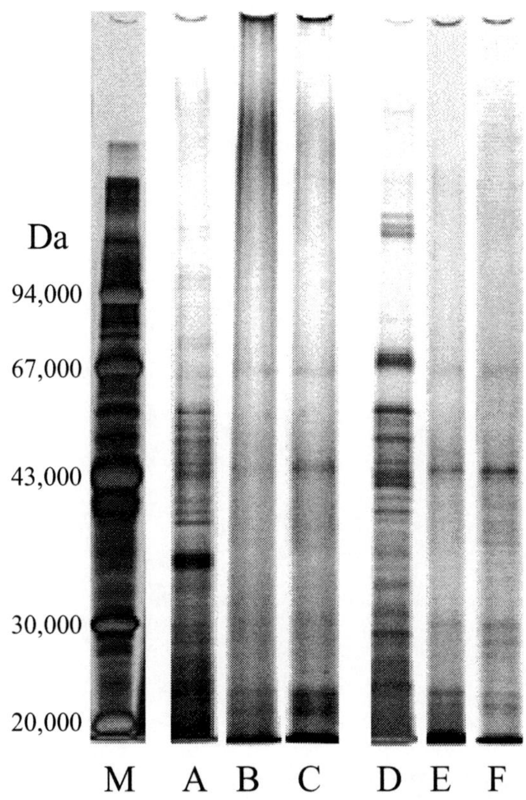

Figure 5. SDS-PAGE profiles of AdVBPs. Proteins were stained by silver. M, marker. Names of the other lanes (A, B, C, D, E and F) correspond to those in the peaks in Figure 4.

It was speculated that AdVBPs in the third peaks (i.e., peaks C and F) have stronger binding ability to AdV particles than those in the other peaks, because a higher concentration of the elution buffer was required to strip these AdVBPs out from the affinity column. In order to confirm the binding ability of AdVBPs to AdV particle, an enzyme-linked immosobent assay (ELISA) was performed by using infectious virions of AdV3 and AdV41. The affinity fraction including AdVBPs in each peak was concentrated by a dialysis against ammonium bicarbonate and a rotary evaporator as described elsewhere [Sano et al., 2004] and applied to ELISA. The average values of AdVBPs in the concentrated samples of peaks A, B, C, D, E, and F are 260, 80, 60, 950, 200 and 110 mg/L, respectively. Figure 6 shows the signal to noise (S/N) ratio for AdVBPs in each peak obtained in the affinity chromatography. The S/N ratios of AdVBPs in all peaks were significantly larger than those of the AdVBP-negative well, which means that AdV particles were firmly adsorbed to AdVBPs in all peaks. The relatively smaller values of the S/N ratio and the larger amount of AdVBPs in the first peaks (peaks A and D in Figure 4) imply that the binding ability of AdVBPs in the first peaks was weaker than those in the other peaks. These results can be explained by the affinity chromatographic profile indicated in Figure 4, in which AdVBPs in the first peak were recovered from the AdV-peptide immobilized column with the injection of the relatively lower concentration of the elution buffer. On the other hand, a significant difference was not observed between S/N ratios of the second and third peaks. Especially, AdVBPs for AdV40/41 in the second peak (peak E) exhibited larger S/N ratio than those in the third peak (peak F). This could be attributed to the difference of the recovery amount of AdVBPs. The concentration of AdVBPs in peak E was 200 mg/L, whereas that in peak F was 110 mg/L as described above. The amount of immobilized AdVBPs in the ELISA well is influenced by the amount of AdVBPs introduced to the well. The lower amount of immobilized AdVBPs in peak F than that in peak E decrease in the S/N ratio.

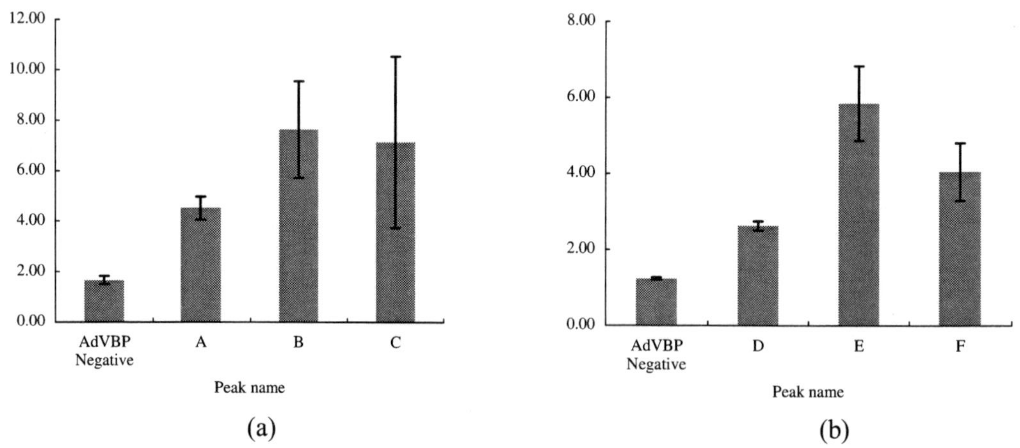

Figure 6. Signal to noise ratios (S/N ratios) in enzyme-linked immunosobent assay (ELISA) for evaluating the binding ability of Adenovirus-binding proteins (AdVBPs) to Adenovirus (AdV) particles. (a) S/N ratio in ELISA using AdVBPs for AdV type 3. (b) S/N ratio in ELISA using AdVBPs for AdV type 41. Error bars indicate standard errors (N=6). The peak name corresponds to that in Figure 4.

Table 2. Amino acid sequence of ADVBPs for adenovirus types 3 and 40/41

Spot number*		amino acid sequence	
1	1	QDAFSYAKGSATXAHTKSDYVG	22
2	1	QDAFSYAKGSAT	12
3	1	ADYSGDIHKNDYKXMQFNVMHTIDQ	25
4	1	ADYSGDIHKNDY	12
5	1	QDAFSYAKG	9
6	1	ADYTGDIHKNDY	12

* spot number corresponds to that in Fig. 7.

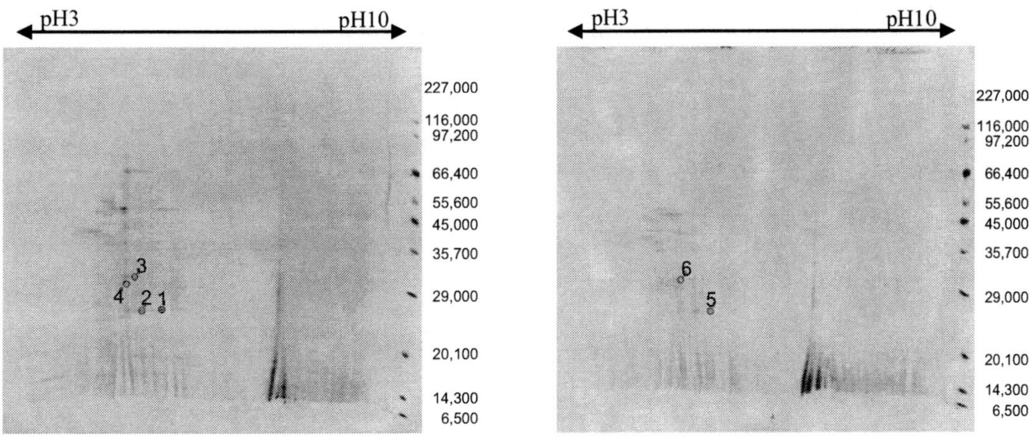

(a) (b)

Figure 7. Two-dimensional electrophoretic profilse of AdVBPs for adenovirus types 3 (AdV3, (a)) and 40/41 (AdV40/41, (b)). Amino-terminal amino acid sequences of AdVBPs indicated by the numbered circles were determined.

The results of ELISA showed that AdVBPs in the second and third peaks can strongly bind to AdV particles. In order to identify the AdVBPs, proteins in the third peaks (peaks C and F) were applied to two-dimensional electrophoresis (2DE), and N-terminal amino acid sequences of several AdVBPs were determined. Figure 7 shows the 2DE profile of AdVBPs for AdV3 and AdV40/41. The isoelectric point (pI) of almost all AdVBPs was lower than 6, which was also observed in our previous study with regard to PoVBPs [Sano et al., 2004]. Six spots were randomly selected, and their N-terminal amino acid sequences were determined (Table 2). AdVBPs in spots 1, 2, and 5 had the same N-terminal amino acid sequence, and those in spots 3, 4 and 6 had the same sequence. Only one hypothetical protein (AHA_1098 from *Aeromonas hydrophila*) was retrieved with the sequence identity of 77% to the AdVBP in spots 1, 2 and 5 by using BLASTP at the NCBI databases [Altschul et al., 1997; Schaffer et al., 2001]. On the other hand, a number of outer membrane proteins of bacteria were retrieved against the AdVBP in spots 3, 4 and 6. A similar sequence was also obtained in our previous study with regards to PoVBP [Sano et al., 2004]. The N-terminal peptide flanking this sequence is known as a signal peptide for outer membrane protein of gram-negative bacteria, which is necessary for membrane proteins to be appropriately located [Inoue et al., 1995; Arkowitz and Bassilana, 1994]. It is implied that AdVBPs are expressed as outer membrane proteins and exhibit the binding ability to AdV particles.

Gene Acquisition of Virus-Binding Protein

Acquisition and cloning of the VBP gene is absolutely necessary for the characterization of VBP. In our previous study, the PoVBP gene was acquired from a genomic DNA library of activated sludge microorganisms by a colony hybridization technique using a digoxigein (DIG)-modified DNA probe based on the N-terminal amino acid sequence of PoVBP [Sano et al., 2005]. The colony hybridization technique is the straightforward approach to obtain the objective gene according to its N-terminal amino acid sequence, but the acquisition of the objective gene with the colony hybridization becomes harder if just a tiny part of the amino acid sequence is obtained. In order to obtain the objective gene on the strength of a small part of the amino acid sequence, a PCR-based method was employed for the gene screening from a genomic DNA library of activated sludge microorganisms [Sano et al., 2006a]. In the PCR-based method, the degeneracy was reduced by employing the consensus-degenerate hybrid oligonucleotide primer (CODEHOP) method [Rose 1998]. With the CODEHOP method, each primer contains one of the possible coding sequences across a 3− 4 amino acid motif at the 3' end (degenerate core). Each primer also contains a longer sequence derived from a consensus of the possible coding sequences 5' to the core motif (consensus clamp). Thus, each primer has a different 3' sequence coding for the amino acid motif and the same 5' consensus sequence. Hybridization of the 3' degenerate core with the target DNA template is stabilized by the 5' consensus clamp during the initial PCR amplification reaction. Hybridization of primers to PCR products during subsequent amplification cycles is driven by interactions through the 5' consensus clamp [Rose, 2005]. The touchdown-PCR was also employed to circumvent spurious priming during gene amplification [Don, 1991].

In the PCR for seeking the objective gene from a genetic DNA library of activated sludge microorganisms, seminested PCR should be employed in order to effectively screen the objective gene, if two sets of degenerate primers can be designed as sense primers from the N-terminal sequence of VBP. Namely, a set of degenerate primers from the N-terminal side of determined amino acid sequence was used as the sense primer in the first PCR, and the other set of degenerate primers from the C-terminal side of the determined amino acid sequence was used as the sense primer in the second PCR. In this case, unreacted primers in the first PCR have to be removed with a column such as MicroSpin S-200 HR Column (Amersham Bioscience) prior to the second PCR. Since the utilization of degenerate primers affects the specificity in PCR, inosine-incorporated primers should be used as much as possible for reducing degeneracy. A consensus primer derived from a vector is useful as an anti-sense primer when neither a midterm nor C-terminal amino acid sequence of VBP was obtained.

The schematic representation of the described approach for gene screening is depicted in Figure 8. Since primers in the first and the second PCRs are designed from the midstream of the N-terminal amino acid sequence, obtained clones from these PCRs do not have the upstream region of the objective gene. The upstream region was acquired with the third PCR in which an anti-sense primer designed from the obtained clones in the second PCR was used. A primer derived from a vector was used as the sense primer, and a genomic DNA library of activated sludge bacteria was used as the template in the third PCR. Then, sense and anti-sense primers can be designed from upstream and downstream regions of the objective gene, respectively. These primers were used for the fourth PCR, in which the full length of the objective gene is amplified. This approach allowed us to successfully obtain the gene of heavy metal-binding protein (HMBP) from a genomic DNA library of activated sludge microorganisms [Sano et al., 2006a]. Such an approach would be useful to isolate genes of VBPs for several pathogenic viruses on the strength of a small part of the amino acid sequences of VBPs.

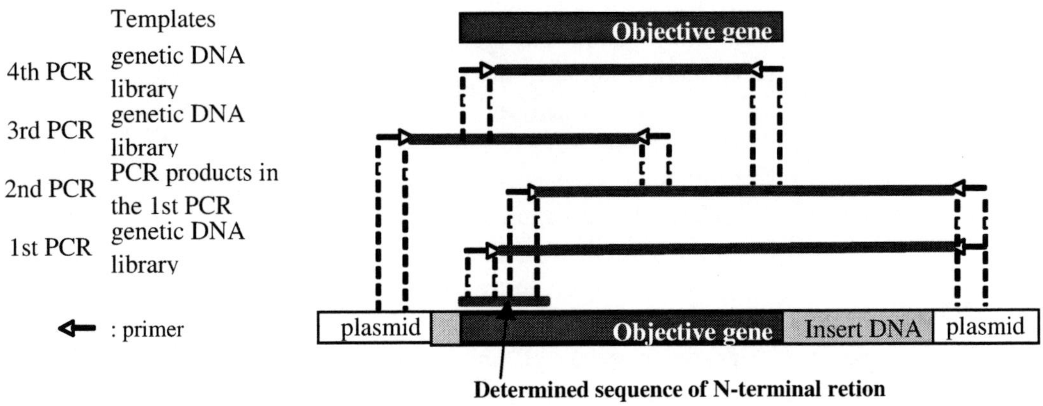

Figure 8. Schematic representation of the strategy for acquiring VBP gene with PCR from a genomic DNA library of activated sludge microorganisms.

Future Applications and Perspectives of Virus-Binding Protein

VBPs were estimated to be stable under the conditions of water environments, because these proteins were originated from activated sludge in the aeration tank of a wastewater treatment plant. This means that it might be possible to stably utilize VBPs as specific viral adsorbents in several technologies of virus removal, concentration and detection from environmental water contaminated by pathogenic viruses. The utilization of novel bioactive materials acquired from environments has not been familiar in water and wastewater treatment engineering, while environmental-origin materials have been valuable in the drug, antibiotics and biocatalysts industries [Zhang et al., 2005; Daniel, 2004]. However, the application of functional biomaterials like VBPs might create new horizons in research and development in the fields of water and wastewater treatment engineering in the near future, so it would be worthwhile to put VBPs into practical use.

The use of immunoassay technology including radioimmunoassay, solid-phase enzyme immunoassay, fluoroimmunoassay and microarray in clinical, food safety and environmental analysis will continue to grow [Vikholm, 2005]. These antibody-based technologies are available to detect very specific and tight binding between antibody and antigen. An immunomagnetic method for concentrating viruses from environmental samples also utilizes antibodies for objective antigens [Schwab et al., 1996]. VBP might be feasible and inexpensive antibody surrogates for concentration and detection of viruses, since the binding specificity is one of the important traits in VBP. The superiority of VBPs to antibodies is simplicity of the preparation, because VBPs can be produced by transformed *E. coli* cells and purified by a single step affinity chromatography. On the other hand, production of hybridoma is required to create a monoclonal antibody, and the hybridoma may be genetically unstable [Chambers 2005]. Furthermore, an immunoglobulin fragment called scFv can be synthesized as a recombinant antibody by *E. coli* cells, but one of the technical problems with scFv is that they are relatively unstable and tend to multimerize [Chambers 2005].

One of the other potent applications of VBP is as a specific adsorbent in virus detection from a large *Water SA*mple. Generally, contamination of environmental water with human viruses usually occurs at low concentrations (several particles per litter or less) [Rutjes et al., 2005]. Especially, the virus contamination level in seawater is as low as the detection limit of the conventional method, but viruses in seawater can be accumulated by cultivated sea products such as oysters, and bring about several diseases among consumers of sea products [Ueki et al., 2005]. Virus detection at the concentrations of several viral particles per more than 10 liter is required to regulate virus contamination in environmental water. It is desirable to utilize VBP as a facile and economical adsorbent for building a new scheme for the monitoring and removal of pathogenic viruses in water environments.

In order to utilize VBPs as viral adsorbents in various technologies as described above, it is necessary to prepare VBPs for a variety of pathogenic viruses. It would be possible to recover VBPs for other viruses such as Noroviruses (NoVs), Rotaviruses (RoV) and Astroviruses (AstV) with the same approach described in this chapter. However, it is not practical to find VBPs for all pathogenic viruses in water, because there are more than 100 species of viruses responsible for waterborne diseases. One practical way is to obtain VBPs only for key viruses as etiological agents. For example, NoVs categorized into genogroup II (NoV GII) are more important etiological agents than those into genogroup I (NoV GI) at the present, which means that VBPs for NoV GII should be isolated. The other way is to discover VBPs with broad affinity to several species of viruses. Although the accomplishment of the isolation of VBPs with broad affinity goes against the mechanism of the affinity chromatography, the employment of an appropriate viral capsid peptide might make it possible to find such versatile VBPs.

The existence of VBPs for a variety of pathogenic viruses means that these viruses could take advantage of these bacterial proteins to survive in water environments. The attachment of human viruses to bacteria harboring VBPs could protect viruses from inactivation factors such as ultraviolet and reactive oxygen species [Schaper et al., 2002; Sinton et al., 1999: Kohn and Nelson, 2007]. The finding of VBPs could lead to the elucidation of the pathway of pathogenic viruses in water environments.

CONCLUSION

Virus-binding proteins (VBPs) are found from a culture of activated sludge bacteria, which can bind human viruses in water environment. Adenovirus-binding proteins (AdVBPs) were successfully isolated with affinity chromatography assay in which an adenoviral fiber head peptide was used as a ligand. Several techniques including the consensus-degenerate hybrid oligonucleotide primer (CODEHOP), touchdown PCR, seminested PCR and inosine-incorporated primers are employed to acquire an objective VBP gene from a genetic DNA library of activated sludge bacteria. VBP-based technology for virus concentration and detection can be developed in the way that VBPs are used as viral adsorbents in water environment. It is necessary to prepare VBPs for key viruses responsible for waterborne infectious diseases, or discover versatile VBPs with a broad affinity to several species of pathogenic viruses.

REFERENCES

Adrian, T., & Wigand, R. (1989). Genome type analysis of adenovirus 31, a potential causative agent of infants' enteritis. *Arch. Virol., 105,* 81-87.

Altschul, S. F., Madden, T.L., Schaffer, A. A., Zhang, J., Zhang, Z,, Miller, W., & Lipman, D. J. (1997). Gapped BLAST and PSI-BLAST: a new generation of protein database search programs. *Nuc. Acid. Res., 25,* 3389-3402.

Arkowitz, R. A., & Bassilana, M. (1994). Protein translocation in *Escherichia coli. Biochem. Biophys. Acta, 1197,* 311-343.

Bewley, M. C., Springer, K., Zhang, Y.-B. Hreimuth, P., & Flanagan, J. M. (1999). Structural analysis of the mechanism of Adenovirus binding to its human cellular receptor, CAR. *Science, 286,* 1579-1583.

Biziagos, E., Passagot, J., Crance, J. M., & Agbalika, F. (1987). Concentration of hepatitis A virus. *Wat. Res. 21*, 683-686.

Block, J. C, & Schwartzbrod, L. (1989). Waterborne viruses in water systems. New York: VHC Publishers, Inc.

Brown, M. (1990). Laboratory identification of adenoviruses associated with gastroenteritis in Canada from 1983-1986. *J. Clin. Microbiol., 28,* 1525-1529.

Chambers, R. S. (2005). High-throughput antibody production. *Curr. Opin. Chem. Biol., 9,* 46-50

Damgaard-Larsen, S., Jensen, K. O., Lund, E., & Nissen, B. (1977). Survival and movement of enterovirus in connection with land disposal of sludges. *Wat. Res., 11,* 503-508.

Daniel, R. (2004). The soil metagenome – a rich resource for the discovery of novel natural products. *Curr. Opin. Biotech., 15,* 199-204.

Don, R. H., Cox, P. T., Wainwright, B. J., Baker, K., & Mattick, J. S. (1991). 'Touchdown' PCR to circumvent spurious priming during gene amplification. *Nuc. Acid. Res. 19,* 4008.

Fiore, L., Ridolfi, B., Genovese, D., Buttinelli, G., Lucioli, S., Lahm, A., & Ruggeri, F. M. (1997). Poliovirus sabin type 1 neutralization epitopes recognized by immunoglobulin A monoclonal antibody. *J. Virol. 71,* 6905-6912.

Forrest, J. C. & Dermody, T. S. (2003). Reovirus receptors and pathogenesis. *J. Virol., 77,* 9109-9115.

Foster, D.M., Emerson, M.A., Buck, C.E., Walsh, D.S., & Sproul, O. J. (1980). Ozone inactivation of cell- and fecal-associated viruses and bacteria. *J. Water Poll. Control Fed., 52,* 2174-2184.

Guttman-Bass, N., Hostovsky, T., Lugten, M., & Armon, R. (1985). A comparison of current methods of poliovirus concentration from tap water. *Wat. Res. 19,* 85-88.

Haramoto, E., Katayama, H., Oguma, K., & Ohgaki, S. (2005). Application of cation-coated filter method to detection of Noroviruses, Enteroviruses, Adenoviruses, and Torque Teno Viruses in the Tamagawa River in Japan. *Appl. Environ. Microbiol., 71,* 2403-2411.

He, J. W., & Jiang, S. (2005). Quantification of Enterococci and human Adenoviruses in environmental samples by real-time PCR. *Appl. Environ. Microbiol., 71,* 2250-2255.

Hogle, J., Chow, M., & Filman, D. (1985). Three-dimensional structure of poliovirus at 2.9 A resolution. *Science, 229,* 1358-1365.

Inoue, T., Matsuzaki, S., & Tanaka, S. (1995). Cloning and sequence analysis of Vibrio parahaemolyticus ompK gene encoding a 26-kDa outer membrane protein, OmpK, that serves as receptor for a broad-host-range vibriophage, KVP40. *FEMS Microbiol. Lett., 134,* 245-249.

Jalal, H., Bibby, D. F., Tang, J. W., Bennett, F., Kyriakou, C., Peggs, K., Cubitt, D., Brink, N. S., Ward, K. N., & Tedder, R. S. (2005). First reported outbreaks of diarrhea due to Adenovirus infection in a hematology unit for adults. *J. Clin. Microbiol., 46,* 2575-2580.

Kohn, T., & Nelson, K. L. (2007). Sunlight-mediated inactivation of MS2 coliphage via exogenous singlet oxygen produced by sensitizers in natural waters. *Environ. Sci. Technol., 41,* 192-197.

Makino, A., Shinojima, M., Miyazawa, T., Kato, K., Tohya, Y., & Asashi, H. (2006). Junctional adhesion molecule 1 is a functional receptor for feline calicivirus. *J. Virol., 80,* 4482-4490.

Nasser, A. M., Glozman, R., & Nitzan, Y. (2002). Contribution of microbial activity to virus reduction in saturated soil. *Wat. Res., 36,* 2589-2595.

Pancorbo, O. C., Scheuerman P. R., Farrah, S. R., & Bitton, G. (1981). Effect of sludge type on poliovirus association with and recovery from sludge solids. *Can. J. Microbiol., 27,* 279-287.

Rose, T. M., Schultz, E. R., Henikoff, J. G., Pletrokovski, S., Mccallum, C. M., & Henikoff, S. (1998). Consensus-degenerate hybrid oligonucleotide primers for amplification of distantly related sequences. *Nuc. Acid. Res., 26,* 1628-1635.

Rose, T. M. (2005). CODEHOP-mediated PCR – A powerful technique for the identification and characterization of viral genomes. *Virol. J.*, 2, 20.

Rutjes, S. A., Italiaander, R., van den Berg, H. H. J. L., Lodder, W. J., & Husman, A. M. R. (2005). Isolation and detection of enterovirus RNA from large-volume *Water SA*mples by using the NucliSens miniMAG System and real-time nucleic acid sequence-based amplification. *Appl. Environ. Microbiol., 71,* 3734-3740

Sano, D., Matsuo, T., & Omura, T. (2004). Virus-binding proteins recovered from bacterial culture derived from activated sludge by affinity chromatography assay using a viral capsid peptide. *Appl. Environ. Microbiol., 70,* 3434-3442.

Sano, D., & Omura, T. (2005). Construction of a cloning system for the mass production of a virus-binding protein specific for poliovirus type 1. *Appl. Environ. Microbiol.,* 71, 2608-2615.

Sano, D., Myojo, K., & Omura, T. (2006a). Cloning of heavy metal-binding protein derived from activated sludge bacteria. *Appl. Environ. Microbiol.,* 72, 6377-6380.

Sano, D., Ueki, Y., Watanabe, T., & Omura, T. (2006b). Genetic variation in the conservative gene region of Norovirus genogroup II strains in environmental and stool samples. *Environ. Sci. Tech., 40,* 7423-7427.

Schaffer, A. A., Aravind, L., Madden, T. L., Shavirin, S., Spouge, J. L., Wolf, Y. I., Koonin, E. V., & Altschul, S. F. (2001). Improving the accuracy of PSI-BLAST protein database searches with composition-based statistics and other refinements. *Nuc. Acid. Res.,* 27, 2994-3005.

Schaper, M., Duran, A. E., & Jofre, J. (2002). Comparative resistance of phage isolates of four genotypes of F-specific RNA bacteriophages to various inactivation processes. *Appl Environ Microbiol., 68,* 3702-3707.

Schwab, K. J., Leon, R. D., & Sobsey, M. D. (1996). Immunoaffinity concentration and purification of waterborne enteric viruses for detection by reverser transcriptase PCR. *Appl Environ Microbiol., 62,* 2086-2094.

Schwede, T., Kopp, J., Guex, N., & Peitsch, M. C. (2003). SWISS-MODEL: an automated protein homology-modering server. *Nuc. Acid. Res., 31,* 3381-3385.

Siehnel, R., Martin, N.L., & Hancock, R. E. W. (1990). Sequence and relatedness in other bacteria of the *Pseudomonas aeruginosa* oprP gene coding for the phosphate-specific porin P. *Mol. Microbiol., 4,* 831-838.

Shields, P. A., Berenfeld, S. A., & Farrah, S. R. (1985). Modified membrane-filter procedure for concentration of enteroviruses from tap water. *Appl. Environ. Microbiol., 49,* 453-455.

Sinton, L. W., Finlay, R.K., & Lynch, P. A. (1999). Sunlight inactivation of fecal bacteriophages and bacteria in sewage-polluted seawater. *Appl. Environ. Microbiol., 65,* 3605-3613

Sobsey, M. D., & Glass, J. S. (1980). Poliovirus concentration from tap water with electropositive adsorbent filters. *Appl. Environ. Microbiol., 40,* 201-210.

Ueki, Y., Sano, D., Watanabe, T., Akiyama, K., & Omura, T. (2005). Norovirus pathway in water environment estimated by genetic analysis of strains from patients of gastroenteritis, sewage, treated wastewater, river water and oysters. *Wat. Res., 39,* 4271-4280.

Vikholm, I. (2005). Immunosensing based on site-directed immobilization of antibody fragments and polymers that reduce nonspecific binding. *Langmuir, 21,* 6473-6477.

Wyn-Jones, A. P., & Sellwood, J. (2001). A review: Enteric viruses in the aquatic environment. *J. Appl. Microbiol., 91,* 945-962.

Worobec, E. A., Martin, N. L., McCubbin, W. D., Kay, C. M., Brayer, G. D., & Hancock, R. E. W. (1988). Large-scale purification and biochemical characterization of crystallization-grade porin protein P from *Pseudomonas aeruginosa. Biochim. Biophys. Acta, 939,* 366-374.

Zarate, S., Romero, P., Espinosa, R., Arias, C. F., & Lopez, S. (2004). VP7 mediates the interaction of Rotaviruses with integrin αvβ3 through a novel integrin-binding site. *J. Virol., 78,* 10839-10847.

Zhang, L., An, R., Wang, J., Sun, N., Zhang, S., Hu, J., & Kuai, J. (2005). Exploring novel bioactive compounds from marine microbes. *Curr. Opin. Microbiol., 8,* 276-281.

In: Environmental Microbiology Research Trends
Editor: G. V. Kurladze, pp. 273-287
ISBN: 978-1-60021-939-9

Chapter 10

ADVANCES IN MARINE BACTERIAL POLLUTION MONITORING

Gabriella Caruso, Rosalba Caruso[1], Ermanno Crisafi and Giuseppe Zappalà

National Research Council, Institute for Coastal Marine Environment (IAMC), 98122 Messina, Italy

[1]University Hospital Agency "G. Martino", Via Consolare Valeria, 98121 Messina, Italy

ABSTRACT

Coastal aquatic environments often suffer from anthropogenic pressure, posing severe threats to human health related to presence of pollutants in seawaters. Recent trends in environmental monitoring aiming at public health preservation highlight the need of a deep revision of the standards up to now used in the assessment of seawater quality, focusing the importance of new bacterial indicators, more reliable than those previously used, in the control of short and large scale-occurring pollution phenomena. Selected bacterial species (*Escherichia coli*) or related parameters are currently included in monitoring programs of marine environmental quality; they allow to track the occurrence and evolution of bacterial pollution events, and prevent human health risks related to the use of polluted waters. Moreover, several limitations intrinsic to culture methods traditionally used to detect bacterial pathogens (long response times, low specificity, high costs) confirm their inadequacy for coastal monitoring, stressing the need for updated standard analytical procedures. In response to this, several research efforts at the CNR - IAMC have recently been devoted to improve technical equipments and methodologies for the assessment of microbiological quality of seawater. The chapter reviews recent advances in coastal microbial pollution monitoring achieved in the framework of projects funded by the Italian Ministry for Scientific Research, addressing the detection and enumeration of *Escherichia coli* in seawater as an indicator of faecal pollution. A summary of the innovative methodologies (the fluorescent antibody method, the β-glucuronidase assay and Real time PCR) developed and optimised at the IAMC laboratory for monitoring bathing waters is reported, which allowed the high-resolution quantitative measurement of target bacterial molecules and accurate quantification of faecal pollution phenomena. These methods provided results significantly related to plate counts within a few hours from sampling, highlighting the main advantages (rapidity and specificity) related to the detection of bacterial antigens or molecules as markers of faecal pollution. New combined fluorescence-viability staining protocols were also set up, capable to detect bacteria which persist into seawater under different physiological states, maintaining intact living properties, and therefore have a pathogenic potential. The proposed methods proved to be rapid and specific analytic approaches for the screening of coastal areas with various degrees of pollution; therefore they offer new interesting perspectives to prevent outbreaks of waterborne diseases. Data obtained by these new analytical procedures encourage the use of *E. coli* or related parameters as successful tools for early warning of seawater bacterial pollution.

Keywords: marine pollution, coastal monitoring, *Escherichia coli*, fluorescent antibodies, viability staining, β-glucuronidase assay

INTRODUCTION

Assessment of the Microbiological Quality of Seawater: Importance of Coastal Monitoring

Coastal marine environments are very vulnerable ecosystems, exposed to the impact of anthropogenic activities; they receive organic and bacterial inputs from urban and industrial settlements, tourism, fishing activities. Pollution arisen from these sources is a function of the anthropic pressure over these areas; the consequences of the impact of pollutants over the coastal environment range from local alteration of natural ecological equilibrium to severe deterioration, posing severe threats not only to aquatic organisms but also to human health.

The main sources of faecal pollution are point sources, consisting of urban wastewaters discharged without adequate treatment; in addition, coastal environments may receive diffuse sources of pollution such as surface run-off, stormwater overflows, bathers, wastes from boats, agriculture wastes, bird droppings, and all these sources may escape to control or their occurrence can hardly be prevented. Sewage outfall has a significant impact on coastal areas, causing deterioration in seawater quality and consequently severe public health and socio-economic consequences (i.e. limiting their use for recreation, aquaculture and other uses).

In recent years, the incidence of waterborne diseases (gastroenteritis, otitis, wound infections) related to the use of contaminated waters has frequently reached alarming proportions, due to several potential causes among which the resistance showed by some microorganisms to disinfection, the exchange of antibiotic resistance factors among bacteria and the spreading of emerging microbial pathogens associated with the increase of international tourism. Therefore, rapid and effective coastal monitoring is a topic of public concern and also a critical step for safeguarding the hygienic-sanitary quality of seawaters.

Why the Need for Advanced Technologies and Rapid Methods?

An important criterion for assessing the potential health risk of recreational waters to bathers is to evaluate the density of bacteria associated with faecal contamination. Recent trends in environmental monitoring aimed at public health preservation highlight the need of a deep revision of the standards up to now used in the assessment of seawater quality. In fact, bacterial indicators (i.e. total and faecal coliforms) previously used for detecting pollution proved to be inadequate as indicators of faecal pollution [1], stressing the importance of new, more reliable, bacterial indicators for the control of short and large scale-occurring pollution phenomena. Selected bacterial species (Escherichia coli) or related parameters (target genes or molecules) are currently included in rapid laboratory protocols as effective bioindicators for marine quality monitoring; they allow to track the occurrence and evolution of bacterial pollution events, and prevent human health risks related to the use of polluted waters.

In addition, culture methods currently used for bacteriological controls are often time- and labour- consuming, and characterised by low sensitivity and specificity, inability to detect stressed or viable but nonculturable bacteria (viable but not culturable cells, VBNC); these limitations frequently lead to an underestimation of bacterial loading and to bias in seawater quality assessment, making these methods inadequate for coastal monitoring [2, 3]. Another important issue concerns the assessment of bacterial viability, since enteric bacteria released into natural waters may overcome adverse conditions entering a VNBC state as a survival strategy [4, 5]. In this state, they become undetectable by current methodologies, but may retain their pathogenic potential [6, 7]. Therefore, all these considerations have stimulated interest towards the development of more sophisticated techniques and systems of bacterial detection and enumeration, suitable for use in early warning of faecal pollution episodes and compatible with basic laboratory facilities [1, 8, 9, 10].

Escherichia coli as the Main Bacterial Indicator of Faecal Pollution

Bacterial indicators of faecal pollution allow to early identify the occurrence of pollution events and sources in order to immediately set up proper protection/recovery actions. Recent European Environmental Agency directives [11] also promote the request of synthetic indicators for a better management of hydrological resources in a sustainable way by the decision makers. The recent European Directive concerning the suitability of bathing waters (EEC Directive (COM (2002) 581) recognises Escherichia coli, a faecal coliform common member of the intestinal microflora of humans and warm-blooded animals, as the main bacterial indicator of faecal pollution, due to its long persistence in the aquatic environment and to its low sensitivity to disinfection practices. The detection of this bacterium in seawater provides information about the potential, but not actual, health hazard related to the occurrence of enteric pathogens.

Expertise Developed at the CNR- IAMC- Messina in the Field of Rapid Methods for the Detection of Bacterial Indicators

Since 1989, the Thalassographic Institute, CNR of Messina, now Institute for Marine Coastal Environment, has gained experience in the field of coastal marine assessment, devoting several efforts to upgrade methods and technologies for the detection of bacterial indicators. Recent advances in this context have been achieved in the framework of the "Advanced Monitoring Systems" SAM Project (2001-2004), funded by the Italian Ministry for Scientific Research. Within this project, research was addressed to the development of new analytical protocols for assessing the bacterial quality of seawater, through the detection and enumeration of *E. coli* using the modern tools of biochemistry and molecular biology. In particular, three methodological approaches, the fluorescent antibody (FA) method, the measurement of the β-glucuronidase activity (by fluorogenic MUG assay) and a molecular approach (Real time Polymerase Chain Reaction, Real time PCR) were chosen for the experimentation, since their characteristics (high specificity, rapidity of detection) match the requirements of environmental monitoring. Their analytical protocols were set up and compared with the standard method as new attractive strategies for *E. coli* determination.

Aims of the Chapter

The specific aims of this chapter are: 1) to review the innovative methodologies developed and optimised by our laboratory for monitoring bathing waters; 2) to report some of the results obtained by the application of these new rapid methods to the analysis of coastal Sicilian waters; and 3) to provide a "practical guide" to their use for environmental monitoring, highlighting their main advantages and disadvantages.

MATERIALS AND METHODS

Monitoring Area

The monitoring program covered the shoreline near Messina town; this coastal area is affected by river runoff carrying some illegal urban effluents not properly treated. The particular hydrodynamism of Messina Straits is characterised by the mixing between the coldest and saltiest Ionian waters and the warmest Tyrrhenian waters which flow in opposite directions. A stream called "montante" flows northwards from the Ionian Sea and alternates with another one, called "scendente", flowing southwards from the Tyrrhenian Sea; this generates intense turbulence phenomena and affect the distribution patterns of organic inputs along the coasts. Higher levels of bacterial concentrations were generally found during "montante" current [12]. During four years of coastal monitoring, surface samples were taken at stations which exhibited different pollution levels, in order to follow the extent and spread of anthropic inputs.

FA Method

Basically, this method relies on the antigenic structure of *E. coli* cells and on the labelling of surface "antigens" with specific immune sera (containing specific "antibodies"), thus producing an antigen-antibody complex that is detected using a secondary antibody (goat anti rabbit IgG) conjugated to the fluorochrome fluorescein isothiocianate (FITC). FA method is used in bacterial diagnostics [13] as well as for the detection of bacterial strains of environmental significance (such as *Nitrosoccoccus oceanus* and *Synechococcus* spp. [14, 15].

FA procedure includes the concentration of the sea*Water SA*mple by filtration through a Nuclepore black membrane (0.22 mm pore size), followed by incubation for 30 min at room temperature with immune sera (*E. coli* agglutinating sera, Murex Biotech, mix of pools 2+3+4) specific for enteropathogenic (EPEC) and enteroinvasives (EIEC) *E. coli* serotypes. After rinsing with phosphate buffered saline to eliminate background fluorescence due to unlabelled serum, the filter is then incubated for 30 min at room temperature with an appropriate dilution of the secondary antibody (goat anti rabbit IgG-FITC conjugated). The filter is mounted on a slide with a drop of FA mounting fluid (pH 7.2, Difco) and observed. *E. coli* cells labelled with fluorescent antibodies are detected with an epifluorescence Axioplan 2 microscope (Carl Zeiss Inc.), equipped with the blue light (BP 490, LP 510, FT 520) filter set; green fluorescing, rod shaped cells are counted (Figure 1). Microscope counts are reported as the number of cells ml^{-1}.

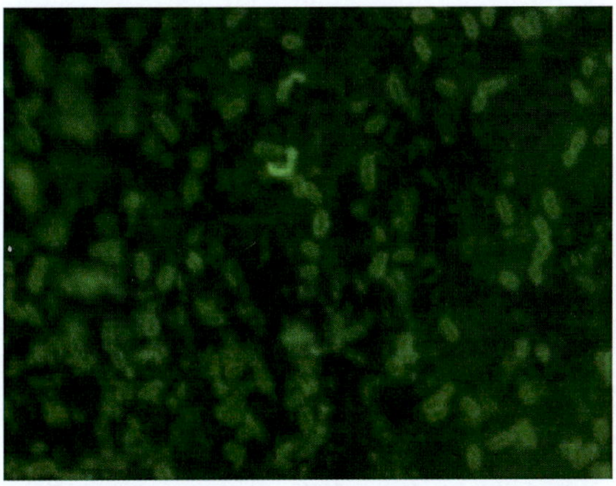

Figure 1. *Escherichia coli* cells labelled using Fluorescent Antibody method.

Combined FA–Viability Staining Protocol

As an improvement of the FA method, a FA labelling and viability staining procedure was further developed, which combines the use of specific immune sera for enteropathogenic serotypes with the viable stains propidium iodide (PI), marker of membrane-damaged (or dead) cells, or 5-cyano-2, 3 ditolyl tetrazolium chloride (CTC), marker of actively respiring cells. The steps of the FA-viability staining procedure are schematised in [7, 9].

In the FA-CTC staining procedure, after incubation with CTC (Polysciences; final concentration, 5 mmol l^{-1}), the sample is filtered through a 0.22 µm polycarbonate black membrane (Nuclepore) and then the filter is treated according to FA procedure. In the FA-PI staining procedure, sample amounts of 100 ml or less are filtered through a 0.22 µm polycarbonate black membrane (Nuclepore) and then incubated with propidium iodide (PI, Sigma; final concentration, 0.1 mg ml^{-1}). The abundance of actively respiring cells as well as of membrane damaged cells is determined with an epifluorescence microscope, using FITC (blue light, BP 490, FT 520) and rhodamine (green light, BP 510-560, FT 580, LP 590) filter sets. Depending on the staining procedure (FA-CTC or FA-PI), within the total (living + not-living) FA-labelled *E. coli* population, appearing as fluorescent green rods under blue light excitation, it is possible to distinguish the fraction of dead or membrane-damaged cells (scored as PI-positive [PI+] cells), red fluorescing due to the intracellular penetration of PI (emission peak: 617-623 nm), or the one of viable, actively respiring cells, showing intracellular CTC-formazan crystals with bright red fluorescence under green light excitation, and thus scored as CTC-positive [CTC+] cells.

β-glucuronidase Activity Estimates

β-glucuronidase activity assay (MUG assay) relies on the determination of the potential activity of β-glucuronidase, an enzyme specific of *Escherichia coli* and *Shigella*, Enterobacterium closely related to *E.coli*; this enzyme catalyses the hydrolysis of β-D-glucopyranosiduronic derivatives into D-glucuronic acid.

The fluorogenic substrate methylumbelliferyl-β-D-glucuronide is a synthetic compound that is not fluorescent by itself, but it is cleaved by β-glucuronidase into the fluorescent product methylumbelliferone, with the release of fluorescence.

The biochemical assay involves the addition of increasing amounts of the fluorogenic substrate 4-methylumbelliferil-β–D-glucuronide (MUG) to 10 ml sub-volumes of a 10 times concentrated sample, according to the procedure reported in detail by [16, 17]. Measurements of the released fluorescence are performed with a fluorimeter at time 0, immediately after the addition of the substrate, and after 3 hours of incubation at 44°C, at 365 and 440 nm excitation and emission wavelengths, respectively. Calibration of the instrument is performed with the standard methylumbelliferone. The increase in fluorescence intensity is converted, using the Lineweaver Burke linear transformation, into nanomoles of methylumbelliferone released per hour and per 100 ml of sample.

Real-time PCR

Real-time PCR offers a rapid and sensitive method to detect and quantify *E. coli* in environmental samples, through the high-resolution quantitative measurement of target bacterial molecules, in this case the *uidA* gene, which codifies for the enzyme β-glucuronidase. SYBR Green I dye intercalates into double-stranded DNA, producing a fluorescent signal [18], whose the intensity is proportional to the amount of dsDNA present in the reaction [19].

Table 1. Specificity of the used immune sera

Tested strains	Murex
E.coli O125 (Sclavo)	+++
Pseudomonas .spp.	---
Vibrio spp.	---
V. metschnikovii	---
Aeromonas hydrophila	---
Escherichia vulneris	---
E. hermannii	---
Shigella flexneri	++-
Klebsiella pneumoniae	---
Enterobacter agglomerans	---
Proteus mirabilis	---
Yersinia. enterocolitica O:10	---
Y. enterocolitica O:3	---
Citrobacter freundii	---
Salmonella. arizona	---
S. panama	---
S. blockley	---
S. bovis morbificans	---
S. gallinarum	---
S. typhimurium	---
S. enteritidis	---
S. typhi	---
S. paratyphi B	---

Table 2. Primers designed and synthesised for Real-time PCR, which identify a fragment of about 150 bp within the *uidA* gene.

Primer	Oligonucleotide sequenze	Position on *E. coli* DNA
UidA-MCF Middle Coding region, Forward	*GGC AGT GAA GGG CGA ACA G*	*1000*
UidA-MCR Middle Coding region, Reverse	*GAG GTA CGG TAG GAG TTG GC*	*1145*

Conserved regions of the genomic *E. coli* DNA, consisting of 20 base pairs, were first identified from GenBank molecular database and tested for specificity with the Check Probe programme; specific oligonucleotide probes (UidA-MCF + UidA-MCR) complementary to these regions were then designed to be used as primers in the amplification reaction performed by Taq DNA polimerase [20]. Their sequences and the location recognised on the genomic DNA of *E.coli* are reported in Table 2.

Real-time PCR amplification was carried out in a GeneAmp 5700 (Applied Biosystem), using a qPCR Core kit for SyBr Green I (Eurogentec) and a Master mix containing: 5 µl 1X reaction buffer (Eurogentec), 0.2 mM dNTP, 50/50 nM primers (Forward to Reverse ratio), 10 ng DNA, 0.1 mg BSA, 1u Taq DNA polimerase native (Fermentas), SyBr Green I (final reaction volume: 50 µl). PCR conditions were: initial denaturation step (95°C x 10min), followed by 45 cycles (95°C x 30 sec, 60°C x 1 min, 72°C x 2min) and final extension (72°C x 10min); hold at 25°C. Known amounts (15, 10, 5, 1 and 0.1 ng) of *E. coli* DNA were included in the amplification reaction, both as a standard (in triplicate) and unknown sample (in duplicate). An axenic culture of *E. coli* O125 reference strain, from which DNA was extracted with RNA/ DNA mini kit (Qiagen) and quantified through a Biophotometer reading at 260nm, was used to optimise the reaction conditions. Different combinations of the primers UidA-MCF + UidA- MCR (in terms of concentrations, in nM) were also tested and the combination 50/50 nM (Forward to Reverse ratio) was chosen as working concentration. Real time amplification results were converted into bacterial concentrations using a standard curve obtained from serial decimal dilutions (up to 10^{-6}) of target DNA with known concentrations of the target molecule (25, 15, 10, 5, 1 and 0.1 ng).

Culture Counts

In order to compare the performances of the new rapid and standard methods, culture counts of *E. coli* (in colony forming units, CFU 100 ml^{-1}) were performed filtering suitable volumes of seawater (10, 100 ml) through gridded Nuclepore membranes (0.45 µm pore size); filters were placed on m-FC agar plates and allowed to incubate at 44.5°C for 24 h [21]. Presumed *E. coli* colonies were confirmed by indole production test.

RESULTS

FA Method

An example of microscopic counts obtained by FA is reported in Figure2, compared with plate counts. Culture method generally underestimated *E. coli* abundance, producing counts that were about 1-2 orders of magnitude lower than microscopic counts. This quantitative discrepancy suggested that cells were mostly under VBNC state, so estimable only using microscopic observation.

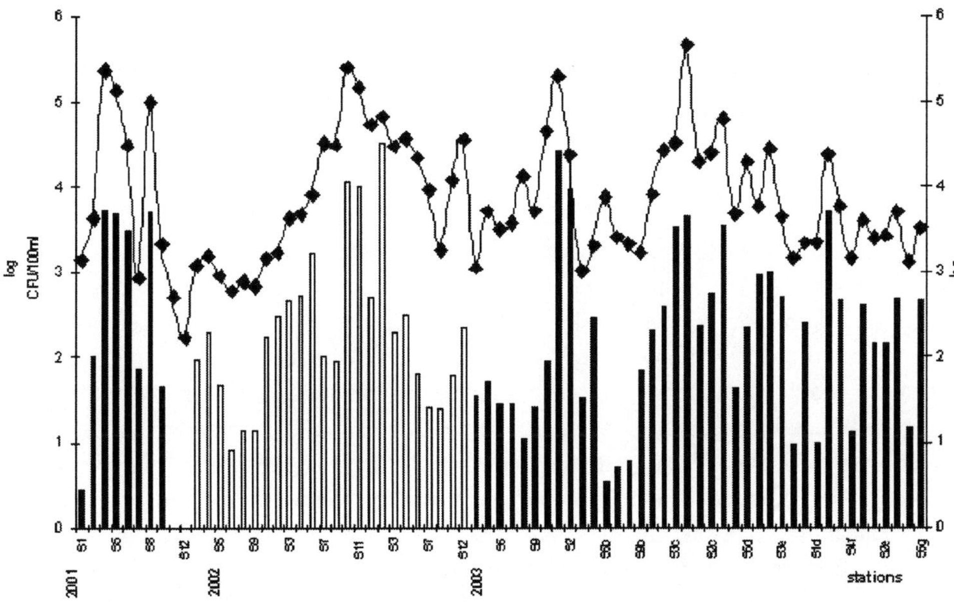

Figure 2. Microscopic (line) and plate (bars) counts performed in Messina Straits.

FA method provides results significantly related to plate counts within a few hours from sampling. However, before using immune sera it is necessary to check their specificity, to exclude any possible cross-reactions towards a range of clinical and environmental bacteria.

Results of the specificity assay performed on the used immune sera are reported in Table 1. They were highly specific to E.coli, although some cross-reactions were observed with Shigella flexneri; sera did not react with environmental strains such as Pseudomonas, Vibrio or Aeromonas.

Among the limitations intrinsic to FA, the high occurrence of particulate detritus in sea*Water SA*mples sets a limit to the volume of sample that can be filtered through the membrane and frequently filters are obtained by filtration of a seawater volume less than 100 ml. Sample pre-filtration on membrane with higher porosity (8 μm) could increase the amount of filtered sample, but cells associated with particulate matter could be removed by this treatment, thus leading to underestimation of the effective bacterial abundance. On the other hand, FA method is not able to detect *E. coli* at a concentration lower than 100 cells per 100 ml, that represents the threshold value to the application of this method. Disadvantages include also the narrow range of reactivity of the sera and the subjectivity of readings.

Combined FA–Viability Staining Protocol

FA-viability staining method allows to determine the degree of viability of the bacterial cells and the presence of different physiological states within the bacterial population; however, this method is affected by the same limitations as those reported for FA method. The study of *E. coli* viability showed the occurrence of seasonal variations in the concentrations of CTC+ and PI+ cells; conversely, the concentration of total FA labelled *E. coli* cells did not display seasonal changes, ranging from 4.17 x 10^5 (summer) to 3.68 x 10^5

cells 100 ml^{-1} (winter) and decreasing in spring only (Figure 3). In summer, culturable *E. coli* accounted for a low percentage (0.22%) of total FA counts, while their contribution to total *E. coli* population reached a maximum of 57.80% in winter. In summer, a high percentage of target bacteria was hypothesized to survive in seawater in a viable, but not culturable (VBNC) form, due the high discrepancy between plate and microscopic counts. On average, total-FA labelled *E. coli* counts exceeded by one order of magnitude the culturable (m-FC) counts. Actively respiring (CTC+) cells were detected in concentrations ranging from 7.60 x 10^3 (winter) to 2.14 x 10^4 cells 100 ml^{-1} (summer), when they represented, respectively, 20.67 and 51.30% of the total *E. coli* population. Dead or membrane damaged cells were found in concentrations comprised between 1.48 x 10^3 (autumn) and 7.79 x 10^3 cells 100 ml^{-1} (summer), accounting for 3.79 and 18.69% of the total FA labelled *E. coli*, respectively. The seasonal study provided evidence that in winter the bacterial cells within the total *E. coli* population were mostly membrane damaged (increase of PI+ cells) or entered a phase similar to quiescence or stationary phase, reducing significantly their active respiration (decrease of CTC+ cells). These metabolic changes allowed them to overcome adverse environmental conditions. During this season, however, the importance of continental run-off as a source of pathogens was suggested by the peak concentration of culturable cells detected. In spring, when environmental conditions became favourable to bacteria, cells recovered their living properties, as suggested by decreased PI positivity and increased CTC positivity. The sum of the percentages of culturable, actively respiring and dead cells gave values lower than the total abundance (100%) of *E. coli*, suggesting the existence of a fraction of bacterial cells that showed living attributes different from those detected in our study (i.e. other metabolic characteristics), therefore remaining still undetectable by our methods.

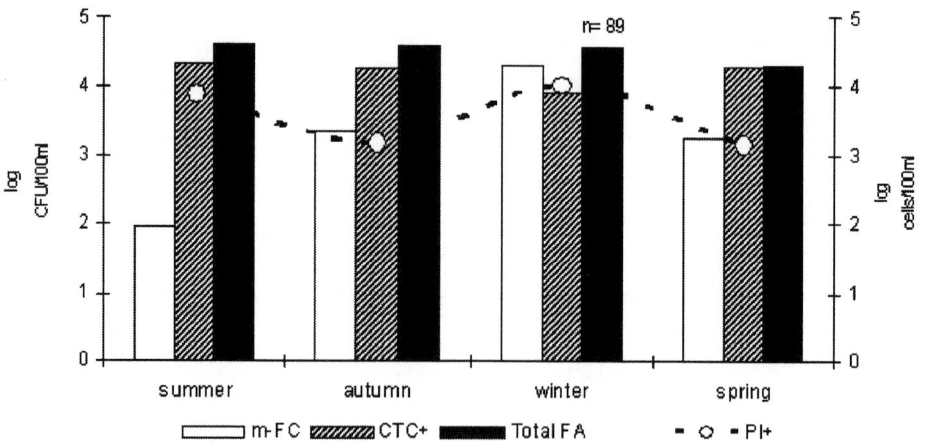

Figure 3. Seasonal variation of *E. coli* viability in Sicilian bathing waters. Reported are: on the left axis, culturable counts on m-FC agar (white bars), total FA cell counts, calculated as the mean value obtained by both CTC-FA and FA-L/D staining procedures (black bars); actively respiring cells (CTC+ cells, ruled bars); on the right axis, dead or membrane damaged (PI+) cells (white circles).

β-glucuronidase Activity Estimates

The application of MUG assay to environmental samples showed that enzymatic data correlated significantly with culture (m-FC) counts; the significance of this statistical relationship increased at high pollution level (Figs.4a, b) [16, 17]. In fact, the regression analysis performed on all samples regardless of their pollution level gave a better relationship between mFC and FA counts (R^2=0.3802, n=113, P<0.05), compared with that found between mFC and MUG (R^2=0.1195, P<0.05). Considering the most polluted samples only, whose plate counts exceeded 10^2 CFU/100ml, the statistical significance of the relationship obtained between mFC and MUG increased (R^2=0.3838, n=34, P<0.05), reaching values similar to those found between mFC and FA (R^2=0.4221, P<0.05). A possible explanation for this finding could be that in heavily polluted conditions, a high number of cells keep metabolic activity thanks to the high content of organic matter, while in oligotrophic conditions a low amount of organic matter is available to support bacterial viability; consequently, the greatest presence of injured/damaged bacteria could account for the poor relationship between MUG and mFC.

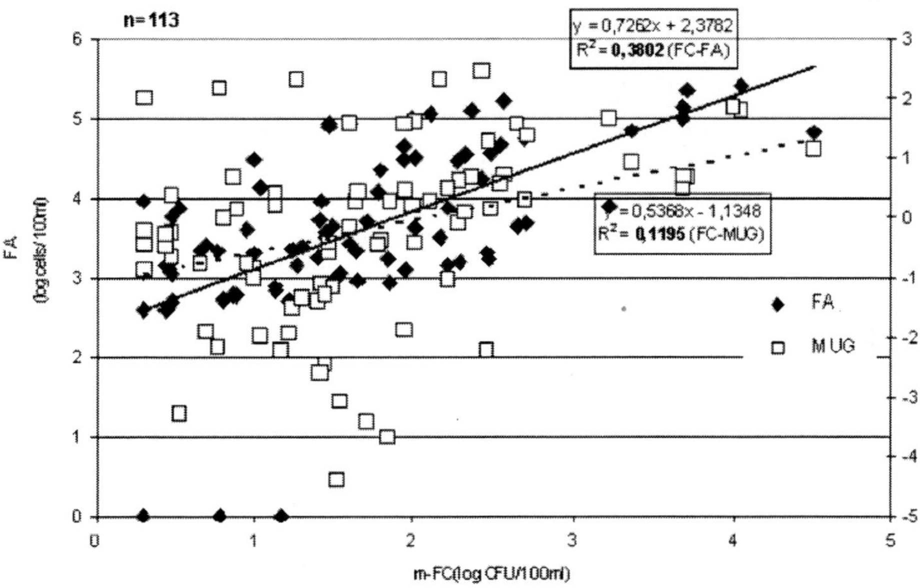

a

Figs. 4. (continued on next page).

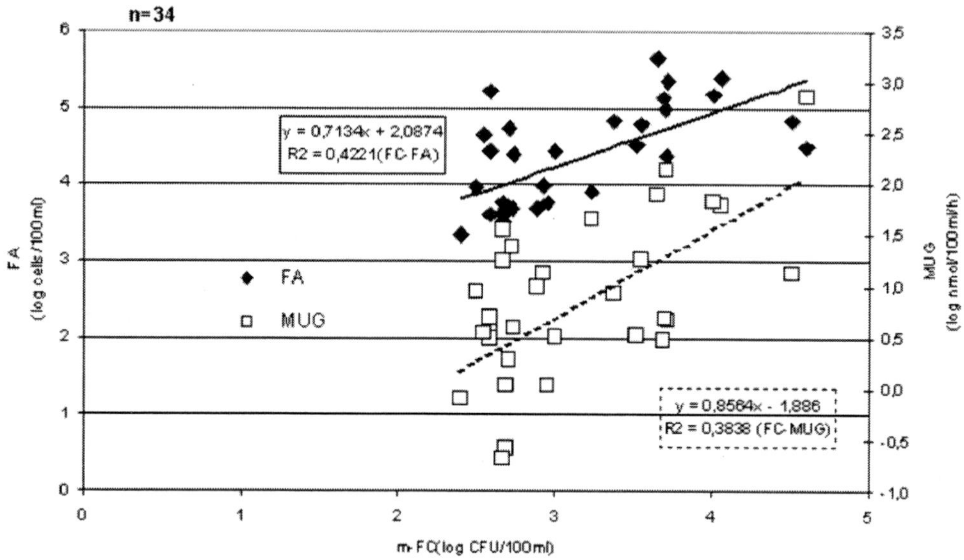

b

Figs. 4(a, b). Regression between culture (m-FC) counts, enzymatic (MUG) values and Fluorescent Antibody (FA) counts; a, all the samples; b, heavily polluted samples.

The MUG assay represents an indirect method to estimate the faecal pollution and provides a measure of the potential β-glucuronidase activity rates of *E. coli* cells, that are not directly comparable with bacterial counts. In general, the threshold value required to obtain a positive result is 10^2 cells 100 ml^{-1}. The main advantages related to the use of MUG assay are its reduced analysis and response times, low reagent costs, and the detection of VNBC cells. This may lead to a more accurate estimate of the actual bacteriological quality of seawater. However, the possibility of false positives (*Shigella* spp.) and negatives (β- glucuronidase negative *E. coli* strains) must be kept in mind [16, 17], as suggested also by other authors [22].

Real-time PCR

The specificity of PCR, assessed using axenic cultures of Enterobacterial strains other than *E. coli* (*Shigella flexneri*, *Klebsiella pneumoniae* and *Shewanella putrefaciens),* showed negative results for all these strains, except for *Shigella*, according to their close taxonomical relationship.

The standard curve obtained by Real-time PCR of *E. coli* O125 is reported in Figure 5. The threshold cycle (C_T, i.e., the cycle yielding a positive amplification result) was proportional to the logarithm of initial DNA concentration.

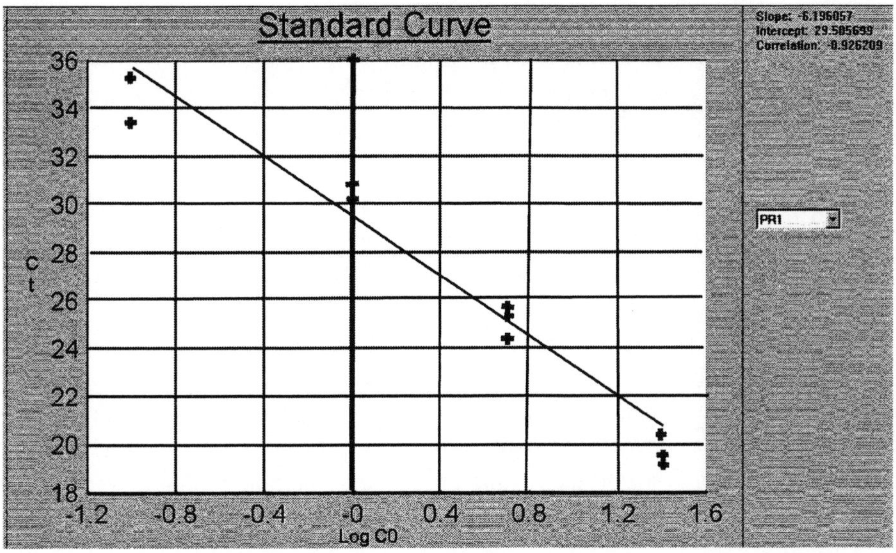

Figure 5. Standard curve for Real-time PCR measurements. DNA concentration (x-axis) is plotted against the threshold cycle value (y-axis).

The detection limit of the reaction (the minimum number of cells identified by DNA amplification), evaluated on serial dilutions of a pure culture of *E.coli* O125, was found to be 7 cells. Therefore, the Real-time PCR approach was preferred to Fluorescent In situ Hybridization (FISH) method, using fluorescently labeled rRNA-directed oligonucleotide probes, which could result in biased estimations in presence of low pollution conditions such as those usually found along Messina shoreline (*E. coli* concentrations generally 10^4-10^5 CFU 100 ml^{-1}).

Real-time PCR of natural sea*Water SA*mples showed values significantly related to culture counts (Tab. 3).

Table 3. Comparison between Real-time PCR and Plate counts of two representative samples

Samples	Real-time PCR (Cells 100 ml^{-1})	Plate count (CFU 100 ml^{-1})
Station Pagliarisi	$2.0x10^5$	$6.9x10^5$
Station Vela	$8.0x10^4$	$1.8x10^4$

CONCLUSION

Data obtained by these new analytical procedures indicated that *E. coli* or related parameters may serve as early warning tools of faecal pollution and encourage the use of bacteria or their molecules in bathing waters monitoring for revealing potential environmental risk to human health. The proposed methods proved to be very effective for the survey of coastal areas showing various pollution levels and therefore they offer new interesting perspectives to prevent waterborne disease outbreaks.

The potential of the new systems for environmental monitoring lies in their high sensitivity and speed, which enable to develop an immediate response for the safety and/or recover of human impacted marine sites.

The analysis of the antigenic cell determinants (FA method) or of the metabolic pathway signatures (MUG assay) proved to be highly sensitive and suitable for the detection of *E. coli* cells in natural marine waters [8]. Real-time PCR was also suitable for the fast detection and quantification of *E. coli* in seawater [20]. Moreover, the detection of bacterial viability with the combined FA- viability staining method is a promising approach for the assessment of *E. coli* cells retaining living attributes (active respiration or metabolism) in seawater, which better reflects the potential health hazard related to its use [7, 9]. In fact, this operational approach can provide a strategy of primary significance to adapt the development of better risk assessment programs to the effective amount of bacteria retaining potential pathogenicity. Appropriate combinations of these methods and integration with physical and hydrological parameters are suggested, to obtain more complete bathing water profiles.

Rapid laboratory methods based on new reagents or probes with potential applications in environmental monitoring will be improved in the near future; however, besides the technical development, the microbiological safety of waters must be guaranteed by a series of actions including implementation of active surveillance and technology transfer. Advanced approaches for rapid data collection and analysis and the integration between environmental monitoring and health surveillance represent the challenge for future developments in the field of seawater quality assessment.

REFERENCES

[1] Ashbolt, N, Grabow, WOK; Snozzi, M (2001). Indicators of microbial water quality. In: Fewtrell L, Bartram J editors. Water quality: guidelines, standards and health. London: International Water Association; 2001; 289-316.

[2] Sartory, D.P., & Watkins, J. (1999). Conventional culture for water quality assessment: is there a future? Journal Applied Microbiology Symposium Supplement, 85, 225S-233S.

[3] Caruso, G; Zaccone, R; Crisafi, E. Use of the indirect immunofluorescence method for detection and enumeration of *Escherichia coli* in sea*Water SA*mples. Letters Applied Microbiology, 2000, 31, 274-278.

[4] Roszack, D. B. and Colwell, R. R. (1987). Metabolic activity of bacterial cells enumerated by direct viable count. Applied and Environmental Microbiology, 53, 2889–2893.

[5] Rozen, Y., & Belkin, S. (2001). Survival of enteric bacteria in seawater. FEMS Microbiology Reviews, 725, 1-17.

[6] Pommepuy, M., Butin, M., Derrien, A., Gourmelon, M., Colwell, R. R. and Cormier, M. (1996). Retention of enteropathogenicity by viable but nonculturable *Escherichia coli* exposed to seawater and sunlight. Applied and Environmental Microbiology, 62, 4621–4626.

[7] Caruso, G; Mancuso, M; Crisafi, E. Combined fluorescent antibody assay and viability staining for the assessment of the physiological states of *Escherichia coli* in seawaters. Journal Applied Microbiology, 2003, 95(2), 225-233.

[8] Caruso, G; Denaro, R; Genovese, M; Giuliano, L; Mancuso, M; Yakimov, MM. New methodological strategies for detecting bacterial indicators. Chemistry and Ecology, 2004a, 20(3), 167-181.

[9] Caruso, G; De Pasquale, F; Mancuso, M; Zampino, D; Crisafi, E. Fluorescent antibody-viability staining and β-glucuronidase assay as rapid methods for monitoring *Escherichia coli* viability in coastal marine waters. Journal Immunoassay Immunochemistry, 2006, 27, 1-13.

[10] International Water Association (IWA). Rapid microbiological monitoring methods: the status quo. In: International Water Association, The Blue Pages; 2000; 1-13.

[11] European Environment Agency (EEA). Indicator-based state of the environment report prepared by the EEA for the conference of environment ministers of all European countries in Kiev (May 2003). Kiev Report, Technical report No. 66. European Environment Agency Publisher; 2003.

[12] Caruso, G; Zaccone, R; Monticelli, L; Crisafi, E; Zampino, D. Bacterial pollution of Messina coastal waters: a one year study. Microbiologica, 1999, 23, 297-304.

[13] Caruso, G; Crisafi, E; Mancuso, M. Immunofluorescence detection of *Escherichia coli* in seawaters: a comparison of different commercial antisera. Journal Immunoassay Immunochemistry, 2002, 23(4), 479-496.

[14] Zaccone, R; Caruso, G; Azzaro, M. Detection of *Nitrosococcus oceanus* in a Mediterranean lagoon by immunofluorescence. Journal of Applied Bacteriology, 1996, 80, 611-616.

[15] Acosta Pomar, MLC; Caruso, G; Maugeri, TL; Scarfò, R; Zaccone, R. Distribution of *Synechococcus* spp. determined by immunofluorescent assay. Journal of Applied Microbiology, 1998, 84, 493-500.

[16] Caruso, G; Crisafi, E; Mancuso, M. Development of an enzyme assay for rapid assessment of *Escherichia coli* in seawaters. Journal Applied Microbiology, 2002b, 93(4), 548-556.

[17] Caruso, G; Crisafi, E; Mancuso, M. (2004b). Coastal monitoring by MUG assay to the detection of seawater pollution. 37 th CIESM Congress, Barcelona (Spain), June 7-11, 2004, p.269.

[18] Wittwer, CT; Herrmann, MG;. Moss, AA; Rasmussen, RP. Continuous fluorescence monitoring of rapid cycle DNA amplification. Biotechniques, 1997, 22, 130-138.

[19] Heid, C., Stevens, J., Livak, K. and Williams, P. (1996). Real time quantitative PCR. Genome Research, 6, 986–994.

[20] La Cono V., Denaro R., Giuliano L., Iakimov M., Caruso G. (2004). Rapid detection of *Escherichia coli* by Real-time PCR. 6° Convegno FISV, Riva del Garda, 30 settembre - 3 ottobre 2004.

[21] American Public Health Association (A.P.H.A.). Standard Methods for the Examination of Water and Waste Water. 18 th Edition. Washington, DC: American Public Health Association; 1992.

[22] Farnleitner, AH; Hocke, L; Beiwl, C; Kavka, GG; Zechmeister, T; Kirschner, AKT; Mach, RL. Rapid enzymatic detection of *Escherichia coli* contamination in polluted river water. Letters in Applied Microbiology, 2001, 33, 246-250.

INDEX

B

C

D

E

F

G

H

I

N

O

P

S

U

V

W

X

Y

Z